D0481229

DATE DUE

THE TRIALS OF
LENNY
BRUCE

THE TRIALS OF
LENNY
BRUCE

The Fall and Rise of an American Icon

RONALD K.L. COLLINS & DAVID M. SKOVER

SOURCEBOOKS MEDIAFUSION™
AN IMPRINT OF SOURCEBOOKS, INC.®
NAPERVILLE, ILLINOIS

Published by Sourcebooks, Inc.
P.O. Box 4410, Naperville, Illinois 60567-4410
(630) 961-3900
FAX: (630) 961-2168
www.sourcebooks.com

Library of Congress Cataloging-in-Publication Data

Collins, Ronald K.L.
    The trials of Lenny Bruce : the fall and rise of an American icon / Ronald
K.L. Collins and David M. Skover.
        p. cm.
    ISBN 1-57071-986-1
    1. Bruce, Lenny—Trials, litigation, etc. 2. Trials
(Obscenity)—United States. 3. Freedom of speech—United States. 4.
Censorship—United States. I. Skover, David M. II. Title.
    KF224.B78 C65 2002
    345.73'0274—dc21

                                                    2002003139

Printed and bound in the United States of America
        LB 10 9 8 7 6 5 4 3 2 1

To the Men in Our Lives

RONALD COLLINS   DAVID SKOVER

Lee Collins   Alex Skover
Michael Collins   Philip Bice
Ronald Hathaway   Philip Calderone
Michael F. Jacobson   John G. Murphy Jr.
Hans Linde   Jon O. Newman
Michael Ormond   Sean Patrick O'Reilly

and, of course, Lenny Bruce

CONTENTS

ABOUT THE AUDIO

LENNY BRUCE WAS one of America's most famous comedians, an outlaw social critic, and eventually a free speech martyr and cultural icon. All of this was due, in large part, to the words he spoke on stage. It is hard to imagine a more fitting subject for a book with an integrated audio component.

We carefully compiled the audio for the CD that accompanies this book so as to enhance your understanding of Lenny Bruce and his struggles for free speech. It is not intended, however, as a "Best of Lenny Bruce" collection. Rather, it follows the text, presenting Lenny's performances and interviews with others in the context of his obscenity-law story as it unfolded. The CD will help you to understand Lenny's humor—his exposure of unspoken truths and his breach of social taboos, as he experimented with comedy and commentary.

Some of the recordings on the CD are taken from performances for which Lenny was arrested and tried. In other cases, however, Lenny's routines come from other shows. As the text explains, Lenny often performed the same bits differently from one appearance to the next. For several of the "bust" performances, no audio—or no usable audio—exists. But we felt strongly that there were enough similarities in theme, style, and/or content to warrant inclusion of routines that were alleged to be "obscene" in other performances.

One note on the New York trial tape excerpts (tracks 38–40): as these tapes were made secretly by Lenny during his New York trial, with a tape recorder concealed in his briefcase, the sound is muffled and coarse, at best. Repeated listening may be necessary to understand everything that is said. To assist you, there are partial transcripts of two of those excerpts in the book (Dorothy Kilgallen, p. 262, and Rev. Forrest Johnson, p. 258-9). In addition, you can read the transcript of Richard Gilman's cross-examination online at www.trialsoflenny bruce.com. At the same site, you can also hear other related audio clips, including more of the interview with George Carlin.

Above all things, Lenny wanted to be heard. To that end, listen to this CD and judge for yourself if he should have been silenced.

CD TRACK LIST

CD *This symbol throughout the book denotes text that corresponds to audio on the CD.*

WHEN OUTLAWS
BECOME HEROES

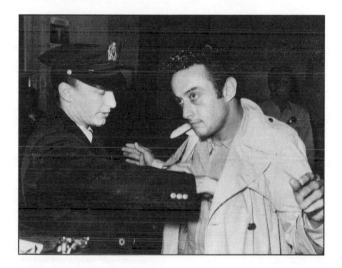

In order to give value to his gestures of defiance, [Lenny]
did need a lot of opposition....If you are going to break
a taboo, it has to be a taboo.

—*Harry Kalven Jr.*

People v. Bruce

HE WAS A man with an unsettling sense of humor. Uncompromising, uncanny, unforgettable, and unapologetic…every outrageous step of the way. He entertained America with disturbing frankness. His words crossed the law and those in it. He became intolerable to people too powerful to ignore. When it was over, not even the First Amendment saved him. He died convicted—a comedian condemned for his words. He was Lenny Bruce.

Censorship, arrests, trials, convictions, and appeals. Police, lawyers, judges, and jurors. The state versus the individual; the old guard versus the *avant garde*. It's all there, nonstop for five years, in the drama stamped *People v. Bruce*. Here is the story of comedy on trial, a story without rival in the annals of American history. It is the story of Lenny Bruce's struggle for free speech.

Words were his catalyst to fame; to failure, as well. Words were his power, his incomparable gift, his way into the unexplored realms of life and law from which there is seldom safe return. He tore into the planks of conventional morality like a furious buzz-saw: "My concept? You can't do anything with anybody's body to make it dirty to me. Six people, eight people, one person—you can only do one thing to make it dirty: kill it. Hiroshima was dirty." Daring to make public jokes about private matters, he satirically ridiculed hypocritical religious and legal authorities: "Respectability means under the covers," he explained, "I [am] pulling the covers off." His words cost him, in dollars, freedom, and sanity. His words—comical, critical, distasteful—put America's First Amendment principle to the test: Can offensive speech *really* be free?

The trials of Lenny Bruce are like no other in the history of our law. His free speech story is no dry recitation of lawyerly argument and mundane judicial precedent. From microfilm pages and dust-covered court records emerges a remarkable account of a man who was the magnet for enough prosecutors (twelve or more) to staff an entire state attorney's office, enough defense lawyers (twenty-three) to fill a small law firm, and more trial and appellate judges (some thirty) than have presided over any single body of First Amendment litigation. And all of this for *misdemeanor* offenses.

Lenny Bruce—born Leonard Alfred Schneider, a Jewish kid from Mineola, New York—was a comic criminal. He was prosecuted by the likes of Johnnie L. Cochran Jr., and defended by the likes of Harry Kalven Jr., one of the great free-speech scholars of the twentieth century. Thurgood Marshall, before becoming a justice on the Supreme Court, once sat in judgment over Bruce. Nat Hentoff, the liberal columnist, testified on his behalf, just as Ernest van den Haag, the noted conservative commentator, testified against him. Steve Allen, the celebrated TV talk show host, also spoke out for Bruce—from the beginning, throughout his trials, to the end. Judy Peabody, a noted New York socialite, and Phil Spector, the infamous rock-and-roll record producer, stood by Lenny as well—they subsidized him and his work at a time when virtually everyone else had abandoned him.

In his own lifetime, this comic outsider's speech was castigated by well-meaning conservatives and demeaned by well-meaning liberals. Major newspapers were relatively silent, and never ran editorial protests. Years after his death, feminist Susan Brownmiller lashed out against Lenny Bruce in a campaign to support his New York prosecutor for district attorney of Manhattan.

He had his defenders, too—among them Max Lerner, Woody Allen, Gore Vidal, Norman Podhoretz, Paul Newman, Elizabeth Taylor, James Baldwin, John Updike, and Susan Sontag, to name but a few. They once signed a petition in his defense: "Whether we regard

Bruce as a moral spokesman or simply as an entertainer, we believe he should be allowed to perform free from censorship or harassment."

And then there is the remarkable story of Justice William Brennan Jr. The obscenity opinions he wrote over four decades ago figured prominently into Lenny Bruce's struggles for free speech. The evolution of Brennan's view of the First Amendment was central to the handling of *People v. Bruce*. It explains how Bruce was prosecuted, defended, once exonerated (on appeal), and how he may have been legally vindicated if only he had lived longer.

Incredibly, the Bruce story is virtually absent from the recorded history of the First Amendment. There is no celebrated Lenny Bruce precedent, because his cases have been virtually forgotten. True, Lenny Bruce has become a cultural icon. But in the world of the law, his life and legal struggles are nothing; it is as if he had never existed. Such legal inattention is folly, however. For in the comic and tragic turns of this life, there is a great legal story to be told. It is a story of the poignant and perverse sides of free speech and the way that speech plays to people and power. It is a true story, but one clouded by myths and complicated by paradoxes.

The Living Dead

THE BEST YEARS of Lenny Bruce's life came after his death. "Dirty Lenny" became "Saint Lenny." Where the law once had prosecuted him, the culture now hailed him. Lenny was, according to Albert Goldman, the "greatest comic talent in modern times." Goldman, Bruce's ruthless biographer, labeled him "one of the culture-makers of the modern age." Indeed. On Broadway, on the big screen, on a Beatles album cover, on records (by Miles Davis, Bob Dylan, Grace Slick, Nico, Tim Hardin, and R.E.M.), in books and documentaries, in reissued recordings, CDs, and posters, in comedy clubs, in college classes, in the Columbia University archives, in the Museum of Television and Radio, and on the Internet, America continues to honor its unabashed hero of free speech. So strong is this sentiment that Saint

Lenny could return, if only in celluloid form, to the city that once had made him an outlaw—New York.

On the evening of October 21, 1998, Lenny Bruce (never R.I.P.) ventured back to the West Village for a triumphal performance. What a mind-twist of an evening, the night that Robert Weide's documentary, *Lenny Bruce: Swear to Tell the Truth*, opened in Manhattan. To a packed house of die hard fans, Lenny banged out on film some of his most controversial bits—"Christ and Moses," "Eleanor Roosevelt's Tits," and "Selling Out Your Country" (or "The Hot-Lead Enema"). Flippantly, he boasted about his notoriety: "I have been on television…mostly newsreels." Pausing for a reflective moment, he added: "The reason I've been busted a lot these last couple of years is because of religious point-of-view. That's what it's all been about." Satirical and serious. Time to tell how his comedy came to be on trial. To that end, Weide's documentary replayed a powerful excerpt from John Magnuson's 1965 *Performance Film*:

> I figured out after four years why I got arrested so many times. Dig what happens—it's been a comedy of errors…I do my act at, perhaps, eleven o'clock at night; little do I know that at eleven A.M. the next morning, before the grand jury somewhere, there's another guy doing my act who's introduced as Lenny Bruce *in substance*. "Here he is: Lenny Bruce, *in substance*." A peace officer…does the act. The grand jury watches him work, and they go: "That stinks!" But *I* get busted. And the irony is that I have to go to court and defend *his* act.…
>
> Now the cop is going to do the act before the judge who never heard of Lenny Bruce before.…"I don't remember the whole act, your honor, but I made these notes.…Ah, let's see now: 'Catholic,' 'asshole,' 'shit,' 'in the park,' 'tits,' 'n 'shit,' 'n 'Catholics,' 'Jews,' 'n 'shit.' That's about all I remember. That's about the general tenor of the act." **CD**

That night of the living dead was his. The outlaw had become hero. So sweet the revenge, now to be canonized in film with the routines and words that once had condemned him in court.

They all sat there, packed into the Film Forum theater, cheering and crying as the documentary brought the "sick" comedian back from the dead. Jack Sobel, who had managed Lenny in the early years, was there to pay tribute, even though his faithful and skillful work was once repaid by Lenny's devious 1962 plot to ditch him, with a letter signed "Love," no less. Don Friedman, the guy who staged Lenny's historic 1961 Carnegie Hall Concert, gladly joined in the chorus of praise—forgetting the fact that Lenny once betrayed him by letting someone else "cut into" his nightclub booking action. It was ninety-four minutes of pure ACLUism…the disturbing agony, the eternal lesson, and the postmortem triumph. When it was over, well-wishers lined up to shake the hand of Martin Garbus, one of many lawyers Lenny had hired and then fired. They were all there, Nat Hentoff (the devoted columnist), Judge Allen G. Schwartz (the dedicated friend and lawyer), and Richard Kuh (the ardent New York obscenity prosecutor)—one big First Amendment family.

Explanations

HOW COULD ALL of this happen? How could a comic, vilified by the state and abandoned by so many, be resurrected as a free speech hero? There are at least four explanations.

First, commercial exploitation—the repackaging of Lenny's words and image. Example: his album *To Is a Preposition, Come Is a Verb* was posthumously renamed *The Story of Lenny: What I Was Arrested For*; the record company even slipped the disc into a new cover with a station-house mugshot. In time, the Lenny Bruce story became ripe for commercial transformation. As a *Los Angeles Times* critic observed: "The ingredients are all there: the hip philosopher, the junky saint, the crusader against hypocrisy, the lynch victim, the martyr to free speech." Alive, Lenny Bruce was the target of the criminal law; dead, he is the object of intellectual property. Yesterday's comic prophet became today's commercial profit.

Second, there is Hollywood romanticism—showbiz readily taps into "Bruce's lingering cult appeal," as the *New York Times* once billed it. Thus tinsel-town *re*created Lenny when it created *Lenny*, the 1974 movie starring Dustin Hoffman. With the appeal of a docudrama, Lenny Bruce was offered up in heroic black-and-white. In the words of a *Newsweek* film reviewer: "[T]one him down, sweeten him up, and turn this hard-driving hipster into a good guy's truth crusade"—that's how they did it. Alive, Lenny was a reality-check; dead, he is a celluloid fantasy.

Next, there is the generational explanation—the phenomenon of the rebellious ways of '60s hippies easing into the accepted beliefs of new millennium yuppies. In the "battle between the hard hats and the peaceniks, the over-thirties and the youth, [the] law-and-order [and] the libertarians," as Bruce's New York prosecutor described the intergenerational conflict, the counterculture won out. Those who once grooved to Julian Barry's psychedelic play, *Lenny* (1971), were now comfortable with E! TV's 1998 adoring rendition of Lenny as a cultural maverick. A new generation was no longer offended by his attacks on traditional values. It is a case of embracing the prodigal son, but *only* after he enters the mainstream. Alive, Lenny was antiestablishment; dead, he is Establishment.

And finally, there is cultural schizophrenia—the inability to tolerate the dissenter during his lifetime versus the compulsion to love him after his death. "Posthumous sainthood," a *Ramparts* article on Bruce declared, "comes only to those whom the living could not face." Shortly after Lenny died, the public embraced the guilt-laden message of Simon and Garfunkel's "7:00 News" (1966). The song's words were set to the accompaniment of "Silent Night": "In Los Angeles, Lenny Bruce died of what was believed to be an overdose of narcotics." Shortly after the peak of his prosecutions, Lenny released his autobiography (1965); it bombed. Yet by 1972, six years after his death, a published volume of his bits sold a half million copies. Alive, Lenny was a clear and present danger; dead, he is socially redeeming value.

No single explanation suffices; the reality of Bruce's resurrection is colored by all of them. Nonetheless, individually and collectively, these explanations reveal a peculiar and pathetic notion of freedom—that First Amendment liberty requires martyrdom. In other words, society's free speech rights evolve at the expense of cultural outlaws, as death eventually vindicates their crusades to liberate our language and open our minds. A kind of baptism by burial. Then, and only then, can we accept the Lenny Bruces of the world.

But need life and law be this way? Could *People v. Bruce* have been decided differently in Lenny's lifetime—without castrating his comedy? These questions demand that we reconsider the relationship between law and subversive comedy, and between how Lenny's case was argued and decided and how it might have been argued and decided. Simply, things may well have ended differently—at least as a matter of law.

So much of the myth and hype about Lenny Bruce and his struggles for free speech ignore some basic complexities—for example, how hard he made it for his lawyers to defend him and the courts to acquit him, and how radically different his conception of the judicial system was from the ways it actually operated. This does not mean that it would have been impossible to have saved him, just difficult.

Honey Harlowe, his free-spirited ex-wife, once chastised him: "You're defying the court so openly that they *have* to make an example of you."

Lenny replied, "You want to bet *who wins?*"

It was a rigged wager, for Honey understood the larger point: "Well, that depends on what you call winning."

He was *the* confrontational comic. The need to be outspoken, even offensive, was part of Lenny's genetic makeup. It was an adrenaline rush for him. It was also key to his faith in free speech: "[T]he First Amendment is…the only strength our country has….A country can only be strong when it knows all about the bad—the worst, worst things. When it knows about the bad, then it can protect itself." Implicit in this is a core principle of freedom. If the First Amendment is worth anything, its worth must derive, in important part, from our commitment to protect the cultural outlaw while alive, while offensive, and while extreme to the point of blaspheming every damned thing deemed sacred. Just how that is to be done, if at all, is what makes the *People v. Bruce* story so relevant.

Lenny Bruce was a comic who cared less about being a dead First Amendment hero than about being a living performer, free of censorship. "I really don't want to be the great wounded bird, flying and trying to break through those weights so we can bring free expression to everybody. I'm a guy who has to work." He sought free speech *for the living*. What follows, then, is the complex and tragic story of a free speech hero who didn't want to be one.

1

COMEDY AS COMMENTARY

We comedians are all entertainers because we entertain. But there is an artist at work in some of us, as well. And the artist is involved with interpreting the world—interpreting the universe around us through his filter, through his prism. Same as a painter does. Same as a composer or a serious writer does. He looks at the values that the culture presents to him, and he has a take on that. The comedian who does that is more than just a comedian. He's something of a commentator.

—*George Carlin*

Obscenity or Blasphemy?

Sydney has never seen...a public performance of such blasphemy.
—*Sydney Sun* (September 7, 1962)

HIS GIG AT Sydney's Aarons Hotel opened Thursday night. Come Friday morning, it was history, cancelled due to a "blasphemous account of the Crucifixion" and a "steady stream of dirty words." Lenny, so the complaints ran, had breached both the law and the people's faith. The commands of God and man could not countenance such comedy.

Blasphemy had been illegal for ages. "Profane scoffing," observed the great seventeenth-century British jurist William Blackstone, long had been a crime warranting "fine and imprisonment, or other infamous corporal punishment." No laughing matter.

The ancient Greek philosopher Anaxagoras was cast into a dungeon when he mocked the popular gods as fanciful playthings. And then there were all those other blasphemers from Jesus to the Quakers. As late as 1971, two Pittsburgh shopkeepers were charged with blasphemy for displaying publicly a "wanted" poster of a hippie Christ. So, Lenny Bruce was bucking the lessons of history when he hit Sydney with his raw line of satire: "We Jews killed Christ, and if he comes back, we'll kill him again!" 🔘

But Australia is not America. We have the First Amendment. Our comics—including those who ridicule religion—are to be protected. It is the American creed.

Ephraim London, one of Lenny's lawyers, made it his business to defend that bedrock American principle. In 1952, London took on the National Legion of Decency and Cardinal Francis Spellman when he challenged an attempt by New York officials to censor a "sacrilegious" movie denounced by moralists. The Supreme Court sided with the "blasphemers": the state "has no legitimate interest in protecting any or all religions from views which are distasteful to them. It is not the business of government in our nation to suppress real or imagined attacks" upon religion.

That should have settled it. Whatever the laws of Sydney, Lenny Bruce's American acts were beyond prosecution *for blasphemy*. And, in a way, they were. For Lenny was never formally charged with blasphemy. His sin, if there were one, was obscenity—that cousin of blasphemy. According to the official record, the State had no objection to the comedian's frontal attacks on organized religion. What purportedly bothered officialdom were all the "motherfucker" and "tits-and-ass" remarks, those verbal offenses committed in dark, smoke-filled jazz and folk clubs.

The words, then, and not the parties against whom they were directed, landed Lenny in jail. That, at least, was the prosecutors' line. For them to prevail in court, a Lenny Bruce bit could only be dirty words: vulgarity divorced from any redeeming social value.

From Godfrey to Gazunka!

The basic division in current American and British topical satire
is between Lenny Bruce and all the others.
—Nat Hentoff (1963)

LENNY BRUCE WASN'T always a social critic-comic. When he appeared on *The Arthur Godfrey Show* in 1948 (a year after he changed his name from Leonard Schneider and three years after he was discharged from the Navy for wearing women's clothing), Lenny and his act were hokey. He was a living black-and-white Brylcreem ad: greased-down hair, bow-tie, wide lapels. His movements only slightly exaggerated the stock-in-trade gestures of comic impersonators. There he was, doing Cagney and even Hepburn: "Kiss me Gregory. Naaaaw, kiss me Gregory. Naw Gregory, naw you can peck!" For the most part, Lenny echoed his burlesque-comedian mother's routine—virtually the same act that Sally Marr did in a 1942 USO show for sailors (with seventeen-year-old Lenny sitting among the uniformed members of the audience). He mimicked Sally's zany impressions, such as Bogart talking in a German dialect: "All right, Veagah! Drop the schmeagah!" Not political, not philosophical, not satirical, and certainly not controversial…but enough to put his name on the marquee of New York's famous Strand Theater in 1949.

In time, clean-cut gave way to raunch, when Lenny worked Southern California's strip-joint circuit from 1953 to 1956. He found comic liberation in those "burlesque shithouses," as he called them. Comedy born in the bump-and-grind of Downey's Cup & Saucer and in the debauchery of The Cobblestone, that libidinal honky-tonk at the wrong end of Lankershim Boulevard. Both the act and the marquee had changed. Now, the lights bore the names of "China Doll," "Lora Lei," and "Marnee," the dancers ogled at L.A.'s Strip City. Taking a trade-cue from his wife, Hot Honey Harlowe, a stripper he met in Baltimore, Lenny upstaged "the girls" when he emceed clad in *nothing* but black socks and shoes at Duffy's Gaieties, with Honey singing *Granada* and mother Marr keeping a watchful eye on the raincoat clientele. Such Freudian frenzies were a far cry from the family-friendly "Ka-zam!" magic routines he had performed with Honey only a few years earlier in New York. And by any measure, his new calling was not the podiatrist's life that his father, Mickey Schneider, had envisioned for him.

Lenny's new reputation spread wildly: a nude comic in new demand. "The cheesier the dive, the freer Lenny became." His wild stage life resonated with all those crazy sex and drug parties at his Palm Avenue house—really a one-bedroom cottage with a picket fence and pink satin bedroom drapes, thanks to Honey the "seamstress."

But the days at the dives were ending; physical crassness would give way to cerebral pointedness—and verbal crassness.

Steve Allen: "We've decided that, once a month, we will book a comedian who'll offend *everybody*....[He's] a man who will disturb a great many social groups. I'm serious. His satirical comments refer to many things not ordinarily discussed on television...." With those words, Steve Allen—the gutsy critic of the Blacklist Era in Hollywood—introduced the new comedian to the new medium. "So, ladies and gentlemen," continued the host of *The Steve Allen Show*, "here is a very shocking comedian, the most shocking comedian of our time, a young man who is skyrocketing to fame—Lenny Bruce!" While nowhere as shocking as his strip-club highjinks, Lenny's act was daring for his late '50s TV audience.

"I have a reputation for being sort of controversial and irreverent," he admitted. And then he showed why: "There are words that offend me. Let's see: Governor Faubus, segregation....The shows that exploit homosexuality, narcotics, and prostitution under the guise of helping these societal problems." ⓒⅾ Blending serious commentary with fanciful comedy, he did a drug bit, the tale of an adolescent who accidentally gets high on airplane glue. "I'm the Louis Pasteur of Junkiedom!" the stoned boy proudly exclaims.

What Steve Allen dared to present, however, was received much more cautiously by other television celebrities. For example, in a November 26, 1958, letter to Lenny's manager, Ed Sullivan expressed his concern that once Lenny took to the cameras he would mouth "whatever he damn well pleases." That very much troubled the Great Stone Face. He needed assurances; indeed, he *demanded* them. He insisted that Bruce prepare an advance script of "exactly" everything he planned to say on the show. Only with such "built-in safeguards" would Sullivan present Lenny Bruce to the world. Of course, such "safeguards" were anathema to Lenny. No deal. He never appeared on the "really big show." Even so, his *shticks* were drawing more and more attention, though no one was quite sure about Lenny Bruce and what he was doing.

It caught on. *Time* later gave it a name, "sick comedy," and featured Lenny. He was a "sicknick," one of those comedians who dispense "social criticism liberally laced with cyanide…[with] jolly ghoulishness…[and with] a personal and highly disturbing hostility toward all the world." He was not only a "sick comedian," he was the "high priest of the sick comedians." At last, he was ready to move his comedy to another level.

Just as TV had momentarily tamed Lenny, the jazz scene permanently released his inhibitions. He did burlesque gigs with jazz accompanists such as Red Mitchell, Hampton Hawes, Philly Joe Jones, Elmo Hope, Lorraine Geller, and Carl Perkins. Sometimes, as at The Cobblestone in Southern California, he had his own combo with whom he performed: Kenny Drew on the piano; Joe Maini, tenor sax; Herb Geller, alto sax; Lawrence Marable, drums; and Leroy Vinnegar, bass. Jazz's jumble and jive suited him. He liked the "loose," "funky," and "soulful" forms that are the trademarks of jazz, and read about those forms and the jazz lifestyle in *Down Beat* and Ralph Gleason's *Jazz Quarterly*. Lenny was so inspired by jazz as an art form that he borrowed much from it for his evolving kind of stand-up comedy. In the clubs, up to one half or more of his bits were sometimes pitched to the guys in the band—if the audience came along, fine; if not, that was fine, too. He socialized with the jazz set; he loved the jazz life with its alien ethos, its ebb and flow spirit, its menacing eclecticism, its chaotic atmosphere—in short, its *freedom*.

The nightclubs brought out the hipster, the drug user, and the troublemaker in him. Black music, white powder, and blue comedy mixed to make stage acts that challenged the gods of heaven and earth. It was Cab Calloway, Miles Davis, Charlie Parker, and Little Richard all tumbled into one, verbalized in ways light years beyond the clever imagination of Mort Sahl. "Conveying the particular impact of Bruce," as Nat Hentoff described it, was "almost as difficult as verbalizing about Thelonious Monk, Ornette Coleman, or those few other jazzmen who move in a distinctly personal nimbus and who have to be seen and directly felt to be fully believed." You had to *hear* and *see* him to believe him, to sense what his *live* stand-up, shoot-down, blow-up, zig-zag comedy was like. His records, by and large, could only convey a part of the extraordinary dynamic that first made him famous, and then infamous.

At a time when *The Nun's Story* was debuting in movie theaters and below-the-knee hemlines were popular, Lenny Bruce was busting through the walls of predictability. He was, in his own prophetic words, "chang[ing] the architecture" of comedy in America. Ad-lib and *spritzes*, combined with unheard-of candor, were the buttresses of that new art form. In the fall of 1959, at the Hungry i in San Francisco, Lenny laid it out autobiographically in his famous, but little performed, twenty-minute bit titled "The Palladium." There, he took aim at the status quo in show business; he "castigated its whoring after status, its preposterous smugness, its crybaby sentimentality, and its secret contempt for the public it fawns." To do that, he hurled comic grenades at the edifices of hypocrisy in the hope of leveling the past and reconstructing the future along the lines of something radically more honest, more human, and more provocative. As "The Palladium" bit reveals, he was quite aware of the personal and professional costs of such provocations. But that would not stop him.

Lenny Bruce was making a case for a new kind of comedy. "[M]y humor is mostly indictment," he explained. And indict he did—with charges leveled against the officialdom of Rome, Hollywood, Washington, Vegas, or any sanctimonious potentate. In a more reflective moment, he added: "I am part of everything I indict." Lenny Bruce, the comic inquisitor, would indict anybody, any institution, or any cause for a (pensive) laugh.

People couldn't believe their ears. He gave public voice to their most guarded thoughts about religion, prejudice, sex, and violence. He violated taboos with murderous impunity. There was never a safe seat in the house, no place for the detached observer to avoid the shock of recognition. "The expectancy in the nightclub [was always] laced with anxiety," Hentoff stated. "How far will he go *tonight*?" Rather like an "intimidating panther," observed Arthur Gelb, Bruce prowled and bit sharply, "leaving the stage strewn with carrion."

He loved to walk the fine line, that place forever undefined between the heaven and hell of what is deemed socially acceptable. "Are there any niggers here tonight?" he would ask in the middle of a bit. Shocked silence. Then, the hum of whispers: *What was that?* Before the people's jaws dropped to their knees, he'd say it again: "Are there any *niggers* here tonight?" He was making liberals—his defend-ers—uncomfortable: *Does he really have to go that low for laughs?* Yes. Because it was all part of a comic campaign to bleed racist words of their poisonous meaning. By bringing the *N*-word into the open, Lenny filched it from bigots and redefined it on his own we-are-all-created-equal terms. A "strategy of subversion," is how Harvard Law Professor Randall Kennedy tagged it almost four decades later in his book, *Nigger*. Part of that strategy was to be an equal-opportunity "bigot." Within no time, the bit moved to "kikes, spics, guineas, greaseballs, Yids, Polacks," and even "Irish micks." Bigotry knew no bounds. The result: there was no one left to single out. He thus stunned his listeners into thinking about unthinkable things.

Lenny stalked reality, and then staged it. He invented *comic real-ism*: "Let me tell you the truth," he once said. "The truth is what *is*. And what should be is a fantasy, a terrible, terrible lie someone gave the people long ago." High ideals, mighty truths, or core beliefs: they were shams. Behind the curtain stood a man, not a wizard—a con man, a hustler who fools himself and others about his should-be world. "We're all hustlers. We're all as honest as we can afford to be," he declared. And so the hustler and his hypocrisy became the butts of Lenny's comedy, the target of his attack on the *zug gornischt* (say nothing) culture.

One of the prime targets of his relentless indictments was institu-tionalized religion. Take, for example, his "Christ and Moses" bit. ⓒⒹ The skit opens with the two biblical figures standing in the back of St. Patrick's Cathedral; Cardinal Francis Spellman is deep into his ser-mon. When Archbishop Fulton Sheen interrupts him, Spellman protests: "Stop bugging me." Informed of their heavenly visitors, Spellman panics: "Did Christ bring the family? What's his mother's name?…Mary Hail? Hail Mary? Hairy Mary?…Oh, Christ, look at the front door. The lepers are coming!" Flesh is falling on the polished floors. Spellman is frantic. He calls Rome: "Hullo, John? Fran, in New York. Listen, a coupla the kids dropped in….Yeah, you know them." Once the pope realizes who the two VIPs are, Spellman explodes: "Well, we've gotta do something….Put 'em up in your place….What am I paying protection for?…Look, all I know is that I'm up to my ass in crutches and wheelchairs here!…They're in the back, way in the back…*Of course, they're white!*" All said, Lenny had reduced the Church hierarchy to hucksterism; equality to bigotry; compassion to intolerance. The vernacular became vulgar.

He was crossing the line. Rude assaults on religion and the Catholic Church would cost him, but not by way of any formal blasphemy charge. What would bring on the heat, what would enable his prosecutions, were those ribald references to "cocksuckers" (S.F.), "*schmuck*" (L.A.), "tits" (Chicago), and "fucking" (New York). Those junkie-induced *shticks*—the jazz drummer's riffs on the verb "to come," the unrestrained exposés on "dykes" and "fags," the lurid tale of the Lone Ranger *doing* Tonto, and Silver, too!—all would contribute to the charge of "obscene Lenny."

Whatever his defense lawyers would claim, Lenny Bruce was surely no Jonathan Swift ("I never heard of Jonathan Swift," Lenny once said) or François Rabelais. Rather, what he did in life vacillated wildly between two poles: call them good and evil, moral and nihilistic, pure and dirty, or lawful and lawless. Psychologically, Lenny was torn between the "impulse to be a saint and the temptation to be a criminal." Philosophically, he aspired for the best in humankind (maybe), while he was prepared to accept the worst (definitely). For Nat Hentoff, his friend and defender, Lenny was neither a cynic nor a pessimist. If anything, his philosophy was solipsism—"You don't know anything about anybody but you. Just you live in that thing. You always live alone," is how Bruce once verbalized it. From this singular vantage point, he became increasingly preoccupied with the "elusiveness of any absolute, including absolute truth." Pursuing the big T kind of truth, he believed, gave us not only a false sense of reality, but in time it made us confident in ways that we cannot be, righteous in ways that we could not ever be, and hypocritical in ways that we could never admit to being.

In his everyday life, too, Lenny played out this split-take on living, this unexplainable tension between life as valued and life as lived. "I am heinously guilty of the paradoxes I assail in our society," he readily admitted. Indeed, Don Friedman, his friend and producer, thought as much: "There were two sides to Lenny. On the one hand, he was such a con man. On the other hand, he was human and funny, wanting to reveal lies in the subconscious in order to bring them to the light of consciousness." Though he was torn, Lenny spoke out, mindful of the inconsistencies life imposes. In all of these ways and many others, the comedy of Lenny Bruce was deeply rooted in political, social, and religious commentary. Without them, there could be no Lenny Bruce bits.

To some, Lenny was a "sort of white James Meredith in that metaphysical Mississippi called Puritanism." He was a comic sage, "a scholar of sleaze," who revealed "the gap between the real and the official." "Un-coded comedy" is what Jack Sobel, his manager, called it. Hentoff described Lenny's technique as a "verbal sleight of hand": "By stringing together enough Yiddish firecracker jazz jargon" and various other devices, "he reaches his audience with his more serious assaults before they are quite aware that they themselves are also included among his targets." Boldly, Lenny unmasked the masked man; he "delighted in exploring why certain words were forbidden—and then demystifying them," Hentoff added. He challenged "community standards" by questioning whether the community *actually* held to its Sunday standards. "What I want people to dig," Lenny said, "is the lie." ⓒⅅ Social conventions of speech sheltered the lies; vulgarity, by contrast, outed them; it served up life in its raw and raunchy form. Rebelliously, satirically, and honestly, he took aim—time and again—at the "should" world with vivid reports from the "is" world. "He hated hypocrisy," Harry Kalven Jr.—one of Lenny's lawyers—remarked, "he was almost insanely honest." Lenny put it as only he could: "I'm pissing on the velvet, that's what I'm doing."

To others, Lenny cut too hard, too close, and too often. "I'm a surgeon with a scalpel for false values," he once quipped. He specialized in humor with an edge, so much so that a London *Times* obituary claimed that some felt "Bruce sought to disturb rather than amuse." Kenneth Tyson, the *London Observer* critic, put it this way: "He goes out to do a rush job of psychoanalysis on the audience. He…root[s] out their deepest inhibitions, their deepest repressions, all the things they're scared of, the things that are never talked about. And [he] holds them up to the most relentless scrutiny, analyzes them, tries to force the audience to come to terms with reality, actual unspeakable reality." Less charitably, *Commonweal* reported that Lenny was viewed as a "child who could not accept the careful accommodations of adulthood, the arranged pretenses and self-protective structures of grown-up life...."

Lenny Bruce's comedy always invited diverse assessments. His fans were unfailing in their dedication to him and his work, no matter how controversial. Conversely, his enemies were unfailing in their antagonism toward him and his work, no matter how commendable. Hentoff captured something of that divided sense in 1963 when he wrote: "After an encounter with Bruce on one of his more demonic nights...you may look at the mirror with gnawing doubt that you indeed know who you are, or rather, what you really feel. About sex. About justice. About Negroes. About being a Jew." *Demonic...gnawing...look in the mirror*—tough words from an admirer of Lenny Bruce's *comedy* underscore how it affected his audiences.

His devil-may-care mindset provoked the best, conservatives and liberals alike. Take, for example, the felt need of the American Guild of Variety Artists, the entertainers' union, to reprimand him. While his obscenity prosecutions would surely be seen by Guild artists today as part of the harassment of the arts, back in 1960 that same body of liberal performers tagged Lenny's antics as a "vulgar display of bad taste." In the early 1960s, Lenny once opened a show for the noted singer Mel Tormé. During Bruce's performance, as a *San Francisco Examiner* critic described the incident, Tormé turned to a friend and said, "'Who is this disgusting creep? I'm ashamed to be on the same bill with [him].' Bruce overheard just enough, inserting a quick, 'You're ashamed? How do [you think] I feel?'" But the Mel Tormés were not the only ones who took exception to Bruce's comic quips. His bits could even offend the likes of angry hipsters such as Jack Kerouac, who said of Lenny, "I hate him! He hates everything, he hates life!"

However his critics labeled him, Lenny redefined the relations among comedy, the human experience, and the law. When Lenny made private talk public, when he tapped into the taboos, he became prey for prosecutors. Lenny was now uninhibited, robust, and wide-open—wide-open to all sorts of attacks.

The wit, the drama, the irony, the Yiddish nuance (*oy vey!*), the finger-popping spontaneity were for naught once the vice-hounds got a whiff of those four-letter (and ten-letter) words. Never mind the message: "If God made the body, and the body is dirty, the fault lies with the manufacturer." Never mind the social value of comic commentary: "What's wrong with appealing to the prurient interest? We appeal to the *killing* interest." This was sex talk; these were dirty words; it was all *obscene*.

Lenny was demanding conversational freedom as his constitutional right. His "comedy of dissent" openly proclaimed a "right to be disgusting." The nightclub was the free speech podium where he brought that right to life. But, take free speech to that point, and one thing is certain: the Law will demand its due. As Kalven—a noted First Amendment scholar—observed: "To be as honest as he was, and as perceptive as he was at the same time, was a dangerous combination....In a sense, he was bound to be arrested." Or as Jimmy Breslin put it: he said "bad words...in a nightclub and they screamed for the cops." "They" were typically prosecutors, not patrons. It was as though the system had proclaimed: "Cuff him, and don't worry about the fine points—let the courts deal with the constitutional details." That was just about how it went in the cities where he was busted.

No Laughing Matter

THE FUNNY THING about Lenny Bruce is that he was, at times, *not* funny.

"I wasn't very funny tonight. Sometimes I'm not. I'm not a comedian, I'm Lenny Bruce." So he confessed at the close of a San Francisco performance—the one he gave right after his first obscenity bust. By design, his bits were not always funny. That is part of what distinguished him from the comic pack. Funny or not, what Lenny Bruce did on stage defies simple definition. That is why his audiences were uncertain, his critics never quite sure, and his prosecutors often at a loss about what to make of his routines as a matter of law.

The obscenity busts took their toll. They wore him down, trial by trial, dollar by dollar, year after year. Between 1961 and 1966, he gradually became a pathetic caricature of the *Time* magazine man he once was. From the Nehru to raincoat to denim jacket periods, he took more drugs and more chances. Now, the law was his main routine.

Lenny summoned the proceedings of the courtroom onto the stage, while he tried to do his stage *shticks* in court. "He lost his sense of reality and no longer knew where he and his art left off and the rest of the world and the law began," observed Edward de Grazia, one of his lawyers. Toward the end, "[h]is bits lost spirit, originality, spontaneity, energy; they became boring, even depressing; often they did not provoke laughter or thought anymore." Well, not entirely.

A surviving video from his August 1965 performance at Basin Street West in San Francisco evidences Lenny's Dostoyevskian obsession with the law and comic madness. Even this late in his life and in the dark dungeon-like atmosphere of the club, one could still sense his comic and satirical greatness, though it came more slowly and not as often now. A badly beaten man, he read from trial transcripts, did truncated and misplaced bits from his famous acts, and capped the show by hustling pedestrians near the offstage door: "Hello, how are you? Dirty Lenny in here. Dirty Lenny is going on soon."

Only a few years earlier, before depression claimed him, he didn't have to barker. He was so much more alive (even "romantic") when he closed an act: "And so, because I love you, fuck you and good night!"

2
THE FORCE OF
AN OPINION

The First Amendment does not protect "speech which is
outrightly lewd and indecent."

—*William J. Brennan Jr.*

Previous page: Supreme Court Justice William J. Brennan Jr., who wrote the major-ity opinion in the landmark First Amendment case, Roth v. United States *(1957)*

Aiding and Abetting

SOME OF THE trouble Lenny Bruce had with the law traces back to what Justice William J. Brennan Jr. penned decades ago. In his early years—both as a justice on the New Jersey Supreme Court and as a junior justice on the U.S. Supreme Court—Brennan displayed an ambivalence about the strength of First Amendment rights in the arena of erotic expression. While there was a good measure of free-speech sensitivity in his opinions, there were concessions to the power of the State to regulate morality. Those concessions were sometimes troubling, sometimes ill-defined—in ways indicating that Brennan, for all his advanced thinking, was still a man of his times.

"There are 'narrowly limited classes of speech' which are not given the protection of the First Amendment....By universal agreement one such exception is speech which is outrightly lewd and indecent." So Brennan put it in a 1953 obscenity opinion for the New Jersey high court. There, he granted that the state's authority to preserve "decency and good order" was broad enough to prohibit any show with a "dominant effect" of dispensing "dirt for dirt's sake." He was careful, nonetheless, to articulate a variety of speech-protective norms to guard against censorship based on a "highly subjective view of morality." Hence, he asked:

> Does every reference to...the sex relationship *ipso facto* classify the presentation as lewd and indecent?

Does the presentation become such if the censor's view is that the subject matter or its treatment is not fit for commercial exhibition to patrons of places of public entertainment while suitable for presentation before medical societies or under educational or social welfare auspices?

Can the presentation be banned in toto as lewd and indecent because a part—even a minute part—is coarse, vulgar, or profane?

Those were precisely the questions that would be raised a decade later in the obscenity prosecutions of Lenny Bruce. Unfortunately, in 1953, Brennan's answer was more rhetorical than useful: "These and like questions have not always been answered the same way."

· When William Brennan took his seat on the U.S. Supreme Court, he entertained the same questions, and "answered" them with much the same ambivalence. He did so in his majority opinion in *Roth v. United States*, the controversial 1957 precedent that, in a way, enabled the prosecutions of Bruce and countless other moral-code breakers.

The story of *Roth* is complicated, and much needs to be told before its nuances and its relationship to Lenny Bruce are understood. Here, then, is how that story begins.

SAM ROTH, A New York publisher of risqué literature, was sentenced to five years and fined $5,000 for sending an "obscene, lewd, lascivious, and filthy" publication called *American Aphrodite* through the U.S. mail. David S. Alberts, a Los Angeles book distributor, was placed on two-year probation on condition of serving sixty days and paying a $500 fine—this for distributing and advertising such "obscene and indecent" books as *Sword of Desire*, *She Made It Pay*, and *The Business Side of the Oldest Business*. On appeal, both Roth and Alberts stipulated to having violated their respective state obscenity laws, though they challenged the constitutionality of those statutes. The two cases were consolidated, and came to be known by the single and famous title, *Roth v. United States*.

Back in 1956, before his case had come to the Supreme Court, David Alberts was on trial in the Beverly Hills Municipal Court. Not far away—up Santa Monica Boulevard to Cahuenga, turn left—Lenny Bruce was busy doing the dives where comedy was squeezed in between shots of bourbon and shots of flesh. Duffy's Gayeties was the parlor of the moment. The owner of the club, Rocky Lo Fusello from Chicago, had given Lenny full reign; the place sorely needed a jolt of life. So Lenny went to work: for starters, a five-piece junkie jazz band and a half-dozen hooker/strippers. Then, spotlights perched, sin-red curtains hung, sawdust on the floors, he banged out new and dirty material. Just to give the act a little more class, Lenny wore a tux...at least that's what he wore when he didn't dart out nude, pissing into a knothole on the stage floor. He mixed it up, the band whooped it up, the crowd ate it up, and Rocky had a heart attack.

In those days before L.A.'s raving-mad traffic, it was only a twenty-minute drive from Duffy's, where Lenny was performing, to the Beverly Hills courthouse, where David Alberts was defending himself against obscenity charges under Section 311 of the California Penal Code. Several years later, Lenny would make his debut in that same courthouse on Crescent Drive—charged, like Alberts, with a Section 311 violation. Stanley Fleishman, Alberts's lawyer, was the same man whom Lenny would call frantically eight years later to assess the trial tactics of his lead New York attorney. At this point, however, Lenny was too occupied with his own stage antics to bother with somebody else's day in court.

Sweet Victory or Disaster?

MONDAY, APRIL 22, 1957: thirty-two days after he was confirmed by the Senate—with Joe McCarthy railing against him—William Brennan took his seat on the Supreme Court as it heard oral arguments in case Nos. 582 and 61, *Roth v. United States* and *Alberts v. California*. He was the junior player sitting alongside constitutional giants: William O. Douglas, Hugo Black, John Harlan, Earl Warren, and Brennan's former Harvard Law School professor, Felix Frankfurter.

The Court Chamber, where the *Roth–Alberts* oral arguments took place, is a monumental paean to the law's grandeur. Under the forty-four-foot ceiling supported by twenty-four columns of Italian marble, the constitutional dialogue began just as Justices Tom Clark and William O. Douglas quietly distributed pornographic materials to their colleagues on the bench, out of the sight of the people in the Court gallery. Prior to oral arguments, the Justice Department had shipped those materials to the Court to demonstrate what kind of filth would be legitimized if the Justices were to reverse the convictions of Sam Roth and David Alberts. Hence, in the very quarters where decorum and propriety were the rule, some of the Justices eyed "stroke" mags as they listened to the nuances of American procedural and constitutional law. If only Lenny Bruce had known, it might have made a great bit.

Justice Frankfurter dominated the dialogue, peppering the parties with procedural, evidentiary, and jurisdictional questions. With professorial fervor, he tried repeatedly to pin Roth's counsel down to *exactly* what his position was. The more he asked, the worse it got. Exasperated, the Justice said: "You can't just swim in the midst of the Pacific Ocean in these matters. You've got to get some footing on some...terra firma." Frankfurter also chided Alberts's attorney, Stanley Fleishman, for raising arguments not properly addressed in the lower courts.

Throughout the exchange, Brennan spoke only once, and not for very long. He asked the Deputy District Attorney from California how to identify the offending frame, namely, that point at which an erotic movie crosses the line from the constitutionally protected to the legally obscene. The response was non-responsive—no defining point, just common knowledge: "Every man in the street knows what obscenity is."

When all was said and done, these were the kind of oral arguments that made it all too easy for the audience to drift off and stare at the sculpted marble panels surrounding the chamber. No one reasonably could have guessed either the outcome of the case or the landmark status it would later attain.

Maurice Rosenfield, Hugh Hefner's attorney, had submitted an *amicus* brief in support of Sam Roth, whose conviction the Court upheld (7 to 2 vote) along with that of David Alberts (6 to 3 vote) on Monday, June 24, 1957. While the judgment of the Court and some of the language in Justice Brennan's majority opinion surely must have troubled Rosenfield, there were aspects of the decision that promised a new measure of First Amendment freedom. But, on this busy day, Rosenfield could not have imagined how all of this would affect one of his future clients—Lenny Bruce. Years later, Rosenfield would be part of a dynamic team of appellate lawyers who would represent Lenny before the Illinois Supreme Court.

Positioned on the far right of the bench, under two figures depicting the "majesty of the law" and the "power of government," Justice Brennan announced the Court's judgments and opinion in *Roth–Alberts*. It sounded like a tribute to the Roman god Janus, the great gatekeeper with two faces gazing in opposite directions.

There was the conservative face. Of this side of the opinion, Charles Rembar, a leading First Amendment expert, observed: *Roth* was "hailed as a sweet victory by the proponents of censorship, and regarded as a disaster by libertarians." Here is why, to quote from Brennan:

> [T]his Court has always assumed that obscenity is not protected by the freedoms of speech and press.
>
> [I]mplicit in the history of the First Amendment is the rejection of obscenity as utterly without socially redeeming importance.
>
> There are certain well-defined and narrowly limited classes of speech, the prevention and punishment of which have never been thought to raise any constitutional problem. These include the lewd and obscene....It has been well observed that such utterances are no essential part of the exposition of ideas, and are of such slight social value as a step to truth that any benefit that may be derived from them is clearly outweighed by the social interest in order and morality.

Obscenity was, by definition, worthless—no analysis or balancing necessary. For prosecutors, that meant that, if they succeeded in branding a book, movie, play, or performance "obscene," that was typically the end of the matter—off to the local holding-tank with the moral offender. Such a fate awaited Lenny at the hands of some judges all too willing to find that his *shticks* were no essential part of the exposition of important ideas.

In contrast, there was the liberal face. Of that side of the opinion, Charles Rembar also remarked: "[*Roth*] contained within it (nearly hidden, and at the time unnoticed) the seed of future freedom-giving cases." Here, to quote from Justice Brennan, is the language that inspired that assessment:

> [S]ex and obscenity are not synonymous....
>
> [Obscene material is] material having a tendency to excite lustful thoughts....
>
> All ideas having even the slightest importance—unorthodox ideas, controversial ideas, even ideas hateful to the prevailing climate of opinion—have the full protection of the guaranties, unless excludable because they encroach upon the limited area of more important interests.

The upshot? Messages about sex were no longer categorically obscene. Moreover, the suggestion was strong that a finding of obscenity hinged on evidence that a work pushed the libidinal buttons. Finally, when messages about sex commingled with social commentary, they ranked higher on the First Amendment scale. For Lenny, all that would prove promising in the hands of some judges sensitive to the nuances of his unorthodox and controversial *shticks*.

That, then, was Justice Brennan's "insoluble enigma"—one that left the judiciary "lost in a wilderness," according to constitutionalists John Nowak and Ronald Rotunda. It pleased conservatives and liberals alike, even as it troubled them.

THE MOST MEMORABLE portion of the *Roth* opinion—the words that would find their way into so many state and federal obscenity statutes—was Justice Brennan's famous (or infamous) formula for determining obscenity:

> [1] Whether to the average person, [2] applying contemporary community standards, [3] the dominant theme of the material taken as a whole [4] appeals to prurient interest.

Each of these four prongs had its peculiar relevance to Lenny Bruce.

Take "the average person" standard: Lenny's bits were not to be judged either by the thin-skinned sensibilities of shocked Shriners or by the hardened ways of tattooed sailors. Identifying the mindset of that "average person," obviously, could be a Herculean task.

The "contemporary community standards" criterion meant, for example, that Lenny's acceptability in Manhattan was not to be governed by the norms of Peoria, and vice-versa. Lenny thus took his chances when he went national, when he ventured from San Francisco to St. Louis…all at a time when mores were fixed in some places and fluid in others. And then there is the insightful point made by Justice Douglas, dissenting in *Roth*: "[I]f the First Amendment guarantee of freedom of speech and press is to mean anything…it must allow protests even against the moral code that the standard of the day sets for the community." Douglas had anticipated the problem Lenny would face: the social dissenter who contests the very community standards by which he will one day be judged.

The next prong suggested that Lenny's routine could not be evaluated by a few isolated and offensive phrases—for example, Eleanor Roosevelt's bodacious "tits," or "shoving" a funnel of hot lead "up the ass." Of course, the underlying assumption was that a work could, indeed, be considered as a *whole*—an assumption challenged by some of Lenny's future prosecutors.

The final criterion was, by far, the most problematic. On the one hand, "prurience" was synonymous with inciting lustful thoughts; or, as Lenny translated it, "I must get you horny—that's what it means. If I do a *disgusting* show…that's not obscene." Bruce was half right. But buried in a footnote in *Roth* was a passage that Lenny's prosecutors would stress time and again: prurience includes "a shameful or morbid interest in nudity, sex, or excretion" described in a manner going "substantially beyond customary limits of candor." With that footnote, the *Roth* opinion blurred the distinction between vulgarity (i.e., coarse and offensive language) and obscenity (i.e., sexual immorality)—a dichotomy emphasized by the Supreme Court as early as 1895.

For Justice Harlan, the Court's cerebral conservative, Brennan's constitutional handiwork was but a series of "disarming generalizations" destined to create "a number of problems." For Chief Justice Warren, a moderate on the matter, the *Roth* opinion moved too far, too fast, and in ways too far removed from the context of particular circumstances. And for Justice Douglas, the free speech absolutist writing in dissent, the Court's test was "too loose, too capricious, [and] too destructive of freedom of expression to be squared with the First Amendment." Right, center, left—*Roth* was an opinion that bothered all.

But for Lenny, unsophisticated in the niceties of constitutional exegesis, the opinion was pure bliss. "It's a beautiful law. They give you this leeway, and the language is so beautiful. If your stuff is utterly without any redeeming social importance, then it's obscene. Otherwise not." Ironically, Lenny was confident in adding: "That's the problem I've had, that I'm too conscious of the law."

Withhold Judgment

WOULD WILLIAM BRENNAN, an Irish Catholic of dignified demeanor, have appreciated—or defended—Lenny's lowest-brow bits? Whatever the speculation, Brennan was not in Los Angeles at The Slate Brothers' 1957 New Year's Eve celebration on La Cienega Boulevard to test his First Amendment tolerance for Lenny's most bizarre best:

> A kid looks up at his father and he says, "What's a degenerate?" The father says, "Shut up, kid, and keep sucking!" *And that's what I say to you people out there!*

The audience was aghast. One could almost hear the question racing through their minds: Did he *really* say that? But nobody spoke a word. Lenny flipped around, shook his *tuchas*, and then raised the Italian high-salute. "Good-bye," he screamed as he headed for the exit. For extra measure: "And *fangoola-da-mama*."

With that behind him, Lenny moved to San Francisco, to North

Beach where life was hip, where City Lights Bookstore stayed open until three A.M., where bohemians hung out at the Co-Existence Bagel Shop, and where the bereted Henri Lenoir personally greeted newcomers to his Vesuvio Café. It was the land of the Black Cat, the Purple Onion, Tosca Café, and Enrico Banducci's famous Hungry i. And it was there on Broadway, fifty feet east from the Matador, that Lenny debuted on the velour-bedecked proscenium stage of Ann's 440 Club. Early countercultural, it was a safe-haven for "dykes," "fags," "drag queens," and those who affirmed their lifestyles. Just as Ann Dee could boast of having launched Johnny Mathis's career, now she was about to do the same for Lenny Bruce.

A local billboard announced: ANN'S 440. HEAR LENNY BRUCE. CENSETE ITA IN CONDITIONEM NON (loosely translated, "withhold judgment"). The warning was appropriate. At Ann's 440, Lenny revealed a new comic consciousness, one not dependent on raunchy pranks. Now satire was his tool—searing social commentary of a much more sophisticated character. He challenged his audience as he amused them with routine after routine, including one that was to become a Lenny Bruce classic, "Religions, Inc." CD

At the Madison Avenue headquarters of Religions, Incorporated, America's new "religious leaders" have gathered—including Oral Roberts, Billy Graham, Danny Thomas, and Jane Russell—to hear the latest marketing report. With a deep Southern drawl, the sales hustler declares: "Faw the fust time in twelve yeuhs, Catholicism is up nine points, Judaism is up fifteen. The Big P, the Pentecostal, is stahtina move, finally." Introducing the season's tie-in products, he chimes: "[W]e got the kiss-me-in-the-dark mezzuzha...an these wunnerful lil cocktail napkins with some helluva sayings theah—'Anuthuh mahtini faw Muthuh Cabrini.'" Eventually, Oral Roberts takes a phone call from the newly installed Pope John XXIII: "Hello Johnny! What's shakin' baby? Boy, it's really been an election month, hasn't it, sweetie? Yah, the puff of white smoke knocked me out." Passing onto business, Roberts complains: "They're buggin' us again with that dumb integration. Nah, I don't know why the hell they wanna go to school, either....They say, get the religious leaduhs, make 'em tawk about it....I know it, but they're gettin' hip....No, they don wan' no more quotations from the Bahble. They wan' us to come out an say things. They wan' us to say: 'Let them go to school with them.'" Roberts winds up with the pitch: "When ya comin' to the coast?...I can get ya the Sullivan show the nineteenth....Wear the big ring....Okay, sweetie....No, nobody knows you're Jewish!"

The trade press raved. The review in *Variety* opened: "[A] wildly insane comic whose material is beyond surrealism, farther out than Mort Sahl, and devastating in its attacks on the pompous, the pious, and the phony in American culture." The reviewer confidently predicted that "Bruce is a good bet for any jazz club in the country." That certainly seemed a safe bet, as Lenny's booking fees increased steadily to $3,500 a week; but it overlooked the animosity that such commentary could generate.

Ralph J. Gleason, a columnist and jazz critic, authored that review. Four years later, he would be called to the stand as a defense witness in Lenny's San Francisco obscenity trial. There, his expert observations would be offered to demonstrate that Lenny's material had enough socially redeeming value to warrant First Amendment protection under the *Roth* test. By the time Gleason took the stand, however, the meaning of *Roth* already had begun to develop—in San Francisco, and in another famous obscenity trial. It was in that 1957 trial that Justice Brennan's mixed messages first would be deciphered and given coherence in ways directly germane to Lenny Bruce.

3

FREE SPEECH IN
NORTH BEACH

In 1957, I was one of Lawrence Ferlinghetti's lawyers in the "Howl" obscenity case. Five years later, I represented Lenny Bruce in the retrial of his first obscenity case. For all the free-thinking that had come to the Bay Area, the struggle for freedom was by no measure won.

—Albert Bendich

Holy Howl

IN THE BEGINNING, there was Ginsberg.

Before comedy, there was poetry. Before comic "obscenity," there was poetic "obscenity." Before Lenny's "To Is a Preposition, Come Is a Verb," there was Allen's "Howl." Before Bruce's words collided with the law, there were Ginsberg's words.

Holy, Holy, Holy. Holy Ginsberg. Holy Kerouac. Holy Burroughs, Whalen, and Lamantia. Holy Orlovsky, Snyder, and McClure. Holy Rexroth, Ferlinghetti...and Lenny Bruce? Holy, Holy, Holy.

They were loosely tagged the "Beats," the mid-century generation of iconoclasts who envisioned a world stripped of hypocrisy. The Beat movement was, in one sense, catapulted to fame with a poem—a long and uninhibited poem by Allen Ginsberg.

Ginsberg's legendary poem was first performed at 6 Gallery, a carriage house built in 1906. That station for stagecoaches was reworked in the 1950s into an automobile repair shop, which was thereafter converted into a "cooperative art gallery." From carriages to cars to canvasses, it was long journey in time and mind. (Today, the San Francisco gallery—located at 3119 Fillmore Street, between Filbert and Lombard—is the site of Silkroute Oriental Rugs.) Around eight P.M. on October 7, 1955, some 150 poets, painters, professors, bohemians, anarchists, cynics, and communists journeyed to the

"Negro section" of the city to hear six poets at 6 Gallery. Noncon-
formists all, they passed through the wide doors of the "gallery" clad
in "various costumes, worn-at-the-sleeves corduroy jackets, scuffy
shoes, [and] books sticking out of their pockets." They stood under a
big-beamed ceiling, and mingled alongside seven pillar beams that
ran up and down the center of the space. They passed around, com-
munal style, gallon jugs of California burgundy and waited. And then
it came, at around eleven o'clock. From the prophetic lips of one of
those poets they heard what became a great poem, lyrics that would
deconstruct and then reconstruct "the world lost." Poignant and personal. Words of rage and indignation. It was a poetic declaration of
discontent, decay, and debasement, coupled with dreams of mystical
survival borne in love...in homosexual love, to be precise. It was
"Howl."

"Unscrew the locks from the doors! / Unscrew the doors themselves from the jambs!" Thus, the epigraph to the poetic manifesto of
the Beat movement. Slightly intoxicated, the curly haired Ginsberg
rose from his folding chair. He walked a few feet on the cobblestone-
like floor, and then stepped onto a makeshift dais. Clad in Levis and a
navy sweater, he unleashed "Howl"'s opening line:

> I saw the best minds of my generation destroyed by madness,
>   starving, hysterical, mystical, naked,
> dragging themselves through the Negro streets at dawn looking for
>   an angry fix,
> angelheaded hipsters burning for the ancient heavenly connection
>   to the starry dynamo in the machinery of night...

Jack Kerouac was ecstatic beyond containment. "Go! Go! Go!" he
shouted in cadence. The audience responded with more shouts, more
wonderment, and (to be sure) more jug wine. It was Bacchanalian.
Ginsberg's public candor was unprecedented:

> ...who let themselves be fucked in the ass by saintly motorcyclists,
>   and screamed with joy,
> who blew and were blown by those human seraphim, the sailors...

"Go! Go! Go!" More applause, more spontaneity, more reorientation and disorientation. Through the lenses of his horned-rimmed glasses, Ginsberg envisioned a fallen world:

> *...Time, & now Denver is lonesome for her heroes,*
> *who fell on their knees in hopeless cathedrals praying for each*
>   *other's salvation...*

Relentless. Merciless. Wondrous. It was the manifesto that broke the barrier between culture and dissent. Life itself—with its mortals, gods, and weaponry—had been "outed." The unspoken had been spoken.

Afterwards, the poets ate at Sam Wo's Chinese restaurant, then gathered at The Place for yet more drink...cocksure that a corner to the counterculture had been rounded. "We had gone beyond a point of no return," recalled Michael McClure, one of the six poets. "[A]nd we were ready for it, for a point of no return," he added. Lawrence Ferlinghetti, North Beach bookstore owner, poet and publisher of "suspect" literature, was similarly confident, though he did not join his friends. Rather, he returned to his second-floor apartment on Chestnut Street where he hurried upstairs straight to his study. In the historical shadow of Emerson's celebrated response to Whitman's *Leaves of Grass*, he composed a telegram to the nearby Ginsberg: "I greet you at the beginning of a great career. When do I get the manuscript?" That telegram would put into motion a history waiting to be born. And, in time, it would form a link to still another history yet to be played out—the trial of Lenny Bruce.

JUDGE CLAYTON W. HORN was a Sunday school Bible teacher. He was a man who cared about the moral character of his world and those in it.

Before he presided over Lenny Bruce's 1962 obscenity trial, he was in the national limelight twice. First, there was the case of five women shoplifters. Having found them guilty as charged, Judge Horn sentenced them to serve time at the cinema. They were confined for 219 minutes in a local theater for a court-ordered movie-viewing of

The Ten Commandments. The cinema sentence did not end with the ladies watching Cecil B. DeMille's epic film starring Charlton Heston (Moses), Yul Brenner (Pharaoh Rameses), and Anne Baxter (Nefertiti). No. They had to put pen to paper and discuss, in essay form, the moral lessons to be drawn from the movie.

The judge's sentence drew harsh criticism from the editorial page of the *San Francisco Chronicle*: "Municipal Judge Clayton Horn's freewheeling excursion into movie-reviewing and *belles lettres* in weighing penalties for five petty shoplifters fills us with wonder and no little trepidation." Worse still, that lesson in morality, the editors emphasized, required the five misdemeanants to sit through a film filled with "violence, lust, sex, and orgies." Ironic. It was also "cruel," "unusual," and "unconstitutional." Alongside the editorial was a derisive cartoon of Horn clad in holy garb and sandals, holding a graven tablet that declared: THOU SHALT NOT MISS "THE TEN COMMANDMENTS"—JUDGE CLAYTON HORN.

The Honorable Clayton Horn was famous for a second reason, one bearing more immediately on Lenny's future. The Bay-area jurist, who resembled the actor Gene Lockhart, presided over the much-publicized trial of Lawrence Ferlinghetti. It would be the first major case to apply the test of *Roth v. U.S.*—a precedent later to prove important to Lenny Bruce.

In the fall of 1956, Lawrence Ferlinghetti, a tall and lean man with a receding hairline and European features, did what he long had yearned to do; he published Allen Ginsberg's *Howl and Other Poems* as part of his "Pocket Poet Series." (When City Lights first opened in June 1953, its name was City Lights Pocket Book Shop—a place where one could buy a variety of inexpensive "pocket" paperbacks.) Within a few months, the poem was seized. On March 25, 1957, Customs officials took custody of the booklets as they were being shipped to San Francisco by the English printer, Villiers. (Shortly before that, Customs officials had seized *The Miscellaneous Man*, sent by the same printer.) According to a report in the *San Francisco Chronicle*:

> Collector of Customs Chester MacPhee continued his campaign...to keep what he considers obscene literature away from the

children of the Bay Area. He confiscated 520 copies of a paper-bound volume of poetry entitled *HOWL* and other poems…."The words and sense of the writing is obscene," MacPhee declared. "You wouldn't want your children to come across it."

Ferlinghetti, a man who relished a row with officialdom, would not be bullied. He contacted the ACLU, which had already been recruited to give advice on the legality of printing the poem. The seizure would be contested on First Amendment grounds. Meanwhile, a new edition of *Howl* (with exactly the same text) was printed in the U.S., thereby removing it from the jurisdiction of Customs. Ferlinghetti next took to the press. Writing as a guest in William Hogan's *San Francisco Chronicle* book column, the poet defended "Howl" with bravado as "the most significant long poem to be published in this country since World War II…"

The poet-publisher was ready for constitutional battle. But, it never came. The U.S. Attorney refused to commence condemnation proceedings against *Howl*. Accordingly, the books were released on May 29, 1957. A victory for poetry and publishing!

The victory proved short-lived, however. For the bold and feisty autobiographical poem proved too much for Captain William Hanrahan of the Juvenile Division of the San Francisco Police Department. The captain knew when words crossed the penal line: "When I say filthy I don't mean suggestive, I mean filthy words that are very vulgar." True to that conviction, he ordered two officers to go to City Lights Bookstore and purchase a copy of *Howl*. The officers then took the material back to the stationhouse, examined it, and returned on May 21, 1957, to City Lights with a warrant for the arrest of Ferlinghetti, the store owner. They also had a "John Doe" warrant for his sales clerk Shigeyoshi ("Shig") Murao. The two men were charged with selling unlawful poetry…or as the authorities saw it, for publishing and selling obscene material.

The First Amendment was under attack in North Beach…of all places! In no time, a petition was circulated by twenty-one of San Francisco's leading booksellers; it called on Mayor George Christopher to "use all the power of your office" to end such police harassment. "This sort of censorship has no place in a democratic society," they declared in unison. The same day that news of the petition broke, the trial in *People v. Ferlinghetti* began.

The ACLU took charge, assembling a formidable team of defense lawyers. Lawrence Speiser, legal director of the Northern California chapter of the ACLU, continued to work on the *Ferlinghetti* case as it entered its latest phase, the trial. Albert M. Bendich, a bright twenty-eight-year-old lawyer, was called in to work as staff counsel on the case. The final member of the team, Jacob Wilburn Ehrlich, took the lead both in the trial and in the limelight. Jake "Never Plead Guilty" Ehrlich, or "the Master" as he was popularly known, was a California lawyer with a big ego and a national reputation. He had won hundreds of murder cases and represented celebrities in civil cases; names such as Errol Flynn, Billie Holiday, and even Howard Hughes were among his better known clients. (His career was fictionalized in *Sam Benedict*, a popular TV series.)

The trial began on August 17, 1957, with Judge Clayton Horn presiding. The courtroom was packed. Henry Miller, the novelist, was there to show his support for the First Amendment. Unknowns did the same, as they brought copies of *Howl* into the courtroom. (Copies of the book also remained in the window of, and for sale at, City Lights.) The defendants waived a jury trial, so the outcome was in the hands of the Sunday School teacher. Raising defenses based on the California statute, the California Constitution, and First Amendment freedom of press, the ACLU team squared off against Ralph McIntosh, the San Francisco assistant district attorney with an established track record for prosecuting nudie rags and dirty movies. The prosecution called three unimpressive witnesses (a police officer, an English professor, and a teacher), while the defense called nine impressive ones (six college professors from different disciplines, a newspaper book editor, and two noted authors).

The *Ferlinghetti* trial was a cause célèbre for the San Francisco literati. Grand literary poobahs—Mark Schorer and Kenneth Rexroth, among others—testified in defense of *Howl*'s merits against the prosecutor's accusations of its "filthy, vulgar, obscene, and disgusting language." At the request of defense counsel, and to familiarize himself better with past obscenity challenges, Judge Horn actually read *Ulysses* together with the court decisions about it; he then studied *Howl.* In the course of things, Ehrlich colorfully argued to the court, Speiser quietly prepared the witnesses, and Bendich thoughtfully submitted the all-important constitutional arguments to the judge. (By late August, it became clear that the charges against Shigeyoshi Murao would be dismissed as the prosecutor had failed to prove that he had the requisite knowledge of the allegedly obscene nature of the materials sold at City Lights Bookstore.)

On Thursday, October 3, 1957, Clayton Horn handed down his opinion, in *written* form (rare for municipal judges). The opinion left little doubt where this jurist stood on questions of free speech: "The authors of the First Amendment knew that novel and unconventional ideas might disturb the complacent, but they chose to encourage a freedom which they believed essential if a vigorous enlightenment was ever to triumph over slothful ignorance....The best method of censorship is by the people as self-guardians of public opinion and not by government." It was pure John Stuart Mill, pure Louis Brandeis, pure Hugo Black, pure protection for dissident expression:

> [L]ife is not encased in one formula whereby everyone acts the same or conforms to a particular pattern. No two persons think alike; we are all made from the same mold but in different patterns. Would there be any freedom of the press or speech if one must reduce his vocabulary to vapid and innocuous euphemism? An author should be real in treating his subject and be allowed to express his thoughts and ideas in his own words....

Judge Horn buttressed his rhetoric with legal analysis, carefully applying the rule of *Roth.* The San Francisco jurist was impressed with a point Al Bendich had made in one of his arguments; as Bendich stressed, "the majority opinion in *Roth* requires a trial court to...decide in the first instance whether a work is utterly without social importance, *before* it permits the test of obscenity to be applied..." That crucial point would be lost in many of Lenny's future trials, but it was the *first* of twelve points Judge Horn listed for applying the law of *Roth* to the facts of the *Ferlinghetti* case. "If the material has the slightest redeeming social importance it is not obscene," Horn wrote. That point alone readily could have ended the prosecution's case. Yet, the judge went on to elaborate eleven other points that needed to be considered before a work could be deemed obscene and therefore illegal. Among other things, the words contested must excite lascivious thoughts or arouse lustful desire to the point where they "present a clear and present danger of inciting antisocial or immoral action." Moreover, if the words used are "objectionable only because of coarse and vulgar language which is not erotic...in character, [they are] not obscene."

Not surprisingly, then, the court ruled for the defense. *Howl* did, indeed, have "redeeming social importance," which meant that it was no longer criminal to sell Allen Ginsberg's lyric in San Francisco. It was poetic justice. The elated audience in the packed courtroom welcomed the ruling with applause and cheers.

A major victory for the cultural outsiders: Ginsberg (then vacationing in Paris) was vindicated, Ferlinghetti liberated, and the cause of free speech celebrated. The Bible-teaching judge had done it; he had demonstrated how *Roth* could be applied in ways faithful to full First Amendment freedoms. Admirably, this municipal judge, whose daily routine was traffic offenses and other petty infractions, had developed complex points in *Roth* that would take U.S. Supreme Court Justice Brennan more than a decade to work out in a multitude of First Amendment cases. Of course, the defense lawyers had assisted Judge Horn by educating him in law and literature.

More than any other single work, Judge Clayton Horn's opinion in *People v. Ferlinghetti* reveals how Lenny Bruce would come to view his free speech freedoms. That understanding became a sort of constitutional gospel for him. The problem was that there were *other*, less protective, ways to interpret *Roth*.

The uncertainties of the future were still far away. In 1957, however, the landmark *Ferlinghetti* opinion signaled freedom in North Beach. When his day in a San Francisco court came five years later, Lenny ultimately would benefit from that generous measure of freedom. But things didn't start out that way.

What Kindava Show Is It?

IT WAS A purple and blue building, across the street and down from Finocchio's, at 475 Broadway. From the 1950s on, The Jazz Workshop was one of the big North Beach clubs, along with the Blackhawk, Basin Street West, and the Downbeat. John Coltrane, Miles Davis, Lou Rawls, Dizzy Gillespie, and Cannonball Adderley all had performed there. Now, Lenny Bruce, too—appearing on a bill with Ben Webster, the great tenor saxophonist, and pianist Paul Moor.

"Yeah, you heard about it. I got busted in Philly." There was Lenny, opening at The Jazz Workshop on Tuesday, October 3, 1961, at ten P.M.—a comic hustling laughs with a fast spin on his recent drug arrest.

I'm sick in the hotel. In bed. Two A.M. Don't want to be disturbed, dig? Comes a knock on the door.

Lenny: Go away.
Police: Mr. Bruce, please open up.
Lenny: Go away.
Police: Mr. Bruce, this is for your own good.

So I pick up the phone. "I want the police." And foom! The door opens and there they are.

Forever the hipster, decked out in a black Nehru jacket, he jived with a young crowd of hipster wannabes. Giving it his own gloss, he downplayed the narcotics charge:

I've had a virus, two, three months. My two doctors prescribed the stuff for me....[The charges will be dropped] as soon as they analyze the stuff and make sure it's what the doctors prescribed, not something I've been making.

Then it was on to more familiar material—bits on sex, religion, and bigotry in 1960s America. The following day, the local paper covered his opening in a matter-of-fact way, with nary a hint of indecency.

Surely, nothing much here to raise the attention of the foot patrol of Police Beat 17—who kept the nightlife on Broadway, from Mason to Battery, within the bounds of decency—except for an *alleged* complaint from an unidentified patron offended by Lenny's language.

The next night, Lenny was cookin'. He loved this city, ever since he played Ann's 440. So why not reminisce about it with some comic flair? Why not tell them about the agent's phone call that brought him to the 440?

> *Lenny*: What kindava show is it, man?
>
> *Agent*: Well, ya know.
>
> *Lenny*: Well, no, I don't know, man…
>
> *Agent*: Well, it's not a show. They're a bunch of cocksuckers, that's all. A damned fag show.
>
> *Lenny*: Oh. Well, that is a pretty bizarre show. I don't know what I can do in that kind of show.
>
> *Agent*: Well, no. It's…we want you to change all that.
>
> *Lenny*: Well—I don't—that's a big gig. I can just tell them to stop doing it. **CD**

He ripped up the joint. Art Auerbach, the owner—who charged a door fee ($2.50) for the first time in the club's history—might have felt that he was getting his money's worth from the "sick" comedian. Lenny, always the haggler, had arranged a complicated deal whereby he hoped to make as much as $5,000 for a week's worth of double-show nights.

With comrades in the audience such as columnist Ralph Gleason and Saul Zaentz of Fantasy Records (Bruce's record company), Lenny was full-throttle, five hundred miles-per-hour, for forty-plus nonstop minutes. True to the name of the club, he gave them a jazz riff—accompanying himself on a drum and cymbal:

> Tooooooooo is a preposition …
>> Commmmmmmme is a verb! …
>> To is a preposition,
>> Come is a verb, the verb intransitive.
>> To come.

To come.

I've heard these two words my whole adult life and as a kid when they thought I was sleeping.

Toooo Commmmme....

It's been like a big drum solo.

Did you come?

Did you come?

Good.

Did you come good?

Did you come good? ...

I come better with you, sweetheart, than with anyone in the whole goddamn world.

I really came so good.

I really came so good 'cause I love you.

I really came so good....

But don't come in me.

Don't come in me.

Don't come in me.

Don't comeinme, don't comeinmeinmeinmeinme.

Don't comeinmeinmeinme....

I can't come.

'Cause you don't love me, that's why you can't come...

What has that got to do with loving? I just can't come, that's all.

Now, if anyone in this room or the world finds those two words decadent, obscene, immoral, amoral, asexual—the words "to come" really make you feel uncomfortable—if you think I'm rank for saying it to you...you probably can't come. And then you're of no use because that's the purpose of life, to recreate it. 🄲🄳

There were more bits, all kinds of bits, going in all orbits. There was also a strange tale about a man, leaning against a ticket booth with a sign hanging from his penis, which read: "When we hit fifteen hundred dollars, the guy inside the booth is going to kiss it."

James Ryan, a San Francisco policeman, was there to witness it all. He had been directed by his superior, Sergeant James Solden, to attend the Jazz Workshop performance to see if there was anything of a "lewd nature" going on. Ryan was stationed in the back of the club. After hearing some of Lenny's bits, Officer Ryan was *shocked* at what he had just heard. "Jeez, you know," he told his sergeant shortly afterwards, "I can hardly believe this myself. The man is up there on stage and he's performing and he's taking the term 'cocksucker' and using it." To make matters worse, the suspect had "made several references about the same thing, only he didn't use the word." Unbelievable. In a nightclub, in North Beach, rough language in the presence of men and women—too much! A few minutes before the performance ended, Officer Ryan stepped outside to confer with his sergeant. Assuredly, there were grounds for an arrest, they readily concluded.

You Break It Down by Talking about It

THE FIRST HALF of his night's work was done. Shivering and tugging on a white trenchcoat, Lenny sat down with Gleason and a friend as folks filed out. About that time, Sergeant Solden came in and asked to speak with Mr. Auerbach. He informed the club owner that they were there to take Lenny Bruce into custody for performing an obscene show.

"Where is he?" asked the sergeant. Auerbach informed him that Lenny was in the rear of the club. Before the officer turned away, however, Auerbach asked, "Couldn't you overlook this? We'll clean up the show." Too late. The crime already had been committed—in the presence of the police. Auerbach then went over to Lenny to break the bad news: he was going to jail. They then escorted the suspect outside. "Cold night," Lenny said. "Yes," Ryan replied. "You understand the sergeant wants to have a word with you." Conversing, they bore the elements en route to the police call box, in front of Enrico's cafe.

"I took exception. I took offense," Solden exclaimed. Likely reacting to Lenny's semantic defense, the sergeant turned philosophical: "We've tried to elevate this street. I'm offended because you broke the law. I mean it sincerely. I mean it. I can't see any right, any way you can break this word down, our society is not geared to it."

With realist insight, Lenny rejoined, "You break it down by talking about it....How about a word like 'clap'?"

Straightening his back, the sergeant rationalized: "Well, 'clap' is a better word than 'cocksucker.' "

"Not if you get the clap from a cocksucker," Lenny countered.

The sergeant yelled into the call box. Three squad cars and a paddy wagon finally arrived. Lenny was whisked away to the old Hall of Justice. There, he was booked on misdemeanor charges for violating Municipal Police Code Sections 176 and 205. Once the paperwork was completed, Lenny was taken to the basement of the Hall of Justice where he was fingerprinted, photographed, and locked up in a dark cell with a pee-stained mattress on the floor.

While Auerbach (also a lawyer) hustled down to the station to pay Lenny's $367.50 bail, the patrons and waitresses remaining in the club discoursed for two hours about free speech in North Beach. By the time the dialogue died down, Lenny was back from the city jail, ready for his one A.M. performance.

"I better keep the coat on this time," Lenny opened, as he walked onstage still wearing his trenchcoat. "You'll never guess where I've been. I've been busted."

Someone in the audience yelled out, "We read about it in Philly."

"No, no," Bruce explained. "I mean now. Right now. Right after the first show. I just came from the stationhouse." As was his way, he folded reality into *shtick*. Officers Ryan and Solden became the targets of the biblical injunction, "Let he who is without sin amongst ye cast the first stone."

In a moment of frank public self-analysis, he spoke a simple truth: "I'm sorry if I'm not very funny tonight, but I'm not a comedian, I'm Lenny Bruce." It would become one of his classic lines.

He couldn't even sleep off this nightmare. Only several hours later, the management of the Clift Hotel showed him the door. "We don't want people like you here," declared the manager. Leave! "Right this minute, or we'll call the police and have you thrown out!"

"It wasn't what you would call my day," a weary Bruce conceded.

Quickie Trial

IN RETROSPECT, LENNY was lucky. Had the wheels of justice continued to turn the way they started, he likely would have been convicted, sentenced to the max, and forced to appeal. But fate was kind and gave him a second chance—with a different lawyer, a different judge, and a different outcome.

"In a million ways, I felt that this was going to be a lark," Seymour Fried recalled. The young Fried was Lenny's L.A. lawyer who handled such matters as his business dealings and his 1957 divorce from Honey. He was Lenny's first line of defense in San Francisco. Whatever Fried's abilities as a civil lawyer, he had no real experience as a criminal litigator. Even so, he agreed to represent Lenny, if only because he did not think that this misdemeanor charge would be very difficult to beat. "I told that to Lenny. He wanted a trial. He felt that the publicity of a trial would help his career tremendously. So we were going to have a trial. I told him that I felt that we'd be silly to have a jury trial. He took my advice on that."

This was the *first* case in the line of obscenity cases to be named *People v. Bruce*. It was the Genesis ("In the beginning"), the grand start of things ("We the People"), the initial turning point ("When, in the course of human events") in the troubled history of Lenny Bruce's comic and tragic career. His life in the law would never be the same after what began in San Francisco on Friday, November 17, 1961, in Department 10 of the Municipal Court of the City and County of San Francisco. Alexis J. Batmale, the official court reporter, took it all down for later generations to appreciate just how the American legal system first dealt with its madcap comic dissident, Lenny Bruce.

"Nuance" was not a word that came to mind when the name Albert A. Axelrod arose in conversation. The sixty-one-year-old had a rather take-charge personality, a man more concerned about the adjective than the noun in the phrase "speedy justice." Statutory law, common law, constitutional law—it all didn't matter to the man educated at the University of California, Hastings Law School. What mattered was how facts matched up with his subjective sense of fairness. For better or worse, Albert Axelrod was the first jurist assigned to hear *People v. Bruce*.

What Lenny and Seymour did not know that Friday, when they made tracks down to the Hall of Justice at 850 Bryant Street, was that Axelrod had little tolerance for foul-mouthed comics. The chemistry of Axelrod and Bruce was combustible: one was serious and severe, the other flip and carefree; one was moralistic and judgmental, the other relativistic and compassionate.

All of this would become apparent in the few hours it took to conduct this "quickie trial." No expert or lay eyewitnesses required. A grand total of three people testified—two for the prosecution and one for the defense. Assistant District Attorney Arthur M. Schaefer called Officers Ryan and Solden to the stand to recount what they had heard at The Jazz Workshop, and Seymour Fried called Lenny to the stand in his own defense. (In a letter of November 8, 1961, Fried had asked Ralph Gleason, a noted San Francisco culture critic, to testify as a witness for the defense. For whatever reason, Gleason was not then called as a witness.)

The prosecution presented disjointed and fragmented accounts of three of Lenny's routines to establish that he had violated Municipal Police Code Sections 176 and 205 (unlawful presentation of an "obscene, indecent, immoral, or impure" performance) and California Penal Code Section 311.6 (knowingly speaking "lewd or obscene" words "in any public place"—the state actually amended its complaint, over the objection of the defense, to include prosecution under the then newly revised §311.6). There were three bits that gave rise to these charges: 1) "the club was overrun with cocksuckers" bit; 2) "the man in the front booth is going to kiss it" bit, and 3) the "don't come in me, don't come in me" bit. The strategy was simple: present the officers' testimony of what transpired, their official reactions to it, and their opinions that it was obscene—arresting witnesses, expert witnesses, and "community standards" witnesses all conveniently combined in the testimony of Ryan and Solden.

Seymour Fried, for the defense, was more sophisticated. In concluding that the show was obscene, he inquired, had the officers considered the work *as a whole*? In considering if the performance appealed to "prurient" interests, had they taken the entirety of Bruce's show into account? If they did, could they recall it *all* and *precisely*? It would not satisfy the commands of the First Amendment to focus—as the prosecution, witnesses, and court were doing—on isolated words taken out of context, argued Fried. This line of argument pointed in two directions: first, it could establish a constitutional basis for dismissing the case; second, and alternatively, it could establish a foundation for introducing the actual audiotapes of Lenny's Jazz Workshop performance in order to refute the recollections of the two officers.

"[I]t is our opinion," Fried stressed, "that it is distinctly unconstitutional and it has been held so, to pick excerpts from a given piece of material, given piece of work, and to rely upon that excerpt in determining whether or not the material is obscene....[Y]ou cannot take an excerpt from [Mr. Bruce's performance] and use that portion of the excerpt to show it is obscene."

But counsel was wasting his breath on Judge Axelrod, who didn't want to hear the "whole" of the matter: "You don't have to have the whole performance to be obscene. I think that the way any word is used or spoken during that performance which has an obscene meaning within that definition, that there is a violation. I take a different point of view." The judge then added: "Now, if you are discussing a book, then you may have to take perhaps the whole meaning, but we are not talking about that. We are talking about a specific word." Put another way, the *whole word* was enough. Move on!

Then came the infamous tapes of Lenny's performance at The Jazz Workshop. Begrudgingly, the judge allowed them to be played in the courtroom. The quality of the reel-to-reel audiotape was poor, and there were technical troubles. To no avail and to Bruce's dismay, the tape recorder's speakers failed before the Ann's 440 bit played out; the recorder could not be repaired immediately.

It wasn't just the technical problems and the quality of the sound that troubled the irritated jurist, it was also the poor quality of the words Lenny Bruce chose to use. "I think I've heard enough," he snapped after hearing a part of the tape. Besides, "if the Supreme Court doesn't think it is obscene, then I don't know." Good omen for reversal on appeal, but a bad omen for a trial court victory. Fried repeated his objections. A frustrated Axelrod yielded: "[The word he used] is enough in my book. I mean, if you want to play the rest all right....I don't want to hear any more, but go ahead. That is your privilege. I can't stop you; it is a matter of testimony."

Ironically, the very idea of playing the tape was to persuade the court of the legality of Lenny's performance. But Axelrod was saying he wouldn't be persuaded, tape or no tape. Given that, Fried indicated that he was prepared to "withdraw our offer to play the tape and offer it in evidence."

> *Judge:* Do I understand that you are not offering the tape now?
> *Fried:* Well, we are not offering the tape in evidence, if the Court feels that the playing of the tape would not serve any purpose.

Defense counsel had called the court's bluff. As a consequence, Axelrod allowed the tape to be introduced into evidence and agreed to listen to it *if* the quality were such that he could understand it.

After a few hours of direct and cross-examination concerning Bruce's act, Judge Axelrod was ready to rule, convict, and sentence...even *before* Lenny could take the stand. When the State rested, Seymour Fried again raised his *Roth*-based objections. But an agitated Axelrod would have no part of it; he didn't need Supreme Court precedent to tell him what was or was not obscene:

> I don't need any points and authorities to tell me that this language which was used and which was quoted by the officer and the context in which it was used is obscene. Now, if the Supreme Court takes a different view, that is up to them. But to me, it is obscene and I certainly wouldn't let my grandchildren sit in and listen to a show like this. Now, that is my viewpoint.

So much for judicial acumen and deference to the highest court in the land. Incredibly, all of this transpired *before* Lenny approached the witness stand.

By the time the black-clad Bruce took the stand—in tight black pants, black linen jacket buttoned at the neck, and shiny black boots—his mood mirrored his clothing. Protesting that he had been misunderstood, Bruce in effect argued that obscenity is in the ear of the hearer. He claimed to be maintaining community standards, so much so that (curiously) he had "the children's interests at heart." Axelrod snapped: "I'm glad my children are not raised under the same standards as yours." (Of course, all of this was irrelevant, insofar as children and grandchildren were barred, quite properly, from The Jazz Workshop.)

On, then, with Lenny's direct examination testimony. The main purpose in calling the defendant was to have him authenticate the tape Fried wanted to introduce into evidence. Lenny Bruce's answer, however, could not be so readily confined:

> *Fried*: Mr. Bruce, at this time I'd like to know if this is the tape that is in the machine?
> *Bruce*: …Is this the tape that I made to question a father's concept of God, [the God who] made the child's body but qualified the creativity by stopping it above the kneecaps and resuming it above the Adam's apple, thereby giving lewd connotation to [the] mother's breast that fed us and [the] father's groin that bred us, then this is the tape, yes.

The audience—the people in the *courtroom*, that is—must have loved Lenny's clever "bit." Predictably, objections followed and the parties and the court went back and forth.

Fried really didn't ask much more of Lenny; he was more interested in playing the audiotape. The tape, however, was not easy to understand and the recorder continued to malfunction. "Frankly, this is rather indistinct," complained Axelrod. "I mean, I can't understand it. Parts of it I get, parts I don't. If this is being played for my benefit, you are wasting your time because it is not getting over to me. I'll be very frank with you."

Arrangements were then made to get a different tape player along with a transcript of the performance. Accordingly, Judge Axelrod granted a thirty-day stay so that Fried might arrange to have the performance tape transcribed and to submit legal memoranda. Mindful of Bruce's upcoming Curran Theater concert, Axelrod had some final and not-so-grandfatherly words for Bruce: "It is my understanding

[Mr. Bruce has] a show Sunday. If there is any repetition of this conduct, I'll deal with him accordingly. I want to caution you right now that if I get a report in the interim that you repeated any of the language or anything obnoxious, you will take the consequences. Is that clear?" To which Bruce responded: "You will specifically do this to me if I repeat these words?" Axelrod was stern: "Repeat anything that is obscene. I'll take it into consideration when I finally dispose of the case. Let that be a warning to you. From your testimony here, I just have a little feeling that the lesson hasn't gotten home." (The popularized account of Axelrod's warning, which first appeared in a local newspaper from the time, runs as follows: "I'm cautioning you now that if you say anything obscene at your performance, I'll hear about it....[I]f I get a report you have repeated this language, you'd better bring your toothbrush with you when you come to court again." Lenny would use that account in his Curran Theater performance.)

The good Judge was off to Phoenix to visit his grandchildren. And the "bad boy" comic was off to the nearby Curran Theater on Geary Street—for what Hal Zeiger, the promoter, billed as "An Evening for Those Who Prefer Lenny Bruce."

Inviting Contempt

HE WAS FREE-FORMIN' and ad-libbin', rip after rip into the judge.

"Dig Axelrod. 'I warn you, Lenny Bruce, if I hear those words...' If he hears from somebody else that I talked dirty tonight, then I'll be in court again."

Lenny mocked him; he taunted him; he challenged his heterosexual masculinity.

"'If I hear it, you'd better bring your toothbrush.' Hmm... now...bring your toothbrush. This means two things to me. The first thing...that we were compatible, because a toothbrush is an intimate thing, everybody knows that." CD

Two days on the heels of Axelrod's stern admonition, Lenny was tempting fate with comic abandon at his Curran Theater concert. At

8:45 P.M. that Sunday night, Lenny took to the stage before an audience of three hundred or more who paid $3.50 to $5.50 a seat and trekked through torrential rains to hear him. Art Schaefer, his prosecutor, was there, too.

Lenny flirted with contempt of court. Spliced in between some of his recognized bits were Axelrod *spritzes*. He intended to give the judge some of the same treatment that he had imparted one month earlier to that corrupt "son of a bitch" Magistrate E. David Keyser in Philly, who offered to fix his Philadelphia narcotics rap for a cool ten grand. Lenny courageously blew the whistle on the crook and his cronies, holding a sidewalk press conference outside the magistrate's courtroom on October 9. Now, he aimed to expose—in a comic *tour de force*—the fault-lines in Judge Axelrod's character.

Bruce portrayed Axelrod as a man without patience or compassion, a judge who reamed a welfare recipient for buying a car:

Judge: I've given you every break in the world.
Defendant: But your Honor.
Judge: Shut up!
(*Lenny*: What kind of power does this cat got?…And he keeps yellin'…)
Judge: I don't want to hear that. I've given you every break in the world.
(*Lenny*: No, you didn't give him every break in the world. If you did, they wouldn't take his car away.)
Judge: I've given you every break in the world. Ninety days.
(*Lenny*: That's not every break in the world.)

His stream of consciousness next flowed to a satirical treatment of the forbidden word for which he had been busted at The Jazz Workshop. Lenny's devious mind had to find a way to say "cocksucker" without saying "cocksucker." He reveled in the triumph of form over substance. Referring to a "vulgar term" that the court assumed was "related to homosexuals," Lenny mused:

That's funny…because I don't know if they're hip to it, that's not only a homosexual practice but the practice of every good wife who is contemporary....

"Sucker": one who is a pawn, an unaware person, who can be taken advantage of. And since the "cock" is the male, the feathers, I assume [the compound word means] many transvestites who are pawns for baubles, beads, and feathers....So then, we must go to the *American Dictionary of Slang*. Dig what it says, this is beautiful.... "One who plays the female role in a homosexual relationship."

Now, Lenny upped the ante. "Do you want to hear a beautiful fantasy I had to 'do in' Axelrod?" he asked. "This is genius." The devilish comic transformed the judge's sensitivity about sex talk around his grandchildren to the judge's insensitivity in having sex with one of his grandchildren. In the routine, Lenny's ex-wife, Honey Harlowe, ensnares the judge by pretending to faint in his presence, and asking him to take her to a hotel. Five minutes later, they're in the sack.

> *Honey*: Will you talk hot to me? Tell me that I'm your granddaughter.
> *Axelrod*: Okay, you'll get it, granddaughter.
> *Honey*: Get up there, Axelrod.
> *Axelrod*: Okay, sweetie....You didn't think your old man had it, huh?

Honey springs the trap when she asks Axelrod to fix her hit-and-run case. He all too willingly agrees. Throughout, she has secretly recorded the incestuous pedophilia and the corruption of justice. The only thing that remained was to air the tape at prime time on the Jack Paar program.

What a performance it was—nonstop for three hours, seven minutes, and twenty-eight seconds! Introspectively, Lenny explained to his audience: "I see things in a ludicrous sense, and I report that kind of scene." Indeed, that was the magic of the Curran concert.

The magic moments, however, were coming to an end. For it was twenty-seven days and counting until "Toothbrush D-Day," when Lenny had to return to Judge Axelrod's courtroom.

You Can't Win a Case Based on "Cocksucker"

LENNY HAD BEEN asking around, looking for a powerhouse mouth-piece, preferably someone who was "hip" to First Amendment law. Predictably, Albert Bendich's name came up. "Hi, Al Bendich? This is Lenny Bruce. Do you know my work?" Bendich paused. He knew the notorious name, but not the notorious work, not really.

It was a Saturday, the day before the Curran performance, and Lenny called Bendich at home. With an Axelrod conviction all but sure, Fried was out of the picture. Lenny wanted a legal *starker*, and he wanted him now. When Bendich agreed to meet with him, Lenny pressed to come over that night after his show. He offered to bring the Jazz Workshop tape and the trial transcript.

"When Lenny arrived with a friend, he was clearly stoned out of his head," Bendich recalled. They went upstairs and listened to the tape. Bendich was impressed. (He admired Lenny's work even more the next evening when he attended the Curran concert.) Bendich was confident that the act was constitutionally protected. Even so, there was a fly in the ointment—what to do about Axelrod.

The move was brilliant. Bendich made a motion for a new trial based on Judge Axelrod's failure to advise Lenny of his right to counsel at the arraignment. It worked. The same judge, who only a few weeks earlier was prepared to throw the book at Lenny, was now releasing his grip on him. As luck had it, the case was reassigned to none other than Judge Clayton Horn—the same judge who acquitted Ferlinghetti some four years earlier with Albert Bendich as co-counsel for the defense. The hope was that history would repeat itself, this time in Lenny's favor.

Given the liberal bent that Judge Horn revealed in the *Ferlinghetti* case, it seemed that he would be an ideal judge for the defense in yet another "dirty words" case. Why take a chance with an unknown jury when there is a judge with a known track record? Forego the jury trial and let Judge Horn decide—true to his constitutional commitment to free speech. It was a logical choice. But Lenny, as in so many other instances, was not about to let logic rule. No, "he was afraid of judges," Bendich explained. Fried had convinced him to go with Axelrod, and look how that story ended. Moreover, Lenny "wanted the public attention that would come with a jury trial." After all, the publicity would be good for him. Bendich preferred the jury trial option for more legalistic reasons: it would permit appropriate instructions to be given to the jury and allow for appeal if the instructions were inappropriate.

Before the trial began, Bendich got a call from Lenny's manager, Jack Sobel. Sobel asked Bendich to persuade Jake Ehrlich, his co-counsel in the *Howl* case, to represent Lenny in the new trial. Bendich agreed to intercede, with a categorical condition: "If Ehrlich says no, I won't pick up the pieces. I won't represent [Lenny]. You'll be on your own."

Ehrlich did say no. "Al," he declared, "you can't win a case based on 'cocksucker.'" Now that Jake Ehrlich had declined to be Lenny's San Francisco mouthpiece, Bendich was about to follow suit. Despite his earlier condition, Bendich capitulated to the pressure of Sobel calling from New York and of Lenny calling from Miami. There was still one condition, however: "You must let me argue the case alone, and you must not interfere with my handling of the case." On this point, he would never capitulate. Lenny agreed, and Bendich—Ferlinghetti's lawyer, and the former ACLU staff attorney—remained his new San Francisco counsel.

The Letter of the Law

THINGS STARTED BADLY that Monday, March 5, 1962.

Only a few moments into the jury selection, a messenger approached the bench with a letter for Judge Horn. After glancing at it, Horn recessed the court, and ordered defense counsel, defendant, and the court reporter into his chambers. Lenny made himself at home, slumping into the Judge's leather divan. "Stand up, Mr. Bruce," the judge ordered. Horn was perturbed, for there in his hands was a letter to him from none other than Lenny Bruce, the defendant.

To make the matter official, Horn read the 132-word "illiterate" letter into the record. In part, the awkwardly drafted document stated:

> The monstrous rumor "Judge Horn feels the defendant takes the matter lightly" motivates this letter. Odious is the matter, my arrest for obscenity has enfilmed my career with a leperous stigma that St. Francis could not kiss away at ethereal peak. Objectivity is impossible for me....This inference you would prejudge is the fear of the courts as a result of Axelrod Palace. His statement "I don't understand a thing on this tape but, as far as I am concerned, he's guilty"—without hearing one witness.

Lenny had told his lawyer about the letter only *after* he sent it. A dumbfounded Bendich quickly assured Judge Horn that he had not in any way authorized or encouraged Bruce's actions. " 'Axelrod Palace' refers to Judge Axelrod, obviously," Judge Horn objected. Lenny assured the judge that it was not his intent to display disrespect for the court. And Bendich strove to explain that the letter merely demonstrated the anxiety of a person who did not understand judicial protocol.

Notwithstanding the defendant's apologies, Lenny was held in contempt. Judge Horn, however, deferred sentencing until the end of the trial. He nonetheless assured Bruce and Bendich that this episode "will not affect my feelings as far as the conduct of the trial is concerned." Lenny, forever the skeptic, was unsure:

> *Bruce*: You are completely divorced from this? I felt that perhaps you felt a hostility toward me....
> *Horn*: No, I don't feel any hostility toward you. My rulings will be just the same as though this hadn't happened.
> *Bruce*: That I know, but I feel that you are prejudiced, definitely.
> *Horn*: That's up to your attorney....Whatever you want to do....
> *Bendich*: Your Honor. I don't share that opinion, but I think that because this has arisen it is necessary for me to consult with Mr. Bruce about the matter....I would just like to make this one comment: Mr. Bruce turned to me and told me a moment ago, "I really

don't understand this. It's perfectly legal to write a letter to the President."…I mention this only because I think it reflects the defendant's understanding of the situation and his attitude. I believe sincerely, your Honor, that he did not intend any contempt.
Bruce: It was not sassy.
Horn: Well, regardless of what he intended, Mr. Bendich, he'll just have to learn that there are certain things he can't do, and that letter is one of them.

Lenny ended up deferring to his lawyer's judgment that the Court would not be prejudiced against him. With the contempt matter over for the time being, the process of empanelling a jury began. Question after question, both sides strove to select those tried-and-true citizens most sympathetic to their side of the story. Miss Settle, the *Reader's Digest* devotee—excused by Bendich. Mr. Witherspoon, a well-dressed middle-aged black man—excused by the new prosecutor, Deputy District Attorney Albert Wollenberg Jr. And so on. The result: four men, eight women, two alternates. Varying ages. All white. All conservatively dressed.

Prosecutor Wollenberg called only two witnesses for the State. He appeared to build his case on the shock value of the arresting officers' accounts. No expert witnesses—no literati, no sociologists, no stage critics.

Officer James Ryan took the stand. He set the backdrop for the State's case, providing his sketchy recollections of Lenny's act on the night of the bust. Attempting to describe the jazz-riff bit, for example, Ryan truncated the routine and drained it of all its alleged artistry:

Ryan: Later in the show he went into some kind of a chant where he used…a cymbal and a drum for a tempo, and the dialogue there was supposed to be—
Bendich: I'll object to what the witness infers the conversation or dialogue was supposed to import, your Honor. The witness is to testify merely to what he heard.
Horn: Sustained.…
Wollenberg: Can you give us the exact words or what your

recollection of those words were?

Ryan: Yes. During that chant he used the words, "I'm coming, I'm coming, I'm coming."

Wollenberg: Did he just do it two or three times, "I'm coming, I'm coming, I'm coming"?

Ryan: Well, this one part of the show lasted a matter of a few minutes.

Wollenberg: And then was anything else said by the defendant?

Ryan: Then later he said, "Don't come in me. Don't come in me."

Wollenberg: Now, did he do this just one or two times?

Ryan: No. As I stated, this lasted for a matter of a few minutes.

Wollenberg: Now, as he was saying this, was he using the same voice as he was giving this chant?

Ryan: No. He used higher and lower pitch to his voice.

Wollenberg: And when would he change the pitch of his voice?

Ryan: Well, this particular instance where he was saying, "I'm coming, I'm coming," he was talking in a more normal tone of voice. And when he stated, or when he said, "Don't come in me"…he used a little higher-pitched voice.

And so on. The absurdity of Ryan's portrayal of Bruce's act was patently apparent to Lenny, his lawyer, and his fans in the courtroom.

Bendich now cross-examined Officer Ryan, with three purposes in mind: to establish the "community standard" for the clubs in North Beach, to demonstrate that Lenny's performance did not appeal to prurient interest, and to evidence the common usage of vulgarity. Through all this, there was a subtext—a strategy counter to Wollenberg's. The more the word "cocksucker" was used, the more the jury would be desensitized to it.

Leading Ryan down a primrose path, Bendich inquired about one after another of the flesh joints on the officer's beat. There was Moulin Rouge, and its amateur strip night for housewives; there was Finocchio's, and its drag-queen black-net-stocking-and-brassiered cabaret. When testimony turned to the scanty details, Wollenberg objected: "Oh, if your Honor please….We're not trying Finocchio's here today."

Replied Bendich: "We're certainly not trying Finocchio's, but we are trying Lenny Bruce on a charge of obscenity, and we have a

question of contemporary community standards that has to be established, and I am attempting to have Officer Ryan indicate what the
nature of the community standards on his beat are."

The judge agreed, but asked Bendich to keep it short: "I don't
think we want to take inventory of Finocchio's performers. I don't
think we have to start with the shoes and work all the way up."

On to prurience. Section 311.6 of the California Penal Code,
under which Bruce was charged, required the government to demonstrate that an obscene work appealed to prurient interest. Bendich
went straight to the point: "Were you sexually stimulated when you
witnessed Lenny Bruce's performance?" Again, Wollenberg
objected—"Irrelevant and immaterial, especially as to this officer,
your Honor." The judge disagreed: "Overruled." Ryan then
answered, "No sir."

"Officer Ryan, you're quite familiar with the term 'cocksucker,' are
you not?" the defense counsel asked. Ryan answered affirmatively.
"Well, as a matter of fact, it is frequently used in the police station, is it
not?" Yet again, Wollenberg objected: "That's irrelevant and immaterial, if your Honor please. What's used in a police station or in private
conversation between two people is completely different from what's
used on a stage in the theater." Judge Horn was unconvinced: "Well, a
police station, of course, is a public place....[T]he objection is overruled." Finally came the answer that all expected from Ryan: "Yes, I
have heard it used."

Sergeant James Solden was the second and final witness for the
prosecution. Seemingly, the deputy D.A. aimed to expose just how
callous and flippant Lenny was in his use of vulgarity. Wollenberg
asked whether Solden had conversed with Bruce on the evening of the
bust. "I had a conversation with Mr. Bruce as we led—took him from
The Jazz Workshop to the patrol wagon....I spoke to Mr. Bruce and
said, 'Why do you feel that you have to use the word, 'cocksuckers,' to
entertain people in a public night spot?" And Mr. Bruce's reply to me
was, 'Well there's a lot of cocksuckers around, aren't there? What's
wrong with talking about them?'" This line of questioning suggested
that the mere *mention* of the word was enough to establish guilt under
the obscenity statute.

With that, the State rested. Perhaps it was not so meager an offering, given that this was a *misdemeanor* matter. Wollenberg handled it that way. But Bendich would not.

Reasonable Doubt

HE HAD SAVED his opening statement until the prosecution was done. Now, Bendich methodically took apart the State's case. What Lenny Bruce did that night at The Jazz Workshop was social criticism aimed at exposing the hypocrisy and greed of the clergy; it was political commentary on racial discrimination and animosity toward homosexuals and other minorities; it was a satirical slap at the Establishment and self-righteous liberals. And all of this was done, the jury was told, consistent with the great literary traditions of Chaucer, James Joyce, and Aristophanes.

"I'm going to object," Wollenberg broke in. "Aristophanes is not testifying here, your Honor." Bendich retorted: "Your Honor, I didn't say I would call Mr. Aristophanes." Horn chuckled despite himself: "I don't think you could, very well."

The defense counsel promised that he would demonstrate how Lenny used comedy as commentary, and had neither the intention nor the effect of being obscene:

> We will present evidence, ladies and gentlemen, which will prove, I
> believe to your satisfaction, that Mr. Bruce had the soundest basis
> for believing that the nature of his performance was in no way an
> appeal to prurient interest, in no way an attempt to excite sexual
> interest, erotic arousal, and that he had the firmest foundation and
> basis for feeling, thinking, and knowing that the material which he
> based his show upon and that the character of his show was serious
> in intent, artistic in execution, and socially significant.

Bendich called nine witnesses and Lenny to the stand. He started with Ralph Gleason, a local figure and something of a giant of a cultural commentator. Perhaps the first critic anywhere to review opening nights at folk, jazz, and pop clubs, Gleason joined the *San Francisco Chronicle* in the late 1940s, where he interviewed the likes of Hank Williams, Elvis Presley, and Fats Domino. He was also a correspondent for *Variety*, and was among the first to appreciate the talents of Bob Dylan, Miles Davis, and Lenny Bruce, whom he admired personally and professionally. Only a few months before he testified, Gleason wrote a glowing review of the Curran concert, which he tagged as "great, possibly historic."

When Bendich called Gleason, he hoped to establish the thematic integration of Bruce's varied bits and to elevate the intellectual stature of those bits. Gleason did not disappoint; he spoke of Lenny's act at The Jazz Workshop as a literary critic would lecture on James Joyce's *Finnegans Wake*. "The theme of the performance on the night in question was a social criticism of stereotypes and of the hypocrisy of contemporary society....He attempted to demonstrate to the audience a proposition that's familiar to students of semantics," Gleason declared. "[That] is that words have been given in our society almost a magic meaning that has no relation to the facts, and I think that he tried...to demonstrate that there is no harm inherent in words themselves."

Quick to object, Wollenberg reminded the judge that Officers Ryan and Solden were not allowed to give their opinions of Bruce's work, and therefore neither should Mr. Gleason.

> *Horn*: The officers were not here as experts.
> *Wollenberg*: Well, this witness is an expert on what, your Honor?...
> *Horn*: Well, I think if you listen, you'll find out.

The counsel for the defense next had to confront the very problem Jake Ehrlich identified when he declined to represent Lenny: "You can't win a case based on 'cocksucker.'"

"Mr. Gleason," Bendich asked, "do you have an opinion concerning the use of ['cocksucker' with regard to] its artistic relevance to the work of Mr. Bruce?" Irrelevant and immaterial once again, Wollenberg protested. He deemed it unnecessary to probe into the literary or artistic importance of "cocksucker" in the context of an obscenity trial. Judge Horn, who had presided over the *Ferlinghetti* obscenity trial, reminded the deputy D.A. that he had heard this same issue "argued at length before me in the *Howl* case, and I'm very familiar with it. Overruled." Gleason proceeded to explain the societal hypocrisy of tolerating "cocksucker" in some settings but not in others.

Sensitive to what Justice Brennan had written in *Roth v. United States*, Bendich inquired as to whether or not a Bruce routine needed to be "considered as a whole" to be fully appreciated:

> *Bendich*: Mr. Gleason, you have just indicated that the performance must be taken as a whole. In your judgment, is a Lenny Bruce performance a work which has integration and which must be taken as a whole and as an entirety if it is to be understood properly?
> *Wollenberg*: Same objection [as irrelevant and immaterial], Your Honor.
> *Horn*: Overruled.
> *Gleason*: Yes, I think it has to be taken that way, sir.

Immediately, Bendich changed direction in his examination of Ralph Gleason. The cultural critic had maintained an extensive file of reviews, interviews, and news stories concerning Bruce, and the defense counsel now intended that the jury hear some of the analytical praise that Lenny had garnered. Albert Wollenberg's objection notwithstanding, Gleason read to the jury a lengthy excerpt of a Nat Hentoff article written for *Commonweal*, a Catholic weekly magazine. A noted New York music critic and another Bruce enthusiast, Hentoff "testified" to Lenny's artistry and sociopolitical importance: "It is in Lenny Bruce—and only in him—that there has emerged a cohesively 'new' comedy of nakedly honest moral rage at the deceptions all down the line in our society....Coursing through everything he does, however, is a serious search for values that are more than security blankets." There was Bendich making his case that Lenny was a modern-day Jonathan Swift. That was the dominant theme—comedy as commentary.

Wollenberg desperately strove to block Bendich's defense strategies, but time and again his objections—*irrelevant and immaterial, your Honor; inadequate foundation, your Honor; beyond the scope of the witness's expertise, your Honor*—were overruled. One embarrassing incident for the assistant district attorney interrupted the normal course of proceedings, as if a premonition of things to come. While Wollenberg quizzed Gleason about one of his newspaper clippings, Judge Horn cut him off with a smirk: "I'd like to carry on the trial without further levity. But at the sake of being facetious, your shirt tail is out." Somewhat rattled, the prosecutor responded curtly: "I don't think it is terribly relevant to the issues here, your Honor." To the contrary, the symbolic meaning of the episode merely eluded Wollenberg: like his sartorial style, his legal suit was beginning to come undone. At the close of the second day of trial, it was already evident to the trained legal mind that the defense had cast reasonable doubt into the prosecution's case.

Now Lenny could rest more easily...this time at the St. Francis Hotel.

A Throw-Away Line?

BEFORE LENNY WAS busted, City Lights Bookstore proudly displayed his *Stamp Out Help...and Other Short Stories*—a wacky self-published work featuring Lenny and others in various hallucinatory states of pot consciousness. Unlike Ginsberg's book *Howl*, which was also in the window, *Stamp Out Help* was a photo album of sorts, with costumed Lenny posing as everything from a cop to a rifle-toting cowboy in a toilet graveyard.

Al Bendich called witness after witness, expert and lay alike, to knock out the elements of the California obscenity statute, one by one. There were the Browns: Kenneth, a Daly City High School English teacher, and Mary, housewife and mother, who were together at The Jazz Workshop on the night of Lenny's arrest. To Mr. Brown, the Bruce performance was an experience in "aesthetic pain"—softening by laughter the raw truths of social dysfunctionality—and certainly not an experience in sexual stimulation. Ms. Brown affirmed her husband's assessment that the show did not appeal to prurient interests. Ditto from Clarence Knight, a former deputy district attorney for San Mateo who had evaluated more than two hundred potential pornography cases, and who had witnessed the entirety of Lenny's Jazz Workshop act.

An assistant professor of English from U.C. Berkeley, Robert Tracy, was called for his expertise in drama and American comedy. Reciting passages from Anglo-American literary masterpieces, he maintained that blue language was part and parcel of classic novelistic writing. With Tracy as their mouthpiece, Geoffrey Chaucer and James Joyce also "testified" for the defense. The jury heard a raucous excerpt of "The Miller's Tale" from Chaucer's *Canterbury Tales*: "The night was dark as pitch or as coal / And at the window out she put her hole, / And Absalom felt no better or no worse / But with his mouth he kissed her naked arse / Full savorly before he was aware of it. / Back he jumped and thought something wrong, / For he knew perfectly well that a woman has no beard."

The "grand lit" lesson continued with another of Professor Tracy's selections, this one from Molly Bloom's soliloquy in Joyce's *Ulysses*: "there's the mark of his teeth still where he tried to bite the nipple...they are so beautiful of course compared to what a man looks like with his two bags full and his other thing hanging down out of him or sticking up at you like a hat rack." Thus, Bendich continued his assault on the prosecution's case by emphasizing yet another element of California Penal Code Section 311.6. If Chaucer's and Joyce's indecent language did not deprive their works of "redeeming social importance," by implication, then, why should Bruce's indecency be treated otherwise?

The defense needed to tie Bruce's Jazz Workshop act back to the high literary styles that the jury had just heard. Grover Sales, a performing arts publicist, took the stand to do just that. He attested to the changing nature of Bruce's comedy over the years. By the time of the Jazz Workshop performance, Lenny had entered into a new phase of "free-form or free-association, very much in the same style as the passage that was read out loud from James Joyce, the Molly Bloom soliloquy."

Mr. Wollenberg detected an opportunity to strike back. On cross-examination, he asked Sales whether, when Lenny was recalling his appearance at Ann's 440, he merely had interjected the phrase "over-run with cocksuckers" into his narrative. "Well, 'interjected,' I'd say, is the right word, because this material was an aside or an interjection on Mr. Bruce's part," noted Sales. "This is what he would call in his profession 'a throw-away line.'" It was exactly what Wollenberg wanted to hear. If Lenny's "cocksucker" reference were only a throw-away line, then it could not be an integral part of his artistic work "considered as a whole." And, if that were the case, Wollenberg might defeat one of Bendich's major arguments under the obscenity definitions in the California statute and *Roth*.

Seizing on the phrase, Wollenberg inferred: "You say a 'throw-away line.' It didn't have any meaning to the show, is that what you are telling us?" Unfamiliarity with show-biz lingo now disserved the deputy district attorney. Sales quickly corrected the prosecutor's mis-impression: "No, that's not the meaning of a 'throw-away line.' A 'throw-away line' dramatically is a line that is not stressed or given emphasis, but is merely tossed off in a *sotto voce* fashion, as though it's just an afterthought....[A]nything Mr. Bruce sees fit to put in his show is necessary to that show." A strong point of prosecutorial contention had been weakened significantly. So much so that Wollenberg's efforts to dent Bruce's defense had barely scratched it.

Bendich also relied on Louis Gottlieb, the witty Ph.D. front man for the folk trio, The Limeliters. The defense wanted to drive home the point that contemporary standards of candor in local nightclub entertainment could and should tolerate Lenny's comic assaults on social prejudice. "I feel that the social effect of [his] themes...are only beneficial," Gottlieb opined. "He creates sympathy...within his audience for socially produced problems such as racial and religious bigotry, perhaps even narcotics addiction, the problems of inverts and other people whose problems...must be regarded sympathetically." Putting the finishing touches on his portrait of Lenny's comic perspective, Gottlieb declared: "Mr. Bruce's point of view is one of the great comic points of view in literature and in history, I would say, and it has been characterized as laughter through tears, or laughing to keep from crying....Mr. Bruce is able to evoke that by virtue of his approach and his skill."

INDEED, DIVERSIONS AND distractions had become the common fare—both inside and outside of the courtroom. For example, a nineteen-year-old student from San Francisco City College, Jefferson Poland, created a commotion in the courthouse hallways as he distributed leaflets authored by one of his friends. Their printed First Amendment message:

WELCOME TO THE FARCE!

Lenny Bruce, one of America's foremost comedians and social critics, is at this moment playing an unwilling part as a straight man in a social comedy put on by the City and County of San Francisco...

Forgive Lenny's language. Most of us use it at times; most of us even use the things and perform the acts considered unprintable and unspeakable by the authors of [§311.6 of the California Penal Code], though most of us are not nearly frank enough to say so.

Lenny has better things to do than play in this farce; the taxpayers have better uses for their money; and the little old ladies of both sexes who produce it should have better amusements.

With a nostalgic sigh, let's pull down the curtain on People v. Bruce and its genre; and present a far more interesting and fruitful play called "Freedom of Speech." It would do our jaded ears good.

Unwittingly, Mr. Poland found himself playing the part of a rather flustered and remorseful "extra" in Lenny's "farce." Hauled before Judge Horn on the third afternoon of the trial, the young actor was subjected to a dressing-down:

Horn: Don't you know that these might get into the hands of a juror?...Someone might leave it around or just hand them one, then the damage is done.
Poland: I see.
Horn: You see what you're up against here. You are actually in contempt of court for interfering with the processes of the court.
Poland: Oh.
Horn: Because if this got into the hands of a juror...this might affect the course of the trial....[Y]ou are not permitted under any

circumstance to distribute literature of this type in a courthouse where a trial is taking place.

Poland: Oh. I see....

Horn: Well, I'm not going to do anything about it this time, although this conduct of yours constitutes contempt of court. Because of your age, because of the fact that I don't know as yet whether or not this will influence the course of the trial, I'm not going to take any action at this time....But if it should develop that these pamphlets have some effect on the course of the trial, why, then we'll have to take this up again.

Lucky for Jefferson Poland that he was standing sheepishly before Clayton Horn, rather than before Albert Axelrod! Lucky, too, for him that the trial proceeded with no further incidents related to the leaflets.

INSIDE THE COURTROOM, Lenny himself did plenty enough to disrupt decorum. Throughout the trial, he bombarded his counsel with questions, suggestions, and corrections. He furiously took notes and passed them. From time to time, he burst out with editorial ejaculations. This pent-up energy stemmed, in real measure, from the fact that Lenny could not argue his own case. He had, after all, struck a deal with Bendich—he, not Lenny, was to do the talking. But now, at long last, Lenny Bruce the entertainer was about to take center stage.

Dressed in his third striking outfit of three days—this one, very tight white pants, faded blue denim jacket, and white boots—Lenny may have been the most insignificant of the witnesses Bendich had called. His testimony largely consisted of banter about what he *actually* had said. For example, Lenny insisted that his *shtick* about the ticket-booth sign ended "kiss it," rather than "eat it" (as it earlier had been reported). When Bendich inquired whether there was any meaningful difference, Lenny replied: "Kissing my mother good-bye and eating my mother good-bye, there is a quantity of difference." If nothing else, it made for good theater.

So did the tape recording of the Jazz Workshop show, when eighteen minutes of its most critical content were played to the jury the next day. In the process, Lenny had staged his act in the Hall of Justice. The courtroom became his theater—but not an unrestrained and boisterous one. When Albert Bendich cautioned Judge Horn that the spectators were likely to hoot at the high comedy, the court would have none of it:

> *Bendich*: The request which I wish to have your Honor consider is this: I think in all sincerity, your Honor, that there are portions of this tape which are going to evoke laughter in the audience.
> *Horn*: I anticipated you; I was going to give that admonition.
> *Bendich*: Well, what I was going to ask, your Honor, is whether the audience might not be allowed to respond naturally, given the circumstances that this is an accurate reproduction of a performance which is given at a nightclub; it's going to evoke comic responses, and I believe that it would be asking more than is humanly possible of the persons in this courtroom not to respond humanly, which is to say, by way of laughter.
> *Horn*: Well…this is not a theater and it is not a show, and I am not going to allow any such thing.…I am now going to admonish the spectators that you are not to treat this as a performance. This is not for your entertainment. There's a very serious question involved here, the right of the People and the right of the defendant. And I admonish you that you are to control yourselves with regard to any emotions that you may feel during…the reproduction of this tape.

There were smirks and repressed giggles, but no waves of laughter. Lenny's act played on, but before a strangely sober audience—surely the most silent that he had experienced ever before.

The closing arguments were a case study in contrast. On the one hand, Albert Wollenberg appealed to the jury's sense of common decency, unaffected by the nuances of law or the high-brow opinions of the elite. "Now, the question isn't what the University of California professors or the high school teachers from Daly City feel is literature or comedy…not the top of the community educationally, those people over in the ivory towers.…[I]t is what the people on the street, the conglomerate average, feel." This was a call to populist jurisprudence.

On the other hand, Albert Bendich appealed to the jury's oath to apply the law, whatever their populist predilections. Point by point, he outlined the defense's case; jot by jot, he demonstrated how the state had failed to prove its case *as a matter of law.* "On any and all of the four points of this code, Mr. Bruce is innocent beyond any question....I ask the jury to return the only verdict consistent with the law as it has been worded and as it has been interpreted to you by this court, not guilty." It was a call to honor the letter of the law.

Judge and Jury

HAD THE CLOCK stopped at the end of the lawyers' closing arguments, the prosecution could have won its case, given the makeup of the jury. That, however, would have discounted the critical role that Judge Horn played in the final stage of the trial. For some thirty minutes, he instructed the jury on the relevant law and how it should be applied. As in the Ferlinghetti trial, Horn understood the governing law in a way consistent with a liberal interpretation of *Roth.* Among the most pertinent of the instructions were the following:

—Sex and obscenity are not synonymous.

—In order to make the portrayal of sex obscene...the portrayal must be such that its dominant tendency is to deprave or corrupt the average adult by tending to create a clear and present danger of antisocial behavior.

—The law does not prohibit the realistic portrayal by an artist of his subject matter, and the law may not require the author to put refined language into the mouths of primitive people.

—The use of blasphemy, foul or coarse language, and vulgar behavior does not in and of itself constitute obscenity.

—If the performance is merely disgusting or revolting, it cannot be obscene, because obscenity contemplates the arousal of sexual desires.

—A performance cannot be considered utterly without redeeming social importance if it has literary, artistic, or aesthetic merit, or if it contains ideas, regardless of whether they are unorthodox, controversial, or hateful, of redeeming social importance.

—[I]n the crime charged here, a necessary element is the existence in the mind of the defendant knowing that the material used in his production on October 4, 1961, was obscene....In determining whether the defendant had such knowledge, you may consider reviews of his work which were available to him, stating that his performance had artistic merit and contained socially important ideas.

In essence, these were the same free speech points Horn had made in his *People v. Ferlinghetti* opinion four and a half years earlier. And, in a real sense, these were direct and unambivalent answers to the questions Justice Brennan posed in his 1953 obscenity opinion for the New Jersey Supreme Court. Now, they were to direct the jury's judgment in *People v. Bruce*.

The jury retired. Clearly, the eight men and four women struggled with Judge Horn's instructions; first, they requested Horn to restate them orally, and subsequently they asked for written copies. On the first ballot, the jury split 9 to 3 in Lenny's favor. But, after a total of five hours and twenty-five minutes of deliberation, unanimity was reached.

The court clerk announced the verdict: "We, the jury...find the defendant not guilty of the offense charged, misdemeanor, to wit: violating Section 311.6 of the Penal Code of the State of California." In reply to the judge's question, "Ladies and gentlemen of the jury, is this your verdict?" the jury foreman, George H. Casey III, answered in the affirmative. For safe measure, Judge Horn asked the question a second time. The answer was the same.

"WE HATE THIS verdict," one juror admitted. "But under the instructions there was nothing we could do but give the 'not guilty' verdict." George Casey III added: "That's the way all of us felt, and I hope your newspaper people will report this, that we all felt the law should be tightened." Later, when the jury was polled by the Center for the Study of Law and Society, one thing was certain: "The 'law,' as expressed in the judge's instructions, made a decided difference." The overall jury sentiment, it was reported, could best be articulated as such: "Under the law, as we the jurors understand it, based on the judge's instructions, and in as much as we feel that the law should be changed to prevent such behavior from occurring, Mr. Bruce is not guilty."

Al Bendich—someone who seemed quiet, humble, and never more visible than necessary—had done it again. He had beaten back the forces of censorship, though this time by the grace of a begrudging jury. Lenny Bruce's freedom hinged on the fact that, in the name of the First Amendment, the members of the jury tolerated what offended them. Less tolerant, perhaps, was the indignant San Francisco chief of police, Thomas Cahill. To him, if Bruce's acquittal meant "that we allow this type of language in public performances, then we stoop to a new low." He called for the law to be changed—free speech should not be *that* free.

THE EPILOGUE TO *People v. Bruce* played out at an eleven PM courtroom session. Not one to forget a contempt citation, Judge Horn conducted a hearing, listened to Bendich's arguments, took Lenny's testimony, and ruled—this time, against the defendant. He imposed a $100 fine, a far cry from his original inclination to jail Bruce for five days. A friend picked up the tab.

LENNY BRUCE CLEARED was the banner headline for the March 9, 1962, edition of the *San Francisco Chronicle*. There, on the front page, was a photograph of an elated Lenny whooping it up with one of the women jurors. It had been 156 days since the bust on Broadway, 350 pages of costly trial transcript, and $2,100 in Bendich's fees alone. Two trials, two judges, two prosecutors, two lawyers, two jury votes, and two grand—too damn much.

San Francisco now looked glorious again. As he played to the press, Lenny emoted: "I'm very grateful to the city of San Francisco....[W]e're coming to a delightful renaissance when intellectualism and virility are not at separate ends." With an irony that then escaped him, he added: "I'm never going to say any four-letter words again. I'm bored with the dirty word aspect and I'm off for a bigger mission." The thirty-six-year old comedian then rushed to catch a red-eye to New York.

Meanwhile, rumors spread that Lenny Bruce was again *persona non grata*, this time with the Los Angeles authorities with whom he previously had run-ins. An idle matter then, but soon enough rumor would become reality.

4

L.A. STORY

It hasn't always been a circus, the [story] of Los Angeles,
but it has always been interesting. Relentlessly interesting.
                                                    —*Gordon DeMarco*

Eye Candy

FREE AS THE bohemian life was in North Beach, Lenny Bruce found more fertile ground for uninhibited comic creativity in Los Angeles. There, he had become an unhinged comedian with an ever-developing flair for far-out, freak-out, and stream-of-consciousness humor of all imaginable sorts—long before the 1962 rumors that L.A. authorities were growing more hostile to his shenanigans. The L.A. story begins in 1950...in one of those many "toilets" that Lenny worked so cavalierly.

Near the L.A. intersection of Pico and Western, Maynard Sloate traded in taboos and paraded firm flesh. It was not Sin City, though it might have been. It was Strip City, where a two-drink minimum ($1.50) was a gent's pass to an eyeful of tits 'n ass; it was all prurient appeal designed to get the guys horny. There, in Sloate's happy-hormone club, Lenny Bruce once performed. And there, too, he met two men who would come to play leading roles in his free speech struggles in Los Angeles—Burton Marks and Seymour Fried.

Sloate was a twenty-five-year-old agent booking highbrow gigs for Sarah Vaughan, Ella Fitzgerald, and Count Basie and lowbrow acts for a Sunset Strip burlesque house when he decided to make more money by opening his own club. With two partners, the brown-haired and bespectacled young man bought a failed nightclub located at 1301 Western, across the street from Scriveners, a drive-in. Having little money to decorate, the new owners mounted a vertical neon sign trumpeting STRIP CITY. They also covered the two large front glass windows with photos of strippers, sure to grab any stroker's eye. The clientele loved the tease of sex. Voyeurism being what it is, business boomed in no time. As Sloate recalled: "When we first opened, the police said we'd draw attention by calling it 'Strip City.' About a month later, the police decided that we needed a raid. Three cops from the Wilshire District Police Department synchronized their watches to converge upon the stage at a preordained time. I asked, 'What's this all about?'"

Reminiscent of Captain Louis Renault in *Casablanca*, a Sergeant McFarland answered Sloate: "I am shocked and embarrassed."

Then, Sloate related, "I asked again, 'Well, what happened? What did you see?' 'I was shocked and embarrassed.' You understand, he had been programmed to utter only those...words."

The next thing Maynard knew, he was in the slammer to be bailed out by his parents, and he had a criminal record for conducting a lewd and indecent show. The lesson learned? "We then started to pay off everybody in the city of Los Angeles." It worked; the heat never returned.

Strip City wasn't a plush purple palace, or a lush red velvet cabaret; it was a shit-brown joint for working stiffs. Strip City wasn't a place where the dancers blew the band, caressed the clientele, or humped a pole. No, nothing *that* uninhibited or ribald. It was vanilla erotica starting with stage costumes and ending with pasties and g-strings. Through five acts every hour until two A.M., black-skirted and white-bloused waitresses oiled the audience with drinks; the young Burton Marks manned the old National Cash Register at the bar; and the cook, Mary Lou, fried steaks and chicken for the few who dined. Meanwhile, Don Raffel, the band leader, wailed on his tenor sax, Frank Devenport banged on his piano, and Kenny Hume tried to catch the girls' bumps and grinds with rim shots on his drums. On weekends, as many as 250 gawkers crowded the semicircle of tables around the dance floor, hooting and howling as the lusty ladies strutted their stuff.

In 1953, the owl-eyed Sloate saw Bruce for the first time. Lenny and his wife, Honey Harlowe, had recently arrived in Southern

California; he was working the Cup and Saucer, a dive in rural Downey, and she was working the Colony Club, a burlesque house in Gardena. Bruce's agent, Lou Dorn, brought Maynard to see Lenny's routine at the Cup and Saucer. Here was a comedian who wasn't doing a hackneyed Army act; he was doing his own original bits, some of which amused Maynard. This fresh comic appeal impressed Sloate enough that he offered Lenny $75 a week to emcee at Strip City. Lenny accepted, in no small part because Honey worked nearby (for $35 weekly) and easily could pick him up in their black Caddy at the end of the night.

Strip City's unadorned marquee billed Lenny along with the names of five strippers. The twenty-eight-year-old comedian was the middleman between the girls on stage and the guys at the tables; he introduced the dancers, one after the other, and then performed longer bits during intermission while the three-piece band took a fifteen-minute break. Because his *shtick* interrupted the gaze, the audience was frequently uninterested. After all, his bits had to compete with female flesh designed to seize male retinas. How could his words, however funny or profound, compete with the bawdy curves of Lusty Busty Brown (a twenty-one-year-old pin-up model who later married Sloate), Gay Dawn (a blonde "girl scout" with a bust job), and Melba "the Toast of the Town" (the plain-looker hired because of her stage name)?

As the girls freed themselves of their wrappings, Lenny began to free himself of his comic restraints, sometimes by design and other times by disaster. There was one night, for example, when a table of newspapermen (reportedly from the *Los Angeles Times*) unexpectedly became a part of Lenny's act. Sloate had comped them in the hope that Strip City would likewise be comped with some favorable ink in their paper. Drinking with abandon, one of them got rowdy and began heckling. It unnerved Lenny, and he spontaneously devised a counter-attack. During his break, he snuck out to Scriveners drive-in; with devious intent, he returned with a pie tin filled with whipped cream. When the heckler resumed, Lenny asked: "Would you stand up a minute?" The newsman was sitting right in front. "Come on, stand up a minute." Rising to his feet, the reporter received a cream facial. It was an old routine now put to comic revenge. The last laugh, however, was the *L.A. Times'*—for whatever reason, the paper never published a favorable review of any Lenny Bruce act during his lifetime.

Maynard Sloate recounted an even more bizarre episode: "The other comic on the show, Rod "Shorty" Rogers, was singing a parody of Bing Crosby's 1936 hit 'Pennies from Heaven' that Rogers tagged 'Bennies from Heaven.'" ("Bennies" was the street vernacular for Benzedrine.) The ever-mischievous Lenny planned to add his own comic touch from on high. "So, Lenny climbs up into the crawl space of a false ceiling, finds a hole in the ceiling above Rogers's head, and begins to drop aspirins, one by one, to signify 'bennies from heaven.'" The gag became hilarious when it took an unexpected and dramatic turn. Instead of bennies, plaster and dust fell from heaven. "Lenny winds up coming through the ceiling." Crack! *Crash!!* CA-BOOM!!! "First we see a foot, then a leg, then his whole body as the false ceiling caves in." Rogers dodged the downpour as a hapless Bruce desperately grabbed for any kind of support. Thus, Lenny's deconstruction of "Bennies from Heaven."

Lenny also appeared on stage at Strip City with the infamous Lord Buckley, although only in "the finale"—Maynard Sloate's theatrical contribution to strip shows. Buckley was the high priest of the hipsters, a comic known for his outrageous comments and conduct. The Lord of Hip invoked audiences' attention with pitches like "Hipsters, Flipsters, and Finger Poppin' Daddies, knock me your lobes!" The elegantly dressed and Salvador Dalíesque wax-mustachioed comedian preferred to be addressed as "His Lordship." Apart from his proper British accent and mannerisms, he was all wildly American. He would say and do almost anything that came to mind. Sometimes speaking in jive-jazz lingo—"hipsemantic," he called it—His Lordship welcomed a good row with his audience: he sprayed seltzer into ladies' cleavage and cut gentlemen's ties. Lord Buckley was Bruce's kind of guy; Buckley's swash-buckled flair for the ridiculous fed Lenny's own appetite for the absurd.

In many ways, "Strip City was like a college of comedy for Lenny," recalled Honey. "For a while, each performance was a credit. It was also Russian roulette. Two shows in a row go fine, then the third show flops. Two shows bomb out, then the next one takes the roof off." But with the company of Lord Buckley and the nod of the band, it didn't much matter what an audience of crude dudes thought—Lenny was in the limelight, and he loved it.

Burton Marks, the weekend cashier at Strip City, liked the antics of the tall Buckley and the short Bruce; they struck his funny bone. Though such comedy revealed a "weird" kind of thinking, Burt was drawn to it, nonetheless. A brother-in-law to Bill Robinson, one of Sloate's business partners, Burt was not yet twenty-one when he began managing the club's money. By the time Lenny arrived on the scene, Burt was of legal age and of a legal mindset—he was a student at UCLA Law School. A young man of average build and affable manner, he studied conventional codes of behavior on weekdays and surveyed unconventional courses of behavior on weekends. In time, Burt's Strip City experiences would affect his attitude toward criminal law in general, obscenity law in part, and Lenny Bruce in particular. Ten years after meeting Bruce, Burt would represent him in one of his L.A. obscenity busts. For now, however, he was amused by Lenny's biting comedy and outrageous exploits with cream pies and ceiling plaster.

Another Sloate connection, this one his close friend and lawyer, was a notable player in Lenny's legal life. He was Seymour Fried. Born on the same day as Lenny but two years earlier, Fried graduated from Southwestern University Law School the very year Strip City opened. Maynard referred Bruce to Fried when the comedian found himself in some legal scraps—involving everything from civil tort actions to corporate transactions to criminal cases. In time, Fried became one of Lenny's faithful fans and First Amendment counselors.

Those lawyer years, when Lenny was up to his stoned eyeballs in legal troubles, had not yet arrived. There was only the present-perfect, *la vida* at Strip City. "Good evening, everyone," he began. "It's a real pleasure to be working Arlington Cemetery tonight." The guys in the band loved it, this slap at the audience. "You're gonna like our show because tonight we have ladies from a Science Fiction Review, performing for your pleasure," he continued. "We'll be starting off with an acrobatic stripper known as the 'Upside-Down Girl,' a six-foot-two towering eyeful, and she'll be sharing star billing with a sensational newcomer, Miss Fifty-four D. If this little lady comes to your house to borrow some sugar, don't let her in! She's got the biggest cups in town!" Again, the band wolfed it up while the audience sat freeze-dried, demanding to *see* the next bust job on stage.

Remarkably, as Lenny's bits became "sicker" and "raunchier," he was never busted in the year and a half that he played at Sloate's club. But those days of uncensored freedom would end soon enough. Though there would be some clubs where Lenny's liberty was unthreatened, he would never again enjoy as long a comic run uninterrupted by vice squads as he did at Strip City.

Building Up to The Crescendo

REALITY IS THE flipside of tease. While the nights at Strip City and the Colony Club were erotically fanciful for Lenny and Honey, their days were economically brutal. They scratched by on a skin-stretched budget, frequently cutting into their savings to cover monthly expenses—rent ($135), car payment ($252), car insurance ($24), groceries ($68), appliances ($21), plus miscellaneous costs such as gas for the guzzling Cadillac. All expenses totaled, they typically found themselves on the red side of the ledger. What to do?

One answer: try to break into Hollywood, while still working the joints. Nineteen fifty-four was the first of Lenny's filmmaking years. Though the very idea of Lenny as a celluloid figure—scriptwriter, actor, producer—seems comic, it was one he pursued seriously. Starting with *Dream Follies* (1954), continuing with *Dance Hall Racket* (1954), and ending with *The Leather Jacket* (1955–1957), Lenny brought his meager cinematic talents to bear on films that have either been lost to history's dustbin or should have been.

Take *Dance Hall Racket*, an excuse for a riveting gangster flick. Lenny wrote the screenplay and starred as a switchblade-wielding goon. The movie's eye-drooping plot revolved around the sinister doings of a dance hall proprietor (who fenced hot diamonds), his duo of henchmen (one played by Lenny), the dance hall hostess (played by Sally Marr), and a coterie of ticket-taking dancers (including Honey).

Everything was a con, from petty larceny to homicide. For that matter, *Dance Hall Racket* itself was a con, what with its puerile script, hokey sets, wooden acting, and home-movie production quality. But Hollywood was not to be conned—the B-movie ran in only one venue, a fleapit theater down on Main Street.

A more promising way for Lenny to make money was to continue doing what he did best—comedy. That meant working better-paying joints and hoping to break into upscale clubs. When his film career flopped, Lenny struck a deal with Rocky Lo Fusello, a retired Chicago pharmacist turned club owner, to perform at Duffy's Gaieties for nearly twice his salary at Strip City. The added revenue was essential, given the birth (November 7, 1955) of his daughter, Brandie Kathleen Bruce; Lenny changed her name to Kitty, since he felt that "Brandie" sounded too much like a stripper's name.

Duffy's, a burlesque club on Cahuenga, was a bacchanalian haven, a place where you could let your libido hang out. Unemployed jazzmen gigged there, hookers cruised there, strippers grinded there, junkies scored there...and Lenny thrived there. From his opening night on New Year's Eve 1955 to June 1956 (and for several weeks in 1957), Lenny plied tired one-liners and more imaginative longer bits. His nine P.M.–to–two A.M. routines, delivered from a stage not much larger than a closet, were chock-full of dope jokes, inspired no doubt by his budding relationship with the jazz saxophonist, Joe Maini, the white-skinned, dark-haired, hook-nosed, ex-con junkman who taught Lenny to mainline. High on hilarity and heroin, Lenny pushed his routines beyond dirty words—entering in the buff, he pissed in a knothole on stage as a "labor protest" for the strippers who bitched about their stilettos getting caught in it. At Duffy's, and other derelict dives like it—Gil Parker's Bamboo Room and the Cobblestone, both in the San Fernando Valley—Lenny became ever more free-wheeling in his approach to comedy. "Lenny probably never had more fun than he had at Duffy's," recalled Maynard Sloate.

Moved by that same free-wheeling spirit, Lenny also had some fun at the expense of the private property rights of others. Early one morning after Duffy's had closed, he hooked up with his friend, Frank Ray Perilli, who was emcee at the Near and Far, a Santa

Monica Boulevard strip joint owned by the mobster Mickey Cohen. Instead of returning to the confines of his apartment, Lenny wanted something more expansive, more luxurious, something with a beach view. As quickly as you could say Malibu, they were off to that spectacular stretch of the coast to sleep a few hours, relax in the sand, and work on their tans. They were to stay overnight at the beach home of one of Lenny's pals—or so Perilli thought. "Lenny was driving around and around; he said he had lost his way," Perilli recounted. "Finally, he pulled into a place where there were a lot of newspapers on the lawn; the people were out of town." When Lenny could find no key under the doormat, "he assured me that it would be alright to break a window to enter. Knowing how devious Lenny could be, I should have caught on that something was seriously wrong." The next thing Frankie knew, there was shattered glass and Lenny was hunting for the bedrooms. "'Don't sleep too late,' Lenny warned me. 'Wake me up, and we're going to hit that beach.' So, I'm sleepin'," Perilli continued, "and then, all of a sudden, I feel somebody shaking my toe. It's the owner of the house. 'Lenny,' I call out, 'your friend is here.' The guy said to me, 'Don't call him. I don't even know who the fuck you two are!'" Caught in the act, a shame-faced Lenny immediately tendered $25 to fix the window and hightailed it out of there. "Luckily," Perilli sighed, "the owner never called the police on us."

Nineteen fifty-seven was a year of mixed blessings for Lenny. On the one hand, he divorced Honey; things got worse for Honey when, that summer, she was sentenced to two years in a federal penitentiary for violating probation in connection with a marijuana bust. Now, Kitty's care was left to Sally and Lenny. On the other hand, *Fortuna* smiled on Bruce's career; he finally got a gig at a class-act club.

Sloate moved up in the world, and so did Lenny. Sloate and one of his business partners, Joe Abrams, sold Strip City and bought into the chic Crescendo at 8570 Sunset Boulevard. They had been invited to do so by Gene Norman, a one-time disc jockey for KFWB and KLAC and the lead partner and ultimate owner of The Crescendo. Formerly a restaurant called "The Chanticleer," The Crescendo was an attractive amber-hued room with crystal chandeliers and large picture windows overlooking Los Angeles. The club played host to such big-name acts as Duke Ellington, Count Basie, Billie Holiday, Ella Fitzgerald, the Four Freshmen, and the Mary Kay Trio. Located at the same site, but one floor above, was a separate and more intimate club called The Interlude. Norman bought The Interlude from a noted Los Angeles criminal defense lawyer, Harry Weiss (who, in the course of his career, would collaborate with Burton Marks on cases not involving Lenny).

Bruce hooked up with Norman through Sloate. "I was Lenny's friend," Sloate explained, "and I was responsible for bringing him to The Crescendo. Lenny wasn't the main attraction in the beginning; he was the opening act for other talent." At first, Sloate remembered, Norman did not appear to dig Lenny's comedy: "When Lenny would go on, Gene would say things like 'Is he funny, Maynard?' Gene and Lenny weren't exactly in tune." Norman himself conceded that he was hesitant to hire Bruce in the beginning: "When I heard what he did, I wasn't that happy with it. Because it was a little bit rough for me. I didn't want to be associated with four-letter words." Nonetheless, Norman was a good businessman and knew a draw when he saw one. As time passed and word spread, L.A.'s hip set could not get enough of the daring Bruce. So, after Sloate left The Crescendo, Norman continued to book Lenny both there and at The Interlude for relatively long stretches between July of 1957 to July of 1962. His runs proved to be so lucrative that, at one point, Norman paid Lenny $4,000 a week. It didn't matter anymore whether or not the comedian was funny—he *was* Lenny Bruce!

Other blessings were bestowed on Bruce in 1957, though he would not come to realize their impact for several years. In June, the U.S. Supreme Court delivered *Roth v. United States*, a significant high court decision that helped to liberalize the First Amendment law of obscenity. Three and a half months later, San Francisco Municipal Court Judge Clayton Horn issued his free-speech-friendly opinion in *People v. Ferlinghetti*, the first California court decision to interpret the mandates of *Roth* for obscenity prosecutions. The Lenny Bruce of this period, of course, was not yet Lenny the Lawyer. So, he could afford to be oblivious to these two legal precedents that would so much affect his future. And, indeed, he was.

On New Year's Eve, 1957, Lenny played two shows on the opening night of The Slate Brothers club…and quickly closed what was to
have been a two-week run. A trendy and posh Hollywood hotspot on
La Cienega that sat 125 people, The Slate Brothers' décor offered
"crystal chandeliers, mirrored walls, and carpet so deep it would shine
your shoes in six steps." The club would come to feature entertainers
such as Don Rickles and Bobby Darin and to cater to celebrities such
as Frank Sinatra and Louella Parsons.

Things didn't get off to a good start that night. As William Karl
Thomas, Lenny's friend and photographer, told it: "The first show,
Lenny was just nervous. When a line failed he'd turn his back on the
audience and play to the band…" Things got worse, all the way to the
end. "After the first show, one of the Slate Brothers came over to [the
publicist, Sam Wall] and said, 'Can't you revive him? He's dying up
there.'" But, in his second show, Lenny finally caught the audience's
attention; in fact, he blew them away. Shortly before Father Time
turned his clock to 1958, Lenny let loose one of the sickest jokes that
he ever told in a chi-chi milieu. In the presence of George Raft,
Georgie Jessel, the Three Stooges, and Bert Gordon (the "Mad Russian" from the Eddie Cantor Show), Lenny did a bit reportedly told by
Buddy Hackett.

"A kid looks up at his father and he says, 'What's a degenerate?'" The
father says, 'Shut up, kid, and keep sucking!'" Stunned silence, then
pandemonium. According to Lenny's sidekick, Frank Ray Perilli:

> Henry Slate, a tough guy, was outside the club on the sidewalk,
> nervous, since it was his opening night. Well, they all come running
> out, saying, "Henry, do you *know* what Lenny Bruce *did*?!" When
> Henry heard *that*, [well] Lenny quit on the spot. Lenny and I ran
> over to Canter's: "Fuck 'em, I don't care," Lenny said. The Mad
> Russian came in: "Lenny Bruce, *what* did you do?" Lenny turned
> to me: "Take me to Western Union." He sent the Slate Brothers a
> telegram: "I love you guys. I'm sorry if I embarrassed you. I really
> didn't mean to bring you trouble." The funny part is that the Slate
> Brothers were willing to give him the opportunity to come back, but
> he never did.

The next day, Lenny made the trades for the first time, as *The Hollywood Reporter* figuratively (and presciently) compared his one-night stand at The Slate Brothers to an arrest: LENNY BRUCE BUSTED FOR BLUE MATERIAL. No matter. For Lenny was off to North Beach for another first run—this time at Ann's 440, where the club owner and crowd did not go zonkers about cocksucking bits. Sometime later he was southeast-bound to Florida, where he hoped his audience would be equally hip.

"Miami Beach is where neon goes to die," Lenny once remarked. When Bruce visited Miami, however, he brought the city to life with his zany electric energy. The young Larry King, then a disc jockey, first met Lenny when the comedian unexpectedly dropped in at Larry's radio station one morning at seven A.M. "I really dig ya," Bruce told King; and Lenny invited him to attend his show. "When Lenny was cooking, down on the floor you went," King recalled. "[W]hen he was good, he was raucous. He was sexual. He had a way of moving his hands, his body." King returned the favor by inviting Bruce onto his new radio show that aired from Pumpernick's restaurant. There, in the glass booth, Larry once had Lenny and Don Rickles together.

In August of 1958, Fantasy Records released Lenny's first LP, *Interviews of Our Time*. It was the debut album in Fantasy's Social Studies Series (that would later include poetry readings by the likes of Kenneth Rexroth, Lawrence Ferlinghetti, and Allen Ginsberg). The thirty-three-minute red see-through vinyl record contained nine bits, of which "Father Flotsky's Triumph" became the most famous. In this brilliant parody of 1940s prison-break movies, Lenny exaggerated the voices, accents, and expressions of stereotypical characters, all to surprising comic effect. There is Warden (the hard-nosed prison superintendent willing to maintain order at any cost, including the sacrifice of "four or five prisoners as an example"); Dutch (the deranged and desperate convict unwilling to bargain with the warden or to answer his demands with anything other than inarticulate roars: "yahdudeyah-dudeyah!!"), Father Flotsky (the Irish-American priest, mimicking the actor Pat O'Brien's brogue and behaviors, who is the model of pastoral forgiveness: "Killing six children doesn't make you *all* bad."), and the

Negro Prisoner (the Death Row optimist who is preparing himself for the afterlife: "Soon Ih'm gwine up ta hebben. Yessuh."). Apart from a few politically incorrect moments, "Father Flotsky's Triumph" was tame stuff compared to his contemporaneous acts at clubs like Chicago's Cloister and San Francisco's Ann's 440 and Facks II. Playfully, the flip side of the album cover warned: "Suitable for air play ONLY if station plans to terminate broadcasting activities."

Shortly after his first album's release, Lenny met Herb Cohen, yet another player in the comedian's future L.A. obscenity battles. Herb owned the Cosmo Alley coffeehouse, located on Cosmo Street between Ivar and Cahuenga. The house sponsored musical acts such as Theodore Bikel, The Limeliters, and Maya Angelou, "the greatest nightclub chanteuse of her time" according to Cohen, and stand-up comedy as well. Cosmo's manager, Ben Shapiro, knew that Bruce had a faithful following, and so urged Herb to speak to Lenny about coming on board. "We sat at Cosmo talking for about an hour," Herb recounted, "and Lenny described material that sounded so completely zany that I loved it—a new and different form of comedy that we had never offered before. It sounded odd enough to be the kind of Beat act that we should be doing." Chalk up another quirky venue for the whacked-out comedian.

They were packed in like an L.A. traffic jam at Lenny's Cosmo Alley debut, and the place was never empty through the entire run of two shows a night for a month. Lenny breathed gutsy new life into the building that once had housed "Harout Marimar," an Armenian restaurant. "The nature of his show," Cohen stressed, "was absolutely astounding for the times. Here was a guy talking about the pope, Rabbi Weiss, the establishment, the corruption of politics and religion, the concept of putting homosexuals in jail with a lot of other men—and people were speechless. No one else had said such things, not on the stage." Though Cosmo Alley was not as stylish as The Slate Brothers or The Crescendo (it had all the charm of a tenement house), it was filled with electricity. The Cosmo clientele was different, too. "Look who was there," Cohen exclaimed. "Hollywood types, artists, hookers, bartenders, the non-conforming, non-normal sectors of society." The man was in his milieu.

What a time it was. Bobby Darin's "Mack the Knife" topped the charts; Buddy Holly, Ritchie Valens, and the Big Bopper died in a plane crash; the Supreme Court held *Lady Chatterley's Lover* non-obscene; Chuck Berry was charged with violating the Mann Act; and Lenny Bruce lived through one of his most promising and potentially perilous years—1959. His life ledger for that year included credits and debits: an attention-grabbing article in *Time* magazine versus bad publicity about a drug bust at The Crescendo; an appearance on *The Steve Allen Show* and the release of his second album versus threats by the LAPD concerning his performances at Club Renaissance. It was all so typically Lenny: success laced with danger.

While *Time* took much of it in descriptive stride (billing Lenny as the "most successful of the newer sickniks"), the mainstream magazine nonetheless noted Bruce's tendency to shock ("much of the time he merely shouts angrily and tastelessly at the way of the world"). It wasn't just the language anymore, it was also the *content* of his routines that unnerved people. Now, heaven forbid, he was going after religious leaders like Oral Roberts and the pope; he mocked them with unrestrained license. He amused most, outraged many, and once even got into a pissing match with Herb Caen, the celebrated *San Francisco Chronicle* columnist. "Sure I say things that may offend people," Lenny admitted to a *Globe-Democrat* reporter during his September 1959 gig at The Crystal Palace in Saint Louis. "But they don't have to pay to listen to me." To the *St. Louis Post-Dispatch*, he added: "I'm not a moralist. I don't object to any of the sins of today. I just object to people who don't admit their sins." Lenny summed it up: "I've always been a rebel, and I'm still a rebel." It was precisely that rebel *attitude* that brought him notice and notoriety. And it was precisely that willingness to *offend* that led to Lenny's very first real run-in with the law over the content of his comedy.

Ben I. Shapiro, the former manager of Cosmo Alley and the current owner of Club Renaissance, was on the receiving end of legal shrapnel meant to drive Lenny Bruce out of town. In late August of 1959, Shapiro advertised for an upcoming Bruce one-week engagement (September 10–17) at the Renaissance. Two days prior to Bruce's opening, recalled Shapiro, a pair of LAPD guys paid him a visit. If Lenny Bruce dared to perform at the Renaissance, they warned him, "there would be much trouble."

The message was intimidating but vague. Shapiro loved Lenny, however, and was not about to be bullied. Days after the comedian completed his run, Shapiro began receiving suspicious official notices from the Health Department, Building and Safety Department, and even the Fire Department; the club needed "extended improvements immediately." Such costly demands could shut the place down…and they did. Hence, Shapiro moved the Renaissance to another location, but this required an appearance before the Public Welfare Commission in order to transfer his club license. Ben was prepared; he made sure that every wire was covered and every faucet fixed. To his surprise, the commissioners were really not concerned about regulatory compliance; they were troubled by the nature of Lenny Bruce's performance. One commissioner, a Mr. Farrell, opposed the transfer of Shapiro's license simply because of Bruce's appearance at the club. In the end, the license was granted—though with an *ex officio* warning to ditch Lenny Bruce. Again, Shapiro ignored the threat, *but* he did urge Lenny to tone down his bits. Uncharacteristically, the comedian did so this time. The show went on, the newly located Renaissance remained open, and the badges at the Building and Safety Department left Ben alone.

While Lenny was taming his act in one venue, he was testing the limits of tolerance in many other and larger venues. For example, there was the 1959 release of his second Fantasy album, *The Sick Humor of Lenny Bruce*. The cover photo portrayed the very much alive Lenny picnicking in a green graveyard dotted with tombstones. On the cover's backside, Ralph Gleason's liner notes hailed the "colossally irreverent" comedian, the man for whom virtually "nothing was sacred." Gleason readily granted that "it's ribald. Yes, even sometimes rough. But it's real." Actually, it was both real and surreal, as evidenced by track 2 on side 2: Lenny's "Psychopathia Sexualis." It was a "Beat"-like poem backed by a cool jazz accompaniment. Something hip, right out of North Beach. (Decades later, the bit would be included, along with a Lenny Bruce profile, in a 1992 Rhino Records poetry collection entitled *The Beat Generation*.)

Dig: it was Lenny grooving with a Texas drawl on a fling he had with a filly:

> *Psychopathia Sexualis*
> *I'm in love with a horse that comes from Dallas*
> *Poor neurotica me....*
> *She looked so nice against the rail*
> *with her pretty long legs and her pony tail.*
> *I guess against convention I'll never win*
> *I'll probably end up in the loony bin*
> *but in my heart I'll always be free....*
> *I'm paranoid and sublimated*
> *in love with a horse that ain't been spayeded....*
> *We finally got adjusted and I was boss*
> *when I woke one morning and on the lawn found a fiery cross*
> *The Ku Klux Klan said we had to get out that day—*
> *move everything*
> *lock, stock, horse, and carriage;*
> *the Klan wouldn't stand for any mixed marriage...*

However deranged the filly fantasy, it did not disturb most '50s people the way the track that followed it did. "Religions, Inc." became one of Lenny Bruce's best known routines. The ingenious and irreverent bit (almost ten minutes long) was a satirical slam at organized religion and the con-man, big business mindset behind it (see chapter two).

The Sick Humor of Lenny Bruce revealed a ruthless attitude toward everything "decent" in American culture, from the unmentionables of sex to the unmentionables of the sacred. It was a peek at the rotting backside of life's prim white siding, a sordid view of human and holy things. The rebel in Bruce felt compelled to rip the façade off of respectability.

However dark the world appeared in Lenny's comedy, it appeared dazzling from his castle in the sky. In 1960, Lenny purchased a home tucked away high in the Hollywood Hills. The split-level house at 8825 Hollywood Boulevard seemed to be a metaphor for his life. It was hard to access, perched above a risky road of complex curves—a struggle to the top and a roller coaster ride to the bottom. The forty-five-degree angle driveway was sealed off by a tall, black, wrought-iron, electronic gate that often didn't work. "You'd think you were going to see Bela Lugosi," Frank Perilli gibed. The southwest side provided a big-picture view of the world, as its glass walls carried the eye almost to Catalina. Stark in style, the furniture was spare and uncomfortable. "Lenny's sofas were hard as a rock," his buddy Jo Jo D'Amore recalled. "Lenny told me, 'Listen, Jo Jo. If the furniture is good, people who come over will stay. I'll have to entertain them, and I don't want to do that.'" The $65,000 home was sometimes more dysfunctional than functional. "To prevent long-distance calls being made when he was away," Perilli said, "Lenny would take all the mechanical stuff out of the telephone." In time, it became a *de facto* boarding house (the upper floor was rented out for mortgage money), a crowded storage facility (reels upon reels of club performances were stockpiled), and a makeshift law library (trial transcripts, appellate briefs, legal dictionaries, statute books, case reports, affidavits, and memoranda were in abundance).

When Lenny was gigging, the trek from the House on the Hill to the nightclub was slightly more than a mile. Out the double wooden doors, down some fifteen steps onto the carport, then down the forty-five-degree blacktop, a sharp left onto Hollywood Boulevard, around the blind spots at the turns (15 mph posted speed), a quick right onto Queens Road and down the steep street to Sunset Boulevard, then another right to 8572 Sunset—The Crescendo.

The Crescendo period of 1960 was of a different order than the years at Duffy's. It was perhaps Lenny's most creative time, when crass antics gave way to comic art. "He was writing up a storm," Maynard Sloate observed. "He was doing new material and experimenting. I think this was the high point of his career." By August of that year, Lenny had conjured up and was performing some of the bits that became the hallmarks of his comic legacy.

"Christ and Moses" (recounted in chapter one) originated here, as did "To Is a Preposition, Come Is a Verb" (recounted in chapter three). The former was highly offensive (some said blasphemous) because it mocked the hypocrisy of hierarchical Catholicism; the latter was highly shocking (some said obscene) because it challenged the hypocrisy of sexual mores with unrepressed abandon.

The Crescendo routine that most forthrightly emphasized the "dirty word" concept, however, was the famous (some said infamous) "Las Vegas Tits and Ass." Essentially, it was a dialogue about what is deemed to be clean or dirty language:

> *Question*: What is the big attraction [in Las Vegas]?...
> *Answer*: Tits and ass.
> *Question*: *Whaat's that?*
> *Answer*: Tits and ass. That's what's that.
> *Question*: Ahh, just tits and ass?
> *Answer*: Well, they give you an Apache team in between for rationalizion. But, basically, that's what it is, man, tits and ass.
> *Question*: Well, that's just one hotel. Give me the second biggest hotel.
> *Answer*: More tits and ass. CD

The questioner then objects that the words "tits and ass" cannot be plastered nightly on a Las Vegas marquee, because to do so would be dirty. What about the propriety of using synonyms, such as "*tuchuses* and *nays-nays*"? Could those words be used on the marquee? Perhaps. Then, what about foreign words for tits and ass? Say, something austere: "*gluteus maximus* and *pectoralis majoris*." Relieved, the answer is: "That's about the cleanest." To which, the reply comes. "Clean to you, but dirty to the Latins." "Las Vegas Tits and Ass" assailed the hypocrisy of social conventions regarding sex talk; it did so as it openly violated those conventions.

Lenny's delivery of those three controversial bits at Gene Norman's club in the late summer of 1960 did not provoke, for whatever reason, the L.A. County vice squads. Likewise, some of those routines and others did not bring the vice men to his famous Carnegie Hall concerts (February 3 and 4, 1961) in New York. But, in other clubs in Los Angeles and elsewhere, the "sick comic" would not be so lucky. For now, however, Lenny Bruce was at the crescendo of his career.

Trouble at The Troubadour

"ACCORDING TO JUSTICE Douglas's opinion for the Court in *Lambert v. California*, the fact that Mrs. Lambert was guilty of an omission instead of an act appears to be critical. Why is that so?" That was precisely the kind of question that Ron Rothman, a first-year evening student at Southwestern University Law School in 1962, hoped to dodge. Sitting in the second row of his Criminal Law class, Rothman wasn't the hot-shot type eager to volunteer information; he would just as soon have his classmate Julian Dixon (later a U.S. Congressman) field such questions from Professor Hecht.

Ron Rothman was a tall, athletic, good-looking, nice Jewish boy who went to law school. At the same time, he was a deputy marshal with the L.A. County Marshal's Office and a bailiff at the Beverly Hills Municipal Court. "I was an anomaly," Rothman admitted. "I'm this young Jewish liberal in the Marshal's Office in civil service. I mean, there is no such thing as Jews in civil service. Jews don't become deputy marshals or policemen. Jews go out there and become doctors and lawyers." The self-analysis was so candid and comic that it could have been a part of a Lenny Bruce act—or so Rothman might have hoped. For he had plans to pick Rosemary Jonas up in his Corvette and head out to The Troubadour to catch one of Lenny's next shows.

Unknown to the young Mr. Rothman, Professor Hecht likewise had plans to catch Lenny's act. Adjunct law professor by night and a grade-one deputy district attorney for Los Angeles County by day, Richard W. Hecht exemplified the dedicated civil servant. His towering height notwithstanding, Hecht was mild-mannered and understated. He always came across as a *professional*—knowledgeable, conscientious, businesslike, and ever prepared. "If a case came down yesterday," Rothman recalled, "Hecht knew about it today and would use it." The professor-prosecutor was that way in class and in court. No wonder, then, that Sergeant Sherman Block, head of the West Hollywood vice squad, called him from time to time for legal advice. Indeed, it was at the behest of Sergeant Block that Hecht was heading to The Troubadour.

Doug Weston's Troubadour was an "in" place. A gathering spot for an audience of 300—typically North Beach wannabes who grooved to the sounds of folk and jazz—The Troubadour featured the likes of Odetta, Joan Baez, and Peter, Paul and Mary in the early days and the Byrds, Neil Young, and Buffalo Springfield in the late '60s. (Afterwards, Elton John launched his American career at the club and comedians Steve Martin, Bill Cosby, and Cheech & Chong performed there.) It was for many years one of America's most important show-cases for contemporary talent. "The people who play our club are sensitive artists who have something to say about our times," Doug Weston observed. "They are modern-day troubadours."

In more ways than one, The Troubadour was at the crossroads of culture. Located at 9081 Santa Monica Boulevard, this Swiss chalet–looking club lay on the border between wild West Hollywood and sedate Beverly Hills. Rolls-Royces and Mercedes passed by in one direction while '55 Chevys and Jeeps flew by in the other. The well-to-do middle-aged hip hung there with L.A.'s young folkies. The acoustic mixed with the electric. And traditional love ballads blended with modern political protest songs.

But what was Lenny Bruce doing there, booked for a twelve-night engagement starting on Wednesday, October 17, 1962? After all, he didn't warble spirituals and folk odes. Neither was he a guitar hand. He was, however, controversial and way-out. That alone would have appealed to Doug Weston's drugged out, antiestablishment, risk-prone personality. This was a six-foot-three, strapping guy with an *attitude*, and an iron-horse party animal ready to whoop it up. In short, the maverick club owner and the madcap comedian were made for each other.

The evening of October 24, Herb Cohen, once the owner of Cosmo Alley and now of The Unicorn coffeehouse, arrived at the club for Bruce's 8:30 P.M. show. He passed under the marquee—DOUG WESTON'S TROUBADOUR PRESENTS LENNY BRUCE—and beyond a bold disclaimer hung on the varnished front door:

THE TROUBADOUR NEITHER CONDONES NOR CONDEMNS MR. BRUCE'S STATEMENTS SINCE IT IS OUR POLICY NOT TO INTERFERE OR LIMIT IN ANY WAY AN ARTIST'S PERFORMANCE ON OUR STAGE.

Cohen did not proceed directly through the foyer and past the two heavy oak doors, topped with a proscenium-carved sign announcing SHOWROOM. Rather, he took a quick left turn into the nineteenth century–styled barroom with its heavily carved columns and mirrored wall; plopping down on a wooden stool, he leaned against The Troubadour insignia on the stool's iron back, and ordered an orange juice…on the rocks. But, Ron Rothman and his date, Rosemary, didn't take the same detour. Rothman paid the $1.50 admission charge apiece at the ticket box in the foyer and followed Rosemary into the 55-by-50-foot barn of a theater with its open-beamed ceiling, west-wall balcony, and small tables and folding chairs facing a stage straight ahead. Looking around for seats, Rothman was surprised to spot Professor Hecht sitting at one of the rear tables. The ever-businesslike Hecht either did not acknowledge his student or did not see him because he was preoccupied.

Richard Hecht was not at The Troubadour to be entertained; decked in suit and tie, Hecht was on the job. Earlier that day, Sergeant Sherman Block, who had worked vice for two and a half years, had come to Hecht's Beverly Hills office (above a jazz joint called "The Little Club" off Santa Monica Boulevard) to ask a favor. The sergeant wanted Hecht to accompany him and Sergeant James Cline to witness Lenny Bruce's performance that night; and he needed legal advice as to whether Bruce's act violated Section 311.6 of the California Penal Code for speaking obscene words in a public place. Both Officers Block and Cline had seen prior shows, and believed Lenny's act to be obscene; but before making an arrest, they wanted the opinion of an obscenity law expert. (Sergeant Block later acknowledged: "Of course, I did know at the time that [Lenny] had been arrested on a number of occasions for illegal drug possession and use.")

The sergeant explained to his friend Dick that he had attended Lenny's opening night act at The Troubadour on Wednesday, October 17, along with Deputy George Koga and two narcotics officers, Sergeant Joel Lesnick and Deputy John White (who had busted Bruce earlier on a heroin possession charge). Block took some notes of the "dirty words" that Lenny had uttered during his performance. Having once worked at a Jewish delicatessen, the sergeant was familiar with the racy Yiddish terms he now jotted down. Block noted that the comedian had referred to his ex-wife Honey as *fressing* (eating out) a maid in the bathroom, and had laced his bits with *schmuck* and *putz* (cock), and *schtup* (fuck).

Then, six days later—on Tuesday, October 23—Block sent Sergeant James Cline and Deputies Thomas Frawley and Gerald Schayer to observe Lenny's ten P.M. show. (At that point, no fewer than seven undercover officers had monitored Lenny's words at Weston's club.) Sitting among the fifty or so patrons, Officers Cline, Frawley, and Schayer listened to the entire forty-five-minute act, but made no tape recording. They heard variations of "Las Vegas Tits and Ass" and "Adolf Eichmann," another bit on the etymology of "cocksucker" ("taken from the word 'cock' which would be a fowl…and 'sucker' meaning lollypop"), and an anecdote on circus lion–taming (the lion's fear of a tamer's prop arises from the scent of the "numerous assholes [that once had been] seated on the chair"). The officers reported that Lenny's routine "primarily centered around sexual activities of various parts." Characterizing the act as a whole, Officer Schayer recalled later: "In our opinion, it was obscene." But now, the evening of October 24, it was Richard Hecht's turn to look and listen, and render his considered judgment to Block and Cline, the two plainclothesmen seated next to him.

Before he could begin to assess things, however, Hecht had to wait and wait…and wait. The never-punctual Lenny emerged from the dressing room off the balcony next to Doug Weston's office not a moment before 9:30 P.M. In the meantime, Lenny's thin, taciturn black friend, Eric Miller, had entertained the audience on his guitar. When Bruce finally stepped onto the stage, he came out snarling: "Tits and ass, tits and ass, tits and ass, tits and ass, tits and ass, tits and ass, tits and ass, tits and ass, tits and ass, tits and ass," and "tits and ass." Or so Sergeant Block remembered the prelude to "Las Vegas Tits and Ass."

Later, Lenny launched into one of his most popular routines, "Thank You Mask Man." Running seven minutes or so, this version of the then-unreleased comic playlette allowed Lenny to switch with razorsharp speed among a number of hilarious characters. There was the Lone Ranger with his cartoonish Dudley Do-Right of the Mounties intonation, "the man that never waited for 'thank you'"; there was the redneck with a Southern drawl, angry at the good guy in white for refusing to accept gratitude ("You're jus too daamn goood for evvrybaady"); there was also the Jewish *shtick*man, trying to make sense of it all ("What's with that *schmuck*?"). Fed up with the Lone Ranger's refusal to accept their gratitude, the townspeople held him up at gunpoint. Forced to explain, he reasoned that he would have neither the time nor the motivation to do good if he were to wait around for their adulation. This time, they insisted, he *had* to accept a gift, if only this once.

> *Lone Ranger*: Alright. Give me that Indian over there!
> *Redneck*: Tonto?…What the hell you wan' him fer?
> *Lone Ranger*: To perform an unnatural act.…
> *Redneck*: Goddaaamn…The masked man's a fag!! *Blaaaagh!*
> *Lone Ranger*: …While you're at it, I want that horse, too.
> *Redneck*: *Whaafaar?*
> *Lone Ranger*: For the act.
> *Redneck*: *BLAAAAGH!*…daaamn degenerate! Ⓒⅅ

In the end, the townsfolk were in a far less charitable mood. Now that the Mask Man's views and desires were revealed, they were revolted. They drove him out of town.

No doubt, Ron Rothman and Herb Cohen roared, while the crowd jumped up and hollered, "The Lone Ranger's a *fag!* The Lone Ranger's a *fag!*" Some appreciated Lenny's ingenious *tour de force* on the hypocrisy of social etiquette and the corruptive force of conventions; others laughed for far less elevated reasons. Similar responses greeted Lenny's and Eric's joint lampoon of liberal hypocrisy toward race relations in "How to Relax Your Colored Friends at Parties." Other, lesser bits sometimes did or did not hit their mark—for example, Lenny's commentary on indiscriminate rapists who "ball" transvestites even after discovering they are undercover policemen in drag ("This would never stop a real rape artist because some of those cops have pretty nice asses and the rapist might even want seconds"); or his semantic rap on *Life* magazine's use of the word "shit" as a synonym for narcotics ("So, if you shit in a bag and smoked it, it would be

alright"). In and out, and around and between, Lenny flung disconnected zingers.

The three law enforcers sitting in the rear had found little to chuckle
about in those routines. But the moment that really raised eyebrows
around Richard Hecht's table was that in which Bruce reamed the lighting booth operator. Lenny asked that the stage lights be dimmed.
("These lights may be fine for George Shearing [the blind jazz pianist],"
he teased, "but they're too bright for me.") The high beams still kept on
glaring. Staring up at the control booth, Lenny yelled, "You dwarf
motherfucker, turn the lights down!" When there still was no change, he
bent over the table closest to the stage, and said: "The dwarf prick
thinks I'm kidding." Finally getting with the program, the lighting operator reduced the kilowatts. Whether he knew it or not, Lenny's excited
utterances would soon be deemed a part of his act.

When the house lights raised after Lenny's exit, Sherman Block
and James Cline turned to Richard Hecht. "Whadaya think?" Block
asked. "I was deliberately slow in reacting to his question," Hecht
later recollected, "because I was thinking. But I finally concluded
that this *was* an obscene performance under the law as I understood
it at the time." Block wanted to know if he could make an arrest.
"And I thought about it some more," Hecht continued. "I said,
'Yes.'...And I knew this: that by making such a statement to Sherman, the case would be filed and that I had committed myself to it."

Twenty minutes before midnight, Block and Hecht ascended, single file, the twenty steps of the twisting staircase leading to the club's
balcony. They passed by the yin-yang, light-dark wooden door to
Weston's office, and proceeded down the short hall to a nondescript
dressing room into which The Troubadour's sign lights bled through
three curtained windows. Sergeant Cline had preceded them. When
that square guy with officialdom written all over him strode into the
room, the eye contact said it all. Another bust, no doubt. Cline didn't
have to flash his shield for Lenny to figure out why the stranger was
intruding into his zone of privacy. Within no time, the husky Sergeant
Block and the tall prosecutor Hecht were on the scene. The shit was
hitting the fan—*again*! Only nineteen days earlier, he had been
popped at Bobby Coogan's West Hollywood Grand Prix Hobby

Shop for heroin possession. Immediately after the October 10 arraignment for that bust, he had belted a KTLA television cameraman, and was now facing criminal battery charges for that. He was paying money galore for legal fees on these matters, not to mention all the bucks that had been spent to win the San Francisco obscenity trial. Lenny's legal tangles were already interfering with his club bookings. And now *this!*

The officers cuffed the comic criminal, but Doug Weston was left untouched. Hecht detected the obvious: "Lenny was agitated. Controlled agitation, if there is such a thing." They escorted him out of the club and into an unmarked car (one of their own personal vehicles). With the suspect in the back seat, they headed for the nearby West Hollywood station. Lenny got a special billing/booking—the press was given advanced notice of that night's celebrity catch, and reporters eagerly awaited his arrival. That very morning's *Herald Examiner* carried a photograph of Lenny with a banner headline:

"SICK" COMEDIAN BRUCE "SICKER" WITH NEW ARREST.

When Lenny was booked, he was charged with two misdemeanor counts of speaking obscene words in a public place in violation of California Penal Code Section 311.6. The first count was based on his October 23 performance at the Troubadour, and the second on his October 24 performance. The thirty-seven-year-old comedian was released when his mother, Sally Marr, paid the $525 bail; he was "cited out" to appear for arraignment the following week. In the early morning hours, Lenny still found enough energy to make a press statement. The only printable comment: "I'm having money problems. I don't know when or where I'll get an attorney."

Beverly Hills Justice

LIFE IN BEVERLY Hills was so very good. The warmth of a compassionate sun, the sway of dreamy palms, the deep green of God's grass, the charm of Spanish-style buildings, the spic-and-span of sidewalks, and those chic little boutiques on Rodeo Drive.

Four-fifty North Crescent Drive was a part of that world, what with its round basin fountain gushing amidst picturesque palm trees and perfect lawns. There sat an ornately sculpted Spanish-style building capped with a turquoise and gold-tiled dome. In earlier times, it was City Hall. In 1962, it housed the Beverly Hills Courthouse, the police station, and the city attorney's office, in which a lone prosecutor from the L.A. District Attorney's Office worked. In those enchanting quarters, one floor up, justice was handed out in rooms where the ugly face of crime stood before the shining majesty of the law—that was the ideal, anyway.

In the fall of 1962 and winter of 1963, Lenny Bruce's L.A. freedom would very much hinge on the doings of a prosecutor (Ronald Ross), a defense lawyer (Burton Marks), two judges (Robert Dulin and Henry Draeger), and a cast of characters that included a bailiff, jurors, witnesses, policemen, and a club owner (Herb Cohen). Here were the starring actors in the Beverly Hills rendition of *People v. Bruce*:

—Ronald Ross's office was a mere one hundred feet from the entrance to the municipal courtroom. *People v. Bruce* was one of the many case files he found stacked on his desk on the morning of Bruce's arraignment. The thirty-year-old, Missouri-born deputy district attorney had graduated from the University of Southern California Law School and served in the Judge Advocate General's (JAG) Corps before becoming a prosecutor in 1961. Manning the satellite office in Beverly Hills, he handled felonies (from homicide to robbery) and a ton of misdemeanors (from prostitution to parking) that occurred in the city and in the surrounding unincorporated areas such as West Hollywood and the Sunset Strip. *People v. Bruce* was his first real obscenity case. "This is going to be an interesting case," he thought. "We'll find out what the community thinks about obscenity."

—Burton Marks, a criminal defense attorney, thought that *People v. Bruce* would be an interesting case, too. The kid who first met

Lenny Bruce at Strip City while working weekends for Maynard Sloate was now Lenny's lawyer. A tall and heavyset man with bad teeth and a tick in one eye, Burt had come a long way from his rowdy days at the strip club; he was running a successful solo practice out of the Gale-Wilshire Building, a suite of offices owned in part by Sydney Irmas (who would defend Lenny in a different obscenity prosecution). Within less than a decade after graduating from UCLA Law School, Burt had argued no fewer than twenty-seven cases in California's inter-mediate and high appellate courts. Moreover, in April 1962, he had argued *Douglas v. California*, an important right to counsel case, in the United States Supreme Court. (After representing Lenny in the Beverly Hills obscenity trial, Marks would prevail in *Douglas*. One year after Lenny's death, Marks would win a key Fourth Amendment privacy case, *Katz v. United States*. And in 1972, he would argue a landmark obscenity case, *Miller v. California*.) Although Lenny had hired Burt in the past for representation in contractual dealings, he currently needed Burt's expertise for pressing criminal matters. Lenny's $500 retainer secured Burt's defense in three pending prosecutions: the hobby shop heroin possession case; the KTLA cameraman battery case; and, most recently, the Troubadour case.

—"After Robert Dulin was appointed to the Beverly Hills Munici-pal Court bench, his critics said he was about ninety-three years old, while his supporters claimed he was only ninety-one." That was how the kindly Richard Hecht characterized Judge Dulin. "I did not have a high opinion of him," Ronald Ross tactfully put it. "Dulin showed favoritism toward one side or the other in a number of cases. He was not a fair arbiter." Ron Rothman, who occasionally served as Dulin's bailiff, was yet more critical: "He was a terrible judge. His personality was garrulous and offensive." Judge Dulin presided over the pretrial motion stage of *People v. Bruce*.

—And then there was Henry Herman Draeger, the trial judge. Born in 1892, the same year that Grover Cleveland was reelected pres-ident, Draeger had practiced trusts and estate and tort law before becoming a Beverly Hills Municipal Court judge in 1952. He was a well-respected, dignified, and handsome jurist. "With his thin, slicked-back silver hair, and his conservative dress, he's what you would have expected from Central Casting for a judge." Where Dulin was rather inept and arbitrary, Draeger was very competent and fair. He came out of retirement to preside over a variety of cases at the municipal courthouse, including *People v. Bruce.*

—Of course, Lenny was always the producer, director, writer, and lead actor; and so, the drama depended on how and when he scripted things.

Friday, October 26—Arraignment Day: Ron Rothman was the bailiff on duty at the Beverly Hills Municipal Court when Lenny walked in with his attorney, Seymour Lazar, who had been his general counsel and, for a time, his manager. The comedian was there to waive a reading of the state's complaint and of his rights, and to plead not guilty to the two obscenity counts charged in *People v. Bruce.* Rothman wasn't used to seeing Lenny Bruce "play" the court. "What are you doing here?" he asked. "I got busted for dirty words at The Troubadour two nights ago," Lenny told him. "But I saw that show," Rothman exclaimed, "and I didn't think anything was bad about it."

Seymour Lazar said nothing but heard everything. Rothman's story passed to Burton Marks after a perfunctory hearing on December 5, 1962, when Marks substituted for Lazar, who could no longer juggle all of Lenny's legal balls. As quickly thereafter as a subpoena could travel, Rothman was directed to testify on Bruce's behalf. "Somebody at the Marshal's Office warned me that the department wasn't going to be too happy with that," Rothman recalled. "So, the next time I saw Lenny in court—I don't remember which proceeding—he said to me:

> *Bruce*: What's the matter, kiddo? You're not lookin' too happy.
> *Rothman*: I got subpoenaed on your behalf, and the department is giving me heat.
> *Bruce*: Then, you're not going to testify.

Burton Marks took exception to Lenny's generosity. After all, it would have been a nice twist to call as a *defense* witness someone who was a marshal, a law student of Professor Hecht, and an upstanding and sympathetic representative of the local community's standards. "Obviously, Lenny prevailed," Rothman concluded, "because that was the end of it."

December 1962 was a *busy* month for Bruce. A dizzying tornado of club bookings and legal hassles swept the comedian from city to city and his lawyers from courtroom to courtroom. Having begun a scheduled four-week run at Chicago's Gate of Horn in late November, Lenny's act was cut short when he found himself, once again, in the booking station of a police department—this time in the early hours of December 5, charged with violating Illinois's obscenity laws (the Gate of Horn bust, the Ash Wednesday obscenity trial, and the aftermath of the Chicago conviction are discussed in chapter five). No surprise, then, that on Pearl Harbor Day, December 7, Burton Marks returned without Bruce to the Beverly Hills Municipal Court to seek a postponement of the Troubadour obscenity trial, or that Lenny missed his arraignment on December 10 in the Van Nuys Superior Court for the hobby shop drug bust. Jumping the Chicago jurisdiction and forfeiting bail, Lenny was hell-bent to earn some money—if only to meet the monthly mortgage for the House on the Hill, give Sally and Kitty some support, pay the refinancing on his car, feed his drugged-out veins, and make a dent in his accounts payable for attorney's fees (bills for legal representation in 1962 alone totaled over $12,000, an amount constituting approximately 15 percent of his gross earnings for that year). So, first, it was off to Saint Louis for another short series of successful shows at The Crystal Palace, and then to Miami Beach in time for a New Year's Eve gig and a brief run at Le B. He *had* to do those gigs to keep the money flowing, to keep his life floating, and to retain his identity as America's most controversial comic.

Friday, December 28—Pretrial Motion Day: the post-Christmas sales were in full swing on Wilshire Boulevard as Judge Robert Dulin cracked the whip in his court, hoping to get *People v. Bruce* up for trial and off his calendar. But, wanting to dispense with the trial entirely, Burton Marks made a motion to dismiss.

His argument: "It would be a violation of the First Amendment...to hold [that] a person could in one portion of the state be exonerated of guilt in the same circumstances...and then be brought down in a different portion of the state, be arrested again, and tried for substantially the same offense." Essentially, this (double jeopardy–like) argument was premised on the notion that, once a San Francisco jury legitimated Lenny's act, he could not thereafter be prosecuted for performing the same act in California. His words, so the logic went, were already deemed to be *non*-obscene and therefore protected by the First Amendment. The state should, therefore, be "estopped" from prosecuting him. The other prong of Burton's argument was that Lenny could not "willfully" have violated the law in Los Angeles if he believed that his act had been deemed lawful by a San Francisco jury. Another way of saying that, in legalese, was that Lenny lacked the requisite "scienter" required to make an act criminal.

Judge Dulin was unimpressed: the main problem with Marks's argument, as articulated, was that there was no proof that the two performances—the Jazz Workshop and the Troubadour—were the same. Motion denied.

Before the hearing ended, there was one important matter yet to be resolved: whether Lenny had to be present during his Troubadour trial. He wanted to waive his right to be present so that he could perform at various clubs outside of California and attend to his other criminal proceedings. Burton presented a written waiver signed by Lenny, in conformity with a California Penal Code provision. D.A. Ross voiced no objection; and Judge Dulin, eager to proceed, directed that jury selection begin immediately. But there was not time enough to finish voir dire before the weekend began.

New Year's Eve, 1962—Voir Dire: while Dulin was pushing the pedal to the floor, Bruce was putting the brakes on with his latest legal scheming. Never completely satisfied with less than a known name with moxie, Lenny wanted a star-studded lawyer to act as co-counsel with Burton. Why not call his old friend, Melvin Belli, and bring a third defense lawyer into this misdemeanor matter? (Indeed, Melvin Belli's practice was star-studded, having represented—before and after the Bruce trial—such celebrities as Mae West, Errol Flynn, Tony

Curtis, Lana Turner, and The Rolling Stones. He also represented Jack Ruby.) Not surprisingly, Belli was busy when jury selection for the Troubadour trial resumed on December 31, but one of his associates, Charles Ashman, was sent in his stead to seek a continuance.

Dulin would have none of it. The old duffer was not one to let a New Year's celebration stand in his way: "We're going to start the trial, or at least finish jury selection." So, at seven P.M., the jury panel was called into the box. Prosecutor Ross, irritated by Dulin's insensitivity, excused himself for a brief moment to call his wife: "Guess what, dear? I'm not going to be home for a while." The jury pool was restless and annoyed by Dulin's display of swift justice. "After a half hour of this," Ross recalled, "finally cooler heads prevailed, and the case was continued until January 2." Now that he had meddled with their celebratory plans, Dulin was bubbling over with graciousness. "Between now and then," he told the jurors, "have a happy New Year. Have a good time." Everybody, except the slightly bowed and bald-headed jurist, bolted for the doors.

Within twenty-four hours of the USC Trojans' victory (42 to 37) over the Wisconsin Badgers in the Rose Bowl, the jury pool and lawyers in *People v. Bruce* had returned to Judge Dulin's courtroom. Unwilling to share the podium with any co-counsel (including lawyer Lenny), Burton Marks was back in court to take charge. He was prepared, in Lenny's absence, to finish jury selection and proceed to trial. But Judge Dulin had other plans. Unsatisfied with *in absentia* justice, however voluntary, he wanted Lenny's *corpus* in court *now* and for the duration of the trial. Accordingly, with authoritarian dispatch, he directed a bench warrant for Bruce's arrest to be held until February 8 (when Lenny was scheduled to be back from his New York run at the Village Vanguard) and stayed the trial until such time as Lenny appeared in court. As it turned out, Judge Dulin never got around to impaneling a jury or scheduling a trial date. When the legal pandemonium settled and matters resumed, Robert Dulin was no longer in the picture; a new judge had been assigned to the case.

THE DAY BEFORE the anniversary of Lincoln's birth, Henry Draeger traveled the mile from his home on Oakhurst Drive to 450 North Crescent Drive. Confident of himself and his world, Judge Draeger was probably quite blasé about the notorious Lenny Bruce. Having just flown back from New York, Lenny (unwilling to test Dulin's bench warrant) was making a guest appearance in Draeger's court-room late that afternoon.

There was no likelihood, however, that Lenny would be taking the witness stand that day. For Burton Marks hoped to derail the trial by revisiting the motion to dismiss that Judge Dulin had denied. To Marks's dismay, Draeger was no more sympathetic than Dulin to his theories about unconstitutional prosecution for the same act and Lenny's lack of "scienter." Echoing Dulin, Draeger ruled that the Jazz Workshop and the Troubadour acts were *different performances* played to *different localities*.

Marks had yet another card up his sleeve. He moved to dismiss for the court's failure to provide Lenny with a speedy trial. On the one hand, this argument seemed bizarre. After all, it was Judge Dulin who had rushed things along at breakneck speed so that the *People v. Bruce* trial could get underway; and it was Lenny who was delaying the process by changing lawyers and absenting himself. On the other hand, Burton's argument had some nuanced logic to it. After all, Lenny had complied with the waiver statute (California Penal Code §1043); the D.A. had not opposed his absence; Judge Dulin initially appeared to accept Lenny's waiver; and finally, Lenny had provided *bona fide* reasons why his presence at trial would be difficult or impossible for him. Given all that, Dulin's requirement that Lenny be in court before the trial could begin seemed entirely arbitrary. While granting that this was a matter of first impression, Judge Draeger nonetheless denied the motion to dismiss on the grounds that the state waiver statute left it within Judge Dulin's discretion to require his presence. If thereafter Lenny failed to appear, *he* was responsible for delaying his trial. (Of course, were Judge Draeger's ruling incorrect, Lenny would have been denied due process of law—an issue he eventually could take up on appeal.)

February 12 was a national holiday, so jury impaneling was postponed once again. Before adjourning, however, Judge Draeger took the occasion, late in the afternoon, to caution counsel about their conduct during voir dire. "Gentlemen," he declared,

> it sounds as though there is going to be what to many people might be very vulgar words...don't you see? But I think in making your statements to the jury and selecting the jury that you should be permitted to give the words that might come out in evidence...but not to each individual juror or repeat them and so on, because that is just piling on unnecessary things of a character that to many people makes it a rather unpleasant situation....[A]ll the law requires is that the jury is conversant with what they are to confront....But it should not be repeated all the time to the jury...

Understandably, Burton Marks took some objection to this, in that Draeger sounded as though he were prejudging the very matter before him. Admittedly, words like *schmuck*, *putz*, *fress*, and "dwarf motherfucker" might be uncouth or tawdry, but they were not obscene—or, at least, that's what the defense intended to prove. At the end of the day, Marks conceded the point to Judge Draeger: he would not repeat "dirty words" to each and every juror. That might have been a costly concession. In the San Francisco trial, Albert Bendich had employed the strategy of repeating "cocksucker" so as to desensitize the jury to its offensive impact. This was a strategy that Marks either did not appreciate or, if he did, yielded up to his possible disadvantage.

FEBRUARY 12, 1962, was quite a day. Ronald Ross prepared for his case the next morning. The prosecutor knew it was going to be a tough trial; the law of obscenity was so unclear, and even more so as applied to *People v. Bruce*. Sergeant Sherman Block was far less apprehensive—he assigned two of his vice squad men to monitor Lenny's show that evening. Herb Cohen, who owned the club that the vice squad officers visited, really wasn't worried. And Lenny, well, he surely was not going to let more trouble change his comic mind. Put it all together—the prosecutor's reservations, the sheriff's resolve, Cohen's indifference, and Lenny's existential take on life—and what emerged was another bizarre episode in the history of *People v. Bruce*.

The night before his Troubadour trial, Lenny Bruce performed at The Unicorn coffeehouse over at 8907 Sunset (next to what is now the Whisky A Go-Go). It was Herb Cohen's place. Yes, this was the same Herb Cohen who met Lenny years earlier at Duffy's, who booked Lenny at Cosmo Alley, who was at The Troubadour the night of Lenny's bust, and who broke fortune cookies with Lenny at Chinese restaurants. Like Ben Shapiro, who owned Club Renaissance back in '59, Cohen really dug Lenny. And like Shapiro, he was not a man easily intimidated by the police. Herb was more than happy to open his club doors to Lenny Bruce. No badges were going to stand in his way. Hell, they didn't scare Cohen away years earlier when, over police objection, he opened The Lamp, L.A.'s first lesbian bar.

The famous and infamous flocked to The Unicorn to pick guitars, read poetry, discuss Jean Paul Sartre, sip coffee, and ponder the fate of humanity in light of the Cuban Missile Crisis. Before they made it big, Dennis Hopper, Jack Nicholson, Steve McQueen, Dyan Cannon, and a bevy of other notables hung out in its groovy room with red-painted tiles and a black-painted coffee bar, or baked in the sun on its rear patio, or climbed the back staircase to John Fles's Unicorn Bookstore to browse through works on theater, politics, art, or existential philosophy. "Every person who had sandals, black clothes, long hair, beads, and who was out of work, a student, an intellectual, or an aspiring actor was at The Unicorn—followed by the police who couldn't fuckin' believe that all of these people were there to do anything legitimate!" Cohen exclaimed.

Ever since Cohen had opened the doors to The Unicorn in 1957— with a loan from Theo Bikel (the actor) and some handyman work from Victor Maimudes (later, Bob Dylan's road manager)—he faced official harassment in one form or another. "They couldn't believe," Cohen added, "that we were only selling coffee. The cops would come in with flashlights at night, searching the place, while customers were there." When such searches turned up no criminal evidence, Cohen would be cited for serving alcohol without a license (this for the coffee drinks with rum extract) or having entertainment without a license (this for letting unknowns come in and play their guitars). Searches, citations, court—on and on until the night Judge Edward R. Brand visited The Unicorn with his wife and son, Tony. The kid offered to play his guitar. Just as he started to strum, in walked four cops from the Hollywood Sheriff's Office. Judge Brand asked, "What are you doing here?" The cops didn't recognize him and told him to mind his own business or he'd find himself arrested for obstructing justice. After all, there was a possible "crime" occurring, what with unlicensed guitar playing going on. The plainclothes judge replied: "Look, my name is Judge Brand from the Beverly Hills Municipal Court. I want all of you to leave here right now. I want to see your captain in my court on Monday morning. And if I ever find you in this place harassing anybody else, you're all going to find yourselves in jail." Immediately thereafter, the men in blue made a quick exit for the door.

Unfortunately for Lenny Bruce, Judge Brand was not in the audience when he performed at The Unicorn. In fact, Bruce and Cohen speculated about the likelihood of police presence at his upcoming performances. "You know, Lenny," Herb observed, "there is no way you're not going to get busted. The same thing is going to happen again." "Even if I read the San Francisco transcript to them, and I say the 'dirty words' on a public stage, I'll get busted," Lenny replied. So, they came up with a wacky idea, one that they thought might save Lenny under his mistaken interpretation of California's obscenity law. (Unlike the equivalent statute in New York, which then specifically referred to "immoral shows and exhibitions," California Penal Code §311.6 pertained more generally to "obscene" words used "in any public place.")

On the back wall of The Unicorn's showroom, a door behind the stage opened up to Sunset Boulevard's sidewalk. "I'm buying you a forty-foot mike cord," Cohen suggested, "and you're going to walk off that stage and onto the street before you say any of those words. What would the law do to you then?" (Presumably, Burton Marks knew nothing of such "sage" legal advice.) Lenny was prepared to test, yet again, his troubled legal waters.

"Do 'Tits and Ass'!! Do the Lone Ranger!!" they beseeched him. The energized audience at Lenny's ten P.M. show on Tuesday,

February 12, wanted a First Amendment frenzy; they wanted him to move away from the "vanilla" stuff and get *down* to the "dirty brown." In addition to Burt Marks and his wife Jenny, Lenny saw two suspicious middle-aged gentlemen side-by-side at the rear left of the room. "Well, you know," the blue denim-clad comedian told his fans, "we've got a slight problem. If I say the things you want me to say, those gentlemen back there are going to bust me." The audience turned around and, with libertarian fervor, began to boo. "Don't boo them," Lenny admonished, "it's not *their* fault. They're only doing their job. It's *your* fault I'm being busted. Until you change the law, they have to do what the law requires them to do. It's up to *you* to change the law."

Continuing the Brucean lesson in American civics, the wild comic tried to walk the obscenity law tightrope: "The law says that anything you say on stage that might be considered obscene is illegal—even if you say the same things to each other on the street or at home. In other words, if I'm not on stage, the law doesn't apply, which is ludicrous. So, here's what I'm going to do." At that point, Lenny opened the backstage door, walked into the gutter of Sunset Boulevard, and continued to talk to the audience on the microphone:

> I don't know if you folks understand what the word "obscene" means. It means that I make you horny. Now, may I ask you, does the word "motherfucker" make you horny? If it does, you're in pretty bad shape.

"There he was, out on the street," Cohen recalled, "and he was repeating 'motherfucker, motherfucker, motherfucker, motherfucker!'" The one hundred or so in the audience howled, screamed, and cried out for more as Lenny did his gutter routine.

Once back on stage, Lenny couldn't resist delivering a few "pisses" and "shits" in the course of his forty-minute commentary about criminal arrests, marital relations, and other topics. Throughout the performance, he took pains to be solicitous of his undercover guests; at several points, Lenny remarked that he hoped the vice cops were enjoying the show.

Deputies Val Hall and Ken Jones did not enjoy it, however. (At least, they did not then admit to enjoying anything.) At the end of the act, the pair approached Lenny and told him he was under arrest. "Oh, no!" he moaned, "Not again!" As Herb Cohen then recounted: "Nobody but the officers thought his act or words were obscene. He was well received and very funny." The officers agreed to wait outside a few minutes while Lenny talked with Herb and Burt about what to do next. Wearing his long denim coat, Lenny exited The Unicorn and crossed the street where Hall and Jones were waiting.

What followed was becoming "dirty Lenny"'s life routine: cuff the comedian, place him in the back of an unmarked car, transport him to the West Hollywood station, book him, and alert the press. The usual bail ($525) was set and the usual "bail bondsman" (Sally Marr) was called. Then back to the House on the Hill to rest up for the next day's scheduled events: court trial in the A.M. and another gig (at The Unicorn) in the P.M.

LENNY BRUCE JAILED FOR OFF-COLOR NIGHTCLUB JOKES—that was the headline that Ronald Ross might have read in the *Herald Examiner* the morning he returned to work to try *People v. Bruce*.

"It really concerned and troubled me that [Sergeant Block and his officers] would go out and arrest somebody on the night before the trial [in a case concerning] pretty much the same charges that we had," Ross remembered. It was "very frustrating." Prosecutors tend to cut their brethren in the stationhouses a lot of slack. After all, they do work, by and large, the same side of the sociological street. They work together, of course, until the police begin to muck up the D.A.'s cases. And that was exactly what Sherman Block did when he ordered the surveillance of The Unicorn. Besides, Ross had warned him beforehand to cool it: "I had asked those people from the Sheriff's Department, 'Don't do anything more until we get a definitive determination as to whether or not [Lenny Bruce's performance] is obscene. If it's not, you're just barking up the wrong tree. And if it is, we'll just take the next step at that time.'" Ⓒ Ross continued: "I thought we had an agreement that Lenny Bruce wasn't going to get arrested again until we got this case decided."

But Sergeant Block could not wait; he took the "next step" immediately, before the resumption of the trial at which he was scheduled to appear as a state's witness. Ross was pissed, "and I let Sherman Block know that. But I didn't get any reaction from him other than a stone face." Meanwhile, the prosecutor did expect a reaction from Burton Marks by way of a request for another continuance.

Strategies, Satire, and Schizophrenia

BEVERLY HILLS JURIES had the same hue—always white. And generally, they were evenly divided between men and women over fifty. In those regards, the jury for *People v. Bruce* was typical. The task ahead for the jury, however, was atypical. "I questioned the jurors as to whether they would be so outraged or upset by hearing more-or-less indecent language that they would be unable to render a fair verdict," Ross recounted. Burton Marks remembered his voir dire as being a good deal more colorful. He began by asking each juror: "Would it embarrass you to the extent that you could not render a fair and impartial verdict [if you hear] shit, piss, fuck, cocksucker, mother-fucker?" Marks repeated the words, again and again and again; finally, Draeger admonished him to refrain from such liberality in his language. By the morning of February 14, the jurors were impaneled and sworn to do their civic duty as judges of the facts.

One of the amazing features of the two-day trial was how much of it was conducted *outside* of the jury's presence. Upwards of one-fifth of the proceedings were held in secret in Judge Draeger's chambers or at his court bench. This might have seemed peculiar for an obscenity trial in which the law left so many questions for jury determination—for example, whether a work taken as a whole was utterly without redeeming value for the relevant community or appealed to the prurient interest of its average citizens. As things played out, however, the jury's role was significantly narrowed, as judge and counsel marginalized, decontextualized, and sanitized the record for its consideration.

People v. Bruce raised some novel questions of its own, this beyond the more general Sisyphean task of defining obscenity under then existing law. For example, to what extent, if any, could unknown foreign words (*schmuck, schtup*) arouse prurient interest or offend community standards if the vast majority of the community did not know what those words meant? That was precisely the comic point that Lenny had made in his "Tits and Ass" bit. Now it had become an important question of law—curiously, one largely left unexamined in the course of the Troubadour-Unicorn trial. Then there was the question—first raised in the San Francisco trial and subsequently to be raised again elsewhere— of just how Lenny's performance was to be *considered as a whole*. Did the jury, in order to assess the socially redeeming value of his act, have to examine *everything* he said, or was it enough to consider the gist of what he said, or just the "whole" of this or that particular bit? More confusing still, what if his act could *not* be considered as a *unified* whole? That is, what if it lacked any unifying theme beyond the maddening contours of comedy? One reason why Judge Draeger and the counsel in *People v. Bruce* were off the record so much is that they really had no clear idea of how to answer such questions. How could they ask the jury to make factual determinations based on the applicable law if they themselves did not know what that law was? The alternative was to let the jury hear the messy everything—the legal uncertainties and, yes, the repetition of all of those "dirty words" in Lenny's various acts. The very thought of it proved too much for the upright Judge Draeger; he had to keep a lid on things, or so he thought.

The facts and figures of the two-day Troubadour-Unicorn trial reveal much about what Lenny Bruce was up against. The trial involved three misdemeanor counts: the first for performing an obscene act at The Troubadour on October 23, 1962; the second for performing an obscene act there the following evening (October 24), and the third for performing an obscene act at The Unicorn on February 12, 1963. (The very day the trial formally began, the state had to amend its criminal complaint to include the third count.) Given that there were three counts, Lenny's maximum penalty could be a $1,500 fine and eighteen months in jail. Based on what was said at trial, the state prosecuted Lenny for a total of fourteen "obscene" words he used in the course of his two performances at The Troubadour and his single performance at The Unicorn. (Those words were: *asshole, tits, ass, cocksucker, schmuck, motherfucker, prick, putz, balling, clap, fag, piss, cunt,* and *son of a bitch.*

There were also words like *tuchas* and *dwarf motherfucker* [in addition to *motherfucker*] and *dwarf prick* [in addition to *prick*].)

To make the state's case, Ronald Ross called four witnesses (three officers and a D.A. obscenity "expert"). Nothing elaborate, it was a low-profile presentation of the facts. Let the jurors hear the "dirty" words, let them hear the law, and they would convict. In that respect, Ronald Ross approached his case the same way that Albert Wollenberg did when he unsuccessfully prosecuted the San Francisco variation of *People v. Bruce*. Burton Marks called even fewer witnesses: his spouse Jenny and defendant Bruce. (Originally, he told the jury that he would present the testimony of "a few witnesses from the entertainment industry" and "ordinary citizens who have seen the show.")

Marks's approach stood in stark contrast to that of Albert Bendich in the San Francisco defense of Lenny, when Bendich called ten expert or lay witnesses including a recognized cultural critic, a noted professor of English, and people who attended Lenny's contested performance (one of whom was a recognized obscenity prosecutor). Whereas Marks relied on cross-examination to punch holes here and there in the state's case, Bendich methodologically used his witnesses to defeat every element of the state's case and thereby build an unassailable defense.

Generally speaking, Ronald Ross marched along three strategic avenues in developing the prosecution's case: "shock treatment," "divide and conquer," and "common usage." The logic was that when the jurors heard "cocksucker" and "motherfucker," they would be shocked and offended; when the jurors were told of the disconnected blips of crude comedy, they would discount the possibility of any overarching and elevated theme in Bruce's act; and when the jurors considered the "decent" routines of other comedians, they would appreciate just how far beyond community standards Bruce had gone. The anticipated result: "We, the Jury, find the defendant guilty as to all three counts."

Shock treatment, Ross's first stratagem, operated in much the same style for the prosecution's four witnesses, all of whom had seen Lenny perform. Characteristic of this stratagem was the exchange between the prosecutor and Sergeant Sherman Block about the October 24 performance at The Troubadour:

Ross: Would you relate what you recall was said that evening?
Block: [U]pon entering the stage, the first thing that Mr. Bruce uttered were the words "tits and ass, tits and ass, tits and ass," many times.
Ross: How many times would you say he repeated those words?
Block: I would say many times.
Ross: Was there an estimate at all?
Block: I'd say a dozen....
Ross: All right. Continue, sir.
Block: ...He went on to extol the virtues of marijuana over alcohol. Further, [he] discussed the term "shit"; and he said, "shit, shit, shit, shit, shit. Now, don't get excited," he said, "there's a Supreme Court decision that said that 'shit,' when used as a reference to narcotics, is perfectly legal. Therefore, if you shit in your pants and smoke it, you're all right."

Ross's second strategem, *divide and conquer*, was more nuanced. The idea here was to persuade the jury that Lenny delivered scatter-shot bits, chockful of obscenities, rather than any important thematic messages. Illustrative of this approach was Ross's exchange with his colleague, Deputy District Attorney Richard Hecht:

Ross: Now, directing your attention to these individual sequences that you have spoken of, individual events, was there any related theme between them or were they separate in nature?
Hecht: They were separate...
Ross: In your opinion, then, sir, was there any relation in these stories, any time inferred, so to speak, from one to the other? These time sequences.
Hecht: No, sir. They appeared to me to be unrelated, some of them humorous, stories.

Common usage, Ross's third major stratagem, connected the commonplace practices of comedians to the elusive notions of prurience and redeeming social importance in obscenity law. That is, the prosecutor hoped to prove that Bruce's routines were so vulgar and outrageous, as compared to contemporary comic norms, that the defendant exceeded the customary limits of candor in his routines and appealed to a morbid interest in sex or excretion. Ross's questions to Officer Gerald Schayer about the October 23 Troubadour performance captured the essence of this stratagem:

> *Ross*: How many times have you been to nightclubs where there were acts, comedians, or a use of comedians, maybe not as a whole show but just as a part of the show?...
>
> *Schayer*: Crescendo in the Hollywood area....The Largo in the West Hollywood area. Pink Pussycat in the West Hollywood area. I believe the Lake Club, which would be in the Lakewood area....
>
> *Ross*: Now, what about places not in connection with your work? Have you attended others?
>
> *Schayer*: I believe the Moulin Rouge, Coconut Grove, the Seven Seas Restaurant. There are probably more...
>
> *Ross*: During these times that you attended those performances, did you hear any routines that were similar to these routines that you have testified to concerning Mr. Bruce?
>
> *Schayer*: No, I don't believe so....
>
> *Ross*: I am talking about the type of performance he gave, treating those topics and the manner in which those topics were treated, as you have testified.
>
> *Schayer*: No, I don't believe so....
>
> *Ross*: Now, sir, you stated that you were familiar with...the term as defined in the Penal Code of "obscene"?..."That to the average person applying contemporary standards, the predominant appeal of the matter taken as a whole is to prurient interest"?
>
> *Schayer*: Yes.
>
> *Ross*: Now, sir, did you form any opinion as to the matter that you have testified to on examination as to whether or not, using that definition, the matter was or was not obscene?
>
> *Schayer*: Yes. In our opinion [speaking for Officers Cline and Frawley, as well], it was obscene.

To attack the state's case, Burton Marks devised counter-strategies that largely tracked Ross's approaches. Generally, the defense's cross-examination of the prosecution's witnesses moved along several lines of questioning: "innocuous coarseness," "satirical value," "no prurient appeal," and "faulty memory." The reasoning here was that Lenny's "dirty words" were commonplace crudities that could not shock the conscience; that the words were used with a satirical purpose to tickle the funny bone rather than to incite shameful, morbid, or lustful thoughts; that no objective evidence existed to prove an appeal to prurient interests; and that the witnesses could not recall enough of Lenny's routines to evaluate his act "taken as a whole." The anticipated result: "We, the jury, find the defendant not guilty on all counts."

Innocuous coarseness, Marks's first tactic, was a direct counterpart to the prosecutor's attempt to prove the shock value of Lenny's contested words. In that regard, the defense attorney's cross-examination of Officer Gerald Schayer concerning the October 23 Troubadour performance was typical:

> *Marks*: In the course of your activities as a vice officer, you have heard these words before, haven't you?
> *Schayer*: Yes, I have.
> *Marks*: It did not shock or offend you, did they?
> *Schayer*: No, it didn't.
> *Marks*: They did not appeal to your prurient interests, did they?
> *Schayer*: I would say no, sir.

Marks's second stratagem, *satirical value*, tried to undermine any notion that Lenny aimed for sordid or base titillation. Rather, Marks argued, Lenny's purpose was to entertain in a style that mixed the common talk of the street with the classical tropes of satire. The most telling example of that approach occurred in Marks's exchanges with Deputy D.A. Richard Hecht and Sergeant Sherman Block about the October 24 Troubadour show and with Officer Val Hall about the February 12 Unicorn show:

> *Marks*: Is it your opinion that when he called [the light booth operator] that name ["dwarf motherfucker"] he was intending to appeal

to the prurient interest of that man or anybody in the audience?

Hecht: No, sir. Definitely not. He was trying to make that comment to evoke a humorous reaction of some laughter to that audience and still accomplish the results of having the lights dimmed.

...

Marks: Do you agree that Mr. Bruce's work is one in which he moralizes on society and their use of hypocritical situations that arise out of society?

Block: I didn't quite understand that.

Marks: Have you ever heard of the word "a moralist"?...

Block: Yes, sir.

Marks: Would you apply that to Mr. Bruce?

Block: No, sir. I'd say he's more of a satirist.

Marks: Something like a dirty Will Rogers?

Block: I would say you could call him a dirty Will Rogers, yes.

...

Marks: Did you hear the audience laughing?

Hall: At times; yes, sir.

Marks: Well, throughout his act?

Hall: Yes, at various times throughout his act....

Marks: You thought he was funny?

Hall: On occasion.

Marks: Did anything he said make you horny?

Hall: No, sir.

The *no prurient appeal* strategy was the upshot of Burton Marks's preceding two tactics. If Lenny's coarseness were common and not shocking, and his purposes were satirical rather than sordid or sensual, then how could his comedy corrupt the average person by arousing lascivious thoughts or lustful desires? What objective evidence was there to show that any of Bruce's "*fresses*," "tits and asses," or "fucks" got his audiences hot and horny? Essentially, Marks wanted the jury to agree with Lenny's comical characterization of the matter: if words such as *schmuck or putz* "stimulated the Yiddish undercover agent" then "he should see an analyst." Over the prosecutor's vociferous objections and with the court's disapproval, Marks persisted in that approach in cross-examining Sherman Block as to the October 24 Troubadour performance:

> *Marks*: Anybody at that show, after hearing Mr. Bruce, did they masturbate?
> *Ross*: Objection, your Honor. Immaterial.
> *Draeger*: But I will sustain that. Now, there is no excuse for that, counsel, and I do not want you to ask a question like that, which is entirely improper.
> *Marks*: Did you think that on October 24, 1962, at The Troubadour, people were having an orgy by listening to Mr. Bruce?
> *Ross*: Same objection.
> *Draeger*: Sustained.

Though the state's objections had been sustained, Marks's rhetorical questions had been heard by the jury—the red dye had been dropped into the beaker of clear water, forever coloring it.

The fourth of Marks's cross-examination strategies, *faulty memory*, aimed to demonstrate that the state's witnesses focused entirely on Lenny's "dirty words" without any recollection of the socially redeeming context in which the words played a significant, if not essential, role. By this tactic, Marks intended to establish that the prosecution failed the obscenity law's requirement to assess Bruce's acts "taken as a whole." Once again, the defense attorney's exchange with Richard Hecht regarding the October 24 Troubadour performance was instructive:

> *Marks*: Mr. Hecht, did you hear the word "shit" being used that night…and how in one sense the word may be obscene and in another [narcotics] sense the word may not be obscene, depending on its reference?
> *Hecht*: I do not recollect hearing that, Mr. Marks, and I made no notation with respect to that....
> *Marks*: Mr. Hecht, do you remember the full routine regarding "tits and ass"?
> *Hecht*: No, sir; I do not.

Marks: Your Honor, at this time I move to strike all the testimony regarding that routine.
Draeger: The motion will be denied.
Marks: Do you remember, Mr. Hecht, the story about the gentleman in which there was twice a reference to him as an "asshole"?…
Hecht: No sir, I do not.
Marks: Your Honor, at this time I move to strike all the testimony of this witness about that particular routine.
Draeger: Denied.

Marks's *faulty memory* tactic bore little fruit (at least at the trial level) because, during several critical in-chamber sessions, Judge Draeger already had stemmed the defense attorney's efforts to pursue this line of questioning to his advantage. With his eye both on the trial results and, if needed, the appellate record, Marks hammered home the point that the prosecution had to establish its case on nothing less than the *whole* of Lenny's act. If a state witness could not testify on his own recall as to the whole of Bruce's routines, that testimony should be stricken; such testimony could be tendered, however, if and only if Marks were allowed to test the witness's recollection by playing a recorded tape of the whole act; and more generally, if the prosecution could not prove its case based on accounts of Bruce's complete act, then the state had not met its burden of proof. Judgment for the defendant. But, Draeger's evidentiary rulings were tantamount to judgment for the prosecution:

A witness need only testify to a "general sense of…the context of the words" rather than to a complete routine or Bruce's entire act. *Defense motion to strike denied.*

—A witness's recollection of a routine cannot be tested by way of recorded evidence of similar performances by the defendant. *Defense motion to introduce such tapes for cross-examination purposes denied.*

—The prosecution need not establish its case by considering the entirety of the defendant's performance; rather, it is enough that obscenity be established with respect to a complete routine. Bruce's material, Draeger concluded, "is not a book or something like that where the story runs all the way through. Here you have a comedy act made up of different routines....Each routine is complete in itself, purportedly." The phrase "taken as a whole" had been given a new and constricted meaning. *Defense motions to the contrary denied.*

What all this legalese meant is that Ronald Ross could make the state's case by offering a series of dirty words, as if Lenny had taken the stage and blurted little more than a string of vulgarities. Bruce's satirical style, his free-form technique, and his Joycean approach to comedy didn't count for much to Judge Draeger, at least not for purposes of cross-examination.

Burton Marks had lost the opportunity to derail the prosecution at the close of its case, and now had to mount the defense's own case. Certainly, he didn't have much with which to work. His promise to call entertainers and other witnesses did not materialize beyond the unimpressive Jenny Marks and the unhinged Lenny Bruce. But for those two inconsequential witnesses, he only had edited tapes to play to the jury of Lenny's Unicorn performance and two Troubadour performances prior to the October 24 bust. All totaled, the case for the defense would consume but a few hours.

Lenny Bruce looked awful. Having stayed up all night long, he had dark bags under his eyes on the morning of February 15 as he put on his court garb—a bleached prison-blue shirt and a denim jacket. His longish hair was disheveled and his sideburns bushy. Burton Marks had wanted Lenny to do a makeover, but his looks smacked more of a hangover. Sometime after eight A.M., Burt picked Lenny up at the House on the Hill. The two made their way down to 8024 Sunset, the site of the famous Schwab's Drug Store. There, Lenny bought some makeup to disguise the circles below his eyes, and did a quick cosmetic job en route while Burt descended to Santa Monica and drove southwesterly for under two miles to 450 North Crescent Drive.

The quiet elegance of the Beverly Hills courtroom was well suited to the affluent spectacles of its neighborhood: open-beamed ceiling, medium-dark wood paneling, and ten rows of wooden pew-like benches on both sides of the aisle. When Bruce entered the courtroom that morning, he certainly had more than his testimony for the Trou-badour-Unicorn trial to trouble him. The Chicago obscenity trial was coming up in only three days, and the Van Nuys narcotics trial would start the following month. Moreover, with the prospect of no club bookings for the next several weeks, all this legal *drek* could also inter-fere with his chance to play in England in April. After all, Nicholas Luard, the owner of London's Establishment, would soon apply for a permit for Lenny to work at his club.

Lenny Bruce would not take the Fifth: he wanted to be heard; he wanted the tapes of his acts to be heard; and he wanted a jury of his peers to hear every damned second of his bits. But he had to navigate both Marks's and Ross's questions about the accuracy and reliability of the tapes until the court was satisfied:

> *Marks*: I have a series here of seven tapes. Were these made in the course of your performances at The Troubadour or The Unicorn in the month of October?
> *Lenny*: Yes....
> *Ross*: I see, because these are then all your recordations, but can you tell us expressly which of these are from which nights?...
> *Lenny*: No, but...[t]he problem can be alleviated because as soon as you hear the tape, you will hear it match up with what the officer testified. It's crystal clear. You hear the "tits and ass," you hear the bit; you hear the "cocksuckers," and you hear the bit.

After the legal wrangling, the noon recess, and Jenny Marks's per-functory testimony (the sum and substance of which were that she attended Bruce's February 12 performance at The Unicorn, laughed at it, and didn't think it appealed to her prurient interests), Bruce's wish was granted. His act debuted at the Beverly Hills Courthouse, for a one-day, one-hour engagement. No charge. Finally, the jurors were hearing Lenny's bits as performed by Lenny Bruce, rather than by the prosecu-tion's witnesses—his own words for "Tits and Ass," "Thank You Mask Man," "Smoking the Shit," and the other routines. Would it help him?

Would the jury be amused to the point of exonerating him? Or would playing the tapes hurt him? Would the jurors be offended to the point of convicting him? It was hard to tell from their mixed reactions. Throughout it all, Burton Marks guffawed with uncourtly abandon, while Ronald Ross did his best to suppress an occasional urge to laugh.

When taped testimony gave way to live testimony during cross-examination, the mind-skippin', jive-talkin' Bruce had a "ball" with his straight-laced prosecutor. Trying mightily to pin Bruce down to a serious answer, Ross asked questions that all but invited the flip replies he received:

> *Ross*: By "ball," what does that term mean to you?…
> *Bruce*: "I'd like to ball you." Well, it depends what you are balling.
> *Ross*: It would be an act of sodomy or sexual intercourse?
> *Bruce*: Sodomy, no. No, that's weird. I don't see that at all. I'm an honest man. No.
> *Ross*: It would be an act of sexual intercourse?
> *Bruce*: No, it could—no. No, I'm not being facetious. Kiss them, hug them. "Hold me," "dance with me," "swing with me." "It's a ball." "It's a ball." "Mad ball."

Reminiscent of Bob Dylan's infamous interview with a *Time* reporter as captured in Pennebaker's 1965 documentary, Lenny tormented his inquisitor at every conceptual turn. Not to be undone, prosecutor Ross persisted with his line of inquiry on "Balling the Cops"—only to be taunted by the first display of postmodern comedy in a court of law:

> *Ross*: You were trying to convey something to the audience by the use of that term, I am sure, because otherwise—
> *Bruce*: Yes, but it was an abstraction.…It's—it's there—in the ear of the beholder.
> *Ross*: In other words, you were not trying to convey anything to them or just the connotation that they might put on it?…So, in other words, you are trying to convey a thought to another person, yet you are not exactly sure what that thought is. Would that be a fair statement?

Bruce: In a specific statement, I'm not trying to convey a thought. That—just through the incongruous statement—silly. It was ludicrous. That's the point there. Just completely ludicrous...

Ross: Well, would you say it was being ludicrous or was it just non sequitur, or what?

Bruce: No, not non sequitur. Just ludicrous. Completely inane.

Ross: Then it really did not mean anything?

Bruce: No, I—I didn't give it any real heavyweight meaning, no.

Ronald Ross quickly switched ground to "Thank You Mask Man," ostensibly in an attempt to focus Lenny and to draw out something linear. The attempt failed, as Lenny lapsed into his world of fantasy. "Cocking his head to the left, closing his eyes, and sort of hanging his head down," Ross recalled, "and in a different voice...he launched into his act." For what amounted to some forty lines of trial transcript, Lenny reenacted portions of his Lone Ranger routine. Ross hoped to yank him out of his reverie with a direct and pointed comment:

Ross: Well, specifically, you are just talking about...the unnatural act between the Lone Ranger and Tonto...

Bruce: Yes....What's the most ridiculous thing that the Lone Ranger could do? We assume that's completely incongruous....He wants the Indian....To perform an unnatural act. It is silly, you know.....

Ross: In other words, you were not trying to say anything about the unnatural act, then? In other words, it was just for incongruity, then? Was it trying to raise a laugh from the audience? Was that its point?

Bruce: What do you want from me? Tell me—

Ross: Just your answers.

Bruce: I didn't—I didn't want to encourage anyone in the audience to be perverse or to perform any unnatural act.

From where Lenny sat, this whole line of inquiry was "insanity," "an effrontery," a waste of taxpayers' money. Nonetheless, he did leave his prosecutor, the jury, and future generations with a statement of his comic purpose: "Generally I try to make them laugh," Lenny said, "and it seems that my point of view consistently has been that I am inconsistent and that we all are."

So ended Burton Marks's case for the defense. Legally speaking, this was no Clarence Darrow performance. Lenny might have been right about bringing in Melvin Belli. But, the trial had not yet ended.

Sometime near 3:30 P.M., closing arguments began. Although prosecutor Ronald Ross started with some philosophical flair as he bowed to the importance of First Amendment freedoms, his presentation quickly turned workmanlike and tepid. He walked the jury through the definition of obscenity, black-letter element by element; and he argued that Lenny was no satirist like Jonathan Swift, but rather a man who took the dirty language of the "pool hall and the locker room [into] the public place." Nevertheless, Ross displayed no contentious, vindictive, or "civilization-will-fall" attitude toward the defendant. In fact, toward the end of his closing argument, he made a surprising, albeit open-minded, admission: "If you use this kind of thing in front of children, well, it would be pretty bad. Used in front of *avant-garde*, sophisticated adults, all of the time, maybe it is not so bad." Yet, even that liberal concession had to be evaluated by the jury: "As I said without reiterating, ladies and gentlemen, it is for your determination."

"Nobody is like Lenny Bruce. He is unique." So Burton Marks put it to the jury in his closing argument. After all, no other comedian dared to play with the semantic incongruities of our language, particularly our sexually charged language. No other comedian confronted head-on the hypocrisy of our culture, especially our religious creeds, political ideology, and social mores. In short, no other comedian had the balls to contest the system that made inhibition and hypocrisy possible. Marks wasn't quite that colorful, but that's where he was going.

If it makes you laugh, it can't be obscene. That was what Lenny preached in the clubs, and what Burt argued in court. "You just cannot be having lascivious thoughts while your…laughter is aroused," Marks posited. The weakness of his argument was that it portrayed obscenity as limited exclusively to sexual passions, rather than extending to shameful and morbid interest in sex or excretion. The strength of his argument (only implicit in what Marks stated) was that the notion of the obscene or shameful should not be fixed in time, with no possibility for evolutionary cultural liberation of the type that Lenny offered.

There was more, about things like scienter and criminal liability, but nothing really to touch the soul of the jury—except, perhaps, for Marks's paean to the social value of humor: "Ladies and gentlemen, I do not believe that you can conscientiously go into that jury room and decide that if something is appealing to numerous people, it makes them laugh, they enjoy it, that you can state that this material is utterly without socially redeeming importance."

Now the matter was in Judge Draeger's hands. He was about to give his instructions to the jury. Some lawyers believe that instructing the jury is a formalized ritual of no great import, while others believe it to be one of the most determinative points of a criminal trial. In the San Francisco rendition of *People v. Bruce*, it was impossible for any lawyer to believe that Judge Clayton Horn's instructions to the jury did not save Lenny's *tuchas*. Whether Judge Henry Draeger's instructions to the jury were to have a similar impact in the Beverly Hills version of *People v. Bruce* was far less likely.

Among much standard boilerplate about witness credibility, the character of evidence, and burdens of proof, the court's instructions contained a verbatim recitation of California Penal Code Section 311.6 and its subsection defining the word "obscene." However, Judge Draeger did elaborate upon several of the legal criteria for obscenity, focusing on Bruce's controversial routines (rather than the entirety of his performances), the dominant character of those routines, Bruce's purposes in delivering those routines, their probable effects on the relevant audiences, and the specific factors to be considered in assessing all of those things:

—The dominant appeal of the material used, taken as a whole, must have a substantial tendency to deprave or corrupt the average person by inciting lascivious thoughts or arousing lustful desires.

—The material, applying contemporary community standards, appeals to the shameful or morbid interest of the average person in sex or nudity, bearing in mind contemporary community standards. In judging whether the spoken words are obscene, each routine spoken may not be condemned as obscene merely because some isolated word is deemed objectionable. It must be taken as a whole.

—Something is not necessarily obscene merely because it is in bad taste, shocking, disgusting, stupid, vulgar, embarrassing, immoral, or offensive.

—You may not rely on instinct in determining whether the material charged in the complaint is obscene. The ascertainment of obscenity cannot be merely subjective reflection of the taste or moral outlook of individual jurors. The determination of obscenity cannot be made on the basis of personal upbringing or restricted reflection or particular experience of life in individual jurors.

Could such instructions do much more than dizzy the minds of conscientious jurors? On the one hand, they were told that obscenity incited "lascivious thoughts or…lustful desires." On the other hand, they were instructed that obscenity appealed to a "shameful or morbid interest of the average person in sex or nudity." In other words, obscenity could both arouse and repulse. But if it repulsed, it necessarily offended. Yet, they were also instructed that material could not be obscene merely because it was "shocking, disgusting…vulgar… immoral or offensive." Was the point to find something that repulsed but did not shock, disgust, or offend?

Moreover, the jury was told that Bruce's "material must be taken as a whole," but that the "whole" was only a part of a performance, namely, a particular bit. It was a case of the part being larger than the whole. And the jurors—get this!—were not to make those determinations in a "subjective" way; rather, they were to identify some elusive standard of community values, apparently not through their "personal upbringing or…particular experience of life," and then apply it objectively.

It was all rather schizophrenic. No wonder, then, that prosecutor Ross thought his chances of prevailing were no better than "fifty–fifty." No wonder that D.A. Hecht found *People v. Bruce* to be "a tough call." And no wonder that, sometime after the jurors had retired at 4:40 P.M.

to deliberate, they requested the court to reread the definition of obscenity to them.

At 7:05 P.M., the bailiff reported that the jury was of two minds. At first, they had been deadlocked 6 to 6, and now were deadlocked 7 to 5 (although no one knew which way). Frustrated by the late hour and the stalemate, one female juror wanted to write down her understanding of the obscenity definition and present it for the court's approval. "So you can see," Judge Draeger remarked to counsel as they waited, "the impossibility for jurors to get definitions of the law."

Ten to fifteen minutes later, Draeger directed that the bailiff return the jury to the box to be polled. "At that time," Ross explained, "there was an instruction—we used to call it 'the blockbuster'—to encourage the jury to reach a verdict, because the case was never going to be tried any better than this time, and all the evidence was presented, etc....Judge Draeger gave that instruction." The jury was polled immediately, and remained deadlocked 7 to 5 favoring acquittal. "It became pretty obvious when the jury couldn't reach a verdict that Judge Draeger was going to declare a mistrial," recalled Ross—and the judge did.

The trial "ended" late that Friday in the Beverly Hills courtroom. Some saw it as a victory. "I thought it was a victory," prosecutor Ross declared, "[t]hat I could have convinced almost half the jury that saying some dirty words in a club that was open to the public, but basically a private place, could meet the *Roth* test." Likewise, defense attorney Marks thought it a victory for his client, insofar as a clear majority of the jury had validated Bruce's comedy. But, for Lenny Bruce—the guy who got the lawyer's bills and who wanted a *finale*—it was not a *real* victory, a San Francisco–styled victory.

A hung jury meant no closure. The whole mess could burst open again. In the ordinary course of things, a decision to retry a misdemeanor case would have been left to Ronald Ross. But *People v. Bruce* was not an ordinary case. It had generated much public attention. And Sergeant Block's department had an abiding interest in the drug-addicted comedian's affairs. That meant the decision to retry had to be made by the higher-ups in the D.A.'s Office—by William Ritzi and Ted Sten, to be specific. Four months after the Troubadour bust,

Lenny Bruce was still unsure whether he could play L.A. free of the sheriff's heavy hand. He knew that, club owners knew that, and the police knew that. It was a prime example of what Chief Justice Earl Warren had called a "chilling effect" on freedom of speech.

CHILL OR NO chill, Lenny Bruce had no choice but to keep his comedy alive, to keep his name on the marquees, and to keep the rent money coming in. By May 1963, the notorious comedian was back in the papers:

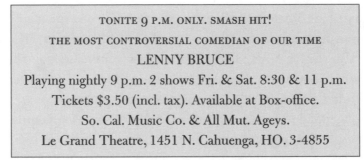

TONITE 9 P.M. ONLY. SMASH HIT!

THE MOST CONTROVERSIAL COMEDIAN OF OUR TIME

LENNY BRUCE

Playing nightly 9 p.m. 2 shows Fri. & Sat. 8:30 & 11 p.m.

Tickets $3.50 (incl. tax). Available at Box-office.

So. Cal. Music Co. & All Mut. Ageys.

Le Grand Theatre, 1451 N. Cahuenga, HO. 3-4855

Here was his name, once again in bold, in the club ad sections along with the likes of Don Rickles (playing The Slate Brothers Club) and Mort Sahl (coming to The Crescendo). But that wasn't all. Splashed across the pages were eye-catching advertisements for "Body Shop Burlesque" (starring Baby Bubbles), "Zomba Burlesque Strip-a-Thon" (eighteen strip shows), and Honey Harlowe's old stomping ground, The Colony Club ("Best of the Undressed"). Ironically, as Lenny's Le Grand ad suggested, his talk of "T & A" was far more controversial than the real displays of T & A.

Between his wild word shows, Lenny was pensive—though always true to his outrageous self—when he talked with Lionel Olay during an interview for *Cavalier* magazine. To his interviewer, the comedian was a "nonpolitical revolutionary," an "authentic hipster hero of the sexual and moral revolution that is taking place in our country..." Lenny was Olay's kind of guy, a man whom the "vested interests like to call a trouble maker." He was a man on the run, a man marked by the law. No matter. Lenny Bruce tested the law inside the clubs and inside the courts—a costly venture in any variety of ways, to be sure. "Why haven't you allowed the Civil Liberties Union to handle your legal defense on the obscenity charges, as it is willing to do without fee, instead of hiring your own attorneys at great expense?" To Olay's question, Bruce responded: "I didn't want that, none of that wounded-bird stuff for me, none of that Help Save Lenny Bruce Clubs that embarrass me." No, he would do it his way with his attorneys and at his expense. He didn't want pity (not yet anyway). He wanted the pride that comes from being the master of one's own fate…even if it meant not mastering that fate. What did he care what others thought of what he said on stage or in court? Lenny Bruce was his own man. Save the kudos and tears for the wimps, for the play-it-safe folks who worship at the altar of public approval.

When the reviews came, the lion's share of the attention did not go to Don Rickles or Mort Sahl—or even to Baby Bubbles. No, the honor was reserved for the proud Lenny Bruce. "Bruce Blasts Off; Verbally, That Is." That headline topped John G. Houser's review of Lenny's debut performance at the Le Grand. "There was another man 'in orbit' last night," Houser began, "and he was flying higher than Astronaut Gordon Cooper. His name is Lenny Bruce and about 150 aficionados of the uninhibited egomaniac caught his opening night act at the Le Grand Theater last night. The act had plenty of explosive fuel to put the crowd into orbit with the Bruce blasts."

But Lenny's high-flyin' bits crashed and burned, in Houser's estimation. Bruce failed to impress his reviewer with his "Thank You Mask Man" and "Religions, Inc." routines or his *spritzes* on Judy Garland, Sophie Tucker, Fidel Castro, Pat Brown, and Richard Nixon. "From the takeoff," Houser continued, "the former comic, who now philosophizes with liberal use of Anglo-Saxon vulgarities, rambled and wandered through more than a score of unrelated subjects. Each was touched with vitriol of his special verbal indelicacies." As if that were not enough, Houser exercised his own free speech rights as a reviewer to the critical max. He was not persuaded by any analogies, so often voiced by Lenny's supporters, that compared Bruce to Jonathan Swift and other famous satirists: "He is not a humorist, an impressionist or a satirist but he uses the façade of each to hammer at what he terms hypocrisy while using the four-letter words to shock an otherwise lethargic audience into attention."

If Houser's review caught the attention of the badges in the vice squad, the Le Grand Theater would be the next stop on their beat that evening. And, to no surprise, it was. LAPD officer Carl Martinez attended Lenny's May 23 act. The recent past repeated itself: the comedian was busted on a familiar Section 311.6 charge, booked, released by Los Angeles Municipal Court Judge Sherman W. Smith on the equally familiar $525 bail, and driven to the theater in time for his next show.

Although the Troubadour/Unicorn mistrial had given Lenny a break from his obscenity woes, that respite was likely to be brief. For all he knew, prosecutor Ronald Ross and his superiors were soon to retry that case, and now he was facing the probability of a new trial for the Le Grand bust. The various and ever-increasing incarnations of *People v. Bruce* were taking their toll on his diminishing income and uneasy sanity. And his popular image, which affected his earning power, was hurting. Only a few years earlier, he could boast of spreads in *Time* magazine. Now, tabloids like *Vice Squad*—that ran "Why the He-She Sex-Change Girl Divorced Her Hubby!" stories—claimed Lenny Bruce with unflattering headlines: VICE COPS CRACK DOWN ON WORLD'S SICKEST "SICK-SICK" COMIC! Strewn with whacked-out pictures of the new Lenny, the call-out text read:

> A year or so ago, Lenny Bruce was the hottest of the sick-sick-sick comics. Today his biggest followers seem to be vice cops who'd like to wash the 4-letter words out of his mouth and chase the monkey off his back!

Admittedly, Lenny was still garnishing notice in some big-name publications. But now those publications, if and when they covered Bruce, reported on how the police were after him, how club owners didn't want him, and how his future looked far less rosy than it once had. "Whether [those] happy days will ever come again is anybody's guess," surmised Robert Ruark in his "Let's Nix the Sickniks" article for the *Saturday Evening Post*. Things were changing, more quickly now, more intensely now, and more for the worse now, or so the L.A. story of Lenny Bruce's life would have led one to believe.

Contrary to popular opinion, Lenny Bruce's free speech persecutions did not begin in San Francisco or end in New York. That dubious honor belonged to the Los Angeles authorities. Between 1959 and 1966, police and prosecutors were almost relentless, either by threats of arrests or actual arrests, or by threats of club closures, or simply by spreading the word that Lenny Bruce was unwelcome in the City of the Angels. Lenny called it "an obscenity circus," a surreal spectacle seemingly without end.

In all of this, the L.A. story was an unruly one. It spilt across other chapters of Lenny's life and compounded the hellish problems he faced elsewhere. Take, for example, what happened in Chicago while Lenny's encounters with California's finest continued to rage on.

5

CHICAGO: THE ASH WEDNESDAY TRIAL

Fighting my "persecution" seems as futile as asking Barry Goldwater to speak at a memorial to send the Rosenberg kids to college.

—Lenny Bruce

The Gate of Horn

"CHICAGO IS SO corrupt," Lenny gibed, "it's thrilling." 🄲

He had good reason to love the Windy City, for it had been kind to him. He debuted in Chicago at The Cloister in July 1958, right after his critically acclaimed run in San Francisco at Ann's 440, and he enjoyed the same success there. That opportunity came to him at the behest of a Chicagoan who played an important role in his comedy career and legal life. The man was Hugh Hefner. Hefner met Bruce in 1958, when he ventured to San Francisco to check out the new comedian about whom he had heard so much. Herb Caen, the noted San Francisco columnist, joined Hefner at Ann's 440 to catch Lenny's act. Hefner loved it, and Lenny loved Hef's open-mindedness…and contacts, money, and *Playboy* lifestyle. Within no time, Hefner arranged a booking for Bruce at Chicago's recently redecorated club, The Cloister. Formerly The Cloister Inn, the club was now hip and swinging—with Lenny Bruce leading the comic charge. Moreover, Hefner had the first performances taped, so that his excitement over the new comedian might be shared with other liberated, fun-loving minds. Word got around quickly, and soon enough Lenny was gigging before enthusiastic crowds at Mister Kelly's and performing twice at The Trade Winds.

He was *soooo* hot that he was melting the ice on Lake Michigan. Studs Terkel interviewed Lenny in February 1959 on Chicago's WFMT radio, billing him as one of the most irreverent, but deft, comedians of the year. That same year, Hefner invited Lenny to guest-star on his television talk show, *Playboy's Penthouse*. Also in 1959, *Playboy* magazine, headquartered in Chicago, featured Lenny in a profile titled "Rebel Without a Caustic Cause," where he jested, "If I haven't any rapport with my listeners in the first ten minutes, I'm dead. But when I'm swinging and I feel that warmth coming up at me, I'd like to ball the whole audience."

Lenny could sing that Chicago was "his kind of town." And The Gate of Horn was his kind of place. It was a two-story brick building, a theater/restaurant located at 1036 North State Street, on the west side of the street. The club's slogan was: "A nightclub for people who hate nightclubs." No wonder, since some of the greatest folk music in the country was performed there. Josh White, Odetta, Judy Collins, The Limeliters, and Peter, Paul and Mary were only a few of the folk giants who strummed and sang at the Horn. Comic talents—including the likes of Shelley Berman and Mike Nichols and Elaine May—brought down that house before they reached national attention. Even Lawrence Ferlinghetti, the poet and publisher of *Howl*, read poetry at the Horn in November 1960.

The Horn was the social center for the local intelligentsia and the post-beatniks/pre-hippies, some dressed in Nehru jackets and turbans and others in gray suits and skinny ties. They came for the thrill of experiencing gifted performers on the rise. How poetically appropriate, since Greek legend held that the dreams that delude pass through the Gate of Ivory, but the dreams that come true pass through the Gate of Horn.

Certainly, Lenny needed to pass beyond the nightmares of his recent L.A. narcotics and obscenity busts when he signed a $3,000-a-week contract with The Gate of Horn for a four-week, double-night gig. They loved him, he loved them, and the critics loved it, too. Lenny Bruce is the "healthiest comic spirit of any comedian working in the United States," wrote Richard Christiansen for the *Chicago Daily News*. Lenny's act, he thought, was "right smack at the center of a true comedy that strips all prejudices and reveals man's inhumanity to man." With similar approval of the comic critic, Will Leonard of the *Chicago Tribune* declared: "Lenny Bruce is here to talk about the phony, frightened, lying world." They were letting Lenny be Lenny…and with their blessings! Best of all, the law left him alone for his first dozen or so performances at the Horn. It looked like Chicago was going to be the "sick" comic's free-speech sanctuary.

If Chicago were a safe haven, its legal culture was to be credited as much as its popular culture. The Illinois obscenity statute—newly amended to take account of *Roth v. U.S.*—appeared to safeguard Lenny in ways that the language of the California law did not. Chapter 38 defined a performance as obscene if:

> ...considered as a whole, its predominant appeal is to prurient interest, that is, a shameful or morbid interest in nudity, sex, or excretion, and if it goes substantially beyond customary limits of candor in description or representation of such matters.

The law qualified the still-confusing definition of obscenity by providing that it be "judged with reference to ordinary adults," and by listing six criteria for establishing a violation. Among them were:

—The character of the audience;

—The effect, if any, [the material] would probably have on the behavior of such people;

—The degree, if any, of public acceptance of the material in this State;

—[And the] artistic, literary, scientific, educational or other merits of the material.

That, then, was the legal yardstick. Anything that Lenny would do at The Gate of Horn would have to be measured against it, *and* against the First Amendment. Meanwhile, no need to think much about the law; after all, Bruce was Hefner's guest at 1340 North State Street, the Playboy Mansion. Life was so good there, so why agonize about troubles elsewhere?

"He Mocks the Pope"

THE LENNY WHO walked onto the stage after midnight on Wednesday, December 5, 1962, was not the slim-trim, Italian-suited, quick-witted, upbeat performer he had been at The Cloister. He was becoming more full-bodied, slovenly-suited, brain-clouded, baggy-eyed, and downbeat, though as the show progressed there were glimpses of the wit and snap of the earlier Bruce.

"Lenny Bruce, ladies and gentlemen," announced the emcee, "Lenny Bruce...let the buyer beware!"

It was the past as prelude when Lenny came out wearing a three-quarter-length black raincoat for his second performance that night at the Horn; it was, after all, the same raincoat look he displayed at the second performance at The Jazz Workshop the night he was busted in San Francisco. "You know what this is? One-day service at the Maryland," Lenny joked, describing the shabby, mismatched garb he was left with when his clothes hadn't been delivered in time at the Maryland Hotel. At first, his speech was slurred and muddled. He rambled and grunted. To some, he may have seemed as high as a Georgia pine.

That night, he did some fifteen bits in fifty-five minutes on the upstairs stage of the Horn. The topical range moved from politics and religion to race and marital relations, from homosexuality to drugs—with King Kong and drag-queen-cop *shticks* thrown in for wild measure. By and large, the audience of some three hundred hung with him. He lost some, however, like "the deuce on the tier" who cared little for his Rock Hudson–homosexuality routine.

Arthur Tyrrell, Michael Noro, and Al Pieper had paid the $2.50 cover charge and certainly were not about to leave early. They arrived at the Horn at 11:05 P.M. and, after ten minutes or so in the downstairs lobby, proceeded upstairs to grab a beer and catch the first show, a folk music trio. They weren't balcony goers; they wanted the choice seats on the main floor—some ten to fifteen feet from the stage with an unobstructed view. This was the evening they longed for, an evening with Lenny Bruce. Lenny did not disappoint them. He ripped things wide open with six bits:

"Paul Malloy and Christianity": Lenny railed against the Chicago columnist Paul Malloy, whom he tagged as "Christ in concrete." Malloy's righteous pronouncements on decency and indecency, good and bad, stuck in Lenny's craw. He always had suspected an intolerable hypocrisy in such moralists. "Mr. Malloy is full of shit," Lenny blasted. Holding up a page from a *Rogue* Girl Calendar, Lenny asked how this "pretty lady" could be indecent. Then, referring to the partially torn photo of the "pink-nippled lady," he registered a forceful dissent: "You see, you defeat your purpose. It's God, your filthy Jesus Christ made these tits. That's all." A few of the faithful exited.

"Adolf Eichmann": Slightly over six months after Eichmann had been hung as a war criminal in Jerusalem, Lenny told the audience that they should have *rochmunas* (sympathy) for the Nazi war criminal. Breaking into an eerie German accent, he played on Thomas Merton's poetic theme when he asked: "Do you recognize ze whore in ze middle of you—that you vood have done ze same if you vere there yourselves? My defense: I vas a soldier." Yes, Eichmann had "vatched through ze portholds," and had seen the Jews "turned into soap." But, he challenged: "Do you people think yourselves bettah becuz you burned your enemies at long distance vith missile vithout ever zeeing vhat you had done to them? Hiroshima *auf Wiedersehen*." **CD**

"War Criminals and Hershey Bars": Reflecting on the cruelty of American war victors to Japanese war victims, Lenny opined why Americans are hated: "You know why? Cause we fucked all their mothers for chocolate bars." American soldiers "*schtupped*" Japanese women in exchange for "stinking coffee and their eggs and their frigging cigarettes." With a satirical stab, he asked the people in the audience whether they really thought the children of war now would say: "There's the fellow who fucked my mother—oh, thank you, thank you, thank you. Thank you for that, and for giving us candy."

"Infidelity": Still working the hypocrisy theme, though in a lighter way, Lenny admitted to having sex with three married women, and then challenged all his male patrons: "Now if I did it—and, Christ, I'm not that unique. Probably every guy in this audience has made it with one married chick or two….And both of us, we didn't pull out." That explains the "brothers and sisters [who] don't look alike."

"How to Relax Your Colored Friends at Parties": This was among Lenny's most famous bits. Its performance at The Gate of Horn, however, was not one of the better renditions. It was like the routine that he had done many times with his close friend, the black guitarist Eric Miller. The bit mocked whites who fancied themselves colorblind, and revealed the lingering racism among the "enlightened" majority. The scene: a party, where a middle-aged white construction worker converses with a black musician: "You know, that Joe Louis, a hell of a fighter….[C]redit to your race….(toasting) [H]ere's to Paul Robeson." Innocently meant, but nonetheless offensive, remarks followed about chicken, watermelon, or raisins, "whatever you people eat." Then, the construction worker acknowledged that he would like to have the musician over to his house, but quickly added: "I got a sister, you know what I mean?…What do you want to hump everybody's sister for?" The satirical rub came in a play on the word "sister."

> *Musician:* Well, no, you missed the vernacular. It's not everybody's sister, but I do it to *sisters.*
> *Construction Worker:* What do you mean, sisters?…You don't mean *sister* sisters?…No kidding, do they put out, those sisters?"

"Christ and Moses": Only a few weeks after the beloved Pope John XXIII convened Vatican II, Lenny did a Marx Brothers variation on another of his classic bits (previously described in chapter one). This routine featured Christ and Moses visiting St. Patrick's Cathedral. The biting humor came with Cardinal Spellman's dilemma: What to do, in the presence of these two holy men, with the lepers polluting the church? On the phone with the pope, Spellman began: "Hey, woppo, what's happening? You were sick, weren't you, fatso? If you'd stop *fressing* so much…" The routine was sprinkled with a few "*schmucks.*"

Inside there was laughter, outside there was trouble. Eight squad car units, with their blue lights flashing, pulled up in front of The Gate of Horn. Before he could finish his *shtick* about a marijuana bust, Lenny noticed two Chicago Blues rise up to halt the performance. "It's the first time they made a bust right in an audience," Lenny chuckled. What happened next smacked of a Bruce bit:

Lenny: Oh shit. (laughing)…Wake up, quick! Out the back way. The bricks move…anything. It's Super-Jew! *Shhoooo*…Okay, the whole place is blocked off.
Police: We're police officers.
Lenny: I knew that, I knew that, yeah.
Police: Show's over, ladies and gentlemen, police officers. Everybody have a seat.…We're checking your ID cards.
Club Manager: Ladies and gentlemen, we now have a new star of our show. 🅒

Perhaps by way of hipster protest, a cool piano and jazz sax played on while Lenny was escorted out of the club. Ditto for Alan Ribback, the coat-and-vested co-owner of the Horn. Also busted were the bartender, a writer from *Swank* magazine, and a non-drinking sixteen-year-old girl charged with violating the curfew laws.

One other patron caught the heat when he was flippant with the police. "Where's your ID?" asked the officer. "I don't believe in IDs," responded the patron. Before he could say George Carlin, he was busted for disorderly conduct. "He sorta grabbed me by the collar of [my] suit and the baggy pant of my ass and bum rushed me down the stairs" and into the paddy wagon. "I'm going to jail," Carlin yelled out to his wife. Once they were both in police custody, Carlin spoke briefly with Lenny. "So what are you doing here?" asked Lenny. "I didn't want to show them my ID," Carlin answered. Lenny was playful: "You *schmuck!*" 🅒 In all of this, Carlin was showing comic support for the man he first had met in 1960, at Cosmo Alley in Los Angeles, where Carlin was then doing an imitation of Bruce as part of his routine. Lenny had loved it so much that he contacted Jack Sobel to encourage General Artists Corporation, a big-time entertainment agency, to extend a contract to Carlin (and his colleague Jack Burns). It had been Lenny Bruce at his benevolent best, for the two comedians never saw much of each other until that fateful night at The Gate of Horn. Now, they were comedians in cuffs.

Patrolmen Arthur Tyrrell and Michael Noro conducted the official honors. The two were family men (with five children between them); they were also undercover officers from the 18th District (with twelve years in the police force between them). The pair made the bust, aided by Officer Pieper. Tyrrell, the primary, worked vice in this city, where there was an abundance of opportunity for anyone in his line of work. Like Officers Ryan and Solden in San Francisco, Officers Tyrrell and Noro were "disgusted" by the evening's performance— clearly, an illegal affront to local morals.

Tyrrell, Noro, and Pieper later provided information for a police report charging Lenny with violation of the Illinois obscenity code (§11-20) for the following reasons:

—Mr. Bruce held up a colored photograph showing the naked breast of a woman and said "God, your Jesus Christ, made these tits."

—"They say we fuck our mothers for Hershey bars."…"I want to fuck your mothers." "Oh, thank you, thank you, thank you."

—Then referring to the good sisters of the Church, he stated, "The sisters cannot like to do it to sisters, fuck, good, good."

—"Everybody's bugging somebody. I bug three married women. All you people out there have at some time or another bugged someone's wife."

—[H]e led into a mockery of the Catholic Church and other religious organizations by using the pope's name and Cardinal Spellman and Bishop Sheen's name.

—Then talking about the War he stated, "If we would have lost the War, they would have strung Truman up by the balls." [This comment came at the end of Lenny's Eichmann bit.]

The police report is remarkable for at least three reasons. First, a comparison between the report and a tape recording of what actually was said revealed obvious police misstatements. (*Playboy* had taped the performance.) Lenny long had complained about having to defend an act that he never had performed. Second, the report lifted Lenny's "dirty words" out of the full context of his bits. By doing so, it did not even recognize the need to consider The Gate of Horn performance as a whole. Finally, the report cited Lenny's animosity and mockery of religion as criminal. The police essentially used the Illinois obscenity statute to arrest Lenny for blasphemy—an "offense" not included within the statute. Given the police report, the misdemeanor charge should have been relatively easy to defeat.

Judge Chester Strzalka released Bruce on $500 bail and transferred his case to a jury court for a December 12 hearing. Meanwhile, Alan Ribback, the president of The Gate of Horn, held a press conference at his club. "The arrest of Lenny Bruce from the stage of The Gate of Horn...for alleged obscenity, raises the issue of The Gate of Horn's position in presenting Lenny Bruce," he began. The reason why Lenny Bruce was given a mike, continued Ribback, was simple and straightforward: "[We] booked because [we] regard him as a serious artist." Much the same way the club had booked the likes of Theo Bikel and Joan Baez. With a firm resolve, Ribback stood his First Amendment ground: "[T]he issues involved in Lenny Bruce's act are the same as those raised in the censorship of the works" of many great literary figures. As with the latter, he added, the thrust of the comedian's work did not appeal to prurient interests, but rather "involves a moral act. Lenny Bruce does not attack believers but rather false believers." Therefore, the show must go on.

The club owner stood up for the comedian. Brothers in arms, in the cause, in the good fight to defend Lenny's right to offend people. Thus, Lenny Bruce continued his appearance at the Horn. No letting down, no "cleaning up his act." No, they would not be bullied. But that did not stop the bullying. For one week after his arrest, Captain McDermott, the head of Chicago's vice squad, paid a visit on Alan Ribback to deliver an official warning: "If [Bruce] ever speaks against religion, I'm going to pinch you and everyone in here. Do you understand?...[H]e mocks the pope—and I'm speaking as a Catholic—I'm here to tell you your license is in danger."

The policeman's prophesy was realized on February 12, 1963, when Mayor Richard J. Daley suspended the Horn's liquor license for fifteen days over three weekends for allegedly offering a "lewd show." Now the law moved beyond mere threats to the reality of suspending business licenses for those who staged Bruce. Such action only could further "chill" the willingness of other club owners to provide a venue for Lenny. As for Alan Ribback, his problems were not yet over.

Legal Problems Galore

IN JANUARY 1963, Lenny sat in an office at 200 West 57th Street, across from Carnegie Hall. He was there to discuss business with Earle Warren Zaidins, an attorney whose name called to mind Chief Justice Earl Warren, the great American constitutionalist.

He was short and stocky, and had curly hair—a bruiser-looking sort of guy. Since the early '60s, Zaidins—an attorney specializing in entertainment law—had handled several contractual matters for Lenny, including a suit against Fantasy Records concerning royalty payments. Zaidins vividly recalled the first time he met Lenny Bruce: "He closed my office door and admitted, 'I'm an addict. Does it make any difference to you?' 'No,' I told him, 'You're speaking to the man who represented Billie Holiday.'"

On that day in January, the usual talk of royalties was not at the forefront of Lenny's mind. Where could he begin? He had *so many* legal problems—there was the pending obscenity trial for the Troubadour and Unicorn busts; there was the pending Van Nuys trial for the narcotics bust; and now there was the pending obscenity trial for the Chicago bust.

Focusing on Chicago, Bruce informed Zaidins that he was covered. George J. Cotsirilos, one of Chicago's prominent criminal lawyers, had made an early appearance for Bruce to set a trial date; but now Sam Friefeld, the lawyer for The Gate of Horn, would represent him. Zaidins questioned the legal prudence of such an arrangement: "Lenny, he might be a great guy and a good lawyer, but you need independent legal counsel. There's a conflict-of-interest problem." He explained that Friefeld's first-and-foremost concern would be to protect the interests of Ribback and The Gate of Horn, even at Lenny's expense. They talked it over. Finally, Zaidins offered to travel to Chicago and find a powerhouse lawyer to represent Bruce. Bruce was relieved.

Lenny prepared to leave New York. His five-week run at one of Manhattan's oldest nightclubs, The Village Vanguard, was nearly over. Max Gordon, the owner, had never been Bruce's biggest fan—"Shit, *putz, schmuck*—what does he need all that horny material for?" he once asked the club manager. Even so, Gordon brought the comic back to the Vanguard because "he fills the room." Every night, Lenny packed the place (in the Village on Seventh Avenue South) with college kids, hookers, gays, and the Harlem and Broadway types—and no one left. Whatever happened in San Francisco, Los Angeles, and Chicago, Lenny felt safe in New York among "my kind of people."

On Sunday, February 10, 1963, he caught a plane for Los Angeles, so that he could appear in the Beverly Hills Municipal Court the next day. One week later, Zaidins and he would have to be in the Circuit Court of Cook County—for yet another obscenity trial.

The Right to Make a Fool of Oneself

THE MARYLAND HOTEL, on Rush Street and not far from The Gate of Horn, served as their sleeping quarters and law offices. Zaidins took a room adjoining Bruce's. On Monday, February 18, Zaidins called around to locate counsel to represent Lenny. He tried in vain to reach, among others, Harry Kalven Jr., a law professor at the University of Chicago. The highly regarded First Amendment scholar was not to be found, at least not by Zaidins.

There was so much to be done with so little time. Even after securing some big-shot Chicago lawyer, the schedule would press: there was courtroom strategy to be developed, motions to be made, witnesses to be called, law to be researched, and audiotapes to be transcribed. Meanwhile, Earle and Lenny settled on an alternate plan: while Lenny worked on finding expert witnesses, Zaidins would appear as his general counsel and ask the judge for a continuance in order to locate a Chicago attorney.

Lenny hoped to have at least three witnesses. He would take the stand, of course; but he also wanted an expert, namely, Dorothy Kilgallen, a celebrated Hearst newspaper columnist who had written favorably about him years before. Even more important, he desired a man of the cloth to testify on his behalf. Father Norman O'Connor, called "the jazz priest," was that man—a Catholic priest who befriended many performers. Earle Zaidins long had known Father O'Connor; the priest had officiated at Billie Holiday's memorial service in 1959, and Zaidins later had arranged a private showing for him of Lenny's self-produced, silent and surreal, unfinished macho-motorcyclist movie from the early 1950s, *Leather Jacket*. The priest promised to testify. But as the trial drew nearer, Father O'Connor sent a profusely apologetic telegram to Lenny at the Maryland Hotel, explaining that his superiors had ordered him not to appear as a witness for the defense. "[W]hat can they do to you? Bust you to nun?" Lenny demanded in frustration.

One month before, Zaidins had brainstormed for a half hour with George Cotsirilos over the telephone, urging him to request an April trial date on the grounds that Lenny had bookings through the month of March. Although Cotsirilos did Zaidins's bidding, he had succeeded only in getting the trial postponed until February 18. In the meantime, Zaidins found Donald Page Moore, a noted ACLU lawyer, to substitute for Cotsirilos. But there was a glitch: Moore agreed to appear only for pretrial matters, but refused to represent Lenny at trial if Bruce insisted on controlling the conduct of the case. That meant Zaidins had a problem. Unless he could persuade Lenny to meet Moore's conditions, Lenny still had no lawyer for the trial itself.

On February 11, 1963, Daniel Page Moore and Sam Friefeld made two pretrial motions on Lenny's behalf. The first, a motion to "quash the information," aimed at throwing the case out of court without a trial on three grounds:

1. The charges against Lenny were "unconstitutionally vague."
2. The charges failed to allege that Lenny had "knowingly" violated the law as required by the Illinois obscenity statute.
3. If the Illinois statute did not require a "knowing" violation, then it was unconstitutional under the free speech and due process guarantees of the federal and state constitutions.

In addition, the two attorneys moved for a "bill of particulars." Since the charges against Lenny were so vague, they could not defend against them unless the prosecution could identify the *specific* portions of Bruce's act that were allegedly obscene.

It was all for naught. On Valentine's Day, Judge Daniel Ryan denied the defense's motion to drop the case. He did, however, allow the state to amend its charges against Lenny in order that they be more specific. Now, the prosecution claimed that Lenny had violated Illinois's obscenity statute when he used certain words. To be precise, there were *seven dirty words or expressions* that proved legally offensive: "Fuck," "Piss," "Tits," "Stumping and Stepping on my dick," "Jag-Off," "Hang Kennedy's balls up," "Fuck their mothers for Hershy [sic] Bars." This amended information also alleged that the comedian had made "gestures indicating masturbation."

Faced with the state's modified charges, Donald Page Moore moved to quash the information once again, this time raising several different legal issues. The Illinois obscenity statute "requires that an allegedly obscene utterance be judged as a whole," Moore argued, but "[t]his information before the court does not plead either the entire utterance or the substance of the utterance." Thus, the state had failed "to lay a proper foundation" for a criminal violation. Moreover, insofar as the Illinois obscenity statute penalized "a morbid interest in nudity, sex, or excretion," it violated federal and state constitutional protections for speech and press. With this new motion to quash, Moore provided the court with alternative grounds for dismissing this case, so that Lenny could get on with his life. Neither rationale hit paydirt, however. Moore's motion was overruled in a summary fashion. The matter was now ready for trial—with all the legal *i*s dotted and *t*s crossed.

Shortly after Bruce and Zaidins arrived at their hotel on the morning of February 18, they conferred with Moore. Not surprisingly, Lenny had refused to render up control of his legal destiny, and so told Moore that he and Friefeld were out of the picture. It was now up to Zaidins and Bruce (the "lead counsel") to take charge and maneuver through the complexities of Illinois procedural, evidentiary, and substantive law, in addition to establishing a record based on the relevant federal law—the First and Fourteenth Amendments to the United States Constitution.

REPRESENTING ONESELF AT trial is always risky. Hence, the old adage: "One who is his own lawyer has a fool for a client."

In Chicago, Lenny Bruce *acted*, for the first time, as his own attorney. More accurately, he was "lead counsel"—the man who called the legal shots. He would orchestrate the trial and how it was to be conducted; and he would rule over the judgment calls (that was his plan, anyway). This was his trial, his freedom, and his right.

It took 186 years of American constitutional history before the Supreme Court recognized an individual right to self-representation. Finding the right in the Sixth Amendment, the Court's 1975 decision in *Faretta v. California* declared: "The right to defend is given directly to the accused; for it is he who suffers the consequences if the defense fails." To force a lawyer on a defendant "can only lead him to believe that the law contrives against him," Justice Potter Stewart wrote for the Court.

The dissenters were appalled; their brethren had opened the criminal justice system "to the whimsical—albeit voluntary—caprice of every accused who wishes to use his trial as a vehicle for personal or political self-gratification." Chief Justice Warren Burger charged that the criminal trial "should not be available as an instrument of self-destruction." And Justice Harry Blackmun complained that "the Court by its opinion today now bestows a *constitutional* right on one to make a fool of himself."

While Lenny Bruce was spending his energy and his money in trial after trial during the early 1960s, the *Faretta* ruling, of course, had not yet been rendered. Though he could claim no federal constitutional right of self-representation, many states already granted his voluntary and knowing choice of self-representation in their courts under their law. Lenny had foregone this option in San Francisco and Los Angeles, yielding begrudgingly to the insistence of his lawyers that he not interfere with their handling of his cases. Whatever his promises, he always managed to meddle in the conduct of his trials, at least in some ways.

By the time of the Chicago bust, however, he was troubled by the spiraling costs of his litigation and paranoid about losing control over his own fate. Now, he harangued and squabbled with his lawyers until they either gave in or gave out. "Of all persons involved in obscenity cases, [Bruce] was the most perverse in his relations with lawyers," claimed Elmer Gertz, a Chicago attorney whom Lenny once almost hired. After the disappointing Beverly Hills hung-jury result, Lenny was much more willing to take on his own defense and test himself against the risks of having a fool for a client. Chicago gave him that opportunity.

TRIAL DAY ARRIVED. No more delays. Without witnesses, without preparation, without anything, Earle and Lenny appeared at eleven A.M. on Monday, February 18, in the Cook County Courthouse, known as "Branch 46." The courtroom was packed with groupies. To the approval of the young onlookers, but over Zaidins's objection, Lenny wore his typical nightclub attire: a denim jean outfit with a mock turtleneck and black boots. "What does a suit and tie have to do with anything?" Lenny scoffed. "The trial is a search for truth, not a fashion show."

Municipal Court Judge Daniel J. Ryan presided. By the time *People v. Bruce* came before him, Ryan had clocked only three years as a municipal judge. To the eye, Judge Ryan—six-foot-four, fair hair interspersed with gray, a reddish nose, forty-six years old—looked like a man of imposing power. He was a "jovial sort, a good-natured Irishman, but when sternness [was] required, look out."

"Ryan was a man who played games," Zaidins recalled. Ironically, Lenny's co-counsel complained that Ryan "thought that Lenny was an addict. When things got a little controversial during voir dire, the judge pulled Lenny into his chambers. Believing the old bromide that a drug addict will not drink hard liquor, the judge offered him a glass of brandy, and Lenny downed it—every drop." Ultimately, claimed Zaidins, "Judge Ryan had one mission: to convict Lenny Bruce." Perhaps he did; then again, perhaps matters were destined to play out to bizarre lengths when this authoritarian judge was pitted against this antiauthoritarian defendant. Bad chemistry can make for bad cases.

Ryan: Mr. Bruce, you are charged with the crime of obscenity in violation of Chapter 38 of the Illinois Revised Statutes, Section 11-20. What is your plea?

Bruce: Not guilty, your Honor.

Ryan: Do you wish to be tried by this court or by a jury?

Bruce: By jury.

Ryan: I wish the record to be quite clear….You are to conduct your defense by yourself with Mr. Zaidins of the New York Bar. Is that correct?

Bruce: That is correct, your Honor.

Ryan: You are entitled to counsel, and you know fully well what you are doing?…You have dispensed with the services of Mr. Moore and Mr. Friefeld. You know fully well what you are doing?

Bruce: Yes, sir.…

Ryan: Send for the jury.

"It was my idea that Lenny be the attorney-of-record, so I could pull out at any time after hiring local counsel," Zaidins later explained. "It was a stall tactic. But, it went to Lenny's head."

When it came to picking a jury, Lenny insisted on taking charge. "But Lenny," Zaidins warned, "You don't know anything about picking a jury."

"Oh yes, I do," Lenny asserted. "I've seen the way Melvin Belli picks juries. I've studied it carefully, and I know how to do it." Pure innocent ignorance, pure Lenny.

Tapping a tactic that Belli never tested, Lenny hit the jury panel with obscene zingers, and asked prospective jurors whether such words offended them. Those who expressed disapproval were automatically rejected. Bruce asked one woman, "Do you consider the word 'son of a bitch' to be obscene?" When she affirmed that she did, Bruce continued: "If the president of the United States were on trial for obscenity and he had used the word 'son of a bitch,' would you consider it to be obscene?" The prosecutor, Assistant Deputy Attorney Samuel V. Banks, objected. Judge Ryan sustained the objection. The juror was excused.

Lenny and Zaidins exchanged words over his selection of one

juror, a feisty Irishwoman. Appearing forty to forty-five years old, puffy-eyed, with "the face of a drunk," she was a choice that Zaidins could not understand. "This is crazy," he exclaimed. But Lenny would not listen. With wild speculation, he told Zaidins: "She's a drunk. When she gets in the jury room, she'll want to keep it short so that she can get a drink." But what did he *really* know about this Celtic matron, or about picking jurors favorable to his case? It was, at best, a wild crapshoot.

The assistant prosecutor, Edward J. Egan, apparently agreed with Zaidin's flippant psychological assessment. In light of what he knew about Lenny Bruce in and out of court, he considered asking Judge Ryan to order a psychiatric evaluation for Bruce. Admittedly, it was a rather crazy voir dire. In the end, eight women and four men were impaneled, and it was time for the actual trial to start.

Lenny the Lawyer

JUDGE RYAN'S FIRST order of business was to remove the children from his courtroom: "Ladies and gentlemen, all of the children will please be escorted from the courtroom during this part of the jury trial. Will the parents please take all children out." And later, when a group of young women from Rosary College entered the courtroom during a tour, Ryan again asked that the spectators leave. Some of the college students were of the same age as the Gate of Horn patrons. What, then, was the jury to infer from the Judge's declaration that Lenny Bruce's trial was unsuitable for the ears of college women? Did the trial's beginning augur its end?

Once the courtroom had been cleared of innocents, the opening arguments began. Prosecutor Samuel Banks spoke to dramatic effect, but in an understated way: "[T]here were certain terms used [in the Gate of Horn act] which are not the acceptable standard of our community....I don't like to use the terms, but I have to. Mr. Bruce, throughout his performance, used the term 'fuck' constantly." He worked the jury's emotions, smoothly: "Truthfully, I'm not permitted to say what I feel. I am sure that you have noticed the perspiration on my nose and my upper lip." After this buildup, he culminated with a searing attack on Lenny's anti-religiosity: "You will hear the mockery of the church, not just any church, not just the Catholic Church, not just the Lutheran Church, but the church *per se*. You will hear mockery that is vulgar and obscene." Zaidins immediately objected, and Judge Ryan sustained the objection. Trying to put the proverbial paste back in its tube, the judge instructed the jury to ignore the prosecutor's characterization of Lenny's crime as blasphemy.

Lenny, "the lawyer," made promise after promise in his opening statement to the jury. Either he didn't realize, or it didn't bother him, that some of these promises could not be honored. He promised to prove that "my intention is not to degradate [sic] the community, to lower the standards." He promised to establish that the state's characterization of his performance was inaccurate and misleading. He promised to demonstrate that the police neither knew the law nor how to apply the law to his comic routine. He promised to call expert witnesses to advance these claims. Finally, he promised to offer into evidence an audiotape recording of the entire Horn act. And all of these promises were made in Lenny's inimitable nightclub manner, with colorfully inapt analogies to eating pork and the wearing of "vulgate" clothing. Not your standard opening statement.

Like prosecutor Albert Wollenberg in the San Francisco trial, prosecutors Samuel V.P. Banks and Willie Whiting (one of the few female assistant D.A.s) called only two witnesses for the state—the arresting officers—during the three days that the state presented its case (February 18, 20, and 21). Like Officers Ryan and Solden in the San Francisco trial, Officers Tyrrell and Noro testified to little beyond their recollection of truncated bits of vulgarity. For example:

> *Tyrrell*: He was talking about the war and if we, the United States, would have lost the war they would have hung Truman up by his balls. Another story which he was talking about. He says, "Look, the waitress just threw up all over her tits." And, "this is no washroom. So, knock it off, *schmuck*."...He stated that he had bugged three married women, everyone must have bugged married women at one

time or another, and that is about all that I can remember about that story. There are other stories of course. Mr. Bruce goes from one thing to another. It is fairly hard to keep up with him.

...

Noro: I recall a story about during the war soldiers were in Europe. As they were marching, they saw some women standing on the road. The soldiers had chocolates. After the war was ended, later we were looking at their children and he said, "We fucked their mothers with Hershey Bars."...He talked about the sisters of the Church. There were stories about doing it with sisters. He stated there is nothing wrong with that.

Unlike defense counsel Albert Bendich in San Francisco, however, the defense counsels in Chicago had no multileveled plan of attack. With nothing but the Gate of Horn tape to introduce as evidence in their main case, the Chicago defense team desperately needed to undercut the prosecution's witnesses on cross-examination. Uncharacteristically, "lawyer" Lenny conceded this all-important task entirely to his co-counsel.

Essential Attacks

EARLE ZAIDINS'S STRATEGY for cross-examination was well-conceived, if not always well-executed.

If he could discredit the officers' testimony on one or more of the essential elements in the statutory definition of obscenity, he might then argue that the state had not carried its burden of proving an obscene performance under Section 11-20. And if, by the time that the state rested, he succeeded in punching enough large holes in its case, he might defeat the prosecution altogether with a motion to direct a verdict for Lenny. To this end, Zaidins's cross-examination moved along four fronts:

The *taken as a whole argument*: establish that the arresting officers never had considered Bruce's performance at The Gate of Horn "as a whole." Here, Zaidins sought to demonstrate that the officers could not recall Lenny's bits in their entirety, but had focused obsessively on isolated words and phrases taken out of a context that was not obscene. One of the most forceful strikes in this regard was directed to Officer Tyrrell:

> *Zaidins*: You likewise recall Eichmann in the voice of the police, stating that he had a defense—that he was a soldier under orders, do you recall that?
>
> *Tyrrell*: Yes, sir, I believe so.
>
> *Zaidins*: You also recall, do you not, for his defense at least, he said that he watched it through the hole and watched these people die in the gas chambers, lethal chambers; do you recall that?
>
> *Tyrrell*: I remember something about gas chambers....
>
> *Zaidins*: In this particular story, up to this point...were there any words that were disgusting words, any words at all?
>
> *Tyrrell*: I could not say.
>
> *Zaidins*: You don't remember.
>
> *Tyrrell*: No, sir, I do not....
>
> *Zaidins*: In fact, isn't it true that you cannot relate the story that Mr. Bruce told, any one of them in which any of these words were used, other than the use of the words? You cannot really relate an entire story or at least the greater portion of a story, can you?
>
> *Tyrrell*: It is pretty hard to follow Mr. Bruce.

The *no appeal to prurient interest argument*: establish that Bruce's performance did not predominantly appeal "to prurient interest, that is, a shameful or morbid interest in nudity, sex, or excretion." Zaidins aimed to undermine Officer Tyrrell's testimony by showing that he neither had appreciated sufficiently nor understood fully that Lenny's performance could not meet the statutory definition of obscenity:

> *Zaidins*: Did you understand what Mr. Bruce meant in relation to the entire scope of the Eichmann story, what was meant by, "If we had lost the war, they would have hung Truman up by his balls." Did you understand?...Is this statement in the context of the story

relating to morbid interest in nudity?…

Tyrrell: Not in nudity, no, sir. I don't believe so.

Zaidins: Sex, sex; morbid interest in sex?

Tyrrell: No, sir, I would say not.…

Zaidins: Did it relate to a morbid interest in "excretion"?

Tyrrell: "Excretion"?

Zaidins: Do you know what "excretion" is?

Tyrrell: Give me a definition of it, please.…

Zaidins: I take it then, that your answer really is that you are not sure of the definition of this word, is that correct?

Tyrrell: That is correct.

Similarly, Zaidins strove to prove that Officer Noro actually believed that Lenny's performance did not appeal predominantly to the prurient interest:

Zaidins: Officer, officer, do you recall testifying, giving testimony in regard to a liquor license issued to The Gate of Horn for the premises located at 1036 North State Street, Chicago?…Such testimony having been given on the date of the 24th of January, 1963, Room 201, City Hall, before Liquor Control Commissioner John F. Cashen. Do you recall testifying before him?

Noro: Yes, I did.…

Zaidins: Do you recall having made the following answer to the following question asked by Mr. Friefeld [attorney for The Gate of Horn, made on cross-examination]? Question: "Did any of the things Mr. Bruce said appeal to your prurient interest?" Answer: "No." Do you recall that?

Noro: Yes, I do.

Zaidins: You have now stated under oath that it was obscene, is that correct?

Noro: Yes, I did.

Zaidins: No further questions.

The *serious value argument*: establish that the character and composition of Bruce's audience at The Gate of Horn ran the full gamut of gender, age, and class, and that this audience recognized and appreciated the serious political and social value in Lenny's comedy:

Zaidins: Let's get back to the audience at The Gate of Horn. There were men there?
Tyrrell: Correct.
Zaidins: There were women there?
Tyrrell: Yes, there were.
Zaidins: There were people of what one might consider of young to middle age, were there not?
Tyrrell: Yes, I would say that....
Zaidins: There were people possibly over the age of fifty?
Tyrrell: I can't recall the ages....
Zaidins: Were these people that you saw on the premises at this particular place, there were some people on the premises that were nicely dressed?
Tyrrell: That is correct....
Zaidins: It is certainly possible that a man may have taken his wife to that place, that night?
Tyrrell: Very possible....
Zaidins: Did anyone on the premises at that time complain to you—not as a result of your questioning, but came to you and said Mr. Bruce's performance is obscene? That didn't happen, did it?
Tyrrell: No, sir.
Zaidins: It did not, indeed. I believe that you testified that there was little laughing, is that correct?
Tyrrell: There was not a great deal, no, sir....
Zaidins: Wasn't it a fact that certain portions of Mr. Bruce's performance were not of a jovial but rather serious nature?...In other words, Officer, if there was any seriousness in the way Mr. Bruce was delivering his presentation, it is conceivable that people who did not laugh thought so, is that not so?
Tyrrell: True.

The *within the customary limits of taste argument*: establish that Bruce's occasional use of "dirty" words or pictures did not exceed "customary limits of candor in description or representation of such matters." Thus, Zaidins inquired into the general availability of "girlie magazines" similar to the *Rogue* calendar pin-up used by Bruce as a prop, and the typical use of vulgarity:

> *Zaidins*: These appear to you, do they not, to be [the *Rogue* Girl] April Calendar, representing that month of the year of 1963, with a figure on each page of the calendar, isn't that what it appears to you?…There are similar calendars being sold at the newsstands and the drugstores in that area, with these pictures?…
> *Tyrrell*: I don't know for sure.…
> *Zaidins*: You don't know if it is sold in the area?
> *Tyrrell*: No, sir.…
> *Zaidins*: Have you seen a *Rogue* Calendar before this time?
> *Tyrrell*: I have seen this type of calendar, but I cannot say that it is this one.
> *Zaidins*: You can buy them at the newsstand?
> *Tyrrell*: I do not know.…
> *Zaidins*: You say that [the word "fuck"] was disgusting to you?
> *Tyrrell*: That is correct, at the time.
> *Zaidins*: You have used the word yourself, haven't you?
> *Whiting*: Object, as irrelevant.…
> *Ryan*: Objection sustained. I think it is immaterial whether or not he has used it.
> *Zaidins*: Have you heard the word used other than by yourself or the defendant?
> *Tyrrell*: I have.

Foiled Again

EARLE ZAIDINS MANAGED to deliver a few body blows to the state's witnesses, but his cross-examination was problematic. Try as he might, Zaidins never demolished the officers' damning accounts of Lenny's purported masturbatory gestures. Officer Tyrrell's testimony on this point ("He...made a motion of masturbation....He pointed to his privates, and went back and forth as such") was never seriously dented by Zaidins's challenge to the offensiveness of the alleged conduct.

Moreover, Zaidins's style of questioning could at times be unfocused and convoluted; his unduly complicated sentences sometimes confused the prosecution's witnesses (and, no doubt, the jury). In one instance, Zaidins failed to convey the meaning of his question in a clear and simple manner, and thus may have forfeited a valuable opportunity to weaken the state's case:

> *Zaidins*: Was there anything in the story itself that was obscene?
> *Tyrrell*: What story is this?
> *Zaidins*: Any story. There was nothing that was obscene in any story, was there?
> *Tyrrell*: Was there anything obscene in any story?
> *Zaidins*: I will rephrase the question. There was nothing in any one of these stories, as a story text, that was obscene, was there? I want you to think a moment.
> *Banks*: Object, and ask that it be read again to the witness. I don't think the witness understands it.
> *Zaidins*: I will rephrase the question and say it slowly. There wasn't anything in any one of the stories that you heard Mr. Bruce perform or relate in relation to them, or the story line itself, that would be obscene, now, was there?
> *Tyrrell*: You mean the beginning?
> *Zaidins*: No, sir.
> *Tyrrell*: The story itself?
> *Zaidins*: I am talking about them. The story itself, not any particular section, but the story itself. The stories, none of the stories, none of the stories themselves, were what in any way might be considered obscene by you, was it?
> *Banks*: If the court please, as to what he thought of the stories as obscene, the State will object....
> *Zaidins*: Your Honor, at this time I would like to point out that the United States Supreme Court has defined obscenity. He is the officer who made the arrest under that state charge. Only he can tell the

court about this, whether he thought it was obscene or not, and
then he must relate it....

Ryan: He may tell what he heard and saw. Not a mental process or
anything else....Objection sustained.

Whether or not Lenny's co-counsel had effectively demonstrated
that the police officers recollected little about Bruce's bits, the prosecution needed to establish that those bits were obscene within the
total context of his performance. The lead prosecutor Sam Banks took
an unorthodox way to shore up the state's case. To the utter surprise
of the defense team, Banks announced that he would present, *as the
state's evidence*, the tape recording made of Lenny's entire December
5 performance at The Gate of Horn.

It was a nervy move. After striving since the beginning of the trial
to authenticate the tape recording in his possession, Zaidins could not
believe what he was hearing, that this *nebbish* was planning to introduce the tape for his *own* purposes. Jumping to his feet, Zaidins asked
that Judge Ryan hear the adversaries in chambers. Outside of the
jury's presence, the assistant state attorneys urged the court to permit
the state to offer the tape as evidence corroborating the police officers'
testimony. "This is the crux of our case, this particular tape recording," Banks pleaded. "[I]t tends to prove the entire performance...[in
that it] describes and tells the exact stories."

Zaidins strongly objected on several grounds. The tape was the
defendant's property, after all: Lenny had paid $200 to the *Playboy*
editor who had recorded his Chicago act for his autobiographical
project with Hugh Hefner's magazine. Moreover, the words on the
tape were Lenny's words, Lenny's testimony, to be offered (or not
offered) as Lenny decided. The Fifth Amendment self-incrimination
guarantee, Zaidins argued, provided no less protection than this.
Although Judge Ryan was ambivalent about the Fifth Amendment
rationale, he finally weighed in with the defense's claim of property
entitlements. Thanks to Zaidins's quick thinking, Lenny had retained
control over whether and when he would "perform" his act in court.

Once the state rested, Zaidins moved that Judge Ryan direct a verdict for the defense. Zaidins believed, of course, that he had exposed

the inadequacies of the prosecution's case sufficiently to deserve a ruling that, as a matter of law, the state could not convict Lenny under the requirements of the obscenity statute. Although Zaidins tried to lay out the logic supporting his motion, his style of oral presentation was not as clear and compelling as those tendered by the prosecution. Sometimes his points were scattered, his rationales disconnected, and his arguments rambling.

Put in its best light, Zaidins's oration scored at least some points. Most important was the argument that the Illinois obscenity statute tracked the First Amendment dictates of Justice Brennan's opinion in *Roth v. United States*, and the state had not met its burden of proving a *prima facie* case of obscenity thereunder merely by eliciting testimony of some dirty words and gestures. As Zaidins explained: "Now the mere words and gestures are not enough. They cannot be enough....[T]he statute gives a definition of obscenity. It shows the *prima facie* issues to be met. [The State] has not met the elements at all."

Lenny's co-counsel had played his strongest hand, but Judge Ryan appeared utterly unimpressed. "I think that the State has set forth a *prima facie* case," Ryan summarily concluded. "The motion for a directed verdict will be overruled." Hoping against hope at this point, Zaidins requested the court to dismiss the action as an unconstitutional application of the Illinois obscenity statute, in violation of Bruce's First Amendment speech rights. Once again, a terse ruling: "Your motion for discharge of the charge is also denied."

Finally, Zaidins made some headway. There was one request that Judge Ryan was willing to grant. Since it was now late on Friday afternoon, Lenny's co-counsel proposed that the trial be recessed so that the defense might collaborate before putting on its case. The court sent the jury home with instructions to reconvene at 10:30 A.M. on Monday, February 25.

It had been an irksome day for Earle Zaidins. His plans for devastating cross-examinations and a preemptive strike had been foiled. Now, the defense was forced to the next stage of litigation. Lenny would have to outshine his co-counsel.

Double Jurisdictional Jeopardy

LENNY WAS DESPERATE to score some stuff, and was having awful luck in Chicago. He needed to get back to his L.A. drug pals. He called long distance from a pay phone at O'Hare Airport, spoke to Honey, and then boarded a TWA flight that Zaidins had arranged for him under an assumed name. Upon arrival at LAX in the early morning of Saturday, February 23, he caught a cab.

What happened next was typical Lenny luck. He had not been in the cab long when the police pulled the car over, purportedly for a defective headlamp. Lenny was ordered out of the back seat. The officers' big black flashlights, panning the rear area of the car, revealed one gram of heroin, three broken syringes on the floor, and a briefcase on the seat containing forty or so methydrine capsules. A syringe and needle were also found in Lenny's pocket. He was under arrest.

By noon of that day, Bruce was released on $2,625 bail. Celes Bail Bond Co. informed him that he could not leave L.A. before the March 7 preliminary hearing. Amazingly, he was facing yet another felony drug rap, this one preventing him from his lawyerly obligations in Chicago.

Monday, February 25, 1963, in Chicago: Standing solo before Judge Ryan, Earle Zaidins alluded to the events of the preceding Saturday. He informed the judge that the defense would be ready to proceed on Thursday. The court's patience was running thin: "Let the record indicate that it is now twenty minutes after one of the 25th day of February, and that the defendant has absented himself from the jurisdiction."

A two-day recess was granted—but not an hour more. The trial would reconvene at 10:30 A.M. on Wednesday, February 27. After panicked phone calls to Lenny, Zaidins realized that the worst had come, and that he would be duking it out alone at trial.

IT WAS THE Wednesday after Quinquagesima Sunday, the first day of the Lenten fast. The Latin name given to that Wednesday, February 27, was *dies cinerum*—commonly known as Ash Wednesday. When

Zaidins, the son of Jewish immigrants, returned to Judge Ryan's court-room that morning, it seemed to him that he had crashed a Catholic religious rite. The judge, the two prosecutors, and *all* twelve jurors appeared bearing a cross of ash on their foreheads. Not a good omen for the Jewish defense team. To his credit, Judge Ryan sensed the problem. He first removed his own spot of ash and then ordered the bailiff to instruct the others to do likewise. It was a scene tailor-made for one of Lenny's bits.

Things were now moving fast-forward. That Wednesday, Zaidins made one motion after another in desperate attempts to decelerate the trial's momentum:

—He moved for a one-day continuance until Lenny could return from Los Angeles. *Denied.*

—He moved for reconsideration of the motion for a directed verdict, based on the legal memorandum submitted two days before (presenting more polished versions of the oral points made in support of his original directed verdict motion). *Denied.*

—He moved that any consideration of the forfeiture of Lenny's bail bond and the issuance of an arrest warrant (technically, a *capias*) be put over until the next day. *Denied.*

—He moved for a change of venue "based upon the prejudice of this Court." *Denied.*

—He moved for the opportunity to call Officer Tyrrell as a hostile witness. *Denied.*

The court had had enough. It would wait no longer; it would not tolerate what it deemed to be stalling tactics. In a remarkable statement for the record, Judge Ryan explained his decision to force the defense to trial—in the absence of the *pro se* defendant:

I want the record to reflect at this time that this court has continued the trial of the defendant, Lenny Bruce, early in the afternoon of February 21 because of the request by the defendant, Lenny Bruce…and the co-counsel referred here today so that they would have a little more time to prepare their defense. Consideration was given the request and the court sent the jury home.

The court is well aware according to newspaper articles that the defendant has been arrested in another jurisdiction, but the court is also aware that no permission was asked of this court to leave this jurisdiction as is required by the bond that Mr. Bruce put up to guarantee his appearance here.

We waited patiently all day Monday for the defendant. At that time a request was made to continue this case. It was continued from the 25th day of February until the 27th day of February.

Mr. Bruce, the defendant, is not in this court at this time, which is now ten minutes before the hour of 12:00 [noon].

The state is ready. The defense counsel has asked for a continuance. The request will be denied. I will give you until 1:30 to prepare your defense.

Now, Zaidins had a hundred minutes to organize his case…and without any help from the lead counsel, Lenny.

That afternoon, Zaidins put on the entirety of the defense's case: he played The Gate of Horn audiotape for the jury. Then the court adjourned. Before he left his chambers that evening, Judge Ryan forfeited Lenny's bail, issued the writ for his arrest, and asked the state's attorney to commence extradition proceedings.

Friday, February 28, was the last day of the Chicago trial.

Zaidins began the proceeding with another futile set of motions. He asked to call Captain McDermott as a defense witness, hoping to compel testimony about the threats that the captain allegedly had leveled against Ribback and his club. McDermott had not been subpoenaed and was not in court, however, and Judge Ryan deemed such post-arrest statements irrelevant to the case. *Denied.*

The defense then requested the removal of a juror and a declaration of mistrial: although the judge had interrogated the jurors about avoiding any news reports relating to the case at hand, he had not similarly instructed them to ignore the news about Lenny's recent narcotics arrest or inquired about their exposure to such reports. Again, Judge Ryan found the matter irrelevant to the case on which the jury needed to pass. *Denied.*

Zaidins had no other cards to play. Explaining that Lenny had given him no further instructions on how to proceed, Zaidins rested the defense's case. "I was left with nothing," he recalled, "I felt like a guy going to a duel without a gun."

"We the Jury Find…"

THE TIME HAD come for the closing arguments. Launching into a summation of the state's case, Sam Banks delivered what might have seemed, to the untrained ear at least, a mundane and plodding retelling of the facts.

He trooped out, one by one, details about the night of the arrest, relating a good deal of uncontroversial data (ticket prices at The Gate of Horn, the all-male trio playing the opening act on the evening of December 4, and so on). Banks did not fail, however, to give his account exactly the right spin to recall Lenny's perverse irreverence against both Catholicism and sex within holy matrimony—and this he presented to jurors who only two days earlier had come to court with ash-marked foreheads:

> *Banks*: During the course of his performance, the defendant went into a series of stories, a series of jokes and anecdotes in which he made reference to various people, to various things. He made reference to the pope; he made reference to the bishops, the nuns, and priests. He made various references to different acts which all people, I assume, I know, consider sacred—a sacred part of marriage.
> *Zaidins*: Your Honor, I am afraid I have to make an objection. The defendant is charged with obscenity, not with blasphemy.
> *Ryan*: The jury has heard the evidence.

Equally effective was the delicacy with which the assistant state's attorney handled the vulgarity in Lenny's act. Banks touched the topic of "dirty" words and gestures…oh, so gingerly, like a butterfly landing on a leaf. With unmistakable clarity, he conveyed the utter disgust that he himself held toward such terms, or toward anyone who would throw them around in a public performance. By his ever-cautious treatment of vulgarity, Banks set the standard for civil discourse that he intended the jury to uphold:

> *Banks*: [The defendant] used certain terms which the State has set forth and which you have heard from the witness stand and which are obscene, and through references made by the defendant—I don't think I have to reiterate them—you heard them three times, now four times….The defendant made these statements knowing full well what they were. It was his act, his performance. You have to assume that whatever he said, he knew what he was saying….Mr. Bruce, at another time, made certain statements in which he gave a story about Germany, I believe soldiers in Germany. During this story…he used a particular term in a particular way. I don't think I have to tell you the term, I think that you recall it. Basically it was…a word that started with an *F* and ended with a *K* and sounded like "truck." Basically you heard the word, you know it, and heard the way that it was used.
> *Zaidins*: I am afraid that I will have to object to that.
> *Ryan*: The jury has heard the evidence. You may proceed.

Although the prosecution had not been permitted to play the Gate of Horn audiotape as part of the State's case, nothing prevented Banks from co-opting its value. After all, the recording provided the prosecutors with the evidence that they could not extract from their own witnesses—the performance-context peppered with Lenny's dirty words that Banks then used to buffer the State's argument:

> This tape recording set out the entire performance by Mr. Bruce. This tape recording only corroborated everything the State said, everything, every word that the State proved from its witnesses.

You sat and heard it. Again [the obscene terms were] reiterated by the defense, through that tape recording. In fact, there were even numerous other statements made on the tape recording which would have been almost impossible for the police officers to remember.

Prosecutor Banks saved his moment of flourish for the very end of his summation. He was talking to the triers of fact, of course, but he did not fail to remind them of the critical function they served as the standard bearers for public morality. "I don't think we have to tolerate this type of performance," he insisted. "I don't think that you people of the jury have to tolerate it, and I don't think that you will tolerate it." Just before sitting down, Banks off-handedly pitched a final comment, meant to clinch the matter: "Just one more thing. The State's evidence stands uncontradicted. Thank you very much, ladies and gentlemen."

It may have been brief. It may have been dry. And perhaps it was even a bit boring. But, Banks's summation was straightforward and coherent. At its best, it was shrewd. The same could not readily be said of Zaidins's closing argument. At times he displayed a style similar to that of his oral presentations during the trial—wordy and obscure. Could the jury understand exactly what points this New York lawyer meant to convey? It was anyone's guess.

A few glimmers of light did emerge from the darkness, however. Zaidins acknowledged that the jury members could not be expected to appreciate Bruce's choices of subject or terminology: "[Y]ou may or may not personally admire his words. You may or may not personally admire what he has to say. You may not even care or you may not even want to hear."

However understandable, such attitudes ought not to govern the jury's judgment of Bruce's performance, Zaidins explained. He reminded them of their civic duty of toleration, invoking the famous maxim attributed to Voltaire: "[W]e have often heard the words, 'I may not agree with what you say, but I will defend to the end your right to say it.' That, perhaps, is what I am trying to do right now, fighting for his right to say it." Zaidins challenged his audience: "We live by these beautiful words. Do we live by them? Do we?"

Aiming at the weaknesses in the prosecution's case, Lenny's co-counsel characterized the prejudicial motivations of the state's witnesses in a rather generalized and unfocused manner:

> You have heard testimony of the two witnesses that there was no one on the premises who complained. Nobody at all. Just two officers, and they couldn't even tell the stories. All they heard were the dirty words. I remember other things from the stories. Long before I met the defendant, Lenny Bruce, I can remember other things, other than the dirty words of the stories. If you wish to remember dirty words, you can remember them.

Finally, Zaidins strove to point up the dire consequences likely to follow a jury verdict of guilty—consequences to the American free speech system, to the American concept of citizenship, to the American way of life: "[F]ind Lenny Bruce guilty, and no one dare use these words again. Where do we go from there? Where is the next step?...[I]f you want to do your duty as a citizen, you will vote to acquit him."

Judge Ryan then instructed the jury; his instructions were nowhere near as sophisticated as those of Judge Horn to the San Francisco jurors. The twelve decision-makers then retired. It took approximately two hours of deliberation: "We, the jury, find the defendant, Lenny Bruce, guilty in the manner and form as charged in the information."

Zaidins now began his post-verdict motions to the court. He requested a judgment of not guilty "notwithstanding the verdict" and for arrest of judgment. *Denied.* A decision on a motion for a new trial was reserved to the day of sentencing.

One last thing: the juror who apparently led the charge against Lenny was none other than the Irishwoman who had been the prize choice of his voir dire.

Love Letters

LENNY THRILLED IN writing "love letters" to the judges who presided over his fate. He had done so with Judge Horn in San Francisco to express his disapproval of Judge Axelrod. That cost him a contempt of court citation. Now, a year later, he wrote two more such letters—these sent by wire—to the already irate Judge Daniel Ryan.

The first of Lenny's telegrams complimented the judge on his impartial handling of the case, but it was a compliment *up to a point*: "To praise you more, I cannot, lest I am scurrious sychopant [sic]." He then begged that the trial be suspended until his return: "I am not contemptuous of the Court....I am not guilty of the charge technically, spiritually, morally, legally....Please have mercy. I do not like, in fact I am quite unhappy when my view is barred." For official measure, the misspelled missive ended, "Respectfully, Counsellor Lenny Bruce."

The other telegram came thereafter, two days before his sentencing. The direction of this letter turned 180 degrees, as Bruce complained about the judge's permitting him to be tried and convicted *in abstentia*. Never one to kowtow to authority, Lenny used his choicest words to make his point: "illegal, unconstitutional, and most fascistic...behavior." What else could he say, short of calling the judge some coarse name?

George C. Pontikes, the lawyer called in to substitute for Zaidins, unsuspectingly found himself in the crossfire on March 14, the day of Lenny's sentencing. As the hearing began, a livid Judge Ryan read both telegrams into the record. At this inopportune moment, Pontikes moved for a new trial. Lenny's fifth Chicago trial lawyer explained that Bruce recently had arranged for an impressive team of three *new* lawyers to defend him: Harry Kalven Jr., Maurice Rosenfield, and William R. Ming Jr. Judge Ryan was indifferent: "We have always granted every due consideration to Lenny Bruce. We have put [the motion for a new trial] over for this day, and there is no Mr. Bruce. He is two thousand miles away, if the telegrams did come from him. At the time he absented himself, his counsel had to return to represent him. The motion is denied."

Lenny's court strategy and letters worked like a charm—maximum sentence: one year in jail, a $1,000 fine. Samuel Banks, the prosecutor, declared: "We will start extradition proceedings. They will be started today." The state dealt Alan Ribback a kinder hand, however, when it dismissed the case against him on March 21, 1963. Still, The Gate of Horn never recovered from the prosecution of Lenny Bruce; its days of glory were over.

What promised to be a sure winner of a case proved to be a sure loser. It seemed that everything that could go wrong did go wrong—thanks in no small measure to Lenny himself. Under both law and facts, the Illinois variation of *People v. Bruce* was an easier misdemeanor case to win than its counterparts in California. Despite this, the Gate of Horn prosecution ended in Lenny's first obscenity conviction. Could that conviction, with its glaring free speech injustices, be reversed on appeal?

Lenny's sole comment to the press about Judge Ryan's sentence: "I think it's quite obscene."

The Great Trio

PEOPLE V. BRUCE had enormous potential to create a new body of First Amendment law. The case appeared to provide the conceptual framework to allow Justice Brennan and his colleagues to rethink *Roth v. U.S.* Now, Professor Harry Kalven Jr., the University of Chicago Law School scholar, could put to the test the ideas he had floated in his seminal 1960 article, "The Metaphysics of the Law of Obscenity," published in the *Supreme Court Review*.

In that article, the highly regarded Kalven was critical, albeit respectful, of Justice William Brennan and the Warren Court for what they had done in *Roth*. He challenged the *Roth* premise that the First Amendment could be divided so neatly into two categories, one of protected speech (e.g., political expression) and another of unprotected speech (e.g., obscenity). He also questioned the soundness of the notion that traditional free speech formulas (such as the "marketplace of ideas") should govern new forms of artistic, literary, and erotic expression. Finally, and perhaps most importantly, he pointed to the two sides of *Roth*—one, rights affirming; the other, rights denying—and suggested how the Court might reinterpret *Roth* to remedy this division and thereby reinvigorate the First Amendment.

Ever since 1957 when *Roth* had been decided, lower courts had to deal with its rather schizophrenic qualities—for example, how could it equate obscenity with "materials having a tendency to excite lustful thoughts" and *also* describe obscenity as materials that reflect a "shameful or morbid interest in nudity, sex, or excretion"? Put simply, *Roth* declared that obscenity could be, at one and the same time, that which excites and that which does not; it could be erotic and non-erotic; it could be appealing and offensive. It was, to borrow from Professor Kalven, all rather "metaphysical." And whatever else the law should be—especially the law of free speech—it should not be something akin to a philosophical exercise. Lenny Bruce's freedom, and that of others like him, should not have to be decided by reference to standards like those found in *Groundwork of the Metaphysics of Morals*, Immanuel Kant's famous 1785 philosophical tract.

People v. Bruce, then, could be the test case to reexamine *Roth*. After all, there was so very much in Lenny's bits that lent itself to full First Amendment protection. For openers, Lenny's satirical comedy had a strong and inseparable *political* character. By ignoring this, lower courts actually had devalued the most cherished form of First Amendment expression. Furthermore, and as the Chicago case brought into bold relief, Lenny was being prosecuted (albeit indirectly) for blasphemy. But the Supreme Court already had made it clear that there was little or no room for blasphemy prosecutions in a world committed to the First Amendment of James Madison. Moreover, the obscenity prosecutions in San Francisco, Los Angeles, and now Chicago were made possible because Lenny's offensive words—all the "cocksuckers," "*schmucks*," and "fucks"—were specifically lifted from his routines. In other words, his message was not being considered *as a whole*.

To help Kalven move from the theoretical to the practical, the noted First Amendment scholar collaborated with Maurice Rosenfield and William R. Ming Jr.—two friends, highly reputable lawyers, and colleagues from their University of Chicago Law School days.

Maurice Rosenfield (who once had coauthored an influential law review article with Kalven) was a partner in the prestigious Chicago law firm of Devoe, Shadur, Mikva, and Plotkin. He counted Hugh Hefner among his prominent clients. (Rosenfield had represented Hugh Hefner in the mid-1950s and the early 1960s. Among the cases he handled were ones in which prosecutors or postal inspectors sought to ban the distribution of *Playboy* magazine.) Six years earlier, Rosenfield had authored an *amicus* brief in *Roth v. United States* favoring an expansive interpretation of the First Amendment.

William R. Ming Jr., the first black professor at the University of Chicago Law School, had been one of Thurgood Marshall's gifted NAACP advisors. A powerful mind and an eloquent advocate, Ming worked with Marshall on the landmark brief presented to the Supreme Court in *Brown v. Board of Education*. By this time, he was a partner in the law firm of McCoy, Ming, and Black.

This distinguished appellate trio was personally and professionally committed to bringing *People v. Bruce* to a victorious end.

But first, they needed to secure an appeal bond so that Lenny wouldn't linger in jail while the case meandered through the legal system. When the three lawyers paid a visit to Judge Ryan's chambers, he received them graciously—that is, until they asked him to grant their client a bond. "For you guys, I'll do anything," the judge conceded. "But, for that cocksucker Bruce, I'll do nothing." Their jaws dropped, so great was the irony.

Lenny's new lawyers had better luck on April 2 with Walter V. Schaefer, a respected liberal justice on the Illinois Supreme Court. The justice imposed only one condition before granting a bond: Bruce must be present in his chambers by the next afternoon.

Of course, as with any matter involving Lenny Bruce, there was a hitch—actually, several. The Illinois extradition order already had been issued, sent, and served; John Marshall (one of Bruce's L.A. drug lawyers) surrendered him to Los Angeles Municipal Court Judge Maurice T. Leader on March 26; the extradition hearing was set for April 25; Lenny was now out on $2,500 bail, and loathe to forfeit it by skipping town ("Bruce told Judge Leader he didn't surrender to Chicago authorities because he would have to wait in Cook County

Jail until Judge Ryan returned [from his vacation in Florida]. 'I'd rather get the gas chamber in Los Angeles than spend a day in jail in Chicago,' Bruce said."). Beyond all this, complying with Justice Schaefer's condition also meant risking arrest in Chicago on the fugitive warrant. So, Lenny and his lawyers developed a plan: Rosenfield was to pick Bruce up at O'Hare that evening, bring him to the justice's chambers the next day, and deliver him back to the airport immediately—all done very secretly.

Predictably, Lenny didn't show at the scheduled time. Nobody knew where he was. Maurice Rosenfield certainly didn't and returned home quite frustrated. With just a few hours of darkness left on the morning of April 3, Lenny telephoned Rosenfield from Milwaukee. He assured his not-so-confident attorney that he would get to Hefner's mansion in due time for the meeting with Justice Schaefer. When Rosenfield met Bruce there later that morning, the lawyer found his client in a disheveled state and demanded that Lenny clean up and put on a respectable coat. After some searching, one of Hefner's guests lent him a sports coat.

That proved to be the easy part. The next challenge—and it was no small one—was to travel through the city in broad daylight. It didn't take long before patrol lights flashed bright blue, and the fugitive Lenny turned bleached white. An officer approached the vehicle, leaned over, and asked Rosenfield for his driver's license—the lawyer had made an illegal left turn. A ticket was issued, Lenny went unnoticed, and the two were back en route to the Justice's chambers.

When they arrived, Kalven and Ming were already there. Lenny was on his best behavior as his lawyers discussed the fine points. In no time it was over. Feeling like a free man, Lenny waltzed down the streets unafraid.

The Chicago Three had scored their first victory over Judge Ryan. Next, they had to move from the man to the merits. They had to formulate some compelling arguments to defend Lenny Bruce's free speech rights and reverse his conviction. There was one immediate obstacle, however: the trial record.

Appellate courts are fastidious bodies when it comes to legal procedure. They are loathe (and that is putting it mildly) to consider issues on appeal that were either not raised at all or not raised properly at the trial level. By that standard, there were major problems with *People v. Bruce*.

The way Judge Ryan had conducted the trial, the way Earle Zaidins had proceeded with the case, and the way Lenny Bruce had *not* argued the matter, it was hard to imagine just what sort of record could be made for an appeal. In the maddening frenzy of it all—with Ryan readily denying motions and Lenny often unreachable in L.A.—the substantive claims of the defense's arguments could not easily be identified and developed. For one thing, no one formally had raised any First Amendment claims. How would Kalven's long-awaited and ideal free speech case become a landmark precedent if the defense actually had never raised the key constitutional claim in the lower court?

Appealing Arguments

LENNY BRUCE WAS not "a mad man writing dirty words on the walls of a public toilet." He was "an original social critic with an unconventional vocabulary."

That was the central theme of the brief filed in Lenny's appeal to the Illinois Supreme Court in its November 1963 term. Maurice Rosenfield and Harry Kalven had worked assiduously in Rosenfield's law office on LaSalle Street to draft the brief, and had passed it to William Ming for his critique. When completed, the brief offered five main arguments:

First, the *social commentary argument*: Lenny's routines were steeped in "bitter social criticism" of unquestionable value. For example, "God, your filthy Jesus Christ, made these tits" (from "Paul Malloy and Christianity") inquired into "the intrinsic goodness or evil of sex and the ambivalence of everyone, including organized religion, toward it." Similarly, the "We fucked all their mothers for chocolate bars" comment (from "War Criminals and Hershey Bars") was a powerful story of "the American conquest of Europe's women by American soldiers armed with the American standard of living." These bits, like other Bruce routines, were not merely dirty words strung together; they were social critique with redeeming value.

Second, the *no erotic effect argument*: fundamentally, Lenny's style involved "the non-erotic use of erotic words." Nothing about "fucking the sisters" (from "How to Relax Your Colored Friends at Parties") was sexually arousing to the audience, either in intent or effect. The same held true with the "hang Truman by the balls" line (from "Adolf Eichmann") or any of the other sex-talk in Lenny's routines. "The listener may be shocked," the Rosenfield-Kalven-Ming brief stated, "he may be offended, he may be amused, he may be bored, but he will never be aroused sexually."

Third, the *no obscenity argument*: as a matter of constitutional law, the non-erotic use of erotic words cannot be obscene. Although citing Supreme Court First Amendment cases for support, the text of the appellant's brief did not once explicitly mention the First Amendment, since it had not been formally invoked at the trial. Lenny's free speech claims turned entirely on analysis of Fourteenth Amendment due process and state law rights. "[N]o case has ever held that the use of the so-called 'dirty' words is *per se* obscene," Lenny's counsel contended. To support this claim, they referred the Illinois Supreme Court to one of its own 1954 opinions authored by Justice Walter Schaefer. This principle was eminently defensible: violation of "language taboos" alone is not criminal. "If it were, the result would be absurd. Can a crime lie in the choice of one synonym rather than another for a sexual organ or a sexual act?" the brief asked.

The brief's fourth and fifth arguments were more procedural. Because the state had failed to prove that the Illinois statute was violated, Judge Daniel Ryan should have found the defendant not guilty at the end of the prosecution's case. And, by completing the trial in Lenny's absence and without representation by counsel, the judge had deprived him of due process.

Rosenfield, Kalven, and Ming came to a powerful conclusion, framed as a challenge: "[T]he police officers listened only for the dirty words Bruce used. The obligation of this court however is to listen for the meaning."

The People's brief was originally assigned to William J. Martin, who was one of the six lawyers working in the Brief Department of the Cook County State Attorney's Office. "I refused to write the obscenity part," Martin said years later. "I could not in good conscience do it. I didn't think it was right." James R. Thompson, who would go on to become governor of Illinois, "was the one who wrote most of the brief." Having argued many such cases, Thompson was known as "the obscenity specialist." With literary flair and formidable legal analysis, the prosecution's brief responded with one counter-argument after another. Though it was not the central point, the state's brief reiterated Lenny's off-color words and did so boldly, replete with a dirty-word count:

shit—used 16 times
fuck, ball, frig, schtup, or lay—used 12 times
schmuck, dick, putz, or pudding—used 16 times

The point, argued Thompson, was that Lenny's "frequent use of obscenity is relevant in determining whether the *real purpose* of such use is the 'necess[ity] to…portray…particular scenes or characters'…or whether it 'represents a calculated exploitation of dirt for dirt's sake.'" If what Lenny did at The Gate of Horn was nothing more than "dirt for dirt's sake," it was unprotected expression.

The state also argued that Lenny's "non-erotic use of erotic words" was, indeed, obscene. Conceding that Bruce's performance did not arouse sexually, the state argued that, nonetheless, the 1961 Illinois Criminal Code had broadened the obscenity definition to include works appealing to "a morbid or shameful interest in sex, nudity, or excretion."

Thus, Thompson urged an interpretation of *Roth* by which obscenity could be censored constitutionally for two reasons—one erotic and the other non-erotic. This rationale offered the Illinois high court a foundation for sustaining Judge Ryan's judgment and sentence. (Rosenfield, Kalven, and Ming also filed a reply brief. In it, they argued that, however offensive Lenny's bits, they were not imposed on an unwilling "captive audience." Moreover, they contended that historical evidence established that *Roth* did *not* have two prongs—one obscenity, the other vulgarity. It had only one—sexually arousing obscenity.)

Two more points were essential to the state's arguments. First, Lenny's act could not (as required by *Roth*) be "considered as a whole," if only because his performance lacked thematic continuity. So many parts were disjointed and unconnected to anything approximating a "dominant theme." Hence, the disjointed portions of the performance—the bits with all those "schmucks" and "tits" and "jerk offs"—were not part of the "work as a whole," and could therefore be judged independently for what they were, namely, constitutionally unprotected obscenities.

Second, the state argued that it was not punishing Lenny for *what* he said (that would be unconstitutional), but rather for *how* he said it. It was the *way* that Lenny expressed himself that was objectionable. While ideas could not be regulated, certainly the manner in which they were presented could be. That, at least, was the state's claim.

As was his custom, legal Lenny pored over the briefs. He then sent a Western Union telegram from his home in Los Angles to his lawyers in Chicago: "With a brief like that, I wouldn't mind loosing [sic] the case....Love Lenny." His lawyers wired back, framing the matter quite differently: "With a client like you, we do mind losing the case."

But Lenny wasn't losing all of his cases—even when he wasn't winning them. Earlier that summer, about four months after the Beverly Hills jury deadlocked in the Troubadour/Unicorn obscenity case, the D.A.'s office relented and the charges were formally dismissed. "I thought it was not really a good case," remarked prosecutor Ronald Ross. "No useful purpose would be served by retrying it. I specifically told my superiors, 'You can try this case until the cows come home, and half the people are going to think it's obscene and half will not.' They agreed, and so we decided to drop the matter." This was a vindication...of sorts: the L.A. authorities were unable to establish that Lenny had crossed the legal line at Doug Weston's Troubadour or Herb Cohen's Unicorn. But the LAPD would not be deterred from investigating Lenny's performances elsewhere. The L.A. story of *People v. Bruce* had by no means ended.

"There Were Adult Women Present"

CHICAGO WAS OUT, for now anyway. Unless Lenny's Gate of Horn conviction were reversed, he could not perform in the Windy City without jeopardy. That meant that he had lost a highly profitable venue, and this at a time when he sorely needed cash.

Where would he go next? He had to make a geographical decision. Back west to San Francisco or east to New York or somewhere in between, say, St. Louis or Milwaukee?

He dreaded working towns like Milwaukee with all those Grey Line Tour types. Too square, too uptight, too goyish. Rather like lime Jell-O and trailer parks—mega goyish! But New York, that was a different story. Yiddish friendly, open-minded, and hip, Jewish big-time. Like latkes. It was a frame of mind, not a religion. He tagged it Count Basie–Ray Charles–Dylan Thomas "Jewish." Manhattan cooked. A real Lenny Bruce Paradise.

There were other paradises, too, like Los Angeles—actually Hollywood. Were palm trees and freeways goyish or Jewish? Who knows? Who cared? This city in the sun was a far cry from Milwaukee. Besides, it had Nate 'n Al's Deli. So, in early 1964, nearly a year after his Chicago conviction, Lenny found himself in L.A., either high in his House on the Hill or down in the city doing the boulevard hangs. But working L.A. was no snap. After all, there had been police hassles at the Club Renaissance in 1959, obscenity arrests at The Troubadour, Unicorn, and Le Grande in 1962–1963, and several L.A. drug busts throughout this period. With the heat Bruce had generated, it certainly seemed he was a *persona non grata* in Southern California. The belated decision of the Beverly Hills prosecutors to dismiss *People v. Bruce* was not enough to calm the fears of a good number of club owners. Absent some more definitive ruling from a local trial court or a state appellate court, few L.A. nightspots were willing to open their doors to him.

One club was different. The Trolley Ho, located at the intersection of La Cienega and San Vincente Boulevards south of 3rd Street, was more than willing to host Lenny Bruce and his wild bits. For Jim and Don Duffin, managers of The Trolley Ho, "Bruce had done them a great favor by being the feature of attraction at their place." Predictably, the favor drew wide public and police attention. The vice-squad crowd—Officers Robert F. McGuire, William Taragan, Paul C. Burks, and Corleen Schnell—got to be regulars there during Lenny's run. And so did many of their silver-badged friends.

The Trolley Ho became the free speech testing site of this latest encounter with L.A. officialdom. The club, which seated some 250 people, featured Lenny since New Year's Eve of 1963, when he packed the place. Around the same time that the "sick" comedian was doing his routine at the Trolley Ho, Lawrence Welk was doing his "champagne music" at the Palladium on Sunset Boulevard—only in America could two so radically different performers appeal to the radically diverse tastes of the same community.

The Trolley Ho deal was a lucrative one for both the financially strapped house and performer. Thus, it continued for a few months—but at a risky price. A police report dated March 16, 1964, revealed the extent to which Lenny's acts were still very much the focus of police attention:

> Sgt. Burks and Officer McGuire attended the Lenny Bruce show at [The Trolley Ho]. During this show [February 22, 1964] Bruce used the following words: "cocksucker," "fuck," "shit," "motherfucker," and frequently made references to homosexuals and their activities. Since this time six (6) teams of officers from this division have viewed the Bruce show and have submitted 15.7s [LAPD report forms] on their observations. Some other obscene words used by Lenny Bruce are as follows: "bullshit," "ass," "asshole," "tits," "penis," "piss," "cocks," "cunts," and [he] also referred to comic strip characters as "Dikes" [sic] and "Fags."

As the report evidenced, seven years after *Roth v. U.S.* was announced, none of L.A.'s finest bothered to consider Lenny's performances *taken as a whole*. They just searched out all the four- or ten- or twelve-letter words, as if they were searching a room for bags of heroin or bottles of amphetamines, as if the words alone were contraband.

And *six teams* of police! No place—not even the local Winchell's donut house—could command that kind of police draw. Night after night, from February 22 through March 13, 1964, they were there on assignment, duly gathering every "cocksucker" or "tits" reference that issued from Lenny's lips. Pens and notepads were typically used, though on three occasions, attempts were made to tape the show. Only one attempt proved at all successful; it produced an hour-long performance audiotape, but one of insufficient quality for evidentiary purposes.

Throughout it all, Lenny remained Lenny: "I see we have some civil servants with us tonight," he proclaimed at the outset of a show. Having introduced the vice officers to the audience, he proceeded to joke about "his past experiences with law enforcement and the courts." According to official reports, Bruce even made "fun of all religions" and of "many people [then] currently in the news." Another report (filed earlier by Lieutenant A.B. Comer of the Vice Division) stressed that the "substance of Bruce's dissertation was primarily based on denouncing religion, God, and the police in general."

One other fact was also regularly reported. All of Bruce's offending words and ideas were spoken before a mixed audience: "During all of the shows there were adult women present...." Here was dirty Lenny denouncing God, defending dykes, and just talking shit in front of *women*! He was asking for—even demanding—trouble.

Lenny took it in stride: "[A]fter tonight, I will probably have a new case," he told one of his Trolley Ho audiences. Indeed, he was not too wide of the mark. For in the reports filed, the city attorney was asked to grant the police an application for a criminal complaint, assuming there were sufficient legal grounds for such action. Permission was granted. On March 17, Officer McGuire filed a complaint charging Lenny Bruce with having performed an obscene show at the Trolley Ho four days earlier. Yet another purported Section 311.6 violation—that number, like *666*, had become the Mark of the Devil in Lenny's life.

For Judge Mario L. Clinco, however, if anything were marked by Satan, it was Lenny Bruce's smutty mouth. An appointee of Governor Edmund G. ("Pat") Brown, and the eventual recipient of the "Judge of the Year" award for his "intense dedication" to L.A. justice, the thirty-six-year-old Clinco was still a junior judge at the Los Angeles

Municipal Court when he heard the full litany of Bruce's "obscene" words. Furthering his intense dedication to the law of Section 311.6, Clinco signed a warrant for Bruce's arrest. The warrant was executed on Thursday evening, March 19. With chilly efficiency, the LAPD ensured that Lenny was arrested, booked, bailed ($500), and released from custody by nine P.M.—all in time for his ten P.M. show at the Trolley Ho.

Meanwhile, Lieutenant Comer was busy moving on other legal fronts. Specifically, he was going after The Trolley Ho's entertainment and dance licenses. In his professional opinion, Lenny's performances at The Trolley Ho were "obscene and offensive" and were therefore "a violation of Board rule No. 6 governing Café Entertainment." With that, the state's *administrative* law was tapped along with its penal law to punish Lenny Bruce and his sponsors.

BEFORE IT WAS The Trolley Ho, it was The Turnabout Theater. Rented by acting troupes doing far-off Broadway plays, the theater offered two stages, one on either side of the building, with old trolley seats for the ticket holders. Typically, Act One was delivered from one stage, and Act Two from the opposite stage; during intermission, the backs of the trolley seats were switched over to face the second stage. The Turnabout's audience thus enjoyed a biblical experience: the last would be first, and the first would be last.

By the time Lenny Bruce played the hundred-seater Trolley Ho club, it had lost much of its antique charm, both inside and out. Now it was a joint with black wrought-iron bars looming ten feet high in front, giving the club the look of a fortress. The imposing fence separated The Trolley Ho from the rest of the world, including La Cienega—the boulevard known as "restaurant row," what with House of Murphy, Stears for Steaks, and Lowry's nearby. Ron Rothman couldn't help but notice the wrought-iron fence as he passed through it to the club's entrance. Still an inveterate Bruce fan years after seeing him at The Troubadour, the law student/bailiff Rothman was excited to catch the comedian's latest act at The Trolley Ho. As the show began, the forbidding gates closed.

Two Lenny Bruce fans of another stripe were also raring to go to his ten P.M. performance on March 19, but they arrived late. Like crazed party crashers, they hurled themselves up and over the iron gate. When Don Duffin spied them, he confronted the suspicious trespassers and inquired as to their purposes. The story they told boggled Duffin's mind: the two were Bruce's arresting officers who, just hours after busting him, had returned to The Trolley Ho to gather *more* incriminating evidence. After all, there was a "dirty word" crime being committed even as they spoke, and they intended to seize evidence of it on tape.

Lenny needed yet another criminal lawyer. He already had hired, sometimes fired, and often not paid a dozen or so attorneys for his obscenity trials alone. Whom should he call *this* time? A celebrity lawyer? A noted defense lawyer? A revered professor? A street-fighting *starker*? Or what about one of those ACLU guys? He settled, for whatever reason, on the familiar—Sydney Milton Irmas.

Sydney—the tall, well-built, handsome, and impeccably dressed criminal lawyer (who became one of Los Angeles's millionaire business executives, philanthropists, and art collectors)—was Lenny's most recent hire. Not infrequently, Lenny's circle of friends (and it was a wide circle) overlapped with his circle of foes (and it was a widening circle). For example, Syd Irmas counted himself among Sheriff Sherman Block's friends (despite the fact that Block had arrested Lenny Bruce for obscenity at The Troubadour). Apparently, Bruce had discovered Irmas when he read a newspaper report of the lawyer's stunning success in a California Supreme Court decision that released a drug addict from the state's rehabilitation center. Bruce first retained Irmas to fight the appeal of his own "Department 95" rehabilitation commitment order associated with his North Hollywood hobby shop drug bust. Now, turning temporarily from Fifth Amendment due process concerns in the Department 95 case, Syd was to cut his First Amendment teeth on Lenny's Trolley Ho case.

Irmas intended to win a free speech victory by pretrial arguments alone, but he needed time to prepare a motion to dismiss and hard-hitting points and authorities. So, at the arraignment on March 20, Syd asked Judge Robert Feinerman of the Los Angeles Municipal

Court to extend Lenny's time for pleading. The matter was continued for several weeks.

By March 1964, then, there was no lingering doubt that Los Angeles had become a hostile and dangerous venue for Lenny Bruce. If the prosecutors could not convict him the first time, they could try again. If the police needed more evidence, they could send in more teams to witness and record more Bruce acts. And if that could not rid the city of this sick comic, the police could go after entertainment licenses, and maybe even shut down the clubs that provided a forum for Lenny. And that did not include the ever-present threat posed by the narcotics squad.

It was time to leave L.A. to accept the offer of a few gigs in a safer city. Time to head for Manhattan, where Lenny's next set of engagements took him.

6

WHAT DOES IT MEAN TO BE FOUND OBSCENE IN NEW YORK?

What does it mean to be found obscene in New York? This is the most sophisticated city in the country. This is where they play Genet's *The Balcony*. If anyone is the first person to be found obscene in New York, he must feel utterly depraved.

—Lenny Bruce

The Man from Outer Taste

NEW YORK WAS the kindest and cruelest of places. It was filled with an inexplicable tension—a conflict between tolerance and intolerance, between creativity and conformity, between freedom and persecution. It both made and destroyed Lenny Bruce.

Signs of this love-hate relationship were apparent early on. Lenny debuted in April 1959 at The Den at the Duane Hotel on Madison Avenue and 37th Street. Manhattan welcomed him with the kind of enthusiasm that intoxicates the young and makes them think of nothing but marquees and money. It all started in the hotel's basement bar located next to a boiler room. The place had the charm of an army barracks.

The Den was a tiny club into which more than a hundred customers crammed themselves like sardines. There was little room to move and barely much more to breathe. Oxygen was in short supply. Yet even that didn't cramp Lenny's wild style. Once he got into it, the place came alive with hipster energy as he did some of his best bits— "Religions, Inc." ("Anuthuh mahtini faw Muthuh Cabrini") and "Father Flotsky's Triumph" ("Give up, Dutch, and we will meet any reasonable demands that you have, except for the vibrators"). They ate it up, every screaming one of them, including jazzman Miles Davis, singer Martha Raye, and columnist Dorothy Kilgallen. Even Lenny's off-color comments—"tits and ass" and "cocksucker"—didn't faze them. He had them bouncing off the low ceiling, laughing so hard they were gasping for breath.

A year later, it was an entirely different scene. For the first time, Lenny drew the audience's ire and caught the city's censorial eye. He had traveled to the Upper East Side to play the chic and prestigious Blue Angel, the aesthetic opposite of boiler joints like The Den. Here the décor was tuft-gray velour walls and red carpeting; just "[l]ike the inside of a coffin," Lenny observed. The manner was continental, the clientele conservative, and the entertainment conventional. So, when Lenny broke out with bits such as "How to Relax Your Colored Friends at Parties" ("I heard you guys got a wang on ya, ya sonofagun, ya!"), some of the customers walked and some of the critics railed:

"[O]bnoxious, arrogant, foul" (Jim O'Connor, *Journal-American*)
"diarrhea of the mouth" (Tim Taylor, *Cue*)
"the man from outer taste" (Bob Sylvester, *Daily News*)

The controversy in the New York dailies was so great that *Variety* credited Bruce's act with the rise of a no-holds-barred genre of café criticism. In fact, one particularly offended columnist registered a formal complaint with the New York Police Department. The next night, Lenny got word that there were special guests in the crowd—cops with armpit microphones hooked to a tape recorder. When told that "[t]here's fuzz out front," he uncharacteristically toned down his act, but to the detriment of his reputation. Word had it that twenty of Lenny's regulars—hookers, potheads, and musicians—walked out in disgust. He hated to make the concession to authority. As for his other Blue Angel critics, he gibed: "There's nothing sadder than an old hipster."

Earl Wilson, a columnist for the *New York Post*, was more pragmatic in his assessment of Bruce: "He is going to become fantastically successful and make several fortunes. That is the direction the world is going today." And, indeed, it seemed so, the Blue Angel episode notwithstanding. Judging by Lenny's rave receptions at The Village Vanguard (April–May 1960), Basin Street East (December 1960), Carnegie Hall (February 4, 1961), and the Village Theater (November 30, 1963), he was untouchable.

For six weeks at the Vanguard, Lenny jammed the joint nightly with his kind of folk: "college kids, hookers, fags, the jet set, Harlem society, the Broadway and Hollywood crowd. Nobody walked out on him." Joan Rivers, like Bill Cosby, had caught one of the Vanguard acts. She tagged it "hysterically funny." With a bit of her own wit, she added, "The children were lined up to be fed. I was seeing Jesus."

His run at one club was banner news for the *New York Times*:

LENNY BRUCE HEADS PROGRAM AT BASIN STREET EAST

While popular, Lenny's comedy was nonetheless seen as controversial; the management billed the act "For Adults Only." Although conceding that Bruce's "lapses in taste are often forgivable," the *New York Times'* Arthur Gelb inquired "whether the kind of derisive shock therapy he administers and the introspective free-form patter in which he indulges are legitimate night-club fare, as far as the typical customer is concerned."

Legitimate or not, on February 4, 1961, Bruce diehards braved a phenomenal snowstorm (up to seventeen inches deep) to attend a packed midnight performance at Carnegie Hall—one conceived and organized by Don Friedman. There was magic in the air as the crowd fled the snow and filed into the big hall to be with Lenny Bruce. According to biographer Albert Goldman, Lenny was "[s]o touched, so moved, so overwhelmed by what the people had done for him that he decided to give them the greatest performance of his entire career." It was unbelievable, uninhibited, and uncensored. Twenty-eight bits in all—covering the gamut from "The Ku Klux Klan" to "Shelley Berman," from "Dykes and Faggots" to "Kennedy's Acceptance Speech," and from "Dear Abby" to "Las Vegas Tits and Ass"—for a concert that finished after two A.M.! New York had paid its highest tribute to the dissident comic.

Two and a half years later, about a week after Lee Harvey Oswald assassinated JFK, Lenny tempered tragedy with comedy at The Village Theater. The old burlesque house—a 2,800-seater as large as Carnegie Hall, situated next to Ratner's, a kosher deli-restaurant—had seen better days. Lenny's appearance brought new life to the place. He walked out on the stage, cringed against the gold-glittered curtain, and remained stoically silent for what seemed like an unbearably long time. With a paranoid fix on the jam-packed audience, he broke the silence: "Don't shoot!" As if on cue, a young man leaped up onto the stage carrying an American flag and screaming, "Fuck Texas!!" But this was not a scripted bit—so, a freaked-out Bruce streaked into the wings. Even after reemerging, the stress was too much for Lenny. He stumbled through his performance, fumbled his bits, and mumbled about his recent legal battles in Chicago and elsewhere. Don Friedman, who had booked The Village Theater gig, charitably billed it "one of Lenny's less successful performances. The evening was a little harrowing, after all." Still, his audience forgave Lenny's display of nerves and remained faithful.

Lenny's popularity suited the emerging freedom of Manhattan's sex life. In the early '60s, Times Square alone sported some twenty porn shops. Taboo after taboo disappeared as strippers pared down their accoutrements, bath houses heated up, and sexual liberty redefined the cultural landscape. In 1963, however, the city began to test the boundaries of its Bacchanalian indulgence. For example, between "April 1963 and August 31, 1964, more than 130 of New York County's 166 obscenity arrests were made in the Times Square area." With the local government's blessing, the campaign to bring decency back was on. Sending strong warnings to the wayward, the NYPD launched its Operation Pornography, aimed at cleaning up the smut centers; in only the first two months of its massive raids, the police arrested 154 porn sellers, leading to eighty-three convictions with stiff fines and jail sentences up to three years. Such efforts received the blessings of Francis Cardinal Spellman, the New York leader of the Catholic Church, who called on the city to establish a "citizens' commission" to pursue "necessary, appropriate, and legal means" to guard against "the influences of salacious literature."

Though once faint, the signals of New York's anxious ambivalence toward the likes of Lenny Bruce were becoming louder and clearer. In all of the Lennymania, it is doubtful that he was listening.

Mr. First Amendment

APRIL 1, 1964. Ephraim London was arguing yet another obscenity case before the Supreme Court of the United States. The Brooklyn-born Brahmin, a partner in a New York law firm established by his father and uncle (a U.S. Congressman), had garnered a well-deserved reputation as a censorship opponent. After all, he had litigated many, many obscenity cases; moreover, he already had beaten the State of New York before the Supreme Court in two obscenity challenges. He defended films banned by the Motion Picture Division of the New York State Board of Regents and denounced as sacrilegious by Roman Catholic authorities. His 1952 case cleared the way for public viewing of *The Miracle*, a film directed by Roberto Rossellini involving an Italian peasant girl convinced that she was bearing a child immaculately conceived with St. Joseph. In a unanimous decision, the Court placed motion pictures squarely within the aegis of First Amendment protections. Perhaps even more famous was his 1959 case, in which a majority of the Court struck down a ban on the filmic rendition of D.H. Lawrence's *Lady Chatterley's Lover* and ruled that New York could not censor films simply because they depicted conduct deemed immoral.

In the 1964 case, however, the constitutional contest was not with New York. London was taking on the state of Ohio, challenging the conviction of a Cleveland movie theater owner, Nico Jacobellis, for showing *The Lovers*, a Venice Film Festival winner that had been praised by New York critics as a work of art. Though the film had played without cut to enthusiastic audiences in other Midwestern cities such as Chicago and Detroit, Cleveland authorities were appalled by "one of the longest and most sensuous love scenes to be seen in this country" that came "as close to authentic *amour* as is possible on the screen."

The tall, stately London was back in his element. He was a natural for this forum, eager to do cerebral battle. Once again, he argued for a broad reexamination of First Amendment obscenity law—one aimed at stopping local governments from imposing their parochial standards on the nation's more generous free speech guarantees. First, he urged the Court to restrict obscenity bans only to "hardcore pornography"—material which is "so flagrantly, patently, blatantly obscene, that there could be no difference of opinion…between reputable people with respect to whether or not the matter is actually obscene." Second, he recommended that the "community standards" prong of *Roth* be tested according to national mores rather than the values of any state or local polity.

The Supreme Court's receptivity to London's rationales was of great importance to Bruce and his Illinois lawyers. Should the Court vote against Jacobellis, its decision certainly would prove a major obstacle to Lenny's appeal of his Chicago conviction, then pending before the Illinois State Supreme Court. In contrast, should the justices accept London's logic, the Illinois high court might well appreciate the soundness of Rosenfield, Kalven, and Ming's views that obscenity cannot be determined by balancing the localized virtues and vices of comic commentary.

Oral arguments in *Jacobellis* were formidable, just the way London liked them.

> *London*: [I]t is still the First Amendment that has become applicable to the states, and the First Amendment right I should not think would vary from state to state.…
> *Justice Stewart*: How do you find out the national standard? Is it the lowest common denominator? Is it some average of all public opinion in each of the fifty states?
> *London*: The question of determining standards, Your Honor, is an extremely difficult one and poses many problems.

Indeed. Determining standards, after all, is what the obscenity debate is all about…unless one is an absolutist.

> *Justice Harlan*: Supposing you were rewriting the *Roth–Alberts* test. How would you reform it?
> *London*: I wouldn't, Your Honor. I'm afraid my opinion would follow Justice Black's [absolute view].
> *Justice Harlan*: You mean obscenity can't be dealt with at all?

London: I believe—that is my own opinion which Your Honor asked for.

In the early hours of that same Wednesday in 1964, before his lawyer-to-be was discoursing in the High Court, Lenny Bruce was putting London's First Amendment views to the test at the Café Au Go Go in New York's West Village. It was the impetus for what was said to be the "longest, costliest, most bitterly contested and widely publicized [obscenity] trial" of its kind.

Going to Au Go Go

HOWARD AND ELLA Solomon loved things French. He was a stockbroker, and she a fashion designer and seamstress; they had fantasized together about opening a discotheque in Paris. The way things turned out, however, the Solomons chose to infuse French influences into a coffeehouse located at 152 Bleecker Street across from The Bitter End, a folk music and comedy club. A bright red domed canopy bearing the name Café Au Go Go hovered over the entrance door, with an illuminated display box on each side.

Once you entered, you went down fifteen steps to a landing, where you paid $3.50 (general admission) or $10 (ringside) to catch Lenny Bruce's act. Then you walked around a ceiling-to-floor curtain as the handsome, tweed-jacketed maitre d', Tony Ponzini, escorted you to your seat. The Parisian décor was unmistakable: twenty papier-mâché masks from the Folies Bergères and twenty-four pink globes, controlled by a rheostat dimmer, hung from a flat black ceiling hued with blown sand; oil-painted murals, portraying show business caricatures, graced the red brick walls; gray studio carpeting covered the floor; fifty pew-like benches with leather-covered seats lined the walls; and original Thonet Bentwood café chairs encircled the center tables with their butcher-block tops.

In the full house, you were among 350 people in a twenty-five-hundred-square-foot room waiting for Lenny to take the sixteen-foot-

by-eight-foot, semicircular stage on this, the fourth night of his scheduled ten-day run at the Café. The terms of the agreement were
sketched out on the back of a Western Union telegram, with Lenny
originally asking for $6,000 a week but ultimately settling for approx-
imately $3,500.

The house lights dimmed, the stage lights intensified, and there he
was in living flesh—all two hundred–plus pounds of him! No longer
the suave, lean, and high-tailored look of the '50s; the Lenny Bruce of
the mid-'60s was bloated and beaten down. The hipster wit of earlier
nights at Ann's 440 now all too often gave way to a patchwork account
of legal troubles occasionally interspersed with comic tales. For three
quarters of an opening hour, Lenny got autobiographical: talk of his
busts, trials, lawyers, judges, and financial problems were a major part
of his "sick" routine.

When not obsessing about his drug and obscenity arrests, Lenny
returned to those tried-and-true bits that once had landed him in station-house cells: "To Come" (San Francisco) and "Infidelity"
(Chicago). But the bulk of his funny material was the "safe stuff"—the
acts for which he had not yet been carted away in handcuffs. The following were among them:

"Eleanor Roosevelt's Tits": In a riff on his celebrated "tits and
ass" routines, Lenny spontaneously declared: "Eleanor Roosevelt had
the nicest tits of any lady in office." Claiming that, as a young man, he
saw her breasts "by mistake standing on a box looking in a window" at
the White House, he play-acted the encounter between the former
First Lady and himself. "You've seen them, haven't you? My tits?"
Eleanor inquired. The young admirer responded: "You have really
nice tits and I oughta tell everybody...how nice they are and how nice
you are for not having me arrested for looking at them." Lenny wound
up the bit by suggesting that, in failing to have him arrested, Eleanor
had aided and abetted the Peeping Tom.

"Hauling Ass to Save Her Ass": Only four months after President
Kennedy's tragic assassination, Lenny mused on a photograph published by *Time* magazine of Jacqueline Kennedy scrambling out of the
backseat and onto the trunk of the convertible in which the president
had been shot. The caption for the photo explained that Mrs.

Kennedy was climbing out to bring help aboard. "That's bullshit, that's a dirty lie," Lenny sneered. Rather, Mrs. Kennedy "hauled ass to save her ass." ⓒⅅ This picture was objectionable, he explained, because it set up a lie: "[W]hen your daughter, God forbid if her husband's face gets shot away and she hauls ass...she'll feel like a piece of shit" because she was not as courageous as the good Jackie Kennedy who remained to help. Railing at the hypocrisy, Lenny cried out: "*None* of you *motherfuckers* ever stayed," and yet they would "sit in judgment and indict!"

"Guys Are Carnal": Perhaps one of the most ludicrous bits that Lenny ever did on the subject of sex drove home the point that men are oversexed by nature and capable of having sex with anything, even a chicken. Were women to appreciate this, they might understand that the proverbial one-night stand is no good reason to end a lifelong relationship. Imagining the scene of a woman returning home to find her husband in bed with a hen, Lenny transformed himself into the incensed wife: "You want dinner? So get your chicken to get it for ya!" The embarrassed adulterer rationalized, "I didn't love her or nothing." At the denouement of the bestial relationship, the dejected husband assured his spouse: "I'm telling ya I don't see her anymore. I just bumped into her in the yard there, that's all."

"The Hot-Lead Enema": Lenny tested the principle that a real, red-blooded American would not betray his country to save his life. Alluding to Francis Gary Powers (the CIA pilot who was received unceremoniously when released from a Russian jail two years after his U-2 reconnaissance plane was shot down over the USSR), Bruce satirized the bravado of the would-be hero, a cryptographer with secret data: "*I'd never* sell my country out." The braggart is placed in full view of another prisoner-of-war, who is about to be tortured. "They're putting a funnel in his ass...what the hell?...What are they heating up that lead for? They're not putting hot lead in the funnel...are they?" Now entirely rattled by what's in store for him, the blowhard changes his tune: "The secrets? *Surprise!* Here they are." No problem explaining away his cognitive dissonance: "[W]hat are you kidding? I don't want a hot-lead enema. [Y]ou take it, *schmuck,* I just don't like it."

Lenny weaved back and forth between legal reality and comic

fantasy, between sincerity and satire, between the political and the scatological—captivating his audience at every offensive turn. No one complained, no one walked out, and no one called the police...no one, that is, who was not an undercover agent.

The Sting

THE NEW YORK District Attorney's office "wanted to hear what Lenny Bruce was all about." The prosecutors desired "to learn whether his performances seemed so obscene that the best available evidence of them ought to be collected for grand jury presentation." But incriminating evidence was needed. And that is when Herbert S. Ruhe came into the picture.

He was once a CIA agent in Vietnam. He was a Missouri-educated Frenchman, a small, dark-skinned, and dapper man with a mustache. He was License Department Inspector Ruhe. March 31, 1964, was the third night of Bruce's run at the Café Au Go Go. Acting on the orders of his superiors, Ruhe arrived there at about 10:30 P.M., paying $4.75 to sit at a table one row back from the stage. He waited patiently, along with an audience of about two hundred, until Lenny came on stage; having sprained his ankle, Lenny was limping and his left foot was in a cast.

Inspector Ruhe was busy at work. He began to make entry after entry into his pocket notebook. Using a "system of memory recall—to put into my notes key words and key phrases which would subsequently assist me in typing up a complete report," Ruhe jotted down terms such as "jack me off," "mind your asses," "fucks us around any more," and "fag man." In addition, he scribbled phrases—regarding the Eleanor bit, "nice tits," "Nice, aren't they?" "Don't touch or play around"; regarding the chicken routine, "has done it to a chicken," "I was drunk," "Go come in a chicken." This was a clandestine operation to gather evidence of a crime—to wit, a misdemeanor.

The next day, the inspector organized his notes into an official report, which he then submitted to Richard H. Kuh, an assistant district attorney. Nicholas Scopetta, a fellow prosecutor, also received a copy. Whereas

Scopetta urged restraint, Kuh took the matter directly to the Manhattan district attorney, Frank Hogan, and recommended investigation.

Frank Smithwick Hogan was a man wed to civility. Prominently displayed in his office was a plaque that read: "Courtesy Is the Golden Key that Unlocks All Doors." Not surprisingly, he was priggish about vulgarity. For example, in the 1940s he actively prosecuted Edmund Wilson's *Memoirs of Hecate County* as a criminally obscene work. The Irish Catholic prosecutor had little tolerance for works that "wallowed in filth." He also respected Richard Kuh's judgment and was predisposed to honor the discretion of a senior staff member. Per Hogan's order, police were assigned to monitor Bruce's act on the night of April 1.

Four plainclothes vice-squad officers—Patrolmen Lane, O'Neil, and MacCambridge, and Lieutenant Russo—infiltrated the Solomons' Parisien quarters to conduct their covert dirty-words operation. Seated at two black marble-topped tables, the vice men waited for Lenny's ten P.M. show. Patrolman Robert Lane placed himself about fifteen feet from the stage, the better to capture Lenny's words on the mini-reel wire recorder strapped to his body. Unlike L.A. Deputy District Attorney Richard Hecht at the Troubadour, New York's Assistant D.A. did not join the police at the club. Instead, the four officers were at the Café as Prosecutor Kuh's ears and were not to lay hands on anybody. No arrests, just evidence.

After Kuh heard the largely inaudible wire recording the next morning, he directed Patrolman Lane to rerecord it onto tape and to transcribe the performance. Joseph Le Page, a hearing reporter for the D.A.'s office, spent hours "translating" the partially intelligible undercover work-product. The typed transcript listed truncated blips of Lenny's vulgarities—at the moment of President Kennedy's assassination, "the wife, hauled to save her ass;" "the sheep aren't safe, that's all, we got enough reports now we gotta make a law...the SPCA will cool it as best it can and that will be it...If you came home and found your husband with a chicken would you belt him, really feel bad, bad, a chicken, ah it's an odd bed."

Patrolman Lane then carried his typed script to the grand jury room in the New York Supreme Court building. Before the body of twenty-three grand jurors, Assistant D.A. Gerald Harris (who doubted the wisdom of pursuing the matter) presented the case for a criminal prosecution. The patrolman testified, as did Inspector Ruhe; the script was handed out, and the tape recording was played. The following day, Kuh instructed the grand jurors on the applicable statutory law. He explained to them his understanding of Section 1140-A of the Penal Law (Immoral Shows and Exhibitions), which prohibited any "obscene, indecent, immoral, and impure drama, play, exhibition, show, and entertainment…which would tend to the corruption of the morals of youth and others."

The first two nights in April, Lenny had made it through his performances without interference by the NYPD. It was a different story the very next morning.

Always courteous, Howard Solomon asked: "May I help you?" He wanted to know the business of the two men who apparently were trying to enter his club at 10:30 A.M. William O'Neil led Solomon to believe that he and Officer McCambridge were investigating "a complaint." Solomon, by contrast, recalled no such notice. "They just presented themselves as Lenny Bruce fans, eager to learn more about him," he later recounted.

What followed was a seemingly innocent conversation, but one pregnant with prosecutorial possibilities. Inviting the officers/fans in for a tour of the club, Solomon engaged them. "Do you know Lenny Bruce?" O'Neil asked. "He's a pure genius. One of the most brilliant comedians I've ever heard," Solomon affirmed, explaining that he had followed Bruce's career for years. Aware of the ongoing grand jury investigation, Officer O'Neil's questions became more focused: "Have you seen Mr. Bruce's performances at your club?" Unaware that his answer could incriminate him, Solomon boasted: "I've seen every one." To encourage the officers to behold this comic genius in action, Howard comped them a pair of tickets for the Sunday matinee performance. "I gave them the best seats in the house; they were ten-dollar tickets," Solomon recalled later, "What a fool I was!" Of course, as part of their official duties, O'Neil and McCambridge already had observed Lenny's genius. Now, it was into the squad car and back to the D.A. Within no time, Patrolman O'Neil was testifying before the grand jury.

The twenty-three grand jurors had heard all of the prosecutors' evidence. What they may not have heard, however, was how exactly and how much the First Amendment should factor into their deliberations. But, no matter; for by the close of April 3, they issued a criminal information against Lenny Bruce and Howard Solomon, accusing them of violating Section 1140-A. Prosecutor Gerald Harris reflected back on the grand jury matter years later: "I half-expected the 'conscience of our community' to tell us to lay off. To my mild surprise, the grand jury voted to file charges."

Given his history, Lenny had good reason to believe that all of the police snooping signaled trouble. Yet, this was New York, and while he had been harassed before he had never been busted for obscenity. So, let the show go on!

A capacity crowd waited for Lenny to come onstage for the ten P.M. gig on April 3. The show never happened; he never appeared. Shortly before the scheduled performance, Lenny and Howard Solomon were collared in the dressing room. A bench warrant charged them with giving an indecent performance. When Lenny inquired as to the charges, the plainclothes officer told him, "Section 1040." More informed than his captors, Lenny protested, "But...that's prostitution." "Aw, Lenny," whined the patrolman, "don't be technical. It's one of them numbers." Hauled to the Sixth Precinct headquarters on Charles Street, the comedian and his club sponsor were booked, fingerprinted, and incarcerated.

Sometime thereafter, Bentley Kassal, a civil law attorney who handled the Café Au Go Go's legal matters, received a call for bail help from Howard Solomon. Kassal arranged for a bondsman and contacted Arthur Markewich, a friend and a New York appellate judge. In the middle of the night, Kassal went to the judge's home on Riverside Drive, where bail was fixed and bonds approved. Around two A.M., Kassal left the station with the two alleged misdemeanants. Later that morning, a TV news reporter interviewed an aggravated and fatigued Bruce. "It seems that it's taken eight years for [the local authorities] to finally, I guess, understand what I was saying," Bruce said sarcastically. "They found it was obscene enough to put me in a jail cell....And the thing I wish they would do is tell me which words were obscene."

Bruce and the Solomons were determined to continue their contract. Lenny would not be intimidated; he would return to the stage. His strategy for the April 4 performances was to *spell* out forbidden words rather than pronounce them. That "ingenious" idea occurred to him on the very same day of his arraignment in Weekend Court before Judge Vincent P. Rao. The judge had released Bruce on $1,000 bail and Solomon on the recognizance of his lawyer. If Lenny were "not guilty"—as he had pled—for saying obscene words, then surely he could not be guilty for spelling them. At least, that was the bent of his mind. Perhaps this technique had fortuitous merit, if only because the spell-binding act never produced a criminal complaint.

More Heat

MAURICE ROSENFIELD AND his wife, Lois, were visiting New York on April 7. While there, they had gone to the Drake Hotel to check out its new "happening" discotheque, Shepherds. Kibbitzing with a couple of their friends, they were interrupted. A tall man came to their table and asked, "Where's Rosenfield? Which one is Rosenfield?" After identifying himself, the Chicago lawyer was told: "Lenny Bruce *needs* you." Lenny was calling from the Café Au Go Go. Concerned that he might be busted again, he wanted advice as to whether he should perform that night. Within moments, Rosenfield and his party were in a cab traveling the two and a half miles down Park Avenue, over west and south again to Bleecker Street, arriving at the red canopied entrance to the Café.

Rosenfield proceeded immediately to the office behind the stage. There, he joined a conference in progress. Bruce and the Solomons were already brainstorming with a team of dark-suited lawyers—Herbert Monte-Levy and Allen Schwartz—both of whom soon would represent the defendants in some capacity. (The comedian "Professor" Irwin Corey, Lenny's backup act, was also there.) The discourse was anything but comic, as they discussed the recent bust at the Café, the appeal pending in the Illinois Supreme Court, the New York statute, and the *Roth* ruling. The legal decision was unanimous: despite their concerns, Bruce and Solomon were counseled to stand on their First Amendment rights. Rosenfield was particularly resolute that Lenny test the constitutionality of the law. Bruce deferred. The legal talk done, now it was time to raise the curtain. Howard Solomon, however, would miss the show; he had seen enough, and opted to leave the Café.

In the dressing room just before Lenny's first scheduled performance, Ella Solomon asked him whether he really wanted to chance it by speaking his mind. He replied with some earnestness: "Do you tell an artist what colors to choose from his palette?" Ella agreed, and the show ran its course in the presence of several suspicious, well-dressed gentlemen. Licensing agent Herbert Ruhe had returned with his notepad, this time accompanied by three different NYPD officers: Inspector Powell, and Patrolmen Hahne and La Piedra, the latter outfitted with a Minofon recorder.

Midway through the show, Lenny spotted someone taking notes. Screeching to a halt, he gibed: "Ha! Now, dig how paranoid I get." Referring to "that fellow writing," he prodded, "I don't think you're writing home....But, you wouldn't be that blatant. Or would you? That's really balls." Cheekily dismissing the officer-scribe, Lenny asked: "[W]hat if he's writing a shopping list just to screw up the paranoia?" Although sensing the heat in the audience, Lenny did not temper his act. Four years earlier, at The Blue Angel, he had been more timid in the presence of police with wires. Now he was less risk-averse.

The scene was like something right out of one of Lenny's old skits: "[F]irst place, they're two guys working....They have ties on and they're dressed. They're two guys together. Yeah, that's heat....[T]hey have a feeling of belonging anywhere. It's amazing....*Pchung!* Done. That's all." True to form, comedy became reality. Officer La Piedra arrested Lenny, while Officer Hahne arrested Ella Solomon. What followed was even more routine. A courtesy ride to the Charles Street Station, a photo-op session, and private quarters. This time, Howard Squadron picked up Lenny's bail tab of $350, and sprung him in the middle of the night.

That very day, the poet Allen Ginsberg was still fuming about Bruce's first bust. The author of *Howl*, the "indecent" work that led to the Ferlinghetti trial in 1957, saw the Bruce incident as the latest of several sanctimonious attacks on New York's avant-garde artistic freedom. Earlier, there had been the controversial New York Coffee House Law, enacted in 1962 but not really enforced until 1964. When the law was used in February 1964 against the owner of the Café Le Metro who hosted a poetry reading by Jackson MacLow, that episode was seen by many as a way of harassing the unwashed and radical elements in the Village. Worse still was the obscenity charge against filmmaker Jonas Mekas for screening Jack Smith's *Flaming Creatures* and Jean Genet's *Un Chant d'Amour*, an event viewed as yet another and characteristic attack on the arts. Committees were formed, marches were organized, and protests were scheduled; the "resistance" had begun.

When Lenny Bruce was arrested a *second* time at the Café Au Go Go, it was really all too much—a word-crime bust at a *coffeehouse*, no less. Immediate action had to be taken; the troops had to be called out. Ginsberg formed an "Emergency Committee against the Harassment of Lenny Bruce." Hence, "brigades of absolutists in the war on censorship joined the avant-garde"—at least, that is how prosecutor Richard Kuh described it. Beyond the avant-garde, there was the press; it had to be rallied, too. So, the angry poet prepared a news release outlining Bruce's legal hassles and quoting some of his plaudits from the American and foreign literati. When reports of the campaign reached Lenny, he was comically contrary: "The problem of people helping you with protest is that historically they march you straight to the chair."

"Get Me Somebody Who Swings with the First Amendment"

FISHING FOR LAWYERS should have been an art by now. Not counting his business deals or drug busts, Lenny had an unprecedented amount of experience in selecting attorneys. But for him, litigation skills were never as important as reputation. His instinct was to go with the big-name lawyer, and to impress the court and public. In San Francisco, he wanted Jake Ehrlich, Billie Holiday's lawyer; in Los Angeles, he wanted Melvin Belli, Zsa Zsa Gabor's lawyer; in Chicago, he frantically hunted with Earle Warren Zaidins for a local luminary. Each time, the effort failed, sometimes for better, sometimes for worse.

In New York, too, Lenny scouted for a headline-grabber—but this time in First Amendment law. He leaned on Albert Goldman, a pop-culture writer who taught English at Columbia University, to dig up a distinguished professor or practitioner from the law school. When Goldman suggested a bright, young admirer of Bruce with up-and-coming potential, Lenny whined, "No, man, I'm tired of breaking in these twerps. Get me somebody who swings with the First Amendment."

Bruce's first choice was Morris Ernst, the seventy-five-year-old attorney who had succeeded in clearing Radclyffe Hall's *The Well of Loneliness* from New York obscenity charges in 1929, and who did likewise in 1933 for James Joyce's *Ulysses*. Additionally, Ernst had just coauthored *Censorship: The Search for the Obscene*. Bruce visited the noted ACLU lawyer at his Fifth Avenue apartment. There, he played a tape (made by Solomon at Bruce's insistence) of his April 3 performance at the Café Au Go Go. Ernst listened and branded it as "the stuff you see on bathroom walls." Nonetheless, he was willing to defend Bruce for free. But Lenny would have none of it. He turned down Ernst's offer, for the old man had gotten under his skin.

Nat Hentoff, who had written enthusiastically about Bruce since the early San Francisco days, urged his friend to "swing" with Ephraim London. In Hentoff's mind, the fifty-two-year-old London seemed the ideal attorney: he was "the best First Amendment lawyer I knew at the time," "a scholar of the Constitution," and "a man of utter self-confidence." Prior to his death, London would argue and win nine cases before the U.S. Supreme Court; by 1964 alone, London already had litigated more than 250 obscenity cases in fifteen states. Now, he agreed to be the lead counsel of record in *People v. Bruce*. He asked Martin Garbus, a young associate in the firm of Brennan, London, and Buttenwieser, to assist him. The thirty-year-old NYU Law grad had seen Bruce perform several times, usually at The

Village Vanguard. With Garbus, the attraction to Lenny seemed natural; with London, just the opposite. London "sensed right from the start," Garbus recalled, "that he and Lenny would not mix well. London—meticulous and refined, Lincolnesque in appearance and formal in manner—and Lenny—by now looking frayed and harried, strung out on drugs and drained dry by almost two years of legal harassment—would indeed have made an odd couple." But, of course, that was just an unseasoned lawyer's opinion.

Ella and Howard Solomon needed their own lawyer. Unlike Art Auerbach (San Francisco's Jazz Workshop) or Doug Weston (Los Angeles's Troubadour) or Herb Cohen (Los Angeles's Unicorn), the Solomons were arrested for hosting Lenny Bruce's show. Unlike Alan Ribback (Chicago's Gate of Horn), who was also arrested, the Solomons actually were prosecuted. Notably, they would be the first and last of Lenny's club owners and operators to stand trial.

The couple picked a former Manhattan assistant district attorney, Allen G. Schwartz, to represent them. (Earlier, Lenny had considered hiring Schwartz, but the deal fell through.) Ephraim London's lofty credentials notwithstanding, he lacked at least one significant thing that Schwartz had—a working knowledge of his former colleague, Prosecutor Richard Kuh.

Frank Hogan's office initially had assigned the prosecution of the State's case to Assistant District Attorney Gerald Harris. In addition to the presentation to the grand jury, he had handled some important preliminary matters—the arraignment and one early hearing. But, when it came to the trial itself, Gerald Harris finally withdrew. Like his colleague Nicholas Scopetta, Harris considered Bruce's performance to be "funny" and "on target." He was unwilling to pursue the matter any further: "I told my bureau chief and District Attorney Frank Hogan that I could not, in good conscience, continue." Like William J. Martin (the Illinois lawyer in the State Attorney's office), Harris had First Amendment problems with going forward with the matter.

The case would be reassigned entirely to Richard Henry Kuh, who had played a significant role in the criminal investigation and grand jury presentation of the Bruce case. He was the most formidable of any of Lenny's prosecutors. He not only had attended Harvard Law

School, but had been a member of its prestigious law review before graduation. The assistant D.A. had served in Frank Hogan's office for eleven years before *People v. Bruce*. Not infrequently, Hogan praised Kuh's brilliant legal mind, characterizing it as one of the best in the entire D.A.'s office. The chief of the Criminal Courts Bureau, Kuh had an impressive track record. To some who observed him at trial, he was a man who "gloried in combat." As for Gerald Harris's prosecutorial reservations, Kuh later declared: "I think that [Harris] misconstrued his obligation as an assistant prosecutor....It is not up to each assistant to say, 'I don't want to handle this kind of case.'" For Kuh, prosecuting Lenny Bruce was a duty, and one not to be shunned. However characterized, this much was certain: Dick Kuh was a man to be reckoned with, a dangerously coiled opponent—a man whose very manner warned, "Be careful!"

Though other counsel occasionally entered and exited *People v. Bruce* and *People v. Solomon*, these were the lawyers who claimed the lion's share of the cases on their course to judgment.

Make-It-or-Break-It Proceedings

ARRAIGNMENT. THE WORD is derived from the Latin adjective *a* ("to") and noun *ratio* ("account for," "reason"); the word means "to indict," "to accuse," or "to call a person to answer a criminal charge before a court." This much Lenny undoubtedly knew from the early days when he read *Black's Law Dictionary* in Melvin Belli's San Francisco law office. Of course, he also had plenty of firsthand experience with arraignments. On Monday, April 13, before Judge Manuel A. Gomez of the New York Criminal Court, Bruce and the Solomons were called to answer for their alleged crimes. That day, the charges were never read, and the defendants never pled. Rather, lawyerly wrangling began—a struggle over legal complexities that would last nearly two months.

The devil is in the details. The pretrial matters alone involved six hearings before three different judges (the Honorables John

Murtagh, Frederick Strong, and Manuel Gomez), prosecuted by two assistant D.A.s (Richard Kuh and Gerald Harris), and contested by seven defense attorneys (Ephraim London, Martin Garbus, Howard Squadron, and Lawrence Rogovin for Bruce; Allen Schwartz, Herbert Monte-Levy, and Bentley Kassal for the Solomons). These six hearings generated a total of some five hundred pages of transcript—a sum almost as large as the transcript for the entire Chicago obscenity trial. And all of this fracas over continuances, evidentiary rulings, and motions to dismiss—the very kind of details that could prove to be determinative.

Judge Gomez was no different than other judges; he wanted to move the cases along and clear his docket. Besides, this was not the Rosenberg trial; it was another in a long line of misdemeanor cases. But, mindful of their Sixth Amendment rights to counsel of their choosing, the defendants were not in such a hurry. They moved to substitute new attorneys for their original counsel, and therefore requested a continuance. The prosecution, however, would have none of it:

> *Kuh*: If new counsel is ready, I have no problem with their substitution. If new counsel claims they can't be ready because of short notice, I would ask that prior counsel not be relieved....
>
> *Garbus*: We were retained last night. The case is somewhat unusual....I can't see any way how the D.A. can be prejudiced by a delay to May 8. We cannot possibly prepare a case of this magnitude in less than that....
>
> *Schwartz*: I came into this case only this weekend....[T]he case is of such great importance that it requires preparation, and I ask your Honor please permit the substitution of counsel and to allow us a reasonable time to prepare this case....
>
> *Judge Gomez*: You know, we cannot play this game of Russian roulette, changing attorneys continuously and not having a disposition in the case....[Mr. Bruce] cannot come to court and say, "Well, I want adjournments *ad infinitum*," for the simple reason that, insofar as a performance of this questionable nature is concerned, it must be adjudicated.

Prosecutor Kuh stressed the delicate nature of this case, one that required acceleration of judgment. But, not wishing to appear unreasonable, he offered a compromise:

> *Kuh*: [T]he People are certainly not in a position of censors, and not in a position of stopping or starting performances. In the light, however, that Mr. Bruce, after the first arrest, performed on at least three separate evenings…substantially the same show that a grand jury found was obscene, I think that it is in Mr. Bruce's interest, and certainly in the interest of the people in this community where a World's Fair opens next week, that whether or not this is an indecent show be promptly adjudicated.…Now, if Mr. Bruce wants a delay until May 8 or May any day, then it seems to me he…should volunteer and his counsel should urge upon the court that it will not produce any sort of a show that is an indecent show until the issues of indecency could be disposed of.…
>
> *Garbus*: I resent Mr. Kuh's making this a condition of the adjournment. Mr. Bruce has been appearing in this state for eight years. He's appeared in Town Hall; he's appeared in Carnegie Hall. I don't think that as a condition of this adjournment he should be required to stop his performances.…
>
> *Judge Gomez*: [T]his defendant is in no position to be asking for adjournments…while he has what might be considered, in most charitable terms, a questionable performance which might be given.…I can mark the hearing for tomorrow. If it's a question of a trial, I can put the trial over for two weeks.

When the dust settled, attorneys Monte-Levy, Kassal, and Squadron were out; attorneys London, Garbus, and Schwartz were in; and the new defense counsel had overnight to prepare for a preliminary hearing, with the trial date yet to be set.

The thorniest pretrial issue was the struggle over evidentiary use of tapes of Bruce's April 1 and 7 performances at the Café Au Go Go. The day after Lenny's second arrest, a lengthy column appeared in *The Village Voice*, reporting that Bruce had played "tapes of the shows for which [he] was arrested" at "the Fifth Avenue apartment of a prominent civil libertarian." (With legal naïveté, Lenny had invited Stephanie Gervis Harrington, the reporter, to hear all of this "incriminating evidence" at the same time that he was consulting with Morris Ernst, his potential counsel.) "This was welcome news," prosecutor Kuh later gloated. The D.A.'s office possessed a usable tape of one performance, recorded on April 1 by Patrolman Lane, but that account was only partially audible; the prosecution's case could be made more easily by quoting from a clear and complete audiotape. The D.A. subpoenaed the tapes, but the defendants refused to hand them over.

The contest over the tapes was played out from April 13 to 15 before Judges Gomez and Strong consecutively. The defense counsels were adamant that the tapes were the personal property of their respective clients; hence, to force production of the tapes would violate their constitutional rights.

> *London*: [W]e believe that the production of those tapes, since they are the property of the individual defendants, would be a violation of their rights under the Fifth Amendment—it would be compelling them to testify against themselves, and it is for that reason we object to the production of those tapes....
>
> *Schwartz*: May I say, your Honor...the Fifth and Fourteenth Amendments [bar the State from compelling a person] to come forth and [proffer] the very evidence of the crime of which he is accused, the actual facts....
>
> *Garbus*: Whether [the tapes] are used in open court is one thing; whether the district attorney uses them in the preparation of the case is quite something else. I am concerned about the district attorney...using tapes that belong to Lenny Bruce in the preparation of his case against Lenny Bruce....

However compelling those arguments, there was one potential problem, a *serious* problem. Richard Kuh argued vociferously that the Café Au Go Go *corporation*, not the defendants, owned the tapes; accordingly, the subpoena must be honored and the tapes produced, since corporations (unlike individuals) cannot claim the Fifth Amendment privilege. To establish corporate ownership, the prosecutor needed to call an officer of the corporation to the stand. Howard Solomon was that officer most knowledgeable about the contractual relationship between Lenny Bruce and the Café.

However compelling Kuh's argument, there was one potential problem, one *major* problem. For his purposes, could the prosecutor split Solomon's identity as corporate officer with no constitutional rights from his identity as a criminally accused with constitutional rights?

> *Schwartz*: Mr. Solomon is the only person in the corporation who has knowledge of the way these tapes came into being, and, accordingly, I have directed him that if called as a witness, he has a perfect right to refuse to answer on the ground that it may tend to incriminate him.

The prosecutor angrily dismissed all such "Tweedle Dee," "Tweedle Dum" arguments as frivolous:

> *Kuh*: I think we are facing here a specious effort to separate and to create the distinction between the role of one Howard Solomon, who, if you will, was an alter ego of the corporation, and one Howard Solomon, private citizen, who chooses to engage in criminal conduct.

Later, Kuh added, "It seems to me that this court is being imposed upon with…double-talk."

In the Ping-Pong game of establishing ownership, Howard Solomon repeatedly took the Fifth at the advice of his attorney—even to the point of invoking the right when his *own* lawyer questioned him. The standard colloquy was:

> *Solomon*: I refuse to answer on the grounds that it would tend to incriminate me.
> *Judge Strong*: I direct you to answer.

Throughout this hearing, the colloquy was repeated one hundred times, each time infuriating the prosecutor more and more:

Kuh: [T]o prolong this hearing that should have taken a few minutes, to last all day, when a court is as busy as this court...is petti-
fogging interference with the normal business of this court.

"*That's* obscene," Lenny Bruce murmured to himself. Nothing
much had been heard from Bruce all day. In fact, Lenny seemed rather
blasé and bored about the cheek-to-jowl tussling over the tapes. Slumped
on a back bench in the courtroom, he remained in a semi-dormant state,
with his head dangling and eyes closed. "I've been through all of this
before," he droned, "Chicago, Los Angeles, and other places..."

When all was said and done, Howard Solomon answered every
question under the judge's orders, to Kuh's advantage: the tapes
belonged to the corporation, the judge ruled, and they now had to be
turned over to the prosecution.

LENNY WAS NOWHERE to be seen when the preliminary hearing
took place before Judge Strong on the afternoon of April 15. This was
highly uncharacteristic of him; Bruce typically insisted on participating
actively at each stage of his legal proceedings. His lawyer explained:
Lenny was at his hotel room in bed, fighting off an attack of pleurisy.

The defendant's absence was troubling to the prosecutor, Gerald
Harris, who questioned whether the hearing should proceed at all. "I
just hope," stressed Harris, "that we are not later confronted with a
demand by him that he has been denied some important opportunity
to be present when the charges against him were sired." By contrast,
Ephraim London was not so troubled. While granting that Lenny had
not given him specific authority to waive his appearance, London was
nonetheless emphatic: "I am his attorney. I am in charge of the case. I
believe that it's proper for us to proceed."

However understandable, London's attitude was a bit too cavalier
for the court. Judge Strong urged him to call Bruce and obtain permission. Probably, London's attitude would have been equally cavalier, if only in style, for Lenny's tastes. After all, by this time "Lenny
Bruce, Counselor" was presenting his own arguments to judges, as he
had done recently with Judge Ryan in Chicago.

The preliminary hearing was a make-it-or-break-it proceeding. For the state, it was the crucial test of a *prima facie* case to go to trial. For the defense, it was the critical opportunity to end the prosecution by way of successful motions to dismiss. For Lenny, it was everything. If the hearings continued beyond this point, he would become more vulnerable to the kind of criminal sentence he had just suffered in Chicago.

There was also the nagging problem of money: Lenny could not afford a full-blown trial, particularly given London's rates and the specter of countless billable hours. (He had yet to pay the $350 chump-change that he owed Squadron for bail, let alone Squadron's attorney's fees.) And most important of all, winning the preliminary hearing meant that Lenny could go back to work. For all practical purposes, he was currently unemployable in New York, Chicago, and Los Angeles, where club owners were loath to hire him while his court battles continued. In these ways and others, the protections of the First Amendment were vital to his existence.

Both defense lawyers London and Schwartz argued that the state had not proven that the accused had violated Section 1140-A. Schwartz claimed that Ella Solomon could not be prosecuted under the statute because the Café Au Go Go corporation was the owner of the club, and she had not managed, directed, or participated in any way with Bruce's performances. "[T]he only testimony here," Schwartz declared, "is that there was a [loudspeaker] near where she was standing [at the ticket booth on April 7]. There is…absolutely no testimony to connect her with the show or even with knowledge of the show, your Honor."

For his part, prosecutor Harris believed the State had met its burden on this point, when it introduced testimony from Patrolman Hahne that Bruce's monologue could be heard clearly from the area where Ella was posted, thus establishing her culpability. Judge Strong concluded that the facts favored the State: "As to the responsibility of the defendant, Ella Solomon, I cannot say how I would rule as a member of a trial bench, but for the purposes of this hearing I do find that the People have established sufficient [evidence] in connection with [her] responsibility."

Ephraim London offered three basic reasons (concurred in by Schwartz) why the complaint against Bruce should be dismissed. First, the New York obscenity statute was meant to *protect* performers like Lenny, insofar as it specifically exempted them. London pointed to the text of Section 1140-A; it explicitly declared that "this statute shall not apply" to anyone "participating in a performance merely as an actor." Surely, the exemption pertained to Lenny and his gigs at the Café Au Go Go. "The only evidence we have here," London reasoned, "is that Lenny Bruce appeared as an actor. He delivered the lines. And under the clear language of the statute, he is not within [it]." To the contrary, Harris maintained: by "actor," the statute envisioned a performer who recited material written or prepared by another. "[W]hat the legislature is speaking of," Harris told the court, "is someone who is performing a script, or a play, or a monologue at the behest of someone else, written by someone else….I think the evidence before this court makes it clear that Mr. Bruce was not an actor—'merely an actor,' in that sense." Here too, Judge Strong sided with the prosecution: "[I]t is my view that ['merely as an actor'] refers to persons who are…just hired to mouth the words which have been written by somebody else….[I]t is quite clear, at least *prima facially*, that the material was prepared by Mr. Bruce himself." By this definition, if someone else were to perform *verbatim* Lenny's transcribed gig, vulgarities and all, that person (unlike Lenny) would be exempt from prosecution. In other words, anybody but Lenny could perform his act.

London's next argument, his favorite, was a constitutional one. On its face, Section 1140-A was "clearly void." A violation under the statute was inextricably linked to "the corruption of the morals of youth or others"; this, London contended, was an impermissible standard for obscenity under a 1957 Supreme Court precedent. "The standard must be the average adult of the community," declared London. For the prosecution, the "morals of youth" proviso could be disregarded entirely. Judge Strong agreed, once again, with the State.

"Now let me come to the third point, and the most important one," London announced. "[T]here is nothing that was shown…that, under any stretch of the imagination, could be deemed obscene within the meaning of the law." Here was the distinguished First Amendment lawyer, seven years after Justice Brennan's *Roth* opinion, still litigating the knotty issue of the "schizophrenic" nature of "prurient interest." Did the talismanic phrase refer simply to lustful desires, as Albert Bendich had argued and Judge Horn had ruled in the 1962 San Francisco rendition of *People v. Bruce*? Or, rather, did the term include a shameful or morbid interest in sex, as Samuel Banks had argued and Judge Ryan had ruled in the 1963 Chicago rendition of *People v. Bruce*?

London directed the court's attention to *People v. Wendling*, a 1932 New York high court decision holding that coarse and vulgar language was not, in itself, obscene. For London, that precedent and others meant that only "hardcore pornography" could be regulated. "And God knows," he asserted, "there was nothing" that was said in Lenny's performances "that would arouse sexual desire in the normal average adult of this community." Predictably, Harris echoed the standard prosecutorial line: "prurient interest" was not limited to sexual arousal, but also included morbid curiosity about sex.

Ephraim London played his last card—another First Amendment claim derived from a liberal line in *Roth*. Lenny Bruce's performances of April 1 and 7, however prurient, still had "socially redeeming value" and, therefore, were beyond the pale of prosecution:

> *London*: What Mr. Bruce was talking about were things of genuine interest to the community....He was talking about the exploitation of tragedy, the commercial exploitation of tragedy...He was talking about the cruelty of fighting over the custody of children.
>
> And the mere fact that he uses language which other people consider coarse, which other people consider vulgar, can't possibly make what he said obscene.

Moreover, as if to bear witness to the soundness of his view, and thereby to foreclose any counterarguments, the proud London tendered his credentials:

> *London*: Now Your Honor, I must say that I speak with probably greater experience than any other attorney in the United States on

the question that I have been discussing...There is not the slightest doubt in my mind that any conviction...of this defendant, Lenny Bruce...for violating a law relating to indecency, or obscenity, couldn't possibly stand.

I would stake my reputation on that, Your Honor, and I think holding these defendants, under the proof that has been made out in this case, will only be putting the state to an expenditure which ultimately will be wasted—which must be wasted.

Staked though it was, London's reputation did not save Bruce from being put to the test. The *People v. Wendling* precedent was distinguishable, in the court's view, because it involved theatrical actors, not club performers. And, as for the big constitutional questions, the sixty-one-year-old, Harvard-educated jurist did not feel beholden to London's ostensible expertise. For Judge Frederick Longfellow Strong, his role was a modest one, largely inconsistent with striking down a state law. Accordingly, he punted: "This court will not pass upon the constitutionality of Section 1140-A of the Penal Law. That must be, if it is to be passed upon, must be done in a higher court."

The pretrial hearings were a bad omen. Kuh and Harris had defeated London and Schwartz on virtually every point. Three different judges had ruled against the defense on six different occasions on a variety of issues from tapes to prurient interest. To add injury to injury, the defense had no more success in securing a jury trial in the New York Supreme Court. "Where the results of the prosecution will involve a question of censors," London's motion stated, "the expression of the public judgment should come from the best expression of that judgment—the jury." This motion, too, was denied without opinion on May 13, 1964, by Justice Gerald P. Culkin. Until the U.S. Supreme Court struck down Section 40 of the New York City Criminal Court Act in 1970, misdemeanor trials were decided without a jury. Consequently, as was their right under that law, the defendants elected to have a three-judge panel, rather than the typical single-judge court.

All was not lost, however. The trial might still save Lenny. As in San Francisco, he might march out triumphantly and bathe in the media spotlight. He could be vindicated again. Still, after what had just transpired, Bruce might have felt like Adolf Eichmann in one of his bits: "He'll get the best trial in the world, Eichmann. *Ha!* They were shaving his leg while he was giving his [opening statement]."

The Sick Comedian

AS FATE HAD it, the defendants got their way on one of their requests—postponement of the trial—though not for any reason they had contemplated. On April 22, 1964, Lenny pled not guilty in the Trolley Ho prosecution before Judge Richard Schauer of the Los Angeles Municipal Court. The following day—the same day that the New York trial was to begin—Lenny played host for five hours to a surgeon's scalpel, until a rib was removed and his chest drained of fluid. Pleurisy had racked him with excruciating chest pain at his every breath. Its symptoms (swelling of the membranes lining the chest cavity and lungs, and fluid build-up in between) put him out of action and on his back, literally.

His stay at the Flower and Fifth Avenue Hospital was the semblance of an institutionalized nightclub act. Among the antics in Lenny's room was Tiny Tim penetrating the sterilized air with his signature warbling of "Tip-Toe Through the Tulips." Things got more uninhibited with each passing day, to the point that the staff complained. When Lenny sensed that the white coats and caps weren't hip to his frolics, he split—all the way back to his "House on the Hill." Indifferent to the enormous health risks he just had taken, he now began to recuperate at his two-storied glass-walled home situated near the summit of the Hollywood Hills.

There, gazing over the expanse of Los Angeles that sprawled between the extremes of sea and mountain, Lenny had time and energy enough to dream up promotional schemes. A little more than a month earlier, he was scheduled to appear as a guest on the Saint Patrick's Day broadcast of *The Steve Allen Show* to hawk his self-recorded/self-released album, *The Ballad of Dirty Lenny*. With an infomercial mindset, Bruce had expected that his friend Allen would introduce him with reference to the album, interview him about the album, and then display the album cover on camera along with mail order purchase information. Album, album, album—buy, buy, buy! Much to Bruce's chagrin, the filmed interview never aired. The official reason cited by the UPI: Lenny was bumped in favor of an interview with former President Harry S. Truman. The unofficial, behind-the-scenes reason was revealed in an exchange of letters between Bruce and several NBC executives: ostensibly, Lenny had demanded that his taped interview (replete with his album plugs) run unedited, but NBC would not honor the demand, for whatever reason. There being no meeting of the minds, NBC dropped the interview and the American public never saw the candid dialogue between Bruce and Allen.

Ever the capitalist, Lenny now fantasized about another promotional scheme, this one to raise money for his New York trial. He planned to run an advertisement in New York papers about another of his underground records, *Lenny Bruce Is Out Again*. The ad would invite readers to call a phone number and listen to his message:

> Hello there, this is Lenny Bruce. Get a pencil and write down what I'm going to tell you. Now don't lie to me and say you've written it down, like I do to the long-distance operator. I make believe I'm writing with my finger. Got the pencil? I've got a new record album, and it's called *Lenny Bruce Is Out Again*. If you want it, send $5.00 to my pad, 8825 Hollywood Boulevard, Los Angeles.

While Lenny took pains to publicize his new recordings and suffered pains to mend his fourteen-inch incision, his Los Angeles attorney Sydney Irmas was up to his neck in procedural briars—including demurrer, motion to dismiss, points and authorities, declaration, and discovery motion—concerning the Trolley Ho prosecution. Typically, the defense's efforts failed. It looked as if another *People v. Bruce* obscenity case would be set for trial *unless* a new judge saw the matter in a new light.

Bernard Steven Selber was that judge. Presiding over Criminal Division 21 of the Los Angeles Municipal Court, he heard Irmas's First Amendment motion to dismiss on May 21. (Lenny Bruce was not in court, as Syd had urged him to remain home and rest up.) It then fell on the shoulders of a twenty-six-year-old, Louisiana-born lawyer, who had worked as a deputy city attorney for only sixteen months, to legitimate what the LAPD had done at The Trolley Ho. Having met Sydney Irmas during the Bruce controversy, that D.C.A. would develop a deep professional and personal relationship with him. The lawyer was Johnnie L. Cochran Jr. (In time, "Syd became Johnnie's mentor," Irmas's widow Audrey recollected. "It got to the point where Johnnie used to tell people that he was my oldest son, and some were so naïve that they believed it.")

Complying with the court's discovery order, Cochran played the tape recording of Lenny's March 19 performance. Six months after President Kennedy died in Dallas, Judge Selber listened to Lenny belittle *Time* magazine's portrayal of Jacqueline Kennedy's heroism. And this against the backdrop of laughter. What kind of sick man was this? What kind of perverse audience could find humor in what the First Lady had done? But if the First Amendment couldn't protect an act like "Hauling Ass to Save Your Ass," what good was it?

Judge Selber asked Cochran for any additional evidence before he ruled on the constitutional motion. "No," the D.C.A. replied, "the words are clear and plain." The tape spoke for itself. The attorneys then tendered their arguments. Whereas Cochran urged the judge to entrust the issue of obscenity and community standards to the jury, Irmas pressed the court to do otherwise and to end the matter now. Relying on *Roth v. U.S.* and the California Supreme Court's decision in *Zeitlin v. Arnebergh* (1963), Judge Selber dismissed the case and ordered bail exonerated. "[F]ate and the First Amendment were against me this time," Cochran subsequently conceded.

Not since the San Francisco acquittal had Lenny been vindicated in any of his obscenity trials. It was a new morning. Was the light of the First Amendment finally beginning to shine on his comedy? Was this a sign of better things to come…in Los Angeles (Troubadour/Unicorn), Chicago (Gate of Horn), and now New York (Café Au Go Go)? Bruce was radiating. Sometime later, he dashed off a brief congratulatory note to Irmas, the *pescado grande* in his life. The beneficiary of Syd's talents, Lenny boasted that he was now spoiled. So much so that he could sneer at "Sheriffs' cars as they pass in the night." If the cops hassled him, he'd call Syd, his marvelous mouthpiece.

Of course, his luck could change if the City Attorney's office decided to appeal Judge Selber's ruling to the Appellate Department of the Superior Court. Slightly more than a week later, it did just that. The new morning had ended.

Poetic License

BACK IN MANHATTAN, Allen Ginsberg and his emergency committee had been mobilizing the campaign to save Lenny Bruce. Officially, they were the Committee on Poetry. Their general mission: "to promote freedom of expression where such expression is threatened by social prejudice or outside force..." Appropriately so, the Committee issued a press statement, and an accompanying petition, on behalf of Lenny Bruce.

Along with Ginsberg, two women played key roles in drafting and publicizing the documents. Helen Elliott (who had worked for MCA Records) had ties to celebs, while Helen Weaver had ties to literary figures. The trio lined up some one hundred luminaries to sign the petition on behalf of Lenny Bruce. The press release and petition, issued on Saturday, June 13, were perfectly timed for the Sunday papers. Moreover, both documents had been designed with great care. From the banner headline down through each and every paragraph, the charges were crafted with attentive nuance—announcing the literati's counteroffensive to the "rising tide" of intolerance.

The press release banner began:

ARTS, EDUCATIONAL LEADERS PROTEST USE OF NEW YORK OBSCENITY
LAW IN HARASSMENT OF CONTROVERSIAL SATIRIST LENNY BRUCE

Noted actors, publishers, editors, critics, writers, poets, and scholars all joined in the campaign proclaiming their opposition to censorship and their support of Lenny Bruce's First Amendment rights. Among the most famous names were: Woody Allen, James

Baldwin, Richard Burton, Bob Dylan, Lawrence Ferlinghetti, Dick Gregory, Irving Howe, Alfred Kazin, Max Lerner, Norman Mailer, Henry Miller, Reinhold Niebuhr, Paul Newman, Peter Orlovsky, Norman Podhoretz, Susan Sontag, William Styron, Elizabeth Taylor, Lionel Trilling, John Updike, and Gore Vidal. Try as he may, Ginsberg could not persuade Jack Kerouac, the poet and novelist best known for *On the Road*, to endorse the petition. Kerouac had little sympathy for Bruce, mainly because of the latter's attacks on religion.

The typed press release—issued on Committee on Poetry letterhead and sent to every paper in the nearby universe—described the fate that had recently befallen Lenny Bruce and the signatories' disapproval of his arrest: "Those signing the petition grant that Bruce uses four-letter words"—described in the petition as "vernacular"—"in his monologues, but they maintain that Bruce is a vital modern representative of the satirical tradition of Swift, Rabelais, and Twain."

The body of the petition—the "manifesto," as Richard Kuh tagged it—opened:

> We the undersigned are agreed that the recent arrests of nightclub entertainer Lenny Bruce by the New York Police Department on charges of indecent performance constitute a violation of civil liberties as guaranteed by the first and fourteenth amendments to the United States Constitution.
>
> Lenny Bruce is a popular and controversial performer in the field of social satire in the tradition of Swift, Rabelais and Twain. Although Bruce makes use of the vernacular in his nightclub performances, he does so within the context of his satirical intent and not to arouse the prurient interests of his listeners. It is up to the audience to determine what is offensive to them; it is not a function for the police department of New York or any other city to decide what adult private citizens may or may not hear.
>
> Whether we regard Bruce as a moral spokesman or simply as an entertainer we believe he should be allowed to perform free from censorship or harassment.

The Sunday papers took the bait: 100 FIGHT ARREST OF LENNY BRUCE, was how the *New York Times* headlined the story. The *New York Herald-Tribune* billed it this way: RALLYING TO DEFENSE OF LENNY BRUCE. And focusing on the Hollywood angle, the *New York Post's* banner announced: BURTONS JOIN PLEA FOR LENNY BRUCE. If Lenny Bruce's bust wasn't big news, the campaign to save him certainly was. Ironically, Bruce apparently cared as little for the petition as Kerouac, though not for the same reason. Lenny was suspicious of all icons, liberal ones included. According to his friend, Dick Schaap, he "thought that the petition...was ridiculous. He wanted nothing to do with it."

Unwilling to try his case in the press, Lenny was now set to try his case in court. On Monday, June 15, he walked out the door, went to the Los Angeles airport, boarded a plane, and flew east for 2,300 miles to New York.

7

THE COURTROOM OF THE ABSURD: NEW YORK, PART II

[O]ne gets the feeling of being present at an historical
event—the birth of the courtroom of the absurd.
                                        —*Stephanie Gervis Harrington*

Previous page: Lenny with (from left) Maurice Rosenfield, Howard Solomon, Herbert Monte-Levy, and Bentley Kassal after the Café Au Go Go obscenity bust

Standing Room Only

EQUAL AND EXACT JUSTICE TO ALL MEN
OF WHATEVER STATE OR PERSUASION.

That maxim is chiseled conspicuously on the edifice of the Manhattan Criminal Courts Building. It was the principle that, ideally, was to govern the prosecution of Lenny Bruce. Yet the trial had less to do with idealism than with the *realities* of courtroom justice, less to do with the logic of the law than with the *absurdities* of its execution. At times—and there were many of them—the trial seemed as if it had been scripted by Eugene Ionesco, one of the inventors of the Theater of the Absurd.

The site of the trial was an imposing gray tripartite tower of granite and glass located at 100 Centre Street, South Entrance. The towering triads were depressingly stark. Morning sun hardly touched the lifeless monolith, which was titled simply the "Criminal Courts Building." The building smacked less of compassionate justice than icy indifference. It had all the charm of Stalinesque architecture. The towers were something right out of Allen Ginsberg's "Howl," reminiscent of his poetic description of Moloch, the Canaanite idol to whom human sacrifices were made: "Moloch! Moloch! Nightmare of Moloch....Moloch the heavy judger of men....Moloch whose buildings are judgment!....Moloch whose eyes are a thousand blind windows." Moloch, this sphinx of cold cement.

Within that artless monument to justice, case docket Nos. A4406, A4407, A4623, and A4624 were called. The official title of the trial: *People of the State of New York—against—Lenny Bruce, Howard L. Solomon, and Ella Solomon.*

Public interest in Bruce's trial was running at such an unanticipated pitch that the case had been transferred from a small courtroom on one of the building's lower floors to 535, a larger courtroom generally reserved for felony hearings. To enter Courtroom 535, situated at the right-turn, cul-de-sac end of a long hall, one passed through silver metal doors with small windows and then through wooden doors, also windowed. Once beyond the metal and wood, one came into the chamber. High on three floor-to-ceiling inlaid panels behind the bench, in raised gold letters, was the proclamation "In God We Trust." (Later, reflecting on the absurdity of his trial, Lenny devilishly remarked that the adage should read "No Smoking.") Descending from the divine to the secular, the eye first glimpsed an American flag, a judge's gavel placed in the center of an elevated bench, and a square witness box situated on the left. Five pew-like rows of individualized bench seats lined both sides of the aisle, abutting the walls. The windows, on the right side as one entered, filtered sunlight with a smoke-like tint. There was not much more. The chamber—thirty-five feet long by twenty-five feet wide—bespoke of an impersonal order.

An "SRO" (Standing Room Only) sign was affixed to the door. The seventy-five spectators included members of the press, Bruce friends and foes, court watchers, and prospective witnesses. If nothing else, the air-conditioned atmosphere of the courtroom was a welcome relief from the sweltering heat and staggering humidity.

By any measure, it was absurd: a *misdemeanor* trial that began on June 16, 1964, did not end until December 21. In that six-month period, there were thirteen actual court days. The hearings filled more than sixteen hundred pages of trial transcript—this in addition to the five hundred or so pages from the pretrial hearings. There were a total of six criminal counts under Section 1140-A of the Penal Law: three against Bruce (two April 1 performances and one April 7 performance), two against Howard Solomon (the two April 1 shows), and one against Ella Solomon (the April 7 show). Thirty witnesses (twelve for the state and eighteen for the defense) would be called before it was over. The three defendants never took the stand. In the history of New York, this was the first prosecution concerning *spoken* words in a nightclub. Ironically, in this full-blown trial all about free speech, Lenny was often silenced by his own lawyers.

He wore his usual garb: a black Nehru-like tunic buttoned to the neck. As if to make a metaphorical gesture, Lenny removed his rose-tinted sunglasses from his heavily pouched eyes when he entered the room. The newly bearded thirty-eight-year-old comedian was either physically or philosophically exhausted, or both; at times, his eyes drooping and his hands clasped, he seemed to be sleeping or meditating.

The bailiff called the court to order—with all the commotion, the courtroom was in need of it—as the three black-robed jurists filed in and walked up the three steps leading to the bench. They would witness in the months ahead the expertise and machinations of some of New York's finest lawyers. But there would also be comically absurd moments, as when Ephraim London committed a Freudian slip and referred to his client as "Mr. Crotch," or when Richard Kuh insisted on comparing the "shit" in Henry Miller's *The Tropic of Cancer* with the "shit" in Lenny's monologues. The court contributed its own measure of absurdity, as when Chief Justice Murtagh suggested that "I could ask the witness whether a bicycle has literary merit," or when he averred that he had never heard a single foul word during his four-year stint in the Army

JUSTICE JOHN MARTIN Murtagh, administrative judge of the New York City Criminal Court, was a white-haired, blue-eyed, ruddy-cheeked fifty-three-year-old. He had a reputation for being a hardworking and dedicated public servant, though in 1950 he found himself at the center of a major graft and corruption investigation. Ultimately, the New York County grand jury found that the charges against him could not be sustained. For years thereafter, he went about his duties in his characteristically solemn and controlled way. Nothing too visible, nothing too controversial. Just the day-in and day-out work with prosecutors, defense lawyers, and the criminally accused. Even so, he was not your typical Catholic New York judge.

In 1957, Justice Murtagh called for the legalization of prostitution. "Moral offenses, such as prostitution, that do not under most circumstances militate against the common good, should not be part of the criminal law," he argued. More generally, Murtagh believed that it was "stupid to attempt to legislate morality." Preserving the moral order of society "is the business of the home, the school, and the church—but not of the state..." For that reason he was quite outspoken against "any system of police espionage and entrapment" having to do with the enforcement of morality. Consistent with that view, he felt that the very existence of a "vice squad...is an immorality and a shame." All of this and more he set out in his book *Cast the First Stone*, coauthored with sociologist Sara Harris.

Apparently, Justice Murtagh believed that "[a]ttempts by the State to enlarge its authority and invade the individual conscience, however high-minded, always fail and frequently do positive harm." Not since Clayton Horn in San Francisco could Lenny have imagined a sitting state judge with such open-minded beliefs about life, law, and freedom. Murtagh, it would seem, was an ideal judge to preside over *People v. Bruce*. As the jurist who would assume the dominant role among the three, he was just the man to set things straight again.

The Missouri-born Justice James Randall Creel graduated from both Harvard College and Harvard Law School. After serving as a federal prosecutor for the Southern District of New York, he began his judicial career in the Court of Special Sessions in the late 1940s. The portly and graying fifty-nine-year-old Justice Creel would intervene in the proceedings occasionally with a question or comment.

Justice Kenneth M. Phipps was the most amiable, and the least likely to say anything. He was also the most unpredictable of the three judges. He was one of the few people of color in the courtroom. Forty-seven at the time, Phipps had served on the Criminal Court since 1958, a Mayor Robert Wagner appointee. Before that, he was a politician, having served in the state assembly for four years. As far as his judicial reputation was concerned, the Lenny Bruce trial was overshadowed by another free speech trial over which he presided during the Bruce trial. It seems that some overzealous motion picture press agents had circulated fliers announcing that a "murder will be done" on a certain date at Sixth Avenue and 53rd Street. When murder-day arrived, the police were out in force, only to discover that it was all a publicity stunt. The movie agents were arrested and charged with disorderly conduct. The matter came before Justice Phipps. He suspended the sentence, but only after "bawling out" the two defendants. In other words, he had an equitable streak in him.

Two other things about Justice Phipps. First, he was always mindful of the sensitivities of the presiding justice, and would monitor his behavior accordingly. For example, "[w]henever he felt like laughing" during the Bruce trial, "he would swivel in his chair so his back was to Murtagh and he would cover his mouth with his hand." Second, he would die within four years of the Bruce trial's ending; before he died, however, he offered a purported "confession" about his vote.

Whatever the bent of the bench, Lenny was miffed that he had been denied a jury trial. "Don't you see?" he complained. "It's a part of the conspiracy. Deny him a jury trial. Fuck him." He was also concerned about the ethnic makeup of the bench: "Why is it I never get a Jewish judge?" (The fact is that Albert Axelrod, one of the judges in Lenny's first San Francisco obscenity trial, was Jewish.) Horn, Ryan, and now Murtagh, Creel, and Phipps—all goyish judges. Though it may have been no consolation to Lenny, at least his prosecutor, Richard Kuh, was Jewish-born.

Burt Lancaster for the Prosecution

"YOU'VE GOT TO watch that guy," Lenny warned. "He's a good street fighter; and you got to remember, he's in court *every* day. He's *always* in shape." That's how Bruce sized up his prosecutor. Reporters at the trial described Kuh as having an "athletic build and ram-rod stiff posture," a "year-round tan," a "gleaming white-toothed smile," a "nervous energy" impelling his "brisk movements," a "shrillness that enters his voice when he raises it," and a "righteous glare."

When Jules Feiffer saw the tall, dark-haired, firm-jawed Kuh for the first time, he exclaimed, "My God, he's Burt Lancaster."

At the outset, Kuh did not see *People v. Bruce* as likely "to last as much as a day." For him, this was an open-and-shut case. No need for expert witnesses, no need for documentary evidence by literary and social critics, no need for memoranda on points of law, no need for much preparation time—and definitely no need for defense delays. Nor was there a need for trial judges to agonize over First Amendment questions; the court followed Kuh's advice to leave such esoteric issues to the appeals process and summarily overruled London's motion to dismiss the case because the obscenity statute was unconstitutional on its face. It was a simple case. From the defense perspective, however, such simplicity and "fast-forward justice" would only work to the prosecution's advantage.

To prove his simple case, the prosecutor's basic strategy was three-fold: 1) to establish that, as owners or managers of the Café Au Go Go, the Solomons knowingly produced obscene performances; 2) to establish the reliability of the subpoenaed tapes of the Café shows; and 3) to establish that Lenny Bruce's monologues were obscene because of the vulgar language and dirty gestures. Kuh's case-in-chief relied on seven witnesses, virtually all police or licensing agents. Had the defense lawyers not asked so many irksome questions of his witnesses, this stage of the trial might have ended on the same day that it began. As it turned out, it spilled over to the afternoon of June 17.

In the eyes of the law, Ella and Howard Solomon were as culpable as Lenny Bruce if, as owners or managers of the Café Au Go Go, they *knowingly* put on obscene entertainment. The two were not the formal owners of the club; as the pretrial proceedings had determined, ownership lay in the corporation. Even so, Kuh aimed to demonstrate that, as corporate officers or managers of the club, the Solomons were aware of what they were offering to the public.

Prosecutor Kuh called Patrolman O'Neil to recount his visit with Howard Solomon. As O'Neil first told the grand jury and then Judge Strong, Howard boasted of his familiarity with Lenny's gigs. Ella's complicity hinged on what she was able to hear the night of April 7 while she was sitting behind the curtain that divided the entry from the performing area. Officer Hahne testified that he saw Ella in the foyer and heard Bruce's monologue clearly from that spot. On cross-examination, Allen Schwartz established little more than what had been argued unsuccessfully at the pretrial hearings.

For the Solomons, then, if Kuh had won the day on these points, they were that much closer to losing their club license and their liberty. What stood between them and that fate would only be the legality of Lenny's act.

Inspector Herbert Ruhe was Kuh's key witness. The prosecution depicted Lenny's performance by filtering it through the lens of Ruhe's testimony. It was Ruhe doing Lenny, but in a selective and salacious fashion. He recreated several of Bruce's bits by way of his notes, which consisted mainly of such "fine words" as "bullshit," "fuck you," "ballbreakers," "mind your asses," "*schmuck*," "asshole," and "fag man." This portrayal, this concentration of filth, was offered as the essential Lenny Bruce. If first impressions mattered, Ruhe's performance was significant. It *defined* the acts to be judged.

"This guy is bumbling, and I'm going to jail," Lenny protested. "He's not only got it all wrong, but now he thinks *he's* a comic. I'm going to be judged on *his* bad timing, *his* ego, *his* garbled language." What was for Lenny an artistic abortion was for Ephraim London and Allen Schwartz no less than a constitutional infraction. Ruhe's notes and testimony were fatally incomplete, and in no way captured Bruce's performance "taken as a whole." After London initiated this line of attack, Schwartz developed it:

> *Schwartz*: I refer to page five of [your notes]....Here follows, "some philosophical claptrap about human nature"....Is that something that Mr. Bruce said?
>
> *Ruhe*: That's a conclusion here....
>
> *London*: [Y]ou are not suggesting, sir...that your notes...[were] a true and full report of Mr. Bruce's monologue, [are] you?
>
> *Ruhe*: [T]hey were annotations containing key words, relevant to Mr. Bruce's monologue....
>
> *Schwartz:* When you testified this morning with respect to the April 1 performance and you used your notes to refresh your

recollection…did that…constitute, as you remember it, the substance and bulk of Mr. Bruce's monologue of April 1?"…

Ruhe: To the best of my ability.…

London: I would like to move to strike Mr. Ruhe's testimony.…What we have is a concentration on the parts that were considered by him objectionable. The references to such things as philosophical reflections are dismissed in a single line. The references to dogma and hypocrisy [are] dismissed in the same way. Remarks on semantics summarized by a word, whereas all the discussions that he considered objectionable are related at great length, so that you have a gross distortion of Mr. Bruce's monologue.…

Murtagh: Motion denied.

This ruling was significant. Ruhe's testimony was the only evidence that the prosecution had at the time concerning the April 1 midnight performance. (The police's Microfon recording was largely inaudible, and Kuh doubted the authenticity of the tape Schwartz tendered as the account of the show.) Justice Murtagh's judgment made it possible for the State's counts to stand against Lenny and Howard for that performance.

Ruhe also testified—to the great surprise of Bruce and London— that Lenny had engaged in obscene *conduct*. "Bruce moved the microphone backwards and forwards for a few minutes, something like this," Ruhe asserted, simulating a masturbatory act, "and made a remark something like, 'Don't you get up on me.'" Later, when describing the *Saint Paul* bit, Ruhe claimed: "[H]e was making a gesture towards his crotch, giving up fucking." These allegations, if not rebutted, complicated Lenny's defense; under First Amendment law, speech is typically entitled to more protection than conduct.

Turning to Martin Garbus, Lenny panicked: "That's it! That's the trick! That's how they're going to get me, Martin." He continued, "I would never do anything like that—I know better. It's one thing to talk about tits and asses. But to show how to jerk off—they'd put me away for life." Garbus reassured him that these assertions would not go unchallenged when the defense put on its case.

As the state wound down its case-in-chief, the prosecutor introduced the transcripts and tapes of Lenny's April 1 (ten P.M.) and April

7 performances. Unlike the April 1 (midnight) performance, for which there was no tape, these two shows were aired for the court. In a disadvantaged way, Lenny was doing his latest gigs at the Criminal Court of the City of New York. Room 535 came alive, very much alive, as the spectators burst into laughter—including some junior members of the D.A.'s staff. Frank Hogan was livid. "What are you doing here?" he thundered, when he summoned them into the hallway. "Is there anyone here who doesn't have work to do? If so, tell me and I'll find things to do. I don't want to see you here again."

For a pinpoint in time, the gaiety was reminiscent of Ann's 440, Mr. Kelly's, and The Den at the Duane. But, in this venue, the only audience that mattered was the three black-robed men behind the bench. And they were not laughing. Besides, they were already "familiar" with Lenny's monologues—Richard Kuh and Inspector Ruhe had seen to that.

Where Do We Go from Here?

THURSDAY, JUNE 18, 1964, was a terrible day—another in a line of them, in fact. Having suffered through Inspector Ruhe's amateurish impersonation only the day before, Lenny woke up in physical pain. A relapse of his pleurisy, and he was back in the hospital. Ephraim London explained his client's condition to the court that morning. The trial was then recessed until June 30 to give Lenny time to recover.

On that same Thursday, the Illinois Supreme Court inflicted its own measure of pain. Lenny's conviction in the Chicago criminal court was upheld: 7 to 0. Not even Justice Walter Schaefer, the liberal who had granted Lenny's appeal bond, weighed in his favor.

The ten-page opinion by Justice Robert Underwood emphasized that Lenny's words and phrases were of "a vulgar and revolting nature." So, too, his repeated use of "motions indicating masturbation" was disgusting. Ruling that Lenny's act primarily appealed to "a morbid or shameful interest in nudity, sex, or excretion," the court reasoned that his free speech rights to discuss sexually oriented issues had not been compromised. "The problem here presented relates not to the ideas expressed by the defendant," Justice Underwood wrote, "but to the means used to express them." It was Lenny's choice of words and gestures on which the conviction turned: "[Illinois's obscenity law] is not restricted to that which is sexually stimulating, but may embrace that which is repulsive and disgusting." Here the court, unlike Judge Clayton Horn in San Francisco, embraced the interpretation of *Roth* that vulgarity was a subset of obscenity.

In addition, the Illinois justices rejected the argument that *Roth* protected material with *any* redeeming social importance. Rather, the court reasserted the prevailing rule in Illinois law of balancing a work's obscene aspects against any affirmative values. Notably, Justice Underwood's opinion had ignored virtually all of the powerful free speech, due process, and right to counsel arguments advanced in the Rosenfield-Kalven-Ming brief. Instead, the opinion tracked closely the reasoning of the state's brief.

SOME OF THE finest lawyers in the nation had not saved Lenny Bruce. In the early summer of 1964, it appeared that he was at the end of his legal rope. It looked like he was going to *jail* for a year...for using blue words and speaking ill of the pope. As if that weren't enough, now the Illinois precedent could be used against him in the New York obscenity trial.

Theoretically, Bruce had two remaining options.

First, he could petition the U.S. Supreme Court to review his Illinois Supreme Court case. At best, this was a long-shot, since such review is discretionary and rarely exercised. Moreover, given the procedural posture of Lenny's case, he would face the same problems in appealing constitutional questions to the U.S. Supreme Court that he had in petitioning the Illinois high court. Lenny was unlikely to get his long-imagined chance to "play before the Supremes."

His second option was almost as fanciful. He might hope that the Supreme Court would render a generous interpretation of the First Amendment in *Jacobellis v. Ohio*, an obscenity case that had been argued earlier that Court term and that was likely to be decided soon.

The issues raised in that case might well have a significant bearing on *People v. Bruce*. Even if this happened, there were still other obstacles. The Illinois Supreme Court would have to grant a petition for rehearing, and it would have to reverse its earlier ruling in light of *Jacobellis*. Given this chain of improbabilities, chances were good that Lenny would have to appear soon again before Judge Ryan and surrender himself to begin his one-year term in the Bridewell House of Correction.

ON JUNE 22, 1964, only four days after the Illinois high court had ruled against Bruce, a glimmer of light broke through the darkening clouds. The Supreme Court issued its judgment in *Jacobellis v. Ohio*. By a 6 to 3 vote, the justices determined that *The Lovers* was not an obscene film; accordingly, Nico Jacobellis's conviction for exhibiting it could not stand under the First Amendment.

Although there was a solid majority for the result, the six justices in the majority did not speak with one voice. Four separate opinions were issued to explain the decision: Justice Brennan (joined by Justice Goldberg) announced the judgment of the Court, and Justices Black (joined by Douglas), Stewart, and Goldberg wrote concurring opinions.

Whatever the finer differences among their arguments, the justices apparently coalesced around the following five points:

—An appellate court is not bound by the judgment of a trial court or jury, but must itself determine whether the material condemned as obscene is constitutionally protected.

—The *Roth* test for obscenity still governs: "whether to the average person, applying contemporary community standards, the dominant theme of the material taken as a whole appeals to prurient interest."

—Obscenity is excluded from constitutional protection only because it is "utterly without redeeming social importance." Thus, sexually oriented material that "advocates ideas or that has literary or scientific or artistic value or any other form of social importance" cannot be branded as obscene and denied free speech safeguards.

—Because material with *any* social importance is constitutionally protected, obscenity cannot be determined by "weighing" a work's social importance against its prurient appeal.

—The "contemporary community standards" aspect of *Roth* requires that the constitutional status of allegedly obscene material be determined on the basis of a national standard, and not a state or local community standard.

Ephraim London, the victorious appellate lawyer, had won a battle, but not the war. He did not persuade the Supreme Court to change the law of the land to the position that he held personally. The *Roth* test still stood, after all, and a majority had not adopted the more absolutist views of Justices Black and Douglas. But now, London could point to *Jacobellis* and fairly claim that a work with *any* socially redeeming value could not be obscene, that a balancing approach could not be used to determine obscenity, and that a national Constitution required the enforcement of national standards of value. All in all, that was no small feat, and London reinforced his reputation as an eminent First Amendment lawyer.

Furthermore, London's achievement provided real hope for Lenny Bruce. Now the U.S. Supreme Court's view of the First Amendment was more in line with the liberal approach taken by Judge Clayton Horn and ACLU attorney Albert Bendich that had saved Bruce in San Francisco. More important, *Jacobellis* refuted what the Illinois high court recently held in *People v. Bruce*. Essentially, the U.S. Supreme Court had validated several of the key arguments advanced by Rosenfield, Kalven, and Ming in their Illinois appellate brief. Hence, there was good reason to believe that the federal justices would review and reverse what the Illinois justices had declared.

And, what about the New York obscenity charges? What would be the impact of *Jacobellis* on them? Would it prompt Judge Murtagh and 's brethren to view the Bruce and Solomon cases in a far more sympathetic way? Would it persuade Assistant District Attorney Richard Kuh to reevaluate the constitutional wisdom of continuing these costly and protracted misdemeanor prosecutions?

Predictably, *The Village Voice*, which had followed the New York obscenity trial closely, speculated that *Jacobellis* would influence the proceedings in the defendants' favor. Reasonable minds could differ—at least in Richard Kuh's opinion. Then and thereafter (when he wrote *Foolish Figleaves?* in 1967), the lead prosecutor maintained that the "multiple and clashing opinions" of the *Jacobellis* Court "afforded little light by which a…prosecutor or trial judge might learn what was expected of him." Kuh challenged the view that *Jacobellis* either established a mandate for the "utterly without redeeming social importance" test or rejected a balancing approach for finding obscenity. Such a view, he argued, "mirrors the too common American temptation to escalate, and in so doing to distort sound and thoughtful small steps into dogma." Kuh's bottom-line: *Jacobellis* did not, should not, and would not affect the outcome of this case.

Only time would tell whether *Jacobellis v. Ohio* ultimately would save Lenny Bruce in his free speech struggles—whether in Chicago or New York.

Religions, Inc.

HOWEVER AMBIVALENT THE reactions of press and prosecutors to *Jacobellis*, one group—Operation Yorksville, an interfaith association with strong ties to New York's civic leaders—spoke out unambiguously and bitterly. Its mission: to wipe out smut shops, sex shows, and other pornographic activities in New York City and beyond. Its response to *Jacobellis*: "[R]eligious leaders of all faiths in all communities [must] stand together vociferously decrying the fact that the Court has presumed to recast the moral law."

In a tartly worded statement sponsored by Operation Yorksville, nine clergymen (from the Roman Catholic, Jewish, Mormon, and Protestant faiths) and the President of the New York Board of Trade voiced strong protest. They warned that *Jacobellis* (and the Supreme Court's accompanying decision in the *Tropic of Cancer*) "cannot be accepted quietly by the American People if this nation is to survive. Giving free rein to the vile depiction of violence, perversion, and illicit sex, and consequently to their performance, is an unerring sign of progressive decay and decline." Find a way as they must, they would not let this ruling stand—not without a fight, anyway.

In effect, *Jacobellis* fueled the fires of censorship that Operation Yorksville had been stoking for a while. Founded in October 1962 by Julius G. Neumann (an Orthodox rabbi), William T. Wood (a Jesuit Catholic priest), and Robert E. Wittenberg (a Lutheran minister), Operation Yorksville aimed to combat obscenity generally. Often, however, its spokesmen played up a favorite "hot-button" issue: protecting the youth from pornographic influences. While speaking before community groups, for example, its presenters commonly showed a thirty-minute film, entitled "Perversion for Profit," that featured three mothers displaying some choice examples of the "salacious literature" that might well fall into the hands of children.

Not long after its offices first opened at 44 East 84th Street, Operation Yorksville caught the attention of New York's highest officials. No doubt, the *New York Times* coverage of Monsignor Joseph McCaffrey's early May sermon—decrying "the disgrace that is Times Square," and calling for a "clean-up" crusade in light of the approaching World's Fair—energized City Hall. Shortly thereafter, on July 17, 1963, Mayor Robert F. Wagner advised the organization's secretary, the Jesuit Father Morton A. Hill, that the city would develop a four-pronged program to curb, and eventually eliminate, traffic in obscenity. The mayor pledged: 1) to create a full-time NYPD unit that would crack down on "hardcore" porn sales to minors; 2) to demand that city agencies enforce licensing controls on adult entertainment businesses; 3) to establish a special court for pornography cases; and 4) to request the cooperation of the district attorneys of the city's five boroughs in bringing the purveyors of smut to justice. Then, seemingly, inertia set ̄or months, nothing appeared to happen.

̄wo dramatic events succeeded in kick-starting Operation ̄ille's campaign once again. Following the suggestion of some of its members, Kathleen Keegan, a sixteen-year-old girl, entered Book-case Inc. (651 Lexington Avenue) in September of 1963. There, she purchased a copy of *Fanny Hill*. Although Kathleen did not read the book, her mother perused two pages—enough "to convince me it was horrible filth," Mrs. Keegan asserted. The bookstore owner, Irwin Weisfeld, and the clerk who sold Kathleen the book, John Downs, were charged with violating New York Penal Law 484-H, which had gone into effect only earlier that month. The criminal statute prohib-ited the sale to a person under eighteen years of age of any book that "exploits, is devoted to, or is principally made up of descriptions of illicit sex or sexual immorality."

Much more desperate was Operation Yorksville's strategy to speed things up at City Hall. On Sunday, October 28, Father Morton Hill announced during a sermon to his parishioners at the Church of Saint Ignatius that he had been surviving for two days on nothing but water, and that he would continue the "black fast" until Mayor Wag-ner took some decisive action on the four-point antipornography pro-gram that he had promised three months before. In a *New York Times* interview, reported the following day, Hill protested Mayor Wagner's failure to confront seriously the harms that pornographic literature inflicted on children: it "sows the idea of perversion that soon leads to experimentation and finally fixation," eventually culminating in sexual violence and narcotics use.

A *Times* reporter called the mayor's office that Monday evening for comments on Father Hill's protest fast. The night was not over before Mayor Wagner directed his deputy mayor, Edward F. Cavanagh Jr., to coordinate an antipornography drive and to arrange a meeting with Father Hill and his cohorts. This meeting, Wagner explained, would "make it plain that we want and welcome his help and the help of other religious and civil leaders in rooting out this evil." Informed of the mayor's change of heart, Father Hill happily sat down to his first meal in three days.

A series of moves and countermoves among antipornography and anticensorship forces—all played out on Tuesday, October 29—kept the New York press squarely focused on the politics of pornography. After first consulting with the leaders of Operation Yorksville, Deputy

Mayor Cavanagh scheduled a conference to be held the following Monday, at which city officials and clergymen would plan the course of action for an effective antismut campaign. Then, Cavanagh related to the newspapers that "all concerned" would be invited to the conference—police officials, judges, the five city district attorneys, and the heads of other appropriate city agencies.

Meanwhile, piqued by the headline-grabbing Father Hill, Ralph Ginzburg, the controversial publisher of erotica, was determined to snatch some press attention for the anticensorship cause. Still smarting from his June 14 conviction in a Philadelphia federal court for distributing obscene materials through the mails (then on appeal), Ginzburg announced that he would begin a hunger strike of his own. The editor and publisher of the suspended magazines, *Liaison* and *Eros*, railed against "the obscenity panic that is plaguing our city and the country." Ginzburg warned: "The number of obscenity cases in the courts of the country has increased alarmingly. We're really dealing with something akin to witchery."

Operation Yorksville had overcome the inertia of City Hall, but it soon enjoyed an equally sweet victory with the judiciary. On November 14, 1963, a three-judge panel of the New York City Criminal Court found Weisfeld and Downs of Bookcase Inc. guilty of a misdemeanor for having sold *Fanny Hill* to the young Miss Keegan. The court's opinion was authored by Justice Benjamin Gassman, a short and fleshy man known as a no-nonsense conservative, an avid reader of Talmudic and legal scholarship, who could not be bothered with ribald fiction. "It was due to our judicial duty rather than to idle curiosity that we read this book," Justice Gassman declared. His judgment rang with the tones of a harsh literary critic: "While it is true that the book is well written, such fact does not condone its indecency. Filth, even if wrapped in the finest packaging, is still filth." All this was music to the ears of Operation Yorksville's secretary, Father Hill. "This decision is a recognition that the policy of 'anything goes' is not the community standard of the United States," Hill exclaimed. "By this decision one basic objective of Operation Yorksville has been attained."

The momentum of New York's antiobscenity crusade accelerated steadily throughout 1964—before, during, and after the Lenny Bruce trial. Only two weeks prior to Lenny Bruce's arrests at the Café Au Go Go, the rafters of the New York Statler-Hilton Hotel resounded with the condemnation of "homegrown leftist individuals" responsible for "cesspool publications." The occasion was the annual communion breakfast of the Sons of Xavier; the featured speaker was Dr. William P. Riley, president of the New York State chapter of Citizens for Decent Literature. Before a riveted audience, Dr. Riley charged the American Civil Liberties Union, Ralph Ginzburg of *Eros* magazine, and Hugh Hefner of *Playboy* (all three, of course, were Lenny Bruce defenders) as "people who want to destroy the Judeo-Christian concepts upon which the world has been built."

Moreover, six days before the Bruce obscenity trial began in Courtroom 535, the Roman Catholic Archbishop of New York, Cardinal Francis Spellman, called on the city's officials to establish a "citizens' commission"—involving political, business, labor, educational, and religious leaders—to halt a "powerhouse of perversion." Speaking at Fordham University's graduation exercises, Spellman cautioned that "more than sporadic raids" on "shops and newsstands that feature filth" were necessary to counteract pornography's "assault on our youth…destroying those virtues which will keep America strong."

Cardinal Spellman would have his way. Reacting once again to mounting pressure, on August 6, Mayor Wagner named a twenty-one-member "Citizens' Anti-Pornography Commission" to direct the city's existing campaign against obscenity. The Mayor himself would serve as chair, Deputy Mayor Cavanagh as vice-chair, and prominent civic, business, labor, and publishing leaders as members. With its first meeting scheduled for September 9, the commission would "seek ways to work within existing statutes to spur court considerations of pornography cases and…work closely with prosecuting agencies in such cases," the deputy mayor explained. That same evening, speaking at a Denver convention of the Fraternal Order of Eagles, Spellman complimented city hall for "acceding to our request" in creating such a commission.

In contrast to Deputy Mayor Cavanagh, there was at least one city official who believed that no effective antiobscenity war could be waged under existing state laws. That man was Assistant District

Attorney Richard H. Kuh. On September 21 (in the lull between the Bruce trial and the criminal court's judgment), Kuh testified to his convictions in public hearings before the New York State Legislative Committee on Obscene Publications. To pass judicial scrutiny, Kuh argued, new obscenity legislation was necessary—a statute "limit[ed] to commercial distribution" of materials deemed obscene and "utiliz[ing] language that is highly specific in declaring just what is to be taboo." Explaining his recommendations to the committeemen assembled in the State Office Building at 270 Broadway, the assistant D.A. observed: "We're living in a decade of changing sexual mores and I think the courts' attitudes reflect that change." Kuh advised lawmakers to distinguish between the freedoms of adults and children, but added that the law still should impose some limits on the obscenity to which adults might be exposed. Moreover, Kuh urged a speedier appeals process for those convicted under a new statute; at present, far too many were back on the streets without serving sentences, because their artful attorneys had delayed their appeals.

All things considered, the record is quite clear. In the years preceding and following the Bruce trial, New York City was a feverish hotbed of antiobscenity activity. The excitable clamor of religious authorities shook the halls of political leaders; and the mayor issued multiple directives to the city's district attorneys and licensing agencies to strike out against the venues of erotica.

Martin Garbus and others speculated that the political pressure exerted by Francis Spellman and the clergymen of Operation Yorksville directly influenced the obscenity prosecution of Lenny Bruce. "[Frank] Hogan was an esteemed member of New York's archdiocese," Garbus reasoned, "and I suspected that he and his close friend Cardinal Spellman were more deeply offended by Bruce's frequent references to the church and religious hypocrisy than by the words he used." For Richard Kuh (speaking years later), this was nonsense: "There was never a more independent public official than Frank Hogan," Kuh asserted. "Nobody, be it the cardinal [or any other religious leader], could tell Frank Hogan what can be done." And news of Bruce's prior obscenity arrests "would not have forced my hand or Frank Hogan's hand."

Lenny with his reel-to-reel tape-recording paraphernalia

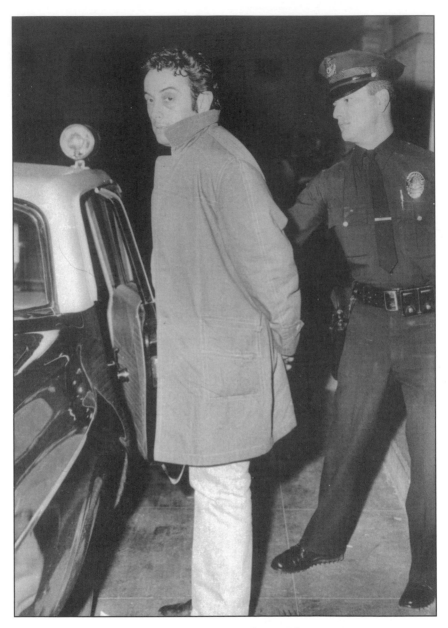

Lenny being booked on a narcotics charge, February 22, 1963

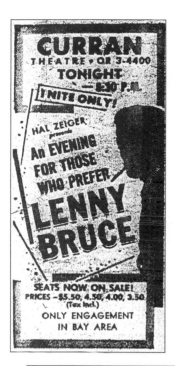

Above: Lenny takes the stand before Judge Clayton Horn in his San Francisco obscenity trial.

Left: A newspaper ad for Lenny's November 19, 1961, Curran Theatre concert in San Francisco

Lenny and Albert Bendich (left) in court at the San Francisco trial, preparing their defense with the aid of Lenny's performance tapes

Lawrence Ferlinghetti, publisher of
Howl and owner of City Lights
Bookstore

Seymour Fried, Lenny's first lawyer
in the San Francisco obscenity trial

The San Francisco Chronicle's *front page announcing Lenny's acquittal by a jury*

Strip City, the L.A. burlesque club where Lenny developed his act in the 1950s. Owner Maynard Sloate is seated in the convertible on the right.

Doug Weston, owner of The Troubadour

Herb Cohen, owner of The Unicorn coffeehouse

Maynard Sloate, handling the rim shots for Sonny Bartlett, a dancer at Strip City

Lenny with (from left to right) Eric Miller, the guitarist who accompanied Lenny in "How to Relax Your Colored Friends at Parties," Paul Krassner, Lenny's friend and editor, and Jack Sobel, one of Lenny's managers

Richard Hecht, a prosecutor who advised Sheriff Sherman Block on whether or not Lenny's act at The Troubadour was obscene

Ronald Ross, Lenny's prosecutor in his Troubadour/Unicorn trial

*Burton Marks, Lenny's defense lawyer for the Troubadour/Unicorn trial,
photographed with an unidentified woman in 1960*

*Sydney Irmas, Lenny's
lawyer for his Trolley
Ho obscenity case*

*A young Johnnie L.
Cochran Jr., Lenny's
prosecutor for the
Trolley Ho bust*

*Bernard S. Selber,
the judge who presided
over Lenny's Trolley Ho
hearing and dismissed
the case against him*

Above: George Carlin, Lenny's friend, performing in the early 1960s. Carlin was busted with Lenny at Chicago's The Gate of Horn.

Left: Lenny shakes hands with Gate of Horn owner Alan Ribback after they were both arrested for obscenity during Lenny's December 5, 1962, show.

Judge Daniel J. Ryan, who
presided over Lenny's Chicago
obscenity case, which became known
as the Ash Wednesday Trial

Earle Warren Zaidins, Lenny's lawyer for
his Gate of Horn obscenity trial in Chicago

Two of Lenny's Illinois appellate lawyers,
Professor Harry Kalven Jr. (left) and Maurice Rosenfield

William R. Ming Jr. (standing), Lenny's third Illinois appellate lawyer

*Don Friedman, who produced
Lenny's historic 1961
Carnegie Hall concert*

*Bentley Kassal, the Café Au
Go Go's business attorney*

Frank Hogan, the longtime New York district attorney who ran the D.A.'s office during Lenny's New York obscenity trial

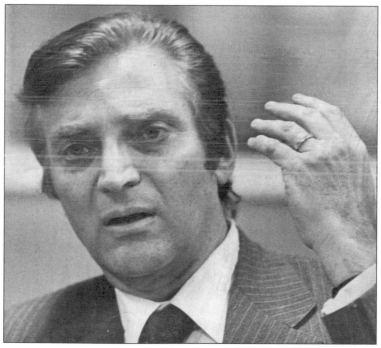

Richard H. Kuh, the New York assistant D.A. who aggressively prosecuted Lenny, and was haunted by it ten years later in his own bid for the district attorney's office

Ephraim London, Lenny's lead counsel for his New York obscenity trial, at a press conference in his office, June 28, 1962

Martin Garbus, one of Lenny's New York defense attorneys

Allen G. Schwartz, the former Manhattan assistant D.A. who defended the Solomons in the Café Au Go Go obscenity trial

John M. Murtagh (right), the presiding justice in Lenny's New York trial, being sworn in as chief magistrate by New York Mayor William O'Dwyer in 1950

100 FIGHT ARREST OF LENNY BRUCE

Arts Leaders Protest, Citing Violation of Free Speech

By THOMAS BUCKLEY

Nearly 100 persons prominent in the arts charged yesterday that the arrest here of Lenny Bruce for indecency violated Constitutional guarantees of free speech.

The text of the statement and the list of signers was released yesterday by the Committee on Poetry, an organization established to protest legal repression of creative activities. It is headed by Allen Ginsberg, the poet.

The entertainer was arrested in April while performing at a Greenwich Village café. A grand jury had handed up a true bill charging that his act was obscene after hearing a tape recording made by plainclothes men.

He is now at his home in Los Angeles, where a similar charge against him was dismissed last week. Mr. Bruce has also been arrested for obscenity in Chicago and in other cities for the asserted possession of drugs.

The 38-year-old performer, who is decribed in the statement as a social satirist "in the tradition of Swift, Rabelais and Twain," uses not only the four-letter words but also the less-frequently heard 10-letter and 12-letter ones in his monologues on religion, the civil rights fight and the battle of the sexes.

'Intended as Satire'

Acknowledging this, the

and Dwight Macdonald, the critic and social historian.

Novelists who signed the statement were Norman Mailer, James Jones, William Styron, Terry Sothern, Harvey Swados, John Updike, Gore Vidal, Joseph Heller, Henry Miller, Elizabeth Hardwick and James Baldwin.

Among the poets were Lawrence Ferlinghetti, John Hollander, Cecil Hemley, Kenneth Koch, Robert Lowell and Peter Orlovsky.

Professor Trilling said he had never attended one of Mr. Bruce's performances but had read transcripts of them. He said that he was most interested in defending the principals of free speech and that he found Mr. Bruce "a very remarkable and pointed satirist."

'Impressed and Depressed'

Mr. Beichman said that he was both "impressed and depressed" by Mr. Bruce, but that this view was irrelevant, as was any judgment as to whether it was necessary for the comedian to use language that is still seldom heard in mixed company.

"I just don't think the police should be impowered to censor words," he said. "It's a matter of principle. For me, there hasn't been a comedian since W. C. Fields."

Mr. Macdonald said he was not so much concerned with the free-speech issue as with the fact that Mr. Bruce's monologues provided "what is genuinely a criticism of our society."

"He uses rough language, but he uses it in a witty, sophisticated and parodic way," he said.

Dr. Niebuhr, reached by telephone at his summer home in Stockbridge, Mass., said that he had signed the statement after hearing about the case from close friends.

"I have never seen Mr. Bruce

Above: Edward de Grazia, counsel for Lenny's §1983 civil rights actions

Left: June 14, 1964, story in the New York Times about Allen Ginsberg's petition protesting Lenny's arrest

William Kunstler, the radical lawyer who once shot heroin with Lenny, was another of Lenny's New York legal advisors.

Nat Hentoff, a friend and one of Lenny's defense witnesses in his New York trial

A newspaper ad for Lenny's 1966 Music Box engagement arranged by Phil Spector

*A poster for Lenny's last concert put on by rock promoter Bill Graham in June 1966
at San Francisco's Fillmore Auditorium*

Bridge:
An Unusual Race Develops For the Mott-Smith Trophy

By ALAN TRUSCOTT

In each spring National Championship, the player with the best performance, measured in master points, receives the Geoffrey Mott-Smith trophy. In Vancouver, British Columbia, last week, an unusual race developed for the honor.

Anyone who flas with one major event and finish second in another is very likely to capture the Mott-Smith. Yet Ron Andersen of Parsippany, N.J., went into the last day knowing that two seconds and a first might not be enough. He had won the men's teams, finished second in the open pairs, and was in the final of the Vanderbilt Cup. But if he failed to win the Vanderbilt, he was likely to be overtaken by Barry Crane of Los Angeles, who had piled up some 250 points by winning the Open Pairs and scoring heavily in secondary events.

As it turned out, Andersen did not win the Vanderbilt, but he did win the Mott-Smith Trophy, because Crane scored relatively poorly in his final event.

An Excellent Start

However, this gave Crane an excellent start in defending his McKenney Trophy title, which goes to the player earning most master points in a year. His signature style is illustrated by the diagramed deal from the Swiss teams in Vancouver, which he won, teamed with Fred Hamilton of Nassau, Ira Rubin, Kerri Shuman of Los Angeles, and Bob Kehoe of Natick, Mass.

In standard bidding methods, North would respond to one no-trump with a Stayman two clubs, planning to raise hearts if permitted and otherwise to bid two no-trump. But Crane has his own bidding ideas, and two no-trump is such a sequence would not be involutional.

The direct two no-trump raise by Mrs. Shuman as North was invitational, but did not deny a major suit. Crane as South might have passed, but chose to accept the strength of his double on the strength of his four aces. He threw in three forcing spade trick—hoping for a three-diamond bid simply and that she had at least one of the major suits, and South led spades and East's little to finish the same.

The contract is a shaky one, but Crane brought it home. After an opening club

NORTH
♠ 7 6
♡ Q 10 3 2
♦ K 10 8 4
♣ Q 9 7 5

WEST
♠ K 10
♡ 10 6 4
♦ A J 8 3
♣ 8 4 3 2

EAST
♠ Q 9 8 4 3
♡ K 6
♦ 10 7 2
♣ J 2 8

SOUTH (D)
♠ A J 5 2
♡ A 9 8 5
♦ 9 5 3
♣ A 10

Both sides were vulnerable. The bidding:

South	West	North	East
1 ♠	Pass	2 N.T.	Pass
3 ♣	Pass	3 ◇	Pass
3 ♠	Pass	3 N.T.	Pass
Pass	Pass		

West led the club six.

lead, he captured East's jack with the ace. He then led a low spade, conceding a trick to West's ten. Another club lead was taken by dummy's king, and the heart queen was led, covered by the king and taken by the ace.

The contract could now have been made by finessing against West's heart ten, since the club nine can be established in the dummy by a club ruff. But Crane found an ingenious line that required much less help from the gods of distribution. At the fifth trick, he made the key play of the diamond king, which West was forced to allow. After a diamond return to dummy's queen, the heart jack was led, forcing West's ten to the master trump. The position was now this:

NORTH
♠ 7
♡ 3 2
♦ 10
♣ 9 7

WEST
♠ K
♡ —
♦ A 8
♣ 8 4

EAST
♠ Q 9 8 4
♡ —
♦ —
♣ Q

SOUTH
♠ J
♡ 9 8
♦ 9
♣ 10

Crane had five tricks at this point, and he proceeded to make five more. He ruffed a club, establishing dummy's nine, cashed two spade tricks and led a spade for a ruff. West discarded a club, and then another ruff established his remaining diamond. West actually refused to ruff, so South ruffed a diamond and played another spade. East discarded his club and dummy made the last three.

Argentine's Art Collection Sold At Sotheby's for $4.7-Million

Special to The New York Times

LONDON, April 2 — Thirty-four French 19th-century and 20th-century tapestries and drawings, owned by Antonio Santamarina of Argentina were auctioned here tonight for a total of £1,973,000 ($4,725,000). The bidding generally was high, and a Daumier, a Delacroix, a Sisley and a Toulouse-Lautrec fetched record prices.

Earlier in the day the Argentine Government had sought a postponement of the sale, holding that the collection had left Argentina illegally. An Argentine Embassy spokesman said that a "letter of request" from a judge in Buenos Aires had been sent to the high court here, seeking a bill for duty. However, in English jurisdictions can be granted only where plaintiffs can show they are likely to suffer damage or be prejudiced by a future act. This did not apply because the court felt no obligation to issue the Argentine Government and no claim title to the works.

The catalogue for the sale did not name Mr. Santamarina, but described the collection as formed by one person between 1895 and 1920. "Mr. Santamarina is a 88-year-old cattle rancher.

Top price paid tonight was £280,000 ($670,000) for a Toulouse-Lautrec painting of a circus ring. It is called "Au Cirque Fernando: Ecuyere sur un Cheval Blanc," and was painted in 1888. It was bought by a London dealer, Colnaghi's, for $504,000. This is a record for a Toulouse-Lautrec, the previous high being $230,000, paid in 1970.

Alfred Sisley's "L'Inondation à Port-Marly," a flood scene dated 1876, brought a record price of $288,000. The previous high for a Sisley was $220,000.

An American identified at 50: Laing, gave $340,000 for Edgar Degas's pastel and charcoal drawing of ballerinas.

A painting by Pierre-Auguste Renoir executed in 1876 was sold to Colnaghi's for $300,000. It depicts four of Renoir's friends at his studio, including the painter Camille Pissarro.

Pissarro's limpid river scene "L'Eclure à Pontoise," of about 1869, was bought for a private collector in Italy for $254,400. The record price of $150,000 was paid for a painting "Christ Descends au Tombeau" by Eugène Delacroix. Martin Mitchelson, a Beverly Hills lawyer, paid a record $144,000 for a famous drawing by the Italian futurist Giacomo Balla. This is in water-color.

LENNY BRUCE ARRESTED!

Ten years ago today, April 3, 1964, Lenny Bruce was arrested at the Café au Go Go in Greenwich Village for violating a statute against "any obscene, indecent, immoral or impure . . . show or entertainment." Mr. Richard H. Kuh, who is now District Attorney of New York County and who was then an Assistant District Attorney, was the prosecutor. After trial the court imposed a four month jail sentence—warranted, in Mr. Kuh's opinion, because Bruce "has shown by his conduct complete lack of any remorse whatsoever."* Forbidden to work as a satirist, and unable to support himself, Lenny Bruce died on August 13, 1966. The criminal court's decision was reversed on appeal eighteen months later.

Mr. Kuh's actions during the course of the Bruce prosecution, and his own published account and present commentary on those actions, raise serious questions about his capacity to properly fill the office of District Attorney in 1974. Consider:

Mr. Kuh's Role: Prosecutor or Persecutor?

In his book, *Foolish Figleaves?* (1967) Mr. Kuh takes pains to assign responsibility for the arrest not to "the police," but to a duly constituted grand jury: ". . . the first Bruce arrest was made, not by police acting upon their own judgment but pursuant to court-ordered warrants, after a grand jury had acted" (emphasis in the original). Mr. Kuh does not inform us, however, of the realities of grand jury procedure. A grand jury is impanelled to hear a variety of cases, and it is the District Attorney and staff, and they alone, who decide which cases are serious enough to merit grand jury scrutiny. The prosecutor has unlimited discretion in the selection of cases, and is under no obligation to try any such every case, merely because a statute is violated (for example, no District Attorney would dream of prosecuting a case of adultery, or bingo playing in church, although statutes against both practices are firmly entrenched in the books). The crucial fact to ponder is that Mr. Kuh decided that the Bruce case was eminently worthy of grand jury presentation and prosecution: the prosecution was his choice, not his obligation. And it was a choice bitterly regretted by one of his fellow Assistant District Attorneys, who was later to say: "We all knew what we were doing. We used the law to kill him."

As artists and art professionals, we are persuaded that the "search and destroy" mentality exemplified by Mr. Kuh as Assistant District Attorney in 1964 is impossible to reconcile with the fairness, balance, and respect for individual artistic liberties essential to the office of District Attorney in 1974.

Mr. Kuh as Art Critic

In his prosecution of Bruce, Mr. Kuh must have been aware that any "social importance" or "artistic merit" in the satirist's performance would protect him against the charge of obscenity. Assuming an unaccustomed role—the Prosecutor as Art Critic—Mr. Kuh sought to erode the defense's claim that Bruce was, indeed, an artist, and that what his opponents found most objectionable was not so much his random scattering of "vulgar" epithets, but, rather, his merciless political and religious satire. In his own account of the trial, Mr. Kuh quotes himself—approvingly, one supposes—as having questioned the artistic component of Bruce's satire in exchanges with various defense witnesses. He argued, for example, that the skit about Jacqueline Kennedy's attempted exit from the car in Dallas lacked "artistic unity"; that the gestures allegedly used in Bruce's skit about his mother and an exhibitionist lacked "artistic value"; that there was, throughout the performance, a lack of "schematic build-up" of "flow" from one incident to another, of "order, or symmetry." There was, instead, "indecency, immorality, and possibly perversion."

The Trial Court, following Mr. Kuh's lead in assuming a function normally reserved for critics, decided that the performances were criminal because they were "devoid of any coherence," were "a series of unconnected items." (Judge J. Randall Creel dissented from this majority decision of the three-person court.) Under Mr. Kuh's aegis, one can easily imagine that certain specific works or performances by artists as diverse as Picasso, Duchamp, Larry Rivers, Robert Rauschenberg, Tom Wesselmann, Jim Dine, Ed Kienholz, and Robert Morris might come under judicial scrutiny. And their good names as artists, or the general conception of artistic liberty, would be of no avail to their defense, because, according to Mr. Kuh, "if artistry is to redeem . . . it must be artistry discernible and definable in the very item under judicial scrutiny" (emphasis in the original).

There is hardly anything so repugnant to the principle of artistic liberty as the spectacle of law enforcement officers proceeding to render esthetic judgments, and to penalize artists who do not conform to their self-appointed standards. Mr. Kuh's eagerness to assume the role of art critic, and to prosecute accordingly in 1964, seems to us to be incompatible with the attitudes and actions essential to a District Attorney in 1974.

Mr. Kuh as Social and Political Analyst, in Spite of Himself

Having argued throughout his prosecution that there was no redeeming social importance to Bruce's monologues, Mr. Kuh freely admits in his book that Bruce was an iconoclastic and effective social satirist: "Bruce, and the sex and scatology of his monologues, crystallized rebellion . . . The cruder and more shocking the pornography, the greater the scorn it expressed for the established. Lenny Bruce provided not only bone-searing talk, but fanfare and a rallying point."

By his own words, then, Mr. Kuh acknowledges that Bruce's monologues were a medium for the communication of dissident and abrasive ideas and attitudes. As such, Bruce's words and gestures, whether "devoid" or not, should have fallen under the protection of the First Amendment. For, under our system of civil liberties, it cannot be a crime to "express scorn for the established," or to engage in "bone-searing talk," or to be a "rallying point" for those who are seeking personal or social liberation.

If Mr. Kuh takes his own words seriously, his prosecution of Lenny Bruce will appear to him, as it now does to us, to have been a misguided attempt at muzzling a vulnerable satirist, as a veritable crusade against artistic liberty. As artists and art professionals, we submit that a man who could carry out such a crusade in 1964, and still consider it a job well done, is not qualified to be a fair District Attorney in 1974.

ARTISTS FOR A FAIR D.A. (AFDA)

*All quoted material is from Martin Garbus, *Ready for the Defense*, Farrar, Straus and Giroux, New York, 1971, and Richard H. Kuh, *Foolish Figleaves?* Macmillan, New York, 1967.

To help us defray the costs of this ad, and continue to scrutinize law enforcement philosophy and practice in relation to artistic liberty, please make your checks payable to AFDA and mail to:

AFDA
c/o Carl R. Baldwin
4 Washington Sq. Village
New York, New York 10012
212-677-6445

Name _____

Address _____

City _____ State _____ Zip _____

An ad taken out in the New York Times on April 3, 1974, as Richard Kuh was running for district attorney, to protest his role in Lenny's 1964 New York obscenity trial

*Lenny being interviewed by Pierre Berton at the Ambassador Hotel
in Los Angeles, January 21, 1966*

Perhaps. But what were the chances that Frank Hogan, Richard Kuh, and their colleagues at the Manhattan District Attorney's Office were then entirely oblivious to the machinations and inter-penetrations of Operation Yorksville, Cardinal Spellman, the Citizens for Decent Literature, Mayor Wagner, and the Citizens' Anti-Pornography Commission?

Curtain Call at The Cork 'n Bib

BY LATE JUNE 1964, Lenny Bruce had been fighting in the free speech arena for thirty-three unbearable months. The costs of defending him-self—the skyrocketing lawyer's fees, the mounting expense for trial tran-scripts, and the related travel and hotel bills—were depressing enough; but those were just monies paid out. What really took his breath away were the lost opportunity costs—all the monies not coming in.

With no accounts receivable, how could he pay for the everyday expenses of life—taxes, mortgage, child support, medical costs, and, of course, the high price of spiking his veins? Admittedly, he had record royalties (sales were way down), book royalties for *How to Talk Dirty and Influence People* (sales slumped), and the occasional check from this or that deal. But the tap was dripping, not flowing as it once had. He was getting ever more desperate, hitting up more friends for more money. "Whew, I got to get some bread," Lenny moaned. "In 1960, before the first bust I ever had for obscenity, I grossed $108,000. This year, I'll be lucky to make $6,000."

Lenny was relieved, then, to get a four-show weekend gig at The Cork 'n Bib in Westbury, Long Island, some twenty miles east of New York City. Two nights for $1,100; not great, but he sorely needed the money. So, with the help of Don Friedman, he closed the deal and ventured to the jazz music bar located at 146 Post Avenue. The place was packed ($6.50 minimum), with the devoted in the front and the blue (seven officers) in the back. Lenny was greeted by Norman Levy, Nassau Rackets Squad chief. He was there on a friendly mission, to make sure that Lenny kept his "act within the bounds of the law." No big deal, stay cool. And by the way, "Do you mind if we record your show?" he asked. "No, I don't mind," Lenny replied (though the thought of it *really* bugged him). The racket-squad team then connected Bruce's microphone to their tape recorder. "Testing. Testing." Let the show begin...self-incrimination and all.

When the two Friday performances ended, the unshaven comedian was warned that he could be arrested the next night if he repeated what he had just said. Lenny's routines were "borderline" material, in the squad chief's opinion. In his conversation with John Hirst, the club owner, Levy made it clear that Bruce's humor could cost Hirst his liquor license. If Hirst had any questions, he could take them up with the district attorney. With that, Levy left, incriminating tapes in hand, en route to the office of Nassau County Assistant D.A. William Kahn.

"I never had such a rotten experience," Bruce protested. As he told reporter Myron S. Waldman, "I picture them sitting in their offices the next day listening to the tapes and drooling—saying, 'That's dirty,' or 'We could charge him for that.'" Hirst, a bearded free-spirit sort of guy, believed that was precisely what the authorities would do. After all, only a few months earlier, Kahn's office had confiscated twenty-one thousand copies of the *Evergreen Review*—a literary periodical allegedly containing "obscene" photographs and dirty four-letter words. (A few months later, a three-judge court in Brooklyn ruled the action to be a "clear violation of the Fourteenth Amendment.") Hirst didn't like to be bullied, but neither did he want to be shut down. What choice did he have? The all-too-predictable result: Lenny was out, and George Crater was in.

The Nassau Assistant D.A. had never seen a live Bruce performance prior to the Cork 'n Bib engagement; he had, however, listened to the Manhattan trial tapes. Later, Kahn confirmed that "we heard the tapes," but refused all further comment. The news got back to Lenny's lawyers. The well-tempered Ephraim London was incensed: "These items are in evidence. I have some very serious questions about the right to use them outside the trial. It's not proper." Richard Kuh buttoned his lip when cornered by a *New York Post* reporter: "If we have a case pending in New York now, adjourned at Mr. Bruce's request, it would be improper of me to make any comment." Eventually, Kuh conceded that he had shared trial evidence with the District Attorney of Nassau County, though he insisted that he had breached no law.

Bruce had not been convicted; yet he might as well have been. Whether or not behind bars, he could not get hired in New York due to the long arm of the law. "Why won't they at least let me work while this is going on," Lenny lamented, "so I can live?"

An Anthro-Lingual-Philo-Jurisprudential Scene

FAMILIARITY BREEDS CONTEMPT. The old adage certainly proved true for Bruce and the Solomons as their trial reconvened on Tuesday, June 30, 1964. When the defense attorneys moved to dismiss, their arguments had a distinctly familiar ring. To a great extent, the lawyers for the defense reiterated the claims that they first raised, to no avail, at the preliminary hearing before Judge Strong; the same claims that they raised a second time, to no avail, by way of demurrer at the beginning of the trial. This third time around, London's and Schwartz's explanations generated, at least from the majority of the three-judge court, no greater enthusiasm or approval.

London replayed his three-pronged strategy. First, the statutory interpretation argument: given the precedent of *State v. Wendling*, no prosecution can lie under Section 1140-A for coarse and vulgar language alone. The statute must be limited to monologues that "excite lustful and lecherous thoughts," London maintained; otherwise, as the New York Court of Appeals reasoned, it would be obscene "to use the language of the street rather than that of the scholar." Second, the facial constitutionality argument: the text of the statute penalized speech that "tends to corruption of morals of youths or others," and this standard violated the U.S. Supreme Court's free speech doctrine. Admittedly, these were dry and turgid legal arguments; but they were precisely the kind of legal arguments that, in time, could win Lenny's freedom.

To these first two points, Kuh offered the State's well-rehearsed answers. On the one hand, *Wendling* involved actors in a play "that had some purpose other than mere dissemination of vulgarity"; on the other hand, Bruce's "cheap and disgusting" monologues—"fifty-minute performances, and the words are some one hundred times or thereabouts in each performance"—involve "vulgarity taken for the sake of shock." Furthermore, the People weren't "resting in this prosecution on the unfitness of Mr. Bruce's material for youths." To the contrary, Kuh maintained, "our case would be equally complete if there was a performance before an audience of two hundred people of the distinguished ages of all of Your Honors."

London's third argument, as per usual, went to *Roth*'s obscenity criteria of patent offensiveness judged by contemporary community standards. This time, however, he took a decidedly different tack. What the district attorney read in the transcripts and heard in the tapes were simply words; any "abhorrence" of such words amounted to "nothing more than a social taboo."

In his elegant and erudite manner, London lectured the court on etymology and philology: "[A]fter the Norman invasion of England, the words that began to be adopted, words of politeness that began to be used in the English language were words of French origin. And those that were of Anglo-Saxon origin tended to be used by the peasant class or the servant class." So now, London explained, "we accept words of French origin because they are words associated historically with politeness"; but, words that come from the "vulgate" of the common people are often considered vulgar. (Quite characteristically, Lenny put it in plebeian lingo: "[W]hen I speak like the people, I speak like the people.")

Bringing the lesson down a notch with a seminal example, London observed: "'Coitus,'...'fornication,'...have come through the French and all are considered proper. The word 'fuck' is not...'[S]hit' is another word of Anglo-Saxon origin from old English." The scholarly lawyer concluded by raising the class-consciousness of the court: "[T]here are three groups that use language of that kind frequently. One is the working class, the lower economic strata. Second is the people of the theater, and third is the upper social strata of the higher economic brackets." One final, personalizing touch: "And I would say this language is language that I have heard throughout my life." The idea was that, if the First Amendment does not protect the language of the people, of working stiffs, what good was it?

All this left Justice Murtagh rather flabbergasted:

Murtagh: Never been subjected to a barrage of [vulgarity] such as appears in [Bruce's monologue].
London: I served four years in the Army. I heard it every day that I was in the Army those four years. Every other person I have spoken to in the Army had the same experience. There were ten million of us.
Murtagh: I did not have any in four years of service.
London: Your Honor, your experience is unique. At any rate, whether or not it is considered a social offense to use that language in certain circles or under certain conditions, I think we must agree that this is a purely social taboo. That it is not obscene to use that kind of language. And that is all that one can say that Mr. Bruce has done here. He has used the language that, perhaps, some believe should be confined to the barroom or the barracks or other groups. But should not be used in certain particular circles....And on that basis alone there should be a dismissal.

This was the combination of the language anthropology of Claude Levi-Strauss and the language realism of Ludwig Wittgenstein, blended with First Amendment authority. The learned London argued as if he were enlightening an appellate court, as if he were addressing Justices Felix Frankfurter, John Marshall Harlan, and William Brennan. But he was not.

However impressed by London's oratory, Allen Schwartz felt the need to beat a different and independent path. His was a conventional, law-to-fact approach—no appeal to anthro-lingual-philo-jurispruden-tial arguments here. Once again, he asserted that the obscenity charges against the Solomons, as the "owners" or "managers" of the Café Au Go Go, must be dismissed. As the tapes controversy had determined, the Café Au Go Go Corporation owned and controlled the club. In no other capacity, Schwartz contended, have the Solomons been proven culpable within the terms of Section 1140-A: "It is the District Attor-ney's obligation of showing...not only that [the Solomons] were investors or shareholders, but they prepared the transcript, advertised the performance, gave the permission, directed it, presented it, or participated in it." Without a shred of evidence to this effect, Schwartz concluded, the prosecution had not established a *prima facie* case against "these two people who, before this court, are innocent."

Nonsense, retorted Kuh. Ella and Howard were corporate officers who "in some capacity present a show when the corporation contracts for the show and presents the show." Moreover, there was "abundant evidence" that Howard and Ella were "in charge" of the business, and knew precisely what they were offering to the public in Bruce's shows.

The rhetoric and legal argument—much of it repetitive—covered virtually everything. Only one topic was largely overlooked. Incredibly, the lawyers for the prosecution and the defense made no more than fleeting references to the one-week-old decision in *Jacobellis v. Ohio*, the very obscenity case that London had argued successfully before the U.S. Supreme Court.

Kuh got some mileage, albeit quite limited, out of *Jacobellis*, by reducing it to the obvious proposition that "obscene terms are not within the constitutional protection of the First Amendment." More importantly, he directed the New York judges to the Illinois Supreme Court's recent ruling in *People v. Bruce*, where a "unanimous" bench held "certain scatological terms somewhat similar to [these here] were vile" and, therefore, unprotected by the First Amendment. In effect, Kuh was arguing that the most relevant law was that of a state court, rather than the high court of the United States—that the Illinois decision against Bruce *trumped* the Supreme Court decision that might have saved Bruce.

Justice Murtagh was ready to rule on the motions. His ruling was short, to the point, and without justification. In its entirety: "Now, as to all three defendants and as to all counts. Motion to dismiss is denied. Judge Creel dissents, who votes to grant the motion as to all three defendants on all counts."

The digression was left to the lone dissenter. "I find as a fact that each of these performances here involved," Creel chastised, is "studiously offensive, insulting to the prevailing and current standard of the average New Yorker...as to decency, propriety, decorum, tastefulness, good manner, good speech." But the jurist tempered his personal disgust with his understanding of his constitutional duty: "I find these performances do not make the grade as to hardcore pornography. I find myself as a matter of law bound, however distastefully, to find that none of these perform-ances [is] obscene." The federal high court had forced Creel's hand, and tied those of the D.A.'s office, in his opinion: "I find that the United States Supreme Court has in fact stricken down the state's police power to defend the citizens from such morbid vulgarness....This the Supreme Court has done in the name of freedom of expression."

Was this an omen? Had Bruce and the Solomons lost their case even before they had put on their case? Three highly able defense lawyers, racking up God-knows-how-many billable hours, could not end this legal nightmare. The way things were going, the defense would have been well advised to start preparing its appeal before it called its very first witness. In fact, London hinted as much to the press, when he expressed more confidence in winning ultimately on appeal, rather than in winning at trial. But that take-it-all-the-way-to-the-top attitude really put Lenny on tilt: "If we can win in an upper court, why can't we win down here?" His nagging question focused on London's potential to turn things around in the remainder of the trial. Was there still hope?

Esteemed Enthusiasts

DURING THE TRIAL, Mort Sahl was playing at the Café Au Go Go. Martin Garbus "thought he would make an ideal witness because he was culturally acceptable in a way Lenny was not..." But Sahl "refused to testify," complained Garbus. "Sahl, who saw himself as an avant-garde political satirist," Garbus continued, "was openly resent-ful of the adulation and respect accorded Bruce by the liberal intellec-tual community, an audience he felt did not take him seriously enough." So, the defense proceeded with only eighteen witnesses.

What an array of résumés. It was like a liberal arts college: literary critic, newspaper columnist, magazine editor, writer, minister, instruc-tor of philosophy, English professor, sociologist, advertising copy-writer, lawyer, journalist, housewife—and even a cartoonist. This cast of superheroes would be called upon to prove that Lenny's act had artistic integrity and social utility; that his words did not appeal to prurient interests, but rather conformed to community standards for nightclub acts; and, finally, that Lenny never engaged in any lewd gestures. Now, this was a formidable phalanx against the State's case.

London, who commandeered the counterattack with the help of his young associate Garbus, stood up to call his first witness. Compared to Kuh, London's physique, posture, and mannerisms were a study in contrast. Tall and lanky, the middle-aged gentleman stooped a bit, striking a pose "resembling that of Abraham Lincoln." Characteristically dignified, pensive, and reserved, there was a highly formal way about him. London reminded Bruce of his father: "I can't talk to him," Bruce later confessed.

Richard Gilman, *Newsweek* literary critic, delivered a testimonial to the artistic integrity of Bruce's comedy—London's first line of defense. "Bruce is not using these words—'motherfucker, cunt, piss, shit in the sink'—with any intention but to liberate those words from the weight of disturbance and the weight of shame that has overlaid them," Gilman explained. "His intention is artistic. His intention is to reveal the truth and his use of that language is a technical matter." With Gilman and those who followed, London elicited evidence of the artistic merit and social utility of Bruce's work. When he called Dorothy Kilgallen, the prim and proper columnist, London had the same purpose in mind. Kilgallen, whom Lenny had wanted to testify at his Chicago trial, now praised him as a "brilliant satirist" whose "social commentary" was "extremely valid and important." Bruce is concerned, she averred, with "almost every moral issue that there is"—religion, civil rights, sex relations.

Nat Hentoff, the bearded staff writer for *New York* magazine, came next. For Hentoff, who had followed Bruce's career since the late '50s, Lenny was "more moral" than any other contemporary comedian. Allan Morrison agreed. The city editor of *Ebony* magazine testified that Bruce's "superb social satire" reflected his "continuing concern for basic issues such as racial equality, bigotry, [and] religious intolerance....His comments on such questions as to oppression, and the discrimination against the Negro people, his references to religious misunderstanding and intolerance, and bigotry point this up well."

And the United Church of Christ minister, Forrest Johnson, carried the compliments to a new level. Bruce was "attempting to probe moral truth through the constant hypocrisy and sham and foolishness of contemporary society." This, Johnson affirmed, was "a moral act"; on this score, "I think he verges on genius."

In the second line of defense, London and Garbus sought to establish that Bruce's language neither appealed to prurient interest nor was patently offensive under contemporary community standards. During Martin Garbus's exchange with Nat Hentoff, the presiding justice intervened on this point:

> *Murtagh*: Would you say Bruce titillates the audience in these performances?...
>
> *Garbus*: Now, Mr. Hentoff, in response to Judge Murtagh's question about Mr. Bruce's attempt to titillate, can you tell us if in any way you were titillated by Mr. Bruce's performances?
>
> *Hentoff*: No...nor have the audiences that have been present....It's like a shock of recognition, very effective. There is a lot of spontaneous laughter, a kind of, both laughter and an attempt to really see what he is trying to say. It is searching....
>
> *Garbus*: Would it be fair to say Mr. Bruce's performances are primarily concerned with arousing sexual thoughts?
>
> *Hentoff*: He is certainly concerned in making people think in sexual terms, I would say, in a rather snickering way.
>
> *Garbus*: Is that the purpose of Mr. Bruce's performances?
>
> *Hentoff*: That is absolutely not the purpose of Mr. Bruce's performances.

To the same effect, Professor Herbert Gans tendered a sociological perspective. (When Lenny heard the full list of Gans's professional affiliations, he quietly joked: "This guy can't hold a job.") Having lived in lower-to-middle-income communities from northern Minnesota to Boston, Gans had heard it all:

> *Garbus*: Have you heard the words, "cocksucker," "shit," "fuck," used in the Boston community?

Gans: Yes, I have.

Garbus: How were they used?

Gans: They were used as words of accusation, of anger....

Garbus: Did they connote sexual imagery?

Gans: No...they didn't....

Garbus: At what point, in the lives of the various people of the community, did they first learn these words?

Gans: I assume they learned them because they were in daily use; the children learned them from other children, learned them from parents, learned them from neighbors....

Garbus: [H]ave you observed [the language] used with groups of women together?

Gans: Yes.

Garbus: And [are the terms] used in mixed company?

Gans: Yes.

Jason Epstein, a vice president for Random House Publishing, had been called primarily to testify to the not-infrequent use of vulgarities in modern literature and drama—a practice relevant to contemporary community standards for artistic expression. He had seen Bruce's performances a few times before, and was generally familiar with his routines. London asked Epstein to comment on the transcripts of the April 1 (ten P.M.) and April 7 shows:

London: In these performances of Lenny Bruce's, that you have read, is there an attempt of shock for shock's sake?

Epstein: No, I think never in the case of Lenny Bruce. I think that's one of his virtues.

London: Is there vulgarity for vulgarity's sake?

Epstein: Never as far as I am concerned.

And so on, down through the list of luminaries—all attesting in various ways to the societal value of Lenny's comedy, to the ability of the community to tolerate his coarse barbs, and to the fact that his routines had nothing to do with sexual arousal.

Finally, regarding the prosecution's charge that Lenny had

engaged in obscene conduct, London launched his third line of defense. He called ten witnesses to the stand, all of whom had been at the performances in question, but had not seen any masturbatory or other objectionable gestures.

Lenny Bruce, the man who lacked a high school diploma, the man with a tattoo on his arm (he got it in Malta in 1942), was the same man who was now the object of paean and adulation by society's elite. What a proud moment. Lenny was moved to tears by the many notables who came to his defense. Even more so with Dorothy Kilgallen. He sobbed quietly, because her support was "a more significant imprimatur than a seal of approval from *The Village Voice* or the American Civil Liberties Union."

The evening of Wednesday, July 1, after Kilgallen's testimony, Martin Garbus visited Lenny in his second-floor room at the Marlton Hotel on Eighth Avenue. If nature abhors a vacuum, Lenny did, too. Lawbooks, legal documents from his earlier trials, drug paraphernalia, and spools of unwound and twisted audiotape were heaped up and strewn about, virtually filling every square inch of space. Even the chenille-covered bed in his pale green room was littered with hypodermic needles, recording equipment, and a gallery of Marilyn pictures that satiated Bruce's Monroe-mania ("I can tell by looking at her pictures what she was on," Lenny bragged to Garbus.) Pointing to his assortment of goodies, Lenny smirked: "The All-American Boy's Bed." That night, Bruce shared a mischievous secret; opening the gray attaché case that he always carried into court, Lenny revealed a portable tape recorder securely affixed to the interior. He had been recording the trial proceedings all along, unknown to everyone. Just as the Manhattan constabulary secretly had taped Lenny, now Lenny was secretly taping Kuh and the court.

Attacking the Person and Performance

TO PUT IT mildly, Richard Kuh was unimpressed with the "expert" testimony he had heard. He put it uncharitably: it was "unadulterated poppycock" born out of "[a]nticensorship zeal." Looking back on his cross-examination of the defense's case, Kuh told filmmaker Robert Weide: "Expert witnesses are not very influential....I had great fun with the experts....They took positions that were absurd."

Watching Kuh cross-examine someone would give any prospective defense witness pause. The courtroom was his forum; he knew its rules and its logic and how to work them to his advantage. He was a high-stakes player who loved to up the ante, whatever the odds. And, depending on the hand dealt, he knew which card to play. The D.A.'s cross-examination strategy was essentially twofold. First, there was the focus on the person—character, qualifications, and bias. Second, there was the focus on Bruce's performance—its unity, offensiveness, and social value. Moving back and forth between the person on the stand and the performance on the stage, he strove to win against one witness after another.

In the *attack-the-person* category, one of Kuh's preliminary stratagems was to challenge the expertise of the expert. That is, how much did this-or-that witness know about nightclub criticism generally and about Lenny's three Café Au Go Go shows specifically? For example, though Allan Morrison of *Ebony* magazine knew about race relations, what did he know about nightclub acts? Or, though Herbert Gans was a sociologist in "city planning and architecture," Kuh asserted, "how that makes [the] man an authority on the use of language is beyond my faintest comprehension." Or, what about Daniel Dodson, the Columbia University English professor? Surely he knew about modern fiction, but what did he know about comedy in coffeehouses? In each instance, Kuh made his point by narrowing the parameters of the relevant subject matter.

On this score (as on others), Justice John Murtagh was quite sympathetic to Richard Kuh's mindset. At one point, Murtagh offhandedly remarked, "I think the record is being overborne with [expert] testimony that is of questionable value." The presiding justice had no qualms in intervening during London's or Garbus's presentation of the case to cross-examine the defense witnesses himself—and in an openly skeptical and argumentative manner. For example, Murtagh sparred with Richard Gilman time and again:

Murtagh: Frankly, you are straining the statement to get that meaning, aren't you?

Gilman: I don't think so, your Honor....I think it is a compressed bit of material here. You can compress a very large meaning and get a large effect. I think Bruce does this constantly. I think that is one of the things that makes it difficult for certain people to follow his intention, the fact that he is so compressed. He moves very quickly from one main point to another.

Murtagh: Doesn't it leave the bulk of the audience with nothing but filth and very little, if any meaning?

Gilman: I can't speak for the bulk.

Murtagh: He may have the greatest intention, but isn't the net effect of the dialogue pure filth and little message?

Justice Murtagh's aggressive interrogation of Gilman culminated in a judgment: "I think that much of the witness's testimony runs contrary to the actual facts that are before the court." This attack on Gilman's testimony eventually provoked the characteristically self-possessed Ephraim London to protest. Thus, the following exchange:

Murtagh: Doesn't there come a time when the overruling purpose [of Bruce's vulgarity] is to simply be obscene...?...

London: I would like to make a comment at this point, your Honors....I think that the court ought to retain an open mind...

Murtagh: I am simply asking the witness a question.

London: Your Honor, it indicates an attitude.

Despite his obvious incredulity, Justice Murtagh typically allowed the defense witnesses' opinions into evidence, overruling Kuh's systematic objections for irrelevancy or lack of expertise. The court, Murtagh declared, must "err" on the side of openness, permitting such testimony "for what it's worth, but we have reservations as to [its] value."

Most objectionable to Kuh was the very notion of an expert in morals. Forrest Johnson, the tall and athletic-looking minister at the Edgehill Community Church in Riverdale, bore the brunt on this score: "Someone testifying as an expert on moral content, that is an area of expertise that I have yet to see recognized in any case, anyplace, any time," Kuh charged. So, too, for Sidney Lanier, the Vicar of St. Clement's Church: "If your Honors please, I object. I'm not sure what he's an expert on. I would gather, like [Forrest Johnson], he's being tendered as an expert on morality. I know of no such field of expertise rightly asked by a court of law." Justice Kenneth Phipps, in one of his rare contributions to the dialogue, added a bit of levity as he reacted to Ephraim London's comments:

> *London*: I think it should have great influence to the court, that a man of the Church considers a particular performance morally proper—a moral performance or an immoral one...
> *Phipps*: Oh, Mr. London....I'm certain your expertise has been broad enough not to suffer delusions, just because he is a man of the Church, that his morals are something or are not.

Once Murtagh allowed for the possibility of moral expertise, the next question was whether the defense witnesses had the requisite credentials to be moral experts **CD** :

> *Kuh*: Now, you say there's no theological restraint on language, that language is a living thing, and we should not be prudish, am I correct in getting down your words?
> *Johnson*: I said so, yes.
> *Kuh*: What is the Fourth Commandment?
> *Johnson*: You'll have to refresh me, sir.
> *Kuh*: On the Ten Commandments, am I correct, you must be refreshed on the Ten Commandments, Reverend, am I correct on that? Is the Fourth Commandment, "Honor Thy Father and Thy Mother?" I didn't hear your answer, Reverend. I still haven't heard your answer, Reverend. Can you answer my question, or is it too difficult?
> *Johnson*: I don't recall whether it's the Fourth or not....
> *Kuh*: Would you say the phrase, and you'll excuse me, Reverend, for using this language, but the phrase "motherfucker" is in accord with that Commandment?

Johnson: I don't think the term "motherfucker" has any relationship to that Commandment....

Kuh: To the uninitiated, to the unsophisticated, to persons other than reverends, Mr. Johnson, might someone misunderstand the word "motherfucker" as having to do with mothers and fucking?

In the same overall category of attacks on the person, Kuh honed in on the difference between general and particular expertise. It was not enough if a witness had worn out a phonograph needle listening to Lenny Bruce records like *The Sick Humor of Lenny Bruce* and *Lenny Bruce: American*, or had followed Bruce from the Village Vanguard to the Carnegie Hall concert, or even had read all four of the autobiographical profiles of Bruce in *Playboy* magazine. All that was important was whether or not the expert was testifying precisely to the three Café Au Go Go performances in question.

Kuh continued along this line, as he took sharp exception when the Hearst columnist, Dorothy Kilgallen, offered her general assessment of Bruce as a "brilliant satirist" who provided "social commentary" that was "extremely valid and important." Her commentary, Kuh declared, should be stricken because it was not tied to the specific performances. Once again, Murtagh "appreciate[d] the limitation of the response," but took it "for what it is worth."

His favorite *attack-the-person* stratagem was to reveal any bias in the defense's expert witnesses. First, there was the purported bias of those who had signed Allen Ginsberg's April petition protesting Bruce's arrest, without any particularized knowledge of the Café Au Go Go acts. The most revealing example was Kuh's cross-examination of the cartoonist and writer, Jules Feiffer:

Feiffer: Sir, I did not see the transcripts or [hear] the tapes, and I might add that after having heard or read them, it really wouldn't have been necessary, because there's nothing in there that I haven't heard Lenny Bruce do in one way or another before...

Kuh: But at the time you signed this statement, you didn't know for certain what was in the tapes, did you, Mr. Feiffer?...

Feiffer: What I'm saying is that I have enough confidence in who the police are likely to arrest in this town in the area of nightclub appearances and general procedures like that, to have more faith in Mr. Bruce than in the opinion of the Police Department.

Kuh: So, Mr. Feiffer, when you signed this, this was your prejudgment about two things: one, a prejudgment about Lenny Bruce, and two, a prejudgment about the police, is that correct?...

Feiffer: It was a prejudgment based on my experience over a number of years, and a deep interest in both Mr. Bruce and the actions of groups representing authority. As you said, I comment quite a bit on these, and the police in New York have come into that also.

Kuh: And it was your prejudgment, then, on Lenny Bruce, and on the police, was it not?

Feiffer: Yes, sir, it was.

Another type of alleged bias concerned the relationship between defense counsels and their expert witnesses. On this score, Kuh tried to corner Nat Hentoff of *New York* magazine:

Kuh: I noted that you came into the courtroom with Mr. London and Mr. Garbus today; did you have lunch with them?

Hentoff: Yes, I did.

Kuh: Was there any talk of the kind concerning any phase or any aspect of the Lenny Bruce prosecution?

Hentoff: No, except for the fact that I suppose as a performer who is not a performer, I simply asked if I were doing competently, and the impression was okay. That's all....

Kuh: You felt the need for someone else to tell you how your own performance was going?...

Garbus: I object to the question. I don't see what relevancy this has.

Murtagh: Sustained. Let's move on....

Kuh: [W]hen did you first meet with either Mr. Garbus or Mr. London about the Bruce case?

Hentoff: We had lunch, oh, about a week after that. I can't give the exact date, at, I think, the NYU Club.

Kuh: Who else was present?

Hentoff: Mr. London, Mr. Garbus, and myself.

Kuh: When did you next meet with either of these gentlemen?

Hentoff: At Mr. London's house on a Monday evening about three weeks ago, I guess.

Kuh: Who else was present there?

Hentoff: Let's see, Mr. Garbus, Mr. London, Richard Gilman, my wife. I'm trying to remember who all else. Jules Feiffer, Jason Epstein....

Kuh: Are you privy to the strategy or the plan of the defense? Did you help plan who was to be called as expert witnesses?

Garbus: I'll object to the question, your Honor.

Kuh: I submit to your Honor on the question of credibility if this man is part and parcel of an operation, it does affect his credibility.

Murtagh: Objection overruled.

Hentoff: Oh, no...what I did was suggest some people, but as far as being part of a plan of defense, no.

THE SECOND GENERAL category of Kuh's cross-examination strategies involved questions about Lenny's *performances*. The purpose, obviously, was to undermine the defense witnesses' evaluations of the Café Au Go Go shows.

One notable stratagem within this category was *divide and conquer*—that is, separate the "dirty" words from their context, and then judge their worth, word by word. For example, Kuh took *Newsweek*'s Richard Gilman through a list of terms—"motherfucker," "fuck," "tits," "cocksucker"—and asked, as to each word individually and out of context, whether Gilman would want to "liberate" the word "from shame." Bruce complained outside the courtroom about what he perceived to be the distorting effect of this technique; thrusting five pages of trial transcript at a reporter, he exclaimed: "Fifteen hundred words! And how many slang words? Thirty-one. That's almost 98 percent pure. Almost as good as a popular soap."

Prosecutor Kuh also aimed to demonstrate that Bruce's crudities lacked any meaningful artistic value. That is, if Lenny's offensive words had no value in their own right, then why did he have to use them? What purpose did they serve other than shock value? And, if Lenny's words contributed nothing much to the artistic integrity of his monologues, did he have a legal right to use them at all? Are artists to be given special license to throw anything into the mix, to say anything they please?

Much the same concern underlay San Francisco prosecutor Albert Wollenberg's 1962 cross-examination of defense witness Grover Sales. Wollenberg had asked: "Mr. Sales, you call it a 'throw-away line.' It didn't have any meaning to the show, is that what you're telling us?" Now, some two years later and two thousand miles away, Richard Kuh was following suit, but with greater sophistication.

The so-called "throw-away" character of Lenny's "dirty" words would be obvious, Kuh believed, by comparing Lenny's LPs with his Café Au Go Go acts, or contrasting the routines of other socially minded comedians with Lenny's off-color bits. This was Kuh's *compare and contrast* stratagem. The prosecutor used this tack against the lady who removed her white gloves before testifying 🔘:

> *Kuh*: [I]f I tell you that all through [the *I'm Not a Nut, Elect Me*] record and these others that I have here, "fuck," "motherfucker," and "cocksucker," and "cunt," and the whole list of them are not used at all, would you say that these records show less genius than the [transcripts of the Café performances] that you have read?...
>
> *Kilgallen*: No....
>
> *Kuh*: Would you say that Bruce is able to get his social satire, his moral values, his artistic ability across fully and ably and unimpeded without the use of these words?...
>
> *Kilgallen*: I don't know whether he can get his meaning across fully, because some of these words, which are objectionable as you put it, are terms that are used by people in real life, and I think to be more graphic he must use them just as a playwright or a novelist would use them....I believe Mr. Bruce is both his own writer and performer, and if he feels it's necessary, I do not object to it.
>
> *Kuh*: Well, are you saying, then, that in your eyes Mr. Bruce can do no wrong?

Years later, Kuh volunteered that he listened to Lenny Bruce albums in his Washington Square apartment. He even granted that he liked them (of course, the LPs were censored). But, he was always quick to add that this was the Lenny Bruce "of yore," not the "inarticulate" Lenny Bruce of the spring of 1964.

Another one of prosecutor Kuh's cross-examination strategies stemmed from Justice Brennan's admonition in *Roth* that a work, to be judged obscene, must be *taken as a whole*. On its face, this seemed to be a straightforward requirement—the work was to be considered from beginning to end. With the finesse of a philosopher, Kuh deconstructed the constitutional requirement. What, exactly, does it mean to consider a work as a whole? Is not "the whole" to be determined by its theme, its plot, its linear links? If so, then it would be difficult, if not impossible, to assess Lenny's Café Au Go Go performances "as a whole"—what with their disconnected blips of improvisation and profanity. This resembled the argument advanced by James R. Thompson in the State's brief presented to the Illinois Supreme Court in 1963. Like Thompson, Kuh insisted that Bruce's rambling monologues were not constitutionally protectible works of unity and artistic integrity.

To test his interpretation of the *Roth* requirement, Kuh asked one of the defense's star witnesses, Nat Hentoff, what the logical link was between two of Lenny's bits. How did the exhibitionism routine connect up with the Jacqueline Kennedy routine that immediately followed it? Hentoff described Bruce's style as creating meaning from the juxtaposition of seemingly unrelated bits:

> *Hentoff*: One of the techniques that Mr. Bruce uses, and it's a technique that is increasingly common in literature, and to some extent in…all drama, is what I call kaleidoscope. There does not have to be in this kind of art, or performance, if you will, an outline, a clear outline of one, two, three. You set a focus on a particular incident that reveals a particular point. Then you move to another point. They are linked because underneath what you are essentially talking about is this: It is one of the ways we live.
> *Kuh*: But you will concede, when you use the word kaleidoscopically, in the old kaleidoscopes, a lot of things can still be jumbled and still come up with the same artistic effect?
> *Hentoff*: No, because it's not absolutely free. You have to make

some decision as to what you're going to use and how you're going to juxtapose them....

Kuh: Would there have been an artistic loss had Bruce gone right from the Uncle Willie and the Apple incident to the Jackie Kennedy incident and omitted the exposure incident?...

Hentoff: To me there would have been, because I was particularly absorbed by that image.

It was yin vs. yang, Bach vs. Charlie Parker, Aristotle vs. Marshall McLuhan. It was a clash of mindsets—one more logical, the other more poetic.

Kuh was more on *terra firma* when he cross-examined the defense witnesses regarding personal use and community tolerance of vulgarity. Repeatedly, he asked questions such as, "Do you use the word 'fuck' in the presence of women who are strangers?" and "Have you ever seen the phrase 'motherfucker' or 'cocksucker' used in any accepted national publication of any kind?" Even more colorfully, Kuh asked the genteel Miss Kilgallen: "[D]o you know any other contemporary American author who uses these words in the profusion that Bruce does, and uses these stories one after another after another—Roosevelt's tits, Jackie Kennedy's ass, chicken in bed, urinating from windows...?"

It may have been funny, but it was a laugh that came at Lenny's expense. If liberal-minded individuals didn't use such language, how in God's good name could their community condone such language? Thus, the prosecutor set out to undermine the defense's claim that Lenny's acts were consistent with contemporary community standards.

Unlike Kuh, Justice James Creel seemed much more insecure about the court's competence to discover contemporary community standards or to judge Bruce's epithets, by use of such standards, as obscene or not. The justice questioned the Random House editor, Jason Epstein, as to the very existence of the nebulous notion:

Creel: Mr. Epstein...I wonder if you could help us. We are having—counsel, both of them, and this trial court are having a little trouble as we grope for the meaning of this word, contemporary community standards. We have heard from experts, we have heard each in their field. You can testify about a small percentage of books. We have heard from commentators of Broadway theaters and nightclubs, and while, I suppose, New York has the largest, it's still small. Are we groping for a nonexistent mirage, a pretty green thing that as you approach it and reach for it and get hold of a part of it, it disappears? Is there such a thing, in your opinion as an expert?

Epstein: I have always thought, in connection with the decisions I have to make in my own work, that there must be a variety of community standards in New York, as there are a variety of communities.

Creel: A community taste varies, some taste would be sophisticated or jaded, others, well, simple, sacred....Does it exist? Is there such a thing as an average New Yorker? Is there such a thing as a New York community standard or a national standard?

Epstein: I have never met an average New Yorker. I wouldn't know him if I saw him.

Apparently, the prosecutor did not suffer such esoteric epistemological doubts. Taking up the cause of community standards of civility, Kuh grilled Forrest Johnson, the minister of the United Church of Christ, who testified:

Johnson: I have used ["fuck"]. As a matter of fact, the other day, I was discussing this case, and my eight-year-old asked, "Did they use the word 'fuck'," and she asked it in a most objective fashion, and I thought in a way that didn't cast any kind of disfavor upon her. I—I'm glad my daughter felt that she could ask that word in company that included my congregants.

Kuh: And when you go home, tonight at dinner, with your daughter, you intend, in order to relieve her of guilt feeling, to use the words, "fuck," "motherfucker," "cocksucker"?

Garbus: Your Honor, I object.

Murtagh: Sustained....

Kuh: Are these words that are socially acceptable in your community, Reverend, in terms of being used in mixed company, ladies, strange women?...

Johnson: I don't consider myself an expert in this matter, but I do know that I have heard such words used, and that I know in society where I have been, they are acceptable…

Kuh: Can you tell me if there's any reason why you haven't leaned on these words in order to make your point strongly [in homilies]?…

Johnson: I would say that I will just consider that these words are not related to the points I want to make.

After watching Kuh's cross-examination, Stephanie Gervis Harrington reported in *The Village Voice*: "[W]hen it's all over, the court record may show that in the course of this trial Kuh has used the words he is prosecuting Bruce for using more than Bruce did in all of the performances of his abbreviated New York run." Then again, this may have reflected the standards operative in Kuh's professional community. Purportedly, Kuh did not have to leave his office at the Criminal Courts building to hear those choice words that Lenny liberated at the Café Au Go Go. As Nat Hentoff recounted it, "[a] young member of the district attorney's staff was laughing in the corridor. Seeing me, he volunteered: 'Talk about community standards. I was just thinking that you ought to hear how some of the cops who come into Kuh's office talk.' He started an imitation, but froze when he realized he was being stared at by a large plainclothes detective."

As for the defense witnesses who testified to seeing Bruce make no obscene gestures, Kuh took a uniform approach. He cross-examined eight of the ten of them, attempting to prove that they lacked any reliable recollection of *exactly* what Lenny was doing with his hands and with the microphone from moment to moment. If their credibility on this score could be impeached, Inspector Ruhe's charge might stick.

The prosecution's cross-examination was always relentless, at times sophisticated; always well-planned, at times effective. Some witnesses, like Nat Hentoff, seemed unscathed by Kuh's assaults; others were more fragile. As Dorothy Kilgallen "stepped down from the witness stand, she touched Lenny Bruce's arm and whispered, 'I hope I haven't hurt your case.'"

Justice Murtagh had delayed his summer vacation long enough. The court stood adjourned for eighteen days.

8

THE COURT ADJOURNED:
NEW YORK, PART III

But it would be a beautiful musical curtain line: the three judges just about to exit, and one turns to the other at the end and says, "See you later, motherfucker."

—*Lenny Bruce*

Gifts from on High

THE ILLINOIS SUPREME Court could not have picked a better moment to withdraw its opinion and judgment in *People v. Bruce*. It happened on July 7, 1964, just before the New York trial court recessed. The Illinois high court made a rare request that the parties file "suggestions" concerning the effect of *Jacobellis v. Ohio* on Bruce's Chicago conviction. Moreover, the court had done this on its *own* motion. Even Lenny, who was used to betting on longshots in his legal struggles, could not have foreseen this extraordinary development.

Naturally, Lenny's Illinois appellate team—Rosenfield, Kalven, and Ming—urged the court to reverse its earlier course. The state justices initially had affirmed Illinois's balancing approach to obscenity questions because the federal high court had never been "unequivocal" in rejecting that approach. *Jacobellis* was now unequivocal in its rejection of balancing. The Illinois high court, it seemed, was obliged to overturn Lenny's conviction if his act had *any* social value. "Whatever one may think of Mr. Bruce's performance, it cannot be said that his work is 'utterly without social importance,'" the appellant team declared.

Not so fast, cautioned the Office of the State's Attorney. The appellant's argument rested on a logical fallacy. Although obscenity is without any socially redeeming importance, the opposite is not true. Put simply, material chockful of hot sex scenes or gross vulgarities surely cannot be immune from obscenity regulation just because it also contains a nugget of social value or the smidgen of an idea. The correct interpretation of *Jacobellis*, the state suggested, must be that, as a general rule, a court cannot weigh the merits of a work against the prurient appeal of its sexy parts. But this still would permit censorship of Bruce's comedy act: whatever the germs of social importance to be detected within his routines, his patently offensive language and manner had soured his act so much that it was "'utterly without social importance' *as a whole*."

Practically, the state's reasoning created an unfortunate catch-22. On the one hand, if *Jacobellis* were read to redeem a work that contained an iota of social importance, "there could be no [real] enforcement of the obscenity laws," as the state argued. On the other hand, if *Jacobellis* were read to allow censorship because of the lewd or disgusting manner of expressing otherwise valuable ideas, there could be no real enforcement of free speech guarantees. Obscenity control, after all, is regulation of "manners." Thus, if the First Amendment were to mean anything in the obscenity context, it must protect ideas of value despite the socially unapproved manner of their expression. Would the Illinois high court appreciate this conundrum?

EVERY SILVER LINING has its gray cloud. The same prosecutor who once had alerted Justice Murtagh and his colleagues to the Illinois Supreme Court's opinion against Bruce was now downplaying the omen signaled by the withdrawal of that opinion. On Thursday, July 9—the very day that Ephraim London called his final witness—Kuh addressed a letter to the three New York justices. His purpose was to "clarify" the significance of the Illinois high court's latest action. Discounting what seemed inevitable, he doggedly emphasized the status quo—the state of things *here and now*. No matter what the speculation, Bruce's Chicago conviction "still stands." As he told the New York justices, their Illinois brethren left Lenny's conviction "intact, where it will remain intact until, or unless the high court acts on it and reverses it." In other words, don't think about tomorrow.

Within twenty-four hours, another gift came from on appellate high, a decision that the lawyers for the defense had been awaiting with some impatience. *Fanny Hill*—John Cleland's novelistic memoir of an English prostitute's sexcapades that had thrown British and American vice men into a twitter for two hundred some years since its 1750 publication—was finally legalized in New York. The state's high court toed the line that had been drawn by the Supreme Court's recent rulings in *Jacobellis* and *The Tropic of Cancer*.

Let New York Chief Judge Charles S. Desmond protest, in his dissent, about the "numerous instances" in *Fanny Hill* "not only of prostitution, but of voyeurism, transvestitism, homosexuality, lesbianism, flogging, seduction of a boy, etc., etc." And let Judge John F. Scileppi complain that Cleland's work "is one of the foulest, sexually immoral, debasing, lewd, and obscene books ever published, either in this country or abroad." Nonetheless, a majority of the New York Court of Appeals found nothing more offensive about *Fanny Hill*'s old-fashioned allusions to engorged "pricks" and "quivering quims" than could be found in Nico Jacobellis's modern exhibition of French-styled *amour* or the "fuck," "cock," and "cunt" in Henry Miller's writings.

Bruce and the defense counsel took heart. "How can they continue this?" Lenny wondered. How could his playful sex-bits and vulgarities be considered any more obscene than the sexiness and crudity of *Fanny Hill* or *The Tropic of Cancer*? Now, surely, Frank Hogan's office must drop the charges against Bruce and the Solomons.

But, Kuh's response to these events? The assistant D.A. already had tipped his hand: in arguing against London's motion to dismiss, Kuh advised the three trial judges that whatever the high "court in Albany" eventually did with *Fanny Hill* "had no impact on whether or not Lenny Bruce is filthy or disgusting." It certainly didn't for Kuh. He wanted the trial to continue—the state had expert witnesses, too.

A Cast of Critics

IT WAS JULY and Lenny was in San Francisco, performing at the Off Broadway by night. By day—always post-noon or later—he wrote letters, read cases and transcripts, and phoned friends from his room at the Swiss American Hotel. San Francisco seemed to be the only venue left open to him, the only place in the nation where his acts were protected by the First Amendment. Freedom by the Bay. He needed it. More importantly, he needed the money he could make there, this at a time when most cities and most clubs were off limits to him. He was increasingly bummed out by the turn of events in New York and Los Angeles. How could he survive? In the basement of the dressing room of the Off Broadway, a depressed Lenny Bruce confided to his friend Ralph Gleason: "All I can see ahead is death and destruction." But he still fought on, at least as long as he could perform and earn a living. So he wrote to Ephraim London, urging him to resume the trial *without* him; he needed the cash. London, understandably, would have no part of it. In a letter dated July 20, 1964, he made it clear that Justice Murtagh insisted on the defendant's presence. Failure to appear would mean that Lenny's bail would be forfeited, and could lead to all sorts of other hellish consequences. Besides, "[w]e have a good trial record and I don't want anything to spoil it," London added by way of a penned postscript. Come soon, come for sure. It smacked of a Lenny Bruce routine, *sans* any humor.

So, Lenny was in Frisco, performing. London was in New York, worrying. Chief Justice John Murtagh was away, vacationing. And Richard Kuh? He was in Manhattan, working. The man who once forecast a one- or two-day trial was busy, with his boss Frank Hogan, rounding up rebuttal witnesses for the State.

Try as he did, he could not persuade Lionel Trilling (Columbia University professor who had signed the Ginsberg petition), Abel Green (*Variety* editor), or Bosley Crowther (*New York Times* movie critic) to join the state's effort to convict Lenny Bruce, Howard Solomon, and Ella Solomon. The prevailing sentiment, however critical of Bruce, was expressed best by Crowther, who wrote: "Although I find the material distasteful and disgusting in the extreme, I feel it would be inconsistent with my concepts of free speech to partici-pate....I deplore the fact that there are people who will listen to such stuff, but I don't feel it would help matters—or be consistent with our democratic principles—to lock up Bruce." Kuh loathed the "sort of reverse McCarthyism" of the liberal intelligentsia that discouraged people such as Crowther from speaking out against trash.

Nevertheless, he managed to gather five impressive rebuttal wit-nesses: Robert Sylvester (*New York Daily News* columnist), Daniel Potter (executive director of the Protestant Council of New York), John Fischer (editor-in-chief of *Harper's* magazine), Marya Mannes (freelance writer), and Ernst Van den Haag (sociologist and psychoanalyst). Kuh relied on them to buttress his case-in-chief, to refute the conclusions of the defense's expert witnesses, and to attempt to satisfy the constitutional requirements for obscenity as recently reformulated in *Jacobellis*.

Unlike Ephraim London, Richard Kuh was less concerned with building a record for appeal than with winning the case before him. Still, he had to be mindful of what Justice William Brennan had declared only one month earlier: though obscenity is "utterly without redeeming social importance," sex-oriented expression that "advocates ideas" or that has "literary or scientific or artistic value or any other form of social importance" cannot be "branded as obscenity." However high the hurdles of *Jacobellis*, Kuh was determined to surmount them. To that end, Kuh devoted two days of hearings to proving that Bruce's acts at the Café Au Go Go lacked socially redeeming value, offended contemporary community standards, and were incapable of being "considered as a whole" because of their alleged discontinuity.

> *Kuh*: Have you an opinion as to the social value, if any, of either or both of these Bruce performances?
>
> *Potter*: In my judgment, I feel there is no positive social values, but there are negative social values in both of these [tapes].
>
> *Kuh*: Can you explain just what you mean by that answer, Reverend Potter?
>
> *Potter*: Well...the constant use of both foul language, the offensive use of words and images would in my judgment...if anything, incite and increase the feelings of hostility towards others in the community...

Later, John Fischer of *Harper's* was called to the stand to corroborate what the Presbyterian clergyman had opined about the utter lack of social value in Bruce's Café Au Go Go performances:

> *Kuh*: Have you an opinion as to the literate manner of the tapes that you heard and the transcripts that you read?
>
> *Fischer*: Any such opinion has to be highly subjective, but I could not see any literary merit in either of them.
>
> *Kuh*: Thank you. Did you see any artistic merit in either of them?
>
> *Fischer*: No, sir.
>
> *Kuh*: Have you an opinion as to whether there is any social value in either of the tapes that you heard or the transcripts that you read?
>
> *Fischer*: None that I could discern. As a matter of fact, it was hard for me to understand quite what point Mr. Bruce was trying to make. The material seemed to me rather incoherent.

Perhaps the best witness for the prosecution on the question of artistic, literary, or social value was Marya Mannes, the sixty-year-old writer who was a frequent contributor to *The New Yorker*, a feature editor at *Vogue*, and an essayist on such subjects as television, film criticism, and political satire:

> *Kuh*: Have you an opinion as to the artistic or literary merit of the two tapes which I supplied?
>
> *Mannes*: Yes. I have an opinion.
>
> *Kuh*: Can you tell us what that opinion is?
>
> *Mannes*: Well, the opinion is that I, in spite of real effort and the intention of being wholly objective about this, could not find artistic value in either the transcripts or the performances.
>
> *Kuh*: And have you an opinion as to any social value contained in either of those transcripts or performances?
>
> *Mannes*: Here again this must be a subjective comment. I personally did not, and I looked for it, but I did not find it.

On cross-examination, Martin Garbus tested Mannes's convictions that Bruce's work lacked *any* socially redeeming value:

Garbus: Do you understand Mr. Bruce's transcripts contain many such social statements? We will go through them piece by piece.

Mannes: There are such statements sprinkled through the scripts....[T]o pick out one or two or five or six sentences as evidence of social content, as far as I can see, is proof of nothing.

Garbus: Your point is the social statement is being made, but it is being lost among other things?

Mannes: Lost, confused, and overwhelmed.

Garbus: There is a social statement?...

Mannes: I said before that there were several statements made which could, I suppose, be called social statements because they refer to society, yes.

Garbus: And these are the statements being made by other people in the community about the same subject?

Mannes: Said in other ways.

Striving to rehabilitate his witness, Kuh asked Mannes to explain when she would accord literary or artistic value to the use of offensive words, and when she would not:

Mannes: [O]bscenity is sometimes necessary in portraying characters who speak this way, which is part of the characterization in their kind of speech, whether it is soldiers or whether it is free wheelers of any kind. Obscenity is part of the nature of their character. My distinction is largely when obscenity has a clear part in the pattern of the writers, when it is essential to dramatic impact, or to the development of character—this, then, is literature. If it is used for shock effect, for an amusement, to get a laugh, or just as Mr. Bruce said, "Let's talk dirty," then I fail to see its redeeming values, either social or artistic.

Kuh: When Bruce uses it...in your judgment, your critical judgment, would you say he uses it for shock value for his brand of entertainment rather than for any literary purpose?

Mannes: He uses it to get a laugh, which is the last resort of the comedian. I have listened to the transcripts carefully and listened to the nightclub, and every four-letter word was followed by a burst of laughter, regardless of context. This is the comedy....I am not one and never have been for censorship. I am not at all sure that the law that is on the books, to which we are now referring, is a clearly definable law. I think it is susceptible to a great many interpretations. However, it is the law, and unless it is changed by repeal or defined more clearly so as to totally avoid all danger of censorship, it seems to me that the major questions which I tried to answer are still valid. Has obscenity, left alone, social and artistic value? And my only feeling is, in both cases, negative.

On to contemporary community standards. Here, Kuh's purpose was to establish that Bruce's strong language was offensive to the New York community in general and to the New York nightclub scene in particular. On this score, whom better to ask than Robert Sylvester, the *New York Daily News* columnist?

Kuh: Can you tell whether you can possibly imagine, in your opinion as a critic, any way in which those performances may be delivered that...would result in their coming out other than being filthy, disgusting, and incoherent?...
Sylvester: Well, they would be objectionable to me.
Kuh: No matter how they were performed?
Sylvester: Yes, sir.

Justice Creel also prevailed on Sylvester's expertise to inquire into the modern nightclub comedian's typical use of vulgarity:

Creel: I would like your opinion, as an expert, as to whether there are other nightclub performers, entertainers, who make this same extensive and liberal use of the vulgarity as does this defendant Lenny Bruce, in these two transcripts? Or is Lenny Bruce unique in his use of vulgarity such as in these two transcripts?
Sylvester: We have several, your Honor, very vulgar comedians. I have heard them use some of the words that are in the Bruce transcripts.
Creel: They make the same extensive use of vulgar words?

Sylvester: Not the same extensive use, but extensive use. I believe you asked me if in my opinion Mr. Bruce is unique....Yes, I think he is unique.

With Daniel Potter and Ernst Van den Haag, the two take-the-gloves-off witnesses on community standards, Kuh's case against Lenny took a more openly hostile turn. Bruce's performances were a "sort of verbal diarrhea," the conservative sociologist Van den Haag observed, "instead of defecating on a stage in a literal sense, he does it through orality." Reverend Potter was similarly unrestrained: "There is only one community I can think of where this would be acceptable, and that would be in the back wards of the Rochester State Hospital, in the mental hospital, where persons for the most part go get on stumps and speak in this kind of random, irrational way and primarily employing filthy and vulgar words and playing on them for the sake of playing on them. This is tolerated....They let them babble on." This line of expert testimony suggested that the defense was invoking free speech rights to protect madness—nothing short of an insane, Marquis de Sade interpretation of the First Amendment.

Still reeling from his kaleidoscopic encounter with Nat Hentoff, Kuh needed to repair the damage the irksome writer had done. Again, he hoped to prove that Lenny's work lacked any unity, and therefore could not be considered "as a whole," per the requirement of *Roth*.

For this, he turned to John Fischer. "[D]o you see any artistic kaleidoscopic unity in those exhibits," Kuh asked. "No," Fischer replied, "I was not able to discern any pattern or any unity." Marya Mannes was of a similar opinion: "[C]ould I, perhaps, put it another way? Do I think these transcripts add up to a coherent social satire or social statement? No, I don't think they do. In fact, I would be very much surprised if the people, after hearing Mr. Bruce, could define precisely what it was that he was trying to tell them."

In so many ways—legal, philosophical, cultural, psychological—the prosecutor's case hinged on demonstrating "that Bruce the iconoclast's iconoclast, Bruce the martyr at hypocrisy's altar, Bruce the brave, was...a far more pallid picture as Bruce the accused." Those were Richard Kuh's exact words.

Censorship Debate and Courtroom Drama

"LITERATURE OR LICENSE?" was the debate. The effect of obscenity censorship on an open society was the topic. Aired on NBC's *Open Mind*, with Princeton Professor Eric P. Goldman as moderator, it featured a panel of distinguished guests, including Arnold Gingrich (publisher of *Esquire*), John E. Lawler (counsel to a New York antiobscenity organization), and Barney Rossett (head of Grove Press). Two other luminaries were there for the intellectual exchange: New York Civil Liberties Union director Ephraim London and New York University professor Ernst Van den Haag. The same two men who were adversaries in a criminal trial before a three-judge bench were now pitting their wits in civil discourse before a nationwide television audience.

The general concept of censorship made eminent sense to the sociologist and psychoanalyst Van den Haag. "There is something that you call 'self-censorship.'...When things tend to arouse too much anxiety," he pronounced, "people in effect repress them. I wish to suggest that censorship as a whole is really this process reproduced in society." London reminded Van den Haag of the personal price that he might pay in such a repressive society: "We can't judge by what the majority feels at any time. If we did, Professor Van den Haag would not be practicing psychiatry today because the people were not ready to accept psychiatry in the past." To London, most obscenity regulations were anathema to principles of democratic self-government. "In a democracy," he argued, "we must assume that the adult is able to determine for himself what he should see, and what he should read, and what he should buy."

Clarifying his position, Van den Haag retorted: "I don't think we have to assume there are people we have to protect. But it seems obvious that people themselves seem to favor such laws....We can try to minimize censorship. But I do not think that we can eliminate it." "Professor Van den Haag," replied London, "in this country we have a tradition of minority rights. It is not only what the community as a whole wants, but it is also what the minority wants....Creations which yesterday were the detested and the obscene become the classics of today."

It was as though the civil libertarian and the conservative pedagogue were rehearsing their roles for *People v. Bruce*. For, when they next met, Ephraim London was cross-examining Ernst Van den Haag on his testimony as a rebuttal witness for the State's case. Bruce's lawyer attempted to undermine Van den Haag's credibility as an expert by demonstrating that he was entirely "out-of-touch" with the nightclub scene and, thus, had no real foundation for evaluating community standards for the use of vulgarity in nightclubs:

London: Dr. Van den Haag, have you ever made a study of nightclub performances?

Van den Haag: No, sir.

London: When did you last attend a nightclub?

Van den Haag: Well, that may be twenty years ago.

London: Then you do not claim to have expertise in what is acceptable or not acceptable in nightclubs, do you?

Van den Haag: No, sir, I wouldn't agree. I do....I do claim some expertise in the sense that I believe you can study something theoretically without having the direct experience of it....One can study prostitution, no doubt, without being a prostitute, and so one can also study the behavior of nightclub audiences and their reactions without being in a nightclub....[Chief Justice John Murtagh no doubt appreciated this argument, if only because in 1957 he had coauthored a book on prostitution.]

London: And your study has been limited to reading what other people have written about nightclubs and speaking to your personal friends?...And when you speak of friends, I assume you are talking of your social friends?

Van den Haag: Yes.

London: People who share your intellectual interests?

Van den Haag: I never find people who do....

London: Have you ever studied the content of any nightclub performer's monologue?

Van den Haag: This is the first....

London: Yet, on the basis of your reading of other people's material, and on the basis of what some other people may have said about

nightclub performances, and without having heard a single nightclub performance in twenty years, you have stated to the Court that
Mr. Bruce, in his nightclub performances, has transgressed the
boundaries?...
Van den Haag: Mr. London, I said the boundaries of community
standards, which I conceded to you before are drawn considerably
more widely in nightclubs than in other parts of the community, but
it seemed to me that Mr. Bruce exceeded the general boundaries
that a community would expect to be respected even in a nightclub.
London: And I say you reached that conclusion without having
attended a nightclub performance in twenty years—
Van den Haag: I reached that conclusion as a member of the community, not of nightclubs....
London: Again, your answer, then, is based on your knowledge of
general community standards, not on your knowledge of whatever is
performed in nightclubs?
Van den Haag: Yes, sir.

London employed the same tactic to undermine the credibility of
other rebuttal witnesses, sometimes to rather embarrassing results:

London: Mr. Potter, when is the last time you went to a nightclub?
Potter: About six months ago....It was the "Hawaiian Club" at the
Lexington Hotel, and I am not certain of the artist's name who
performed.
London: Are you aware that the "Hawaiian Room" is not consid-
ered a nightclub? Are you aware of that?
Kuh: If your Honor please, I don't know who considers it. I think
the question is improper.
Murtagh: The court is well acquainted with what the "Hawaiian
Room" is. I don't think we need to get into a matter of semantics.

Just as prosecutor Kuh had done in his cross-examination of the
defense's expert witnesses, London used several *attack-the-person*
strategies. In addition to challenging a witness's expertise, the defense
counsel favored the *reductio ad absurdum* tactic: push an expert's

opinion to the point where the person appears either absurd or highly biased. This worked most effectively in his cross-examination of Daniel Potter, where London tried to portray the reverend as an inveterate "bluenose" willing to censor literature that was unquestionably protected under the First Amendment:

> *Potter*: As co-chairman of the committee of religious leaders appointed by the mayor, we have had projects of studying community standards from the point of view of newspapers, pictures, magazines, literature, books, and publications...
>
> *London*: [I]s it not true that many books use the word "fuck" with considerable frequency?
>
> *Potter*: I would say some....[T]his is obviously a suggestive word, and in the judgment of our committee this kind of word is not used generally in the average family, in the average group in our community.
>
> *London*: Now, would your same objection be made to the word "fornicate"?
>
> *Potter*: Yes....
>
> *London*: And you would make the same objection to the words "sexual intercourse"?
>
> *Potter*: Yes, "sexual intercourse" is not used—each of these are [used] in varying degrees, I will admit. In other words, the use of the word "sexual intercourse," or the use of that expression relating to cohabitation with the sexes is used in medical terms...
>
> *London*: So that the words "sexual intercourse" is permissible in a medical context or scientific context, but not in a social one?
>
> *Potter*: And it is not acceptable in the social one, the word that you said....
>
> *London*: Have you read the book, *Lady Chatterley's Lover*?...You are aware...the word "fuck" is used quite frequently in that book?
>
> *Potter*: Yes.
>
> *London*: And it is offensive to you even in that context?
>
> *Potter*: Yes.
>
> ...
>
> *Schwartz*: Can you concede on a situation where a performer may take the stage in a nightclub and use the word "shit," and that you

may find it acceptable usage, acceptable for your purposes and for the church's purposes? Could you concede of any such situation?
Potter: This would be very rare. I am not presently able to imagine quite a situation where it would be considered non-offensive or somewhat humiliating, and embarrassing to the average person.

THE AIR-CONDITIONED environment of Courtroom 535 heated up during the controversy regarding the defense counsel's "test of the petition." London read Allen Ginsberg's cry against censorship, and asked several of the rebuttal witnesses if they agreed with any of the statements. This was all too much for Richard Kuh, who charged that London was out of bounds:

> *London*: Now, I show you the [petition], the one I just read, and ask you to read that. If I tell you that Mr. Epstein testified that [the petition expressed] his opinion,…will you state now whether or not you agree with any of the statements in [it]?…
> *Sylvester*: Mr. Epstein is a brilliant man and fully qualified to have any opinion in the world of literature. I am not familiar with Mr. Bruce's act; and that is why I must fail to answer it.
> *London*: Well, will you read the whole statement, please, and see if there is any part of it with which you agree.
> *Sylvester*: I would agree that it is not the function of the police department of New York or any other city to decide what adult private citizens may or may not do.…
> *Kuh*: May I ask that answer be stricken.…May I suggest to Your Honors that what should or should not be the law is properly considered in a legislative hearing, but not a judicial proceeding.
> *Creel*: Are you quite so certain? A lot of judges presume to take over this field.
> *Kuh*: If they have, I think they make a bad mistake.
> *Murtagh*: We will allow it.

By using Allen Ginsberg's petition, of course, London tested the strength of a rebuttal witness's convictions about censoring Bruce. At long last, Kuh spied an opportune moment to checkmate his opponent. London asked Reverend Potter if he would agree with the eminent theologian Rheinhold Niebuhr, who had signed the petition, whether "Lenny Bruce is a popular and controversial performer in the field of social satire in the tradition of Swift, Rabelais, and Twain."

As Kuh well understood, Niebuhr's was "a name to conjure with," and he was hell-bent to prevent the defense from ever conjuring anything with that name. Tipped off by a *New York Times* report that Dr. Niebuhr had endorsed the petition without seeing Bruce's acts or reading anything about them, Kuh went into action in early July, while the defense counsels were still putting on their case. By way of Niebuhr's son, with whom Kuh was acquainted, the prosecutor solicited a letter from the theologian.

"I want to confess that my signature to that petition was ill advised," Niebuhr wrote. "It was prompted by conversations with friends who knew Bruce and who had competence to judge the merits of social satire." Niebuhr continued: "I violated the habit of a lifetime in signing a petition which had to do with some issue about which I had no personal knowledge. I will make no charge against Bruce; but also I will not say anything in his defense."

Now, describing the contents of the letter to the court, Kuh was ready to submit it into evidence to counter "the defense tactic of having wrung [Niebuhr's] name into the testimony as a sort of absent and exalted witness." Attempting to quiet Kuh, London withdrew his earlier question to Reverend Potter about agreeing with Niebuhr's opinion. Kuh, however, would not be silenced:

Kuh: At this point, I will not withdraw. I would like to be heard.
London: If your Honor pleases, I am still cross-examining this witness...This is entirely improper.
Kuh: On a voir dire on this question, in this area, concerning Rheinhold Niebuhr, I think this is the proper time.
London: There is no voir dire of Rheinhold Niebuhr. This is utter nonsense....
Kuh: I think this record should not stand with a misleading and insulting assault on the integrity of a leading churchman in it. And

I think this court should allow this exhibit not on the truth of whether or not Bruce is obscene, but simply to clarify this record concerning the absurd use of the name Niebuhr by this defense....I say, as a member of the bar and as an officer of this Court, that that letter was produced by me after a telephone conversation with Rheinhold Niebuhr, whose telephone number I got from his son, who is personally known to me. And I say that letter is without doubt authentic, and I will vouch for it.

Murtagh: Mr. Kuh is out of order, and the offer is not accepted.

London: He is out of order at the top of his voice.

Phipps: No, no, no.

Creel: Let's get on with it.

Murtagh: This is not the proper time, and his offer is rejected. Proceed.

Never one to be put off lightly, Kuh persisted without flagging. Before reexamining his rebuttal witness, Reverend Potter, Kuh moved the court once again to receive the Niebuhr letter into evidence. During his argument, he read a portion of the *New York Times* article of June 14, reporting on Niebuhr's unfamiliarity with Bruce's routines, thus ensuring that the essence of the theologian's retraction got into the record in any case.

Kuh: [O]n June 14...the *New York Times* says, and I quote, "Dr. Niebuhr, reached by telephone at his summer home in Stockholm, Mass."...Now, in quotes, "I have never seen Mr. Bruce or read anything about him." Close quotes....So, I suggest, here, when Mr. London suggests to this witness that Reverend Niebuhr knew what he was signing when he signed it, I suggest a deceit is being practiced not only upon this witness, but a wilful deceit is being practiced upon this court; and more important, and I say this with respect to this court, a wilful slander upon the name of one of our leading theologians...

The court refused to receive the letter into evidence, but Chief Justice Murtagh noted that "this court certainly can ignore innuendo; and they need no further reference to Reverend Niebuhr..." Still not satisfied, Kuh seized one last chance to have his way on the matter:

Kuh: Reverend Potter, will you tell me whether you agree or disagree with this statement, "But I should not have signed the petition at all, because I have no firsthand knowledge of Bruce's performance, and therefore—"
Murtagh: Mr. Kuh.
London: Objection. I move that the question be stricken.
Murtagh: Sustained. Strike it out.
Kuh: May I just make it clear, if your Honor please, that I would like this as a court's exhibit for the limited purpose for which I expressed its use [i.e., to establish that Niebuhr signed the letter without prior knowledge], and not on guilt or innocence...
London: I object to its being considered as an exhibit, your Honor.
Murtagh: Objection sustained.

Kuh threw in the towel, and the trial proceeded at a less feverish pitch.

BEYOND CHALLENGING THE credibility of the state's rebuttal witnesses, London cross-examined them to establish that Bruce's dirty words were commonplace, well within the bounds of "contemporary community standards." First, London endeavored to show that the expert witnesses themselves used vulgarities in their own conversations, even in the presence of mixed company. Thus, he asked the *New York Daily News* columnist, Robert Sylvester:

London: You spoke, Mr. Sylvester, of strong language. I suppose you mean the words like "fuck" and "shit" and "tits," and the like?
Sylvester: Yes, sir.
London: Those are words that you use in your conversation, are they not?
Sylvester: Yes, sir, many of them, to an invited audience.
London: And, as a matter of fact, you use that language in mixed company, with ladies present?
Sylvester: Not all, sir.
London: Several of them?

Sylvester: Several of them.

London: As a matter of fact, you have used those words in con-demning censorship, have you not?

Sylvester: I have.

Second, London attempted to establish that Lenny's crudities were a customary practice in the New York arena of nightclub entertainment. Again, he cross-examined Robert Sylvester and others to elicit that they had heard other comedians who spouted such vulgarities:

> *London*: You stated a moment ago, Mr. Sylvester, that there were comedians who used some of this language extensively, and by that I mean these words, "fuck," "shit," "tits," and the like. Now, can you give me the names of those performers?
>
> *Sylvester*: Jackie Cannon at the Rat Fink Room carries vulgarity to quite an extreme....
>
> *Creel*: To the same extreme as these two transcripts?
>
> *Sylvester*: No, sir. No, your Honor....
>
> *London*: Have you heard Dean Martin...[u]se the same language or at least some of it?
>
> *Sylvester*: Not to that extent, Mr. London.
>
> *London*: But he does use some of those words?
>
> *Sylvester*: He is vulgar, yes.
>
> *London*: In public performance?
>
> *Sylvester*: Yes, sir.

On Tuesday afternoon, July 28, 1964, Ernst Van den Haag delivered the last critical words on Bruce's comedic words. During redirect exam-ination, the professor concluded: Bruce's "discourse did not offer any-thing much in terms of wit or elegance of speech or poetry or whatever cognitive content. The point must be...the unfamiliar use of taboo words in public when people sort of waited for them but wondered, 'Does he dare, or will he?'" An anticlimactic cross-examination and another brief redirect followed, and Van den Haag left the stand. The People rested.

A BOLT FROM the blue. A flurry of activity from the defense table, and—for the first time during the entire trial—Lenny stood up to address the court:

> *Lenny*: Your Honor, at this time, I would like to ask the court to allow me to speak. I do have counsel that ably represents me but I have a problem communicating with them, and there is evidence withheld from the court and I would—
>
> *Murtagh*: The court strongly advises you to be guided by the wisdom of counsel. You are fortunate in having most distinguished and able counsel.
>
> *Lenny*: This is evidence important to the court and I don't have the opportunity to communicate with—and I don't have the opportunity to—
>
> *Murtagh*: We'll take a short recess to allow you to communicate with the counsel.

Who knows exactly what Bruce and London said to one another during those tense moments? Reports varied. Nat Hentoff later noted that London told Bruce not to testify, lest Kuh bring up his former obscenity busts. London later stated curtly: "Lenny is a real genius, a near-genius, but the most inept lawyer I've ever run across." Kuh later suggested that London advised against Lenny's taking the stand because he thought he "was not articulate." And Bruce later claimed that London told him his "important" evidence would be introduced more appropriately on appeal.

Whatever the reason or reasons, it was clear that London was prepared to withdraw from the case if Bruce did not abide by his advice; during the recess, London packed his briefcase in a huff. Finally, Lenny surrendered, however dispiritedly. On the advice—really, the insistence—of counsel, he forfeited his free speech rights in order to safeguard a right against self-incrimination. Ephraim London spoke up: "If the court please, Mr. Bruce has agreed to be guided by my advice and the defendant Bruce now rests." Allen Schwartz, on behalf of the Solomons, rested too.

The incident was but a passing storm, or so it seemed. The defense counsels renewed their motions to dismiss; the court set dates for legal memoranda; and the trial was over. It had been forty-three agonizing days since the first of thirty trial witnesses took the stand. It would be another ninety-nine anxious days until the parties returned before the court. That would be Judgment Day.

Playing the Court

EPHRAIM LONDON NEVER really listened to Lenny. London ignored him when he whispered suggestions during the trial, or passed notes that he had written furiously with his redflow pens. London patronized him, sometimes treating him like a child; once, when Lenny tried to look at a legal document on the defense table, London slapped his hand right there before the justices. London dismissed him when he argued that the only way to win was to put on the *real* Lenny. "I'll perform my act. They'll see I'm not obscene," Bruce repeated over and over. "They've got to *see* me work. [Otherwise,] it's like judging a foreign film by just the soundtrack."

London slighted all the hot evidence that Lenny had dug up or compiled—like documents on the original meaning of the "actors" exception to Section 1140-A ("I sent to Albany and I got the legislative history"), or a list of numerous damning errors in the state's transcripts of his performances ("One thousand two hundred and seventy-three words omitted and 857 words inserted, clearly a total of 2,130 errors in wording," for thirty-four transcript pages alone). And London disregarded the many long letters that Lenny sent all through the summer from his walnut-paneled office in Los Angeles, requesting that the trial be reopened so that he might testify and the new evidence be introduced.

No more. Lenny had had it up to here. He began to formulate a plan. If London didn't do his bidding, he'd fire him. Then Lenny would take the case over for himself, play the court the way he had played Carnegie Hall, and win.

"There's gonna be a surprise ending to all this," Lenny fantasized. "A big party, where all the judges and all the D.A.s from all the jurisdictions call me into a room decorated with banners and give me medals and prizes for having faith, and understanding the judicial system, and for not paying the $10 or $25 fines for the misdemeanors." It was really something to imagine: "Dick" Kuh, and "Judge John" in his psychedelic fantasy, raising a glass to "brave Bruce" for saving the legal system from itself.

LENNY EXECUTED THE first stage of his plan on September 2, 1964. He wrote a letter to London, lambasting him for disrespecting the trial court as "merely a recording studio waiting to be administered and overturned by the appellate court." "You are an appellantophile," Lenny struck out, "possessed with 'a shameful and morbid' interest in finding statutes unconstitutional on their face."

Now, it was time to tell London off for discounting the evidence that he had compiled to win this case: "And your statement, 'I agree that your transcript of the performance at the Café Au Go Go is better than the one offered in evidence. There is nothing to prevent us from using your transcript…on appeal,' is insanity. What the fuck is the matter with you, Ephraim?" Finally, Lenny delivered his ultimatum: "[S]hould you choose to ignore the following instructions for whatever reason you might have, then I ask you to accept this letter as notice that I don't intend paying you the money I originally promised to pay you….[S]ubmit these transcripts, tapes…AND GET THEM INTO THE RECORD."

London replied with a letter of his own: a bill for services totaling $15,541. The bill showed a paid retainer of approximately $1,000, with some $14,000 still owing. Lenny kept his word: he stiffed London. Within weeks, Bruce was a named defendant in another controversy—this time, a civil action for breach of contract filed by his former lawyer.

Having fired London, Lenny moved to the second stage of his plan. He would inform the court that he wanted to act as his own counsel from this point forward (or "*propria persona*," as Bruce called it), and alert the justices to the important evidence he wanted to introduce. Lenny, the Counselor, was in the habit of writing to his judges;

he had practiced the art with Judge Clayton Horn in San Francisco (for which he was held in contempt) and with Judge Daniel Ryan in Chicago. So, he sat right down and wrote Chief Justice Murtagh a letter, a very long letter.

Dated September 10, 1964, Lenny's mind-boggling missive began: "Dear Judge Murtaugh." Misspelling Murtagh's name in the salutation was no way to impress an already unsympathetic jurist. Lenny asked to proceed *propria persona*, given that he already had dismissed Ephraim London. The reason he gave was that his former counsel "withheld from the Court" some "very important evidence." In his characteristic writing style—with its syntactical loopiness and meandering logic—Lenny expressed his gratitude for the opportunity to arrest this travesty of justice in due time: "[W]hen the Court is deciding they are deciding and they do not make their decisions until they have finished deciding."

The letter proceeded to take the justice on a magical mystery tour through the *Webster's Third New International Dictionary*. Lenny had studied the meanings of each and every word in a list of "purple vocabulary" condemned in the People's brief (filed in opposition to the defense motions to acquit). He noted the distinctions between the "literal" (or original) and the "contemporary" (or slang) meanings of those words. Since the First Amendment protects expression consistent with contemporary community standards, it followed (at least, in Lenny's mind) that public usage of slang words could never be obscene. "All the words I use are considered slang," Bruce informed Murtagh, except for words like "cunt" and "motherfucker." Accordingly, he declared, "Ninety-eight percent of the words I used are correct words in *Webster's Third New International Dictionary* which is the highest authority."

To underscore his point, Lenny provided the literal and contemporary definitions of a few choice words, and demonstrated how his routines made sense only in the context of the slang meanings. "The hyphenated phrase, 'You jive motherfucker,' did not mean, literally, 'You intercourse one's mother, you.'" Lenny tendered *Webster's Third* as preachers do the Bible or lawyers do the Constitution—as the highest validating authority. He offered the results of his definitional exegesis as if he were engaging in a Talmudic exercise. And he submitted his evidence as though he were an *amicus curiae* filing a Brandeis brief. All said, he concluded: "And the last, but most important statement I wish to make to the Court is that my intent is not one of contempt. Communication is my desire." The problem was that Lenny's communication was unique—and often incomprehensible to someone who did not strive to make reason out of ramblings.

Communication between the defendant Bruce and his obscenity judges was two-way. Shortly after his letter was mailed to Justice Murtagh, Lenny received notice of the September 14, 1964, decision of the Appellate Department of the California Superior Court in the Trolley Ho rendition of *People v. Bruce*. The good news: Judge Bernard Selber's June 11, 1964, pretrial ruling in his favor had just been affirmed by a 2 to 1 vote. The bad news: the majority opinion was perfunctory, extremely narrow in scope, and unpublished. Moreover, it had no precedential authority for Bruce's obscenity cases outside of Los Angeles.

The memorandum opinion of Judge Frank G. Swain contained fewer than one hundred words, and read in relevant part: "In the case at bar, the tape recording of the alleged obscene material was played to the trial judge, as the only evidence of the same, but is not part of the record before us. Lacking that, we have no basis for holding that the judge erred. The order of dismissal is affirmed." Judge Sherman W. Smith, the jurist who had released Lenny on bail in the 1963 Le Grand case, concurred. But the third member of the panel, Judge Harold P. Huls, saw the matter differently and dissented. In essence, he argued that the trial court's ruling on the merits "unconstitutionally deprived the People of a jury trial. Had a jury decided that the recording was obscene, we cannot say that the same trial judge would have held that it was not." A philosophically interesting point, but a legally bizarre one nonetheless. Not outraged by the purported denial of their constitutional rights, the People did not appeal the case to the U.S. Supreme Court (which was the only recourse that the prosecution had).

Lenny Bruce could now claim two legal victories, albeit technical ones, in Los Angeles—the dismissals of the Troubadour/Unicorn and

Trolley Ho charges. Those *might* prove enough to ward off *official* harassment by the LAPD and the County Sheriff's Office. But, such Pyrrhic victories were not likely to influence Justice Murtagh much more than Lenny Bruce's letter to him.

MAKING A SPECIAL trip to New York, Lenny appeared briefly before Justice Murtagh on October 5. Accompanied by Martin Garbus, Lenny requested that his defense team be relieved and that he himself be named as counsel of record. Furthermore, he asked that the trial be reopened and that he be allowed to present new evidence. Lenny advised Murtagh that he felt "qualified" to do this because of his "respect for the court." Presiding alone, Murtagh explained to Bruce that the full court was not in session, but that it would take the matter under consideration. Lenny was to make his formal application to the court on November 4, the date proposed for final decision. Predictably, Richard Kuh objected to the month's delay, arguing that he could see no good reason for it. Murtagh, nonetheless, adhered to the date set.

Once again, it was standing room only in Courtroom 535 on November 4 at ten A.M. When Bruce appeared late, friends and foes smirked and whispered among themselves. He had shaved his beard ("There's no sense in making it too easy for them"); and, for the first time since the trial began, he was dressed in a black jacket and tight black pants, and sporting a tie. Inveterate Bruce groupies might well have recalled one of his bits about wearing a suit in court: "How do you spot the crooks? They got the suits on, *schmuck*."

Lenny got off on the wrong foot right from the start. When Chief Justice Murtagh asked whether he was represented by counsel, Bruce reminded him that London and Garbus had been relieved. Murtagh testily corrected this misimpression: "The court clearly advised you at the time that court was not in session. I was presiding alone. I did not rule on any substitution. Ephraim London is still your counsel. If the request is he be relieved, then the court can now consider that request." Request made and granted, Bruce launched immediately into his role as Counselor.

In the Courtroom of the Absurd, Lenny's performance was high drama. Pleading for the court to reopen the case, he begged to be given a voice—to be allowed to speak freely—to be recognized finally for what he *really* was, and not for the filthy and perverse portrayal that had emerged from the distortions of his own counsels' representation:

> *Lenny*: I want to tell you what the performance is, what I do. I am not obscene....If your Honor will allow me to represent some of the gestures....Your Honor, the gestures, masturbations, were gestures of benediction. I did a bit on Catholicism. How perverse Ephraim London would be to defend me for gestures of masturbation. They were meant to be gestures of benediction. I have the right to say "fuck you." I didn't say it. Please, your Honor, I so desperately want your respect. I want the court to know....
>
> *Murtagh*: The court has all of your arguments to that effect before it.
>
> *Lenny*: The court hasn't heard the show....[P]lease let me testify. Let me tell you what the show is about....Finally to talk to the court....I had said these counsel are insane. I must talk to the court. They are defending me, throwing me in with a band of pornographers....I realize I come back before this court as Eichmann before a Jewish judge.

He was getting nowhere, and he knew it. Suddenly, it was meltdown. The typically "scathing, self-lacerating, jivey, *j'accusing*" Bruce dissolved into the submissive, self-pitying, victimized, pathetic Bruce:

> *Lenny*: Don't finish me off in show business. Don't lock up these six thousand words. That's what you are doing, taking three counts, taking away my words, locking them up. These plays can never be said again. You are finishing me up in show business.
>
> *Murtagh*: Mr. Bruce, the case has been closed....The case is on here for decision today....
>
> *Lenny*: I want to know why you won't let me tell you.
>
> *Murtagh*: We must conclude now these proceedings.

THE TRIALS OF LENNY BRUCE

Now, it was Justice Murtagh's cue to take center stage. It was time for the court to speak. Raising his voice over the flagging Bruce, he pronounced judgment:

> *Murtagh:* Appropriate motions have been made to dismiss the information against all three defendants on the ground the People have failed to prove the defendants' guilt beyond a reasonable doubt. Having considered all of the evidence, after due deliberation, all of these motions are denied as to each count with respect to the defendants Lenny Bruce and Howard Solomon. The court, Judge Creel dissenting, finds the defendants Lenny Bruce and Howard Solomon guilty as charged. The court by unanimous vote finds the defendant Ella Solomon not guilty. The court will file its opinion and a dissenting opinion by Judge Creel....[T]he defendants Lenny Bruce and Howard L. Solomon will be sentenced on December 16.

Lenny asked to be sentenced immediately "since I have no more money left to live on in this area. I cannot work, as you know." Justice Murtagh sternly refused his request, and ordered Bruce and Solomon to undergo psychiatric examinations and probation investigation before sentencing. Bruce exited, ignoring the court officer's instruction to wait for fingerprinting.

"I'm like something out of a Kafka novel," Lenny would say. Like Joseph K., the joyless antihero in Franz Kafka's unfinished and fragmentary story, "The Trial," Lenny had struggled, madly at times, to obtain justice from a bureaucratic authority with which he could not communicate effectively. And again like Joseph K., he had ended his trial utterly frustrated, suffering a loss of dignity and respect.

As he left the Criminal Court Building that day, Bruce once again passed by its chiseled precept: "Equal and Exact Justice to All Men of Whatever State or Persuasion." Considering all that had transpired during Lenny's trial, one might well agree with what he once said about justice: "In the Halls of Justice, all the justice is in the halls."

A Court Opinion Unfit to Be Printed

CENSOR: "A PERSON who exercises supervision or judgment over the conduct or morals of others." The word seems so fitting, for so many reasons, for so much of what happened in connection with the trial court opinions in *People v. Bruce*.

Chief Justice Murtagh did not simply announce the court's ruling from the bench as was customary in misdemeanor cases. He also released a mimeographed copy of the majority and dissenting opinions, totaling some five legal-sized, double-spaced typed pages. That was highly unusual for him since only a year earlier, in another obscenity case, Murtagh tried to ban Criminal Court judges from issuing and distributing published opinions. (The controversy arose after a trial judge issued a published opinion declaring that 2 to 1 decisions by the Criminal Court were unconstitutional.) The irony notwithstanding, the mimeographed decision was made public. Now the press and public could read for themselves and decide what they thought of the opinions in *People v. Bruce*.

James M. Flavin, the official state law reporter, decided against publishing any part of *People v. Bruce*. He gave no reasons. Thus, while there were a few mimeographs of the opinions, not a single word graced the pages of the official state reports. Thereafter, the *New York Law Journal* (a widely read legal newspaper) also declined to publish the *Bruce* opinion. That story was a bit more complicated.

In its November 24, 1964, issue, the *Journal* ran a front-page "Notes and Views" column by Justice James Randall Creel. The column was a slightly edited version of his dissent. But where was the "column" for the majority opinion? Subscribers (such as the noted obscenity lawyer Charles Rembar) complained. It was censorship, this unwillingness to publish the majority's opinion—the same opinion that announced the guilt of Lenny Bruce and Howard Solomon for exercising their First Amendment rights. The editors, however, were of a different mindset:

> The majority opinion, of necessity, cited in detail the language used
> by Bruce in his night-club act and described gestures and routines

which the majority found to be obscene and indecent. The *Law Journal* decided against publication, even edited, on the grounds that deletions would destroy the opinion, and without the deletions publication was impossible within *Law Journal* standards.

Such irony. Essentially, the *Journal* would not publish the majority opinion because it was obscene and indecent. (About twenty percent of the opinion consisted of a dry recitation of Lenny's "vulgar" words and bits.) What the majority had written was law, albeit court-law. Hence, the editors' refusal to publish *People v. Bruce* was, in effect, a refusal to publish a statement of the law. Remarkably, the application of the law to the facts had been deemed obscene. Like so much else in *People v. Bruce*, it was unprecedented, if not surreal.

The unpublished majority opinion was *per curiam*, meaning "for the court." That is a fancy Latin way of saying that the author or authors of the decision wished to remain nameless. (It was not, however, *per totam curiam*, meaning for the entire court.) Since Justice Creel dissented, the author of the *per curiam* was either Justice Murtagh or Justice Phipps, or perhaps the work-product of both men. (Most likely, John Murtagh was the main man behind the opinion, or the bulk of it.) What we do know, thanks to Richard Kuh, is that the unsigned opinion drew "substantially from the prosecution's memorandum." In that sense, Kuh was one of the "authors" of the trial court majority opinion in *People v. Bruce*.

It was some twelve hundred words long, the length of an op-ed in a Sunday paper. The unpublished opinion is remarkable for what it said, as well as for what it failed to say. For example, the *per curiam* mentioned only three cases, *Roth* and two New York decisions. It did not mention the U.S. Supreme Court's decisions in *Jacobellis v. Ohio* and *Tropic of Cancer*, or the then recently decided *Larkin v. G.P. Putnam's Sons* handed down by the New York high court. Of course, the last three opinions were all *favorable* to the positions argued and briefed by Ephraim London and Allen Schwartz. In a similar vein, the majority made no mention whatsoever of several of the constitutional claims raised time and again by the defendants. Arguments about due process, for example, were simply ignored.

While the majority was not hesitant to repeat Lenny's dirty words—e.g., "tits," "ass," "fucking," "pissing"—it revealed *nothing* about the context in which many of the words were used. Thus, a bit about false patriotism, about accepted forms of *braggadocio*, was reduced to "'Shoving' a funnel of hot lead 'up one's ass.'" Anything in Bruce's acts resembling socially redeeming value was left unmentioned. It was as if Lenny had taken to the stage for an hour and said nothing but "fuck," "shit," "cocksucker," "motherfucker" and "fuck," "shit," "cocksucker," "motherfucker" and "fuck," "shit," "cocksucker," "motherfucker," nonstop.

The *per curiam* opinion was strong on conclusory pronouncements. For example: "The dominant theme of the performances appealed to prurient interest and was patently offensive to the average person in the community, as judged by present-day standards. The performances were lacking in 'redeeming social importance.'" It announced such constitutional catchphrases in a talismanic fashion, as if their mere mention made them true.

The opinion was as weak on legal argumentation as it was strong on unsupported conclusions. Take its reliance on a 1963 New York opinion, *People v. Fritch*, one of three appellate opinions to which it cited. The author—or authors—of the *per curiam* felt no duty to disclose the fact that *Fritch* had been "overruled," as the New York Court of Appeals had expressly announced four months earlier. However innocent their reliance on a concurring opinion in *Fritch*, they nonetheless should have revealed the legal status of that case.

The majority dispensed with the defense's many constitutional arguments in a summary fashion: "Section 1140-a of the Penal Law is not unconstitutional as contended by defendants. The statute was before the Court of Appeals in *People v. Wendling* (1932), and though the conviction there was reversed, *the court did not declare the statute unconstitutional.*" Though technically true, the statement is highly misleading for several reasons.

The *Wendling* court did not declare Section 1140-A unconstitutional, if only because it had *absolutely* no reason to do so. Since it ruled in favor of the defendants under the statute, the court had no right in logic or law even to consider any constitutional questions. Not surprisingly, the court never said anything about the statute's constitutionality. What the *Wendling* court did say, in an opinion by Judge Cuthbert Pound, was something quite different: "the Court is not a censor of plays and does not attempt to regulate manners." It also declared that "course, vulgar, and profane" words, when used in a "cheap and tawdry" play, do not necessarily violate Section 1140-A. "Unless we say," added Judge Pound, "that it is obscene to use the language of the street rather than that of the scholar, the play is not obscene under the Penal Law, although it might be so styled by the censorious." In short, however "repulsive" the language of the stage, "puritanical ideas of propriety" do not inform the content of the law. Thus, when Justices Murtagh and Phipps invoked *Wendling* in their *per curiam* opinion, they were actually relying on legal authority *favorable* to Lenny Bruce and Howard Solomon.

The *per curiam* opinion was more faithful to the law when it quoted from Justice Brennan's 1957 *Roth* opinion for the proposition that a thing is obscene if it appeals to a "shameful or morbid interest in nudity, sex, or excretion, and if it goes substantially beyond customary limits of candor in description or representation of such matters." Seven years after *Roth* and four obscenity prosecutions later, the counsels for Lenny Bruce were still saddled with Brennan's troublesome language...buried in a footnote, no less. Problematic as it was, enough First Amendment case law had come down in federal and state courts to indicate that such language was insufficient to hang the likes of Lenny Bruce.

Howard Solomon, the majority held, "is equally guilty with the defendant Lenny Bruce" insofar as he "*actively participated in the presentation of performances.*" With Ella Solomon, the case was different. She had done no more, noted the *per curiam*, than "assist her husband." But if she had assisted him as he "actively participated in the presentation of performances," why then was her fate different? After all, she was the president of the Café Au Go Go Corporation; she had advertised the Bruce performances; and she knew of Lenny's routines and had spoken with him about them. The same law that was interpreted so sternly against Lenny and Howard was applied relatively compassionately against Ella. Still, like Howard she had paid her dues for sharing Lenny Bruce with a willing public. Unlike Howard, she did not have to continue paying; and unlike Lenny, she did not have to pay with her liberty.

Justice James Randall Creel's dissent—nearly twice as long as the majority opinion—concluded that "the performances of Lenny Bruce here in question are found not to be obscene." In reaching this conclusion, the judge was duly mindful of the recent federal and state high court rulings that had "materially changed and lowered the legal standards as to obscenity." Even so, he granted that the law of obscenity was unclear to the point that trial judges desperately needed "guideposts and directives from the higher courts." By no measure had Creel made a compelling case for Bruce's free speech claims; nonetheless, his legal conclusion could be readily aligned with the then-existing First Amendment law.

The more one reads of Justice Creel's dissent, however, the more one wonders what possessed him to write some of the bizarre things he did. For example, early on in his opinion he wrote: "I fear we have proceeded not unlike an explorer plunged into a vast uncharted virgin area in pursuit of a mirage of some fabled lost golden city." Or maybe it was his references to the "Delphic Oracle" or his equating *People v. Bruce* with the notorious 1857 *Dred Scott* decision. The message was clear: the judge was wildly veering off the judicial path.

The problem, as Creel saw it, was that appellate judges were asserting too much power, thus obliging lowly trial judges to enforce the "new constitutional theory." And that new theory, at least as it applied to obscenity, was producing a "nihilistic state of Judge-made-law." The result? Something beyond good and evil, pure Nietzsche. Or so Creel suggested. While he probably didn't agree with the direction of such "nihilistic" law, he nonetheless felt obliged to honor it.

What to do? Creel's answer was, as with the Civil War, to convene a constitutional convention to address the problem of obscenity. That way the people, acting through the constitutional amendment process, could remedy the problems created by the "'new constitutional theory which licenses sexual filth...'" And once such a constitutional convention was convened, the people could remedy other constitutional defects...such as the unlawful "ratification of the Fourteenth Amendment" by which the guarantees of due process and equal protection were applied against the states. "Strange" does not adequately capture the oddity of Creel's constitutional handiwork. No, it was nothing short of a jurisprudence gone bonkers.

Absurd as so much was about *People v. Bruce*, it was the law. It had real-world consequences on the lives of Lenny Bruce, Howard Solomon, and others who would speak out in Brucean tongues. One of those consequences was the need for still another *costly* round of appeals. Could Lenny afford it, economically, professionally, and mentally?

Victory in Illinois

NOTABLY, BEFORE JUSTICE Murtagh and his colleagues sentenced Lenny Bruce, Judge Ryan's sentence was overturned. The same Illinois high court that had voted 7 to 0 to sustain Bruce's Chicago obscenity conviction five months earlier, now voted 7 to 0 to reverse and discharge it. On November 24, 1964, the Illinois appellate justices issued a *per curiam* opinion. It consisted of a meager 540 words, only a quarter of which might be called, all too kindly, legal analysis. This throwaway opinion in *People v. Bruce* is the only official account of any of Lenny's obscenity trials in all of the published appellate records. (None of Lenny Bruce's other obscenity cases reached the appellate level. There was, however, a published opinion in the appellate case of Lenny's New York codefendant, Howard Solomon.)

"It is apparent from the opinions of a majority of the court in *Jacobellis*," the *per curiam* decision acknowledged, "that material having any social importance is constitutionally protected." Then, the Illinois justices displayed openly their testy and scornful attitude toward the Supreme Court's ruling: "[W]e would not have thought that constitutional guarantees necessitate the subjection of society to the gradual deterioration of its moral fabric which this type of presentation promotes." Still, the court conceded begrudgingly "that

some of the topics commented on by defendant are of social importance." Accordingly, the justices unanimously held that "[u]nder
Jacobellis the entire performance is thereby immunized." (A ninety-
two-word concurring opinion by Justice Schaefer, the court's purported liberal, echoed the State's brief and proposed a more limited
reading of *Jacobellis*.) The Illinois justices had two final words:
"Judgment reversed."

The *per curiam* was an insult to both sides. It did not begin to
reflect the depth of thought, careful reasoning, and eloquent argumentation set forth in the respective briefs. With its curt reversal of the
judgment, the opinion's precedential value might be dismissed. Perhaps, that is why Lenny was not overjoyed by it. But still, Rosenfield,
Kalven, and Ming had moved the mountain. They won a case that had
been botched at the trial level, left largely bereft of a solid record for
appeal, and presented to an unsympathetic state supreme court. The
Illinois trio first had anticipated *Jacobellis* and then used it to secure
Lenny's freedom.

The decision by the Supreme Court in *Jacobellis*, its application
by the New York Court of Appeals in the *Fanny Hill* case, and now its
influence on the Illinois high court in *People v. Bruce* should have sent
strong signals to the New York judges and prosecutors. At best, their
interpretation of the New York obscenity statute was constitutionally
suspect. The proverbial writing was on the wall.

Civil Rights and Uncivil Words

"IT IS TWENTY-FIVE to four and I speak for the record," Bruce
declared. "Your Honor," he told Chief Justice Murtagh and his two
colleagues, "I would like the bench to appoint a referee. The reason
being I have sued Your Honor personally for $500,000 under Section
1983, as your Honor is aware. You were served personally. I sued
Magistrate Phipps and Magistrate Creel, and the civil suit...is still on.
The temporary restraining order was denied, but there is still a suit,
[which is currently on appeal]."

This was *chutzpah* with a vengeance. It was December 21 at ten A.M., the day of Lenny's sentencing (the original date had been postponed due to the §1983 appeal). And he was in open court, before being sentenced, reminding the justices that he had filed a federal civil rights lawsuit for a whopping half million dollars against each of the men who were about to decide what to do with his life and liberty. He had even served Creel, the lone justice who had voted for his freedom. It was a courageous (and crazy) move.

All that time going over statutes and cases (in the Marleton and Earl hotels), and all of that energy spent on reading legal treatises (in hospitals, on planes, and in his House on the Hill) had brought him to this. "Counselor" Lenny had gone to federal court to enjoin the Manhattan and Nassau District Attorneys' offices from prosecuting him; he had gone there, too, seeking damages against the three justices assigned to his case. To this end, he filed an action under 42 U.S.C. Section 1983, which states:

> Every person who, under color of any statute, ordinance, regulation, [etc.]...subjects, or causes to be subjected, any citizen of the United States...to the deprivation of any rights, privileges, or immunities secured by the Constitution, shall be liable to the party injured in any action at law, suit in equity, or other proper proceeding for redress.

The law came on the federal books in the nineteenth century. More commonly known as the "Ku Klux Klan Act of April 20, 1871," the purpose of the law was to enable Americans, especially people of color, to sue state officials for violations of their Fourteenth Amendment rights, particularly their rights to due process and equal protection under the law. Many Southern sheriffs were the targets of Section 1983 actions for police brutality against blacks. The statute was an essential weapon in the arsenal of civil rights lawyers like William Ming Jr., one of Lenny's Illinois appellate attorneys. Only a few years earlier, in *Monroe v. Pape* (1961), Justice William O. Douglas ruled for the Supreme Court that the statute could be used to sue thirteen Chicago police officers for allegedly violating the plaintiffs' rights to be free from warrantless searches and arrests. Donald Page Moore, one of

Lenny's Chicago trial lawyers, successfully argued that case. Given the *Monroe* case, if others could sue the police for violating their Fourth Amendment rights, why shouldn't Lenny be able to sue prosecutors and judges for violating his First Amendment rights? Bruce decided to try that legal theory when, in early December 1964, he filed his novel Section 1983 action in the federal district court in Manhattan.

Not surprisingly for someone who lacked formal training in the law, Lenny fumbled the filing procedures. His complaint was predictably dismissed by the district court. That's where the appeal, which he mentioned to Justice Murtagh, came in. His next performance—with Lenny debuting as an appellate litigator—would be before the United States Court of Appeals for the Second Circuit. Finally, a new venue, another chance, a new day. But as the big moment drew near, Lenny got cold feet; he now wanted a *real* lawyer to argue the case. Better still, a scholarly law professor could handle the appeal before Judges Henry Friendly, Paul Hays, and Thurgood Marshall. He sorely needed someone who knew how to work the system. But, could he be that someone? As his friend Selma Rovinsky observed at the time: "His mental attitude is more than a little nervous."

Down to Foley Square in lower Manhattan and then up seventeen floors. There, in a spacious and handsomely furnished courtroom, Lenny Bruce would take a deep breath and argue his case before a distinguished panel of three federal judges. What a scene: clad in a white Nehru jacket, Bruce strolled in, armed with law books, legal notepads, and a bulging briefcase. He waited until his case was called; then he stood up, walked to the counsel's table and set down some of his tagged books, proceeded to the podium, laid down a few more books, and finally explained his purpose in being there:

> I want them to stop prosecuting me in the future. I want you to enjoin them from any arrests for my act, and to stop them from putting me in jail. I'll show you some of it so you'll see there is nothing wrong with it.

Lenny's performing before a court was always risky, some would say suicidal. Judge Axelrod had not appreciated his act in San Francisco;

Judge Ryan had not enjoyed it in Chicago; and at least two of the three New York trial judges definitely had not liked it. The fact is, Bruce typically bombed in the courtroom. No matter, he was a taboo liberator; his latest round of judges would understand that.

According to Martin Garbus, who was then present, Lenny "went into a sketch commenting on the kinds of justice all white men can expect from black juries, pointing out that black men would treat whites as badly as they themselves had been treated. He concluded with his imitation of an outraged liberal, saying 'They gave me twenty years for raising my voice—those niggers.'" The ugly *N*-word caught Thurgood Marshall's attention. His "head jerked up immediately....Bruce saw Marshall's face, stumbled, tried bravely to explain the joke, but could not." Ⓒⓓ

On the merits, Bruce's Section 1983 action was really a long shot; "only under extraordinary circumstances would a federal court bar a state from continuing a prosecution it had already begun." Moreover, since Lenny had bungled the case below, he was nowhere near showing that the federal trial court had abused its discretion. While Judge Marshall probably did not value Lenny's *shtick*, there was ample reason to rule against him even without offense to the three-judge panel. And rule against him it did. In the end, Lenny's legal maneuvering failed to impress the federal judges and further infuriated the state judges.

"The Jew Is Not Remorseful"

WITH VEILED DISGUST, Justice Murtagh told Lenny Bruce, "Your motion is denied." He summarily dismissed Lenny's plea that the court recuse itself and appoint a master. Three justices (who had been involved in this overblown misdemeanor trial for eight and a half months) were being asked (after the judgment) to avoid any conflict of interest caused by the lawsuit Bruce had filed against them. The very idea that the defendant could disqualify his judges simply by suing them seemed absurd.

The recusal issue over, the justices were now prepared to take up the business of sentencing. Section 1140-A of the New York Penal

Code authorized the court to impose a maximum sentence of one year in prison and/or a fine of $500 per count. By that measure, Lenny Bruce faced a maximum of three years and $1,500; for Howard Solomon, two years and $1,000. Probation reports and Lenny's psychiatric evaluation were already before the court. Only the mitigation statements might influence the justices' predispositions for sentencing. It was that matter to which the justices wished now to turn.

Bruce derailed the matter—for the next sixty-two minutes, for the next thirty-seven pages of trial transcript. In Lennyspeak, he had another "application" for the court, this one to "arrest" the judgment and introduce new evidence. In lawspeak, Lenny was making a motion to set aside the judgment and reopen the trial.

Counselor Bruce made three major arguments. First, his legislative history research revealed that the court had interpreted Section 1140-A erroneously. Second, the court had misapplied the governing First Amendment law. And, finally, prosecutor Kuh had "encouraged perjury" by introducing inaccurate transcripts of his Café Au Go Go performances. By and large, those were his arguments—as best as can sympathetically be put.

He'd given up on the black coat, tight slacks, and narrow tie look. Now he'd taken on the dirty trenchcoat, torn dungarees, and striped T-shirt look. Not your typical lawyerly garb; but what was forthcoming was not your typical lawyerly argument, either.

In his nightclub act, Lenny talked colorfully about Eleanor Roosevelt's lusty anatomy. In his courtroom act, Lenny lectured seriously about Governor Franklin D. Roosevelt's legal authority. As Bruce saw it, when the court earlier had ruled that the "actor's exception" in the statute did not apply to him, the justices did not have the benefit of his legislative research. Since Ephraim London had not offered any legislative history arguments, it fell to his client to make that case. "I sent to Albany and I got the legislative history, and I would like to read it to Your Honor, it's very short," Lenny assured Justice Murtagh. For the next twenty minutes, he would barrage them with arcania—old letters lobbying the governor, old committee reports, and old assembly bills. All this ostensibly showed that the 1931 amendment to the former Section 1140, which was signed into law by Roosevelt, rendered theater owners or managers alone liable for any obscene shows, not "actors" such as Lenny. "If the Court would not heed this," Bruce warned, "what they're doing, actually, is ignoring Roosevelt. They're ignoring the mandates of Franklin Delano Roosevelt. I assume [this] is a great deal more offensive than saying that the late Eleanor Roosevelt has nice Nays-Nays."

Then came his pronouncements on the state of First Amendment law. With something approximating the "kaleidoscopic" consciousness he had put to good use in his routines, Bruce commingled case names, legal citations, and court rulings in a dizzying mix. Occasionally, there were fleeting insights. For example, Lenny was on the mark when he rightfully attacked Justices Murtagh's and Phipps's *per curiam* opinion for relying on *People v. Wendling* as precedent for the constitutionality of Section 1140-A. But those insights were difficult to discern. Indeed, they were hard to discern for the *Village Voice* reporter then in the courtroom: "Deeper and deeper Bruce went, declaiming decisions, citing citations, lecturing on the law until it became impossible to tell when Bruce was quoting Justice Holmes, or quoting Justice Roberts quoting and commenting on Justice Holmes, or when Bruce himself was quoting and commenting on Justice Roberts quoting and commenting on Justice Holmes."

Proceeding to his last argument, Bruce charged that his prosecutor had encouraged perjury by placing into evidence transcripts ridden with inaccuracies. He claimed to have found thousands of errors when comparing and contrasting his own transcripts of the Café Au Go Go performances to those submitted by the prosecution. For example:

Bruce's Transcripts	People's Transcripts
"a suit three sizes too big"	"a shit three sizes too big"
"Uncle Willie's ruddy palm"	"Uncle Willie's ready"
"You're not getting any secrets"	"You're not giving me any shit"
"the Loew's Pitkin"	"the lowest tit"
"Get us out of here"	"Get us out of her"

"It's a realistic portrayal in prison"	"It's a realistic portrayal that pisses"
"Ladies and Gentlemen"	"Raymond jumps me now"

Though well and good, Justice Murtagh questioned the relevancy of all of this. "The relevancy here, Your Honor," Bruce tried to explain, "has to do with the court's opinion of me….[T]he record is all important, and the fact that Richard Kuh talked Ephraim London into waiving the court reporter when they played the tape, there is nothing on the record." He went a little longer, covering the same ground, before he stated: "That's all I have to say, Your Honors, thank you."

William S. Miller, representing Howard Solomon at the sentencing hearing, preferred a more conventional approach. Essentially, he reminded the court of the significance of the Illinois Supreme Court's recent reversal of Bruce's conviction; he asked the justices to reconsider the verdict in light of that ruling and the *Jacobellis* opinion. Miller then began to offer mitigating circumstances, a point to which he would return.

Always alert to nuance, and always mindful of building a record, prosecutor Kuh declared that, though Bruce was "incoherent" for purposes of his legal argument, he was nonetheless "coherent" for purposes of sentencing (as the psychiatric report established). Phrased differently, the defendant should not be the beneficiary of his irrationality. Reassuring the assistant D.A., Chief Justice Murtagh repeated the old adage: "He reflects nothing more than the fact a person representing himself has a fool for a client."

Harry Hershman was counsel appointed by the court to assist Bruce. He was the seventh of Lenny's New York obscenity lawyers (not counting Counselor Bruce). Hershman wished to address a topic that Lenny had left untouched in this sentencing hearing—the obvious matter of mitigating circumstances. He reminded the court that Bruce had "no prior criminal record, any convictions having recently been reversed." And there was one remaining point that needed to be dealt with: "Your Honors, I would like to add for myself an application to be relieved from further assignment after the sentence of the court."

Unquestionably, the most eloquent and powerful argument to the court on Lenny's behalf was made *in abstentia*. Maurice Rosenfield, Lenny's Illinois appellate counsel, had written a letter on December 8 asking to be heard as a "friend of the Court." Rosenfield's letter urged the justices to set aside their verdict in light of the Illinois Supreme Court's recent reversal of Lenny's Chicago conviction in *People v. Bruce*. "For the completeness of the record," Murtagh noted his receipt of the letter, briefly described the nature of Rosenfield's application, marked it as the Court's Exhibit 1—and perfunctorily denied it. The justice lingered just as long over the defendants' motions: "[With] that statement of the record," Murtagh concluded, "the various motions on behalf of both defendants...are respectfully denied in all respects by the court. Are we ready for sentence?"

Given a last opportunity to plead for the court's mercy, Counselor Miller laid it on thickly. His client faced financial failure with the likely revocation of the Café Au Go Go's license, and that surely was enough of a penalty. "Howard Solomon is married, has two children, his wife is expecting a third child. He's been gainfully employed, he has never been involved in any criminal matter," Miller explained, as he entreated the court to impose no jail sentence.

Bruce said nothing of the like in his defense.

It was now Richard Kuh's turn to talk. "I'm here at the direction of the District Attorney Frank S. Hogan," he began. Indeed, Kuh's presence at the hearing was somewhat remarkable. He had resigned from the D.A.'s office in October. Awarded a grant from the Walter E. Meyer Research Institute of Law, Kuh was then researching controversial issues in criminal law administration. But he excused himself from more scholarly pursuits to return to Chief Justice Murtagh's courtroom—all in the interests of ensuring that a full measure of justice was meted out to Lenny Bruce and Howard Solomon.

"[I] ask on behalf of the People of this County...that Defendant Lenny Bruce's sentence be one of imprisonment." Kuh beseeched the court to recognize that "throughout the trial and since the trial, [Bruce] has shown by his conduct absolutely—a complete lack of any remorse whatsoever." After all, following his first arrest at the Café Au Go Go on April 3, Bruce had proceeded with his run. Kuh also reminded the court that this obstreperous behavior had led to Lenny's subsequent arrest on April 7. Moreover, even after his conviction, Bruce "found, apparently, some other club, some other place of entertainment and advertised in the papers on November 25 that he would be appearing again."

By this oblique allusion, Kuh referred to Lenny's aborted plans to appear in concert with Tiny Tim at The Village Theater. That Thanksgiving eve show, titled "The Return of Lenny Bruce, or See Lenny Bruce Speak for Profit, See Tiny Tim Sing for Love," closed on opening night. The small audience of some thirty diehard Bruce fans were sent away by the theater's owner, Ben Bonus, who refused to risk the loss of his operating license. "I suggest," Kuh maintained, "Your Honors have instances of a notable lack of remorse." As for Howard Solomon, Kuh briefly urged a maximum fine on each count, so as to make his trafficking in obscenity "highly unprofitable."

Lenny could remain silent no longer. In the opinion of the *Village Voice* reporter in the courtroom, Bruce struck out "with a lash as cutting as a bull whip." He turned time around nearly two thousand years when he protested: "I am a Jew before this court. I would like to set the record straight, that the Jew is not remorseful." Why should he be remorseful if he were not guilty? "I come before the court not for mercy, but for justice," Lenny remonstrated. And Howard Solomon's money-making venture could be no more condemned than his words: "[P]rofit is everyone's motivation in this country."

No, Bruce asserted, the real offenses had been committed by Richard Kuh. He had insinuated into Lenny's performances filth that was not there: "All the words I use are in the dictionary." Furthermore, Kuh had waged a personal vendetta against him: "Your Honors are aware of the fact that Richard Kuh is emotionally involved—to come here when he's not working for the District Attorney's Office, he's not getting paid....He doesn't represent the people of New York." Chief Justice Murtagh had heard quite enough. "I suggest that you confine yourself to the merits," Murtagh chided. "We have indulged you considerably. Anything further?"

"No," Bruce replied.

LENNY'S STURM UND *drang* did not appear to move the emotionless Justice Murtagh. Still, Murtagh had his compassionate side. For this was the same man who had written only seven years earlier that "the obligation of a judge of a criminal court is not merely to administer justice but also to dispense charity." Perhaps Murtagh believed he was duly discharging his charitable obligations when he imposed less than maximum possible penalties. Dryly, he intoned the sentences:

—For the defendant Lenny Bruce, "the majority of the court imposes a sentence of four months in the workhouse on each of the three counts, sentence to run concurrently, not consecutively."

—For the defendant Howard Solomon, "[t]he court imposes a sentence on each [of two] count[s] of $500 or thirty days."

Justice Creel, who had dissented from the Bruce and Solomon convictions, announced that he voted to suspend the sentences for both defendants.

The Trial of the Absurd was almost over. After eight and a half months, the curtain was about to descend on the courtroom drama that had begun on April 8 with tortured preliminary hearings over performance tapes, that had continued throughout June and July with a chorus of prominent expert witnesses, and that was now ending on December 21 with Lenny's final plea for justice. Only one small matter needed to be resolved—but, quite predictably, it developed into yet another scene for lawyerly machinations.

In order to appeal their convictions, the defendants needed to apply for certificates of reasonable doubt. Consequently, their attorneys requested a short stay to allow for the appeals procedures. Unless Chief Justice Murtagh were to grant a stay, of course, Bruce and Solomon would be jailed immediately. Ever the technician, Richard Kuh questioned the specific authority of the sentencing court to grant a temporary stay of execution. "If it please the court," Kuh brandished the relevant statute before the justices, "there is express provision for a stay when the application for the certificate is formally before Your

Honors....There being no application, I believe, the court is technically without authority until a proper application is made."

To and fro, to and fro—the attorneys and court debated the meaning of the relevant code and the existence of inherent judicial power to
grant a temporary stay. Ultimately, even the strict constructionist John
Murtagh found Kuh's argument to be over the top. Exercising the
court's discretion, the justice granted a stay of execution and a contin-
uation of bail for Bruce and Solomon until Wednesday, December 23.

Lenny had escaped the clutches of his jailers, at least for the time
being. Allen Schwartz, representing Bruce before Justice Henry Clay
Greenberg of the New York Supreme Court, obtained a certificate of
reasonable doubt and negotiated a $50 bail for Lenny. After posting
his bond in cash, Lenny told the press that he hadn't played a show for
five months, was flat broke, and had to borrow the bail money from
friends. He even claimed that, in order to appeal, he would have to ask
the court for a free trial transcript.

Unwilling to serve on a *pro bono* basis, Allen Schwartz informed
Bruce that he could not argue Lenny's case before the Appellate Term
of the New York Supreme Court. (The Appellate Term of the Supreme
Court is the first level of appellate review in the New York legal system,
not to be confused with the state high court—the New York Court of
Appeals.) In a letter written months after assisting Bruce with his initial
appeals process, Schwartz recommended his friend, Patrick M. Wall, a
young and bright appellate attorney who might work for a nominal sum.
Schwartz thought it "most probable" that Lenny's conviction would be
affirmed in the Appellate Term, thus necessitating another appeal. Ultimately, however, Schwartz believed that Lenny would prevail.

Meanwhile, Schwartz stressed that Lenny must act with dispatch,
lest his appeal be dismissed as untimely. If that were to happen, a warrant would issue and Lenny would find himself on Rikers Island.

Island Retreat

SAFE FOR THE present in his fourth-floor refuge at the Marlton Hotel, Lenny was doing his utmost to avoid doing time at Rikers.

The five-hundred-acre island lies at the head of the East River between Queens and the Bronx. By the early 1960s, Rikers Island Penitentiary, several facilities built only for 2,857 people, held 4,800 men, women, and adolescents who had been sentenced for misdemeanors. New construction completed by February 1964 provided colorful dormitories and cells (lemon yellows, warm tans, turquoise, and strong blues greeted male prisoners upon arrival) for two thousand short-term offenders. In the old branch of the prison, however, the atmosphere was grim, gray, and harsh. And this is where Lenny would end up if Justice Murtagh had his way.

Anxious at the prospect of Rikers, Counselor Bruce had his hands full, as he prepared for his New York appeal and his collateral federal civil rights actions. Like a whirling dervish, he dashed from legal task to legal task—rummaging through unwound spools of trial tapes that laced the hotel floor, rifling through piles of law books in search of citations, and reviewing the legal papers that Selma Rovinsky, his "paralegal," brought to him.

There in his "law office," plans of all sorts were devised. There were plans, if you can call them that, to perform in Chicago on January 2, 1965. He could return to the Windy City *free*, just as he had returned to San Francisco to perform. But Lenny had real reservations. He feared that the Illinois Supreme Court ruling in his favor would be applied narrowly. That is, the police and prosecutors might allow him to perform only one show, *specifically* the show adjudged to be constitutionally protected. If he so much as moved off that dime and ventured a new routine with new words, he could be busted again and the entire process would start anew. At least, that was his concern. What to do? He needed more advice. Call more lawyers, he told Rovinsky. There must be some solution.

So more and more friends and professional contacts ventured in and out of his chaotic and squalid "office." For example, he agreed to be interviewed by a *New York Post* reporter at the Marlton on the midafternoon of the day after his sentencing hearing. Dressed in blue jeans and a striped sweater, the barefoot Bruce railed at the unfairness of the trial proceeding, and ranted over the amazing discrepancies between the performance tapes and the trial transcripts. From one moment to the next, he jumped up to play excerpts from a courtroom scene, bounced over to read a passage from a law book, or stopped himself short to recite from memory the comedy routines misrepresented by the transcripts. "If I had really said that *schmutz* that way," Lenny charged, "the judge should have sentenced me." All said and done, the reporter's verdict was judicious: "No one would accuse [Bruce] of being an adjusted personality….But, neither will New York be a better place if this wild, mild, tortured brilliance, who performed before sophisticated adults, not small children, is smothered in the workhouse."

That sentiment was echoed elsewhere in the press. Most notably, the editorial page of the *New York Telegram & Sun* briefly reflected on the unusual character of Lenny's prosecution and sentence. His jail term, "not too different from the time served occasionally by muggers and hit-and-run drivers…and similar types…seems a little stiff," the editorial opined, "Nobody forced patrons into the Café Au Go Go to hear Bruce. They even paid. And the privilege, if any, was reserved for adults only." A concluding question: "Wouldn't the public, and Bruce, be better served if he received more modern treatment than four months cooped up with genuine criminals?"

Lenny had an answer to this query: "I'm not a crier or a whiner. I respect the law, and it will eventually vindicate me."

9

THE PATH
TO VINDICATION

Posthumous vindication doesn't really mean anything.
—*Phil Spector*

High Hopes, Painful Flops

The ideas I have are now imprisoned within me, and
unless this court acts, will not be permitted expression...
—Lenny Bruce (1965)

HIS MIND WAS on the Supreme Court. For years, he had read, studied, and even memorized passages from the Court's opinions. Finally, he had a shot at his day in that revered tribunal to correct the error he believed was committed by the Second Circuit Court of Appeals. Even if the likes of Circuit Judges Henry Friendly and Thurgood Marshall were unimpressed with his prayer for constitutional relief, surely he could muster up the four Supreme Court Justices' votes needed to hear his case. And then he would deliver his *supremo* performance—one more magnificent than his Curran or Carnegie Hall performances.

In late March 1965, Lenny seemed to be practicing his oral arguments in moot court form at Basin Street West, the San Francisco nightery where he was booked for a week-long run. His club routine focused so strongly on his free speech battles that it sounded more like law talk than comedy talk. Pacing the dimly lit stage, Counselor Bruce tossed out his quirky views on such matters as the tribal beginnings of law and the failures of the American justice system. Jumbled with the grand theory were the details of his New York obscenity trial. Before

Bill Graham (the rock promoter) and others, he recounted facts from the bust, read portions of the transcript, and reflected on the legal meaning of it all. Truncated bits from his famous routines became mere footnotes to the larger legal text of his act. The "Constitution won't permit them to convict me," was how he summed it up in his just-published autobiography, *How to Talk Dirty and Influence People*. Basically, that was the same message he was trying to convey at Basin Street West.

Even after his finale on March 30 at the Basin, Lenny had not tired. Squawking on for hours in his second-floor room at the Swiss American Hotel on Broadway, the shirtless orator lectured his friend, Eric Miller, a companion nightclub musician. It was all highfalutin' babble—semantics, obscenity, freedom. He was almost as high on ideas as he was on pot laced with DMT—the tryptamine psychedelic that produces an effect, according to Zen philosopher Alan Watts, similar to "being shot out of an atomic cannon." The cannon powder was a gift from a friend, who advised: "Smoke this, till *the jewels roll out of your eyes!*" The jewels had rolled shortly before Lenny climbed over the bed and onto the windowsill facing the street to make a dramatic point. (The day before, he stood atop his bed showing how he would address the justices of the Supreme Court.) "This is the way it is," he pronounced, just as the window suddenly gave way. He took the "businessman's trip" (as the DMT experience was known in the '60s) down twenty-five feet to the cement sidewalk. There the broken and bruised comedian lay, in blue jeans and cowboy boots. So much for his moot court experience.

"I tried to grab him, but I couldn't," said Miller, who had raced down to the street to aid him. "I was trying to kiss him warm. We always kiss each other. It's not a sexual thing. We dig each other." But Lenny needed more than warm kisses, as he had suffered a broken arm and legs, fractured hip, and back injuries. When the police arrived, Bruce defiantly started swinging, until the point of being cuffed. "I give up," he uttered as he surrendered to the ambulance crew. At the Mission Emergency Hospital, the sick comic raunched out the medical staff so badly that a doctor muzzled him with a bandage during treatment.

However grave his medical ills, Lenny's legal ills were becoming desperately serious. Within days of his accident, his latest appellate counsel, Edward de Grazia of New York, lamented: "When I try to picture Lenny standing up (as I used to picture him before he fell from his San Francisco hotel room), I see a person for whom the walls are closing in." Two things may well have informed de Grazia's fears. First, there was the real likelihood that the federal district court (acting on the case remanded to it by the Second Circuit) would dismiss Lenny's civil rights action. Next, there was the slim likelihood that Bruce would ever get a hearing in the Supreme Court—*in forma pauperis*, no less, since he was broke.

On April 15, 1965, de Grazia's first fear was realized—the district court in Manhattan dismissed the Section 1983 civil rights case. Within eleven days, de Grazia filed a petition for Supreme Court review in the matter of *Bruce v. Hogan*. The twenty-eight page *certiorari* petition, as the lawyer colloquially described it to Ralph Gleason, argued essentially the following: "All Lenny seeks [is to exercise] those rights which are normally considered inviolate for Americans—the rights to say what you wish and to earn some bread." In more legalistic fashion, the petition raised four constitutional questions, all notably phrased in the negative:

Whether the First and Fourteenth Amendments do not guarantee Petitioner the right to deliver dramatic monologues dealing with subjects of topic importance anywhere in the nation regardless of state lines or varying local standards or conflicting state court decisions and whether such a right may not be declared by a federal court.

Whether the federal courts are powerless to restrain state judicial action when it is being applied against an individual in such a way as to abridge his constitutional right to free speech and deprive him of his livelihood and occupation without due process of law.

Whether the federal courts are powerless to restrain state law enforcement officials from actions against an individual, taken under color of law, when these acts are abridging his constitutional right to free speech and depriving him of his livelihood and occupation without due process of law.

> Whether it is not an abuse of judicial discretion for a federal court to decline to enjoin actions by a state court and/or state officials, taken under color of law, when these actions are shown to be restraining a person from speaking on subjects having topical interest.

Worded as they were, the four questions strongly suggested that Lenny Bruce's claims could fail only if the federal judicial system were powerless to protect fundamental speech liberties against state prosecutions. "The injury to petitioner," de Grazia argued, "was clear and irreparable so long as the federal courts refuse to act, for petitioner…was effectively gagged and his audiences sat to silence." The district court's refusal to grant Lenny's relief, therefore, encouraged a system of "prior restraints" that was "slowly strangling Petitioner's expression." The time for Supreme Court action was now, not after "long, arduous, and expensive" appeals through the state court system. And, in taking action, the high Court should apply "a national standard" to prevent Bruce's acts from being declared "obscene in one state and constitutionally protected in another." In sum, de Grazia concluded: "If no determination of the constitutionality of expression such as this, binding throughout the United States, can be given until a conviction…is appealed through the highest state court to this Court…free speech will wither on the vine, or be plucked of its leaves one by one."

The stage, the ultimate stage, was now set. If the Supreme Court allowed review, Lenny Bruce—ailing, confused, and penniless—would *himself* act as lead lawyer. It was his chance, his opportunity to take his act to the highest court in the land, to stand before the likes of Chief Justice Earl Warren and Justices Hugo Black, William O. Douglas, and William Brennan, and make his case in his own voice. The liberal Court, he was confident, would declare that his acts were not obscene, this after having heard him perform *live*.

"If you appear before the Supreme Court, I'll go back there!" Gleason wrote to Bruce. Twenty-nine days later, Lenny's high hopes were dashed and Gleason's hoped-for trip ditched when a unanimous Court declined to consider *Bruce v. Hogan.* "I am sure you have heard that the Supreme Court denied our Petition for a Writ of Certiorari," de Grazia wrote to Gleason. "Perhaps we raised questions which were too difficult for the Court to be able to summon a majority which would vote the right way on the merits." Alternatively, de Grazia speculated, "I also must suppose that the Court felt that Lenny had a way of relief through the appellate structure of the New York Courts, which it may have seemed he did not attempt to exhaust."

When the justices denied review in the final week of their term, Lenny's chances to play the "Big Court" vanished forever. William Brennan, the author of the *Roth* opinion that had both blessed and cursed Bruce, would never hear Lenny's unorthodox bits like "Psychopathia Sexualis."

Now, Edward de Grazia was more convinced than ever that Lenny's mistake, his "fatal error," was that he believed in the legal system, that he trusted it to vindicate him. But, de Grazia lamented, one may "never be able to live with the law if you go and love it. Lenny may just die for his love of the law. It's a Jewish hang-up, probably. Loving the law like that."

White Christmas

CHRISTMAS EVE, 1965. It was cloudy and mild when Lenny Bruce walked into a Manhattan law office located at 511 Fifth Avenue. A holiday party had just begun down the hall when he entered, dressed in a long, light-colored coat and sneakers. Lenny was there to visit his latest civil rights lawyer. The "sick comedian" had two things on his mind that day: recruiting legal help for his Section 1983 action and getting high, sky high! And so he called on the counterculture's mouthpiece, William M. Kunstler—who, as fate would have it, had known Richard Kuh since childhood.

Kunstler was *the* radical lawyer of his day. In the course of his legal career, he defended antiwar demonstrators, draft-dodgers, Black Power activists, and Leftist "conspirators," among others. He stood side-by-side, arm-in-arm, clench-fisted with some of the leading dissidents of the '60s—Father Daniel Berrigan, Dave Dillinger, Jerry

Rubin, Allen Ginsberg, and H. Rap Brown, to name but a few. But before them, there was Lenny Bruce, the man whose life story first introduced him to the "government's use of the might and power of the criminal justice system to crush dissent."

Bill Kunstler had come into the legal picture late, after Lenny's New York obscenity trial, and worked with him mostly in an advisory capacity. Kunstler originally seemed slated to be the lead lawyer in a new round of civil rights actions.

Early in 1965, Lenny explained how he hooked up with Kunstler. He did so in a taped telephone conversation with his learned friend, Professor Harry Kalven of the University of Chicago Law School. Bruce was asking Kalven about some subtle issues of Fourth Amendment search and seizure law—an area in which Kalven had no special expertise. Lenny was fishing into matters relating to still another Section 1983 action that he planned to file against New York prosecutors. Late in the conversation, Bruce said: "I finally got an attorney to think federal, and his name is *Kuuu*nstler....Now I explained to him what I wanted, the declaratory relief....He was going to call me back; he had to take it sorta under advisement. And I got up and was really *depressed*, ya know. I've been fuckin' around....I'd been in this room for two months. So [later] he called me up and said, ya know, that he would be happy to handle it....[Afterwards,] I called him back and...told him a few more things. And it finally did get *through* to him, and then he bought it."

Bruce's strategy was to perform the same club act for which he previously had been busted, to get arrested again, and thereafter to bring a new civil rights action in federal court seeking monetary, declaratory, and injunctive relief. He envisioned doing the identical routine before a federal judge, and to highlight the inherent ambiguity in his allegedly obscene hand movements: "One person sees them as gestures of benediction with a microphone. The other guy sees them as gestures of masturbation. And I want to ask the court, 'Can gestures be obscene? Are these gestures specifically obscene?'" Moreover, Lenny planned to sell mail-order tapes of his performances, so he wanted a court's declaration that these bits were protected under the Constitution.

This scheme for a second Section 1983 action in New York, ultimately filed against Manhattan and Nassau District Attorneys for $25,000 damages on February 11, was followed by a swell of civil rights litigation—one suit filed in the Sacramento superior court (February 24), a second in Los Angeles federal district court (April 30), a third in San Francisco federal district court (October 13), and still others waiting in the wings. The list of his targets included state judges, court clerks, prosecutors, and police who had been involved in his obscenity and narcotics trials, as well as the agencies regulating nightclub entertainment. The jurisdictional geography moved from the East to the West and back to the Midwest. No state official who had brushed against Bruce was immune from his charges. With the declining interest of lawyers in his cases, and with declining income (Bruce was declared bankrupt in October 1965), counselor Lenny brought the actions himself, *in propria persona*.

What prompted these suits, in large part, was the heat that various state authorities had brought upon the owners of clubs hosting Lenny Bruce. Thus, John Hirst, the proprietor of the Cork 'n Bib in Nassau County, had been threatened in June 1964 by Assistant District Attorney Norman Levy: if Bruce goes on stage, "I'll pull your license from the wall." To greater effect was the costly cancellation of the Thanksgiving 1964 Village Theater show, *The Return of Lenny Bruce*, under the pressure of New York authorities. Moreover, John Misterly, the Sheriff of Sacramento County, threatened Bruce and Daniel Katasaros, the owner of The Tender Trap, with immediate arrest if Bruce "got out of line" by using "filth" that injured "the moral fiber of the community" during his club acts in February 1965. And in Los Angeles, the Department of Alcoholic Beverage Control and the Welfare Commission had commenced license revocation proceedings against two clubs where Lenny worked, The Trolley Ho and The Booby Trap. "No one is willing to hire me any more," Bruce protested, "because they don't want to be closed down." Hence, the need for drastic legal action to release the states' chokeholds.

Bill Kunstler was just the man who could make his Section 1983 actions happen, Bruce believed. What he didn't know then was that, with or without Kunstler, the Section 1983 actions were doomed.

Whether the radical lawyer predicted such a fate is unknown, perhaps because the two men had other things on their minds...and in their veins.

THEIR LAW WORK was now done. It was time to make merry. With "Joy to the World" and such filling the holiday air, Lenny turned to Kunstler as the latter headed for a Christmas party. "Bill, you can never understand what it means to shoot up unless you've done it." Then, the big question: "Have you ever shot up?" When Kunstler replied that he had not, the invitation came: "Let's go to the men's room down the hall." As told by the radical lawyer, this is what followed:

> Like a lunatic, I agreed, and we walked down the hall to the bathroom. Lenny tied rubber tubing around my left arm just above the bend of my elbow. Then he put a needle into my arm and injected me. At first, I felt absolutely nothing, so I went, as planned, to the Christmas party leaving Lenny in the men's room. It was the last time I ever saw him.
>
> Shortly after I arrived at the party, I collapsed. Someone carried me to my office, put me on a couch, and called my wife; I was completely unconscious....I was totally out of it and vomited for quite a long time the following morning. I was capable of locomotion but was sick as a dog....
>
> At the time, I suppose I wanted Lenny to think I was a regular guy and that I understood all about shooting up heroin....[But later] I saw the utter recklessness of what I had done—and vowed never again to be so careless.

It was another hellish Christmas for the Jewish comic. Almost a year ago to the day, he had been sentenced to jail for his words. And despite all of his civil rights machinations, his words were still not free. What little freedom he had came by way of his own kind of White Christmas—a spoon-cooked powder streaming in his veins.

"For My Part, Go to Hell"

MAURICE ROSENFIELD OF Chicago had no interest in or patience for any of Bruce's civil rights actions facilitated by Edward de Grazia, William Kunstler, and others. He was more than willing, however, to lend a paternalistic hand in promoting Lenny's appeal from the New York obscenity conviction. To that end, late in 1965, Rosenfield (who helped win Lenny's case in the Illinois Supreme Court) worked assiduously to vindicate Lenny's First Amendment rights.

The Chicago lawyer had grounds for concern. The clock was ticking away and no formal appeal had been filed in *People v. Bruce*. It was an ideal case for First Amendment review in an appellate court. But all Lenny could think of was his grand Section 1983 actions. Other things could wait. So he kept petitioning the New York appellate courts for extensions, one after another. Delay, delay, more delay. The extensions were granted, though the patience of the court was waning. On May 26, 1965, William H. Schaap (Dick Schaap's brother), who previously had worked for Professor Kalven as his research assistant, wrote to Lenny: "your appeal papers must be finished and submitted sometime in early August, and you will be allowed to argue on the opening day of the term in September. These are the last opportunities you will have for either." Schaap, then a lawyer at Strasser, Spiegelberg, Fried, and Frank, warned Lenny: "[D]on't allow the time you have to pass unused." (Allen Schwartz, who could not represent Lenny for free, likewise urged him to proceed with haste.)

Meanwhile, the Manhattan D.A.'s office was moving fast and furiously. Vincent J. Cuccia, an assistant D.A., was now in charge of the case. He sent airmail letters to Lenny, addressed "Mr. Lenny Bruce, Pro Se." One of those letters to Counselor Bruce was an "Affidavit in Opposition to the Defendant's Motion for an Extension of Time." Sufficient time to appeal already had been granted, argued Cuccia. Besides, the convicted comedian was taking advantage of the system, for no good reason: "The defendant's course of conduct since December 1964 indicates a clear scheme to avoid a normal appellate procedure and it negates any good faith intention to perfect the appeal to this court." No more patience, no more extensions, no more mercy. As Cuccia put it:

> During the entire period since the filing of this notice of appeal [on December 24, 1964], the defendant has not taken any action whatever towards perfecting his appeal. His obstinate refusal to proceed in an orderly fashion in the New York Appellate Courts, coupled with his persistent efforts to seek federal intervention, clearly place him in the position of requesting relief with unclean hands.
>
> We further oppose the motion by the defendant to proceed *in forma pauperis* on the grounds that he has failed to allege any facts justifying this relief other than the bare assertion that he is destitute.

As the prosecution portrayed it, Lenny was rolling in bucks. He had long boasted about making over $150,000 annually; he was getting book and record royalties; he had hired big-name lawyers like Ephraim London; and he often stayed at "the fashionable Marlton Hotel." Hardly the portrait of a destitute. Of course, Lenny was so busy with junk (legal and narcotic) that he could not find the time to prove that he was out of work (except in a few spots in San Francisco), out of royalty checks (neither his autobiography nor his albums were selling), out of luck (London had sued him), and out of the Marlton (he could barely afford to make the mortgage on his Hollywood home).

Such information was not being offered to the judges sitting in the New York Supreme Court Appellate Term, First Department. No, a depressed and desperate Lenny seemed to be fiddling as his Rome burned. And so the deadline passed; the defendant had missed his chance to appeal his conviction.

Rosenfield was livid. *Something* had to be done, *quickly*. *People v. Bruce* could not end that way. Meritorious First Amendment claims— arguments sustained by a jury in San Francisco and a state high court in Illinois—could not be lost in New York, especially for such a ridiculous reason as failing to perfect an appeal. Now, the only thing that stood between Lenny and a Rikers Island cell was a measure of extraordinary relief from the Appellate Term of the New York Supreme Court. Somehow, his case had to be reopened.

Rosenfield approached the forty-one-year-old Jay H. Topkis (a Yale Law grad, a former law clerk to the respected federal Judge Jerome N. Frank, and an attorney at the prestigious firm of Paul, Weiss, Rifkind, Wharton, and Garrison) and the thirty-nine-year-old Howard M. Squadron (a Columbia Law grad and solo practitioner who had done some preliminary work related to Lenny's New York arrest). The two attorneys had the kind of acumen necessary to put Bruce's appeal back on track after he had derailed it.

Rosenfield expressed his concern over the legal difficulties that Lenny had created: "The mess Bruce makes for himself in all his legal encounters creates an illusion of complexity about his problems with the courts." But Rosenfield held the firm belief that "the case rests in the higher courts on a point almost absurdly simple—it is to establish that [Lenny] is not merely a nut scribbling dirty words on toilet walls, but a social critic with a totally unconventional vocabulary. As such he is protected wholly by the Federal Constitution."

Unlike the liberal Ephraim London, who had sued Lenny Bruce for attorney's fees, Maurice Rosenfield never sought to collect the fees that Lenny still owed him from an informal agreement concerning the Chicago litigation. Rosenfield did propose, however, to share half of the account receivable from that agreement with Topkis and Squadron, *if* and when Bruce ever rebounded financially and honored his debt. The duo were open to the prospect of representing Bruce, but only under categorical provisos. As Topkis put it in his November 19 letter to Lenny:

Dear Mr. Bruce:

I write to confirm the arrangements which Maurice Rosenfield, Esq. made with me on your behalf:

1. We will attempt to vacate the dismissal of your appeal from a judgment of conviction in the Court of Special Sessions.
2. If successful in vacating the dismissal, we shall thereupon prosecute the appeal to the Supreme Court, Appellate Term.
3. All decisions as to how these matters are to be handled are to be made by me....Of course, I shall be glad to consult with you, but

> I am authorized to act for you if I am unable to communicate with
> you and I am authorized in any event to take such steps as to me
> seem appropriate for the protection of your interests. Under no
> circumstances are you to communicate in any way with any court.
> . . .
>
> 5. So far as compensation is concerned, Maury Rosenfield has
>   undertaken to assure me that any out-of-pocket expenses will be
>   defrayed...

Proviso No. 3 was the killer. When Albert Bendich made virtually
identical demands in 1962, Bruce had yielded begrudgingly. But those
days were now long gone. By this time, Lenny had dispensed with
numerous lawyers and was accustomed to calling the legal shots. After
all, he was filing *in propria persona* Section 1983 civil rights actions
left and right. Besides, he already had "appellate skills," having
appeared before the Second Circuit. And only a few months earlier, he
was fantasizing wildly about arguing constitutional points before the
Supreme Court. Predictably, Lenny declined the offer.

"I come embarrassed," Rosenfield wrote to Topkis upon learning
of Bruce's refusal. It was a hard pill to swallow: "Now it turns out that
Lenny Bruce rejects all aid by way of appeal." Only a few days before,
Rosenfield and Harry Kalven had spoken by telephone to Bruce for a
full hour, trying to convince him of the error of his ways. But, Lenny
would hear none of it, charmed as he was by the federal civil rights
routes he was taking. Rosenfield continued:

> In his passionate insistence that the federal courts applying federal
> law have taken over the whole field and have obsoleted state pro-
> ceedings and appeals, he is rivaled only by extremists below the
> Mason-Dixon Line. This, mind you, is his position even though he
> is offered a subsidized, costless appeal. It's a pity because ultimately
> he will stand convicted for all purposes with no remedy even though
> we are convinced that he is in fact guilty of no crime.

Though one of Lenny's foremost lawyers, one who had defended
him skillfully and successfully, Rosenfield was so exasperated by this

"crazy" turn of events that he wanted to cut the cord. "[H]e is beyond help, and I am through with Lenny Bruce," Rosenfield told Topkis.

The day before Thanksgiving, November 24, 1965, Rosenfield expressed that same sentiment, but in far harsher terms, to Lenny himself:

Dear Lenny:

I cannot refrain from the last word.

In the Eichmann episode in your act found in the transcript of your Illinois performance, you asked the audience, "Don't you see the whore in you?" Do you see it in yourself? You would stand on your lofty perch on stage and look down your nose at corruption everywhere. But when the chips are down, you are as arrogant ("lawyers do not know the law"), as lying and dishonest (you promised me more than a year ago when I loaned you money that you would never abandon your New York appeal and recently, after your telegram to me, you promised that you would go forward with the appeal without interference), as deceitful, ungrateful (our Illinois decision hurts you, you say), as hypocritical and as corrupt as the rest of us. In the phrase you love so much, "Physician, heal thyself."

And, for my part, go to Hell.

Maurice Rosenfield

bcc: Harry Kalven, Jr.
W. R. Ming, Jr.

When Bill Schaap, who thought the world of Lenny, got wind of Bruce's latest blunder, he wrote to his friend Rosenfield: "I wish he had the sense to let you and Mr. Kalven and Mr. Ming help him; but he has not shown himself to be a leader in the sense department." Schaap, too, thought ill of Lenny's "federal fantasy" litigation—an action destined to lose. And when that day arrived, surmised Schaap, Lenny likely would be pleading with Maury to take his case again...this while the police will be "dragging him through the jailhouse door. You might think now about what you will say then," added Schaap.

Fat chance that Maurice Rosenfield would have anything to do with Lenny Bruce. He was done with the "crazy" comedian...but then again, maybe not. Hardly a week had passed since he had damned Lenny, and Rosenfield was back in his camp with a "new idea." He wrote to Topkis about the possibility of filing an *amicus curiae* brief in support of Bruce's appeal. The problem, of course, was that this would have to be done *without* Lenny's approval. Such an extraordinary action was needed, Rosenfield explained, because the defendant "irrationally refuses to pursue his appeal remedies to establish his innocence." What kind of legal system would we have, he queried, if Howard Solomon were acquitted on appeal, but Lenny Bruce stood convicted because he had not perfected his appeal on a mere procedural point? Wouldn't this be "too odd a result for a decent legal system," Rosenfield wrote, and isn't it the "classic function of an *amicus* to see that the system works properly?"

Sympathetic though he was to civil-liberties justice and respect for the integrity of law, these were still not enough to move Jay Topkis to action. The pragmatic problems seemed overwhelming: at a minimum, they would have to tell the court of Bruce's refusal to appeal, and the prospect of arguing that Lenny's decision should not be determinative was daunting. Though Topkis suggested an alternative course— requesting the District Attorney or the court to open Bruce's default if and when Solomon prevailed on appeal—the skeptical and learned lawyer reminded Rosenfield that even this would require Lenny's consent. "I hope you won't think I am being pigheaded," Topkis apologized. "Perhaps this isn't my day for going too far out of my way to help somebody who won't deviate one inch from his way."

What legal wonders Rosenfield and his colleagues did in Chicago, he could not reproduce in New York. Practically speaking, this meant that Lenny's conviction would stand and he would have to begin serving time at Rikers.

That is, unless he opted to flee Manhattan as a fugitive from justice. And opt he did, as he prepared to return to the House on the Hill with little or no income and with the L.A. narc and vice squads waiting for any chance to put him behind bars.

Only six years earlier, Lenny had taken Manhattan by storm at

The Den at the Duane. Then there were his comic conquests at Basin Street East, The Village Vanguard, and the magical midnight performance at Carnegie Hall. But now it was all of no moment. The Café Au Go Go had proven to be his Waterloo, and Lenny was in full retreat.

Room 417 at the Marlton presented formidable challenges for the moving crew. The quarters that Lenny most recently called home contained the detritus of his life in the law—mounds of trial transcripts and piles of law books stacked everywhere, reels and reels of audiotapes strewn about, and a huge trunk in the middle of the room overflowing with more of the same. Through the narrow door, down the mosaic-tiled hall, into the small elevator, via the mirrored lobby, past the pillared entry, and down the steps onto West 8th Street—it took Carl Montgomery, the hotel manager, and the packers some twelve hours to box and move the law junkie's stuff. As was her generous custom, Judy Peabody—Lenny's New York socialite friend and "sponsor"—picked up the hotel and shipping tabs.

Barring the unexpected, New York had seen the last of Lenny Bruce.

The Specter of a Rebel

REBELLION. PHIL SPECTOR loved the concept. Its romantic abandon and heroic appeal charmed him to no end. Defiant, disobedient, determined—the insubordinate outsider—that was the ideal he lived for. So much so that if he could not find it, he would create it, out of whole flesh.

Spector was one of the key forces behind the rebel yell of the notorious Ramones, the kickstart punk-rock group that jarred the youth world in the 1970s. Before that, he worked with John Lennon to produce rebellious songs like "Imagine" and "Power to the People." Before that, with the Beatles to help create the daring *Let it Be* album. The theme echoed all the way back to 1962, when he produced the Crystals' smash hit, "He's a Rebel"—a passionate tribute to the cultural hero who "doesn't do what everybody else does."

In the fall of 1965, Spector met a real rebel, a James Dean figure come to life. Here was a rebel who had the track marks to prove it, a fugitive status to confirm it, and a roguish take on life to seal it. He was someone who taunted the Establishment, an outlaw with bravado. He was Spector's dream come true; he was Lenny Bruce. Better still, his hero was on the outs—out of work and out of luck. For Spector, it was all hip, beyond imagination hip!

By early 1966, they had become brothers-in-arms, two codependent short guys. For Spector, the record producer with enough fame and fortune to cause a frenzy among sycophants, Lenny was his alterego, someone with whom he could brag of guilt by association. The twenty-four-year-old impresario's dark sunglasses, ruffled shirts, eccentric ways, and loaded-gun temper marked him as different. But it was not enough to allow him to lay claim to a *real* rebel status. That was a life he could only live vicariously, hence Lenny Bruce. Besides, Phil was in a career limbo of sorts, so he could relate to another genius whose talents the public had not appreciated. It made him all the more crazy…this ingrate world that failed to realize the real greatness of the Lenny Bruces and Phil Spectors.

For Lenny, the matter was not as psychologically perplexing—Phil Spector was a cash cow. He could raise the down-and-out comedian's name back up on the marquee; he could help rid his life of carping creditors; he could even release and distribute new albums for him. This was a break beyond belief, beyond even the kindness Judy Peabody had extended to him in those last miserable days in New York. Phil Spector was not just a benefactor, however. He was the perfect man to help Lenny reverse his dead-end fate. Phil could breathe new life into Lenny's dying self.

Vicarious life for Phil, reincarnated life for Lenny. It was a match made in Hollywood…in Phil's office at 9130 Sunset Boulevard, to be precise.

Lenny Bruce, then almost forty, was also a sage rebel in Spector's eyes. "He was like a teacher or philosopher. He was like a living Socrates," said Spector. And so, Spector and his Socrates went about Hollywood in Phil's black Cad limo, to be *seen* in clubs like The Trip. But once there, complained Spector, people such as Bill Cosby and the Smothers Brothers ignored the great comic philosopher. "I don't think they knew what to say to Lenny or how to express themselves," he added.

In those play-it-safe days, few, if any, comics came to Lenny's defense; in those days, the First Amendment was not seen as such a great principle of freedom when it came to Lenny Bruce. Nonetheless, Phil Spector spoke out (though in exaggerated ways). More importantly, he put his money where Lenny's mouth was.

PHIL SPECTOR PRESENTS LENNY BRUCE.

That is how the ads billed Lenny's mid-February 1966 booking at The Music Box Theatre in Hollywood. It was to be a one-man comic talkathon slated for a two-week run, "Cops Willing," the *Variety* headline emphasized. But, it was also to be a comedy gig with a legal angle. Here he was—cleared by a jury in San Francisco, freed by a court in Beverly Hills, vindicated by an appellate court in Illinois, and convicted by a 2 to 1 vote in a New York trial court—using the Music Box performances for yet another legal stratagem. Lenny and his lawyer, Sydney Irmas, planned to file a 42 U.S.C. Section 1983 action to safeguard the Spector-sponsored run. The idea was to prevent the Los Angeles authorities ever from doing what their New York counterparts had accomplished in 1964 at The Village Theater. Indeed, Bruce and Irmas went so far as to publicize their game plan.

On opening night, Lenny *schlepped* onto the stage for the first of two one-hour, thirty-five-minute sets, decked out in a black car coat, faded jeans, and brown suede shoes. "All right everybody, this is a raid!" is how he opened things up. A token-size crowd, bunched down in the front rows, received him. He joked, if that is the word, about such things as life in Dixie and the media's slanting of the news. He rambled on and on about Melvin Belli and Jack Ruby, about Hedy Lamar and the FBI, about the Catholic Church and the film *The House on 92nd Street*, and about birth control pills and cabaret licensing.

But for the most part, he obsessed about his arrests, trials, lawyers, judges, and the law that brought them all together. "Can you imagine some cop trying to do my routine in court?" he asked. "All he'll get down are the four-letter words. What sixty-five-year-old judge can understand those words out of context?" His comedy had become entirely free-association. It was highly disoriented—hit here, hit there, read from a trial transcript, then cut to news item, flashback to this bust or that judge, or this law or that lawyer, or whatever, whomever, or however. His routine was *far* more disjointed than it ever had been. To a *Los Angeles Times* reporter, he appeared to be "in a catatonic state." It was no longer comedy with a jazz style; it was tragedy with a pathetic twist.

Predictably, the audience was bored. He could no longer even offend them. People just sat there: some confused, some frustrated, some anxious to leave, and some just patient out of respect to Comedy's fallen hero.

He bombed. Ralph Gleason, the critic who now let his friendship for Lenny Bruce temper his criticism, put his best spin on it. Lenny, he wrote in *Variety*, was "uncompromising in his exposition." Yes, uncompromising...all the way to the humiliating end. The Sunday matinees were humbling to the point of depression.

"Lenny really hurt himself. I tried to tell him," recalled Spector. Lenny saw it otherwise: the show had not been advertised widely enough. Whatever the explanation, the gig was up—and this time without any covert help from the LAPD. Now it was back to the House on the Hill, where life and living rooms were in disrepair and where a weary Lenny Bruce sat up all night.

Phil was "[w]orried sick about Lenny and too committed to turn away from him, [so he simply kept] plying him with handouts," notes Mark Ribowsky, Spector's controversial biographer. Money, money, money...for legal expenses, trial transcripts, and for everything else from birthday presents for daughter Kitty to cigarettes for father Lenny. Danny Davis, Spector's aide, doled out the money...day after day, week after week, and month after month. Lenny Bruce, who had once boasted a quarter-of-a-million-dollar income, was now begging.

Meanwhile, Philles Records released *Lenny Bruce Is Out Again*. It was the last LP issued in Lenny's lifetime. The title of the album was the same that Bruce had used for his underground record, the one he hawked out of his home. But the Philles Records version was a different LP. Distributed sometime after Christmas 1965, the forty-minute yellow and red labeled album was philosophical, comical, and *uncensored*. On it, Lenny reflected upon and joked about everything from the California Penal Code and the definition of obscenity to the enforcement of marijuana laws. He did some of his popular bits, too, including "Thank You Mask Man."

Lenny Bruce Is Out Again was a tribute to populism and freedom, to the idea that censorship is incompatible with the notion of a self-governing people. "The Supreme Court," Lenny opined, "is concerned with one thing: the First Amendment. And here's their concern...not with anybody saying 'shit.' That has nothing to do with the First Amendment. They're concerned with the *information*, that there's no bar to the communication system." With freedom of speech, the "accent," he added "is not on the 'speech' but on the *right* to say it. And the freedom of the press is the *right* to read it or hear it." The knowledge of the people thus depended on that *right* to hear anything—good or evil, holy or blasphemous, decent or indecent. Such a right even included the freedom to publicly release an LP with words on it such as "crap," "assholes," "shit," "ass," and "*schmuck*." In its own way, parts of the LP were a page right out of one of Professor Harry Kalven's law review articles—precisely the sort of idea Lenny's academic lawyer had hoped to present one day to Justice William Brennan and his colleagues on the high Court.

In offering *Lenny Bruce Is Out Again* for public consumption, Phil Spector did in 1965 something of the same that Lawrence Ferlinghetti did in 1956 when he published Allen Ginsberg's *Howl*. As fate had it, neither Spector nor Bruce was ever prosecuted, though the LP was distributed nationwide and in cities such as New York where Lenny had recently been convicted for mouthing indecent words. Incredibly, pressing vinyl had done virtually as much—perhaps more—for the culture of freedom than decades of court battles and Supreme Court precedents. Another corner in the history of free speech had been rounded, though few seemed to notice.

Spector's commercial success, however, did not rival that of Ferlinghetti's. For the days of comic prophet and profit were over for Lenny. The album died months before he did. As for Phil Spector, his

Lenny Bruce college tour never materialized. The iconoclastic record producer now had his sights set not on a dying comic philosopher, but on a very much alive pop R&B performer—Tina Turner.

"I'm Going to Die This Year"

When things began to get difficult, there was...
a certain self-destructive element within the man.
—Hugh Hefner

LOS ANGELES SUPERIOR Court Judge Benjamin Landis had just ruled. It was in Lenny's trial for possession of heroin. On April 18, 1966, Bruce was given a suspended one-year jail term, fined $250, and placed on two years' probation. The judge did not stop with the terms of the sentence, however. To the convicted man standing before him, he offered words of hope: "I believe you have a spark of talent in the field of your endeavors. If you resolve your conflicts, you may yet ignite this spark of talent into the flame of genius."

With those words, Lenny was a free man again—at least everywhere except in New York. By this time, he had prevailed, in one way or another, in all but one of the obscenity and narcotics actions against him. He seemed to be turning a corner, leaving his law troubles behind. But now his problems were more than legal—his body was battered and bulging, his morale was declining, his psyche depressed, and his creditors were circling. Suffering from emphysema and in severe pain, Lenny would ask his mother to rub ointment into the stitches left from his collapsed lung surgery. In the eyes of Mort Sahl and others, "he looked very, very sick."

Judge Landis's words of inspiration notwithstanding, Lenny might then have felt that he was living the death that his friend, Paul Krassner, had parodied in a 1964 "Obituary for Lenny Bruce," published in *The Realist*. The obituary, however, may no longer have seemed premature. "God, I'm a failure, Ma," Bruce told Sally Marr. "I can't beat that—system. It just seems they want me to go under." Given such depression, Lenny probably had no idea that, only three weeks or so earlier, Justice William Brennan had referred to his Illinois case in a plurality opinion in *Memoirs v. Massachusetts* (1966). The reference implied that Bruce's New York conviction could well be inconsistent with First Amendment law. It was no great victory, but only a hint that there could be light at the end of the tunnel—a light that he was not destined to see.

Lenny already had sequestered himself off from the world. Almost a recluse, he rarely left his Hollywood home except to visit his parole officer or to drive through the Hollywood hills with Lotus Weinstock, his last girlfriend. The blonde, doe-eyed Weinstock recalled a prescient conversation: "I came home one Friday night and he said to me, 'I have something to tell you, and when I say it I don't want you to react or dramatize. I just need to hear myself say it out loud....I'm going to die this year.'" Hoping to alter his mood, Lotus asked, "If I get you some raisin cookies, will you wait a year?" "Yes," he replied. So she ran out, and bought him raisin cookies, "certain that he would keep his end of the bargain."

And, indeed, he appeared—at times, at least—to be trying. Lotus sensed that Lenny was in a delicate balance, half of him yearning to live, the other half waiting to die. "[W]e were going to Hawaii, we were going to get married, we had wonderful fantasies," the effervescent Lotus remembered. "He was even on a healthy macrobiotic diet at the time, trying to lose weight." (Lenny's daughter Kitty, however, recounted that her father's health regime was often supplemented by "six cans of Coca-Cola and some candy bars.")

Lenny could no longer work The Crescendo or The Troubadour, or even The Golden Bear in Huntington Beach. Nobody wanted him anymore; he was too much of a risk. But Bill Graham would have him. "I was not really a great fan," recalled the famed rock promoter. But Graham backed him, because he felt that Bruce "was being denied his rights." "What I wanted to present," Graham added, "was a combination of talent and a martyr. A man who was truly fighting for his sanity and fighting for his life." So he contacted Lawrence Ferlinghetti, and asked him to pass along the word that Graham wanted to book Lenny for a concert.

It was a two-day gig (June 24–25, 1966) at the legendary Fill-more Auditorium in San Francisco. This was the stomping ground of the rock bands on the make, the likes of Jefferson Airplane, Big Brother and the Holding Company, and Moby Grape. Lenny was to share the bill with one of the zaniest of the counterculture bands, Frank Zappa and the Mothers of Invention. "What do *they* do? When are *they* going on? Why do we need *them*?" Bruce asked, when he called from L.A. More important still were the terms of the deal. Lenny drew up a contract in his own handwriting, as was his style: $1,000 per show, plus half of the gross ticket sales over a $1,000. And it had to be in cash.

The deal done, the next step was for Graham to pick Lenny up at the airport. A time was arranged, but Lenny, as was also his style, arrived *very* long after the scheduled hour (about five A.M.). "You're outta your fucking mind," Bruce complained, when Graham arrived in a Karmann Ghia convertible. They drove off and headed for Lenny's destination in the city: an all-night newsstand near the Swiss-American Hotel. Once there, Bruce got out of the small sportscar, walked into the store, hooked up with a guy named Albert, and then left. It was that simple, that bizarre. "No hellos. No good-byes." Just Lenny and Albert, off into the night.

Bruce was "very nervous" the afternoon before his performance—not only about his act, but about his very existence. "I gotta straighten out my life. I hope it goes different from now on," he told Graham and others. He talked, too, about cops, about his mother, and how he had not turned out to be what he might have been for her.

The show was comical, though only in a derisive sense—what with the quintessential '50s jazz hipster playing to the '60s drug-rock generation. When the audience laughed, they laughed less with him than at him. Lenny Bruce, the celebrated high priest of comic dissent, was awful. It wasn't just that he started his act two hours late, or that he was whacked out of his head. It was that everything about him was wretched—his puffy appearance, his deranged ways, and his words that now conveyed the anguish of a defeated man waiting to die. "I'm *not* responsible. I'm not responsible for this," complained a horrified Graham afterwards. And then, the promoter stood back and reflected on what had transpired: "It was the living death of a genius. He took on the law and he lost."

The career that began on an unimaginable high in 1948 when Lenny appeared on *The Arthur Godfrey Show* ended with a nightmarish low on June 25, 1966—the last day of his act at the Fillmore. In a span of eighteen years, he had gone from national television and *Time*, to nightclub marquees and *Variety* ads, to *in forma pauperis* petitions and psychedelic posters...to nothing.

The Fillmore was his last live performance.

WEDNESDAY, AUGUST 3, 1966. It was one of the great moments in the history of pop culture. The coverage was fabulous. No entertainer could expect more or better press. The cameras and lights were everywhere. There was footage galore. From closeups to wide-angles, the message went out over every medium. The press had assembled at the House on the Hill to cover Lenny's final performance—the spectacle of his death.

The police arrived shortly before seven P.M. For over five hours thereafter, they allowed reporters and camera crews to feed on the corpse. (It was reminiscent of the way press photographers covered John Dillinger's death thirty years earlier. The mobster's bullet-ridden body was laid out on a slab for all to see and shoot with cameras.) Not until after midnight did the hearse finally carry Lenny away. The pictures became icons: a bearded Lenny, lying on a diamond-tiled bathroom floor, head tilted to his left side, eyes closed. Naked but for the blue denim trousers gathered at his ankles. A hypodermic needle spiked into his right arm, a blue bathrobe sash loosely tied below his right elbow. A syringe, burned bottle cap, and other narcotics paraphernalia scattered about. That is how America saw its great comic.

Lenny's friends saw him in a much more personal way on that fateful day:

John Judnich (the handyman who lived with Lenny): I came home and called, "Hey, it's John." There was no answer. I went in the bathroom and found him....Lenny was a complete person, the warmest in the world. He was one of those people who told the truth as it was.

Lotus Weinstock: I ran outside and started screaming, "How could you do that?"

Phil Spector (caught in the news frames at the scene): Lenny and I were close friends. He was an artist, a genius, a philosopher and a reporter. He was sixteen million dreams ahead of everyone else.

In the eyes of some (like Sergeant Glenn Bachman of the Police Narcotics Squad), it was a heroin overdose; in the eyes of others, it was suicide; and in the eyes of still others, it was a calculated murder by someone who provided a bad batch of drugs. For Dr. Kenneth Chapman, the coroner, it was acute morphine poisoning caused by an accidental overdose.

Several days after Lenny's death, his tragic plight was viewed in a yet more dramatic and curious way by those who read Phil Spector's ad in *Billboard*:

LENNY BRUCE IS DEAD.

He died from an overdose of police. However, his art and what he said [are] still alive. No one need any longer be subjected to unfair intimidation for selling Lenny Bruce albums—Lenny can no longer point the finger of truth at anyone. In his own words, "were poverty, prejudice, dishonesty, disease, and twisted psychology all erased, I would have nothing to attack, nothing to surprise you with, no function."

His last album, *Lenny Bruce Is Out Again*, was to be the first of many we had planned. It will, without question, tell you exactly where Lenny was at before his untimely death.

After listening, you too will realize that America's foremost, and certainly most truthful philosopher is gone.

As it is so apparent in his last album, Lenny's genius and artistry will live on forever. No, it is not necessary to purchase the album, for that is not my objective. But from one who understood, loved, and will miss Lenny Bruce, I implore you to listen to it.

Thank you,

Phil Spector

Phil Spector's prose aside, death by natural causes would have been the odd way out for Lenny Bruce. Death by spiking—by drug overdosing—seemed far more likely. It was *so* like Lenny. It called to mind something he said to George Crater six years earlier in an interview for *Down Beat*. Crater asked, "What is your favorite instrument?" And Lenny responded, "The one of death..." Flip? Perhaps. But that was the instrument he played that Wednesday in August 1966. Junk jazz journey, all in one. Pure Lenny Bruce: the recklessness, the dramatic statement, and the daring ending, whether consciously or unconsciously executed.

On the one hand, Lenny's body might well have developed a tolerance to drugs that demanded an escalating dosage before he could reach "balance"—the sense of feeling "well." That would have put him in a precarious position, as he approached the infamous "LD/50" value level. (LD/50 is the dosage that will kill 50 percent of users of an injected narcotic.) At that point, Lenny would be walking the death-rope, negotiating the fine line between the hit that would satisfy him and the hit that would kill him.

On the other hand, according to some of his friends, Lenny was shaking off junk. He was starting to get "clean." Ironically, that might be just the moment when the *coup de grâce* comes—when a user temporarily "cleans up," and reduces his tolerance level without knowing it. Should he then shoot up at the previously high dosage level, the effects likely would be immediate and toxic. If that were the risky business that Lenny was transacting, it was likely to be toxic to the point of death.

However Lenny Bruce actually died, the spectacle of his death would feed the myth of a cultural icon. When his body collapsed from a toilet seat onto a cold floor, his spirit crashed through existential barriers and entered eternity. And his mission to liberate words from societal constraints delivered him to the cul-de-sacs of infinity where dead comedians recycle their fate in stand-ups waiting to be born.

IT WENT VIRTUALLY unnoticed, the orthodox Hebrew service conducted for Lenny on August 5 at the Eden Memorial Cemetery in the San Fernando Valley. Sally Marr, Frank Ray Perilli, Jo Jo D'Amore, John Judnick, Lotus Weinstock, Jackie Gayle, Shecky Green, Marvin Worth, and Carl Greenfield (Shecky's father) were there, among a few others. Phil Spector picked up the burial tab.

The chapel service was simple and short. A hearse then transported the coffin to the curb closest to the grave. The pallbearers had to carry the casket down a slight hill, slick from the rain on that summer day. Shecky's father, one of the pallbearers, started to slide and slip, almost dropping Lenny's remains. "Look at this," he complained, "I'm going to get killed carrying this guy and I don't even know him." They made it, not-too-gingerly, to the grave. A few friends and a few strangers, with many friends absent, said their good-byes. John Judnich brought things to a close with a symbolic gesture: he dropped Lenny's microphone into the open grave.

Later, a temporary grave marker added a final irony by misspelling Lenny's birth surname. Thus it came to pass that the man who built a career on satirizing organized religion was laid to rest as "Lenny 'Bruce' Scheider," with all the ritualized blessings of organized religion.

The weekend following Lenny's death, Paul Simon dedicated a song to him. He performed it at the Forest Hills Arena in Long Island. The song: "A Most Peculiar Man."

The Wisdom of Solomon

BLOOD, SWEAT, AND Tears played at the Café Au Go Go the day that *People* v. *Solomon* came down from the Supreme Court of New York, Appellate Term, First Judicial Department—some eighteen months after Lenny died. That Monday (February 19, 1968), Howard

Solomon was out of town, so William E. Hellerstein, his Legal Aid lawyer, had to track him down to share the news of the intermediate appellate court ruling in his case.

Hellerstein was twenty-nine at the time, and had been working on Solomon's case since December 1964. He was the ideal lawyer for the case: a Harvard Law graduate, who had served as staff counsel to the U.S. Commission on Civil Rights *and* had been an associate in Ephraim London's law firm during the Bruce and Solomon obscenity trials. This meant that he was privy to the appellate brief London nearly had completed (but never used) in Bruce's case. So, Hellerstein knew the players—the defendants, lawyers, and even the judges. In fact, in the 1980s, he told Edward de Grazia what he had confided to his wife around the time the verdicts had been rendered in the Bruce and Solomon cases:

> After the trial of Bruce was over, I had a call from Judge Creel, who told me he was intending to resign from the bench. He led me to believe it was because of what happened in Bruce's case. He said Judge Phipps also wanted to acquit Bruce but that [Chief] Judge Murtagh threatened to assign him to traffic court for the rest of his term if he did.

Hellerstein still holds to the account, though it is impossible to confirm, since all three of the New York trial judges are dead. However true, what is undeniable is that Hellerstein worked long and hard to free Howard Solomon from the grips of the New York State prosecutors.

First, there was the battle over whether the Criminal Appeals Bureau of the Legal Aid Society of New York could even represent Solomon, the owner of a nightclub. That battle was settled on October 20, 1965, when the Appellate Term both granted Solomon's petition to appeal his verdict and to proceed as a poor person, thereby entitling him to Hellerstein's services. Next, but by no means last, there was the matter of preparing an appellate brief on behalf of Howard Solomon— a brief that could demonstrate that the defendant had been convicted erroneously, both as a matter of fact and of law.

By this time, all of the main attorneys in the New York obscenity trial—London, Garbus, Schwartz, and Kuh—were no longer involved, and the legal contest was between the young Hellerstein and Harold Roland Shapiro, an aging lawyer in the D.A.'s office who had been there since the 1940s. The case came to Shapiro, recalls Hellerstein, because "no one else in the office would take it."

The appellate brief for the defense was nearly a hundred pages long and consisted of eight main arguments. Hellerstein raised challenges under several provisions to the U.S. Constitution: First Amendment (free speech), Fifth Amendment (self-incrimination), Sixth Amendment (jury trial), and Fourteenth Amendment (due process and equal protection). Among his most colorful arguments were the following:

—The New York obscenity law was unconstitutional on its face: it did not require that allegedly obscene materials be considered "as a whole."

—The New York obscenity law was unconstitutional as applied to Solomon: Bruce's monologues neither appealed to prurient interest nor were lacking in redeeming social value.

—The State failed to prove a *prima facie* case that Bruce's acts were contrary to contemporary community standards.

—The New York statute that denied Solomon a right to a jury trial was unconstitutional.

—When Solomon was compelled to turn over and testify about the Café Au Go Go audiotapes, his rights against self-incrimination were violated.

Where Lenny Bruce's basic position long had been that his bits simply did not violate any obscenity law, Solomon's position was much more complex—a battery of constitutional attacks were made against the New York laws themselves.

Unlike the exchange of arguments between London and Kuh in

the trial court, the exchange between Hellerstein and Shapiro at the appellate level was unevenly matched. Whereas Hellerstein's brief was highly structured, Shapiro's was loosely organized; whereas Hellerstein's brief made precise and critical use of legal authorities, Shapiro's either ignored difficult precedents or spewed an unexplained bevy of legal citations; and finally, whereas Hellerstein's brief was analytically compelling and rhetorically powerful, Shapiro's was often logically deficient and rhetorically overblown. On paper and to the objective eye, it looked like the defense had the better argument.

The briefs had now been prepared and submitted, and the time for oral argument had arrived. The courtroom was packed when Justices Saul S. Streit, Samuel M. Gold, and Samuel H. Hofstadter entered the chamber. Hellerstein, the highly able counsel for the defendant-appellant, was ready to proceed to the podium and commence his argument. And Prosecutor Shapiro, the State's counsel, was likewise ready to go forth. But it was all for naught. To everyone's astonishment, oral arguments were dispensed with and the matter was taken under advisement.

"The issues in the case are too abstruse" for oral arguments; so the bench explained its unusual behavior. Howard Solomon was furious. Was it that his case was too coarse to even argue in a public tribunal, albeit an appellate one? If so, what did this portend for how the three-judge panel would view his conviction? He had lost once already, before a New York three-judge tribunal, and now he was worried that he might well lose again before another trio of black-robed men. It was not, to be sure, a good omen.

When the decision was rendered, the headline and story in the *New York Times* were good news, even if they were erroneous news:

APPEALS COURT VOIDS CONVICTION IN
LENNY BRUCE OBSCENITY CASE

"The conviction of the late Lenny Bruce for giving obscene monologues in a Greenwich Village coffeehouse," the story began, "was reversed yesterday [February 19, 1968] by the Appellate Term of the State Supreme Court."

Howard Solomon's name was not even mentioned until the sixth paragraph of the article, and then only in passing. Perhaps this explains why, in future years, so many commentators would argue that *Lenny Bruce's* unappealed conviction was posthumously reversed on appeal—though it clearly was not. (Years later, even Lenny's New York trial co-counsel Martin Garbus would make the same mistake in his book, *Tough Talk*: "On August 3, 1966, Lenny Bruce died of a drug overdose. Eighteen months later the appellate term in New York reversed his conviction.")

Of course, the real news was that *only* Solomon's conviction had been reversed, by a 2 to 1 vote with Justice Hofstadter in dissent. The unpublished memorandum opinion by Justices Streit and Gold for the majority was some 220 words long. In no way did it reflect the breadth of argument presented in the briefs to the court. Indeed, the ruling was a very narrow one; it was good for this case, and this case alone. It reached none of the grander constitutional claims—no statute was declared unconstitutional. Incredibly, the opinion nowhere explicitly mentioned Lenny Bruce, though it did, of course, have to refer to his act.

In relevant part, the opinion read:

> While the performance presented...contained coarse, vulgar, and profane language which went beyond the bounds of usual candor, basic principles of jurisprudence, however, command us to put to one side all personal predilections, including our distaste for commercial exploitation of sensuality.
>
> In our opinion, the proof failed to meet [the requirements of *Memoirs v. Massachusetts* (1966)]. The court below found that the monologues were "not erotic" and "not lust-inciting"....Moreover, integral parts of the performance included comments on problems of contemporary society. Religious hypocrisy, racial and religious prejudices, the obscenity laws, and human tensions were all subjects of comment. Therefore, it was error to hold that the performances were without social importance.

To support the last proposition, the majority (like Ephraim London had done almost four years earlier) relied on the Illinois

Supreme Court's opinion in *People v. Bruce* and the U.S. Supreme Court's opinion in *Roth v. United States.*

The majority's opinion ended with what appeared to be a *pro forma* order: "Judgment of conviction reversed on the law and the facts and informations dismissed." With those words, Howard Solomon's $1,000 fine or sixty-day jail term had been wiped away. Solomon had been vindicated in practice. Although Lenny was not alive to appreciate it, he, too, was vindicated, but only in principle; had Lenny's appeal not been dismissed, his conviction also would have been reversed. Solomon had stood his ground, and now victory was his, unless the State took an appeal and prevailed.

H. Richard Uviller, assistant district attorney in charge of the appeals bureau, found the Appellate Term's order anything but *pro forma.* He moved the Appellate Term to amend that order so as to apply to *matters of law* alone—as distinguished from matters of *both law and facts.* He feared that New York's high court (which only considers issues of law) might decline jurisdiction over the State's appeal. In that instance, the prosecution's case would be over. He was equally concerned that, even if the state high court accepted the appeal, it could only do one of two things: either rule against the State, or require the State to retry Howard Solomon. Both options were unacceptable to Uviller. What he wanted, of course, was for the New York Court of Appeals simply to reinstate Solomon's conviction. It was all rather technical, but the course of law often turns on such technicalities.

Uviller's procedural points gave rise to considerable wrangling between the prosecution and defense counsels. When the air cleared, the Appellate Term discounted Uviller's strategies, refusing to amend its order or to hear reargument on the issue. But Frank Hogan's office did not concede so readily: it brought the issue before the New York Court of Appeals.

When it came to the merits, the briefs presented to the New York Court of Appeals were not significantly different from those filed below with the Appellate Term. Harold Shapiro seemed to place his greatest stock in the claim—emphasized by his use of capital letters— that Bruce's acts involved obscene public *conduct*:

In addition to the findings of obscene language and imagery, THE MAJORITY OPINION IN THE TRIAL COURT MADE A SPECIFIC FINDING, SUPPORTED BY THE CLEAR TESTIMONY OF THE PEOPLE'S WITNESSES WHICH IT CREDITED, that during the first performance of April 1st, "BRUCE FONDLED THE MICROPHONE STAND IN A MASTURBATORY FASHION," and that "IN THE SECOND PERFORMANCE OF APRIL 1ST, WHILE TELLING OF AN ACT OF EXPOSURE, HE MOVED HIS HAND OUTWARD AND UPWARD FROM BELOW HIS WAIST IN AN OBVIOUS AND CRUDE PANTOMIME OF AN ACT OF EXPOSURE AND MASTURBATION."

On December 3, 1969, the parties went to Albany to present their arguments before the seven-member New York Court of Appeals. Harold Shapiro went first, having lost in the court below. The counsel for the State began his opening arguments on a personal note to Chief Judge Stanley H. Fuld, with whom he had served years earlier in the D.A.'s office. Looking at Fuld, he said: "You know my wife, Mr. Chief Judge. The worst thing about this case is that she had to read a draft of my brief."

Going beyond personal pleasantries, Shapiro got to the meat of his argument. Judge John F. Scileppi expressed considerable interest in the state's claim that Bruce had engaged in constitutionally unprotected conduct. The judge went on and on about Bruce's simulated masturbation. As for his brethren, they asked both counsels about everything from the meaning of Yiddish words (like *tuchas*) to the significance of the Supreme Court's ruling in *Memoirs v. Massachusetts*. By and large, their central concern appeared to be how to construe Section 1140-A in a manner consistent with recent First Amendment rulings. Like the Appellate Term, the Court of Appeals seemed to be focusing narrowly.

"Order affirmed. No opinion." That was it. It took less than a month.

On January 7, 1970, the Court of Appeals voted 6 to 1 in Howard Solomon's favor. Predictably, Judge Scileppi was the lone dissenter. Though the majority of the judges lined up on Solomon's side, they did so for different reasons. Chief Judge Fuld and Judges Francis Bergan, Charles D. Breitel, and James Gibson affirmed on the basis of the Appellate Term's opinion. Judge Adrien P. Burke concurred on the grounds expressed by trial judge James Creel. Finally, Judge Matthew J. Jasen concurred solely on constraint of the *People v. Bruce* (Illinois, 1964) footnote reference in *Memoirs v. Massachusetts* (1966). From this judgment, the State would take no appeal.

"THE DISTRICT ATTORNEY'S office has informed me that they do not intend to proceed further with the case," Hellerstein wrote to Solomon. "Hence it is finally all over and it is as if there had been no conviction." His letter closed on a more personal note: "I only wish Lenny could have been around."

At long last, the battle had ended. Whatever the victory, it could only be bittersweet. For it had taken Howard Solomon some two thousand-plus days, untold dollars, and constant anxiety to come to this point. He could not even celebrate at the Café Au Go Go, as it already had closed its doors.

In a larger sense, the legal victory was humbling. No landmark Supreme Court opinion came of it; no extended opinion issued from the New York appellate courts; and it had virtually no formal impact on the state or national law of obscenity.

When it was all over—when Lenny was dead and Howard out of business—what remained was yet another irony. Maurice Rosenfield's greatest fear had come to pass. One man stood convicted (Bruce) and the other exonerated (Solomon)—for the *same* show.

It made more poignant the irony of Lenny's illusory belief in the legal system: "[T]he law is a beautiful thing."

10

THE RESURRECTION OF
LENNY BRUCE:
1966–1974

He used to say that he was being crucified, and...I'd say,
"Hey, man, but don't forget the resurrection."

—Mort Sahl

Previous page: Dustin Hoffman portraying Lenny Bruce in the 1974 Bob Fosse film, Lenny

Icon and Irony

"DEATH IS THE best publicity agent." Artie Shaw's great line aptly fits the Lenny Bruce story. What a great agent death was for Lenny! After Bruce died penniless, he made it big time. There were court opinions, books, magazine articles, movies, documentaries, plays, records, posters, tributes, and even copyright and trademark lawsuits. And there were all those tales of friends who stuck with Lenny "in thick and thin," and who now spoke out against the evils of censorship.

That is the stuff of which icons are made. And that is the stuff that later helped shape the public thinking about Lenny Bruce. It started in Manhattan in August 1966, with a peculiar memorial service for Lenny.

Any memorial service for Lenny Bruce had to be a strange event. The very idea of such a service was bizarre. "[It] would have, at best, appalled him. His friends knew th[at]," observed Lenny's friend, Dick Schaap, "but they held the memorial anyway; it was held, as memorials are, for the benefit of the living." And so it was, that very strange service conducted at the Judson Memorial Church on Friday, August 12, 1966.

Located in the heart of Greenwich Village, the Judson Church was founded in the late nineteenth century by Edward Judson, the son of a famous missionary father. It was originally a place for progressive Protestants, and stressed the theme of "organized kindness." The Judson became a church for "dissident spirits" and "artistic innovators," such as Yoko Ono. It preached "social change and social service." Reverend Howard Moody, an outspoken critic of obscenity laws, was then its senior minister. Moody had been approached by Alan Garfield, who knew Lenny, with a plan for a church tribute—a way to say good-bye.

The formal "service" was to get underway at six P.M., though the church was packed an hour before. To the best of anyone's knowledge, Lenny had never set foot in the Judson Church. Nor had he ever met Minister Moody. Still, as far as churches went, this antiestablishment house of God with a stage door entrance seemed as fitting as any place of worship *might* be for a solemnized service. The tone for the memorial was set by rock music, *avant garde* poems, and weird routines. Allen Ginsberg—the godfather of poetic dissent, the radical who rallied to Lenny's defense in New York, and the man who began it all with *Howl* a decade earlier—was there, too. Along with Peter Orlovsky, the two recited a Buddhist chant for the dead, accompanied by thumb cymbals, of course. For charity's sake, there was an announcement of a Lenny Bruce Memorial Fund (for Kitty Bruce upon her twenty-first birthday).

Lenny's longtime friend, confidant, and ever-faithful follower, Paul Krassner, presided over the event. Or, as he tagged his role, he was the official "Master of Ceremonies." Comedy and the ways of the stage would thus coexist with worship and the ways of God in this tribute to Lenny. There was, of course, a tension, a sense of "What are we doing here?" Krassner, ever willing to rearrange reality, played on this tension:

> It's a very bizarre situation for me [to be here] because, ah, I kept thinking: What would Lenny have liked? I was trying to imagine how he would feel about something like this and then I realized that…in view of *Time* magazine's obituary [which, among other things, stated that Lenny "viewed life as a four-letter word"], he would like this if nothing else but as an antidote.
>
> We're here for all our own personal reasons. Some of us are here because we want to show that we knew Lenny in some way. Others are here for more complex reasons. It may all be in *very* bad taste, but Lenny would have liked it that way.

John Lee Wilson followed with a jazz/gospel song and piano performance. After that, and before Krassner could make the next introduction, a young man—identified only as "I knew Lenny"—started shouting. He brandished an American flag and wore bright green corduroy pants with a Tom Jones–like shirt. The emcee gave the boisterous intruder "a minute" to perform.

"I was hooked before the Lord Jesus Christ, that Force, visited this Church." Continuing on with his righteous theme, the rebel Christian announced: "All have sinned and come short of the glory of God." With religious fervor, he lambasted his secular co-worshipers, those smug Lefties who now worshipped at the altar of Lenny. "Jesus Christ gave all, Lenny Bruce did not accept it." Laugh as they might, he warned: "You can't cheat God." His minute of glorious fame now well over, Paul Krassner took charge: "Thank you very much. That was John Lennon of the Beatles." But this Elmer Gantry of a man's voice would not be silenced; he could still be heard saying: "You will pay God's dues, just remember that." It was the perfect segue for Krassner, the emcee: "Now, here's Lenny." A Bruce tape, one of his irreverent religion bits ("The True Christian"), was then played in this unorthodox home of the Lord.

What a memorial romp: the Fugs sang "Death Is a Comin'," Allen Ginsberg voiced his "Who Be Kind To" poem, the Tony Scott Quartet performed a jazz set, Jean Shepherd did his uncanny bit about a showbiz memorial, and Paul Krassner asked, "Just out of curiosity, how many people turned on today?" Weaving through it all were Lenny Bruce bits (including one on obscenity). Even an incomplete Lenny Bruce song ("It Doesn't Matter") was read aloud by the emcee: "...Don't worry about convention / Don't worry about disgrace / You'll know it doesn't matter / When they throw that dirt in your face..."

Beyond those few verses, perhaps the only touch of solemnity came from Reverend Howard Moody when he presented his memorial tribute. Speaking in a deep, paced, and decisive voice, the preacher offered Lenny up as a tripartite mortal. First, there was Lenny's *destructiveness*. "He was a comic who demolished our cultural icons with relentless precision. There was no taboo so forbidding, no shibboleth so sacred that it could not be exposed and cut out by his probing, surgical humor." Next, there was his *unbearable moralism*. "Behind the frantic and tragic showbiz life he was a true moralist....Back of all the humor and comedy was the evangelical preacher lashing out in honest rage at all the moral deceptions of a terribly immoral society. He backed religion up against the wall of its presuppositions, and whipped it with the lash of its own confessions." And finally, there was his *pigheadedness*. "He was a man possessed of an innate stubbornness that refused to budge when his comedy became controversy." Destructive, moral, and pigheaded—an annihilator of cultural icons. That was Lenny Bruce, or so the church man preached.

The Judson Church service/spectacle revealed early on just how much of a cultural icon Lenny Bruce had become in the short time since he had spiked his way into eternity only a few weeks earlier. In death, the figure of his life was hip and irreverent, wise and moral, poetic and musical, provocative and innocent, lucent and hallucinatory, and ultimately comic and tragic. He was above irony. He was *Lenny Bruce*.

"May God console those who loved and were loved by Lenny Bruce, may God forgive all those who participated and acquiesced in the deprivation of his livelihood while he lived, and may God grant all of us the 'shalom' that comes from laughing at ourselves." Reverend Moody's call for Christian charity and comic relief went out on that Shabbat evening in 1966. But would it be honored? Could New York's liberal society forgive Richard Kuh, the man who helped turn Lenny Bruce, the destroyer of icons, into an American icon? Forgiveness, of course, comes more easily with time, with the passing of memory.

Essentially Yours

"GENIUS." THAT IS how United Artists Records touted Lenny several months after the Judson Church Memorial service. The record giant had mounted a national advertising campaign to publicize the arrival of *Lenny Bruce*, a release of the famous 1961 Carnegie Hall concert. Magazines, theater playbills, and college newspapers all proclaimed the "genius" of the late, great Lenny Bruce. Never mind that the Carnegie Hall two-record set (an uncommon uncensored release) brought back to life some of the same offensive bits and words for which Lenny had been busted in San Francisco, Los Angeles, Chicago, and New York. Bruce classics—e.g., "Tits and Ass," "The Clap," and "Christ and Moses," among others—were now offered at local record shops everywhere. Ironically, the new album was widely distributed in Manhattan even while Lenny's conviction, and that of Howard Solomon, still stood.

Meanwhile, underground Lenny Bruce tapes—of his club performances, obscenity trials, and drug trials—were being peddled for profit by "friends." Sally Marr, the executor of the Bruce estate, was livid. She hired a staff of New York lawyers to halt the criminal traffic: "These tapes belong to the estate of Lenny Bruce and I feel that anyone using them for commercial gain is acting illegally," she said. Moreover, mother Marr had her own plans for Lenny's recorded legacy, namely, releasing a set of LPs to create "a good image of Lenny." Such motherly love, however, was not left unquestioned. Take, for example, Nico's 1967 "Eulogy to Lenny." In that Tim Hardin ballad with Lou Reed and Jackson Browne on the guitars, Nico (of Velvet Underground fame) lamented the fact that "I've lost a friend / And I don't know why / But never again / Will we get together to die. / And why after every lost shot / Was there always another? / Why after all you hadn't got / Did you leave your life to your mother?" Whatever it meant didn't matter; what mattered was that pop culture had embraced Lenny Bruce as its latest dead hero.

Every hero must have his or her celluloid story, and Lenny would have several in the years following his death. The first of the Lenny Bruce movies was *The Performance Film*, which opened at the Film-Makers Cinematheque on West 41st Street on Sunday, March 19, 1967. This was the film made by John Magnuson in the spring of 1965 at Basin Street West in San Francisco. It was a photographic record of one of Bruce's last performances—sixty-five unedited minutes of Lenny doing a gig. Bruce and Magnuson had prepared for the performance for several months with many takes and run-throughs. Finally, they set things in motion, and recorded a live Lenny Bruce show in August 1965.

Clad in a funky sport coat, a wide-open shirt, and blue jeans, he paced back and forth with mike in hand. The club atmosphere was dark and dungeon-like. (Lenny's failing eyes could only handle so much light.) Still, the camera captured what life and laughter remained in the unshaven, overweight, and baggy-eyed comic. A good part of his act consisted of readings from court papers. "The basic thrust of the performance [was] an attempt to prove that Lenny never actually said the things for which he was tried in New York." *The Performance Film* is the act (or parts of it) that Lenny would have done in open court, had the triers of his fate allowed it. Or it might even be seen as a form of Lenny's "appellate argument," had he ever perfected an appeal. But the performance never found its way to a courtroom. Thus, there was only his *ex officio* cinematic defense, which debuted posthumously in New York. True to Bruce form, the film ran while *People v. Solomon* was still pending before an appellate court. As Vincent Canby described the film in his *New York Times* review, it "is a devastating recapitulation of his New York obscenity trial..." Lenny Bruce was back in the public eye *sans* any threats of Section 1140-A obscenity busts.

What really brought Lenny back to life, however, was the late 1967 release of *The Essential Lenny Bruce*, compiled and edited by John Cohen. Before his gravestone could change hues, he was *essential-ized*—just like Tom Paine, Henry David Thoreau, and Henry Miller. He was pocket portable, just like Dorothy Parker. The "uncut and uncensored" Ballantine Books collection of Lenny's bits would sell some quarter of a million copies within two years. Now, Lenny's words would be discussed in classrooms, pondered in cafés, and read on buses, trains, and airplanes.

"When Lenny Bruce died," wrote Cohen, "he did not know that his life and satire would become a legend to a generation of young Americans who had never seen him perform." Sixteen chapters of Lenny's wit and wisdom were offered to reveal the "hypocrisy of morality," the "spiritual emptiness in much of organized religion," and the "absurdity of our fear of words—particularly words having to do with sex." With biting anger, Cohen proclaimed in the epilogue that "Lenny Bruce did not die of an O.D.; he was murdered" by "the Establishment." If the dead dissident comedian were to be criticized for anything, it was because "he apologized for the agents of his persecution."

In death, Lenny became a new comic for a new generation, a hero for kids weaned on "Captain Kangaroo" when Bruce was doing his race-religion-cocksucker-don't-come-in-me bits in North Beach. It seemed strangely fitting, then, that *Woodstock Nation* was "dedicated to Lenny Bruce." As its author, Abbie Hoffman, put it: "This story is for you, Lenny, from all the Yippies." To the same effect, his words were included in the "thumb-nosing, anti-establishment writings" collected in *The Rebel Culture*—a book with Che Guevara on the cover! There was Lenny's name on the radical honor roll, right alongside those of Malcolm X and LeRoi Jones. Lenny Bruce had become a "brother" radical, someone who fought the system and whose life exemplified the ideal that "disobedience [is] the highest virtue."

It is hard to imagine him embracing such a radical spin. For Lenny Bruce, iconoclastic though he could be, was simply too much of an American of another generation to identify with such a crowd. He defied definition. No matter, he now belonged to the counterculture, which adored his posthumous animated parable, "Thank You Mask Man." On vinyl, in celluloid, and in print, Lenny Bruce was being resurrected *ad infinitum* as a comic with an attitude. He was the quintessential hero of love and freedom—the martyr of free speech, too.

Making Book

BETWEEN 1966 AND 1971, Richard Kuh was very much in the Lenny line of business, though he wasn't doing cabaret acts; and he certainly wasn't billing the dead comedian as either an American hero or a First Amendment champion. Not long after he reincarnated his D.A. credentials to argue the sentencing phase of the Bruce trial, Kuh went to work as a "private consultant on pornography and obscenity," among other things. He became a public speaker, a known writer, and a legislative advocate. An article that he wrote for *The Catholic Lawyer* promoted the use of penal laws "not only to safeguard innocent victims" from obscenity, "but to protect us from our own follies." Kuh admonished: "We are not permitted to go to hell in a handbasket simply because we may wish to do so." And so, he set out to save his world from the plague of pornography.

Foolish Figleaves? Pornography in—and out of—Court was published the year following Lenny Bruce's death. In it, Kuh discussed a number of issues ranging from critiques of the *Roth* and *Jacobellis* cases to a proposed antiobscenity statute. William F. Buckley Jr., writing in the *Washington Post*, was impressed with *Foolish Figleaves?* and prosecutor Kuh's legislative proposals: "I believe that Kuh has made an important contribution to the thought on the subject, and I hope that very soon now his book...will engage the attention of serious legislators."

Richard Kuh worked to make Buckley's hopes a reality. He took steps in the national and state legislatures to help transform his personal ideas into public law. In that capacity, he went to Washington to address a House Judiciary subcommittee on proposed national obscenity legislation. As he had done with the New York Legislature during the *Bruce* trial, he now called on Congress to be *specific* in its lawmaking. For example, "if you feel the showing of genitals during intercourse is obscene, then write the law saying 'there shall be no shipment of materials interstate which show genitals during intercourse,'" he recommended. To the same effect, he served as a special consultant to the New Jersey State Commission to Study Obscenity and Depravity in Public Media.

Yet *Foolish Figleaves?* was not merely future-oriented. It also looked back in time, particularly on Richard Kuh's own life in the law of obscenity. The longest chapter was titled "Live Entertainment." It was about the New York trial of *People v. Bruce*. This was the first book account of what transpired in the greatest obscenity trial of that decade. Carefully tailored to suit his side of the story, the book read like a polished summary of the prosecution's case-in-chief. In his *New York Times* review, Fred Graham aptly noted: "Richard Kuh fudged when he used the title with the question mark." His prosecution and subsequent discussion of the Lenny Bruce case, added Graham, clearly demonstrate that "Mr. Kuh does not consider the law's figleaves foolish."

Richard Kuh maintained, not infrequently then and thereafter, that the "role of the public prosecutor is to take the law as he finds it, and enforce it." Hence, Kuh was simply doing his job in prosecuting the Bruce case. It was not a matter of what he thought right or wrong; it was, rather, a matter of what the law provided and required. The policy call simply was not his. However that claim is judged, by 1967 Kuh had taken a personal position: "As proposed [in my book], the draft [statute] would also ban the Lenny Bruce kind of public show in which a live entertainer regales his audience with the shock humor of massed obscenities and the prurient details of sexual and excretory experiences."

For the record, Kuh endorsed the idea of criminalizing the "Bruce kind of public show." The *"personal* impact of a *live* entertainment on those actually present," he stressed, "is not cavalierly to be undersold." The reason for the law, he noted, was that "[s]pectators become, after a fashion, participants. These personal reactions are compounded when fired by something as personal, as intimate, as sex. Self-conscious excitement may be stirred by an audience's awareness of each others' and of the performers' performance, of the scorning of taboos, and of the daring to do so publicly in the presence of numbers of listeners." This collective breach of taboos, if only in word, was the clear-and-present-danger to which his proposed law was directed. Thus, the need for a Lenny Bruce clause.

In addition to his consulting work, book writing, and testimony before lawmakers, Kuh wrote several articles on the importance of combating obscenity. In *Ladies Home Journal* (in a column titled "Wake Up America"), for example, he wrote of the necessity for more "precise" obscenity laws, especially ones aimed at "penalizing the sale of obscene materials to minors." Later, in yet another article, he argued openly for *"some* censorship—a little censorship, if you will"—when it came to various forms of expression involving sex. "Obscenity censorship…*can*— constitutionally, historically, and practically—exist cheek by jowl with meaningful free expression." A free-speech compromise was required, he felt, if only because the world had become so "either/or," so culturally and generationally divided. "[T]he censorship-pornography battle is, in microcosm," he opined, "the battle between the hard hats and the peaceniks, the over-thirties and the youth, that of law-and-order versus the libertarians." Ideological polarity. Some middle ground was needed, so the argument ran. And Richard Kuh wanted to appear to be just that moderate-man-in-the-middle.

Judging from what Kuh had written in *Foolish Figleaves?*, one could believe that both sound law and policy justified the prosecution of the Lenny Bruces of the world (the Café Au Go Go ones, at least). Of course, "doctrinaire liberals" could never admit that; they were "blind to all else when freedom of speech and press are involved." And yet, by May 1968, Kuh's prescription for liberal censorship (for the progressive "thinking man") had changed in an almost unnoticed, but nonetheless significant way. In an article published in the *Wilson Library Bulletin*, he continued to press for the regulation of "the private (off the street) conduct of adults" in clubs and similar places. But now, unlike what he had argued in *Foolish Figleaves?*, he *confined* his attack on obscenity in clubs to the "display or sale of live or photographed sex in action…" Lenny Bruce routines, like the ones prosecuted in *People v. Bruce*, were henceforth to be beyond the pale of government regulation.

Why the turnabout? Why had Kuh's "liberal thinking man" changed his mind? One possible answer is that several months earlier a New York appellate court had reversed the conviction of Howard Solomon. Kuh never attacked the opinion in writing; he never, as was his style, tried to explain away the decision; and he never argued that the ruling had no applicability outside New York; in fact, he never mentioned the *Solomon* case at all. The *Wilson Library Bulletin* essay would lead one to believe that Kuh's liberal thinker had come to this sound judgment on his own. Whatever the explanation, Richard Kuh was moderating his views, even if he were not too open about it. The times were changing, and so was Mr. Kuh…or so it seemed.

Martin Garbus, of course, saw his legal adversary through a different lens. In his 1971 book, *Ready for the Defense*, the liberal lawyer portrayed Kuh's handling of the *Bruce* case as at times "brutal." He was predictably critical of the "men and forces who prosecuted Bruce." Garbus's essay, like Kuh's, was a selective account of the trial with a personal bias. Notably, the essay made it all too easy to think that Garbus, not London, was the attorney who actually conducted the lion's share of the trial.

Ready for the Defense charged the prosecution with excessive zeal. It emphasized how, in light of then-existing First Amendment law, District Attorney Frank Hogan "could and should have dropped the charges against Bruce....But he did not." Garbus was equally critical of Justice Murtagh. The trial court's findings of obscenity, he argued, simply could not stand. And they did not, he stressed, insofar as the verdict had been reversed in *People v. Solomon* (though not formally applicable to Lenny's conviction). This posthumous victory notwithstanding, Martin Garbus pointed to the need to challenge those who "still hold the power of the law," including those who "prosecuted Bruce."

The most powerful charge in *Ready for the Defense* came by way of a statement from Vincent Cuccia, identified by Garbus as one of the New York assistant district attorneys who helped try the case against Lenny Bruce. According to Garbus, Cuccia said:

> I feel terrible about Bruce. We drove him into poverty and bank-
> ruptcy and then murdered him. I watched him gradually fall apart.
> It's the only thing I did in Hogan's office that I really feel ashamed
> of. We all knew what we were doing. We used the law to kill him.

Murdered. Kill. Strong words. And by a prosecutor, a onetime Kuh ally, no less. Moreover, this alleged prosecutorial wrong was report-edly committed with malice aforethought—"We all *knew* what we were doing." Cuccia's charge affirmed what Garbus reported: first discov-ering that Richard Kuh was handling the State's case, Lenny had assessed the situation quite precisely: "Oh oh, the fix is on."

The Play's the Thing

BY 1971—SEVEN years after Lenny Bruce's New York conviction, five years after his death, and three years after the Solomon reversal— Richard Kuh surely had his fill of Bruce tributes, stories, books, documentaries, and records, all lavishing more and more praise on the fallen free-speech hero. But that did not stop Lenny's arch prosecutor. Kuh, his hair longer now, ventured to the Brooks Atkinson Theatre to see *Lenny*, a play by Julian Barry based on the life and words of Lenny Bruce. The production opened on May 26, 1971, to wide acclaim: "the best original drama on Broadway in some years" (*New York Times*), "a stunning theatrical occasion" (*New Yorker*), "political, anti-religious…and often innocent.…Brilliant" (CBS-TV).

Lenny was revived, *again*—more alive than ever. This was the psychedelic Lenny Bruce, as if he just had stepped down from his place on the cover of *Sgt. Pepper's* with its crowd of pop-culture heroes. The feel of the play was not that of the hipster '50s or the right-on '60s, but of the surreal '70s. It was a psychodrama crammed with fantasies— tribal, sexual, unusual—and staged with bizarre costumes and avant garde props. There was an hallucinatory sense about it. Nonetheless, the dreamlike show had a message about life, law, and Lenny Bruce. Many of the words of the biographical play were Lenny's, some lifted right out of the obscenity trial transcripts.

The Julian Barry rendition of the life of Lenny Bruce traced the comedian's career by splicing Lenny bits—on and offstage, in and out of court—into tales of primitive tribal justice, San Francisco justice, Chicago justice, and New York justice. Throughout, Lenny's once illegal words were repeated: "Can't put a funnel in his ass. Geneva Conference." His racy stories were recounted: "Give up, Dutch, and we'll meet any reasonable demands you've got…except for the vibrators." And his ex-stripper ex-wife was revealed in the flesh (Jane House playing "Rusty" playing Honey Harlowe). True, it was no match for the then-faddish debauchery of Manhattan's Sanctuary club with its Sodom and Gomorrah *shticks* and *shtups*, but it was nonetheless an uninhibited cry distinguished from the common fare found in legitimate New York theaters. It would not, of course, have won the approval of the aging Frank Hogan, still the district attorney of Manhattan. But the law, the supreme law of the land, now made it impossible for him to prosecute another Lenny Bruce act (though the Sanctuary was raided in April 1972).

Its psychedelic melange notwithstanding, *Lenny* was an attack on the triad of societal archetypes the comedian so ruthlessly had thrashed while alive: sexual, political, and religious hypocrisy. And it was in this theater of the absurd, with its towering block as a judge's bench and its masked man atop a floating carousel horse, that the playwright lashed out against the tyranny of the law, especially the law as executed in New York circa 1964.

In Richard Kuh's very town, the production reenacted the same pathetic/sympathetic plea Lenny had made seven years earlier before Justice John Murtagh: "Don't finish me off in show business. Don't lock up these six thousand words." These words left a strong impression on the audience, and particularly on Dustin Hoffman, who himself would one day be cast as Lenny Bruce.

The Ephraim London figure (billed simply as "lawyer") received lukewarm treatment. Thus, Martin Garbus probably would not have been unhappy that he was left out of the cast of characters. For example, there was the following exchange between Lenny (played by Cliff Gorman) and his lead New York lawyer (played by Warren Meyers):

> *Lawyer*: I'm not going through this with you one more day.
> *Lenny*: One more day?? hey, it's been four years [of these trials] for me now…and I hate to bug you baby, but the boat's sailing and if you lose this case I gotta do the time…
> *Lawyer*: Lenny, believe me—the appellate court….You won your case in Chicago on appeal and there's no reason why…
> *Lenny*: But that took two years and everything I had in the bank. You people don't understand…
> *Lawyer*: You want to be an attorney? You want to go in and work the court? You want to play the big room, Lenny? Fine, I've had it with you…
> *Lenny*: They don't understand. I just can't make my attorneys understand.

Comical in some ways, ribald in some parts, and penetrating in some respects, *Lenny* brought the dirty dissident back to New York and hung him up high on a psychedelic neon cross. Fact or fiction, utopia or dystopia, no matter. For *Lenny* was the negation of conformist culture and the affirmation of a newborn freedom. It worked. Even Richard Kuh now sensed that: "I am not sure that, today, questions of pornography and of its suppression are of overriding significance."

Leaving London

EPHRAIM LONDON WAS out of the picture by July 1972, even though he had almost two more decades of life left in him. Literally, he was left out of the picture of Fred and Barbara Baker's documentary, *Lenny Bruce Without Tears*. And "Mr. London," as his wife called him, would be absent from every documentary made henceforth. Not even his *name* would receive honorable mention. Bruce's "final attorney," as the Baker documentary mistakenly billed him, was Martin Garbus. From that point onward, with an occasional protest from Kuh, Garbus was Lenny's New York lawyer...for all publicity purposes, that is.

Lenny Bruce Without Tears was not just a celluloid biographical profile; it was not just an artsy-fartsy film; it was a *political statement*. When the Elgin Theater took out newspaper ads for the film, the commercial caption read:

NEW YORK'S THEATRICAL PREMIER	
TWO MAJOR PROPHETS	
The Murder of	*Lenny Bruce*
Fred Hampton	*Without Tears*
by Howard Alk & Mike Gray	by Fred Baker

Here was the life story of Fred Hampton, the Black Panther "murdered" by the FBI and the Chicago Police, being told alongside that of another radical "prophet," Lenny Bruce. Hampton's trademark phrase—"You can kill a revolutionary, but you can't kill the revolution"—seemed especially fitting for his comic comrade.

The first half of the seventy-eight-minute, black-and-white documentary sketched Lenny's career with voiceover excerpts from his bits, pitched to footage of strip joints, civil rights arrests, gangster films, Spaniards' landings, tribesmen's gatherings, animals in the wilderness, Nazi brutality, Honey and Kitty home photos, cathedral scenes with Bishops, and Vatican scenes with the pope. There were also clips of Lenny doing *The Steve Allen Show* and Lenny at his Philadelphia narcotics trial, the latter involving actual courtroom film footage. The theme of an unjustly prosecuted Lenny Bruce continued throughout the film, whether made by the noted social commentator Malcolm Muggeridge complaining that "[b]ringing the action against Bruce [was] completely absurd," or advanced by the noted drama critic Kenneth Tynan asking, "How can any sane, civilized human being be scared of four-letter words?"

The remainder of *Lenny Bruce Without Tears* held out the image of a battered comic struggling tooth-and-nail to retain his very being, in the face of a relentless State bent on punishing dissident artists. For example, the documentary had some splices of a 1963 *Close Up!* interview that Nat Hentoff did for the Canadian Broadcasting Company at The Village Vanguard, one of the Manhattan clubs Lenny used to haunt. An empty club, a lone interviewer (the young Hentoff with a dark close-cropped beard), a cameraman, and a disheveled, depressed, and obviously stoned subject—Lenny Bruce. Amid the clouds of cigarette smoke, there was this:

Hentoff: Why in the last year or so has the pressure been increased against you?
Bruce [closing his eyes as he began to answer, and then answering forcefully]: I don't know, but stop it! I hate it! It's chic to arrest me.
Hentoff: But why did it suddenly accelerate?
Bruce: Because I gotta a little, um...I'm not restricting myself as much as I used to.

The interview also contained a raw example of psychological vulnerability, a grown man *pleading* for another life, another chance, a way out of his misery. With the pan of a withdrawing lens, the overweight comedian *schlepped* over to a piano, banged recklessly on the keys for a moment or two, and then crashed to the floor and "played a song" to himself, this time with his legs flying in the air and his boots pounding on the keyboard. *Bang, bang, bang*—Lenny Bruce was history.

Then, the cinematic story moved to the trial, the New York prosecution. There were mentions of the other obscenity busts, but they were preludes at best. The New York version of *People v. Bruce* was the feature episode. First Frank Hogan, Manhattan's D.A. His puzzled face flashed on the screen, thanks to an old news clip. "I sometimes wonder what has happened to our moral values," he lamented. Immediately thereafter came Martin Garbus, looking rather Marx/Lennon-like (as in the bearded, wire-rimmed Beatle).

"Bruce said a lot of things about the Catholic Church, about obscenity prosecutions, and about pornography," Garbus declared, and they all hit "very close to home with Hogan." Not to leave the matter there, he spoke of history, of context, and of why he thought Lenny Bruce had been prosecuted and persecuted:

> If you will remember, in '64 and '65 New York was in the midst of an antipornography wave. You had something called "Operation Yorkville [sic]." Father Hill, Rabbi Neumann...had formed a rather strong pressure group. As a matter of fact, there were many set-up cases that Hogan's office had been involved in.

The implication was clear: *People v. Bruce* was a "set-up" case—Church and State working hand-in-hand to abridge freedom of speech. As if the prosecution were not unjust enough, there was the injustice of the court's sentence. "Assuming the guy were convicted of every possible charge," protested Garbus, "he shouldn't have gotten a minute of time, and they gave him four months."

Richard Kuh was not in the cast of *Lenny* characters. No dramatic equal time. But so what? For Garbus's statements could be dismissed as those of a cranky loser, the junior associate of a duo that *lost* the Bruce case. Sour grapes, that's all. Surely, even this new John Lennon generation could glean that. Well maybe, but there was more damning evidence against the State, this time by way of cinematic testimony from one of its own.

"I was wrapped up in the prosecution," Vincent Cuccia admitted. The former assistant D.A.—so clean-cut, so square, so believable— was now repeating and elaborating upon what he had told Garbus in *Ready for the Defense*. Speaking in the protest tongue of the day, Cuccia broke ranks with his fellow prosecutors. He confessed:

> There was community pressure, and there was public pressure in the sense that the overwhelming perception of...the silent majority wanted Lenny Bruce prosecuted, and they wanted him punished because his words were offensive and because his ideas hurt the Establishment and wounded the Establishment. He said things the Establishment didn't want said. And for that reason there was a compulsion to prosecute and punish him, and we did it.

The Elgin Theater audience may not have detected all the generalities. No matter, the die was cast—The Establishment had killed Lenny Bruce.

By way of a satirical sort of presentation, the Baker documentary had WOR radio comedian Jean Shepherd forewarning against the dangers of Lenny's legacy: "I don't think Lenny Bruce, himself, is dangerous. I think, however, the *threat* of Lenny Bruce is." And, just what was that threat? "[A] new kind of Jew burning. I think it could lead to a new kind of gas oven. The gas ovens and the new Jews, of course, being the unhip, those who dared to say that they did not greatly admire Bruce or his types. In short, it's going to be the great war of the sensitives versus the insensitives. And the insensitives are *defined* by the sensitives." In this flight of fancy, probably unrealized by most viewers, Lenny Bruce was being billed as the patron saint of a counterculture that had no tolerance for conformist culture.

The documentary moved quickly to the gruesome and by now classic scenes of the dead Lenny lying nude and face-up on a bathroom floor, as photographer after photographer marched by police to get a final shot for the next day's tabloid. The film then cut to a memorial ceremony and Reverend Glenesk: "He was a man uptight against an artificial world, [a man] who shattered its façades." As the credits rolled, there was a trailer message, in bold relief:

> at last a four-letter word for lenny:
> DEAD at 40…and that's obscene.
> —Dick Schaap

Granted, the documentary was fringe stuff. But it came at a time when the fringe elements in society could still claim public attention, and sometimes even public sympathy. Fringe records, fringe books, fringe plays, fringe documentaries…the fringe was closing in on public opinion. The name Lenny Bruce was becoming, if it had not already become, synonymous with free speech martyrdom.

Man of the Moment

FEBRUARY 5, 1974. Sitting in the governor's office that day, Richard Kuh was a proud, a *very* proud man. It was one of the happiest days of his life. Not since the *Miranda* decision was handed down on June 13, 1966, was he so joyful—that landmark ruling, he always recalled, was released on the same day of his engagement to Joyce Marks Dattel.

Here he was with his wife in Malcolm Wilson's office, sitting as the governor sang praise after praise—a flag in the background, a smiling couple in the foreground, and press and photographers all around. There in picture-perfect reality was the touch of Richard's hand on Joyce's. It said it all: his day had arrived. Richard Henry Kuh was now to be the district attorney of Manhattan, the first new holder of the office since 1941.

All of those years of hard work (he came to the D.A.'s office in 1953), all of those years of trying to keep many of the Warren Court's criminal justice and obscenity rulings in prosecutorial check, and all of those years of professional struggle, they were all behind him. He was in charge now. "My son, 'Dick,'" Kuh's mother explained that day, "has high ideals, and you have to meet them, period." And meet them they must, those two hundred lawyers and two hundred staff who then made up the D.A.'s office with its $5 million annual budget.

In the joy of it all—on that day of good cheer with family and friends—came a question from Laurie Johnston, a *New York Times* reporter. What about Lenny Bruce? Typical of his mixed-message style, Kuh responded that while the *Bruce* case was a part of his reputation he would prefer to "tone down," he nonetheless had "no serious regrets" about how he had prosecuted *People v. Bruce*. Seemingly annoyed, he added, "everybody brings it up." A decade after the case and people were *still* asking about Lenny Bruce. But why? he must have wondered.

What made it incredible for the fifty-two-year-old district attorney designate was the fact that it was "the least significant thing I did on either side of law enforcement." Besides, it was all past-tense now, just irrelevant history: "Today, any prosecutor that spent two minutes on whether Bruce should be prosecuted ought to have his head examined….That aspect of the world—contemporary community attitudes—is way, way different than it was when we got the police and License Bureau complaints on Bruce."

The same issue of the *New York Times* that ran Laurie Johnston's largely favorable profile also contained an editorial about the newly appointed D.A. "[I]ntelligent, articulate, and energetic," is how it characterized Richard Kuh. The editorial noted the "sensitivity he has repeatedly demonstrated to the dehumanizing deficiencies that pervade the criminal justice system." Good news for the man designated to move the wheels of justice, and good news for the people of Manhattan, too. But, as with other evaluations of Mr. Kuh, the editorial was notably tempered in its praise. "He is also assertive in ways that many find abrasive," it added. "And civil libertarians are worried about the hard line he has taken on many issues…" Kuh's handling of *People v. Bruce* was, of course, a prime example of his "hard line" approach to civil liberties. It was an odd editorial, characterizing its subject as *both* sensitive and abrasive.

Three days later, Kuh had a reporter over for dinner for yet another profile of the man-of-the-moment. "To spend an evening with Richard Kuh," observed Judith Michaelson of the *New York Post*, "is to be presented with a kaleidoscope of mood, from defensiveness to aggressiveness, from humor to anger." And what, on that occasion, prompted such mood swings? The mere mention of the name was enough to put the prosecutor in psychological motion: "Would you like to see my collection of Bruce records?" he casually asked one moment. The next moment he changed; he became severe: "Eleven years I was a prosecutor and nine years in defense, and supposedly able newspaper and TV people, all they do is concentrate on one unimportant subject [Lenny Bruce]." And if the subject of Lenny Bruce *had* to be broached, it must be remembered that the prosecutors (or at least the New York ones) certainly were not to blame. Such a charge, he stressed, "does not even remotely resemble the truth." Given that, why pursue the matter? Besides, he told Michaelson with icy reproach, "I don't want this session to turn hostile."

Soon enough, the air lightened at the Kuh home, his voice softened, and the veal casserole became more enjoyable. But the peaceful interlude did not last, for it soon gave way to the dreaded "manufactured issue." The tall, dark-haired host now deliberately returned to the topic; he all-too-gladly lambasted those "self-styled liberals" who really didn't want a "strong imaginative, daring, venturesome D.A." Perhaps the Scotch-and-soda—"We don't drink that much, it's not a nightly occurrence"—made the words come faster, but never fully: "If Kuh can be destroyed—not destroyed, I'm not saying that—but if the D.A. can be frustrated, if his effectiveness can be sapped…" Before his voice had trailed off, Kuh conceded that maybe "I should have kept my mouth shut." Joyce concurred: "You said it just right." Kuh had not yet been sworn into his new $39,100 post, and the specter of Lenny Bruce was defining him again.

However defined, Richard Kuh—deliberate, demanding, and determined—had to forge ahead; he really no longer could afford the luxury of listening to Lenny Bruce records in his penthouse terrace apartment off Washington Square. He had to be about his new job.

As Nat Hentoff (Kuh's nemesis) always insisted, Richard Kuh was the city's *temporary* or *interim* district attorney. He had not yet, after all, been duly elected by the people. Governor Wilson, New York's conservative Republican, had appointed (some say with a devious political purpose) the "lifelong Democrat" to fill out the remainder of Frank Hogan's term, which meant that Kuh could hold the office without challenge for the next ten months. But, to remain in charge after that meant that he had to weather the political storms of both primary and general elections. Could he do it?

"He Sees the Law as a Weapon"

TO ADMIT IN 1974 to being the man who prosecuted and convicted Lenny Bruce was no longer a badge of honor; in fact, it was a badge best hidden. For the would-be elected district attorney of Manhattan, the Bruce "victory" was best ignored (no comment), or explained (the times were different), or clarified (the grand jury charged him), or justified (the judges convicted him), or simply presented as a public official doing his job, however difficult.

There were other matters, more important ones, to consider in evaluating the man who courted the public's support as district attorney of Manhattan. For starters, there was the issue of qualifications for the post. Could anyone match those of the newly appointed D.A.? Richard Kuh thought not, and said as much in a *Newsmakers* WCBS Sunday interview on February 17, 1974:

> I think the staff realizes that there is no one in the state and—excuse the vanity—no one in this country…better qualified to head this great office than Dick Kuh….I am satisfied the person who will be the District Attorney for the next four years is sitting here talking with you gentlemen.

Maybe the "staff" in the D.A.'s office knew that, or maybe not. About that same time, there was a story in the *New York Post* that "[t]hree more top aides in the Manhattan District Attorney's office are reportedly considering resigning to protest Gov. Wilson's appointment of Richard H. Kuh as D.A." While such reports were "publicly denied" by the aides, the denials were questioned. Moreover, the story reported that one senior assistant in the office felt that Kuh's alleged unpopularity had to do with the belief that "[h]e was too puritanical and rigid."

The short month of February 1974 had not yet run its course when Nat Hentoff published *three* lengthy consecutive weekly columns on the man he loved to hate, Richard Kuh. The running title—critical of the Laurie Johnston *New York Times* article with a similar title—had a self-inserted "sic" that said it all: "The Idealistic [sic] Prosecutor." Hentoff, the man who wrote so often and favorably of Lenny Bruce; Hentoff, the man who was quoted in the legal papers written by Lenny Bruce's attorneys; Hentoff, the man who testified for Lenny Bruce; Hentoff, the man who locked horns with the D.A. prosecuting Lenny Bruce; now, that same Hentoff went on the offensive. It was payback time.

Among other things, Hentoff was incensed by Kuh's unchallenged statement to *New York Times* reporter Johnston that it was the police and License Bureau who instigated the obscenity action against Bruce. According to Hentoff, this was simply untrue:

> The D.A.'s office *initiated* those complaints. My sources are a number of people who were assistants to Frank Hogan at the time, as well as former assistants who still kept in touch. They also tell me that Kuh was directly involved.
>
> "A week before Bruce was busted," one of them says, "Kuh told some of the lawyers in his Criminal Courts Bureau that Bruce was going to be arrested…"
>
> Three lawyers in Kuh's bureau, appalled at Bruce being set up…begged Kuh to hear Bruce for himself, and *then* decide whether Lenny ought to be busted. Kuh, with his customary flexibility, refused, adding, "Stay out of this unless you want to be switched to the Rackets Bureau."

Hentoff then quoted Allen Schwartz, a onetime Kuh colleague and later the attorney for the Solomons. Schwartz told him about a dinner conversation he and Kuh allegedly had one evening at an Italian restaurant on Baxter Street. Schwartz, also a former prosecutor, was bewildered why charges were being brought against Howard and Ella Solomon.

"Kuh, flushed, leaned across the table. 'Do you know what he [Bruce] *said*?' Kuh asked rhetorically, and with more than a little passion. 'He said Jackie Kennedy hauled ass—during the assassination—to save her own ass.'" Frustrated that Kuh had not addressed himself to the question, Schwartz asked again: "But what about the Solomons?...Why bring charges against them?" Kuh is reported to have answered: "Those who live by the sword...shall die by the sword."

The first *Village Voice* installment went on to quote various unnamed sources, all of whom said quite critical things about the Richard Kuh they knew—e.g., "truly obsessed," "zealot," "rigid." When Hentoff asked then-Congressman Ed Koch what he thought of the "idealistic prosecutor" and why the Bruce case continued to be such an albatross for Kuh, the reply was poignant: "Well...it's not easy for people to forget that a man was tortured to death."

In the next two installments, Hentoff was equally relentless. "Kuh would exhaust the considerable resources of [the D.A.'s office] for the most petty misdemeanor. Whatever the case, he was going to *get* the defendant....Mr. Kuh's whole outlook on the law is atrocious. He sees the law as a weapon." (So one unnamed "Black lawyer" is reported to have told Hentoff.)

There are "no holds barred when Kuh goes into battle....[T]here is a quality almost of craziness in [the way he] lung[es] for the jugular....It makes me wonder how much Kuh can have changed since [his days as an Assistant D.A.]. Can that kind of pathology, if you want to call it that, be moderated or modified over a period of time? Who knows?" (So asked an unnamed judge.) "I think Kuh's urge is to prosecute. That's his nature, he can't help it," added the unnamed judge. By way of another unnamed lawyer, there was this: "Kuh? That one is dangerous. I sometimes think he feels not only that he's God's helper, but he may know more than the Old Man, since the Creator may be getting a little senile."

Thus it went in Nat Hentoff's stinging trilogy—one not-for-attribution dig after another. Was it suspect? Was it ambush journalism? Or was it rather an indication of how much the New York bench and bar then feared Richard Kuh, the man who wielded more power than ever before?

Old Foes, New Battles, and Artists

KUH HAD HOPED to avoid a challenge in the Democratic primary. After all, he was the incumbent; he was ably qualified; and he was a Democrat. The party nomination, therefore, should have been his as a matter of right. Yet, and true to his fate in 1974, there was a fly in the ointment—actually, there were a few flies. One of those flies bore the name "Lenny Bruce."

The charge: Richard Kuh would make for a "very bad District Attorney." The reason: Kuh lacks the temperament for office; he has the "law-and-order mentality" of Nixon and Agnew. So Martin Garbus put it. It was a strong allegation, especially coming as it did in the year of the Nixon impeachment proceedings. But that did not stop Garbus, the former associate director of the ACLU, from launching into Kuh. Moreover, it was precisely the kind of statement one would expect from Garbus, who in March 1974 announced that he would oppose his old adversary for the Democratic nomination for district attorney of Manhattan. The thirty-nine-year-old radical lawyer—he had defended Cesar Chavez and Attica prisoners—was busy assembling a staff and raising money to defeat the man who had defeated him a decade earlier in the courtroom. And if he could not defeat him, at least Garbus could publicly debate Kuh, and thereby revive the story of the prosecution of Lenny Bruce.

Kuh would not "stoop to answer" the Garbus charges. On that point he was emphatic. Forever confident, he would only say: "I will match my record with any lawyer in the city in terms of nearly nine years as a defense lawyer, in terms of successes, in terms of compassion for defendants and in terms of helping the criminal justice system." He would, in other words, stand on his record taken as a whole, and not let one isolated incident—for which he had no remorse— sully that record. Here again, Kuh wanted to put Lenny Bruce behind him. Martin Garbus, however, was determined to make the past forever present.

As if the Garbus move were not vexing enough, still other liberal Democrats let it be known that they, too, wished to oppose Kuh in the primary. William Jacobus vanden Heuvel, a man well known in

Democratic politics at the time, was considering entering the race. Vanden Heuvel had run unsuccessfully for the U.S. Senate in 1958 and for Congress in 1960. Thereafter, he worked in the Kennedy Justice Department in 1963. A decade later, vanden Heuvel won the Democratic nomination in a bid to unseat Frank Hogan as district attorney. He lost to Hogan, but only after Hogan's in-house supporters insisted that Kuh "divorce himself completely from any Hogan-office campaign." The concern centered around Kuh's role in the Bruce case.

Despite his political setbacks, vanden Heuvel was sounding more and more like a candidate. He was very outspoken. Vanden Heuvel, chairman of the Board of Corrections, felt that Governor Wilson had "invited a divisive political battle" by nominating Richard Kuh to be acting district attorney. He also believed that Kuh had substituted "prosecutorial zeal for prosecutorial fairness" in his handling of *People v. Bruce*. Like Garbus, vanden Heuvel wanted the Lenny Bruce story back in the news.

Robert M. Morgenthau was another man considering his electoral options. Unlike vanden Heuvel and Garbus, however, Morgenthau was a powerhouse, a man not lightly dismissed. He was the former U.S. attorney and the man whom the Democratic Party had offered as its candidate for governor of New York in 1962. As for credentials, Morgenthau could match Kuh—in fact, Morgenthau once had litigated a criminal case against Kuh and had beaten him.

Before the newspaper ink could dry, vanden Heuvel threw his support to Morgenthau, who by mid-March 1974 had announced that he would seek the Democratic nomination. Now, Kuh had a formidable opponent. But would that opponent, that former prosecutor, echo the charges of others and bring the Lenny Bruce issue into the campaign?

At a time when Kuh seemed to be battling one Lenny Bruce charge after another, he received some small but unexpected support from one of Lenny's New York obscenity lawyers. Herbert Monte-Levy wrote to the *New York Times* to defend Kuh's record against the kind of charges being aired by Garbus, vanden Heuvel, and others. Kuh, stressed Monte-Levy, "was a prosecutor, not a persecutor." And he had "handled the prosecution [of Lenny Bruce] in the best tradition of the bar." The law, not the man once called upon to enforce it, was to blame. "Given 1964 times and standards," wrote Monte-Levy, "the prosecution of Lenny Bruce...was almost inevitable." Incredibly, one of Lenny's defenders was now defending his most fervent prosecutor. While Monte-Levy played only a very minor role in Bruce's New York defense, and while he never really was involved in the trial, he was nonetheless part of the initial "team"—and he was also a former ACLU staff counsel (1949–1956). That was enough to suggest, in some minds anyhow, that Kuh might have been treated unfairly by his critics.

MEANWHILE, MANHATTAN'S ACTING D.A. was eager to be about the business of the present. Richard Kuh had to demonstrate that he was taking charge, and charging into a brave new world. In such a world, there was little time or warrant to turn back and lament this or that prosecutorial action, especially a misdemeanor action like *People v. Bruce*. Taking charge of the D.A.'s office meant at least two things: First, building on the remarkable record of his predecessor, Frank Hogan, a.k.a. "Mr. District Attorney." Second, distancing himself from some of the more controversial and questionable positions the elder prosecutor had taken, including Hogan's 1968 prosecution of hundreds of Columbia University students involved in campus protests at his alma mater. So, when Frank Hogan died on April 2, 1974, Richard Kuh had to pay his homage to the fallen public servant (age seventy-two), while at the same time steering clear of controversy, including the Lenny Bruce imbroglio.

He was a "second father," said Kuh at a memorial tribute held in a chamber of the Criminal Court building where Hogan had his office for thirty-two years. His former boss, added the interim D.A., "had the compassion of a Darrow." Faithful to such public sentiments, Richard Kuh was among the honorary pall-bearers when a high requiem mass was held for Hogan at St. Ignatius Loyola Catholic Church (more than a thousand attended).

But even the mighty and "fatherly" Hogan was not immune from criticism when it came to his office's handling of *People v. Bruce*. Amid paragraphs of praise upon his death, the *New York Times* nonetheless reported: "His critics cited his office's 1964 prosecution" of Lenny

Bruce as evidence that Hogan had gone too far. (Hogan's biographer, Barry Cunningham, subsequently noted that "the Lenny Bruce case was probably the first in which the D.A.'s office stepped across the line that separates honest prosecution from official harassment.") Moreover, such criticism did not stop with Frank Hogan. For while the *New York Times* story reported that Hogan's office had won the case against the dissident comic, it also noted that Richard Kuh's "victory was reversed on appeal. 'It was error,' the court said, 'to hold the performances were without social importance.'" The culpability for the Bruce prosecution, then, rested with the late Frank Hogan and his successor-in-blame, Richard Kuh.

The very same day the story of Hogan's death ran, a full-page ad also appeared in the *New York Times*. It was a paid political ad to oppose Richard Kuh's candidacy for D.A. The timing was exquisite. A bold and screeching banner proclaimed:

LENNY BRUCE ARRESTED!

The substance of the text was bolder still; it began:

Ten years ago today, April 3, 1964, Lenny Bruce was arrested at the Café Au Go Go in Greenwich Village for violating a statute against "any obscene, indecent, immoral, or impure...show or entertainment." Mr. Richard H. Kuh, who is now District Attorney of New York County and who was then an Assistant District Attorney, was the prosecutor. After trial the court imposed a four month jail sentence—warranted, in Mr. Kuh's opinion, because Bruce "has shown by his conduct complete lack of any remorse whatsoever."...

Mr. Kuh's actions during the course of the Bruce prosecution, and his own published account and present commentary on these actions, raise serious questions about his capacity to properly fill the office of the District Attorney...

The ad was taken out by "Artists for a Fair D.A." (AFDA), and was signed by some 128 artists, including David Epstein, Jules Feiffer,

Jonas Mekas, Claes Oldenburg, Larry Rivers, George Segal, and Tom Wesselmann. According to Carl R. Baldwin, who was listed as the contact person on the ad, the idea came from Tom Wesselmann. "Tom approached me," he recalled. "He was upset about Kuh running for D.A. and said to me, 'My God, Lenny Bruce was arrested ten years ago and the guy who prosecuted him wants to be the next D.A.'" A campaign was then launched with Wesselmann reportedly doing much of the organizing, and Baldwin drafting the text of the ad, which was run by Aryeh Neier of the ACLU to clear any potential libel problems. The money for the ad was raised by an auction held at the gallery of Ivan Karp, with various artists contributing their art works.

The AFDA ad recited one charge after another against Kuh—all having to do with his handling of the Lenny Bruce case. For example:

> The crucial fact to ponder is that Mr. Kuh decided that the Bruce case was eminently worthy of grand jury presentation and prosecution; the prosecution was his *choice*, not his *obligation*…
>
> As artists and art professionals, we are persuaded that the "search and destroy" mentality exemplified by Mr. Kuh as Assistant District Attorney in 1964 is impossible to reconcile with the fairness, balance, and respect for individual and artistic liberties essential to the office of the District Attorney in 1974…
>
> There is hardly anything so repugnant to the principle of artistic liberty as the spectacle of law enforcement officers proceeding to render esthetic judgments, and to penalize artists who do not conform to their self-appointed standards.

The biting attack on the interim District Attorney closed with no less vigor:

> [Mr. Kuh's prosecution of Lenny Bruce appears] to have been a calculated attempt at muzzling iconoclastic satire…a veritable crusade against artistic liberty. As artists and art professionals, we submit that a man who could carry out such a crusade in 1964, and still consider it a job well done, is not qualified to be a fair District Attorney in 1974.

Much as writers had come to Lenny Bruce's defense in 1964 with their own full-page ad in the *New York Times*, now artists were airing a similar free speech message, though this one took the offensive rather than the defensive.

The Ghost of Lenny Bruce

WRITING IN THE *San Francisco Chronicle* in January 1974, Ralph Gleason predicted: "1974 will be a heavy year for the ghost of Lenny Bruce." And indeed it was, as Richard Kuh found out at one turn after another. While the Lenny Bruce issue by no means defined the 1974 election for district attorney of Manhattan, it was nevertheless a recurring point in the campaign, and one made in such a wide variety of ways.

The legacy of Lenny Bruce as a free speech hero, which had begun almost immediately upon his death, was very much kept alive by works such as Frank Speiser's one-man, two-part show, *The World of Lenny Bruce*. The play—advertised as "No Expletives Deleted!"— was a rather tame rendition of the electric Lenny Bruce. Still, it was so popular in April 1974 that the Bitter End Theater held it over for another run before it opened at the Players Theater on MacDougal Street. (The show continued in different venues for almost a quarter of a century before it finally closed in Philadelphia.) Here was the specter of the hipster Lenny returning to the Village, acting out his club (circa 1959) and courtroom (circa 1964) *shticks* and *spritzes*. Here, for all liberal eyes and ears to witness, was the hell of the New York obscenity trial being reenacted with license. *The World of Lenny Bruce*, and works like it, were now putting Richard Kuh on trial.

But Kuh had his sympathizers and Lenny Bruce his critics. Albert Goldman, a forty-seven-year-old writer who always could be counted on to provoke public attention, was one such critic—the same Albert Goldman who in 1964 signed a petition on Lenny's behalf. In the midst of all the glorification of the dead comedian, Goldman, aided by Lawrence Schiller's research, released his *Ladies and Gentlemen— Lenny Bruce!!* Authorship of the biography was awkwardly billed as "by Albert Goldman from the journalism of Lawrence Schiller." Apparently, a good portion of the drafting and preparation of the legal materials in the Goldman-Schiller biography was done by Richard Warren Lewis.

The five-hundred-plus-page Random House publication was engaging, though sometimes too much so, thanks to imaginative literary devices; and while the work was impressively researched, it was generally undocumented. Goldman's biographical style was relentlessly negative and penned in an impressionistic novel-like style. Responding to his critics—and he had many—Goldman once declared: "My books are a cold dose of reality."

His biographical profile of Lenny Bruce was a dark account of its antihero. By Goldman's nihilistic measure, America's great comedian was a "junky" with a "flea-skip mind," who in the early years told "inside dope jokes" while serving as a drug "snitch" for the police. Then, he became the "kamikaze of the angry comics," the "alienated conservative," the stand-up with a strong command of the "nigger hipster jazz idiom." As for his ideals, Goldman took the liberty (and it was that) of claiming that "Hitler was Lenny's ultimate hero." No wonder that Goldman's Jewish comic had a "growing obsession with suicide." Albert Goldman would have his readers believe that this, and not the popular image of Lenny's "befuddled liberal allies," was the true Lenny Bruce. (For Nat Hentoff, the book was no more than a "veritable cornucopia of factual errors and a nearly total transmogrification of Lenny.")

While Goldman lacked any real training in the law, he wrote at some length about Lenny's obscenity trials, especially the New York trial. His account of them was equally dark, and penned in an alluring prose style that relied more on literary impression than on legal analysis. Goldman could grant, though it was unusual, that the New York law under which Lenny Bruce was prosecuted "was quite possibly unconstitutional." Consistent with his signing of the 1964 public petition in support of Lenny Bruce, he suggested that the New York prosecution was essentially a way to "harass...the defendant." But such lines were buried in an avalanche of fault heaped upon Bruce, as if his personal proclivities and lifestyle were determinative in resolving his free speech claims. Consistent with that biographical take, Goldman, for example, devoted no more than a single parenthetical line to inform his readers that the New York appellate courts ultimately rejected the prosecution's case.

When it came to Richard Kuh, whom Goldman had interviewed, the pitiless biographer was curiously and relatively tempered. The prosecutor's views were held out as a "perfectly understandable and respectable aversion to change," and his key contentions were characterized as "solid legal argument." Kuh's book, *Foolish Figleaves?*, was depicted as a "very able study of obscenity." (In that very work, Kuh had quoted approvingly a 1964 Goldman article to the effect that Bruce's "use of obscenity has begun to resemble the twitching of a damaged muscle.") Rarely did Goldman describe the assistant D.A. in words sharper than "relentless and resourceful" (though he did allege, without named attribution, that Kuh was out to get Bruce because he "ridiculed Mrs. Kennedy"). If Kuh had any fault, it was that he "was on the wrong side so far as the liberal intellectual audience was concerned."

However damning the Goldman account of Lenny Bruce, and however flattering or forgiving its portrayal of Richard Kuh, it could only hurt Kuh in his election-year bid for district attorney. For in the novel attempt to debunk the myth of Lenny Bruce, Albert Goldman had, by some grand measure, given new and tantalizing staying power to that myth. Bad publicity, after all, is still publicity. But that, as Goldman must have known, is how the myths of popular culture work. The final *spritz* was therefore Lenny's. It was Lenny's, as popular interest in him grew, as the sales of books about him continued to generate interest, and as a major Hollywood movie-in-the-making would reveal soon enough. Would the name, Lenny Bruce, never vanish from the minds of men and the marquees of Manhattan?

IN THE WAKE of all this Bruce publicity in the newspapers and elsewhere, Robert Morgenthau busily built his "no politics" campaign for D.A. "The city is plagued with crime," he stressed as he challenged Kuh. By late May 1974, it became increasingly apparent that Morgenthau would win major Democratic endorsements, including those of black leaders such as Borough Representative Charles B. Rangel (who later would become a Congressman). In contrast, Kuh (like Garbus) had "little visible Democratic organization support." Things looked so bleak for the acting D.A. that, four months before the primary, news reports claimed that Kuh would be the likely *Republican* candidate for the head prosecutor's office come November—a prediction that assumed, of course, that the Democrat Kuh would fail to win the nomination of his own party.

Throughout, the interim D.A. forged ahead and continued to act his role. Thus, he announced a prosecutorial program in which small-scale, illegal sellers of methadone might plead to a misdemeanor rather than face the severe mandatory life sentence stipulated by state law. Whatever some may have alleged about his past insensitivities to the individual caught in the criminal justice system, proposals such as those suggested that he had a liberal, even compassionate side.

Whatever his liberality, it was always hard to move into the future, when the *New York Times* and other papers kept printing headlines such as:

MANHATTAN D.A. RACE BEARS IMPRINT OF THE PAST

Below that June 1974 banner was a subheading: "Bruce Casts Shadow." It was 120 or more days into his term, and the press was still hounding him with ever more Lenny Bruce headlines—and this despite his attempts to launch any variety of innovative prosecutorial programs. Tom Buckley wrote for the *New York Times*:

Almost from the moment of his appointment, it has been clear that the most serious handicap Mr. Kuh faced was the memory of a misdemeanor prosecution he conducted in 1964 while he was an assistant district attorney in charge of the Criminal Courts Bureau...

Since his death...in 1966, [Lenny] Bruce has come to be regarded in some circles as a genius whose life was shortened by such prosecutions...

Thrown on the defensive, Mr. Kuh can only say that the use of dirty words was regarded more seriously 10 years ago than it is now and that, in any event, he was only 43 years old when he prosecuted the case and has matured since then.

The good news for Kuh was that, by June 1974, Martin Garbus was out of the race—he had thrown his support to Morgenthau. That meant that Kuh no longer would have to be hassled at debates by Garbus's pestering recollections of *People v. Bruce*. The bad news, to borrow from Tom Buckley, was that Kuh seemed destined to be judged by "his ghost of prosecutions past."

"Feminists Here Split Over an Endorsement of Kuh"

WITHIN A FEW short weeks, the headlines were of a different order, though the focus remained on Lenny Bruce. Now, a *New York Times* story cast Kuh's handling of the Bruce case in a different light:

> A group of feminists, asserting that Lenny Bruce was a "sexist dirty-joke comedian" whose material was demeaning to women, has endorsed Manhattan District Attorney Richard H. Kuh…
>
> In a 750-word letter mailed last week to 1,300 members of the Manhattan Women's Political Caucus, two feminist writers, Susan Brownmiller and Barbara Seaman, called for support of Mr. Kuh on several grounds, including his recent moves to appoint women to several positions in the District Attorney's office.
>
> But the letter asserted, in particular that "on the much debated obscenity issue, Dick Kuh's consciousness and concern are similar to our own, and we applaud many of the stands he has taken."

The story was accompanied by photographs of Bruce and Brownmiller and text pitting old free-speech norms against new brands of feminism. Here were two outspoken and prominent feminists throwing their lot to a man who made many Manhattan liberals uncomfortable. And they were driving a wedge between Lenny's liberty and their equality—precisely the kind of thing that had long troubled self-respecting liberals. It was a new day, and Richard Kuh was a new hero for women, at least for some of them. (Some of the support for Kuh in feminist circles may have been due to Joyce Dattel Kuh, who as an editor worked with the columnist Barbara Seaman at the *Ladies Home Journal*.)

The year before Susan Brownmiller would publish her groundbreaking feminist tract—*Against Our Will: Men, Women, and Rape* (1975)—she spoke out against Lenny Bruce and in favor of Richard Kuh. More than that, she told the *New York Times* reporter about new and heretofore unimagined alliances between divergent groups of women:

> "When Kuh was appointed," Miss Brownmiller said, "all my liberal friends said, 'That's the man who sent Lenny Bruce to his death.' What are they talking about? Lenny Bruce was a foul-mouthed comedian who died of his own addiction and his own paranoia. Should we, as feminists, think automatically that prosecutors are bad guys? Of course not. On this issue I can foresee a whole new alliance with conservative women."

Stressing that feminists "have no sympathy [with]...the attempt to elevate a sexist dirty joke comedian to the level of a tragic hero," the Brownmiller-Seaman letter also protested against what it believed to be a "peculiar engagement between the political issues of civil liberties and freedom of speech."

Such a stance might be expected from Brownmiller, given what she had written a year before in a *New York Times* op-ed applauding the Burger Court's *Miller v. California* (1973) obscenity decision. The ruling was, she wrote, "wholly consistent" with "other rulings on women's rights." The Manhattan feminist emphasized that, when "word[s]...are strung together with hostile intent and deliberately flung in our direction, there is no mistaking that we are on the receiving end of a duly phrased obscenity that was meant to degrade and offend." But this seemed more like an attack on words in the service of

sexual harassment than on words used in a comedy routine. For
Brownmiller gave nod to the radical and comic idea of a "pro-female
pornographic idiom" that would reduce men to their sexual parts. It
was, after all, something that could be "devilishly funny in the way that
any switcheroo can cause our unexpected laughter." It was also a leaf
out of a Lenny Bruce book.

Still, there seemed to be a larger point here, one Brownmiller
would make clear later in *Against Our Will*. She took feminist exception there to how pornography and other forms of sexist expression
had been "so thickly glossed over with the patina of chic," and this "in
the name of verbal freedom." She objected to the "deliberate devaluation of the role of women through obscene, distorted depictions."
Moreover, Brownmiller targeted ACLU-type liberals who "now fer-
vidly maintain that the hatred and contempt for women that find
expression in four-letter words...are a valid extension of freedom of
speech that must be protected as a constitutional right."

By this logic, certain of Lenny Bruce's bits—say, his "Eleanor
Roosevelt's Tits" routine—were as objectionable, and therefore as
constitutionally unprotected, as *Deep Throat* or the raunchiest of
S&M rape fantasy flicks then playing at any of the sleazy 42nd Street
moviehouses. (Of course, there is the question: What about other bits
such as "Tits and Ass," in which Bruce satirized a society that nor-
malized the sexual objectification of women, or his "Dykes and Faggots" bit that criticized discrimination against gays and lesbians?)

If Richard Kuh embraced Susan Brownmiller's views of the First
Amendment, he never did so in public. Still, he must have been glad
to have the Brownmiller-Seaman feminist endorsement.

For Stephanie Harrington, the *Village Voice* reporter who never
gave Kuh any kind ink, the Brownmiller-Seaman "feminist" flap was
surreal. Could this be? Could a Democrat appointed by a conservative
Republican win his liberal party's nod with the help of reform-minded
feminists who espoused reactionary rhetoric? What was this postmodern world coming to? What was happening to liberalism? To support Richard Kuh was, in her mind, the most "drastic" "anti-obscenity
measure" ever proposed. It was contrary to the creed of free speech, if
not of constitutional liberty itself. And, as for Kuh's admirable record

on bringing more women into the D.A.'s office and the priority status he assigned to prosecuting rape cases, Harrington did not believe the facts were that clear, and surely not convincing enough to endorse Kuh over Morgenthau.

There was something more that deeply troubled Harrington. She pointed to the sexist strain in Kuh's prosecution of the Bruce case. That is, Kuh "repeatedly asked expert witnesses if they would use Bruce's language in mixed company that included women who were strangers. This is a feminist question?" Harrington asked rhetorically. The new feminist indictment of Lenny Bruce and endorsement of Richard Kuh were premised, the *Voice* reporter argued, on blind antagonism to the former and favoritism to the latter. "If it is not fair to tax Kuh for assuming a double standard five years before feminist definitions were incorporated into liberal etiquette," she asked, "is it fair to call Lenny Bruce sexist when he died before he ever had the chance Kuh has had to have his consciousness raised?"

Brownmiller and Seaman also overlooked another important point—the real-world consequences of their approval of Kuh's anti-obscenity campaign against Lenny Bruce. They were, in effect, endorsing the very kind of prosecutions that were used in the past, and would again be invoked in the future, to censor the voices of rebel women. Just consider, Harrington wrote, what Gloria Steinem had recently noted in *Ms.* magazine: "The long history of anti-obscenity laws makes it very clear that such laws are most often invoked against political and lifestyle dissidents." Surely, Barbara Seaman could understand this point from her own personal experience (her 1972 book, *Free and Female*, once had been banned in some cities); and Susan Brownmiller was likewise sensitive to the problem, having issued a cautionary warning in a *New York Times* op-ed, in which she wrote: "To avoid a tragic misuse of censorship it is imperative that 'the average person applying contemporary community standards' to works in question must not be personified by or limited to the respectable businessman of local repute who has been the traditional guardian of public morals. For who else but he has fostered the hypocritical double standard that has led to our present state of confusion?" What about male judges such as the ones who presided over *People v. Bruce*?

The case, be it libertarian or feminist, against Richard Kuh was strong—in Ms. Harrington's mind, that is. The *Village Voice* writer lashed into Kuh:

> Kuh displayed a prosecutorial temperament so pristine he some-
> times gave the impression he was prosecuting not a mere human
> being but evil itself. Obsessive zeal in defense of an individual
> against the state cannot upset the balance of justice. But the idea of
> such zealousness combined with the power of the District Attor-
> ney's office is precisely what makes us unable to forget Richard
> Kuh's prosecution of Lenny Bruce.

For all her carping against him, Kuh did not really have to fear the opinions of one woman writing for a small alternative newspaper. What was far more important was the public's awareness of just where Kuh planned to take the D.A.'s office in the future. Thus, he welcomed the widespread media attention given to the press confer-ence he held announcing the creation of a consumer protection bureau in the district attorney's office. With cameras flashing and lights glaring, the consumer-friendly Kuh sat proudly alongside State Attorney General Louis J. Lefkowitz and Consumer Affairs Commis-sioner Eleanor Guggenheimer. Also in the picture was Assistant Dis-trict Attorney Leslie Crocker Snyder—the *woman* he had appointed to head the new office.

Tempers, Gentlemen

SEPTEMBER DREW NEAR. The primary was now six weeks away.

Richard Kuh became more visible and more outspoken. For example, he held a news conference announcing that he was opti-mistic about getting a federal grant to set up a sex-crimes prosecution unit. And ever mindful of his opponent's strong standing in the polls, the acting D.A. took forceful aim at Robert Morgenthau. "He's not a very good lawyer," Kuh charged. Not only that, Kuh continued, he was an inept administrator and someone who changes his views with the advent of a new political wind. "I'm ready to go on television with him and say that he had the worst record for [a backlog of] cases in America." Kuh was throwing down the gauntlet—he wanted to debate Morgenthau on television. But no, he charged, Morgenthau would not agree to a televised exchange (a charge the latter denied).

Kuh responded quickly and spoke rapidly when, in July, he met with reporters and editors from the *New York Times*. Sometimes, for emphasis, he would pound the table with his fist. At one point, he launched into a meltdown assault on Morgenthau, but then caught "himself in mid-sentence and [said] he could hear his wife's admonition: 'Don't get on a negative note.'" Ever himself, however, he returned to the offensive.

"He has the backbone and spine of a banana," Kuh claimed. Those words were borne out of the charge that women prosecutors were not allowed to try criminal cases in Morgenthau's office. The banana-backbone critique was directed against his opponent's purported claim that the policy was dictated by the head of Morgenthau's criminal division. "Damn it," continued Kuh, "I am the district attorney. My Criminal Court bureau chief isn't....I am able to make these decisions. And I don't say this with vanity, but with reality—the buck stops here." Kuh, as he portrayed himself, was someone who would always be personally accountable, a man who never would saddle others with responsibility for his own actions.

By Robert Morgenthau's measure, these were the telltale signs of a desperate candidate, one out of control once again: "Richard Kuh's lack of restraint and fairness in attacking me is part of a pattern of conduct. He has repeatedly taken extreme positions and has been involved in violent confrontations with judges and lawyers." Still months before the election, a confident Morgenthau predicted that, in the final weeks of the primary, the "temperament" of the two men would "become a major consideration in the campaign." And, indeed, it did, as it became apparent when the two prosecutors met in late August at the offices of the *New York Times*.

It was a two-hour, nine-minute debate. Throughout it, they snapped at one another—accusations, interruptions, and harsh words were all part of the rough-and-tumble between Kuh and Morgenthau as they sat at the conference table dividing them. Their manner grew tense at times: eyes rolled, hands trembled, and voices rose. From 11:11 A.M. until 1:20 P.M., they vied for the final word. The issues were ones that they had debated before—plea bargaining, sentencing, hiring more women, victims' rights, etc.—and would debate again. They even did so in print, in a lengthy exchange in the *New York Law Journal*. The contest between them, however, became particularly uninhibited when the topic turned to Lenny Bruce:

> *Morgenthau*: I don't think an assistant D.A. should do what Mr. Kuh did when he was an assistant D.A., and that is try to muscle the judges into giving jail sentences. The Lenn[y] Bruce case is an excellent example of that, where Mr. Kuh said Bruce show[ed] no remorse....Mr. Kuh did try and did muscle those judges in a misdemeanor case into sending Bruce to jail.

It was a rare moment. For here was a former prosecutor and candidate for district attorney of Manhattan charging the acting district attorney with being too aggressive in a criminal case, in an obscenity case no less. Kuh was unnerved:

> *Kuh*: One of the things that bothers me—and Mr. Morgenthau has used this forum to do it—is that Mr. Morgenthau's associates in this campaign of his, have dredged up and attacked me bitterly, based on a case that he chose to bring up today, the Bruce case.

While Kuh might have been surprised that Morgenthau breathed the Bruce name at this moment, it was hardly a topic that needed to be "dredged up"—it had been in the papers and elsewhere since day one of his stint as interim D.A. It was *the* issue he could never entirely duck. Thus, Kuh's response was similar to others he had tendered many times before, but now with a new dig at his opponent:

> *Kuh*: It was ten years ago, a case in which I acted under Frank Hogan's direction, a case when standards of obscenity were so

different that Mr. Morgenthau was trying to keep the public of this country from seeing a picture like *I'm Curious Yellow* and a picture like *491*, and tried to keep those out, although he was unsuccessful.

Kuh skirted the Bruce sentencing issue and, as he had done before, denied responsibility for prosecuting the case. Besides, Morgenthau was no guardian of the First Amendment, had he acted as Kuh charged.

If anything, Richard Kuh's quarrelsome replies only brought on more of the talk he madly abhorred. Sensing this was not an issue to abandon, Morgenthau replied in kind:

> *Morgenthau*: Well I think it was not only the trial of that Bruce case but it was the harshness with which Mr. Kuh tried it. He tried to prevent Bruce from getting bail and in trial he opposed a certificate of reasonable doubt after convictions, and Mr. Bruce could not get bail pending appeal....And he [tried the case] against the advice of the obscenity experts in the office, who told him there was no case.

Morgenthau now sounded like Nat Hentoff or one of Lenny's New York defense lawyers. Joining the chorus of Hentoff and others, Morgenthau alleged that there was something unusual, something peculiarly severe, about the way Kuh went after Lenny Bruce. This was really too much for Kuh. The Bruce matter had to be put to rest. And this ruthless and unfair condemnation of him had to stop:

> *Kuh*: I just want to button this up. One of the things I find a low blow—I might suggest the Morgenthau..."dirty tricks"...department—has consisted of circulating ugly stories about the Bruce case and my role in it.
>
> Your statement that I opposed releasing Mr. Bruce in his own custody, or low bail—I forgot what it was—after he was convicted, is false—F-A-L-S-E.
>
> And I refer you to the court records in which, after conference with Frank Hogan, the decision was made that we would not oppose what is called a certificate of reasonable doubt.

The New York Civil Liberties Union was unimpressed...with *both* candidates. Said Ira Glasser, its executive director: "The point is, since each is making civil liberties such a prominent part of his campaign and attacking the other for his shortcomings in that area, that it seems to me important to point out that neither candidate has a distinguished civil liberties record....[T]he bottom line on both of them is that when they had prosecutorial power, they abused it to the detriment of civil liberties." The Citizens Union, a government watchdog group had a different impression. It found both men to be "highly qualified" and "superb prosecutor[s]." Having said that, it gave its endorsement—its "preferred" rating—to Robert Morgenthau. And so did the *New York Times*: "Robert Morgenthau [is] the distinctly preferred candidate in Tuesday's primary."

The Sunday before the primary election, Richard Kuh went on *Newsmakers*, a WCBS-TV program. Among other things, he said that his campaign spending was under $50,000—way below the $250,000 he reckoned Morgenthau had spent (the latter countered that the figure was nearer to $140,000).

That September Sunday was a sunny one. So, Dick Kuh went bicycling in Central Park with Joyce and their two children. The Kuhs were a family together, at one with their world in the park.

Wide Margins

SEPTEMBER 10, 1974. Richard smiled as he looked into Joyce's eyes and placed his arm around her shoulder. It seemed odd, the photograph taken that Tuesday evening at 845 Third Avenue, the site of Kuh's campaign headquarters. The look seemed peculiar in a nearly empty room with a "downcast secretary" and a top aide who was reduced to near silence. But it was the ten P.M. face he wore when the "bad news" arrived—Richard Kuh, the acting district attorney, had been defeated soundly by Robert Morgenthau in his bid to obtain the Democratic nomination.

For progressive Democrats such as Mario Cuomo (Lieutenant

Governor), Robert Abrams (Attorney General), and Jacob Fuchsberg (Court of Appeals), the evening was a night for celebration, since all three had won the right to represent their party in the general election. For Kuh, however, it was a different story. He had been defeated by a humiliating 3 to 1 margin; he lost every one of the thirteen Manhattan Assembly districts, too. As if that were not enough, "four Kuh assistants showed up at Morgenthau's campaign headquarters on primary night." They were jumping ship even before the new (Republican) campaign was launched.

Kuh would not be discouraged. Standing on a chair at his headquarters, Kuh called on his supporters to fight on, to go into battle one more time. What had happened that evening at the polls was due to "Democratic disgust at Watergate developments," which had caused many of his supporters to stay home. As for his concession of defeat, Kuh congratulated his opponent, but in his own signature way. He telegrammed Morgenthau, inviting him to join in "a regular and frequent dialogue" in the local news to prove who "can better serve" as Manhattan's D.A.—Kuh, the "lifelong Democrat with Republican support," or his opponent.

The contest ahead seemed destined to be even more bitter than the one that had just ended. Of course, Morgenthau could take comfort in the political fact that the "Democratic nomination is usually tantamount to election in Manhattan races." Or, as the *Daily News* put it in a tabloid sort of way: Kuh's chances seemed "as slim as that of a three-time loser facing a hanging judge."

Now the lifelong Democrat would run as a Republican in that, the year of Watergate.

"I CAN'T GET worked up about politics. I grew up in New York....I have no illusions. You believe politicians, what they say? It's a device to get elected." Lenny Bruce could be so cynical. He was so caught up with exposing the lie that he may have doubted the possibility of finding the truth...in God, country, or in local politics.

It was an unexpected headline, even coming as it did a mere twenty-seven days before the November election: "SCRUTINIZE POLICE,

KUH ORDERS STAFF." The unpredictable Richard Kuh had done it again; he had out-liberalized his liberal opponent.

Prompted into action by several recent police shootings, the acting D.A. called a press conference to announce the issuance of a directive entitled "Improper and Illegal Police Conduct." Flanked by Bayard Rustin, a black community leader (and someone Kuh once had defended successfully in a criminal case), Kuh read from portions of the directive. "There can be no such thing as a policeman's white lie."

Incredible. A prosecutor—*the* district attorney—was erecting a wall of purity between prosecutors and police. Unprecedented. "We are not a brotherhood," he continued. "We are not a club jointly with the police in which we must fight to the death for the good name of a particular policeman who may have abused his trust. We have no obligation to protect that abuser." Aryeh Neier of the ACLU could not have put it better. (Of course, Mr. Neier and his ACLU colleagues were quite critical of Kuh for his active support of stop-and-frisk and no-knock laws—the kind of practices that, in their view, either reflect or lead to police abuse.) Mr. Rustin was very impressed: "I look upon this document as being of extraordinary significance to the poor, to minorities and particularly for Blacks..."

Get over Lenny Bruce! That was all past tense. *Now*, liberals could count on Richard Kuh to do the right thing, no matter what the Establishment might think. If need be, he announced he was also prepared to go after the presiding justice of the Appellate Division to end the kind of corrupt practices that allowed the wealthy to avoid jury service. Along the same lines, he spoke out against unlawful wiretaps, the kind of practice he alleged Morgenthau condoned two decades earlier when, as a private lawyer, he hired a professional investigator to conduct illegal taps on behalf of a client.

Forget Lenny Bruce! If the people of Manhattan wanted a *real* public servant sensitive to civil liberties, race, gender, poverty, corruption, consumer and victims' rights, then they need look no further than their man in office, District Attorney Richard H. Kuh. "He had performed ably since his appointment by Governor Wilson last

February," editorialized the *New York Times*. And yet they threw their support to Mr. Kuh's opponent, to the man "with warm human sympathies and a deep understanding of needed reforms in the criminal justice system."

The subtext was clear.

Landslide. Robert Morgenthau again triumphed over his opponent in the November election. This time, however, Richard Kuh would not concede defeat formally, not even with one of his ambiguously worded "congratulatory" telegrams. His days in public office were numbered. He had tried valiantly to hold onto Frank Hogan's seat. He failed due to his character, his opposition, the times, and yes, due to the ghost of Lenny Bruce—a phantom that never ceased to haunt him.

It was time to close shop, forget the past, spend time with family and friends. Catch a good movie, even.

Cinematic Justice

Dustin Hoffman plays Lenny and Valerie Perrine plays me!
Outrageous, our lives immortalized in celluloid! Lenny and I have
become historical figures!...A few years ago, Society screamed,
"Destroy him!" Today, Lenny's screen character is a highly coveted
role, played by one of the hottest names in cinema.
—Honey Bruce

OTHER THAN ALBERT Goldman, could anyone have imagined in 1964 that Lenny Bruce would become a celluloid superstar? Had Lenny thought it possible, he surely would have sold off future shares in the "action." But back then, he struggled with the very *idea* of his future.

After all, a court had just convicted him; his creditors were foreclosing on him; his lawyers were suing him; most of his friends had abandoned him; and few clubs in America would have him. From where he then stood in the squalor of his Marlton Hotel room, Hollywood fame seemed unattainable in his life or the next. Hell, if society had no *rochmunas* for him, how likely was it that the public would one day wildly applaud him?

And so when *Lenny*—produced by Marvin Worth and directed by Bob Fosse—came to Manhattan in late 1974, it was contrary to what might have been expected back in the days of Ruhe, Kuh, and Murtagh—the men who finally brought him down. How ironic. In the same city where he was once a social outcast, he was now a celebrated cultural figure. Yesterday, he was a criminally obscene comic; now, he was a free-speech icon. The Cinema I Theater on Third Avenue at 60th Street was Lenny's latest venue, where he was received as a hero of the culture wars.

The United Artists release was R-rated. *Lenny* was filmed in Florida in early 1974, with some of the club scenes being performed at Miami nightspots before invited audiences. It was a black-and-white dramatized documentary with Dustin Hoffman in the lead role. Hoffman, who had pored over his studies of the stand-up comedian and met with Sally Marr, struggled with the Lenny role. As Hoffman would later note, Bob Fosse "had me doing this routine where Lenny is talking lickety-split. Take after take, he said, 'Faster, Faster.' I said nobody talks like this. I got very angry at him. It was like twenty takes." Trying to do fast-paced Lenny bits in front of a live audience (of carefully selected strangers) was intensely trying, sometimes causing the frustrated actor to blow-up. Nonetheless, when the sixteen weeks in Florida were done and the editing completed, *Lenny* was set to claim a profitable share of box-office receipts.

The work was filmed as a make-believe documentary, though based on real-life events. Hence, it depicted an "interviewer" taping the recollections of actors playing Honey Harlowe, Sally Marr, and one of Lenny's managers. As each of the three offered this or that memory, the film cut to a parallel club scene or life situation. For one hour and fifty-two minutes, the audience witnessed Lenny's comic and tragic life unfold as the zany Dustin Hoffman and the sultry Valerie Perrine took them from Baltimore (where they met) to Hollywood (where Bruce died).

"The point is the suppression of words," said a bearded Lenny at the outset of the movie. While the film began there, it really didn't return there until some time into the production. Rather, it was more like an imaginary biographical profile of Lenny and Honey as told from the perspective of his "*shiksa* goddess." Their fun times, their wild times, their drugged-out times, and their dangerous times were all acted out as the plot progressed from Honey's near-fatal car accident to her lesbian loves, to her drug arrest and conviction in Hawaii, to everything that followed.

Finally, the film moved into the free-speech realm. "The suppression of the word gives it the power," said the hipster Hoffman, playing the hipster Bruce as he did the infamous "Are There any Niggers Here?" bit. Then, onto the "We Killed Christ" routine. (However make-believe the movie, Worth and Fosse did take their chances, even in the '70s, when they ventured into such sensitive areas.) The next thing the audience witnessed was Lenny—the great defender of gays and lesbians—being busted in San Francisco for mouthing the word "cocksucking." Though not without agony, he won his first trial. Shortly afterwards, the audience saw him driving down a highway in a sports car convertible with Honey beside him. She congratulated him on the jury's verdict. But he was not satisfied: "I wanted to win it on the First Amendment." Great scene, pure fiction.

The drama built as an increasingly pathetic Lenny was busted in Chicago, and then in New York. "This obscenity circus has been going on for about four years now, man. It's like a three-ring circus, starring the district attorney, the lower courts, and the Supreme Court. And I'm like some *schmuck* who fell off a high-wire right in the middle of it, and it's killing me." In no time, the police took our hero away from the club and into a New York courtroom, presided over by a single judge.

An unnamed prosecutor (apparently Kuh) then hammered the State's case, while Lenny feared for his fate. Cut to a recess, a bathroom scene. There with his two New York trial lawyers (one of them, of course, is black), Lenny was assured of victory: "These lower courts are meaningless; they don't mean a damn thing....We'll appeal to the state supreme court and you'll get relief there." As fictional as the scene and its text were, they did capture a familiar theme in the man's legal life. True to Lenny's sentiment, though not to his actual words in context, Dustin Hoffman turned to his lawyers and yelled: "I'm like a nigger in Alabama lookin' to use the toilet. By the time I get some relief, it's going to be too late. I don't want to go to jail." He then fired them. Next, he pleaded with his last judge: "I so want your respect..." And then he was convicted. Cut to another bathroom, this one in the House on the Hill in Hollywood.

The emotionally drained audience was left with dark images of Lenny's corpse as the film reenacted the famous Lenny Bruce death scene—a naked body lying on the floor, while reporters circled and cameras flashed. Soon, it was over and the credits rolled. Meanwhile, a Miles Davis horn played as the audience exited.

Powerful. Gripping. Hard-hitting. Predictably, movie award nominations—Academy Award, Golden Globes, New York Film Critics Circle—followed, as did a *Lenny* soundtrack and *Lenny: The Real Story* (a rather unreal book based on the movie). Within five months of its release, *Lenny* had grossed over $11 million from engagements in 316 theaters.

Despite the numerous rave reviews and box office receipts, Dustin Hoffman felt *Lenny* was "a flawed work." True Lenny Bruce fans, like Andrew Kopkind, were more critical. "Bob Fosse's movie," he wrote, "is a disappointment [in part]...because it will now define and describe Lenny Bruce and his comedy for all those who have no means to know better. What they see is a trendy, liberal, middle-class, gentile translation of a life and art that was perverse, radical, lower-class, and unassimilatedly Jewish." Given such a characterization, how could Dustin Hoffman (the "post-*Graduate*") portray Lenny Bruce honestly? How could he possibly convey to the public just what a "threat" Lenny was considered to be? Indeed, many of Lenny's former prosecutors would have agreed.

AS THE GLORY, misery, and cinematic fantasy of 1974 ran their course, Richard Kuh packed his books and his memories. Twenty-one years earlier, he had begun his life in public service, in the Criminal Courts Building at 100 Centre Street. In that sixteen-story granite monolith—where Frank Hogan rose to fame and Lenny Bruce fell to infamy—he held the title that his predecessor held for thirty-three years. Kuh's reign, however, lasted only a little more than three hundred days. But, over a quarter of a century later, Robert Morgenthau remained in office.

Kuh's run was ending, just at the time when yet another Lenny Bruce incarnation was beginning. In death, the stand-up comic had outlasted and outwitted his relentless prosecutor. Mort Sahl was right—Lenny had resurrected.

11

EX OFFICIO
JUDGMENTS

My experience with Lenny Bruce…was the first time I saw in action the government's use of the might and power of the criminal justice system to crush dissent.

—*William M. Kunstler*

Lenny's Legacy

THE LEGACY OF *People v. Bruce* is unparalleled in the history of American law. When it was over, really over, the prosecution of Lenny Bruce for misdemeanor obscenity:

—Involved at least eight obscenity arrests (for Bruce alone)

—Entailed six obscenity court cases in four cities

—Took over four years and some 3,500 pages of trial transcripts

—Required eight state trial judges (not including the numerous judges who heard bail matters and preliminary motions, etc.)

—Involved more than a dozen state attorneys and double that number of billable-hour defense lawyers

—Prompted legal actions by Bruce in federal courts in New York, Los Angeles, and San Francisco

—Consumed untold man-hours and amounts of public monies

—Involved appeals and/or petitions to state courts, federal appellate courts, and the U.S. Supreme Court (presided over, in total, by twenty-five state and federal appellate judges, plus nine more judges in *People v. Solomon*)

—And bankrupted Bruce, who once made nearly $200,000 a year in the early 1960s.

And this virtually unprecedented exercise of government power—what was it for? The answers are equally bewildering:

—To enforce laws that, even *at the time*, were constitutionally suspect or unconstitutionally applied in light of then new United States Supreme Court free speech rulings

—To invoke criminal laws in factual situations where it was not entirely clear that prosecution was required

—To prosecute cases in which the public interest was dubious

—And to apply the sanctions of criminal law against a cultural dissenter whose work, when *taken as a whole*, was clearly of a political or social character (though not simply that).

Ultimately, Lenny Bruce was vindicated…in principle, if not always in practice. However coarse his performances, however brazen his actions in court, and however bizarre his life, the fact remains that his speech was allowable *as a matter of law*. First, in San Francisco a jury acquitted him. Second, in Los Angeles no jury was able to convict him—charges dropped or dismissed. Third, in Illinois the State Supreme Court reversed his conviction. And fourth, in New York the state appellate courts finally sustained the principle of his free speech claims, though not in his case or his lifetime. The tragedy, of course, is that though his speech was legal, he died a convicted man. In the formal annals of recorded law, then, he remains a criminal.

It is beyond ironic, the notion that a First Amendment hero is outside of the law. After all, the First Amendment *is* law; it is a key component of the supreme law of the land. And yet, James Madison's great contribution to the Constitution was trumped in Bruce's lifetime by mere misdemeanor statutes—laws misused, or misapplied, or mis-construed, or mistakenly invoked, or whatever, to convict America's foremost comic critic.

He was a criminal whose "crime" was irreconcilable with Ameri-can constitutional justice.

Outlaw?

BELOW THE SURFACE of the irony just mentioned is another far more perplexing one. It is the irony—resolutely defended by some artists—that Lenny Bruce could not have remained within the law and remained, at the same time, true to himself as an artist. For them, Lenny's standing conviction is a badge of dissident honor. Hail Lenny Bruce, the lawbreaker!

Seymour Krim makes the argument, although in abbreviated fash-ion, for the artist as outlaw. For him, dissident artists must necessarily exist *outside* the bounds of the law's protection. Thus, his comments on Lenny Bruce:

> [T]he society he has willfully baited now pesters him...it makes his life a small hell of red tape and harassment. And it's just in this arena that our sympathy grows tough. Mature artists and rebels through-out the well-known ages have assumed, early on, that they were in opposition to their times and that they would be suffering from pic-ture postcards in the brain to expect kindness from the social order they ridiculed.

Krim's argument is powerful. Or, it seems so, because it respects the integrity of the dissident artist. It does not attempt to co-opt the artist by portraying him or her as society-friendly. Essentially, it respects Lenny as lawbreaker, and virtually no other way. It is a picture of the artist as outsider—proud, uncompromising, ready to stand up to the state, and if need be, willing to accept its life-denying wrath. It is the artist as Joe Hill, the dissident poet shot before a firing squad in Utah (circa 1915). Hill's fiery legacy: "Don't mourn, organize!" Undoubtedly, there are those who see Lenny Bruce through Joe Hill lenses. The late Albert Goldman—Bruce's uncanny and controversial biographer—seems to have been one of those people.

While Goldman's early articles on Lenny Bruce once were used by lawyers to defend the dissident comic (for example, in the Illinois Supreme Court), his take on the matter was far more complicated. In a 1965 essay, for example, Goldman was critical of Lenny's New York defense. For him, Ephraim London and Martin Garbus paraded "critics, columnists, editors, professors, and clergymen" through the trial to demonstrate that there was "nothing offensive in the comedian's language, gestures, and fantasies." Yet Lenny's style, added Goldman, constituted "one of the densest scatological textures ever exposed on an American stage." Such defense witnesses were, at best, "deliberately overstating their position to protect the defendant from what they regarded as a prejudiced and ill-informed tribunal."

Taking issue with that tack, Goldman understood that Lenny had to be offensive to convey his message; he had to transgress community standards in order to attack the hypocrisy behind them. Hence, if Bruce had to be judged by community norms, then he was outside of the law. End of case.

With a cultural critic's insight, Goldman then made a compelling point: "Bruce's defenders were in one sense less firmly in contact with his work than his judges, who felt at least the shock of outrage." By that measure, Lenny's life as an artist required that he offend not only his nightclub audiences, but also the very judges and juries assigned to decide his legal fate. Goldman's portrayal of Bruce was not one of a blameless artist, a hapless victim, or a misunderstood man. No, his was a portrayal of a man who traded in taboos, so much so that he would neither allow his lawyers (he fired them) nor the law (he "violated" it) to mollify his message. Consistently, Goldman feared that applying the law to the satirist was an action "fraught with problems and paradoxes."

There is an intoxicating quality about such an either/or portrayal of Bruce and his trials. It is also a captivating argument: to defend a rebel artist under law is to deny his or her art. Ultimately, so the argument goes, the integrity of the artist cannot coexist with the integrity of the law. At some point, art and law must forever war if each is to be true to itself.

Without denying the centuries-old problem of the contest between art and the social order, we think the Krim-Goldman view shortsighted. It depends far too heavily on a dangerously mistaken notion of the First Amendment. The notion is that an artist's use of word-taboos must be judged, at least in significant part, by community standards. Though we think the claim erroneous, it is nonetheless understandable. For Justice Brennan implied as much in *Roth*; Judge Ryan did as much in the Chicago trial; Richard Kuh argued as much and Justices Murtagh and Phipps held as much in the New York trial.

The notion of the community judging art *as a matter of law* is premised, however, on an idea that Justice Brennan ultimately rejected, that Judge Horn and attorney Bendich renounced in San Francisco, that counsels Rosenfield, Kalven, and Ming challenged in Illinois, and that London would have contested had he represented Lenny in an appeal of his New York conviction. They believed that an artist's use of word-taboos is dissident expression that is *not* to be judged by community standards, however defined. Accordingly, the criminal law never could penalize the artist for transgressing them.

By this measure, art and law need not war, at least not in the facts presented in *People v. Bruce*. When Lenny was ribald, raunchy, irreverent, and tasteless, he was an American standing on his rights. When Lenny was unseemly, unrestrained, and unrepentant before his judges, he was a Madisonian dissident demanding his constitutional due. And when Lenny was unremorseful in prosecutor Kuh's judgment, he was a fearless citizen teaching the state's attorney a civics lesson. Under this admittedly bold view of the First Amendment, comedy of that kind never again should be put on trial.

All of this is not, of course, to place Lenny Bruce on the same rhetorical plane as, say, Aristophanes. Nor is it to claim that all of what Bruce did in his club acts *always* represented the elevated side of the First Amendment, for surely it did not. To allow a man or woman to stand proudly on his or her constitutional rights does not mean, of course, that society must or should applaud the expression that gave rise to the need to invoke constitutional protection. And, yet, reasonable minds can sense that there is something very risky about venturing to apply criminal sanctions against Bruce, while attempting to remain within the boundaries of a viable and vibrant First Amendment. As we pointed out in chapter two, William Brennan, while still a member of the New Jersey high court, sensed this as early as 1953.

If anything, the Lenny Bruces of the world need to stand *outside* of the community (though not the law), if only to alert those within the community to that which they cannot see. And standing outside means, obviously, that criteria such as community standards should be inapplicable to judge such expression. In the end, what *People v. Bruce* reveals is the need to protect such dissident comic expression as we would protect political expression. (Of course, certain time, place, and manner restrictions might nonetheless come into play, subject always to First Amendment limitations.)

We freely grant the oddity of someone defying community standards (always elusive) while still remaining within the law. But that oddity, if you will, is the greatness of our constitutional system of free speech. It makes us better than ancient Athens, if only because under our supreme law the state has no right to take Socrates' life…or even the liberty of Lenny Bruce, a comic philosopher.

Such are our fundamental reasons for thinking that Lenny Bruce did not stand outside the law in his obscenity cases. These core philosophical reasons are, we believe, buttressed by more practical reasons having to do with just how unmanageable (and, therefore, unfair) were the legal "tests" used to allege or determine guilt in *People v. Bruce*.

Community Standards, Then and Again

I don't think Lenny Bruce would be arrested today in New York...
—William F. Buckley Jr. (1970)

BUCKLEY PROBABLY HAD it right. His *Playboy* interview concession had less to do with vindicating Lenny Bruce than with condemn-
ing the culture that first created and then canonized "dirty Lenny."
After all, what was civil society coming to if such filth, such blasphemy,
and such disrespect for societal norms were now deemed tolerable, let
alone fashionable? Buckley's answer: "A society that abandons all of
its taboos abandons reverence." Nonetheless, if society wanted to go to
hell in a handbasket, that was its democratic right—a right Bill Buckley granted, though grudgingly.

The Harvard-educated Richard H. Kuh was like the Yale-edu-
cated William F. Buckley Jr. in this respect. He, too, felt that the times
had changed, no doubt for the worse, to the point where the words of
Lenny Bruce became immune from criminal prosecution. Here again,
realism informed his judgment. Thus, a decade after the Bruce conviction, Kuh was confident that the law would view Lenny Bruce in a
different light: "Today, any prosecutor that spent two minutes on
whether Bruce should be prosecuted ought to have his head examined," is how he put it in 1974.

In politics, nuance is critical. In law, it is essential. In both, it is
what distinguishes the relevant from the irrelevant, or from what is at
least seen as irrelevant. Whatever else, Richard Kuh was a man learned
in the art of nuance. He knew well how to distinguish this from that
fact, or this from that precedent, or this from that argument, or even
this from that bygone time with its lingering truths.

His 1974 campaign statements exemplify this. Recall that, as a
candidate for the office of district attorney, Kuh tried to put the
Bruce case behind him, *forever*. Law and life had changed so
much, he argued, that there was no longer any warrant to prosecute
the likes of such sick comics. It seems logical enough, almost as if
Buckley had said it himself. It seems logical, that is, provided one
never pauses to consider the logic by which Kuh originally argued

People v. Bruce. By that measure, his argument fails. It fails for several reasons.

At the outset, there is the claim that First Amendment law had changed so much by 1974 that it was virtually impossible to prosecute the likes of Lenny Bruce. The fact is, however, that the United States Supreme Court actually had curbed certain categories of free speech rights in the years since Bruce's death. That is, the Court's 1973 obscenity rulings were more *conservative* than was the constitutional rule in place in 1964 when Bruce was tried and convicted. Hence, the 1973 Court rulings would *not* have made it any more difficult for Kuh to prosecute Bruce in 1974 than in 1964, given how he originally had presented his case, and given the judges before whom he had presented it.

Essentially, the Court's two 1973 obscenity rulings—*Miller v. California* and *Paris Adult Theatre I v. Slaton*—reaffirmed the basic principles of *Roth v. United States* (1957), except that Chief Justice Warren Burger's majority opinions abandoned several of the more constitutionally protective pre-1973 glosses on *Roth*. The Burger Court, in other words, reined in the increasingly liberal interpretations of *Roth*. Justice William O. Douglas, the Warren's Court's preeminent liberal, thus complained: "Today the Court retreats from the earlier [liberal] formulations of the [*Roth*] test..."

Had Kuh prosecuted Bruce in 1974—say, without a jury and before the same three-judge panel—the *law* as announced by the Supreme Court would have made his job somewhat easier (though still as constitutionally suspect in 1974 as in 1964). As Nat Hentoff rather curtly put it: "Mr. Kuh, as a self-styled expert on obscenity law, knows that."

But there was more than the status of the law; there was also the matter of its application in contemporary times. On that score, Kuh argued, and with some justification, that *community standards* had changed in a decade. In his own words: "That aspect of the world—contemporary community attitudes—is way, way different than it was when we got the police and License Bureau complaints on Bruce." And, so the argument continued, since community standards became more liberal with the passage of time, it would have been absurd to prosecute Lenny in the permissive '70s.

Well, yes and no. Surely, it would have been hard to imagine that Lenny's Café Au Go Go performances were entirely beyond the pale of community standards circa 1974. But, it must be remembered, the community-standards point was also a difficult one to argue in Bruce's own day given how sexually lax Manhattan was for the times. Easier in '74 than '64, yes—but that is not necessarily what would have proven determinative.

Key to the Kuh prosecution of Lenny Bruce was the *method* by which the prosecutor sought to establish that the comedian's bits were contrary to community standards of decency. That method, had it been employed in the same manner and before the same panel of state judges, could well have produced the same result in 1974 as in 1964. Here is why.

Remember how prosecutor Kuh went about establishing his argument that Lenny Bruce's Café Au Go Go performance was inconsistent with community standards. Consider, for example, the following lines of his prosecutorial logic:

Prosecutor Kuh: Do you use the word "fuck" in the presence of women who are strangers?

...

Have you ever seen the phrase "motherfucker" or "cocksucker" used in any accepted national publication of any kind?

Or recall his line of questioning to Miss Dorothy Kilgallen:

Prosecutor Kuh: [D]o you know any other contemporary American author who uses these words in the profusion that Bruce does, and uses these stories one after another after another—"Roosevelt's tits," "Jackie Kennedy's ass," "chicken in bed," "urinating from windows"...?

He asked similar questions of Reverend Forrest Johnson:

Prosecutor Kuh: And when you go home, tonight at dinner, with your daughter, you intend, in order to relieve her of guilt feeling, to use the words, "fuck," "motherfucker," "cocksucker"?

. . .

Are these words that are socially acceptable in your community, Reverend, in terms of being used in mixed company, ladies, strange women?

If such lines of questioning convinced the two judges who ruled against Bruce in 1964—Justices John Murtagh and Kenneth Phipps— it is difficult to see why the same questions would not convince them again in 1974. For example, in 1974 were men in New York engaging in conversation with women so freely that the term "cocksucker" could be used openly and repeatedly at a dinner party?—e.g., "Does anyone here know if Sue or her husband are cocksuckers?" Or for that matter, was the always proper Dorothy Kilgallen more inclined in 1974 to discuss Lenny's chicken jokes in her newspaper columns?— e.g., "Lenny Bruce has this wonderful bit about a woman coming home to find her husband in bed fuckin' a chicken." Or what about Reverend Johnson and his Sunday sermons?—e.g., "Bless all the motherfuckers and cocksuckers, for they, too, are the children of God." In all likelihood, the answer is "no" to such questions. But if that is so, then again we ask: Given that Kuh's "community standards" arguments won the day before Murtagh and Phipps in 1964, why would they fail in 1974?

That Kuh the candidate viewed *People v. Bruce* differently than Kuh the prosecutor is not surprising, especially when the political fate of the former so readily could be ruined by the legal actions of the latter. Far more important is what all of this reveals about the manipulability and duplicity of the "community standards" test in First Amendment law, and why it should be rejected.

The larger point is that the "community standards" test was a threat to artistic expression in 1964 and in 1974, and would be again in 2004 and 2014. This is especially true if, as in *People v. Bruce*, other constitutional criteria (e.g., the "considered as a whole" requirement) likewise were manipulated. From this vantage point, the law of obscenity will always place comic rebels like Lenny Bruce in jeopardy. That a liberal culture may be unlikely to condemn them does not mean that a particular illiberal community would not prosecute them. After all, if Lenny Bruce's comedy were not legally safe in uninhibited Manhattan in the '60s, who could say with certainty that it would be safe in a more inhibited city, like Moab, Utah, in the twenty-first century?

What makes "community standards" dangerous in this context is not simply narrow-minded intolerance, but also the law that legitimates such intolerance. That takes us back to some problematic First Amendment principles announced in 1957, and still in place today.

"Perhaps It Has Been My Fault"

THE CHARGE ALREADY has been leveled: the prosecution of Lenny Bruce was due, in part, to some of what Justice William Brennan wrote in *Roth v. United States* (1957).

Admittedly, there was much in the *Roth* opinion that cut in Bruce's favor...ultimately, we think, far more than not. And yet, what Brennan wrote—especially in a footnote—was enough to encourage prosecutors in four different jurisdictions to seek Bruce's conviction for violating state obscenity laws. Indeed, they relished quoting Brennan as support for their cases against the dirty dissident.

The prosecution of Lenny Bruce, it must be remembered, was not made possible simply by the doings of moral conservatives, or status-quo defenders, or of others purportedly insensitive to the demands of the First Amendment. No, Justice Brennan, in his own peculiar and indirect way, helped them along. He (unwillingly) gave their arguments a measure (albeit, a small one) of constitutional respectability— though again, we stress that even by *Roth*'s standards, faithfully applied, Lenny should not have been tried at all. A door ajar does not allow a trespass, however much it may invite it.

NOT LONG BEFORE he stepped down from the Supreme Court after thirty-four years of distinguished service, Justice Brennan granted Nat Hentoff an interview. In the course of that interview, the eighty-four-year-old jurist reflected on his career in the law, including his attempt to reconcile the law of obscenity with the First Amendment. "I put sixteen years into that damn obscenity thing," he complained. "I tried and tried, and I waffled back and forth, and I finally gave up," he admitted. Ultimately, it was of no use; he had, in his mind, attempted the impossible. "If you can't define it, you can't prosecute people for it. And that's why...I finally abandoned the whole effort."

The thought of his obscenity jurisprudence continued to plague the ardent defender of free speech at least until the year before his death. For Brennan again publicly expressed his frustration, this time to Jeffrey Leeds, writing for the *New York Times Magazine*: "I do wish we had found a solution to the definitional horror of obscenity," he lamented. The Warren Court had blundered. It was "a very difficult issue which we seemed to have not gotten quite right." On a more personal note, he confessed: "Perhaps it has been my fault..."

Indeed, Brennan had struggled and, by his own measure, failed. From 1957 through 1966 (the year of Bruce's death), the justice had penned no fewer than seven obscenity opinions. Sometimes for the majority, sometimes in dissent; sometimes for the party claiming the First Amendment right, sometimes against him. Thus, in a plurality opinion for three Justices in *Memoirs v. Massachusetts* (1966), Brennan suggested that Lenny Bruce's acts probably could not be prosecuted in a manner consistent with the demands of the First Amendment—but it was only a hint in a footnote and long after the time had passed to appeal Lenny's New York conviction.

The justice employed his famous skills of gentle persuasion in an attempt to build liberal consensus, but failed by and large. He tried again and again to fashion all sorts of procedural safeguards to protect against legislative, executive, and judicial excesses. Yet, here too, they were insufficient to safeguard First Amendment freedoms. By 1973, Brennan had had enough, and gave up:

[A]fter 16 years of experimentation and debate I am reluctantly forced to the conclusion that none of the available formulas [for obscenity]...can reduce the vagueness to a tolerable level while at the same time striking an acceptable balance between the protections of the First Amendment...[and] the asserted state interest in regulating the dissemination of certain sexually oriented materials.

Succinctly, Brennan could not define obscenity in a manner consistent with our free speech freedoms.

Liberals all too readily ignore Justice Brennan's admission that he was *reluctant* (but, nonetheless, finally willing) to extend First Amendment protections to trump most, if not all, obscenity laws. This reluctance can be traced to his idea that the First Amendment protected *political speech*, first and foremost. The following statement from his *Roth* opinion explains his original belief:

The protection given speech and the press was fashioned to assure unfettered interchange of ideas for the bringing about of political and social changes desired by the people.

Thus understood, the First Amendment existed to ensure this Enlightenment function, one essential to the well-being of civil society. From that perspective, "prurient interest" expression could be hard to defend. And that, we submit, may well help to explain why Justice Brennan's obscenity journey was such an arduous one.

Importantly, the various *People v. Bruce* cases illustrate well the difficulty of categorical divisions between protected and unprotected expression. That is because Lenny's bits—e.g., his "Christ and Moses" routine or his "Infidelity" ("sex with a chicken") story—cannot so readily be pigeonholed, and surely not if his work were to be *considered as a whole.*

Lenny Bruce's comedy was *compound* expression, having both political and so-called indecent elements. It was not simply one or the other. Neither the liberals who defended him as a modern-day Jonathan Swift nor the conservatives who prosecuted him as "dirty Lenny" could see this, let alone grant it. One of Lenny's lawyers, however, could. And he long had sought to change the law, its rationale, and the thinking of the young Justice Brennan. That man was Harry Kalven Jr.

As early as 1960, Kalven was keenly aware of the shortcomings of Brennan's constitutional handiwork in *Roth*. As we noted in chapter five, the University of Chicago law professor identified three major faults with the opinion. First, *Roth* was predicated on a "two-level theory of free speech." Expression is either protected (e.g., political expression) or unprotected (e.g., obscene expression). The theory was that elementary, that white-or-black. Speech was either valuable or valueless. Of course, the matter was not that easy if the speech in question was Lenny Bruce's acts at The Jazz Workshop and the Café Au Go Go, for example. It is what Kalven called—even before he met Lenny Bruce—the "problem of the mixed utterance."

The next problem Kalven identified with Brennan's *Roth* opinion was the implication that speech should not be protected unless it somehow contributed to the "marketplace of ideas." This rationality-focused aspect of *Roth* did not portend well for protection of artistic, literary, or other forms of emotive expression. Here, too, some of Lenny Bruce's comedy, to the extent that it was akin to jazz, could be classified (again, we believe, erroneously under *Roth*) as outside the sphere of First Amendment protection.

Professor Kalven's final concern with *Roth* was that the opinion could be interpreted by government to restrict free speech. And, of course, that is precisely what happened in some of the *People v. Bruce* cases, though ultimately *Roth* and its progeny vindicated Brucean styles of expression.

Here was one of the great teachers of free speech instructing one of the great judicial defenders of free speech. It is a lesson that should have been appreciated then, and should be heeded now by those who venture to enforce the obscenity laws—laws still judged by *Roth*-like standards.

People v. Bruce was, thus, an ideal case for Kalven to litigate in the Supreme Court. It gave the professor the perfect opportunity to demonstrate to Justice Brennan and his colleagues the problematic character of *Roth*. More importantly, *People v. Bruce* could be the catalyst to transform the antiquated First Amendment into a modern and vibrant First Amendment, if only because it so well depicted both. On the one hand, it surely had a societal protest component. On the other hand, it also had a sexually indecent component. Combine them, protect them, and what results is a First Amendment released from the shackles of eighteenth-century notions of free speech liberty—a First Amendment with a bold new breadth. That, in any event, is where *People v. Bruce* might have taken the Supreme Court, had the case ever been argued there. And the Court might have vindicated the First Amendment perspective of Kalven, who said: "We have very few really free spirits, and I think we should cherish all of them."

But what, then, would Justice Brennan have made of Professor Kalven's arguments? Would these arguments have prompted him to reform obscenity law or to abandon it altogether? We think the former, for surely the justice did not mean to suggest—and his opinions bear this out—that all expression, however ribald, was protected no matter what its form, to whom it was presented, and no matter what the forum in which it was featured. That being so, where was the obscenity line to be drawn? That question was raised by those who prosecuted Lenny, as well as by those who defended him. But it was never satisfactorily answered during Lenny's lifetime.

If the First Amendment couldn't provide real refuge for Lenny Bruce, could another constitutional guarantee save him?

Taking the Fifth

I'll tell you now, I would never plead any Fifth.
—Lenny Bruce

BY THE TIME he met his maker, Lenny Bruce had learned a lot of law—the hard way. He taught himself the vernacular (he loved the Latin) and much of the substantive law found in various state criminal obscenity statutes. He had friends, acquaintances, and "secretaries" find and photocopy statutes and Supreme Court opinions for him, which he read and then stacked alongside the mounds of tapes and transcripts in his Marlton Hotel room. Lenny familiarized himself with the First Amendment opinions of Justices Holmes, Douglas, Black, and Brennan. And as the police ventured more and more into his Hollywood home and other private quarters, necessity moved him to study the constitutional law of search and seizure. When he died, the last, incomplete words in his typewriter were "Fourth Amendment."

For all of his preoccupation—practical and fanciful—with the law, Lenny Bruce had no real interest in the Fifth Amendment and its great privilege.

The privilege against compulsory self-incrimination is one of the fundamental guarantees of American constitutional freedom. It commands: "No person shall be...compelled in any criminal case to be a witness against himself." Essentially, it is a right to remain silent. And when invoked in a courtroom, its exercise cannot be equated with guilt or any adverse inference. The Fifth Amendment privilege is a command to the state to prove its own case without any help from the criminally accused.

The right against self-incrimination traces back to ancient times, though the critical event in its evolution was the trial of John Lilburne, an outspoken anti-Stuart Leveller. In 1637, Lilburne was tried in the infamous Star Chamber in England. By oath, he was bound to answer all questions posed to him. He refused, and what followed made history. The Parliament abolished the inquisitorial Star Chamber, and the Colonies later gave staying power to Lilburne's refusal by recognizing it, first, in our common law, and then in our Bill of Rights.

Lenny Bruce was no John Lilburne. He was no Fifth Amendment comedian. His very being and entire career railed *against* the idea of remaining *silent*. Lenny always wanted to speak out and give voice to that which had been silenced for far too long.

When it came to his obscenity prosecutions, the matter was no different. Thus, in San Francisco, his attorney, Albert Bendich, never invoked the privilege. In fact, both Bruce and Bendich went to great lengths to offer his words into evidence for the judge and jury to hear. They wanted the court to hear his taped remarks from The Jazz Workshop. Much the same was true for the Los Angeles and Chicago obscenity trials. In all of those proceedings, Lenny volunteered his recorded words to the court and *insisted* that judge and jury hear them. He believed, correctly or not, that his freedom depended not on silencing his words, but rather on proclaiming them.

In New York, however, things were different. It was the first time that Lenny—or more appropriately, his lawyers and Solomons' lawyer—took the Fifth to exclude audio evidence of Lenny's performance. As it turned out, the claim failed...and we think probably for the best. Here is why.

Recall that there was a fierce pretrial battle in the New York courts over whether or not the prosecution could subpoena the Café Au Go Go tapes. The defense counsels were adamant that the tapes were the personal property of their respective clients; hence, to force production of the tapes would violate their constitutional rights.

> *London*: [W]e believe that the production of those tapes, since they are the property of the individual defendants, would be a violation of their rights under the Fifth Amendment—it would be compelling them to testify against themselves, and it is for that reason we object to the production of those tapes.
>
> ...
>
> *Schwartz*: May I say, your Honor,...the Fifth and Fourteenth Amendments [bar the State from compelling a person] to come forth and [proffer] the very evidence of the crime of which he is accused, the actual facts.

Howard Solomon alone, as we already have noted, invoked the Fifth some one hundred times. Ultimately, the tapes were held to be admissible for use by the prosecution.

Question: What if the New York trial court had granted the defense's Fifth Amendment motion to suppress the admission of the Café Au Go Go tapes?

Surely, it would have made Richard Kuh's case much harder to present and win. For all the prosecution would have had then would be mostly inaudible mini-reel wire recordings, the largely incomplete notes of Inspector Ruhe, and the vague recollections of a few police officers. With just that, how could the prosecution ever hope to establish that Lenny's performances *taken as a whole* were obscene? For these reasons, prosecutor Kuh probably was grateful when he first learned of the existence of the Café au Go Go tapes from Stephanie Gervis Harrington's article in *The Village Voice*.

Assume, then, that the cases against Bruce and the Solomons

could not have proceeded because critical evidence had been dismissed on Fifth Amendment grounds. What then?

Lenny Bruce probably would have wanted to go back to work at the Café Au Go Go to finish out his run. If he had performed—at the Café, or elsewhere in Manhattan—it is highly likely that the D.A.'s office would have sent inspectors or police down to record the performance in its entirety and in an entirely audible manner. The State then would have presented this fresh evidence to the grand jury (in audio and transcribed forms) for criminal prosecution. Subsequently, Lenny, Howard, and Ella would all be arrested, booked, and charged *again*. Back to square one—this time with added attorney's fees!

Of course, the Solomons (like any other Manhattan club owners) might well have paused before they let Lenny return to the stage. Having once felt the strong arm of the state, they understandably may have opted not to repeat things. They just may have paid Lenny, and wished him well, *sans* any more performances. If so, where would that have left Bruce? Would any New York club owner hire him with the knowledge that Frank Hogan and his staff stood ready to raid the place at the first sight of Lenny holding a mike?

In light of this, the Fifth Amendment argument may have been good for the Solomons (it might have kept them out of court), but not really as good for Bruce. For what Bruce gained in the short-run (dismissal of criminal charges), he would have lost many times over in the long-run—namely, the ability to perform freely in New York. A Fifth Amendment victory, then, was synonymous with a First Amendment defeat. And this battle the State would have won without ever having had to contest the matter in court!

When all the legal dust finally settled, Lenny's only hopes were his free speech claims—i.e., that he either had not violated the obscenity statute, or that the statute was unconstitutional on its face, or unconstitutional as applied to him. This is not, however, to fault the defense counsels for raising any and all arguments, including Fifth Amendment arguments, on behalf of their respective clients. It is, rather, to point out that different constitutional claims (Fifth vs. First) can sometimes affect the respective parties (Bruce and the Solomons) differently, and can likewise produce different results. As long as a client is adequately apprised of such possibilities, the call remains (as it should) with that client.

As a criminally accused defendant, Lenny may have benefited from the Fifth Amendment. But as a comedian, his future lay with the First Amendment—the right to speak freely and openly. Some of his liberal lawyers seemed not to appreciate that fully. That does not mean, of course, that they were responsible for the fate that befell him. Yet, at least one of Lenny's liberal friends blamed his liberal lawyers for—of all things—his death.

Who Killed Lenny Bruce?

Every age needs a Lenny Bruce
and every age will try to kill him.
—Peter Hall

SIX YEARS AFTER Bruce died, Larry Josephson of Pacifica Radio asked Richard Kuh: "Why do you think Lenny Bruce died?...Would you care to speculate about any other reason than the direct cause of death?"

Understandably, Kuh had little patience for such "Did you kill him?" kind of questions: "Mr. Josephson, I'd be delighted to specu late with you over a beer some night for hours and hours. I thought we were to talk about obscenity here, and about censorship. And I'd like to talk about them."

Vincent Cuccia, who served in the D.A.'s office during the New York prosecution and who opposed Bruce's appeal, answered the question freely: "We drove him into poverty and bankruptcy and then murdered him....We all knew what we were doing. We used the law to kill him."

For Sherman Block, who busted Lenny in Los Angeles, the question evoked sad sentiments: "My only regret is that a man that talented saw a need to engage in illegal activity to the point that it ultimately destroyed him—not the obscenity, but the narcotics certainly destroyed him—and I think that overall, it was probably a loss." In responding to the question that the trials killed him, Block was emphatic: "That's baloney. He was heavily into drugs long before he was ever arrested for his performances [in S.F. and L.A.]."

One of Lenny's lawyers, the young associate Martin Garbus, found fault elsewhere: "[H]is death was in large part due to inner turmoil, frustration, and [the] overwhelming feeling of helplessness he had experienced as he fought the law during his last five years."

The *Herald Tribune* columnist Dick Schaap saw the matter in his own personal-philosophical way. Of the friend he had known since 1960, when they went to see the Yankees play the Pirates in the World Series, Schaap once wrote: "The real trouble with Lenny Bruce is that he [was] alive. He [was] not a book or a movie or a painting." Such things are "nice and dependable" for this or that cause. But Lenny Bruce, he was in no one's ideological tent. Different and difficult he was. He offended all, liberals and conservatives alike, as he poked holes in their lofty principles. He did so to the point of endangering his own freedom, his own life. Everything and everybody be damned: all that mattered was *the Law*. As Harry Kalven told Schaap in November of 1964: "What disturb[s] me [is] that it's almost as though he's more interested in the legal points now than he is in himself." And so it came to pass: when Lenny Bruce met his maker he was more concerned about the letter of the law than about the length of his life. It should be no surprise, then, that the last words typed on his typewriter were the letters of the law, of the Fourth Amendment to be precise.

For the always dramatic Phil Spector, the answer to the "How did Lenny die?" question was bold and metaphorical: "He died of an overdose of police."

William M. Kunstler, the radical lawyer who did some work for Lenny, blamed the authorities for tempting Lenny's already weak hand: "I believe Lenny OD'd deliberately....The government hounded Lenny until his single-minded drive to vindicate himself took precedence over everything else. Fighting the government is appropriate, but Lenny's manic fixation destroyed him." Life and death looked still more complex through Lotus Weinstock's lenses. For the beautiful, new-age-type woman who had been with Lenny during his final year, the answer was rather paradoxical: "I think he surrendered....There was a part of him that wanted to die; he couldn't bear the thought of being an old hippie....He may have played a part in it, but I don't think he ever intended to do that....He wanted to live, [but he also] wanted to end the agony."

Irving Howe, the noted scholar of Jewish history and coeditor of *Dissent* magazine, saw things in a more philosophical light: Lenny Bruce's humor bore "a heavy weight of destruction; in Jewish hands, more likely self-destruction, for it proceeds from a brilliance that corrodes the world faster than, even in imagination, it can remake it....He fell back, deeply back, into a Jewish past that neither he nor his audiences could know much about—a reborn Sabbatai as a stand-up comic."

The "Who killed Lenny Bruce?" question has many answers, depending upon whom you ask and from what vantage point you consider the matter. In a physical sense, Lenny killed himself; he spiked the poison into his veins (we are pretty sure). Then again, the fix, unknown to him, may have been poisoned. In a psychological sense, the answer is less clear, for though Lenny certainly had a strong self-destructive streak in him, it is hard to imagine how his obscenity prosecutions would not have depressed any mortal deeply. So Lenny's depression could well have contributed to his self-destructive tendencies, to the point of killing him.

Of course, one may wonder what value, if any, such inquiries have. Maybe, in the end, they are no more than convenient devices for assigning blame in sensational ways. However that may be, one answer to the question stands out from the rest, and does deserve serious consideration. It was an answer from one of Lenny's own, a man who knew him from the early days.

True to his contrary character, Mort Sahl had a novel take on the "who killed Lenny?" question. Plain and simple, it was the *liberal lawyers*; they were to blame for what happened to Lenny that fateful Wednesday in August 1966.

The comedian and self-billed friend of Bruce saw it this way: "[H]e was led down the primrose path because of those lawyers in Greenwich Village who told him, 'let's test the law, let's break it.'" Pouring fuel onto the rhetorical fire, Sahl added: "They're guys who are not…Trot-skyites *politically* but their social attitude is Trotskyite. 'Let's throw some sand in the gears. Maybe if they can't produce any Chryslers, that'll bring the factory to its senses.'" Then Sahl went on to describe just how cowardly those "Trotskyite" lawyers were: "'Let's you and him fight,'" he had them figuratively saying. "'I'll hold your coat.'"

Lenny "bought it," Sahl told Robert Weide in that interview. The result: "They killed him." And why? Because "[t]hey *need* a victim. They need a victim to indict the system, and they don't want to be the victim. Or as we used to say, 'when they're talkin' about free lunch, they're goin' to serve you with an apple in your mouth.'"

It was pure Mort—provocative, plausible, and punitive. It is the kind of statement that deserves a more thoughtful answer than what Phil Spector offered up: "That's a lot of shit," he once said. Spector aside, Sahl's statement is plausible, but only if one ignores Lenny's life and its relation to law and lawyers.

Lenny Bruce certainly didn't need any "Greenwich Village" lawyers to make his life hell. He did that quite well himself, as wit-nessed by his bonkers handling of his Chicago trial. As for being the puppet of liberal lawyers, that claim surely would have surprised many of those same lawyers who felt that Lenny was an impossible client making impossible demands—the kind that, when unmet, resulted in a "you're fired." And recall, when Lenny had bungled his New York appeal beyond belief, it was the liberal lawyers, in the persons of Rosenfield and Kalven, who offered to represent him *pro bono*. Lenny refused. He wanted to go the fight alone. He did, and he lost.

There is another, far more troubling, problem with Mort Sahl's drive-by philosophical hit. How, exactly, could Lenny avoid "throwing sand in the gears?" How could he avoid that, and remain Lenny Bruce? Was Sahl suggesting that Lenny become a Milton Berle clone? Or that he become more Mort-like, and clean up his act? If so, Sahl's point resembles that of Lenny's Illinois prosecutors, who argued that it was not what he said, but how he said it that was objectionable.

Yet, that begs the question. Lenny Bruce's struggles for free speech were about precisely that—the freedom to say not only *what* he wanted, but also to say it *the way* he wanted. That principle was confirmed by a jury in San Francisco, affirmed by the Illinois Supreme Court, and ultimately reconfirmed by New York's highest court in *People v. Solomon*. It should now become a part of our national law and our culture of free speech.

In the end, arguments like Mort Sahl's foster a caution that belies hardy First Amendment values. Whereas Justice Brennan once counseled that speech be "uninhibited, robust, and wide-open," the common way is to be restrained, to play it safe, even to be quiet. The danger is that Sahl's caution will collapse into cowardliness, into a willingness to self-censor. When that happens, the prospects for a vibrant First Amendment are weak. For lack of courage, one loses voice; and losing voice, one loses liberty; and having lost liberty, not much remains.

Whatever Lenny Bruce's failings—and he had many—he was not without courage. He was not afraid to speak his mind, by the light of his own truth and with the force of his own voice.

ONLY WORDS

So will Bruce end up a hero in the book of history, or a self-destroyer naïvely surprised that people, including cops, seek revenge when you foul their most precious ideals, or call them illusions?

— *Robert J. Landry*

Free Speech Zones

LENNY BRUCE IS dead. Hype cannot change that. Nostalgia cannot clone him anew. His DNA code has vanished and his brain (unlike Einstein's) was not preserved for clinical study. It's over. Curtains.

Our story, however, does not end here. For hereditary traces of Lenny can be found among those who congregate in comedy clubs. Put them together—traces and places—and you can get a sense of Lenny's world. It's a world created in his own rogue image.

Of course, Lenny's admirers and other rebel types need a Lenny Bruce fix. So, the first thing they do is to make him an icon, if only a romanticized one. Then they reincarnate him in the persona of one or another new foul-mouthed stand-up. But no one today can rip into an audience *and rock* the system like Lenny did.

"I get so ugly when I fuck. I don't care. And if you care what I look like when you fuck me, you shouldn't be fuckin' me in the first place." Margaret Cho was in her element that night in February 2001 at the Improv. She was a card, the queen of their hearts. The audience's love for her was almost cultish, a combination of Princess Di veneration and *Rocky Horror Picture Show* mania. Her M.O.: ultra-raunchy and darkly hilarious. Her style: sweet and subversive. Her manner: calm and volatile. Through the yin-yang of it all, she was *very* introspective. "I feel like such an outsider, which brings in so many people," was how she explained it. Pure Cho.

Admittedly, Margaret Cho is no Lenny Bruce. And the Improv—

where three hundred eclectics, alternatives, and straights alike had braved Washington, D.C.'s rare snows to hear their comic hero—is not Strip City. Part of what is radically different is the absence of *danger*, the threat of the big bust, the specter of a comedian being hauled off to jail and the audience rousted. And yet, today's outsiders find a place for themselves in the dark of comedy clubs. Now that *is* Brucean—the idea that people can come together, revel in taboo, and laugh at the hypocrisy of their lives and their society. Dirty words and unfashionable ideas today enjoy a safe harbor in clubs.

The forum matters. Only in rare public places can perversion, subversion, and aversion to the status quo be celebrated. That is why Margaret Cho is so at home in a comedy club. "You go in and discuss things openly, without fear," the thirty-two-year-old comedian put it. "Everything gets broken down....I don't think there are any taboos for me....I haven't come across any yet." Her performances are a testament to her unorthodox convictions. They reveal, in stark form, her authentic mindset: "I don't think it's possible to get too personal....I tell the truth because I am not afraid to. I tell the ugliness to show you the beauty."

In such unconventional quarters there is a trace, an echo of Lenny Bruce—the stand-up who said that you break things down by talking about them. Cho seemed to acknowledge that connection at the Improv as she threw out an aside at the end of her menstruation routine: "If he had a period, would Lenny Bruce talk about it? I think he would. I have no doubt about it."

Yes, he probably would have. In essence, and beyond all of the maddening chaos of his life, Lenny Bruce hoped to liberate words...about anything. Don't hold back, don't sugarcoat, and don't be hypocritical. Speak life as it *is*. That was the splendor and grime of his comedy. That was the reason and risk of his humor. That is one notable link to Cho and others like her.

"Comedy has had a great impact," observed critic Amelia David, "not only on entertainment, but also on freedom of speech." By that measure, August 3, 1966, marked a turning-point in America's free speech history. The date of Lenny Bruce's death is as good a marker as any of the moment when words alone—any performance words spoken in comedy clubs—ceased to be targets of prosecution. More than any legal precedents, the possibility of endless harassment culminating in death changed the First Amendment culture. After John Judnick tossed Lenny's mike into his grave, future comedians could say anything into their club mikes without fear of arrest. And once Eternity claimed Lenny Bruce, everybody knew that.

> *Ralph Gleason*: So many taboos have been lifted and so many comics have rushed through the doors Lenny opened. He utterly changed the world of comedy.

> *Lawrence Schiller*: [H]is self-sacrifice had opened the doors for others to freely communicate whatever sentiments might move them, no matter how offensive or inflammatory.

> *Arthur Gelb*: Lenny Bruce…set the stage for every comedian to follow him.

> *George Carlin*: Lenny opened all the doors, or kicked them down.

> *Barry Sanders*: Lenny Bruce brought about a revolution in comedy.

> *Joan Rivers*: Lenny Bruce was the turning point for me.

> *Margaret Cho*: Lenny Bruce gave me permission to do what I do.

> *Peter Hall*: He remains the patron saint of stand-up.

Such are the testaments to Bruce's legacy. America's five hundred or so comedy clubs have become *free speech zones*, public places where First Amendment freedom is virtually unrivaled. It is a given of contemporary American culture: only in a comedy club can one get a full and saucy taste of freedom. Hear it live, see it face-to-face, savor it.

The accolade of free speech hero, if that is the term, does not go to Lenny Bruce alone. For it was not just what Lenny said, but also what others did that changed history. There are the forgotten ones, the club owners who placed their liberty and their licenses on the line so that Lenny could do bits like "Christ and Moses" and "Las Vegas Tits and Ass." No one remembers them: Art Auerbach of San Francisco's Jazz Workshop; Doug Weston of West Hollywood's Troubadour; Herb Cohen of Hollywood's Unicorn; Alan Ribback of Chicago's Gate of Horn; Jim and Dan Duffin of Los Angeles's Trolley Ho; and Howard and Ella Solomon of New York's Café Au Go Go. They and their kind made conversational directness possible in public places. And they passed the freedom of that venue along to future generations of nightclub owners so that traces of Lenny Bruce might survive in a reconfigured world.

Comedy clubs—those free speech zones—have made it possible to say what cannot be said in most other public places and to hear what cannot be heard on radio or on network television. They have come to symbolize, in Margaret Cho's words, "the freedom to do whatever I want—to do what I do, what we comedians do."

Coming Out of the Free Speech Closet

FREEDOM OF SPEECH is not easily closeted. The pursuit of such liberty does not readily respect boundaries. Bluntly put, its operative logic is: give an inch, take a mile. For example, ever since 1735, when a jury of his peers exonerated publisher John Peter Zenger on charges of sedition, there has been an evolving expectation of *more* freedom. The center of the First Amendment forever expands. Hence, over the course of some two centuries, the pre-revolutionary hero's name has been invoked time and again to justify an ever-growing expanse of First Amendment liberty. Such expectations give our system of free expression much of its meaning and its staying power...albeit at some risk.

At two o'clock on the afternoon of October 30, 1973, WBAI-FM pushed the limits of toleration. The New York radio station (a Pacifica station) took the vernacular that Lenny Bruce had liberated in comedy clubs, and attempted to liberate it in a new arena, namely public radio. The very words for which Lenny had been busted were now broadcast (preceded by an advisory warning) on the airwaves for all to hear, including a father driving with his young son. The protective father and his vulnerable son heard the following that day: "shit, piss, fuck, cunt, cocksucker, motherfucker, and tits." Of course, those words alone were not the act, they were delivered in a context:

> Okay, I was thinking one night about the words you couldn't say on the public, ah, airwaves, um, the ones you definitely wouldn't say, ever....The original seven words were "shit, piss, fuck, cunt, cocksucker, motherfucker, and tits." Those are the ones that will curve your spine, grow hair on your hands and maybe even bring us, God help us, peace without honor, um, and a bourbon.

Those were not the words of Lenny Bruce. No, they came from the mind and mouth of George Carlin, the same man who once imitated Lenny in a 1960 bit at Cosmo Alley, and who was arrested with Lenny in 1962 at The Gate of Horn. Taking a page from the master, Carlin's routine—"Filthy Words"—played humorously with society's hang-ups over "dirty words." As Carlin expressed his purpose: "The words themselves are not harmful. They can be used that way by people in an indecent moment—but the words are harmless. That was the point of my monologue." Besides, Carlin cleverly added, he had learned those words from the "male members of my family, many of whom were policemen and servicemen in the Second World War, people I was taught to respect and look up to."

However elevated Carlin's intent, the irate father was far less philosophical when it came to the comedian's vulgarities. He was unwilling to push the free speech limit to allow Carlin's elaboration:

> Now the word "shit" is okay....At work you can say it like crazy. Mostly figuratively. *Get that shit out of here, will ya? I don't want to see that shit anymore. I can't cut that shit, buddy. I've had that shit up to here. I think you're full of shit, myself. He don't know shit from Shinola, you know that?* Always wondered how the Shinola people felt about that. *Hi, I'm the new man from Shinola....Boy, I don't know whether to shit or wind my watch. Guess I'll shit on my watch....*

And, as if that were not enough:

> The big one, the word "fuck," that's the one that hangs them up the
> most.....What does it mean? It means to make love. Right?...[I]t's
> also a word that we really use to hurt each other with, man. It's a
> heavy.... *Oh, fuck you man. I said, fuck you. Stupid fuck.....*It would
> be nice to change the movies that we already have and substitute the
> word "fuck" for the word "kill," wherever we could, and some of
> those movie clichés would change a bit. *Mad fucker still on the loose.*
> *Stop me before I fuck again. Fuck the ump, fuck the ump, fuck the*
> *ump....Easy on the clutch, Bill, you'll fuck that engine again.*

A cultural line had been crossed. "Dirty words" were no longer
closeted. By its bold action, WBAI had taken Carlin's comic message
outside of nightclubs and record shops, and released it to the ether.
Public radio now exceeded what KBLA (Los Angeles) had dared in
August of 1959 when it aired Lenny Bruce's racy "Can I Touch It?"
and "Your Dyke Alert Bulletin" commercials for the Zeidler & Zeidler
clothing store. (The head of the local PTA reportedly complained to
the store.)

No sooner had WBAI crossed the line than the Federal Communications Commission was petitioned to force the station to retreat. It
took only a lone complaint, filed by the offended father. In response,
the FCC issued a prospective prohibition against the use of "seven
dirty words" by the broadcast media and threatened to fine or revoke
the license of any station that aired Anglo-Saxon epithets during day-
time or early evening hours. Pacifica Foundation, the parent corporation for WBAI, refused to submit quietly to the FCC's censorial hand;
it challenged the order in the U.S. Court of Appeals for the District of
Columbia. The fight was on.

Whereas Lenny Bruce's numerous "dirty words" were judged in
criminal courts, George Carlin's "seven dirty words" were to be
judged in a civil court—but now the emphasis was on cabining the
words instead of convicting the man. In March 1977, virtually a full
year after *Pacifica Foundation v. FCC* was argued before the appellate
court, Carlin's words were legitimated by a 2 to 1 decision (with Judge

Jacob Leventhal dissenting). A former FBI agent, Judge Edward A. Tamm, wrote for the majority and sided with WBAI. Although the opinion turned on the FCC's abuse of its statutory powers, Tamm's rhetoric appealed to loftier First Amendment principles: "Despite the Commission's professed intentions, the direct effect of its *order* is to inhibit the free and robust exchange of ideas on a wide range of issues and subjects by means of radio and television communications. In fact the *order* is censorship, regardless of what the Commission chooses to call it." Even more stirring was Judge David Bazelon's socio-historical critique, made in his concurring opinion, of the FCC's position that the greater a medium's power and influence, the greater a government's reasons to monitor its risky behavior: "This is the traditional argument made in the censor's behalf; this is the argument advanced against newspapers at the time of the invention of the printing press. The argument was ultimately rejected in England, and has consistently been held to be contrary to our Constitution. No compelling reason has been predicated for accepting the contention now."

Eleven years after Lenny Bruce's death, his language-liberation movement appeared to be garnering constitutional respect. One of the nation's most esteemed federal circuit courts had proclaimed, with some hesitation, that government enforcement of word taboos was inconsistent with American speech rights. The medium didn't much matter. It was a Brucean moment, one that affirmed his earnest belief that "there is no such thing as First Amendment punishment, just protection." That moment was short-lived, however.

Washington, D.C., U.S. Supreme Court chambers, spring 1978: "We'll hear arguments, next, in FCC against the Pacifica Foundation. Mr. Marino, you may proceed when you're ready. You may bear in mind that we are familiar with the facts in the case, and get directly to your arguments, if you wish." With those words, Chief Justice Warren Burger introduced the oral arguments in *FCC v. Pacifica*. As court-watchers knew all too well, the chief's admonition to skip the facts and proceed immediately to the law was a euphemism for "Don't repeat any dirty words in *this* court!" It was an omen of things to come—a 5 to 4 endorsement of the government's power to confine "indecent" words to places like comedy clubs.

In the minds of a majority of the Court, the medium very much mattered. That is, the breadth of First Amendment protection was linked to the medium of communication. What was legal in clubs and theaters need not be legal on radio and television. "We have long recognized that each medium of expression presents special First Amendment problems," asserted Justice John Paul Stevens for the Court. "And of all forms of communication, it is broadcasting that has received the most limited First Amendment protection." Thus, the FCC was well within its power to silence Carlin's "seven dirty words" during the most popular listening hours.

Notably, the bow-tied justice from Illinois failed at that time to muster a majority for a far more daring proposition. Stevens would have had the Court create a category of minimally protected speech— namely, "indecent" expression—that consisted of words not *legally obscene* but nonetheless *offensive* to accepted standards of morality. Indecent words, so he reasoned, "lie at the periphery of First Amendment concern"; they are not entitled, therefore, to much constitutional protection. Tellingly, had that category of "indecent speech" been firmly established at the time of Lenny's prosecutions, the whole knotty question of obscenity could have been circumvented. Prosecutors, ranging from Albert Wollenberg in San Francisco to Samuel Banks in Chicago, surely would have branded Lenny's bits as "indecent" expression, and thereby increased the likelihood of convicting him. In the end, because Stevens's focus on the *message* did not prevail, the majority's focus on the *medium* became the decisive factor in determining when and where Brucean comedy would be constitutionally protected.

"The Big Daddy," as Lenny called the Supreme Court, had quartered "dirty" comedy. No radio or network TV performances for the foul-mouthed likes of Lenny Bruce, George Carlin, Richard Pryor, and Margaret Cho. Legally speaking, the liberate-the-language, expand-the-liberty campaign was having trouble taking off...until 1997.

That was the year that the First Amendment embraced the Internet. The most democratic and diverse medium of communication created since Gutenberg's printing press, the Internet enabled the masses to participate more fully than ever before, as both producers and receivers of information, in a free forum. The burning question on every cybercitizen's lips, of course, was whether America's free speech law would extend its highest level of protection to the Internet, or would permit government to treat it like radio or television, as in *Pacifica. Reno v. ACLU* was the Supreme Court's first answer, a stunning one, to that question.

The controversy that provided the grist for the Court's free speech mill was a challenge brought by the American Civil Liberties Union, and others. The object of their disdain was the Communications Decency Act of 1996 (CDA), which prohibited the computer transmission of obscene, indecent, or patently offensive material to any person under eighteen. The CDA was Congress's attempt to turn Internet service providers into vice cops, investigating cyber-materials for dirty content; if they failed to patrol the Net, service providers could be criminally prosecuted.

The dangers to the free speech culture of patrolling indecency in that manner were obvious to cyber-libertarians such as Mike Godwin, counsel to the Electronic Frontier Foundation. If the Supreme Court upheld the CDA, Godwin opined, "the broad protections of the First Amendment would be confined mainly to face-to-face speech and to materials published in ink on dead trees. In a world in which we increasingly communicated, and received content, via computer networks...the First Amendment would be marginalized— maybe even made irrelevant." If that happened, furthermore, the messages of George Carlin and his likes would never reach billions of Internet users worldwide.

To Godwin and his colleagues, the Supreme Court's *Reno* decision was an occasion for wild applause in the chat rooms of cyberspace. For all practical purposes, the ruling delivered a serious blow to pro-decency forces that viewed the CDA as just the sturdy club that government needed to curb vulgarities in all new electronic mass media, not just radio and network television. A unanimous Court struck down the CDA's "indecency" and "patently offensive" provisions as too vague for a regulation of speech content. Moreover, in order to deny minors access to potentially harmful speech, Congress effectively had suppressed a large amount of expression that adults have First Amendment rights to send and receive from one another. The majority opinion acknowledged that, in a former ruling, "we remarked that the speech restriction at issue there amounted to 'burn[ing] the house to roast the pig.' The CDA, casting a far darker shadow over free speech, threatens to torch a large segment of the Internet community."

Incredibly, it was Justice John Paul Stevens who penned those words as the author of the opinion of the Court in *Reno*—the same Justice Stevens who had urged his colleagues in *Pacifica Foundation* to treat indecent speech as a constitutionally inferior and lesser protected category of expression. Granting that the CDA would regulate "any of the seven 'dirty words' used in the *Pacifica* monologue," Stevens nevertheless distinguished the Carlin case narrowly on its facts. *Pacifica* had turned on the limited First Amendment protection accorded to broadcasting, but the Internet was not broadcasting. Among other reasons, its users were not likely to be surprised by objectionable material, and technological means (like filtering programs) were readily available to protect children.

Among many other things, the *Reno* legalese meant that the racy text and audio files of routines like those Lenny Bruce had done at The Gate of Horn, Trolley Ho, or Café Au Go Go could be cybercast to the world without fear of censorship. Thanks, after all, to Justice Stevens, now the black-clad, bad-boy George Carlin could take his satirical raunch off his LPs and CDs and place it into the cyber-homes of America. And Carlin did just that. He exercised his newfound First Amendment rights and launched his own website: *www.georgecarlin.com*.

He was breaking rules, breaching civil pieties, and busting out in ways that other electronic media did not allow. Consider, for example, the tongue-in-cheek advisory and the obligatory "click-ons" by which Carlin's audience was invited onto his website:

WARNING

This web site contains real human language.

This is an early warning system for the faint of heart.

Apparently, there are many people unable to cope with spoken and written language as developed by humans up to this point.

This is for you.

CLICK HERE

to evaluate your language tolerance level.

Then onto forbidden words, even one for which Lenny had been busted:

COCKSUCKER

If this offends you, ask yourself why.

Every woman is a cocksucker, and so are many men.

The men who aren't cocksuckers seem to have no problem with
the women who choose this activity, but have big problems with
the men who do so. Why would this be?

Could it be that all these men are afraid they might
be potential cocksuckers?

If this does not offend you,

CLICK HERE

From Bruce's perspective, the idea of using "cocksucker" freely in a public medium was astounding, a wet dream come true. But now Carlin had taken the legitimate-the-language "crusade" to a frank and fearless world.

Admittedly, Carlin's controversial words already had been made public, thanks again to Justice Stevens, who had included them in an appendix to *FCC v. Pacifica*, which was published in the *Supreme Court Reports*. But now they were catching the attention of a far wider audience, one larger than those of many local radio and TV stations. Reminiscent of the jabs that Lenny had poked at established religions, Carlin flirted with blasphemy when he claimed that the most offensive obscenity in life is

RELIGION

If this offends you, welcome to the world of sane and
realistic critical thought.

More harm has been done to the collective human psyche

by religion than by all the fucking and cocksucking since the dawn of time. By the way, many religious people (including the ordained) fuck and suck each other's cocks all the time.

CLICK HERE

to get back to reality.

"I believe you can joke about anything" is how Carlin justified it in his bestselling book, *Napalm & Silly Putty*. With that mindset, he could be outrageously irreverent, even insensitive to holy figures ("Boy, am I glad to finally be rid of that fuckin' Mother Teresa."). Ironically, *Reno v. ACLU* gave Carlin the opportunity that *Pacifica* had denied him—the ability to use a powerful electronic medium to reach a mass audience. On his website, Carlin fans, young and old alike, can now *listen* to the "7 Dirty Words" that the FCC had banished. They can also buy CDs and videos of that routine, and even T-shirts with two thousand "filthy words" on front and back, or posters with as many as 2,443 such words. It is all rather like a public invitation commercial to a "dirty word" lovefest.

The liberate-the-language forces had taken the beaches…and were advancing steadily toward the citadels of respectability. There were indecent books, CDs, rap concerts, websites, and, of course, indecent bits in comedy clubs. With President Ronald Reagan's deregulation of the FCC, more and more indecency found its way to the public airwaves. There were, for example, filthy TV and radio "shock" programs like the Jerry Springer and Howard Stern shows. Their brazen antics were typically just a syllable short of indecency or a pastie short of obscenity. Indecency had come out of the First Amendment closet.

As for Lenny Bruce, the Internet was not yet an entirely free medium for his ribald routines. For example, in August 2000, America Online, the giant Internet service provider, declared a Bruce bit on drugs "inappropriate" and deleted portions of it from an AOL website. But the order would not stand; the times had changed. Upon reflection and protest, an AOL spokesman later found Lenny Bruce to be a "unique case," so much so that the service provider rescinded its action. Except for broadcast TV and radio, Lenny Bruce's dirty time had really arrived, or so it seemed.

"We Want It Stopped!"

ON THE EVE of the millennium, a full-page ad ran in newspapers across the nation. In bold letters, the paid political ad demanded: WE WANT IT STOPPED! What the Parents Television Council wanted stopped, what so disgusted those decent people, was the "filth, vulgarity, sex, and violence TV is sending into our homes." America had become a "perverse" society in which "steamy unmarried sex situations, filthy jokes…vulgarity, foul language, violence, [and] killings" were becoming the media norm. This putrid state of affairs had to end. The nation deserved better. Something must be done.

The man whose photograph appeared prominently in the ad was Steve Allen. The honorary chairman of the grassroots campaign for a return to decency in American television entertainment was Steve Allen. The person to whom the cutout protest form, at the bottom of the ad, was to be sent was Steve Allen. The one at the vanguard of the crusade to combat "vulgarity" was, again, Steve Allen.

A year earlier, in November 1998, America's thoughtful entertainer made much the same point in a strongly worded op-ed in *The Wall Street Journal:* "In today's Anything Goes culture it sometimes seems that our entire society has become one massive occasion for sin," he complained. The seventy-six-year-old performer spoke out against the "profoundly disturbing realities of our present social predicament." He was "horrified" at what had happened to the "beautiful and socially necessary art of comedy." Something had to be done to halt "the sleaze and classless garbage of recent years."

That was the *same* man who was once just as thoughtful and outspoken in his defense of Lenny Bruce. It was Steve Allen, after all, who brought Lenny into the late-night living rooms of America some four decades earlier. Indeed, it was Steve Allen who in 1964 so courageously attempted to air a nationally broadcast interview with Bruce during his obscenity prosecutions in California and Illinois. And it was Steve Allen who, as late as 1992, lent his name to endorse a boxed-set issuance of the *Performance Film*, Lenny's controversial 1965 club act captured on celluloid. That was the performance in which Lenny made his comic point by using words such as "ass," "balls," "cocksucker," "cunt," "fuck," "motherfucker," "piss," "shit," and "tits." In Allen's endorsement of the commercially distributed video, he described his close friend as a "philosopher" with "superior intelligence" and a man who said things that were "always insightful." To prove his point, Allen offered the following observation by Lenny Bruce:

> Show me the average sex maniac, the one that takes your eight-year-old, *schtups* her in the parking lot, and then kills her; and I'll show you a guy who's had a good religious upbringing.
>
> You see, he saw his father or mother always telling his sister to cover up her body, when she was only six years old, and so he figured, one day I'm going to find out what it is she's covering, and if it's as dirty as my father says I'll kill it.

More ironic still, during Allen's national decency campaign, HBO aired Robert Weide's documentary, *Lenny Bruce: Swear to Tell the Truth*. That cable TV program contained audio clips of "dirty Lenny" giving voice to words such as "cocksucker," and saying things such as "Eleanor Roosevelt had the nicest tits of any lady in the White House." Lenny Bruce, Steve Allen's philosopher-comic, was the prime mover—the force behind latter-day foul-mouthed comedians like George Carlin, Richard Pryor, Eddie Murphy, Chris Rock, Margaret Cho, and all those other "vulgar" funny freaks.

Had the years so changed Steve Allen that he, like Cephalus in Plato's *Republic*, could only turn to virtue in old age, when the flame of his youth had been extinguished? Is this just another case of a young rebel maturing into an old conservative? The answer was: "No, not at all"—for Lenny Bruce was *different*, Allen maintained. Lenny was never out for "cheap, shock laughs....He was always saying something." And when he did use four-letter words to make such socially redeeming points, he "would never have dreamed of doing anything vulgar on television." His posthumous work, *Vulgarians at the Gate*, elaborates the point:

> The absurd attempt is sometimes made to defend [Howard] Stern and others of the toilet talk fraternity on the same grounds that were quite legitimately employed on behalf of comedian Lenny Bruce. The crucial difference, of course, was that Bruce was a satirist, a brilliantly talented and original comic thinker who used the device of stand-up comedy to make often penetrating, philosophical observations. The same cannot be said of most of the present vulgarity specialists.

Steve Allen's conclusion: The man, his message, and the medium were all different. That being so, the societal response could be different, even censorial.

Mindful of First Amendment liberties, Steve Allen astutely conceded that "the right to produce garbage" is constitutionally protected. But that, he emphasized, is not the end of the matter. "[T]hose of us who are shocked and revolted by some of what we see have the same constitutional right to raise hell about it," he added. "We are not allowed to bomb clinics or shoot people the way some of the idiots of the Far Right do these days, but we sure can raise hell."

In that regard, the learned comedian reiterated a basic tenet of American constitutionalism, namely, that the Supreme Law of the Land only bars the *government* from censoring speech. It does not, by contrast, bar private citizens or corporations from refusing to give a forum to objectionable expression. Thus, both Allen and his campaign were entirely within their rights in pressuring the captains of communication to bring decency back to America.

If liberal free speech advocates threatened to swamp America with indecency, then the liberal remedy to curb such excesses could be found in Allen's agenda. At bottom, it rested on the First Amendment notion that *more* speech—this time, protests against commercially subsidized vulgarity and violence—was better. The motivating belief was that the citizenry hears both sides of the debate, and thereafter rationally determines its own course of private action. "Don't support Corporation X if it sponsors indecency" becomes tantamount to

"Don't support Corporation X if it invests in apartheid-ridden South Africa."

"Certainly," Allen reasoned, "no society has ever become so thoroughly depraved, while claiming to respect freedom, that it preaches there must be no limitations on freedom whatever." In other words, Allen was inviting something censorial—public or private—to separate the wheat from the chaff.

"I'm Not a Comedian, I'm Lenny Bruce"

TWO OTHER STEVE Allen contemporaries (and Lenny Bruce admirers) also saw vulgarians at the gate, although through different lenses. Like Allen, both men had reached the pinnacles of success in their respective artistic careers; like the veteran entertainer, both had fought First Amendment battles; and like him, both appreciated the complexities of the age-old tension between liberty and license. But Hugh Hefner and George Carlin had vastly different responses to what so irked Steve Allen.

First Hefner. It was a beautiful summer day in the promised land…at the Beverly Hills mansion on Charing Cross Road. Clad in his signature custom-made clothes (black silk pajamas and burgundy silk smoking jacket), Hugh Hefner sat in the comfort of his private movie viewing room. As he sipped on some chilled spring water (bottled with a Playboy label), he paused before commenting on Allen's anxieties:

> Well, it is the way of things. After all, Pandora didn't know what was in the box. What do you get with freedom? Excesses! Exploitation! And what does one say to that? "A small price to pay. If you don't like it, don't listen to it, don't read it, don't watch it." Without free communication, including the vulgarians, we don't have a free society. Our democracy is based on it. The First Amendment is the first because it is the most important. Everything else comes from that. **CD**

Hefner had special reason to boast about the First Amendment. He had just won a First Amendment victory in *United States v. Playboy Entertainment Group* (2000), a Supreme Court case concerning sexually-oriented cable programming. And in that case, Justice Anthony Kennedy made something of the same point as Hefner, observing that the "history of the law of free expression is one of vindication in cases involving speech that many citizens may find shabby, offensive, or even ugly." The fundamental guarantee bequeathed to us by James Madison would allow no less.

George Carlin was less idealistic. "Part of me doesn't give much of a shit about this stuff. The First Amendment is a nice thing to have—besides refrigerators, which are good, too." So much for James Madison's legacy, according to the cynically flip Carlin. In the calm of his dressing room at the Las Vegas MGM Hotel before his wired, May 20, 2001, ten P.M. performance, Carlin turned more pensive once he thought about Steve Allen's cultural critique. "Well, certainly it's an accurate description of things," he conceded. "Howard Stern caters to the simplistic tastes of young males full of testosterone and limited critical thinking." More troubling for Carlin was the fact that Howard Stern "really picks on the underdogs. You know, his targets are women, homosexuals, immigrants, and those who are the underdogs in society. I think the role of comedy is to go after the powerful people, to puncture the pretentiousness and pompousness of the privileged. That's what comedy and satire have always been about, it seems."

Carlin agreed with Allen that Lenny Bruce and the Howard Sterns of the world really are different comic creatures: "Howard Stern is a creature of the commercial media, which will always appeal to the lowest common denominator. Lenny Bruce wasn't doing that. He was appealing to the people who paid to come in and see him on a given night, who knew about him and shared some of his values, no doubt, and who wanted to hear his latest thoughts." Nonetheless, the plebe-garbed comedian (signature black T-shirt, faded blue jeans, and black sneakers) would not yield to Allen's brand of censorship: "I think you have to defend both of them—Lenny Bruce and Howard Stern....But I don't think in the parlor you defend them the same way."

With his mind fixed on distinctions, the elder Allen seemed overly generous to the comedian the younger Allen once said could "offend *everybody.*" He had it right in 1959 when he introduced Lenny Bruce onto his show: "Ladies and gentlemen, here is a very shocking comedian." Indeed, Lenny "experimented with extremes," as Tony Hendra rightfully observed. In his own time and in his own unique ways, Lenny was as shocking as Howard Stern, Jerry Springer, or any other of Allen's gate-crashing vulgarians. And even when Lenny Bruce aimed more directly at the cerebrum, he undeniably peppered his socially redeeming ideas with socially shocking terminology. In fact, there was something intrinsically shocking about his whole enterprise to liberate language from social constraints.

Granting for the moment Allen's differentiation of Bruce's foul-mouthed philosophy from Stern's toilet-talk humor, what purpose is really served by the differentiation? For example, did Allen really believe that Bruce's comedy had not *at all* paved the way for the vulgar entertainers who followed him? In addition, if a differentiation is to be made, how exactly can we distinguish between the worthless Jerry Springer and the valued Lenny Bruce? Can there ever be a clear and satisfactory line? Is it not one of the essential goals of a vibrant democratic society, moreover, to create a culture of toleration conducive to the *widest* possible measure of free speech?

It is one thing to be critical of the shock-jocks, but it is quite another thing to promote advertiser and media executive boycotts of such entertainers. However portrayed, Steve Allen's agenda was a call for censorship, though privately imposed. He asked us, in the private sector, to ensure that certain voices and messages were never heard in the "family hours" broadcast marketplace. (Cable TV, even during the same "family hours," was another matter.) Furthermore, he asked us not to be troubled by the fact that the censorial order would be enforced by the barons of commerce, rather than by government. What Allen's libertarianism prevented him from appreciating, however, was that freedom of expression is threatened almost as much, though in different ways, by corporate conglomerates now as by government authorities in the past. Does it make any difference if a Lenny Bruce could not appear on *The Steve Allen Show* because of governmental disapproval or because of disapproval by the show's sponsors? Either way, Lenny's "Religions, Inc.," "Tits and Ass," and "Is Sex Dirty?" bits would be silenced. The spirit of the First Amendment, not just its letter, is honored when censorship is eschewed in both public and private spheres. That, anyway, is one postulate for a fully vibrant free speech system.

Steve Allen's concern about the debasement of culture and what to do about it could occupy social theorists and political philosophers for centuries to come. Thoughtful minds could agree or disagree with him on the wisdom of pressuring the private sector to censor indecent words or ideas. What his liberal critics failed to appreciate, however, was the extent to which Allen's agenda hoped to prevent *government* censorship. On that score, he had no real quarrel with his Brucean brethren. For the increasingly conservative Allen, the predictably liberal Hefner, and the incorrigibly cynical Carlin *all* agreed that government censorship of indecent expression was anathema. Comedians should not be imprisoned for their words. The life of Lenny Bruce is a great cautionary tale about why First Amendment freedom must be the rule rather than the exception.

If Lenny Bruce were a free speech martyr (as a *Hustler* ad once portrayed him), what was he a martyr for? Was he a martyr for a kind of First Amendment absolutism that Justice William Brennan (the author of *Roth v. United States*) never formally accepted and Professor Harry Kalven Jr. (one of Lenny's Illinois lawyers) never entirely granted? Perhaps. Maybe the best way to put it is that the comedian, the justice, and the professor all wanted to extend free speech as far as possible in a given era and context, with the realistic understanding that there probably would be artificial limits at some point. That is a kind of pragmatic absolutism, a refusal to abridge speech absent the most immediate, real, and compelling kinds of dangers. It was precisely that vision of speech that animated San Francisco Municipal Court Judge Clayton Horn's remarkable 1957 unpublished opinion in *People v. Ferlinghetti* and his 1962 jury instructions in *People v. Bruce*. It is freedom as the default position.

LENNY BRUCE WASN'T always funny. He told his San Francisco Jazz Workshop audience as much hours after his first obscenity bust. "I'm not a comedian," he avowed, "I'm Lenny Bruce."

There was paradoxical truth to his declaration. On the one hand, Lenny Bruce was obviously a comedian. One of his main purposes was to make people laugh about the absurd in life. On the other hand, Lenny Bruce was obviously not just a comedian. Another of his central purposes was to make people think about the pretenses of life. More-over, his mission to liberate words was often amusing, as many of his bits reveal. That same mission was equally risky, however, as his per-secution and prosecution demonstrate. In the end, the courtroom became his stage, and the stage became his courtroom. The comic Bruce was, at one and the same time, the tragic Bruce.

Lenny understood, like no other modern comedian, that comedy could and should be dangerous. He was no play-it-safe Joey Bishop or even Mort Sahl. He cooked, especially when the heat was in the audi-ence. He was a risk-taker. That was an essential part of what made him so exciting, so outrageous, so offensive, and so threatening. He mocked the hypocrisy of religious faiths, of political beliefs, and of puritan ethics. In his own words, "I'm pissing on the velvet, that's what I'm doing. It's comedy." Little wonder, then, that politicians, police, prosecutors, judges, and a host of other do-gooders could not stomach his defilement of conventional mores. In some important respect, he paid for his comedy with his life.

Thankfully, those days are over. Contemporary comedians need not follow in Lenny's paradoxical footsteps. Nat Hentoff, who testified on Bruce's behalf in 1964, put it succinctly: "[P]erformers can work, most of the time, without fearing that an undercover cop, sitting in the dark, will be taking notes on their acts. And they don't have to fear that the hidden cop will then stumblingly read from those blurred notes in court as evidence that an obscene performance has been given." Instead, stand-ups can take their liberating cue from George Carlin: "I like to find out where the line is drawn, and then drag the audience across the line with me, and make them happier for the experience." In clubs across America, comedians can cross the line with hilarious abandon thanks to yesterday's "sick comic."

Robert Landry was probably right: Lenny Bruce was naïve to think that people would not seek revenge when he attacked their most precious ideals. There is certainly abundant evidence in the historical/psychological/sociological records to bear that point out. Then again, maybe he didn't care, or maybe he was too drugged out to care, or maybe that was simply his genetic makeup. Any of the same could probably be said of some of our pop-culture icons. In that regard, too, Landry was probably correct when he suggested that Lenny Bruce would end up a "hero in the book of history"—and, his critics notwithstanding, with some real justification. For Lenny Bruce, to his credit, *did* create new free speech zones for Americans. In comedy clubs across the country, the unstated can be stated, the unheard can be voiced, and the unholy can be exposed. What a tribute to unabashed speech freedom. It may have unsavory ramifications, as Steve Allen well understood (though he refused to hold Lenny accountable).

We must pay the toll to travel the roads to freedom. Lenny Bruce too much loved the venture to allow for detours or safe returns. His own Socratic maxim was that the unobjectionable life is not worth living. With or without crediting him, Lenny's creed has much become the American creed, at least in places where people speak their minds without looking over their shoulders.

Freedom works best when, like air, it is invisible. Today, freedom of speech is a given in comedy clubs. The sacrifice has been made. Lenny paid the dues. Hence, performers do not have to be Lenny Bruce; they're free to be themselves, uninhibited comedians. Or as Margaret Cho put it: "I don't want to end up like [Lenny Bruce], but I want to be like him." 🄲🄳 In that respect, Lenny Bruce's greatest legacy is that the most brazen of performers can take mike in hand and say confidently, with a liberating twist on the legendary comedian's own words: "I'm not Lenny Bruce, I'm a comedian."

APPENDIX A

ATTORNEYS, JUDGES, AND CLUB OWNERS

We drove him into poverty and bankruptcy and then murdered him. We all knew what we were doing. We used the law to kill him.

— *Vincent Cuccia*

Defense Attorneys

San Francisco

Albert M. Bendich (second Jazz Workshop obscenity trial)

Seymour Fried (first Jazz Workshop obscenity trial)

Los Angeles

Melvin Belli (represented by his associate, Charles Ashman, for pretrial matters in Troubadour obscenity case)

Sidney M. Irmas (Trolley Ho obscenity case)

Seymour Lazar (pretrial matters in Troubadour obscenity case)

Burton A. Marks (consolidated Troubadour and Unicorn obscenity trial)

John Marshall (Illinois extradition order in Gate of Horn obscenity case)

Chicago

George J. Cotsirilos (pretrial matters in Gate of Horn obscenity case)

Samuel Friefeld (Gate of Horn attorney originally retained to represent Bruce and Alan Ribback in obscenity case)

Harry Kalven Jr. (appeal of conviction in Gate of Horn obscenity case)

William R. Ming Jr. (appeal of conviction in Gate of Horn obscenity case)

Donald Page Moore (pretrial matters in Gate of Horn obscenity case)

George C. Pontikas (sentencing hearing in Gate of Horn obscenity case)

Maurice Rosenfield (appeal of conviction in Gate of Horn obscenity case)

Earle Warren Zaidins (Gate of Horn obscenity trial)

New York

Martin Garbus (Café Au Go Go obscenity trial)

Edward de Grazia (§1983 civil rights actions)

Harry Herschman (sentencing hearing in Café Au Go Go obscenity case)

William M. Kunstler (advisory capacity in §1983 civil rights actions)

Ephraim London (Café Au Go Go obscenity trial)

Lawrence H. Rogovin (appears for Howard M. Squadron in pretrial matters in Café Au Go Go obscenity case)

Allen G. Schwartz (certificate of reasonable doubt for appeal of Café Au Go Go conviction)

Howard M. Squadron (bail and bond for arrest and pretrial matters in Café Au Go Go obscenity case)

New York: Attorneys for Bruce's codefendant, Howard L. Solomon

Milton Adler (appeal of Café Au Go Go conviction)

William E. Hellerstein (appeal of Café Au Go Go conviction)

Bentley Kassal (bail and bond for arrest and pretrial matters in Café Au Go Go obscenity case)

William S. Miller (sentencing hearing in Café Au Go Go obscenity case)

Herbert Monte-Levy (pretrial matters in Café Au Go Go obscenity case)

Allen G. Schwartz (Café Au Go Go obscenity trial)

PROSECUTORS

San Francisco

Arthur Schaefer (first Jazz Workshop obscenity trial)

Albert C. Wollenberg, Jr. (second Jazz Workshop obscenity trial)

Los Angeles

Johnnie L. Cochran, Jr. (pretrial hearing on motion to dismiss Trolley Ho obscenity case)

Ronald Ross (consolidated Troubadour and Unicorn obscenity trial)

Chicago

Samuel V. Banks (Gate of Horn obscenity trial)

Edward J. Egan (Gate of Horn obscenity trial)

William J. Martin (appeal of conviction in Gate of Horn obscenity case)

James R. Thompson (appeal of conviction in Gate of Horn obscenity case)

Willie Whiting (Gate of Horn obscenity trial)

New York

Vincent J. Cuccia (procedures for appeal of Café Au Go Go conviction)

Gerald Harris (grand jury and pretrial matters in Café Au Go Go obscenity case)

Richard H. Kuh (Café Au Go Go obscenity trial)

New York: Prosecutors for Appeal of People v. Solomon

Harold R. Shapiro (appeal of Café Au Go Go conviction before New York Supreme Court, Appellate Term)

H. Richard Uviller (postjudgment motions before New York Supreme Court, Appellate Term)

JUDGES

Note: This list names the judges who sat on Bruce's free speech cases, but it does not include the names of all the intermediate appellate judges, state high court justices, and U.S. Supreme Court justices who presided over Bruce's other court cases.

San Francisco

Albert A. Axelrod, San Francisco Municipal Court (first Jazz Workshop obscenity trial)

Clayton W. Horn, San Francisco Municipal Court (second Jazz Workshop obscenity trial)

Los Angeles

Mario L. Clinco, Los Angeles Municipal Court (arrest warrant in Trolley Ho obscenity case)

Henry H. Draeger, Beverly Hills Municipal Court (consolidated Troubadour and Unicorn obscenity trial)

Robert M. Dulin, Beverly Hills Municipal Court (pretrial matters in Troubadour obscenity case)

Robert Feinerman, Los Angeles Municipal Court (arraignment in Trolley Ho obscenity case)

Harold P. Huls, Appellate Department of the California Superior Court (appeal of Trolley Ho obscenity dismissal)

Richard Schauer, Los Angeles Municipal Court (plea hearing in Trolley Ho obscenity case)

Bernard S. Selber, Los Angeles Municipal Court (pretrial hearing on motion to dismiss in Trolley Ho obscenity case)

Frank G. Swain, Appellate Department of the California Superior Court (appeal of Trolley Ho obscenity dismissal)

Sherman W. Smith, Los Angeles Municipal Court (bail hearing after Le Grand Theater obscenity arrest) and Appellate Department of the California Superior Court (appeal of Trolley Ho obscenity dismissal)

Chicago

Joseph E. Daily, Illinois Supreme Court (appeal of Gate of Horn obscenity conviction)

Harry B. Hershey, Illinois Supreme Court (appeal of Gate of Horn conviction)

Byron O. House, Illinois Supreme Court (appeal of Gate of Horn obscenity conviction)

Ray I. Klingbiel, Chief Justice, Illinois Supreme Court (appeal of Gate of Horn obscenity conviction)

Daniel J. Ryan, Cook County Circuit Court (Gate of Horn obscenity trial)

Walter V. Schaefer, Illinois Supreme Court (appeal of Gate of Horn obscenity conviction)

Roy J. Solfisburg Jr., Illinois Supreme Court (appeal of Gate of Horn obscenity conviction)

Chester Strzalka, Cook County Circuit Court (bail hearing after Gate of Horn obscenity arrest)

Robert C. Underwood, Illinois Supreme Court (appeal of Gate of Horn obscenity conviction)

New York

James R. Creel, New York Criminal Court (Café Au Go Go obscenity trial)

Gerald P. Culkin, New York Supreme Court (trial jury motion in Café Au Go Go obscenity case)

Henry Friendly, U.S. Court of Appeals, Second Circuit (appeal of §1983 civil rights action against New York prosecutors and judges)

Manuel A. Gomez, New York Criminal Court (pretrial matters in Café Au Go Go obscenity case)

Henry Clay Greenberg, New York Supreme Court (certificate of reasonable doubt for appeal of Café Au Go Go conviction)

Paul Hays, U.S. Court of Appeals, Second Circuit (appeal of §1983 civil rights action against New York prosecutors and judges)

Kenneth M. Phipps, New York Criminal Court (Café Au Go Go obscenity trial)

Thurgood Marshall, U.S. Court of Appeals, Second Circuit (appeal of §1983 civil rights action against New York prosecutors and judges)

John M. Murtagh, Chief Justice, New York Criminal Court (Café Au Go Go obscenity trial)

Vincent P. Rao, New York Criminal Court (arraignment for charges relating to April 3, 1964, arrest in Café Au Go Go obscenity case)

Frederick L. Strong, New York Criminal Court (pretrial matters in Café Au Go Go obscenity case)

New York: Judges for Appeal of People v. Solomon

Francis Bergan, New York Court of Appeals

Charles D. Breitel, New York Court of Appeals

Adrian P. Burke, New York Court of Appeals

Stanley H. Fuld, Chief Judge, New York Court of Appeals

James Gibson, New York Court of Appeals

Samuel M. Gold, Supreme Court Appellate Term, First Judicial Department

Samuel H. Hofstadter, Supreme Court Appellate Term, First Judicial Department

Matthew J. Jasen, New York Court of Appeals

John F. Scileppi, New York Court of Appeals

Saul S. Streit, Supreme Court Appellate Term, First Judicial Department

CLUB OWNERS

Note: This list includes the owners of all the clubs in which Lenny Bruce was arrested for obscenity, and those owners who were arrested, threatened with arrest, or threatened with club license revocation or suspension.

San Francisco

Art Auerbach, The Jazz Workshop (Bruce arrested on October 4, 1961)

Los Angeles

Herb Cohen, The Unicorn (Bruce arrested on February 12, 1963)

Weldon and Christina Emerson and Charles Davis, The Trolley Ho (Bruce arrested on March 19, 1964; administrative threat in April of 1964 to suspend or revoke the entertainment and dance license)

Ben Shapiro, Club Renaissance (police warning on September 10, 1959, of administrative trouble for club; after Bruce's one-week engagement, administrative notices for extended and costly improvements effectively force the club's closure)

Doug Weston, The Troubadour (Bruce arrested on October 24, 1962)

Sacramento

Daniel Katsaros, The Tender Trap (police warning in February 1965 of Bruce's and Katsaros's arrests)

Chicago

Alan Ribback, The Gate of Horn (Bruce and Ribback arrested on December 5, 1962; liquor license suspended on February 12, 1963, for fifteen days over three weekends)

New York

Howard and Ella Solomon, The Café Au Go Go (Bruce and Howard Solomon arrested on April 3, 1964, and Bruce and Ella Solomon arrested on April 7, 1964)

Long Island

John Hirst, The Cork 'n Bib, Westbury, Long Island (Nassau County District Attorney Office threatens license revocation on June 26, 1964, if Bruce's engagement continues)

APPENDIX B

A FREE SPEECH CHRONOLOGY

A large number of sixties people were tied up with costly, protracted legal struggles that prevented them from doing anything else. Some fought legal battle after legal battle; as soon as one case was over, they would be arrested on other charges, and the battle would begin again.

—*William M. Kunstler*

Note: What follows is a chronology of Lenny Bruce's free speech struggles. References to Bruce's other run-ins with the law (e.g., narcotics arrests and trials) are not always included, unless they affected the course of his obscenity trials. Most of the information provided here derives from official court documents and newspaper or magazine accounts from the period.

1925   October 13: Leonard Alfred Schneider is born in Mineola, New York. (He changed his name to Lenny Bruce in 1947.)

1957   June 24: U.S. Supreme Court delivers its judgment in *Roth v. United States* (354 U.S. 476 [1957]). Justice William Brennan's opinion for the Court defined the First Amendment standard for state obscenity regulation that governed during the period of Bruce's obscenity prosecutions. Brennan's opinion had a "Janus-like" quality, in that it blurred the distinction between vulgarity (i.e., coarse and offensive language) and obscenity (i.e., sexual immorality).

October 3: San Francisco Municipal Court Judge Clayton W. Horn hands down his opinion in *People v. Ferlinghetti*, the first major case to apply the new First Amendment standard in *Roth v. United States* for state obscenity regulation. Horn's decision determined that Allen Ginsberg's poem, "Howl," had "socially redeeming importance," and that Lawrence Ferlinghetti, the owner of City Lights Bookstore, had not violated California's obscenity statute by selling the poem. Albert M. Bendich, ACLU staff counsel working on the Ferlinghetti defense team, would later represent Bruce in his San Francisco obscenity trial before Judge Horn.

1959   September 10: Ben Shapiro, owner of the Club Renaissance, is warned by two Los Angeles police officers that there will be "much trouble" if he does not cancel Bruce's prospective one-week engagement. Bruce performs at the club September 10–17. Shortly thereafter, Shapiro receives official notices from the Los Angeles Health Department, Building and Safety Department, and Fire Department demanding costly and extensive improvements. Shapiro transfers the club to another location, and appears before the Public Welfare Commission to transfer his club license. The transfer is granted but with an unofficial warning to refrain from featuring Bruce.

1960   March: Noted columnist files complaint with New York police about Bruce's performance at The Blue Angel. The next night, police are present in the audience with a tape recorder.

Fall: Bruce performs at Basin Street East in New York. Plainclothes police from special squad are in attendance. After the performance, they ask Ralph

Watkins, the owner, to see the record of Bruce's cabaret card. Since Bruce's card had previously been revoked, he had to go to the police station to obtain a new card. Bruce is subjected to a strip search and interrogated before receiving a new cabaret card.

1961 **September 29:** Bruce is arrested in Philadelphia at the John Bertram Hotel for illegal possession of narcotics. Bail is set at $1,500.

October 4: First obscenity arrest. Bruce is arrested at The Jazz Workshop in San Francisco for obscenity violations of California Penal Code §311.6 and Municipal Police Code, Pt. II, Ch. VIII, §176 and §205. After being booked at the Hall of Justice, Bruce returns to the club for his 1:00 A.M. performance.

October 9: During the course of his Philadelphia drug trial before Magistrate E. David Keyser, Bruce holds a sidewalk "press conference" in which he exposes graft and corruption in the Philadelphia legal system. The story receives wide coverage on television and in newspaper reports.

November 17: San Francisco Municipal Court bench trial for The Jazz Workshop obscenity bust begins, with Judge Albert Axelrod presiding. Seymour Fried represents Bruce. Although Axelrod deems Bruce's words to be obscene, he grants a thirty-day continuance for the defense to transcribe The Jazz Workshop performance tape that had been submitted into evidence and to submit a memorandum of legal points and authorities.

1962 **January 22:** Albert M. Bendich, Bruce's new San Francisco obscenity trial attorney, moves for a new trial, based on Judge Axelrod's failure to advise Bruce of his right to counsel at the arraignment, and requests a jury trial. The motions are granted, and the case is reassigned to Judge Clayton Horn.

March 5: The second San Francisco Municipal Court trial begins with Judge Clayton W. Horn presiding. In his chambers, and before Bruce and his attorney, Albert Bendich, Judge Horn reads into the record a letter sent to him by Bruce that criticized Judge Axelrod. Horn holds Bruce in contempt of court but defers sentencing until the close of the trial.

March 7: Bruce takes the stand in the San Francisco obscenity trial.

March 8: An audiotape of portions of Bruce's October 4, 1961, performance at The Jazz Workshop is played in the San Francisco trial. Closing arguments are given and Judge Horn instructs the jury in a way consistent with a liberal interpretation of *Roth v. United States.* The jurors' first ballot: 9 to 3, not guilty. Ultimately, jury returns a verdict of not guilty. Bruce is fined one hundred dollars for contempt of court for the letter he sent to Judge Horn.

July 31: Bruce performs at Isy's Supper Club in Vancouver. Chief Licensing Inspector Milton Harrell, his assistant Ernest Akerly, and two morality squad detectives demand that Bruce show be canceled. They threaten that if the show is not canceled, the club's operating license will be suspended. Bruce's show is canceled by the owner of club, Isy Walters.

August 1: Bruce is scheduled to appear at the Inquisition Coffee House in Vancouver. After learning of that, Chief Licensing Inspector Milton Harrell threatens to suspend the club's license should Bruce perform. Bruce signs a pledge that he will never again perform in Vancouver (and appears on television to announce this).

September 10: After newspaper criticism of Bruce's performance at Aaron's Hotel in Sydney, Australia, the Australian Broadcasting Company refuses to air an interview that it had scheduled with Bruce for the *People* show.

October 17: Bruce opens at The Troubadour in West Hollywood, California. A disclaimer posted on the front door reads: "The Troubadour neither condones nor condemns Mr. Bruce's statements since it is our policy not to interfere with or limit in any way an artist's performance on our stage." Sergeant Sherman Block and Deputy George H. Koga of the Los Angeles Sheriff Department's vice squad attend the performance, along with Officers Joel Lesnick and John White, who had arrested Bruce twelve days earlier on a narcotics charge.

October 23: Sergeant Sherman Block sends Sergeant James Cline and Deputies Thomas Frawley and Gerald Schayer to attend Bruce's 10:00 P.M. performance at The Troubadour. No arrest is made, although Bruce was subsequently charged for an obscenity violation for that performance.

October 24: Bruce performs at The Troubadour. Los Angeles Deputy District Attorney Richard Hecht witnesses the performance, accompanied by Sergeants Block and Cline. Bruce is arrested and charged with two counts of obscenity in violation of California Penal Code §311.6 for the October 23 and 24 performances.

October 26: Represented by Seymour Lazar in the Beverly Hills Municipal Court, Bruce pleads not guilty to the two obscenity counts charged for his performances at The Troubadour.

December 5: After a week of performances at The Gate of Horn in Chicago, Bruce and club owner Alan Ribback are arrested for obscenity by Officers Arthur Tyrrell, Michael Noro, and Al Pieper.

December 5: Burton Marks appears in Beverly Hills Municipal Court in place of Seymour Lazar, who had resigned as Bruce's defense attorney in The Troubadour obscenity trial.

December 7: Criminal complaint is filed against Bruce for violating the Illinois obscenity law, Ill. Rev. Stat. 1961, chap. 38, §11–20(a)(2).

December 13: Captain McDermott, head of the Chicago Police Department's vice squad, warns Alan Ribback, owner of The Gate of Horn, that his license will be revoked if Bruce performs there again. The officer complains of Bruce's comments about the pope. Bruce performs later that night.

December 28: The Troubadour obscenity trial begins in the Beverly Hills Municipal Court with Deputy District Attorney Ronald Ross handling the State's case and Burton Marks representing Bruce before Judge Robert M. Dulin. Marks argues a motion to dismiss the two obscenity counts, and Dulin denies the motion. Jury selection begins.

December 31: Hired by Bruce to represent him as co-counsel with Burton Marks, Melvin Belli sends Charles Ashman, an associate for his firm, to the Beverly Hills Municipal Court to seek a continuance of The Troubadour trial. Judge Dulin denies the motion to continue, and resumes jury selection. After one-half hour, the impaneling of the jury is continued until January 2, 1963.

1963 **January 2:** Voir dire recommences in the Beverly Hills Municipal Court. Refusing to collaborate with co-counsel, Burton Marks alone represents Bruce. Bruce voluntarily waives his appearance at the trial, as he is performing a New York run at The Village Vanguard. Although the prosecutor agrees to proceed without Bruce, Judge Dulin refuses to try Bruce in abstentia. Dulin directs a bench warrant for Bruce's arrest to be held until February 8 (the scheduled date of Lenny's return from New York) and stays the trial until such time as Bruce appears in court, without scheduling a new trial date.

February 11: The Troubadour obscenity trial begins again in the Beverly Hills Municipal Court, now before Judge Henry H. Draeger. Burton Marks raises motions to dismiss the obscenity charges, but Draeger denies the motions.

February 11: Daniel Page Moore and Sam Friefeld, representing Bruce and Ribback in The Gate of Horn obscenity case, appear before Judge Daniel J. Ryan in the Cook County Circuit Court to argue pretrial motions to dismiss the charges brought under Illinois' obscenity law and, in the alternative, for a bill of particulars. Three days later, Ryan denies the motion to dismiss but allows the prosecutor to provide greater specificity in an amended criminal information.

February 12: The Gate of Horn's liquor license is suspended for fifteen days over three weekends for presenting a "lewd show."

February 12: Bruce performs at Herb Cohen's coffeehouse, The Unicorn. Los Angeles Sheriff Deputies Val Hall and Ken Jones attend the 10:00 P.M. show and arrest him after the performance for violation of California Penal Code §311.6.

February 13: The consolidated Troubadour and Unicorn obscenity trial proceeds in the Beverly Hills Municipal Court. Jury selection begins.

February 14: Jury selection is completed in the Beverly Hills Municipal Court trial. Deputy District Attorney Ronald Ross begins the State's case, calling Sergeant Sherman Block, Officers Gerald Schayer and Val Hall, and Deputy District Attorney Richard W. Hecht as witnesses for the prosecution.

February 15: Troubadour and Unicorn performance tapes are played in the Beverly Hills Municipal Court trial, and Bruce takes the stand in his own defense. The jury deadlocks 7 to 5 favoring acquittal in the Troubadour and Unicorn obscenity trial. Judge Draeger declares a mistrial, setting February 25, 1963, as the date to hear a motion for a new trial.

February 15-25: Deputy District Attorney Ronald Ross, in consultation with his superiors, elects not to reprosecute the Troubadour obscenity case.

February 18: The Gate of Horn obscenity trial begins in the Circuit Court of Cook County, Chicago, before Judge Daniel J. Ryan. Assistant Deputy Attorney Samuel V. Banks conducts the case for the State, with Edward J. Egan as assistant prosecutor. Having dismissed Sam Friefeld and Donald Page Moore, who had demanded complete control of the case without Bruce's interference, Bruce acts as his own counsel, with the assistance of Earle Warren Zaidins. The jury is impanelled, opening statements given, and Officers Tyrrell and Noro are called as State's witnesses. Zaidins conducts the entire cross-examination of the State's witnesses, and moves for a directed verdict at the end of the prosecution's case, which is denied. Trial is recessed until February 25.

February 23: After arriving in Los Angeles from O'Hare Airport, Bruce is arrested in a cab for narcotics possession, and released on $2,625 bail. Bruce cannot leave Los Angeles before the March 7 preliminary hearing in the felony drug case.

February 27: Cook County Circuit Court Judge Daniel Ryan denies Earle Zaidins's motion for another continuance until Bruce can return to Chicago and requires Zaidins to put on the defense's case without Bruce at the trial. Zaidins plays The Gate of Horn performance tape for the jury, and the court recessed. Before leaving his chambers, Judge Ryan forfeits Bruce's bail, issues a bench warrant for his arrest, and asks the State's attorney to commence extradition proceedings.

February 28: Last day of the Cook County Circuit Court trial. Judge Ryan denies Earle Zaidins's motions to remove a juror and declare a mistrial. Zaidins rests the defense's case, and closing arguments are given. Less than one hour after the jury retires, it renders a guilty verdict against Bruce.

March 1: Bruce sends a telegram to Cook County Circuit Court Judge Daniel Ryan.

March 12: Bruce sends a second telegram to Judge Ryan, accusing him of "illegal, unconstitutional, and most fascistic...behavior" for trying him in abstentia.

March 14: Representing Bruce at the sentencing hearing for the Gate of Horn obscenity case, George C. Pontikes moves for a new trial. Judge Ryan sentences Bruce to one year in jail and a fine of one thousand dollars, and Assistant Deputy Attorney Samuel Banks starts extradition proceedings.

March 19: Bruce's Illinois appellate attorneys, Maurice Rosenfield, Harry Kalven Jr., and William R. Ming Jr., visit Judge Ryan in his chambers to seek an appeal bond. Ryan refuses to grant the request.

March 19: Illinois fugitive warrant is sent to California requesting Bruce's extradition.

March 21: The case against Alan Ribback, owner of The Gate of Horn, is dismissed without trial.

March 26: John Marshall, one of Bruce's Los Angeles drug lawyers, surrenders him to Los Angeles Municipal Court Judge Maurice T. Leader, and the extradition hearing is set for April 25.

April 2: Bruce's Illinois appellate attorneys meet with Justice Walter V. Schaefer of the Illinois Supreme Court in an attempt to obtain an appeal bond. Schaefer requires that Bruce be present in his chambers the next afternoon in order that the appeal bond be granted.

April 3: Bruce flies from Los Angeles to Chicago and appears in Justice Schaefer's chambers. Justice Schaefer grants an appeal bond.

April 8: Bruce is barred from entering England at Heathrow Airport and returns to New York.

April 13: After flying to Dublin and then to London, Bruce attempts to perform at The Establishment. Plainclothes police return Bruce to the London airport, where he is deported the next day under authority of the British Alien Act.

May 23: Bruce arrested for obscene performance at Le Grand Theater in Los Angeles and charged with violation of California Penal Code §311.6.

June 20: Los Angeles Superior Court Judge William A. Munnell of Department 95 of the Psychiatric Court orders that Bruce be confined in the State Rehabilitation Center at Chino, California, for narcotic addict's rehabilitation.

July 1: The Troubadour obscenity case is dismissed on the State's motion in the Beverly Hills Municipal Court, the prosecution having decided not to retry Bruce.

1964 **January:** Detroit Board of Censors prohibits Bruce's performance at The Alamo club.

March 4: Los Angeles Lieutenant A. B. Comer of the Administrative Vice Division files a report with the Los Angeles Police Department noting that, on February 22, 1964 at 1:00 A.M., Officers Paul C. Burks and Robert F. McGuire attended Lenny Bruce's performance at The Trolley Ho for about ten minutes and observed him using obscene language in "violation of Board Rule No. 6 governing Cafe Entertainment."

March 7: Los Angeles Lieutenant A. B. Comer of the Administrative Vice Division files a report with the Los Angeles Police Department noting that, on March 6, 1964, at 11:00 P.M., he attended a Lenny Bruce performance at The Trolley Ho. Officer Corleen Schnell accompanied him.

March 16: Los Angeles police officers Robert F. McGuire and William Taragan file a report noting that they had attended and audiotaped Bruce's performances at The Trolley Ho. The surveillance period is recorded as February 22, 1964 through March 13, 1964.

March 17: Police report of Officers McGuire and Taragan is submitted to the Los Angeles City Attorney with "an application for a complaint." Complaint filed by Officer McGuire charging Bruce with having violated California Penal Code 311.6 by conducting an obscene performance at The Trolley Ho on March 13. Judge Mario L. Clinco of the Los Angeles Municipal Court issues a warrant for Bruce's arrest.

March 19: Bruce is arrested on The Trolley Ho obscenity charge, booked, bailed (five hundred dollars), and released from custody, all in time for his 10:00 P.M. performance at the club.

March 20: Sydney M. Irmas represents Bruce at the arraignment in the Trolley Ho obscenity case before Judge Robert Feinerman of the Los Angeles Municipal Court. Feinerman extends Bruce's time for pleading and continues the case for several weeks.

March 31: License Department Inspector Herbert S. Ruhe attends Bruce's 10:30 P.M. performance at Café Au Go Go in Greenwich Village, where Bruce had been performing since March 29. Ruhe takes notes on Bruce's performance and subsequently submits an official report to the Manhattan District Attorney's Office.

April: Los Angeles Department of Alcohol Beverage Control issues an administrative complaint to suspend or revoke the entertainment and dance license of The Trolley Ho Club in Los Angeles, owned by Weldon Harlin Emerson, Christina Jane Emerson, and Charles Davis.

April 1: Bruce's attorney-to-be, Ephraim London, argues *Jacobellis v. Ohio* before the U.S. Supreme Court.

April 1: New York District Attorney's Office orders police to monitor and record Bruce's act at Café Au Go Go. Four plainclothes vice squad officers— Patrolmen Lane, O'Neil, and MacCambridge, and Lieutenant Russo—attend Bruce's 10:00 P.M. show.

April 1-3: New York grand jury hears evidence against Bruce for his performances at Café Au Go Go. Assistant District Attorney Gerald Harris presents the case to the grand jury, which is instructed on New York Penal Code §1140-A ("obscene, indecent, immoral, and impure" entertainment).

April 3: Criminal information filed against Bruce and Howard Solomon, accusing them of violating New York Penal Code §1140-A. Shortly before the scheduled 10:00 P.M. performance, both Bruce and Solomon are arrested in the Café Au Go Go dressing room and booked at the Charles Street Station.

April 4: Judge Vincent P. Rao grants Bruce bail in the amount of one thousand dollars, after he pleads not guilty. Howard Solomon pleads not guilty and is released on the recognizance of his lawyer. Bruce returns to the Café Au Go Go to perform before a full house.

April 7: Criminal complaint is issued against Bruce, Howard Solomon, and Ella Solomon.

April 7: Attorneys Maurice Rosenfield, Herbert Monte-Levy, and Allen Schwartz consult with Bruce, Howard Solomon, and Ella Solomon about continuing Bruce's run of scheduled performances at Café Au Go Go. The legal decision is unanimous: Bruce will continue to perform and test the constitutionality of the New York obscenity law as applied to his act. Bruce performs before licensing agent Herbert Ruhe, Police Inspector Powell, and Patrolmen Hahne and La Piedra. At the end of the evening's first performance, La Piedra arrests Bruce, and Hahne arrests Ella Solomon for violating New York Penal Code §1140-A.

April 8: Hearing before New York Criminal Court Chief Justice John M. Murtagh. Lawrence H. Rogovin appears for Howard H. Squadron, representing Bruce. Herbert Monte-Levy represents Ella and Howard Solomon.

April 12: Bruce hires Ephraim London to represent him. Martin Garbus, a young associate in London's law firm, becomes co-counsel in the Café Au Go Go obscenity case.

April 13: Hearing before Judge Manuel A. Gomez of New York's criminal court. Herbert Monte-Levy, Bentley Kassal, and Howard Squadron withdraw as counsel for defendants and Ephraim London (representing Bruce) and Allen G. Schwartz (representing the Solomons) substitute as counsel for the defendants. Arraignment is deferred.

April 14-15: Criminal contempt hearing before Judge Frederick Strong concerning Howard Solomon's refusal to surrender subpoenaed tapes of Bruce's performances at Café Au Go Go. Strong rules that the tapes belong to the Café Au Go Go corporation, not to Bruce or Solomon, and must be handed over to the prosecution as subpoenaed evidence.

April 15: Preliminary hearing before Judge Frederick Strong on the defendants' motion to dismiss the charges against Bruce and Ella Solomon arising from the April 7 criminal complaint. Ephraim London and Allen Schwartz argue that the state cannot prosecute both of the accused under New York Penal Code §1140-A: Ella Solomon had not managed, directed, or participated in any way with Bruce's performances; Bruce, as a performer, was exempted from the purview of the statute; and, in any case, §1140-A is facially unconstitutional as applied to coarse and vulgar language under *People v. Wendling* (N.Y. 1932) and to comedic commentary with socially redeeming value under *Roth v. United States* (U.S. 1957). As to all bases argued, Judge Strong rules against dismissal of the complaint.

April 22: Bruce pleads not guilty in the Trolley Ho obscenity case before Judge Richard Schauer of the Los Angeles Municipal Court, and he requests a jury trial.

April 23: Café Au Go Go obscenity trial postponed because Bruce is hospitalized for pleurisy.

May 13: Defendants' motion for a trial by jury in the Café Au Go Go obscenity case denied by New York Supreme Court Justice Gerald P. Culkin.

May 21: Judge Bernard S. Selber of the Los Angeles Municipal Court hears pretrial argument on defendant's motion to dismiss the complaint in the Trolley Ho obscenity case. Sydney Irmas represents Bruce in absentia and Deputy City Attorney Johnnie L. Cochran Jr. represents the state. Relying on *Roth v. United States* (1957) and the California Supreme Court's obscenity ruling in *Zeitlin v. Arnebergh* (1963), Judge Selber dismisses the cause on First Amendment grounds and orders bail exonerated.

May 29: Los Angeles City Attorney's Office appeals Judge Selber's ruling in the Trolley Ho case to the Appellate Department of the California Superior Court in Los Angeles.

June 13: A press release and a petition in defense of Bruce—drafted and publicized by the Committee on Poetry and signed by noted artists, journalists, actors, writers, physicians, and musicians—are issued. Among the notable signatories are Bob Dylan, Nat Hentoff, Norman Mailer, Theodor Reik, Susan Sontag, Elizabeth Taylor, Lionel Trilling, Irving Howe, Paul Newman, and Michael Harrington. The next day's New York Sunday papers headline the campaign story.

June 16: Café Au Go Go obscenity trial begins in New York Criminal Court before a three-judge court: Justices Kenneth M. Phipps and James Randall Creel, and Chief Justice John M. Murtagh, presiding. Bruce and Howard Solomon enter pleas of not guilty to the criminal information against them, and the cases against Bruce and the Solomons are consolidated. Assistant District Attorney Richard H. Kuh begins the prosecution's case, relying on testimony by License Inspector Herbert Ruhe and police witnesses.

June 17: Prosecutor Kuh completes the State's case-in-chief and introduces the transcripts and tapes of Lenny's April 1 (10:00 P.M.) and April 7 performances at Café Au Go Go. The tapes are played in open court.

June 18: With Justice Robert C. Underwood writing for a unanimous court, the Illinois Supreme Court affirms the Bruce conviction rendered by the Cook County Circuit Court in the Gate of Horn obscenity case (*People v. Bruce,* #37902, no published opinion).

June 18: Bruce returns to the hospital with a relapse of pleurisy, and the Café Au Go Go obscenity trial is recessed until June 30 to give him time to recover.

June 22: U.S. Supreme Court renders its decision in *Jacobellis v. Ohio* (378 U.S. 184 [1964]) and a per curiam decision in *Grove Press, Inc. v. Gerstein* (378 U.S. 577 [1964]), argued by Edward de Grazia (*Tropic of Cancer*). Although a majority of the Court determines that the *Roth* standard for obscenity still governs, the justices find that sexually stimulating material with any social importance is constitutionally protected, that obscenity cannot be adjudged by "weighing" a work's social importance against its prurient appeal, and that the constitutional status of allegedly obscene material must be established on the basis of a national standard.

June 26: Having heard a copy of the Café Au Go Go performance tapes from the New York criminal trial, Assistant District Attorney Norman Levy of Nassau County, N.Y., informs John Hirst, the owner of The Cork 'n Bib, a nightclub in Westbury, Long Island where Bruce performed two shows, that the club's license will be revoked if Bruce continues to perform there. The weekend gig promptly ends.

June 30: With the resumption of the New York Café Au Go Go obscenity trial, Ephraim London moves to dismiss the case on three grounds: (1) given the precedent of *State v. Wendling,* no prosecution can lie under §1140-A for coarse and vulgar language alone; (2) the statute penalized speech that "tends to corruption of morals of youths or others," and thus is facially unconstitutional; and (3) Bruce's routines could not be deemed patently offensive under contemporary community standards. Allen Schwartz moves to dismiss the case against the Solomons on the basis that the Café Au Go Go corporation owned the club and its managers had not been proven to direct, present, or participate in Bruce's performances. The court denies the motions to dismiss on all counts.

June 30-July 9: Eighteen defense witnesses are called in the Café Au Go Go obscenity trial to prove that Bruce's performances had artistic integrity and social value; that his words did not appeal to prurient interests, but rather conformed to community standards for nightclub acts; and that he never engaged in any lewd gestures. Among the notaries called for the defense, and cross-examined by prosecutor Kuh, are Richard Gilman, *Newsweek* literary critic; the newspaper columnist Dorothy Kilgallen; Nat Hentoff, staff writer for *New York Magazine* and contributor to the *Village Voice*; Allan Morrison, editor of *Ebony*; sociologist professor Herbert Gans; Jason Epstein, vice president for Random House Publishing; the cartoonist Jules Feiffer; and a United Church of Christ minister, Forrest Johnson.

July 7: Illinois Supreme Court vacates its opinion of June 18, 1964, orders reargument in *People v. Bruce,* and requests the parties to submit "suggestions" regarding the effects of the U.S. Supreme Court's decision in *Jacobellis v. Ohio* on Bruce's Chicago conviction.

July 9: Richard Kuh submits a letter to Chief Justice Murtagh and Justices Creel and Phipps to "clarify" the significance of the Illinois Supreme Court's actions of July 7. Kuh argues that, no matter what the speculation, Bruce's Chicago conviction "still stands."

July 10: The New York Court of Appeals rules 4 to 3 that *Fanny Hill* is not obscene in *Larkin v. G. P. Putnam's Sons* (14 N.Y. 2d 399, 200 N.E. 2d 760, 252 N.Y.S. 2d 71 [N.Y. 1964]). The Court also strikes down 4 to 3 the antiobscenity law with regard to minors in *People v. The Bookcase, Inc.* (14 N.Y. 2d 409, 201 N.E. 2d 14; 252 N.Y.S. 2d 433 [N.Y. 1964]).

July 20: Replying to Bruce's request that the Café Au Go Go obscenity trial proceed in his absence while he plays San Francisco's club scene, Ephraim London writes a letter explaining that Chief Justice Murtagh insists on the defendant's presence at trial, and that his failure to appear would result in forfeiture of bail and otherwise work to Lenny's legal deficit.

July 27-28: The Café Au Go Go obscenity trial resumes with five rebuttal expert witnesses called by the prosecution and cross-examined by the defense: Robert Sylvester, a *New York Daily News* columnist; Daniel Potter, executive director of the Protestant Council of New York; John Fischer, editor-in-chief of *Harpers* magazine; a freelance writer, Marya Mannes; and sociologist and psychoanalyst Ernst van den Haag. Richard Kuh relies on their testimony in an effort to prove that Bruce's acts at the Café Au Go Go lacked socially redeeming value, offended contemporary community standards, and were incapable of being "considered as a whole" because of their alleged discontinuity.

July 28: Final day of trial in the Café Au Go Go obscenity case. Out of order, Bruce briefly addresses the bench, requesting to testify as to "evidence withheld from the Court." After a short recess, Bruce accedes to his attorney's insistence that he not take the stand. No closing statements are delivered, but written briefs are to be submitted to the court.

August 3: Bruce sends a letter to New York Criminal Court Justice Creel, asking whether there was "such a thing as hard core vulgarity," and suggesting that crude and vulgar terms are the vernacular of the masses.

September 2: Bruce writes to Ephraim London, firing him as his attorney.

September 10: Bruce writes a letter to Chief Justice John Murtagh, requesting that the Café Au Go Go obscenity trial be reopened so that Bruce might argue his own case.

September 14: Appellate Department of the California Superior Court in Los Angeles affirms 2 to 1 Judge Bernard Selber's pretrial ruling that dismissed the complaint in the Trolley Ho obscenity case.

September and October: Ephraim London sues Bruce for more than $14,000 in attorney's fees and related costs.

October 5: In a brief hearing before Justice Murtagh, Bruce announces his dismissal of Ephraim London and Martin Garbus, and asks to be allowed to act as his own counsel. Murtagh determines that Bruce is to make a formal application to the Court on November 4, the day of judgment.

November 4: Bruce's application to proceed as his own counsel is granted. He requests that the three-judge bench of the New York Criminal Court reopen the trial to permit him to testify, but Justice Murtagh denies the request. Murtagh pronounces judgment, finding Bruce guilty as to the Café Au Go Go obscenity charges. The decision is 2 to 1, with Justice J. Randall Creel dissenting in an unpublished opinion. By the same vote, Howard Solomon is also found guilty. A unanimous court finds Ella Solomon not guilty. Sentencing is set for December 16.

November 24: *New York Law Journal* runs a front-page "Notes and Views" column by Justice James Randall Creel, consisting of a slightly edited version of his dissent in the Café Au Go Go obscenity case.

November 24: Illinois Supreme Court reverses and discharges Bruce's obscenity conviction in *People v. Bruce* (202 N.E. 2d 497 [Ill. 1964]) in a per curiam opinion, with concurring opinion by Justice Walter V. Schaefer.

December 4: *New York Law Journal* explains its refusal to print the New York Criminal Court's per curiam opinion in *People v. Bruce* on the grounds that it was filled with indecencies (152 *New York Law Journal*, no.108, p. 1).

December 8: Maurice Rosenfield, one of Bruce's Illinois appellate counsels, writes a friend-of-the-court letter to the three-judge bench of the New York Criminal Court in *People v. Bruce*, urging the justices to set aside their verdict in light of the Illinois Supreme Court's recent reversal of Bruce's Chicago conviction.

December 14: Manhattan federal district court rules against Bruce's complaint requesting prospective injunctive relief against New York State prosecutors and judges in *Bruce v. Hogan*, the first of his §1983 civil rights actions.

December 16: U.S. Court of Appeals for the Second Circuit (Judges Henry Friendly, Thurgood Marshall, and Paul Hays, presiding) affirms the federal district court's denial of Bruce's request for an injunction against New York State prosecutors and judges in *Bruce v. Hogan.*

December 21: Sentencing hearing in the New York Criminal Court on the Café Au Go Go obscenity convictions. For over an hour, Bruce addresses the court, essentially arguing a motion to set aside the prior judgment and reopen the trial. Bruce contends, first, that legislative history demonstrates the court's misinterpretation of New York Penal Code §1140-A; second, that the court had misapplied the governing First Amendment law; and, third, that prosecutor Kuh had "encouraged perjury" by introducing inaccurate transcripts of Bruce's Café Au Go Go performances. William S. Miller, representing Howard Solomon, and Harry Hershman, court-appointed counsel for Bruce, argue mitigating circumstances. After reading Maurice Rosenfield's friend-of-the-court letter into the record, Chief Justice Murtagh denies the defendants' various motions. Once again representing the New York District Attorney's Office, Richard Kuh argues for Bruce's imprisonment, given his "notable lack of remorse," and a maximum fine for Solomon, to make his trafficking in obscenity "highly unprofitable." Bruce responds to Kuh's arguments, demonstrating that "the Jew is not remorseful" and that "I come before the Court not for mercy, but for justice." Murtagh declares the court's sentences: "four months in the workhouse" for Bruce, and "$500 or thirty days" on each of two counts for Solomon. Against Kuh's advisement, Murtagh grants a temporary stay of execution to allow the defendants to undertake appeal procedures.

December 21-23: Represented by Allen Schwartz, Bruce seeks a certificate of reasonable doubt that will enable him to appeal his criminal conviction to the Appellate Division of the New York Supreme Court. New York Supreme Court Justice Henry Clay Greenberg issues the certificate.

1965 **February 11:** Bruce files a second §1983 civil rights action in federal district court against the district attorney's offices of New York and Nassau County.

February 18: Bruce contracts with Daniel Katsaros for a run at The Tender Trap in Sacramento, California. John Misterly, Sheriff of Sacramento County, orally threatens Katsaros and Bruce with an obscenity arrest if Bruce "gets out of line" by using profanity or filth harming "the moral fiber of the community."

February 24: Bruce files a state civil rights action, *Bruce v. Misterly,* in the California Superior Court of Sacramento County against Sheriff John Misterly for injunctive relief against obscenity arrests for future performances at The Tender Trap.

February 24: Hearing before the Los Angeles Public Welfare Commission to suspend or revoke the entertainment and dance license of The Trolley Ho Club in Los Angeles.

April 15: On remand from the U.S. Court of Appeals for the Second Circuit, Bruce's first §1983 civil rights action against New York prosecutors and judges, *Bruce v. Hogan,* is dismissed by the federal district court.

April 30: Bruce files a §1983 civil rights action, *Bruce v. Draeger,* in Los Angeles federal district court.

May 25: Manhattan Assistant District Attorney Vincent Cuccia opposes Bruce's motion for an extension of time to appeal his New York Criminal Court conviction and for authorization to proceed in forma pauperis.

June 1: U.S. Supreme Court denies Bruce's petition for certiorari in *Bruce v. Hogan,* (381 U.S. 946 [1965]), filed on his behalf by Edward de Grazia and Ernst Liebman.

July 21: Bruce writes a letter to Miami Beach lawyer Richard Marx, inquiring into the possibility of bringing a §1983 civil rights action against the sheriff of North Bay Village for harassing Marvin Dubin, the owner of Le B where Lenny had performed. Allegedly, the sheriff had pressured Bruce to sign a document swearing that he would not use any "dirty words" during his club appearances, and the police had monitored the show with recording equipment.

October: Bruce is declared bankrupt.

October 13: Bruce files a §1983 civil rights action in forma pauperis in the San Francisco Federal District Court to seek an injunction against future arrests for his performances and any criminal complaints "without probable cause" by the police of New York, Chicago, Los Angeles, and San Francisco. He also seeks to have his New York four-month jail sentence enjoined.

October 20: The New York Supreme Court, Appellate Term grants Howard Solomon's petition to appeal his verdict and to proceed in forma pauperis. William E. Hellerstein, a lawyer with the Criminal Appeals Bureau of the Legal Aid Society of New York, represents Solomon in the appeal process, and Harold Roland Shapiro takes over the case for the New York District Attorney's Office.

November: Maurice Rosenfield, one of Bruce's Illinois appellate attorneys, strives to arrange for top-notch New York legal counsel to represent Bruce in reopening his case on appeal from the Café Au Go Go obscenity conviction. Jay H. Topkis (from the Paul, Weiss firm) and Howard M. Squadron (who had done some preliminary work related to Lenny's New York arrest) offer to seek to vacate the dismissal of Bruce's appeal and to prosecute the reinstated appeal on the condition that Lenny not mettle with their efforts or communicate with the court. When Bruce rejects this offer of assistance, Rosenfield writes a letter to Bruce on the day before Thanksgiving: "In the phrase you love so much, 'Physician, heal thyself.' And, for my part, go to Hell."

1966 **February 9:** Bruce speaks on pornography and other subjects at UCLA as first guest speaker in ASUCLA Speakers Program.

August 3: Bruce dies of a morphine overdose in his home in the Hollywood Hills.

August 5: Bruce is buried in Eden Memorial Cemetery in the San Fernando Valley.

1968 **February 19:** *People v. Solomon* (Supreme Court Appellate Term, First Judicial Department) rules 2 to 1, with Judges Samuel S. Streit and Samuel M. Gold for the majority and Judge Samuel H. Hofstadter, dissenting (no published opinion), to reverse the judgment of the New York Criminal Court on the obscenity of Bruce's Café au Go Go performances, and overturns the conviction of Bruce's codefendant, Howard Solomon. (Since Bruce's own appeal was never perfected, his New York conviction is not formally reversed and still stands.)

March-May: H. Richard Uviller, the chief of the appeals bureau at the New York District Attorney's Office, moves the Supreme Court Appellate Term to amend its order to apply solely to matters of law, in order that the prosecutor's appeal of that order to the New York Court of Appeals might result in a simple reinstatement of Solomon's conviction. The Appellate Term refuses to amend its order or to hear reargument on the issue.

1969 **December 3:** New York District Attorney's Office argues *People v. Solomon* before the New York Court of Appeals, urging the court to reverse the judgment of the intermediate court. William E. Hellerstein and Milton Adler represent Howard Solomon.

1970 **January 7:** In *People v. Solomon* (26 N.Y. 2d 621, 255 N.E. 2d 720, 307 N.Y.S. 2d 464 [NY 1970]), the New York Court of Appeals affirms the intermediate court's judgment overturning Howard Solomon's conviction. Chief Judge Stanley H. Fuld, and Judges Francis Bergan, Charles D. Breitel, and James Gibson sign the opinion of the court. Judge Adrian P. Burke concurs on the grounds expressed in the dissenting opinion by Justice James Randall Creel of the trial court. Judge Matthew J. Jasen concurs solely on the basis of *Memoirs v. Massachusetts* (383 U.S. 413, 419). Judge John F. Scileppi dissents and votes to reverse on the grounds expressed in the trial court's prevailing opinion.

NOTES

PROLOGUE

Epigraph: Eileen Sheehan, Unpublished interview with Harry Kalven Jr., Fall 1974.

People v. Bruce

3   "Hiroshima was dirty": Lenny Bruce, quoted in John Cohen, editor, *The Essential Lenny Bruce* (New York: Ballantine Books, 1967), p. 288.

3   "Pulling the covers off": Lenny Bruce, quoted in Martin Garbus, *Tough Talk: How I Fought for Writers, Comics, Bigots, and the American Way* (New York: Times Books, 1998), p. 38.

4   Petition: Thomas Buckley, "100 Fight Arrest of Lenny Bruce," *New York Times*, June 14, 1964, p. 75.

The Living Dead

5   Goldman on Bruce: "Between the Lines," *New York* magazine, 1972, p. 4.

5   Bob Dylan: A Bob Dylan 45-rpm single was titled "Lenny Bruce" (England: Columbia Records, 1981); this song was also included on Dylan's *Shot of Love* album (Columbia Records, 1981).

5   Hero of free speech: Remarkably, Lenny Bruce was listed as among the five hundred people (he ranked 473) who most changed history in the past one thousand years. "It's the Ultimate and Most Controversial List of the Millennium," *The Mirror*, January 1, 2000, p. 28.

6   "I have been on television": Lenny Bruce, from *Lenny Bruce: Swear to Tell the Truth* (Studio City, CA: Whyaduck Productions, 1998), written and produced by Robert B. Weide and narrated by Robert DeNiro, aired on HBO TV, August 1999 (with excerpts from *The Steve Allen Show*).

6   "Police Testimony" bit: Lenny Bruce, from *The Lenny Bruce Performance Film* (Santa Monica, CA: Rhino Home Video, 1992), produced by John Magnuson.

7   Bruce "fired" Garbus: Martin Garbus, *Ready for the Defense* (New York: Farrar, Straus, and Giroux, 1971), p. 129.

Explanations

7   Ingredients for commercial exploitation: Robert Kirsch, "A Schtick-in-the-Mud Looks at Lenny," *Los Angeles Times*, June 16, 1974, p. 60.

7   "Bruce's lingering cult appeal": Bruce Weber, "The Iconoclast as Icon: Filling Lenny's Shoes," *New York Times*, July 24, 1992, sec. B, p. 3.

8   Review of *Lenny*: Paul D. Zimmerman, "Citizen Bruce," *Newsweek*, November 18, 1974, p. 105

8   "Battle between the hard hats and the peaceniks": Richard H. Kuh, "Censorship
      with Freedom of Expression," in Harry M. Clor, *Censorship and Freedom of Expres-
      sion: Essays on Obscenity and the Law* (Chicago: Rand McNally, 1970), p. 145.
8   *Mysteries and Scandals: Lenny Bruce*, aired December 28, 1998 (Los Angeles: E!
      Entertainment Television cable channel), produced by Daniel L. Abrams and nar-
      rated by A.J. Benza. An equally, if not more exaggerated and negative portrayal of
      Bruce appeared several months later on the same cable station in *E! True Hollywood
      Story: Lenny Bruce* (Los Angeles: E! Entertainment Television cable channel), aired
      April 25, 1999.
8   "Posthumous sainthood": Gene Marine, "Lenny, You *Meshugginah*, You Can't Play
      the Hero!" *Ramparts*, June 1972, vol. 10, p. 60.
8   "7:00 News/Silent Night": Simon and Garfunkel, *Collected Works* (New York:
      Columbia Records, 1981), disk 2, cut 12.
9   Lenny and Honey Bruce, quoted in Honey Bruce with Dana Benenson, *Honey:
      The Life and Loves of Lenny's Shady Lady* (Chicago: Playboy Press, 1976), p. 296.
9   "Only strength": Canadian TV interview taped in Los Angeles, CA on January
      21, 1966; Lenny Bruce, quoted in Pierre Berton, *The Cool Crazy Committed
      World of the Sixties: Twenty-One Television Encounters* (Toronto, Canada:
      McClelland and Stewart Ltd., 1966), p. 94.
10   "Great wounded bird": Nat Hentoff quoting Lenny Bruce, from *Lenny Bruce With-
      out Tears* (New York: Fred Baker Film & Video Co., 1992), narration and continu-
      ity by John Parsons and narrated by Fred Baker.

1. COMEDY AS COMMENTARY
Epigraph: Interview with George Carlin, May 20, 2001.

Obscenity or Blasphemy?
13   Epigraph: Lenny Bruce, quoted in "Lenny Bruce Show Closed Amid Criticism in
      Sydney," *New York Times,* September 8, 1962, p. 16.
13   "Profane scoffing": William Blackstone, *Commentaries on the Laws of England and
      of Public Wrongs* (Boston: Beacon Press, 1962), p. 55.
13   "We Jews killed Christ": Lenny Bruce, quoted in "Lenny Bruce Show Closed
      Amid Criticism in Sydney," *New York Times*, September 8, 1962, p. 16.
14   *Burstyn v. Wilson*, 343 U.S. 495, 497–506 (1952).

From Godfrey to Gazunka!
14   Epigraph: Nat Hentoff, "The Humorist as Grand Inquisitor," *Liberation,* May
      1963, p. 27.
15   Hepburn imitation: Lenny Bruce, from *The Arthur Godfrey Show* as reproduced in
      Lenny Bruce: Swear to Tell the Truth (San Fernando, CA: Whyaduck Productions,
      1998), written and produced by Robert B. Weide and narrated by Robert De Niro,
      aired on HBO TV, August 1999.
15   Bogart imitation: Lenny Bruce, quoted in Jane Wollman, "Mother of Modern Com-
      edy," *Newsday*, October 15, 1989, p. 21.
15   "Burlesque shithouses": Lenny Bruce, quoted in Honey Bruce with Dana Benen-
      son, *Honey: The Life of Lenny's Shady Lady* (Chicago: Playboy Press, 1976), p. 213.
15   "The cheesier the dive": Robert De Niro, narrator, from *Lenny Bruce: Swear to Tell
      the Truth* (San Fernando, CA: Whyaduck Productions, 1998), written and pro-
      duced by Robert B. Weide, aired on HBO TV, August 1999.
16   "A comedian who'll offend everybody": *The Steve Allen Show*, April 12, 1959,
      excerpted in *Lenny Bruce Without Tears* (New York, NY: Fred Baker Film & Video
      Co., 1992), narration and continuity by John Parsons and narrated by Fred Baker.
16   "Louis Pasteur of Junkiedom!": Lenny Bruce, from *The Steve Allen Show*, April 10,
      1959, excerpted in *Lenny Bruce Without Tears* (New York, NY: Fred Baker Film &

Video Co., 1992), narration and continuity by John Parsons and narrated by Fred Baker.

16 Sullivan's need for reassurances: Letter from Ed Sullivan to Frank Ray Perilli, dated November 26, 1958.

16 Bruce's growing reputation: "The Sicknicks," *Time,* July 13, 1959, p. 42; Robert Ruark, "Let's Nix the Sickniks," *Saturday Evening Post,* June 29, 1963, at p. 39.

17 Interview with Lenny Bruce regarding jazz: Ed Sherman, "George Crater Meets Lenny Bruce," *Downbeat's Music,* 1960, pp. 56-7.

17 Thelonious Monk and Ornette Coleman: Nat Hentoff, "The Humorist as Grand Inquisitor," *Liberation,* May 1963, p. 28.

18 "The Palladium": Lenny Bruce, *I'm Not a Nut, Elect Me!* (Berkeley, CA: Fantasy Records, 1960, No. 7007).

18 "Castigated its whoring": Albert Goldman and Lawrence Schiller, *Ladies and Gentlemen—Lenny Bruce!!* (New York: Random House, 1974), p. 244.

18 "I am part of everything I indict": Lenny Bruce, quoted in "The Playboy Panel: Hip Comics and the New Humor," *Playboy,* March 1961, p. 38.

18 "How far will he go *tonight*?": Nat Hentoff, "The Humorist as Grand Inquisitor," *Liberation,* May 1963, p. 27.

18 "Intimidating panther": Arthur Gelb, "Comic Gives Shocks with Moral," *New York Times,* December 8, 1960, p. 44

18 "Nigger" bit: Lenny Bruce, quoted in John Cohen, editor, *The Essential Lenny Bruce* (New York: Ballantine Books, 1967) pp. 15-6.

19 "Strategy of subversion": Randall Kennedy, *Nigger: The Strange Career of a Troublesome Word* (New York: Pantheon, 2002).

19 "The truth is what *is*": Lenny Bruce, from *Lenny Bruce: Swear to Tell the Truth* (San Fernando, CA: Whyaduck Productions, 1998), written and produced by Robert B. Weide and narrated by Robert De Niro, aired on HBO TV, August 1999.

19 "We're all hustlers": Lenny Bruce, quoted in Gilbert Millstein, "Man, It's Like Satire," *New York Times Magazine,* May 3, 1959, p. 30.

19 "Christ and Moses" routine: Lenny Bruce, "Christ and Moses," transcribed from *Carnegie Hall Concert* (United Artist Records, 1972), side 2, cut 3.

20 "I never heard of Jonathan Swift": Lenny Bruce, quoted in Lionel Olay, "The Trials and Tribulations of L*nny Br*ce," *Cavalier,* October 1963, p. 83.

20 "Impulse to be a saint": Albert Goldman, "What Lenny Bruce Was All About," *New York Times Magazine,* June 12, 1971, sec. VI, p. 20.

20 "You always live alone": Nat Hentoff, "The Humorist as Grand Inquisitor," *Liberation,* May 1963, p. 29.

20 "Elusiveness of any absolute, including absolute truth": Nat Hentoff, "Satire, Schmatire," *Commentary,* July 7, 1961, p. 377.

20 "Heinously guilty of the paradoxes": Lenny Bruce, *How to Talk Dirty and Influence People* (New York: Fireside, 1992) p. 97.

20 "There were two sides to Lenny": Interview with Don Friedman, March 9, 2002.

21 A "sort of white James Meredith": Lionel Olay, "The Trials and Tribulations of L*nny Br*ce," *Cavalier,* October 1963, p. 12.

21 "Scholar of sleaze": Tony Hendra, *Going Too Far* (New York: Dolphin/Doubleday, 1987), p. 129.

21 "Un-coded comedy": Interview with Jack Sobel, February 19, 1999.

21 "Verbal sleight of hand": Nat Hentoff, "Where Liberals Fear to Tread," *The Reporter,* vol. 22, June 23, 1960, p. 52.

21 Demystifying words: Nat Hentoff, "Lenny Bruce, Redeemed," *Washington Post,* December 29, 1990, sec. A, p. 19.

21 "What I want people to dig is the lie": Lenny Bruce, quoted in Nat Hentoff, *Free Speech for Me—But Not for Thee* (New York: Aaron Asher / HarperCollins, 1992), p. 325.

Notes

"He hated hypocrisy": Eileen Sheehan, Unpublished interview with Harry Kalven Jr., Fall 1974.

21 "Pissing on the velvet": Lenny Bruce, quoted in John Cohen, editor, *The Essential Lenny Bruce* (New York: Ballantine Books, 1967), p. 118.

21 "Surgeon with a scalpel for false values": Lenny Bruce, quoted in "Lenny Bruce Show Closed Amid Criticism in Sydney," *New York Times*, September 8, 1962, p. 16.

21 "Disturb rather than amuse": Lenny Bruce's obituary, *The Times* (London), August 5, 1966, p. 12.

21 "A rush job of psychoanalysis": Kenneth Tyson, from *Lenny Bruce Without Tears* (New York, NY: Fred Baker Film & Video Co., 1992), narration and continuity by John Parsons and narrated by Fred Baker.

21 Bruce viewed as child: Michael Murray, "Bruce Confronts the Lie," *Commonweal*, vol. 101, November 29, 1974, p. 214.

22 "With gnawing doubt that you indeed know who you are": Nat Hentoff, "The Humorist as Grand Inquisitor," *Liberation*, May 1963, p. 28

22 "Vulgar display of bad taste": 1960 letter from Jackie Bright of the Guild, quoted in Albert Goldman and Lawrence Schiller, *Ladies and Gentlemen—Lenny Bruce!!* (New York: Random House, 1974), pp. 284-5.

22 "Disgusting creep": Mel Torme, quoted in Philip Elwood, "Smooth Genius of Jazz: Mel Torme's Style Forged an Era of Vocal, Instrumental Music," *San Francisco Examiner*, June 6, 1999, sec. C, p. 7.

22 "I hate him": Jack Kerouac, quoted in Gerald Nicosia, *Memory Babe: A Critical Biography of Jack Kerouac* (Berkeley, CA: University of California Press 1994) p. 664.

23 "The fault lies with the manufacturer": Lenny Bruce, from *Lenny Bruce: Swear to Tell the Truth* (San Fernando, CA: Whyaduck Productions, 1998), written and produced by Robert B. Weide and narrated by Robert De Niro, aired on HBO TV, August 1999.

23 "We appeal to the *killing* interest": Lenny Bruce, quoted in John Cohen, editor, *The Essential Lenny Bruce* (New York: Ballantine Books, 1967), p. 283.

23 "Comedy of dissent": Ralph J. Gleason, Jr., Liner Notes for *The Sick Humor of Lenny Bruce* (Berkeley, CA.: Fantasy Records, 1959).

23 "Right to be disgusting": Lenny Bruce, quoted in John Cohen, editor, *The Essential Lenny Bruce* (New York: Ballantine Books, 1967), p. 286.

23 "To be as honest as he was": Eileen Sheehan, Unpublished interview with Harry Kalven Jr., Fall 1974.

23 "Bad words in a nightclub": Jimmy Breslin, "Artist of the Pen and Heart," *Newsday*, January 6, 2002.

No Laughing Matter
23 "I'm not a comedian, I'm Lenny Bruce": Lenny Bruce, quoted in Ralph J. Gleason, Liner Notes for *Lenny Bruce Live at the Curran Theater* (Berkeley, CA: Fantasy Records, 1972). Bruce repeated those words at the Curran concert in San Francisco on November 19, 1961.

24 "He lost his sense of reality": Edward de Grazia, *Girls Lean Back Everywhere: The Law of Obscenity and the Assault on Genius* (New York: Random House, 1992), pp. 476-7.

24 "Dirty Lenny": Lenny Bruce, from *The Lenny Bruce Performance Film* (Santa Monica, CA: Rhino Home Video, 1992).

24 "Fuck you and good night!": Lenny Bruce, quoted in Ralph J. Gleason, Liner Notes for *The Real Lenny Bruce* (Berkeley, CA: Fantasy Records, 1975).

2. THE FORCE OF AN OPINION

Epigraph and text quotations: *Adams Theatre Co. v. Keenan*, 96 A.2d 519, 521 (N.J., 1953).

Aiding and Abetting

27 *Roth v. United States*, 354 U.S. 476 (1957).
29 Duffy's Gayeties: William Karl Thomas, *Lenny Bruce: The Making of a Prophet* (Hamden, CT: Archon Books, 1989), p. 15.

Sweet Victory or Disaster?

30 Clark and Douglas distributing pornographic materials in Court: Kim Eisler, *A Justice for All* (New York: Simon & Schuster, 1993), p. 142.
30 "Every man in the street knows what obscenity is.": Leon Friedman, editor, *Obscenity: The Complete Oral Arguments before the Supreme Court in the Major Obscenity Cases* (New York: Chelsea House Publishers, 1970), pp. 15, 38–40, 54.
31 *Roth* as a sweet victory/disaster: Charles Rembar, "Introduction," in Leon Friedman, editor, *Obscenity: The Complete Oral Arguments Before the Supreme Court in Major Obscenity Cases* (New York: Chelsea House, 1970) p. xv.
31 *Roth*: *Roth v. United States*, 354 U.S. 476, 481, 484, and 485, quoting *Chaplinsky v. New Hampshire*, 315 U.S. 568, 571–2 (1942).
32 "Seed of future freedom-giving cases": Charles Rembar, "Introduction," in Leon Friedman, editor, *Obscenity: The Complete Oral Arguments Before the Supreme Court in Major Obscenity Cases* (New York: Chelsea House, 1970) p. xv.
32 *Roth*: *Roth v. United States*, 354 US. 476, 484, 487 note 20.
32 "Insoluble enigma": John Nowak and Ronald Rotunda, *Constitutional Law* (St. Paul, MN: fifth ed., 1995), p. 1199.
32 "Lost in a wilderness": *United States v. Klaw*, 330 F.2d 155, 168 (Second Circuit, 1965).
33 "Contemporary community standards": *Roth*, 354 U.S. 476, 489.
33 Douglas's dissent: *Roth*, 354 U.S. 476, 513.
33 "I must get you horny": Lenny Bruce, *How to Talk Dirty and Influence People* (Chicago: Playboy Press, 1965), p. 159?
33 "Substantially beyond customary limits": *Roth*, 354 U.S. 476, 487 note 20, quoting A.L.I. Model Penal Code §207.20 (2) (Tent. Draft No. 6, 1957).
34 Vulgarity vs. obscenity: *Swearingen v. U.S.*, 161 U.S. 446 (1895). See also Morris L. Ernst and Alan U. Schwartz, *Censorship: The Search for the Obscene* (New York: MacMillan Co., 1964), pp 42–4.
34 *Roth*, 354 U.S. 476, 496 (Justice Harlan concurring and dissenting in part); 495–6 (Chief Justice Warren concurring); 512 (Justice Douglas dissenting).
34 "Too conscious of the law": Lenny Bruce, quoted in Jerry Tallmer, "Lenny Bruce: No Help Wanted," *New York Post*, April 7, 1964, p. 6.

Withhold Judgment

34 "And *fangoola-da-mama*": Albert Goldman and Lawrence Schiller, *Ladies and Gentlemen, Lenny Bruce!!* (New York: Random House, 1974), p. 186.
35 "Faw the fust time in twelve years": Lenny Bruce, "Religions, Inc.," transcribed from *The Sick Humor of Lenny Bruce* (Berkeley, CA: Fantasy Records, No. 7003, 1959).
36 "Wildly insane comic": Ralph J Gleason, "Ann's 440, S.F.," *Variety*, April 9, 1958, p. 111. Gleason (1917–1975) was a noted jazz and rock critic who wrote for various publications, including the *San Francisco Chronicle* and *Variety*. He wrote the liner notes for several Lenny Bruce records released on the Fantasy label (Gleason was vice president of Fantasy). He was also one of the cofounders of *Rolling Stone* magazine.

3. Free Speech in North Beach
Epigraph: Interview with Albert Bendich, March 18, 2002.

Holy Howl

39 Quoted passages of "Howl": A variation of Ginsberg's "Footnote to Howl" in Allen Ginsberg, *Howl,* edited by Barry Miles (New York: HarperPerennial, 1995), p. 99.

40 References to "Howl" and the description of its original delivery: Allen Ginsberg, *Deliberate Prose: Selected Essays, 1952-1995,* edited by Bill Morgan (New York: Perennial/HarperCollins, 2001), pp. 229-42; Jack Kerouac, *The Dharma Bums* (New York: Viking Press, 1958), pp. 13-5; Michael McClure, *Scratching the Beat Surface* (San Francisco: North Point Press, 1982), pp. 11-34; Allen Ginsberg, *Howl,* edited by Barry Miles (New York: HarperPerennial, 1995), pp. xi, 3, 4, 5, 99, 164-8; Michael Schumacher, *Dharma Lion: A Biography of Allen Ginsberg* (New York: St. Martin's Press, 1992), pp. 188-216; Barry Silesky, *Ferlinghetti: The Artist in His Time* (New York: Warner Books, 1990), pp. 61-6; interview with Ferozan Ibrahimi, July 29, 2001 (co-owner of San Francisco's Silkroute). See also various accounts in Ann Charters, editor, *The Portable Beat Reader* (New York: Penguin Books, 1992), pp. xxvi-xxviii, 48-52 (Jack Kerouac), 227-8 (Ann Charters), 283 (Michael McClure); Ann Charters, editor, *Beat Down to Your Soul* (New York: Penguin Books, 2001), pp. xvii-xix (Ann Charters), 204-21 (Allen Ginsberg), 236 (John Cellon Holmes), 370-7 (Michael McClure), 516-9 (Gary Snyder); and Steven Watson, *The Birth of the Beat Generation* (New York: Pantheon, 2000), pp. 183-248.

41 Judge Horn decision in case of women shoplifters: Donovan Bess, "Court Rules on Biblical Essays—1 Wins, 1 Loses," *San Francisco Chronicle,* August 7, 1957, p. 1.

42 "Freewheeling excursion into movie-reviewing": Editorial, "Creative Writing in Horn's Court," *San Francisco Chronicle,* August 8, 1957, p. 20.

42 "Thou Shalt Not Miss": Political cartoon, *San Francisco Chronicle,* August 8, 1957, p. 20.

42 Customs battle and *San Francisco Chronicle* quote: Lawrence Ferlinghetti, "Horn on *Howl,*" *Evergreen Review,* vol. 2 (1957), pp. 145, 145-7. Also contained in *Howl and Other Poems* were: "Footnote to Howl," "A Supermarket in California," "Transcription of Organic Music," "Sunflower Sutra," "America," "In the Baggage Room at Greyhound," and some earlier poems—"An Asphodel," "Song," "Wild Orphan," and "In the Back of the Real."

43 "The most significant long poem": Lawrence Ferlinghetti, quoted in William Hogan "Between the Lines," *San Francisco Chronicle,* May 19, 1957, p. 34.

43 "Filthy words": Captain William Hanrahan, quoted in Allen Ginsberg, *Howl and Other Poems,* Barry Miles, editor (New York: HarperPerennial, 1986), pp. 170, 171.

43 "Use all the power of your office": "Bookmen Ask Mayor to Ban Cop Censors," *San Francisco Chronicle,* August 16, 1957, pp. 1, 4. In 2001, City Lights Bookstore was declared a landmark by the City of San Francisco.

44 Description of trial: Carolyn Anspacher, "'Howl' Trial Starts—Big Crowd," *San Francisco Chronicle,* August 17, 1957, pp. 1, 6; Carolyn Anspacher, "Dismissal for 'Howl' Clerk Indicated," *San Francisco Chronicle,* August 23, 1957, p. 4. An incomplete version of the *Ferlinghetti* trial transcript—with many of the oral arguments of Lawrence Speiser and Al Bendich omitted—is presented in J.W. Ehrlich, *Howl of the Censors* (San Carlos, CA: Nourse Publishing, 1961).

44 Lawrence Speiser: Later, Speiser was the successful petitioner and lawyer in a free speech/due process case that went to the Supreme Court. See *Speiser v. Randall,* 357 U.S. 513 (1958).

44 Description of Ehrlich's career: "Jake Ehrlich, Criminal Lawyer Who Won Murder Cases, Dies," Obituary, *New York Times,* December 25, 1971.

45 Justice Clayton Horn's decision: *People v. Ferlinghetti* (October 3, 1957), quoted

in Allen Ginsberg, *Howl*, edited by Barry Miles (New York: HarperPerennial, 1986), p. 174.

45 "The majority opinion in *Roth*": Albert Bendich, quoted in Allen Ginsberg, *Howl*, edited by Barry Miles (New York: HarperPerennial, 1986), p. 170 (emphasis in original).

45 Obscenity standard: *People v. Ferlinghetti* (October 3, 1957), quoted in Allen Ginsberg, *Howl*, edited by Barry Miles (New York: HarperPerennial, 1986), p. 174.

46 End of trial: David Perlman, "'Howl' Not Obscene, Judge Rules," *San Francisco Chronicle*, October 4, 1957, p. 1.

46 In addition to sources already cited, some of the information set forth above derives from Barry Miles, *Ginsberg: A Biography* (New York: Simon & Schuster, 1989), pp. 227–32; Edward de Grazia, *Girls Lean Back Everywhere: The Law of Obscenity and the Assault on Genius* (New York: Random House, 1992), pp. 327–38.

What Kindava Show Is It?

47 Opening of Jazz Workshop act: Robert Hardin, "Lenny Bruce Here—Smilin' Through," *San Francisco Chronicle*, October 4, 1961, p. 9.

47 Ann's 440: Trial Transcript, *People v. Bruce* (San Francisco City Municipal Court: Dept. No. 11: County of San Francisco) March 8, 1962, p. 16 (bit transcribed from Jazz Workshop audiotape).

48 Five thousand a week: Lenny Bruce, from *Lenny Bruce: Swear to Tell the Truth* (San Fernando, CA: Whyaduck Productions, 1998), written and produced by Robert B. Weide and narrated by Robert De Niro, aired on HBO TV, August 1999.

48 "To Come" : Trial Transcript, *People v. Bruce* (San Francisco City Municipal Court: Dept. No. 11: County of San Francisco), March 8, 1962, pp. 299–301 (bit transcribed from Jazz Workshop audiotape).

49 "Kiss It" : Trial Transcript, *People v. Bruce* (San Francisco City Municipal Court: Dept. No. 11: County of San Francisco), March 8, 1962, p. 295 (bit transcribed from Jazz Workshop audiotape).

49 Officer Ryan's reactions: Trial Transcript, *People v. Bruce* (San Francisco Municipal Court: Dept. No. 10: County of San Francisco), November 17, 1961, p. 14 (Officer Ryan re: "lewd nature"), pp. 32–3 (Officer Ryan rei numerous references to "cocksucker").

You Break It Down by Talking about It

50 The arrest account: Trial Transcript, *People v. Bruce* (San Francisco Municipal Court: Dept. No. 10: County of San Francisco), November 17, 1961, pp. 3–7 (Officer Ryan's testimony), pp. 27–34 (Officer Solden's testimony); Ralph J. Gleason's Liner Notes in *Lenny Bruce: Live at the Curran Theater* (Berkeley, CA: Fantasy Records, 1970); Ralph J. Gleason, "Lenny Bruce's Obscene Language Pinch in Frisco after Philly Rap," *Variety*, October 11, 1961, pp. 61, 64; "Cops Seize Lenny Bruce—'Dirty Talk,'" *San Francisco Chronicle*, October 5, 1961, pp. 1, 8; Ralph J. Gleason's Liner Notes in *The Best of Lenny Bruce* (Berkeley, CA: Fantasy Records).

51 "I'm not a comedian, I'm Lenny Bruce.": Lenny Bruce, quoted in Ralph J. Gleason, "Lenny Bruce's Obscene Language Pinch in Frisco after Philly Rap," *Variety*, October 11, 1961, pp. 61, 64; Ralph J. Gleason's Liner Notes in *The Berkeley Concert* (New York: Reprise Records).

51 "We don't want people like you here": "Hotel Heave-Ho Caps Lenny Bruce's Day," *San Francisco Chronicle*, October 6, 1961, pp. 1, 5.

Quickie Trial

52 "In a million ways": Interview with Seymour Fried, June 6, 2001.

52 Albert A. Axelrod's profile: Kenneth James Arnold, *California Courts and Judges*

Handbook (San Francisco: California Law Book Co., 1968), p. 257.

53 Request to testify as a defense witness: Letter from Seymour Fried to Ralph Gleason, November 8, 1961.

53 Axelrod trial account: Trial Transcript, *People v. Bruce* (San Francisco Municipal Court: Dept. No. 10: County of San Francisco), November 17, 1961, p. 30 (Fried argument re: performance "as a whole"), p. 36 (Axelrod re: whole word), pp. 38–9 (Axelrod re: "I've heard enough"), pp. 36–7 (Axelrod re: points and authorities), p. 40 (Axelrod re: children's interests), p. 41 (Bruce's testimony), p. 43 (Axelrod re: "wasting your time"), p. 49 (Axelrod's parting words); see also Michael Harris, "Lenny Bombs in Court Scene," *San Francisco Chronicle*, November 18, 1961, p. 3; "Encore in Court for Lenny Bruce," *San Francisco Examiner*, November 18, 1961, p. 15.

57 "You'd better bring your toothbrush": Michael Harris, "Lenny Bombs in Court Scene," *San Francisco Chronicle*, November 18, 1961, p. 3.

57 Ad for Curran Concert: *San Francisco Chronicle*, Nov. 19, 1961, p. 2.

Inviting Contempt
57 Curran concert passages: *Lenny Bruce, Live at the Curran Theater* (Berkeley, CA: Fantasy Records, 1970); our account of the Curran Concert is also based on information contained in Ralph J. Gleason, "A Tour de Force by Lenny Bruce," *San Francisco Chronicle*, Nov. 21, 1961, p. 36.

58 Alleged corruption of Magistrate E. David Keyser: "Lenny Bruce Charges Shakedown Attempt in Narcotics Case," *Philadelphia Inquirer*, October 10, 1961, p. 16; "Lenny Bruce in Philly Alleges 10G 'Fix' Offer to Quash Narcotics Rap," *Variety*, October 11, 1962, pp. 1, 68.

You Can't Win a Case Based on "Cocksucker"
60 The material for this section derives primarily from interviews with Albert Bendich, June 9, 1999, and August 27, 2001. Bendich (like many of Lenny's subsequent obscenity attorneys) had been an ACLU lawyer; he (again, like others) did not represent Bruce in a *pro bono*–ACLU capacity. The ACLU did not represent Bruce formally in any obscenity case. Of course, since Bruce would not always pay his lawyers in full, their work effectively became *pro bono*.

The Letter of the Law
61 In-chambers session: Trial Transcript, *People v. Bruce* (San Francisco City Municipal Court: Dept. No. 11: County of San Francisco) March 5, 1962, pp. 2–10; George Murphy, "Lenny—His Typist's Language?" *San Francisco Examiner*, March 6, 1962, p. 3; "Bad Day in Court for Lenny Bruce," *San Francisco Chronicle*, March 6, 1962, pp. 1, 10.

63 Officer James Ryan's testimony: Trial Transcript, *People v. Bruce* (San Francisco City Municipal Court: Dept. No. 11: County of San Francisco) March 5, 1962, pp. 16–28 (Ryan's direct examination), pp. 25–8 (Ryan's account of the jazz-riff bit). Officer Ryan's courtroom "performance" of the jazz-riff bit later led Grover Sales, who testified for the defense, to write and audiotape a dramatic performance based on the San Francisco trial. In it, Sales interjected into the trial testimony a fictional outburst from an outraged Lenny Bruce: "I'm being busted on the basis of this *putzo* doing my act!" See Grover Sales, *The Trial of Lenny Bruce* (audiotape performance based on San Francisco trial).

64 Bendich's cross-examination of Officer Ryan: Trial Transcript, *People v. Bruce* (San Francisco City Municipal Court: Dept. No. 11: County of San Francisco) March 6, 1962, pp. 44–9 (re: Moulin Rouge and Finocchio's), p. 49 (re: sexual stimulation), pp. 50-1 (re: "cocksucker").

65 Sergeant Solden's testimony: Trial Transcript, *People v. Bruce* (San Francisco City

Municipal Court: Dept. No. 11: County of San Francisco) March 6, 1962, pp. 61–3.

65 For further information about the trial, see Michael Harris, "Bruce Jury's Gaudy Tour," *San Francisco Chronicle,* March 7, 1962, p. 2.

Reasonable Doubt

66 Bendich's opening statement for the defense: Trial Transcript, *People v. Bruce* (San Francisco City Municipal Court: Dept. No. 11: County of San Francisco) March 6, 1962, pp. 65–8.

67 Review of Curran Concert: Ralph J. Gleason "A Tour de Force by Lenny Bruce," *San Francisco Chronicle,* November 21, 1961, p. 36.

67 Ralph Gleason's testimony and cross-examination: Trial Transcript, *People v. Bruce* (San Francisco City Municipal Court: Dept. No. 11: County of San Francisco) March 6, 1962, pp. 68–120 (Gleason's direct examination), pp. 78–80, 83 (Gleason's testimony on theme of Jazz Workshop performance), p. 82 (Wollenberg's objection to Gleason's opinion of Bruce's work), pp. 86–7 (Gleason's testimony on artistic relevance of "cocksucker"), pp. 89–90 (Gleason's testimony on "taken as a whole"), pp. 100-3 (Hentoff's *Commonweal* article), pp. 104–5 (Wollenberg's shirt tail).

A Throw-Away Line?

69 *Stamp Out Help* is reproduced in Lenny Bruce, *The Almost Unpublished Lenny Bruce* (Philadelphia, PA: Running Press, 1984), pp. 46–85. On January 23, 1963, Bruce sent Ferlinghetti a telegram ordering him to immediately stop sale of *Stamp Out Help* and to remove all existing copies from the shelves at City Lights Bookstore and destroy them (see *High Times* magazine, October 1976, at p. 47 for a reproduction of telegram). Bruce's (exaggerated?) fears may have stemmed from the then-pending narcotics trial in which he was involved.

69 The defense's case: Trial Transcript, *People v. Bruce* (San Francisco City Municipal Court: Dept. No. 11: County of San Francisco) March 7, 1962, pp. 181, 188, 196–7 (Kenneth Brown's commentary on "aesthetic pain" during direct examination), pp. 214 (Mary Brown's direct examination on prurient interest), pp. 217–9 (Clarence Knight's direct examination), pp. 229–33 (Robert Tracy's testimony on Chaucer), pp. 240–5 (Robert Tracy's testimony on Joyce), pp. 266–7 (Grover Sale's testimony on changing nature of Bruce's comedy), pp. 274–6 (Grover Sale's cross-examination testimony on "throw-away line"); March 6, 1962, pp. 131–2 (Gottlieb testimony on direct examination), p. 134 (Gottlieb testimony on cross-examination).

72 Jefferson Poland's leaflets: Trial Transcript, *People v. Bruce* (San Francisco City Municipal Court: Dept. No. 11: County of San Francisco) March 7, 1962, pp. 204–9.

73 Bruce's periodic interjections and disruptions: Trial Transcript, *People v. Bruce* (San Francisco City Municipal Court: Dept. No. 11: County of San Francisco) March 7, 1962, p. 182.

73 Lenny Bruce takes the stand: Trial Transcript, *People v. Bruce* (San Francisco City Municipal Court: Dept. No. 11: County of San Francisco) March 7, 1962, pp. 278–82 (Lenny Bruce's direct examination), p. 279 ("kiss it" vs. "eat it"); March 8, 1962, pp. 283–9 (Lenny Bruce's direct examination completed).

73 Playing of Jazz Workshop audiotape: Trial Transcript, *People v. Bruce* (San Francisco City Municipal Court: Dept. No. 11: County of San Francisco) March 8, 1962, pp. 288–301.

74 Closing arguments: Trial Transcript, *People v. Bruce* (San Francisco City Municipal Court: Dept. No. 11: County of San Francisco) March 8, 1962, pp. 303–14a.

74 See also Lenny Bruce, *How to Talk Dirty and Influence People* (New York: Fireside, 1992), pp. 114–28; Grover Sales, *The Trial of Lenny Bruce* (audiotape perform-

ance derived from trial transcript in *People v. Bruce*, San Francisco Municipal Court, March 5, 1962); Michael Harris, "Lenny Bruce on the Stand—And Says He Said It," *San Francisco Chronicle,* March 8, 1962, p. 4; George Murphy, "Star-Studded Bruce Trial," *San Francisco Herald-Examiner,* March 7, 1962, p. 3.

Judge and Jury
75 Judge's instructions to the jury and verdict: Trial Transcript, *People v. Bruce* (San Francisco City Municipal Court: Dept. No. 11: County of San Francisco) March 8, 1962, pp. 314a–31 (instructions), pp. 331–2 (verdict).
77 Jurors' reactions: Michael Harris, "Lenny Bruce Cleared," *San Francisco Chronicle,* March 9, 1962, pp. 1, 12; George Murphy, "Bruce Not Guilty of Obscenity," *San Francisco Herald-Examiner,* March 9, 1962, pp. 1, 12; Letter from Sheldon L. Messinger, vice chairman of the Center for Law and Society, to Professor Harry Kalven Jr., dated April 25, 1963 (on file in the Kalven Papers at the University of Chicago Library).
77 "We stoop to a new low": "Acquittal of Lenny Ires Chief," *San Francisco Examiner,* March 10, 1962, p. 3.
77 Contempt hearing and fine: Trial Transcript, *People v. Bruce* (San Francisco City Municipal Court: Dept. No. 11: County of San Francisco) March 8, 1962, pp. 332–50.
77 Contempt hearing: Michael Harris, "Lenny Bruce Cleared," *San Francisco Chronicle,* March 9, 1962, pp. 1, 12.
78 Bruce's post-trial statements: "Acquittal of Lenny Ires Chief," *San Francisco Examiner,* March 10, 1962, p. 3; George Murphy, "Bruce Not Guilty of Obscenity," *San Francisco Herald-Examiner,* March 9, 1962, pp. 1, 12; Michael Harris, "Lenny Bruce Cleared," *San Francisco Chronicle,* March 9, 1962, pp. 1, 12; Ralph Gleason, "Lenny Bruce's Obscene Language Pinch in Frisco after Philly Rap," *Variety,* October 11, 1961, pp. 61, 64.

4. L.A. Story
Epigraph: Gordon DeMarco, *A Short History of Los Angeles* (San Francisco: Lexikos, 1988), p.1.

Eye Candy
81 Strip City: Notably, in his autobiography, *How to Talk Dirty and Influence People*, Bruce made no significant references to any of the numerous Los Angeles clubs in which he performed or to his many run-ins with the L.A. authorities over issues of obscenity. The descriptions of Strip City derive largely from interviews with Maynard Sloate, May 20, July 25, and August 3, 2001; Honey Bruce with Dana Benenson, *Honey: The Life and Loves of Lenny's Shady Lady* (Chicago: Playboy Press, 1976), pp. 213–8, 222; *Lenny Bruce: Swear to Tell the Truth* (Studio City, CA: Whyaduck Productions, 1998), written and produced by Robert B. Weide and narrated by Robert De Niro, aired on HBO TV, August 1999.
84 Descriptions of Lord Buckley: Phil Berger, *The Last Laugh: The World of the Stand-Up Comics* (New York: Limelight Editions, 1985), pp. 34–64; Samuel Charters, "Hipsters, Flipsters, and Finger Poppin' Daddies: A Note on His Lordship, Lord Buckley, the Hippest of the Hipsters," in Ann Charters, *Beat Down to Your Soul* (New York: Penguin Books, 2001), pp. 97–109; Oliver Trager, *Dig Infinity!: The Life and Art of Lord Buckley* (Lanham, MD: Welcome Rain Press/NBN distr., 2001).
85 Descriptions of Burton Marks: Interviews with Maynard Sloate, May 20, July 25, and August 3, 2001; see also Albert Goldman Papers, Butler Library, Columbia University, New York, Box 7, File "Marks, Burt, Attorney" ("weird" thinking).
85 Descriptions of Seymour Fried: Interview with Fried, June 6, 2001.

Building Up to the Crescendo

86   Expenses: Lenny Bruce, *How to Talk Dirty and Influence People* (New York: Fireside, 1992) pp. 74–5; Honey Bruce with Dana Benenson, *Honey: The Life and Loves of Lenny's Shady Lady* (Chicago: Playboy Press, 1976), pp. 208–9.

86   Lenny Bruce's movies: *Dance Hall Racket* (1954) (Phil Tucker, director; Psychotronic Film Society Archives, distributor); William Karl Thomas, *Lenny Bruce: The Making of a Prophet* (New York: Archon Books, 1989), pp. 55–60; Albert Goldman and Lawrence Schiller, *Ladies and Gentlemen, Lenny Bruce!!* (New York: Random House, 1974), pp. 130–3, 145–7.

87   Kitty Bruce: Honey Bruce with Dana Benenson, *Honey: The Life and Loves of Lenny's Shady Lady* (Chicago: Playboy Press, 1976), p. 225.

87   Duffy's Gaieties: William Karl Thomas, *Lenny Bruce: The Making of a Prophet* (New York: Archon Books, 1989), pp. 14–5; Albert Goldman and Lawrence Schiller, *Ladies and Gentlemen, Lenny Bruce!!* (New York: Random House, 1974), pp. 141, 160–4; Honey Bruce with Dana Benenson, *Honey: The Life and Loves of Lenny's Shady Lady* (Chicago: Playboy Press, 1976), pp. 229–31; Interview with Maynard Sloate, May 20, 2001.

88   Malibu Beach break-in: Interviews with Frank Ray Perilli, May 29 and June 1, 2001.

88   Honey's penitentiary term: Honey Bruce with Dana Benenson, *Honey: The Life and Loves of Lenny's Shady Lady* (Chicago: Playboy Press, 1976), pp. 235–46.

88   Lenny's gigs at The Crescendo and Interlude: Interview with Maynard Sloate, May 20, 2001; Interview with Gene Norman, July 24, 2001.

90   Performances at The Slate Brothers: Interviews with Frank Ray Perilli, May 29 and June 1, 2001; William Karl Thomas, *Lenny Bruce: The Making of a Prophet* (New York: Archon Books, 1989), pp. 27–9 (quoting *The Hollywood Reporter*).

91   "When he was good, he was raucous": "The Comics: Lenny and the Great One," in Larry King with Peter Occhiogrosso, *Tell It to the King* (New York: Putnam's Sons, 1988).

91   "Father Flotsky's Triumph": *Lenny Bruce's Interviews of Our Times* (Berkeley, CA: Fantasy Records, No. 701, 1958). As with many other routines, there were several renditions of this live club bit. In 1961, Fantasy released an unexpurgated version of "Father Flotsky's Triumph" in *Lenny Bruce—American* (Berkeley, CA: Fantasy Records, No. 7011, 1961). Unlike the 1958 release, its 1961 counterpart contains, among other things, the hysterical dialogue between the effeminate Kiki, the prison hospital attendant, and Dutch.

92   Cosmo Alley: Interviews with Herb Cohen, April 4 and 7, 2001.

92   The man was in his milieu: Subsequently, Lenny launched a musical revue, "A Wonderful Sick Evening with Lenny Bruce," at the Highland House. Relying on gimmicks, the show was advertised by way of several large posters on the front of the building—including a Charlie Chaplin poster reading "Welcome, Legionnaires" and a Der Führer poster announcing "Coming Attractions, Adolph Hitler." Interviews with Herb Cohen, April 4 and 7, 2001; Interviews with Frank Ray Perilli, May 29 and June 1, 2001.

93   Chuck Berry: Jane and Michael Stern, *Encyclopedia of Culture* (New York: HarperPerennial, 1992), p. 54.

93   *Steve Allen Show*, April 12, 1959: excerpted in *Lenny Bruce Without Tears* (New York, NY: Fred Baker Film & Video Co., 1992), narration and continuity by John Parsons and narrated by Fred Baker.

93   "Most successful of the newer sickniks": "The Sicknicks," *Time*, July 13, 1959, p. 42.

93   Caen "pissing match" and Crescendo drug bust: Albert Goldman and Lawrence Schiller, *Ladies and Gentlemen, Lenny Bruce!!* (New York: Random House, 1974), pp. 254–5, 257–63; Interview with Officer Joel Lesnick (ret.), May 25, 2001.

93 "I say things that may offend": Lenny Bruce, quoted in Joe Pollack, "Non-Conformity Brings in 'The Bread,' Comic Says," *St. Louis Globe-Democrat,* September 16, 1959.
93 "I'm not a moralist": Lenny Bruce, quoted in Dickson Terry, "Lenny Isn't 'Sick,' He's Just a Rebel," *St. Louis Post Dispatch,* September 13, 1959.
93 Putting the squeeze on Club Renaissance: Affidavit of Ben I. Shapiro, signed and notarized on June 2, 1965 in Los Angeles County, CA.
95 "Psychopathia Sexualis" and "Religions, Inc.": excerpts transcribed from *The Sick Humor of Lenny Bruce* (Berkeley, CA: Fantasy Records, No. 7003, 1959).
96 House on the Hill: Interviews with Frank Ray Perilli, May 29 and June 1, 2001; Interviews with Jo Jo D'Amore, May 16 and 18, 2001; Authors' visit to 8825 Hollywood Boulevard, July 24, 2001.
97 "Las Vegas Tits and Ass": excerpts transcribed from *To Is a Preposition, Come Is a Verb* (Douglas Records, 2000) track 5.
97 Three controversial bits: Notably, none of these bits appeared on Lenny's third Fantasy album, *I'm Not a Nut, Elect Me* (Berkeley, CA: Fantasy Records, No. 7007, 1960), on his next Fantasy album, *Lenny Bruce—American* (Berkeley, CA: Fantasy Records, No. 7011, 1961), or even on his posthumous Fantasy double LP, *The Real Lenny Bruce* (Berkeley, CA: Fantasy Records, No. 79003, 1975).

Trouble at the Troubador
98 Southwestern University Law School experiences: Interviews with Ron Rothman, June 4 and 6, 2001.
98 Richard W. Hecht: Years later, Hecht was one of the prosecutors involved in the *Watergate-West* case; the case concerned Nixon's "plumbers" who broke into the office of Daniel Ellsberg's Beverly Hills psychiatrist, Dr. Lewis Fielding. See Michael Parrish, *For the People: Inside the Los Angeles County District Attorney's Office 1850–2000* (Santa Monica: Angel City Press, 2001), pp. 156–7.
99 Troubadour history: Eve Babitz, "Honky Tonk Nights: The Good Old Days at L.A.'s Troubadour," *Rolling Stone,* August, 1979.
99 History of club and "modern-day troubadours" quotation: "Doug Weston Dies at 72, Owned Influential L.A. Club," Obituary, *Washington Post,* February 16, 1999, sec. B, p. 8.
99 Troubadour description: Authors' visit to 9081 Santa Monica Boulevard, July 23, 2001. Doug Weston's original Troubadour, located on La Cienega east of Doheny, closed circa 1961 when Weston moved his club to its Santa Monica Boulevard site. He colloquially referred to the latter establishment as Troubadour II.
99 Troubadour disclaimer: Albert Goldman and Lawrence Schiller, *Ladies and Gentlemen, Lenny Bruce!!* (New York: Random House, 1974), pp. 387–8. Curiously, this disclaimer, noted only in the Goldman-Schiller biography, is nowhere mentioned in the Troubadour trial transcript. One would assume that such a disclaimer, allegedly posted on the advice of Doug Weston's lawyers, would have been raised by the defense.
100 Meeting with Sherman Block: Interview with Richard Hecht, July 16, 2001.
100 Section 311.6 of the California Penal Code: At the time, the relevant part of §311.6 of the Code provided: "Every person who knowingly sings or speaks any obscene song, ballad, or other words, in any public place is guilty of a misdemeanor." §311.6 (a) defined "obscene" more particularly: "Obscene means that to the average person, applying contemporary standards, the predominant appeal of the matter, taken as a whole, is to prurient interest, namely, a shameful or morbid interest in nudity, sex, or excretion, which goes substantially beyond customary limits of candor in description or representation of such matters and is matter which is utterly without redeeming social importance." A San Francisco jury found Lenny not guilty of violating this same section (see chapter 3).
100 Sergeant Block's knowledge of prior drug arrests: Sherman Block, from interview

with Larry Josephson, "Modern Times with Larry Josephson," WBAI Radio (CA: Santa Monica, 1989) audiocassette, side 2.

100 Block's experience working in a Jewish delicatessen: "Very First Person; Requiem for a Heavyweight; Sherman Block's Insatiable Desire to Lead Drove Him Until the Very End," Obituary, *Los Angeles Times Magazine,* December 20, 1998, p. 18.

100 Account of Lenny's October 17 Troubadour performance: Troubadour arrest record, File No. Z-849-573, October 24, 1962, Albert Goldman Papers, Butler Library, Columbia University, New York, Box 2, File 16.

101 Account of Lenny's October 23 Troubadour performance: Trial Transcript, *People v. Bruce* (Beverly Hills Municipal Court: County of Los Angeles), February 14, 1963, pp. 37–40 (lion-taming), p. 41 ("Las Vegas Tits and Ass"), p. 42 ("cocksucker"), p. 79 ("Adolph Eichmann"), p. 90 (Schayer's testimony re: "act was obscene").

101 Account of Lenny's October 24 Troubadour performance, arrest, and booking: Trial Transcript, *People v. Bruce* (Beverly Hills Municipal Court: County of Los Angeles), February 14, 1963, pp. 123–4 (Lenny late), p. 151 (Eric Miller), pp. 125, 151–2 ("tits and ass"), pp. 152–3 ("Lone Ranger's a *fag!*"), p. 155 ("How to Amuse Your Colored Friends"), pp. 126, 154 ("balling" cops), pp. 41, 154, 157 ("smoking shit"), pp. 126, 153–4 ("dwarf motherfucker"); Troubadour arrest record, File No. Z-849-573, October 24, 1962, Albert Goldman Papers, Butler Library, Columbia University, New York, Box 2, File 16 ("balling" cops); Interview with Richard Hecht, July 16, 2001; Interviews with Ron Rothman, June 4 and 6, 2001; Interviews with Herb Cohen, April 4 and 7, 2001; "'Sick' Comedian Bruce 'Sicker' with New Arrest," *Los Angeles Herald-Examiner,* October 25, 1962, sec. A, p. 3. Lenny Bruce, "Thank You Mask Man" is transcribed from *The Lenny Bruce Performance Film* (Rhino Home Video), produced by John Magnuson. "Now It's Obscenity Two Ways," *Los Angeles Herald-Examiner,* October 25, 1962, sec. A, p. 3 (Bruce press statement); Associated Press Release, Hollywood, October 25, 1962, Albert Goldman Papers, Butler Library, Columbia, New York, Box 2, File 16.

Beverly Hills Justice
105 Beverly Hills courthouse: Interviews with Ron Rothman, June 4 and 6, 2001; Interviews with Ronald Ross, June 20 and July 24, 2001.

105 District attorney's satellite office and *People v. Bruce:* Interviews with Ronald Ross, June 20 and July 24, 2001.

105 Burton Marks: Interview with Audrey Irmas, May 15, 2001; "Burton Marks, 57, Noted Criminal Trial Lawyer, Dies," Obituary, *Los Angeles Times,* June 6, 1987, pt. 4, p. 7; Interview with Allan Lasher, May 17, 2001.

106 Landmark obscenity case: *Miller v. California,* 413 U.S. 15 (1973), oral arguments reprinted in Peter Irons, editor, *May It Please the Court: The First Amendment* (New York: The New Press, 1997), pp. 154–7.

106 Representation in and retainer for three criminal cases: Letter from Burton Marks to Lenny Bruce, dated December 10, 1962, Albert Goldman Papers, Butler Library, Columbia University, New York, Box 7, File "Marks, Burt, Attorney."

106 Robert Dulin: Email from Richard Hecht, May 6, 2001; Interviews with Ronald Ross, June 20 and July 24, 2001; Interviews with Ron Rothman, June 4 and 6, 2001.

106 Henry Herman Draeger: Charles Liebman, *Directory of American Judges* (Chicago: American Directories, 1955); Interview with Joel Lesnick, May 25, 2001 ("Central Casting"); Interviews with Ronald Ross, June 20 and July 24, 2001 (Draeger's competence); Interview with Gerald Schayer, May 22, 2001 (Draeger's retirement).

107 Arraignment: Interviews with Ron Rothman, June 4 and 6, 2001.

108 Postponement to December 28: Trial Transcript, *People v. Bruce* (Beverly Hills Municipal Court: County of Los Angeles), February 11, 1963, pp. 7–8.

484 | *Notes*

108 Continuances and 1962 legal expenses: Albert Goldman and Lawrence Schiller, *Ladies and Gentlemen, Lenny Bruce!!* (New York: Random House, 1974), pp. 399–400.

108 Pretrial motions: Trial Transcript, *People v. Bruce* (Beverly Hills Municipal Court: County of Los Angeles), February 11, 1963, pp. 2–6 (motion to dismiss), p. 8 (motion to proceed in Lenny's absence), pp. 16–7 (written waiver).

109 Melvin Belli, Charles Ashman, and New Year's Eve jury selection: Interviews with Ronald Ross, June 20 and July 24, 2001. For additional information on Melvin M. Belli, see Melvin M. Belli with Robert Blair Kaiser, *My Life on Trial: An Autobiography* (New York: William Morrow & Co., 1976).

110 "Have a happy New Year": Albert Goldman and Lawrence Schiller, *Ladies and Gentlemen, Lenny Bruce!!* (New York: Random House, 1974), p. 400; Interviews with Ron Rothman, June 4 and 6, 2001 (Dulin's appearance).

110 Dulin's bench warrant and stay of trial: Trial Transcript, *People v. Bruce* (Beverly Hills Municipal Court: County of Los Angeles), February 11, 1963, pp. 13–4.

111 Judge Draeger takes over: Trial Transcript, *People v. Bruce* (Beverly Hills Municipal Court: County of Los Angeles), February 11, 1963, pp. 2–6 (denial of motion to dismiss), pp. 6–18 (speedy trial motion), pp. 18–20 (Draeger's caution to counsel).

112 Herb Cohen: Years later, after Lenny's death, Cohen produced a two-LP set entitled *Lenny Bruce: The Berkeley Concert* (Burbank, CA: Reprise Records, No. 2XS 6329).

113 Description of Unicorn and incident with Judge Brand: Interviews with Herb Cohen, April 4 and 7, 2001.

114 Bruce's Unicorn show and bust: Interviews with Herb Cohen, April 4 and 7, 2001; "Lenny Bruce Jailed for Off-Color Nightclub Jokes," *Los Angeles Herald Examiner,* February 13, 1963, sec. A, p. 3; Interview with Officer Val Hall (ret.), May 29, 2001; Interview with Officer Ken Jones (ret.), May 23, 2001.

116 Ross disturbed by Unicorn bust: Interviews with Ronald Ross, June 20 and July 24, 2001.

Strategies, Satire, and Schizophrenia
117 Voir dire: Interviews with Ronald Ross, June 20 and July 24, 2001; Interview with Burton Marks, Albert Goldman Papers, Butler Library, Columbia University, New York, Box 7, File "Marks, Burt, Attorney."

118 Amending complaint to include Unicorn charge: Trial Transcript, *People v. Bruce* (Beverly Hills Municipal Court: County of Los Angeles), February 14, 1963, pp. 24–5.

118 Maximum misdemeanor penalty: California Penal Code §19.

120 The prosecution's case: Trial Transcript, *People v. Bruce* (Beverly Hills Municipal Court: County of Los Angeles), February 14, 1963, pp. 151–2, 154 (Ross's shock value stratagem with Sherman Block), pp. 127–8 (Ross's divide and conquer stratagem with Richard Hecht), pp. 89–91 (Ross's common usage stratagem with Gerald Schayer).

122 Defense's cross-examination: Trial Transcript, *People v. Bruce* (Beverly Hills Municipal Court: County of Los Angeles), February 14, 1963, p. 47 (Marks's innocuous coarseness stratagem with Gerald Schayer), pp. 148–9 (Marks's satirical value stratagem with Richard Hecht); February 15, 1963, pp. 172–3 (Marks's satirical value stratagem with Sherman Block), p. 184 (Marks's satirical value stratagem with Val Hall), pp. 163–4 (Marks's no prurient appeal stratagem with Sherman Block).

122 "They did not appeal to your prurient interests, did they?": A key part of Lenny Bruce's comic mission was to liberate certain sexually charged words from shame and thereby to make them commonplace. "They're in the dictionary now, finally," Lenny remarked. "And the reason they came to the dictionary, finally, was through

continual usage." Lenny Bruce, quoted in John Cohen, editor, *The Essential Lenny Bruce* (New York: Ballantine Books, 1967), p. 256.

123 "Yiddish undercover agent": Telegram from Lenny Bruce to Burton Marks, January 21, 1963, Albert Goldman Papers, Butler Library, Columbia University, New York, Box 2, File 16.

124 Marks's faulty memory stratagem with Richard Hecht: Trial Transcript, *People v. Bruce* (Beverly Hills Municipal Court: County of Los Angeles), February 14, 1963, pp. 137-8, 145-6.

125 In-chamber hearings on Marks's motions: Trial Transcript, *People v. Bruce* (Beverly Hills Municipal Court: County of Los Angeles), February 14, pp. 24-30, 61-76, 100-16.

126 Lenny's appearance and detour to Schwab's Drug Store: Albert Goldman Papers, Butler Library, Columbia University, New York, Box 4, File "Chapter 9 raw ms."

126 Courtroom interior: Interviews with Ron Rothman, June 4 and 6, 2001.

127 London's Establishment…a permit for Lenny: As it turned out, Lenny had good reason for concern. See Sydney Gruson, "Britain Bars Lenny Bruce in the 'Public Interest,'" *New York Times*, April 9, 1963, p. 59; "Britain to Expel Bruce a Second Time," *New York Times*, April 14, 1963, p. 75.

127 Tapes of performances played in court: Trial Transcript, *People v. Bruce* (Beverly Hills Municipal Court: County of Los Angeles), February 15, 1963, pp. 189, 194-5 (Marks's direct and Roth's voir dire on Bruce's tape recordings), pp. 250-1 (playing of the Bruce tapes); Interviews with Ronald Ross, June 20 and July 24, 2001 (jury's and counsels' reactions to the tapes); Trial Transcript, *People v. Bruce* (Beverly Hills Municipal Court: County of Los Angeles), February 15, 1963, pp. 252-4, 257, 261 (Ross cross-examination of Bruce).

128 *Time* reporter's interview with Dylan: D.A. Pennebaker, *Bob Dylan: Don't Look Back* (New York: Valentine Books, 1968), pp. 122-31.

129 Bruce's recitation of Lone Ranger routine: Interview with Ronald Ross, July 24, 2001.

130 Closing arguments: Trial Transcript, *People v. Bruce* (Beverly Hills Municipal Court: County of Los Angeles), February 15, 1963, pp. 265-72, 280-2 (Ross's closing argument), pp. 279-80 (Burton Marks's closing argument).

131 Draeger's instructions to jury: Trial Transcript, *People v. Bruce* (Beverly Hills Municipal Court: County of Los Angeles), February 15, 1963, pp. 292-5.

132 "Fifty-fifty": Interviews with Ronald Ross, June 20 and July 24, 2001.

132 "Tough call": Interview with Richard Hecht, July 16, 2001.

133 Jury deliberations: Trial Transcript, *People v. Bruce* (Beverly Hills Municipal Court: County of Los Angeles), February 15, 1963, p. 229 (jury begins deliberations), pp. 296-9 (rereading of obscenity standards), p. 299 (jury deadlocked), p. 300 (Draeger's remark on jury understanding), pp. 301-2 ("blockbuster" instruction and jury polling); Interviews with Ronald Ross, June 20 and July 24, 2001; Interview with Richard Hecht, July 16, 2001; "Lenny Bruce Trial Winds Up with Hung Jury," *Los Angeles Times*, February 16, 1963, sec. III, p. 8.

133 "I thought it was a victory": Interviews with Ronald Ross, June 20 and July 24, 2001.

133 Decision to retry case left to Ritzi and Sten: Interviews with Ronald Ross, June 20 and 24, 2001.

134 "Chilling effect": Chief Justice Warren, dissenting opinion, *Times Film Corp. v. City of Chicago*, 365 U.S. 43 (1961).

134 Le Grand ad: *Los Angeles Times,* May 24, 1963, sec. IV, p. 13.

134 Don Rickles ad and strip show ads: *Los Angeles Herald Examiner,* May 24, 1963, sec. D, p. 3.

134 "Authentic hipster": Lionel Olay, "The Trials and Tribulations of L*nny Br*ce," *Cavalier*, October 1963, pp. 11, 12, 82.

135 Houser pans Le Grand show: John G. Houser, "Lenny Bruce Blasts Off; Verbally, That Is," *Los Angeles Herald Examiner,* May 23, 1963.

136 Le Grand bust: "Lenny Bruce Arrested Again for 'Obscenity,'" *Los Angeles Herald Examiner,* May 24, 1963; "Lenny Bruce Goes to Court May 31," *Los Angeles Times,* May 25, 1963, sec. III, p. 2.

136 "His biggest followers": Stanley Hill, "Vice Cops Crack Down on World's Sickest 'Sick-Sick' Comic!" *Vice Squad,* vol. 3, no. 2, April 1963, p. 18.

136 "Anybody's guess": Robert Ruark, "Let's Nix the Sickniks," *Saturday Evening Post,* June 29, 1963, pp. 38–9.

137 "Obscenity circus": Lenny Bruce, from *Lenny Bruce: The Berkeley Concert* (Burbank, CA: Reprise Records, No. 2XS6329, 1969).

5. CHICAGO: THE ASH WEDNESDAY TRIAL
Epigraph: Lenny Bruce, *How to Talk Dirty and Influence People* (Chicago: Playboy Press, 1965), p. 184.

The Gate of Horn
141 "Chicago is so corrupt": Lenny Bruce, from *The Carnegie Concert,* disc 2 (New York: World Pacific, 1995: CD), originally performed February 3–4, 1961.

141 Lenny Bruce's start in Chicago: Interview with Hugh Hefner, July 17, 2001; Ralph J. Gleason, Liner Notes for *The Real Lenny Bruce* (Berkeley, CA: Fantasy Records, 1975), p. 3; "Record Ramblings," *The Cash Box,* June 20, 1959, p. 25.

141 Studs Terkel interview: Lenny Bruce, *The Almost Unpublished Lenny Bruce* (Philadelphia: Running Press, 1984), pp. 15–21.

142 *Playboy-Penthouse* program: *Lenny Bruce: Swear to Tell the Truth* (San Fernando, CA: Whyaduck Productions, 1998), written and produced by Robert B. Weide and narrated by Robert De Niro, aired on HBO TV, August 1999.

142 "I'd like to ball the whole audience": Lenny Bruce, quoted in "Rebel with a Caustic Cause," *Playboy,* February 1959, pp. 21, 66.

142 Gate of Horn slogan: Eric Lax, *Woody Allen: A Biography* (New York: Knopf, 1991), p. 144.

142 Gate of Horn acts and patrons: June Sawyers, "Folk Was King at Chicago's Gate of Horn," *Chicago Tribune,* March 15, 1987, p. 11; Allan Ribback's obituary, *Chicago Sun-Times,* September 5, 1993, p. 72.

142 Ferlinghetti at Horn: Barry Silesky, *Ferlinghetti: The Artist in His Time* (New York: Warner Books, 1990), p. 104.

142 Gate of Ivory and Gate of Horn: Homer, *The Odyssey of Homer,* Richmond Latimore, translator (New York: HarperPerennial, 1991), Book XIX, pp. 296–7, lines 560–9.

142 "Healthiest comic spirit": Richard Christiansen, *Chicago Daily News,* November 14, 1962.

142 "Phony, frightened, lying world": Will Leonard, *Chicago Tribune,* November 18, 1962.

143 Illinois obscenity statute: Illinois Criminal Code, Chapter 38, §11–20 (a)(2), (b), (c)(1)–(4).

"He Mocks the Pope"
144 Description of Bruce's performance and arrest at Gate of Horn: excerpts transcribed from *Lenny Bruce Live 1962! Busted!* (Viper's Nest Records, 1995); Transcript of Proceedings to Supreme Court of Illinois from the Municipal Court of Chicago in *People v. Bruce* (Gen. No. 62 MC 66009: First District, Criminal Court Branch 46), February 27, 1963, pp. 347–8, 353 ("Paul Malloy and Christianity"), pp. 357–8 ("Adolf Eichmann"), pp. 353–4 ("War Criminals and Hershey Bars"), pp. 359–60 ("Infidelity"), pp. 360–6 ("How to Relax Your Colored Friends"), pp.

370–6 ("Christ and Moses"), p. 394 (bust); Lenny Bruce, *How to Talk Dirty and Influence People* (Chicago: Playboy Press, 1965), pp. 142–5 (arrest); "Cops Nab Bruce For 'Obscenity' at Chi Gate of Horn," *Variety*, December 12, 1962, pp. 53, 56; "Comedian Lenny Bruce Arrested," *Chicago's American*, December 5, 1962, p. 3; Allan Ribback obituary, *Chicago Sun-Times*, September 5, 1993, p. 72 (arrest account); George Carlin, quoted in *A Toast to Lenny* (Montvale, N.J.: Pioneer Artists, laser disc, 1984), aired on HBO; Interview with George Carlin, May 20, 2001 (1960 meeting with Bruce); Lenny Bruce, *How to Talk Dirty and Influence People* (Chicago: Playboy Press, 1965), pp. 142–6 (police report and Captain McDermott's warning); Associated Press wire report, December 7, 1962 (Judge Chester Strzalka).

145 "Adolf Eichmann": Paul Krassner, a close friend of Lenny Bruce's, was at The Gate of Horn the night Lenny performed. He recalls: "Lenny had been reading a study of anti-Semitism by Jean-Paul Sartre, a statement by Adolf Eichmann that he would have been 'not only a scoundrel, but a despicable pig' if he hadn't carried out Hitler's orders. Lenny wrote the piece for the *Realist*, 'Letter from a Soldier's Wife'—namely Mrs. Eichmann—pleading for compassion to spare her husband's life. Now, on stage, he performed the most audacious piece I've ever seen by a comedian." Paul Krassner, "The Persecution of Lenny Bruce," *High Times*, February 2000, pp. 42, 44.

146 "How to Relax Your Colored Friends at Parties": The routine was conceived in late 1959 while Lenny was working with his black guitarist friend, Eric Miller, at El Patio in Miami. It was first presented in March 1960 at the Blue Angel in New York. Lenny characterized the bit in "Bruce Here," *Rogue*, October 1960, p. 8: "[Eric Miller and I are] currently doing a satire on First Plateau Liberals, the ones who get offended with name-calling but worry about their property losing value if a Negro moves next door to them. (You know the type—they don't care what nationality a guy is as long as he stays in his place.)"

149 "A serious artist": Alan Ribback, Gate of Horn press release, December 5, 1962.

149 Horn's liquor license suspended: "Lenny Bruce Rap Kayos Chi Gate's License Fifteen Days," *Variety*, February 13, 1963, p. 57.

Legal Problems Galore

150 Bruce's suit against Fantasy for royalties: *Fantasy Records, Inc. v. Travelers Indem. Co.*, 283 N.Y.S. 2d 473 (1967, filed in 1963).

150 Accounts of Earl Warren Zaidins's early contacts with Bruce: Interview with Zaidins, May 14, 1999.

151 Lenny Bruce's five-week run at The Vanguard: Max Gordon, *Live at the Village Vanguard* (New York: St. Martin's Press, 1980), pp. 74–8.

The Right to Make a Fool of Oneself

151 Maryland Hotel events: Interview with Earl Warren Zaidins, May 14, 1999.

152 *Leather Jacket:* William Karl Thomas, *Lenny Bruce: The Making of a Prophet* (Hamden, CT: Archon Books, 1989), pp. 54–66.

152 Pretrial motions: Transcript of Proceedings to Supreme Court of Illinois from the Municipal Court of Chicago in *People v. Bruce* (Gen. No. 62 MC 66009: First District, Criminal Court Branch 46), December 12, 1962, pp. 59–61 (Cotsirilos sets original trial date); January 14, 1963, pp. 62–4 (Cotsirilos moves for trial postponment); February 5, 1963, pp. 65–9 (Donald Page Moore substituted); February 11, 1963, pp. 70–2 (original motion to quash and motion for bill of particulars); February 14, 1963, pp. 73–80 (amended information and second motion to quash); February 18, 1963, pp. 86–91 (Moore and Friefeld granted leave to withdraw as Bruce's counsels).

154 The right to self-representation: *Faretta v. California*, 422 U.S. 806, 819–20, 834 (1975), 422 U.S. 836, 839 (Burger, C.J., dissenting).

155 Lenny Bruce's perverse relationship to lawyers: Elmer Gertz, quoted in *Chicago Daily Law Bulletin,* May 5, 1992, p. 5.
155 Description of Judge Ryan: Kenan Heise, "Circuit Judge Daniel Ryan, 'A Big Man' Who Hears Big Cases," Obituary, *Chicago Tribune,* November 9, 1986, sec. C, p. 9.
155 Voir dire and the in-chambers meeting between Lenny Bruce and Judge Ryan: Interview with Earl Warren Zaidins, May 14, 1999; Transcript of Proceedings to Supreme Court of Illinois from the Municipal Court of Chicago in *People v. Bruce* (Gen. No. 62 MC 66009: First District, Criminal Court Branch 46), February 18, 1963, pp. 100–14.
156 Plea and jury selection: Transcript of Proceedings to Supreme Court of Illinois from the Municipal Court of Chicago in *People v. Bruce* (Gen. No. 62 MC 66009: First District, Criminal Court Branch 46), February 18, 1963, pp. 95–8; Lenny Bruce, *How to Talk Dirty and Influence People* (Chicago: Playboy Press, 1965), p. 147; "Eight Women, Four Men Picked to Try Lenny Bruce," *Chicago Tribune,* February 19, 1963, sec. I, p. 19; "Comic Turns Lawyer in Obscenity Hearing," *Chicago Sun-Times,* February 19, 1963, p. 42.

Lenny the Lawyer
157 Opening arguments: Transcript of Proceedings to Supreme Court of Illinois from the Municipal Court of Chicago in *People v. Bruce* (Gen. No. 62 MC 66009: First District, Criminal Court Branch 46), February 18, 1963, p. 116 (courtroom cleared of children), pp. 116–24 (State's opening argument), pp. 124–5 (Bruce's opening argument).
158 Testimony of arresting officers: Transcript of Proceedings to Supreme Court of Illinois from the Municipal Court of Chicago in *People v. Bruce* (Gen. No. 62 MC 66009: First District, Criminal Court Branch 46), February 19, 1963, pp. 127–66 (Officer Tyrrell's direct examination); February 20, 1963, pp. 245–71 (Officer Noro's direct examination).

Essential Attacks
159 Zaidins's cross-examinations: Transcript of Proceedings to Supreme Court of Illinois from the Municipal Court of Chicago in *People v. Bruce* (Gen. No. 62 MC 66009: First District, Criminal Court Branch 46), February 20, 1963, pp. 183–207, 212–39 (Officer Tyrrell's cross-examination), pp. 214–5, 218 (cross-examination on Eichmann bit), pp. 229, 231–5, 282–3 (cross-examination on prurient interest), pp. 185–9 (cross-examination on character of audience), pp. 197–9, 204 (cross-examination on public acceptance of nudity and vulgarity).

Foiled Again
164 Transcript of Proceedings to Supreme Court of Illinois from the Municipal Court of Chicago in *People v. Bruce* (Gen. No. 62 MC 66009: First District, Criminal Court Branch 46), February 20, pp. 152, 216–7 (Officer Tyrrell's direct and cross-examination on masturbatory gestures), pp. 218–20 (convoluted questioning style); February 21, 1963, pp. 285–8 (in-chambers hearing on tape), pp. 169–78 (*Playboy* employee), pp. 291–301 (motion for a directed verdict and supporting arguments), pp. 302 (motion to dismiss).

Double Jurisdictional Jeopardy
167 Description of Los Angeles trip: Interview with Earl Warren Zaidins, May 14, 1999.
167 February 23, 1963 drug bust: "Lenny Bruce Again Seized over Heroin," *Los Angeles Times,* February 24, 1963, sec. C, p. 7; "Lenny Bruce in New Jam," *Los Angeles Herald Examiner,* February 24, 1963, sec. B, p. 1; Lenny Bruce, *How to Talk Dirty and Influence People* (Chicago: Playboy Press, 1965), p. 148. Several of Lenny Bruce's

other drug busts are recounted in Albert Goldman and Lawrence Schiller, *Ladies and Gentlemen, Lenny Bruce!!* (New York: Random House, 1971), pp. 257–63 (Crescendo in Los Angeles, 1959); pp. 316–24 (Philadelphia, 1961); pp. 376–87 (Grand Prix Hobby Shop in North Hollywood, 1962); pp. 408–9 (Los Angeles cab, 1963); see also *E! True Hollywood Story: Lenny Bruce*, an E-TV documentary highlighting Bruce's narcotics involvement, aired on April 25, 1999; *People v. Bruce*, 64 Cal.2d 55, 409 P.2d 943 (1966).

167 Two-day recess granted: Transcript of Proceedings to Supreme Court of Illinois from the Municipal Court of Chicago in *People v. Bruce* (Gen. No. 62 MC 66009: First District, Criminal Court Branch 46), February 25, 1963, pp. 306–9.

168 Spot of ash: Lenny Bruce, *How to Talk Dirty and Influence People* (Chicago: Playboy Press, 1965), p. 147; Interview with Earl Warren Zaidins, May 14, 1999.

168 Trial proceedings on February 27: Transcript of Proceedings to Supreme Court of Illinois from the Municipal Court of Chicago in *People v. Bruce* (Gen. No. 62 MC 66009: First District, Criminal Court Branch 46), February 27, 1963, p. 311 (denial of motion for continuance), pp. 313–7 (denial of motion for directed verdict), p. 326 (denial of motion for continuance on vacating bail bond), pp. 328–9 (denial of motion for change of venue), pp. 318–22 (Judge Ryan's statements for the record), pp. 334–94 (playing of The Gate of Horn audiotape), p. 27 (order to forfeit bond and issue capias).

169 Trial proceedings on February 28: Transcript of Proceedings to Supreme Court of Illinois from the Municipal Court of Chicago in *People v. Bruce* (Gen. No. 62 MC 66009: First District, Criminal Court Branch 46), February 28, 1963, pp. 399–400 (denial of request to call Captain McDermott), pp. 401–9 (denial of motion to remove juror and declare mistrial), p. 400 (defense rests).

"We the Jury Find..."

170 State's closing argument: Transcript of Proceedings to Supreme Court of Illinois from the Municipal Court of Chicago in *People v. Bruce* (Gen. No. 62 MC 66009: First District, Criminal Court Branch 46), February 28, 1963, pp. 410–18 (closing argument), pp. 411–3 (stories of pope, priests, and nuns), pp. 414–5 ("F**k"), pp. 416–7 (tape recording as corroborative evidence for State), p. 418 (conclusion of Banks's summation).

172 Defense's closing argument: Transcript of Proceedings to Supreme Court of Illinois from the Municipal Court of Chicago in *People v. Bruce* (Gen. No. 62 MC 66009: First District, Criminal Court Branch 46), February 28, 1963, pp. 418–37 (closing argument), p. 419 (jury may not care for Bruce's words), pp. 423–4 (Voltaire's maxim), p. 424 (prejudicial attitudes of State's witnesses), pp. 433, 435–6 (consequences of guilty verdict).

173 Instructions and verdict: Transcript of Proceedings to Supreme Court of Illinois from the Municipal Court of Chicago in *People v. Bruce* (Gen. No. 62 MC 66009: First District, Criminal Court Branch 46), February 28, 1963, pp. 442–52 (Judge Ryan's instructions), pp. 452–4 (jury verdict), p. 455 (post-verdict motions).

173 Additional information about the last two days of the Chicago trial: Interview with Earl Warren Zaidins, May 14, 1999; "Fear Lenny Bruce's Chi Obscenity Rap May Cue Tighter Show Biz Censorship," *Variety*, March 20, 1963.

Love Letters

174 Bruce's telegrams to Judge Ryan: Transcript of Proceedings to Supreme Court of Illinois from the Municipal Court of Chicago in *People v. Bruce* (Gen. No. 62 MC 66009: First District, Criminal Court Branch 46), March 14, 1963, pp. 460–4.

174 Sentencing: Transcript of Proceedings to Supreme Court of Illinois from the Municipal Court of Chicago in *People v. Bruce* (Gen. No. 62 MC 66009: First

District, Criminal Court Branch 46), March 14, 1963, pp. 465–6 (Pontikes's motion for new trial denied), pp. 466–7 (sentence given and extradition ordered); Abstract of the Record presented to the Supreme Court of Illinois by Maurice Rosenfield, Harry Kalven Jr., and William R. Ming Jr., *People v. Bruce* (No. 37902, November 1963 Term), pp. 61–4; "Lenny Bruce Gets One Year, Fined $1,000," *Chicago Sun-Times,* March 15, 1963, p. 11.

175 "I think it's quite obscene": "Bruce Free in Frisco," *Variety,* March 20, 1963, p. 86.

The Great Trio

175 Harry Kalven's 1960 article: Harry Kalven Jr., "The Metaphysics of the Law of Obscenity," 1960 *Supreme Court Review* 1, p. 10; *Roth v. United States,* 354 U.S. 476, 487 (1957).

176 First Amendment bar to blasphemy prosecutions: *Burstyn v. Wilson,* 343 U.S 495, 497–506 (1952).

177 Influential law review article: Harry Kalven Jr. and Maurice Rosenfield, "The Contemporary Function of the Class Suit," *University of Chicago Law Review* 8 (1941), p. 684.

177 Rosenfield's representation of Hugh Hefner: See, e.g., *HMH Publishing Co. v. Garrett,* 151 F. Supp. 903 (N.D. Ind., 1957). In one such case, Rosenfield enlisted the help of Harry Kalven and Thurman Arnold.

177 *Brown v. Board of Education*: Richard Kluger, *Simple Justice* (New York: Knopf, 1976), p. 637.

177 Account of the appeal bond process: Interview with Maurice Rosenfield, May 18, 1999.

177 Extradition order: "Lenny Bruce Surrenders on Warrant," *Los Angeles Herald-Examiner,* March 26, 1963.

177 "Bruce told Judge Leader…": "Lenny Prefers L.A. Gas to 'Chi' Jails," *Citizen News,* March 26, 1963.

Appealing Arguments

179 Rosenfield-Kalven-Ming brief: Brief and Argument for Defendant Lenny Bruce, in *People v. Bruce* (Supreme Court of Illinois No. 37902, November Term, 1963), pp. 2–3, 16–20, 23–30, 36–7.

180 Vulgarity alone not obscene: *ACLU v. Chicago,* 3 Ill. 2d 334, 343 (1954), quoting with approval *Swearingen v. U.S.,* 161 U.S. 446 (1896).

180 The People's brief: Brief and Argument for the State of Illinois, in *People v. Bruce* (Supreme Court of Illinois No. 37902, November Term, 1963), pp. 14–5, 16, 17, 18, 19, 21. Assistant Attorney General Fred G. Leach and Assistant State's Attorneys Elmer C. Kissane, William J. Martin, and James R. Thompson were listed as counsel on the brief.

181 Thompson as author of People's brief: Interview with William J. Martin, July 15, 1999.

182 "With a brief like that": Western Union telegram from Lenny Bruce to Maurice Rosenfield, Nov. 18, 1963.

182 "With a client like you": Western Union telegram from Maurice Rosenfield to Lenny Bruce, Nov. 18, 1963.

182 Dismissal of Troubadour/Unicorn charges: Interviews with Ronald Ross, June 20 and July 24, 2001.

"There Were Adult Women Present"

183 Bruce's Jewish and goyish routine: John Cohen, editor, *The Essential Lenny Bruce* (New York: Ballantine Books, 1967), pp. 41–2.

183 Los Angeles police reports: Los Angeles Police Report, March 16, 1964 (signed by

Lt. Comer and Officers McGuire and Taragan); Los Angeles Police Report, March 7, 1964 (signed by Lt. Comer and Officer McGuire); Los Angeles Police Report, March 4, 1964 (signed by Lt. Comer and Officers Burks and McGuire).

185 Judge Clinco's background: "Jurist Mario Clinco; Twice Judge of the Year," Obituary, *Los Angeles Times,* May 17, 1986, sec. 3, p. 19.

186 Arrest warrant: Interview with Sydney Irmas, Albert Goldman Papers, Butler Library, Columbia University, New York, Box 6, File "Syd Irmas, Attorney."

186 Complaint, arrest, bail, and arraignment: Memo on Trolley Ho proceedings, Albert Goldman Papers, Butler Library, Columbia University, New York, Box 2, File 2.

187 March 19 10:00 P.M. performance: Letter of Lenny Bruce to the American Civil Liberties Union, dated March 23, 1964, Albert Goldman Papers, Butler Library, Columbia University, New York, Box 2, File 16.

187 Sydney Irmas's appearance and Bruce's discovery of him: Interview with Audrey M. Irmas, May 15, 2001. Interestingly, years after Bruce's death, Irmas's son, Robert, challenged Block in a primary election campaign. See Kenneth Reich, "Block Squares Off as Formidable Political Force," *Los Angeles Times*, April 30, 1994, sec. B, p. 3.

188 Release of narcotics addict: *In Re Duane J. Johnson*, 59 Cal. 2d 644, 381 P. 2d 643 (Cal. 1963).

6. WHAT DOES IT MEAN TO BE FOUND OBSCENE IN NEW YORK?

Epigraph: Lenny Bruce, *How to Talk Dirty and Influence People* (Chicago: Playboy Press, 1965).

The Man from Outer Taste

191 Lenny Bruce's appearance at The Den: Ralph J. Gleason, Liner Notes for *The Real Lenny Bruce* (Berkeley, CA: Fantasy Records, 1975), p. 4; Nat Hentoff, *Free Speech for Me—But Not for Thee* (New York: Aaron Asher Books/HarperCollins Publishers, 1992), p. 327; Eric Lax, *Woody Allen: A Biography* (New York: Knopf, 1991), p. 150. The reference to "Religions, Inc." can be found in, among other places, John Cohen, editor, *The Essential Lenny Bruce* (New York: Ballantine Books, 1967), p. 62; the reference to "Father Flotsky's Triumph" comes from *Lenny Bruce's Interviews of Our Times* (Berkeley, CA: Fantasy Records, No. 701, 1958).

192 A year later, it was an entirely different scene: Shortly after his New York debut in 1959, Bruce produced a television documentary on New York City, entitled *One Night Stand: The World of Lenny Bruce*. See David Everitt, "On the Trail of Television's Lost Treasures," *New York Times,* April 29, 2001, sec. 2, p. 27.

192 Lenny Bruce's appearance at The Blue Angel: Max Gordon, *Live at the Village Vanguard* (New York: St. Martin's Press, 1980), pp. 61–4; Earl Wilson, "It Happened Last Night: Sick…Sicker…Rich!," *New York Post,* March 11, 1960, p. 10; "Barrage vs. Lenny Bruce Reflects N.Y. Dailies' New-Found Tough Stance," *Variety,* March 23, 1960, p. 50; Albert Goldman and Lawrence Schiller, *Ladies and Gentlemen, Lenny Bruce!!* (New York: Random House, 1974), p. 276; Nat Hentoff, "Where Liberals Fear to Tread," *The Reporter,* June 23, 1960, vol. 22, pp. 50, 52. The reference to "How to Relax Your Colored Friends at Parties" is found in John Cohen, editor, *The Essential Lenny Bruce* (New York: Ballantine Books, 1967), p. 25. See also Robert Ruark, "Let's Nix the Sickniks," *Saturday Evening Post,* June 29, 1963 at p. 39; Earl Wilson, "It Happened Last Night: Sick…Sicker…Rich!," *New York Post,* March 11, 1960, p. 10.

192 Lenny Bruce's appearances at The Village Vanguard, Carnegie Hall, and The Village Theater: Max Gordon, *Live at the Village Vanguard* (New York: St. Martin's Press, 1980), pp. 8–9, 75–8; Joan Rivers, *Enter Talking* (New York: Delacorte Press, 1986), p. 307; Arthur Gelb, "Comic Gives Shocks with Moral: Lenny Bruce Heads Program at Basin Street East," *New York Times,* December 8, 1960, p. 44;

Lenny Bruce, *Carnegie Hall* (New York: United Artists L.P., 1972) (with liner notes by Albert Goldman); "Snow Coats City and Most of East; Cold Sets Record," *New York Times,* February 4, 1961, p. 1 (blizzard on night of Carnegie Hall Concert); "An Evening with Lenny Bruce," *New York Times,* November 24, 1963, sec. X, p. 6 (advertisement); Albert Goldman and Lawrence Schiller, *Ladies and Gentlemen, Lenny Bruce!!* (New York: Random House, 1974), pp. 297–301, 438–41; Interview with Don Friedman, March 9, 2002 (Village Theater); Ronald Sukenick, *Down and In: Life in the Underground* (New York: Beech Tree Books/William Morrow, 1987), pp. 82–3.

194 166 obscenity arrests: Richard Kuh, "Obscenity: Prosecution Problems and Legislative Suggestions," *The Catholic Lawyer* 10 (Winter 1964), pp. 285, 286.

194 "Necessary, appropriate, and legal means": Larry Klein, "Cardinal and the Court in a Pornography Fight," *New York Herald Tribune,* June 14, 1964, p. 24.

Mr. First Amendment

195 Background information on Ephraim London: Glenn Fowler, "Ephraim London, 78, a Lawyer Who Fought Censorship, Is Dead," Obituary, *New York Times,* June 14, 1990, sec. B, p. 13; "Ephraim London: Lawyer Specialized in Censorship Cases," *Los Angeles Times,* June 15, 1990, sec. A, p. 26; Martin Garbus, *Tough Talk: How I Fought for Writers, Comics, Bigots, and the American Way* (New York: Times Books, 1998), p. 29.

195 Other obscenity cases: *Burstyn v. Wilson,* 343 U.S. 495 (1952) (*The Miracle*); *Kingsley International Pictures Co. v. Regents of University of State of New York,* 360 U.S. 684 (1959) (*Lady Chatterley's Lover*); Leon Friedman, editor, *Obscenity: The Complete Oral Arguments before the Supreme Court in the Major Obscenity Cases* (New York: Chelsea House Publishers, 1970), pp. 66–88. The oral arguments of the second Supreme Court hearing in *Jacobellis v. Ohio,* 378 U.S. 184 (1964) are reproduced in Leon Friedman, editor, *Obscenity: The Complete Oral Arguments before the Supreme Court in the Major Obscenity Cases* (New York: Chelsea House Publishers, 1970), pp. 143, 148–51, 155; see also Anthony Lewis, "'Obscenity' Rule Argued in Court: Local Standard Challenged in Case of French Film," *New York Times,* March 27, 1963, p. 5 (report on the first Supreme Court hearing in the *Jacobellis* case).

197 "Longest, costliest, most bitterly contested and widely publicized [obscenity] trial": Albert Goldman and Lawrence Schiller, *Ladies and Gentlemen, Lenny Bruce!!* (New York: Random House, 1974), p. 463.

Going to Au Go Go

197 Café Au Go Go performances: Max Gordon, *Live at the Village Vanguard* (New York: St. Martin's Press, 1980), p. 78; Interview with Howard Solomon, July 25, 2001 (Café Au Go Go appearance); Trial Transcript, *People v. Bruce, et al.* (New York City Criminal Court; Part 2B: County of New York), April 14, 1964, p. 49; Albert Goldman and Lawrence Schiller, *Ladies and Gentlemen, Lenny Bruce!!* (New York: Random House, 1974), p. 445; *People v. Bruce* (Criminal Court of the City of New York, Nov. 4, 1964) (unpublished opinion); Transcript of Café Au Go Go performance of April 1, 1964, 10:00 P.M., Albert Goldman Papers, Butler Library, Columbia University, New York, Box 3, File "Café Au Go Go," pp. 21–2 ("Hauling Ass to Save Your Ass"), pp. 22–3 ("The Hot Lead Enema"), pp. 25–6 ("Guys are Carnal"); Transcript of Café Au Go Go performance of April 7, 1964, 10:00 P.M., Albert Goldman Papers, Butler Library, Columbia University, New York, Box 3, File "Café Au Go Go," pp. 13–4 ("Hauling Ass to Save Your Ass"), p. 14 ("The Hot Lead Enema"), pp. 26–7 ("Eleanor Roosevelt's Tits").

198 "Eleanor Roosevelt's Tits"... "Hot Lead Enema": Variations of these four bits can be found on *The Lenny Bruce Performance Film* (Santa Monica, CA: Rhino Home

Video, 1992), produced by John Magnuson. Some of these routines are commercially available only in the Rhino video-CD set.

The Sting

200 Purpose of D.A.'s office: Richard H. Kuh, *Foolish Figleaves? Pornography in—and out of—Court* (New York: Macmillan, 1967), p. 208.

200 Herbert Ruhe: Trial Transcript, *People v. Bruce, et al.* (New York City Criminal Court; Part 2B: County of New York), June 17, 1964, pp. 148–50, 165–9, 192, 207–10; Stephanie Gervis Harrington, "Supreme Court Decision May Affect Obscenity Rap," *Village Voice*, June 25, 1964, p. 13.

201 Frank S. Hogan: Barry Cunningham with Mike Pearl, *Mr. District Attorney: The Story of Frank S. Hogan and the Manhattan D.A.'s Office* (New York: Mason/Charter, 1977), pp. 240–4.

201 *Memoirs of Hecate County:* Edward de Grazia, *Girls Lean Back Everywhere: The Law of Obscenity and the Assault on Genius* (New York: Random House, 1992), pp. 220–2, 224, 227, 234, 236, 238.

201 Vice squad's attendance at performances: Trial Transcript, *People v. Bruce, et al.* (New York City Criminal Court; Part 2B: County of New York), June 17, 1964, pp. 132–40.

201 Transcribing audiotape: Trial Transcript, *People v. Bruce, et al.* (New York City Criminal Court; Part 2B: County of New York), June 30, 1964, pp. 2–8.

201 Grand jury hearing: People-Appellant's Brief in *People v. Solomon* (NY Ct. App., 1969), pp. 6–8; People's Exhibit 5E (transcription); §1140-A of the New York Penal Law; Trial Transcript, *People v. Bruce, et al.* (New York City Criminal Court; Part 2B: County of New York), June 16, 1964, pp. 64–72.

202 Solomon's interactions with Officers O'Neil and McCambridge: Interviews with Howard Solomon, August 24, 1999, and July 25, 2001.

203 "To my mild surprise": Gerald Harris, "My Brief on Lenny Bruce," *New York Times*, September 19, 1990, sec. A, p. 29.

203 April 3 bust: "Lenny Bruce Seized on Obscenity in Act," *New York Times*, April 4, 1964, p. 12; Nat Hentoff, "Burt Lancaster, Abraham Lincoln, and Lenny Bruce," *New York Herald-Tribune*, December 20, 1964; "Lenny Bruce, in Village, is Jailed for Obscenities," *New York Herald-Tribune*, April 4, 1964, p. 3; "Lenny Bruce Pulled In; Too Salty in His Cellar," *New York Daily News*, April 4, 1964, p. 7; "Bruce Tagged on Obscenity, Run Extended at Café Here," *Village Voice*, April 9, 1964, p. 3.

203 Posting bail: Interview with Bentley Kassal, March 18, 1999; "Lenny Bruce Freed on Bail in Charge of Indecency," *New York Times*, April 5, 1964, p. 48;

203 "And the thing I wish they would do": Lenny Bruce, from *Lenny Bruce: Swear to Tell the Truth* (Los Angeles: Whyaduck Productions, 1998), written and produced by Robert Weide, aired on HBO, August 1999.

204 Judge Vincent Rao: Bruce Lambert, "Vincent Rao, Judge in Criminal Cases, is Dead at Age 79," Obituary, *New York Times*, May 6, 1993, sec. D, p. 23.

More Heat

204 Lawyer conference and Solomon's departure: Interview with Maurice and Lois Rosenfield, December 20, 1999; Interviews with Maurice Rosenfield, May 12 and 18, 1999; Trial Transcript, *People v. Bruce, et al.* (New York City Criminal Court; Part 2B: County of New York), December 21, 1964, p. 45.

205 "Do you tell an artist…": Interview with Ella Solomon (now J.E. Stewart), June 18, 1999.

205 April 7 performance: "DA Presses Bruce Case, As Fair Opening Nears," *Village Voice*, April 16, 1964, p. 2; John Cohen, editor, *The Essential Lenny Bruce* (New York: Ballantine Books, 1967), p. 269.

494 | *Notes*

205 Arrest, booking, and bail: Trial Transcript, *People v. Bruce, et al.* (New York City Criminal Court; Part 2B: County of New York), April 15, 1964, pp. 27–8, 38–9, 46–7, 54; Allen G. Schwartz, "Lenny at the Bar," *Village Voice,* August 11, 1966, p. 23 (date mistakenly reported as March 31, 1964; correct date is April 7, 1964, 10:00 P.M. performance); Letter from Howard M. Squadron to Maurice Rosenfield, November 13, 1965; "Bruce Tagged on Obscenity, Run Extended at Café Here," *Village Voice,* April 9, 1964, pp. 3, 6.

205 Allen Ginsberg's reaction: Michael Schumacher, *Dharma Lion: A Critical Biography of Allen Ginsberg* (New York: St. Martin's Press, 1992), p. 409.

206 New York Coffee House Law: Stephanie Harrington, "City Puts Bomb Under Off-Beat Culture Scene," *Village Voice,* March 26, 1964.

206 "Brigades of absolutists": Richard H. Kuh, *Foolish Figleaves? Pornography in—and out of—Court* (New York: Macmillan, 1967), p. 176.

206 "The problem of people helping you": Lenny Bruce, quoted in Jerry Tallmer, "Lenny Bruce: No Help Wanted," *New York Post,* April 7, 1964, p. 6.

"Get Me Somebody Who Swings with the First Amendment"

207 Lawyer recommendations: Albert Goldman, *Freakshow: The Rocksoulbluesjazzsickjewblackhumorsexpoppsych Gig and Other Scenes from the Counter Culture* (New York: Atheneum, 1971), p. 215; Stephanie Gervis Harrington, "He Will Run Out of Fare to the Supreme Court," *Village Voice,* April 9, 1964, p. 6; Albert Goldman and Lawrence Schiller, *Ladies and Gentlemen, Lenny Bruce!!* (New York: Random House, 1974), p. 454.

207 Morris Ernst: Interview with Maurice Rosenfield, June 8, 1999; Diana Souhami, *The Trials of Radclyffe Hall* (New York: Doubleday, 1999), pp. xviii, 243, 245–9; Morris L. Ernst and Alan U. Schwartz, *Censorship: The Search for the Obscene* (New York: MacMillan, 1964).

207 London recommendation: Nat Hentoff, *Free Speech for Me—But Not for Thee* (New York: Aaron Asher Books/HarperCollins, 1992), p. 330; Martin Garbus with Stanley Cohen, *Tough Talk: How I Fought for Writers, Comics, Bigots, and the American Way* (New York: Times Books, 1998), p. 29.

207 Lead counsel of record: Trial Transcript, *People v. Bruce, et al.* (New York City Criminal Court; Part 2B: County of New York), April 15, 1964, p. 94;

208 London vs. Bruce: Martin Garbus with Stanley Cohen, *Tough Talk: How I Fought for Writers, Comics, Bigots, and the American Way* (New York: Times Books, 1998), pp. 28–9.

208 Harris on Bruce: Gerald Harris, quoted in *Mysteries and Scandals: Lenny Bruce* (Cable TV/Entertainment TV-Los Angeles; December 28, 1998), produced by Daniel L. Abrams and narrated by A.J. Benza; Gerald Harris, "My Brief on Lenny Bruce," *New York Times,* Sept. 19, 1990, sec. A, p. 29.

209 Hogan's view of Kuh: Barry Cunningham with Mike Pearl, *Mr. District Attorney: The Story of Frank S. Hogan and the Manhattan D.A.'s Office* (New York: Mason/Charter, 1977), p. 241. As best we know, Kuh's unsigned student article was titled "The Freedom Writ: The Expanding Use of Federal Habeas Corpus," 61 *Harvard L. Rev.* 657 (1948).

209 "Gloried in combat": Nat Hentoff, "Burt Lancaster, Abraham Lincoln and Lenny Bruce," *New York Herald Tribune,* December 20, 1964; *This Week* magazine, pp. 9, 16.

209 "[Harris] misconstrued his obligation…": Richard Kuh, as quoted in the unaired video interview conducted by Robert Weide in preparation for *Lenny Bruce: Swear to Tell the Truth* (Los Angeles: Whyaduck Productions, 1998), written and produced by Robert Weide and aired on HBO, August 1999.

Make-It-or-Break-It Proceedings

210 Exchange over substitution of counsel and continuance: Trial Transcript, *People v. Bruce, et al.* (New York City Criminal Court; Part 2B: County of New York), April 13, 1964, pp. 1–33.

212 Exchange over the subpoena of tapes: Trial Transcript, *People v. Bruce, et al.* (New York City Criminal Court; Part 2B: County of New York), April 13, 1964, pp. 33–51; April 14 (morning), pp. 3–51(a); April 14 (afternoon), pp. 2–169; Stephanie Gervis Harrington, "DA Presses Bruce Case, as Fair Opening Nears," *Village Voice,* April 16, 1964, p. 2.

212 Fifth Amendment claims: Trial Transcript, *People v. Bruce, et al.* (New York City Criminal Court; Part 2B: County of New York), April 14, 1964, pp. 7, 20; April 28, 1964, p. 26.

213 Solomon's right to plead the Fifth: Trial Transcript, *People v. Bruce, et al.* (New York City Criminal Court; Part 2B: County of New York), April 14, 1964, p. 12.

213 Kuh's reactions: Trial Transcript, *People v. Bruce, et al.* (New York City Criminal Court; Part 2B: County of New York), April 14, 1964, pp. 47, 52, 77; April 28, 1964, p. 27. See also Richard H. Kuh, *Foolish Figleaves? Pornography in—and out of—Court* (New York: Macmillan, 1967), pp. 208–9.

214 April 15 preliminary hearing: Stephanie Gervis Harrington, "DA Presses Bruce Case, as Fair Opening Nears," *Village Voice,* April 16, 1964, p. 2; Paul Hoffman, "Lenny Bruce: An Off-Stage Voice in Court," *New York Post,* April 15, 1964, p. 19; Trial Transcript, *People v. Bruce, et al.* (New York City Criminal Court; Part 2B: County of New York), April 15, 1964, pp. 6, 7, 13–6, 81, 84–97, 106, 111, 114 (preliminary hearing); *People v. Wendling,* 258 N.Y 451 (1932).

215 Schwartz's claim that Ella Solomon could not be prosecuted: Strictly speaking, the preliminary hearing only involved the April 7 arrest of Ella Solomon and Lenny Bruce, which resulted from a criminal complaint. Criminal complaints, unlike grand jury informations, trigger a right to a preliminary hearing. By contrast, informations (such as those filed against Bruce and Howard Solomon for the April 1 performance) could be dismissed only at the commencement of the trial.

218 "The expression of the public judgment": "Bruce's Lawyers Want Jury Trial," *Village Voice,* April 23, 1964, p. 2. Ephraim London's point ultimately prevailed—though not in *People v. Bruce.* Years later, William Hellerstein (one of Howard Solomon's lawyers) successfully argued the same right to jury claim in another case, *Baldwin v. New York,* 399 U.S. 66 (1970) and the U.S. Supreme Court struck down Section 40 of the New York City Criminal Court Act.

219 Eichmann trial: John Cohen, editor, *The Essential Lenny Bruce* (New York: Ballantine Books, 1967), p. 35.

The Sick Comedian

219 Pleurisy: Albert Goldman and Lawrence Schiller, *Ladies and Gentlemen, Lenny Bruce!!* (New York: Random House, 1974), pp. 457–8.

219 Rib removal: "Bruce Trial Adjourned," *New York Times,* June 19, 1964, p. 36.

220 The filmed interview never aired: Portions of the unaired Steve Allen interview with Lenny Bruce appear in *Two Five-Letter Words: Lenny Bruce,* a 1999 documentary that was featured at the Museum of Television and Radio with screenings in Los Angeles and New York.

220 Official reason for canceling Allen interview with Bruce: United Press International, "Truman to Appear with Steve Allen," Albert Goldman Papers, Butler Library, Columbia University, New York, Box 1, File "Steve Allen."

220 Lenny's refusal to have interview edited: Letter from Chet Collier to Lenny Bruce, dated March 13, 1964, Albert Goldman Papers, Butler Library, Columbia University, New York, Box 1, File "Steve Allen."

220 Advertisement for *Lenny Bruce Is Out Again*: "Rallying to Defense of Lenny

Bruce," *New York Herald Tribune,* June 14, 1964, p. 37.

220 *Lenny Bruce Is Out Again*: The front cover of this underground album pictured Bruce sitting outside next to a white marble statue placed in a toilet bowl, holding an open newspaper, and glancing over his shoulder into the eye of the camera. The back cover reproduced a January 13, 1963, letter from the Reverend Sidney Lanier to Bruce, expressing emphatic approval of his comedy; the back cover also included a lineup of many of Lenny's lawyers. See generally William Karl Thomas, *Lenny Bruce: The Making of a Prophet* (Hamden, CT: Archon Books, 1989). The album (LB-3001-02) contained ten bits on Side 1 and four bits on Side 2. Apparently, none of these routines was the subject of an obscenity prosecution. Sometime afterwards, Phil Spector's Philles Records released its own version of *Lenny Bruce Is Out Again* (PHLP-4010).

221 Cochran's involvement in case: Johnnie L. Cochran Jr., with Tim Rutten, *Journey to Justice* (New York: Ballantine Books, 1996), p. 4 (Louisiana birth), p. 67 ("[F]ate and the First Amendment"), pp. 67–9 (Trolley Ho hearing, with verified corrections by authors).

221 Trolley Ho motions and constitutional hearing: Interview with Sydney Irmas, Albert Goldman Papers, Butler Library, Columbia University, New York, Box 6, File "Syd Irmas, Attorney"; Memorandum on the Trolley Ho proceedings, Albert Goldman Papers, Butler Library, Columbia University, New York, Box 2, File 2.

221 Irmas and Cochran's relationship: Interview with Audrey Irmas, May 15, 2001.

221 *Zeitlen v. Arnebergh,* 59 Cal. 2d 901, 383 P.2d 152 (1963).

221 Congratulations on Trolley Ho victory: Undated letter of Lenny Bruce to Sydney Irmas, Albert Goldman Papers, Butler Library, Columbia University, New York, Box 6, File "Syd Irmas, Attorney."

Poetic License

222 Actions of Committee on Poetry: Allen Ginsberg, *Deliberate Prose: Selected Essays, 1952–1995*, edited by Bill Morgan (New York: Perennial/HarperCollins, 2000), p. 190 (statement), pp. 187–9 (preparation of press release and petition), pp. 184–6 (press release). There are conflicting accounts concerning the authorship of the press release and petition: Contrast Michael Schumacher, *Dharma Lion: A Critical Biography of Allen Ginsberg* (New York: St. Martin's Press, 1992), p. 410 (crediting Ginsberg) and Allen Ginsberg, *Deliberate Prose: Selected Essays, 1952–1995*, edited by Bill Morgan (New York: Perennial/HarperCollins, 2000), pp. 186–90 (noting assistance but suggesting primary authorship by Ginsberg) with Albert Goldman and Lawrence Schiller, *Ladies and Gentlemen, Lenny Bruce!!* (New York: Random House, 1974), p. 459 (crediting Helen Weaver, a freelance translator and member of Ginsberg's Emergency Committee).

223 Text of petition and Kerouac's refusal to sign: Michael Schumacher, *Dharma Lion: A Critical Biography of Allen Ginsberg* (New York: St. Martin's Press, 1992), pp. 410–1.

223 "Manifesto": Richard H. Kuh, *Foolish Figleaves? Pornography in—and out of— Court* (New York: Macmillan, 1967), p. 177.

224 Press coverage of petition: "100 Fight Arrest of Lenny Bruce," *New York Times,* June 14, 1964, p. 75; "Rallying to Defense of Lenny Bruce," *New York Herald Tribune,* June 14, 1964, p. 37; Jerry Tallmer, "Burtons Join Plea for Lenny Bruce," *New York Post,* June 14, 1964, p. 20.

224 Bruce's attitude toward petition: Dick Schaap, "The Last Show," *Playboy Magazine,* January, 1967, p. 162.

7. THE COURTROOM OF THE ABSURD: NEW YORK, PART II

Epigraph: Stephanie Gervis Harrington, "How Many Four-Letter Words Can a Prosecutor Use?" *Village Voice,* July 16, 1964, p. 3.

Standing Room Only

227 "Moloch! Moloch!": Allen Ginsberg, *Howl*, edited by Barry Miles (HarperPerennial, 1995), p. 6.

228 Opening day of trial: Marvin Smilon, "Bruce in Court: In Person, In Tape," *New York Post,* June 17, 1964, p. 4; "Bruce's Trial," *Newsweek,* July 20, 1964; Trial Transcript, *People v. Bruce, et al.* (New York City Criminal Court; Part 2B: County of New York), June 30, 1964, pp. 12–3 ("Mr. Crotch"); July 9, 1964, pp. 10–3, 17, 47 ("shit," bicycle with "literary merit")..

229 John Martin Murtagh: Tom Goldstein, "Murtagh's Forty-Year Public Life Was Marked by Stormy Cases," *New York Times,* January 14, 1976, p. 14; John M. Murtagh and Sara Harris, *Cast the First Stone* (New York: McGraw-Hill, 1975), pp. 299, 300 (quoting with approval from a report by the Committee of the Home Office in London).

230 James Randall Creel: Sid Cassese, "J. Randall Creel, 85, Criminal Court Judge," Obituary, *Newday,* July 24, 1990, p. 27; "James Randall Creel, Judge, 85," Obituary, *New York Times,* July 24, 1990, sec. B, p. 6.

230 Kenneth M. Phipps: "Kenneth Phipps, Judge Since 1958," *New York Times,* February 6, 1968, p. 43.

231 Phipps monitoring his behavior: Martin Garbus, *Ready for the Defense* (New York: Farrar, Straus, and Giroux, 1971), p. 121.

231 Phipp's "confession": Edward de Grazia, *Girls Lean Back Everywhere: The Law of Obscenity and the Assault on Genius* (New York: Random House, 1992), p. 479.

231 Jewish judge: Lenny Bruce, quoted in Allen G. Schwartz, "Lenny at the Bar," *Village Voice,* August 11, 1966, p. 23.

Burt Lancaster for the Prosecution

231 Describing Kuh: Stephanie Gervis Harrington, "How Many Four-Letter Words Can a Prosecutor Use?" *Village Voice,* July 16, 1964, p. 3; Nat Hentoff, "Burt Lancaster, Abraham Lincoln and Lenny Bruce," *New York Herald Tribune,* December 20, 1964, pp. 1, 16.

232 Trial proceedings: Trial Transcript, *People v. Bruce, et al.* (New York City Criminal Court; Part 2B: County of New York), April 28, 1964, p. 31 (trial lasting a day); June 16, 1964, pp. 64–6, 77 (O'Neil's testimony), pp. 84–5, 100 (Hahne's testimony); June 17, pp. 149–50, 192–204, 207 10 (Ruhe's re-creation of various parts of Bruce's act), 168–9 (vulgar words), 173–5 ("philosophical claptrap"), 246–7 ("true and full report"), 280–2 ("substance and bulk"), 293–4 (motion to strike); June 30, 1964, pp. 9 23 (demurrer and motion to dismiss); July 2, 1964, pp. 52–3 (articles by artistic and social critics); July 28, 1964, pp. 50–1 (requesting early date for submission of briefs); Marvin Smilon, "Bruce in Court: In Person, On Tape," *New York Post,* June 17, 1964, p. 4; Thomas Buckley, "Lenny Bruce and Two Café Owners Go on Trial in Obscenity Case," *New York Times,* June 17, 1964, p. 46.

233 Bruce's reaction to Ruhe's testimony about bits: Nat Hentoff, *Free Speech for Me— But Not for Thee* (New York: HarperCollins, 1992), p. 329.

234 Obscene conduct: Trial Transcript, *People v. Bruce, et al.* (New York City Criminal Court; Part 2B: County of New York), June 17, 1964, pp. 193, 274–5.

234 Bruce's reactions to Ruhe testimony on conduct: Martin Garbus with Stanley Cohen, *Tough Talk: How I Fought for Writers, Comics, Bigots, and the American Way* (New York: Times Books, 1998), p. 34.

235 Hogan livid: Martin Garbus, *Ready for the Defense* (New York: Farrar, Straus, and Giroux, 1971), pp. 111–2.

Where Do We Go from Here?

235 Adjournment: "Bruce Trial Adjourned," *New York Times,* June 19, 1964, p. 36; Stephanie Gervis Harrington, "Supreme Court Decision May Affect Obscenity

Rap," *Village Voice*, June 25, 1964, p. 13.

235 Illinois Supreme Court decision: *People v. Bruce* (Illinois Supreme Court Case Docket No. 37902; June 18, 1964), subsequently withdrawn in *People v. Bruce*, 31 Ill. 2d 459 (November 24, 1964); Robert Howard, "Court Rules Novel, Bruce Show Obscene," *Chicago Tribune*, June 19, 1964, sec. 1-A, p. 5; Stephanie Gervis Harrington, "Supreme Court Decision May Affect Obscenity Rap," *Village Voice*, June 25, 1964, p. 13.

237 Supreme Court rules *The Lovers* not obscene: *Jacobellis v. Ohio*, 378 U.S. 184 (1964). More than any other reason, *Jacobellis* reached pop-cult status because of Justice Potter Stewart's adage about "hardcore" pornography: "I know it when I see it."

238 Speculation about *Jacobellis*: Stephanie Gervis Harrington, "Supreme Court Decision May Affect Obscenity Rap," *Village Voice*, June 25, 1964, p. 13.

239 Kuh's opinion about *Jacobellis:* Richard H. Kuh, *Foolish Figleaves? Pornography in—and out of—Court* (New York: MacMillan Co., 1967), pp. 60-1, 70-2.

Religions, Inc.
239 Reaction to *Jacobellis*: "Nine Clergymen Score High Court," *New York Times*, September 1, 1964, p. 37.

240 McCaffrey sermon: George Dugan, "Priest Denounces Smut in Times Square," *New York Times*, May 6, 1963, p. 32.

240 Four-pronged program: McCandlish Phillips, "City Opens Drive on Pornography," *New York Times*, October 29, 1963, p. 1.

241 Kathleen Keegan and *Fanny Hill* conviction: "Two Guilty in Sale of 'Fanny Hill,'" *New York Times*, November 15, 1963, p. 24.

241 Father Hill's fast: George Dugan, "Jesuit Begins Fast to Protest Pornography Sales to Children," *New York Times*, October 28, 1963, p. 24.

241 Reactions to Father Hill's fast: McCandlish Phillips, "City Opens Drive on Pornography," *New York Times*, October 29, 1963, p. 1.

242 Antismut conference and tour of bookstores: Philip Benjamin, "City Calls Parley on Sale of Smut," *New York Times*, October 30, 1963, p. 28.

242 Ralph Ginzburg: McCandlish Phillips, "City Opens Drive on Pornography," *New York Times*, October 29, 1963, p. 1.

242 Ralph Ginzburg's conviction for distributing obscene materials: *Liaison* and *Eros*, mailed from Middlesex, N.J., hit America's newsstands in 1962. In a newsletter format, *Liaison* contained articles on such subjects as "Slaying the Sex Dragon," "Semen in the Diet," and "Sing a Song of Sex Life," as well as sex-related jokes and rhymes. *Eros* was a more up-scale publication: a glossy, hardcover magazine, featuring some serious pieces, reproductions of recognized works of art, and photographs (e.g., the last studio portraits of Marilyn Monroe were included in Issue No. 3). Among its racier articles were "'My Life and Loves' by Frank Harris," "Bawdy Limericks," and "Black and White in Color." On March 15, 1963, a Philadelphia grand jury indicted Ginzburg on twenty-eight counts of mailing obscene publications and advertisements in violation of federal law. In a bench trial, Ginzburg was found guilty on all counts. See *U.S. v. Ginzburg*, 224 F. Supp. 129 (E.D. Pa., 1963). The case wound its way up to the U.S. Supreme Court, where Ginzburg's conviction and five-year prison sentence were upheld on March 21, 1966, by a narrow majority of five justices. Authoring the Court's opinion, Justice Brennan reasoned that, even if the publications were not obscene in the abstract, the sordid and brazen manners in which Ginzburg "pandered" his materials in the commercial marketplace were sufficient to support his conviction. "[T]he leer of the sensualist" that permeated Ginzburg's advertising, Brennan concluded, "stimulated the reader to accept them as prurient." *Ginzburg v. U.S.*, 383 U.S. 463, 470-1 (1966).

242 Justice Gassman: "Scholarly Judge," *New York Times*, November 15, 1963, p. 24.

243 Dr. Riley's comments: "Head of Anti-Smut Group Castigates 'Leftist' Foes," *New York Times*, March 16, 1964, p. 63.

243 Cardinal Spellman and Mayor Wagner: "Spellman Seeks Anti-Smut Group," *New York Times*, June 11, 1964, p. 18; "Spellman Assails Court Rulings on Pornography," *New York Times*, August 7, 1964, p. 31; Charles G. Bennett, "New Smut Drive Planned by City," *New York Times*, August 7, 1964, p. 31.

243 Cardinal Spellman speaking at a Denver convention: In the same address, Spellman also echoed Operation Yorksville's cries against the Supreme Court's obscenity rulings in *Jacobellis* and *Tropic of Cancer*. He charged that the decisions reflected an "acceptance of degeneracy and the beatnik mentality as the standard way of American life." Professing to respect constitutional freedoms as much as any man, the cardinal opined, "freedom of the press was never intended to afford protection to the shameless, profiteering, degraded merchants of filth."

244 Kuh testimony regarding need for new obscenity law: "New Law to Curb Smut Sales Urged," *New York Times*, September 22, 1964, p. 41.

244 Spellman's influence: Martin Garbus with Stanley Cohen, *Tough Talk: How I Fought for Writers, Comics, Bigots, and the American Way* (New York: Times Books, 1998); Richard Kuh, quoted in unaired outtake interview with Robert Weide for *Lenny Bruce: Swear to Tell the Truth* (Los Angeles: Whyaduck Productions, 1998), written and produced by Robert Weide.

Curtain Call at the Cork 'n Bib
245 Earnings: Nat Hentoff, "Burt Lancaster, Abraham Lincoln and Lenny Bruce," *New York Herald Tribune*, December 20, 1964, pp. 1, 16.

245 Cork 'n Bib contract: Telegram from Don Friedman to Lenny Bruce, June 8, 1964.

246 Levy question: "Law-Abiding Lenny Doesn't Go to Jail," *Buffalo Evening News*, June 28, 1964.

246 Nassau D.A.: Jerry Tallmer, "Lenny Bruce Tapes Used by Nassau DA," *New York Post*, June 30, 1964.

246 "Rotten experience," George Crater, and *Evergreen Review*: Myron S. Waldman, "Comic Left Reeling After Tale of the Tape," *Newsday*, June 28, 1964.

246 Sharing of evidence with Nassau County D.A.: Trial Transcript, *People v. Bruce, et al.* (New York City Criminal Court; Part 2B: County of New York), December 21, 1964, p. 35.

247 Bruce's lament: Martin Garbus, *Ready for the Defense* (New York: Farrar, Straus, and Giroux, 1971), p. 123.

An Anthro-Lingual-Philo-Jurisprudential Scene
247 London's statutory and factial unconstitutionality rationales: Trial Transcript, *People v. Bruce, et al.* (New York City Criminal Court; Part 2B: County of New York), June 30, 1964, pp. 2–6, 17–22.

247 Kuh's counterarguments: Trial Transcript, *People v. Bruce, et al.* (New York City Criminal Court; Part 2B: County of New York), June 30, 1964, pp. 17–22.

248 London's social-taboo rationale: Trial Transcript, *People v. Bruce, et al.* (New York City Criminal Court; Part 2B: County of New York), June 30, 1964, pp. 9–15; Leonard Harris, "Is It Obscenity or Is It Art?" *New York World-Telegram and Sun*, July 29, 1964, p. 16.

249 Argument and counterargument to dismiss charges against Solomons: Trial Transcript, *People v. Bruce, et al.* (New York City Criminal Court; Part 2B: County of New York), June 30, 1964, pp. 13–6, 24–8.

250 Ruling on motions: Trial Transcript, *People v. Bruce, et al.* (New York City Criminal Court; Part 2B: County of New York), June 30, 1964, pp. 36–8.

251 London's confidence in appeal: "Bruce's Trial," *Newsweek*, July 20, 1964.

251 "If we can win in an upper court": Lenny Bruce, quoted in Nat Hentoff, "Burt

Lancaster, Abraham Lincoln and Lenny Bruce," *New York Herald Tribune,* December 20, 1964, pp. 1, 16.

Esteemed Enthusiasts
251 Mort Sahl: Café Au Go Go advertisement for Mort Sahl, *Village Voice,* June 18, 1964, p. 14; Jerry Tallmer, "Across the Footlights: Mort Sahl and Roger Bannister," *New York Post,* June 21, 1964, p. 20.
251 Sahl refuses to be a witness for the defense: Martin Garbus with Stanley Cohen, *Tough Talk: How I Fought for Writers, Comics, Bigots, and the American Way* (New York, Times Books, 1998), p. 37. When asked "Have you ever worked with Marty Garbus?" Saul is reported to have answered, "No, I never did meet him, but I was a good friend of Lenny's." (AOL Interview with Mort Sahl, www.geocities.com/TelevisionCity/3217/aol.html, 1996).
252 London: Stephanie Gervis Harrington, "How Many Four-Letter Words Can a Prosecutor Use?" *Village Voice,* July 16, 1964, p. 3; Nat Hentoff, "Burt Lancaster, Abraham Lincoln and Lenny Bruce," *New York Herald Tribune,* December 20, 1964, pp. 1, 16.
252 Trial proceedings: Trial Transcript, *People v. Bruce, et al.* (New York City Criminal Court; Part 2B: County of New York), June 30, 1964, pp. 50–1, 58 (Gilman); July 1, 1964, pp. 21, 24, 26 (Kilgallen); July 2, 1964, p. 42 (Hentoff); July 3, 1964, pp. 67–9 (Morrison); July 6, 1964, p. 11 (Johnson); July 3, 1964, pp. 44–6 (Hentoff); Allen G. Schwartz, "Lenny at the Bar," *Village Voice,* August 11, 1966, pp. 23, 26 (Gans); Trial Transcript, *People v. Bruce, et al.* (New York City Criminal Court; Part 2B: County of New York), July 9, 1964, pp. 124–6 (Gans), pp. 33–4 (Epstein).
255 Bruce weeping during Kilgallen's testimony: Allen G. Schwartz, "Lenny at the Bar," *Village Voice,* August 11, 1966, p. 23, 26; Lee Israel, *Kilgallen* (New York: Delacorte Press, 1979), p. 382.
255 Description of Bruce's hotel room: Allen G. Schwartz, "Lenny at the Bar," *Village Voice,* August 11, 1966, p. 23, 26; Nat Hentoff, "Burt Lancaster, Abraham Lincoln and Lenny Bruce," *New York Herald Tribune,* December 20, 1964, pp. 1, 18; Martin Garbus, *Ready for the Defense* (New York: Farrar, Strauss, Giroux), pp. 106–7.

Attacking the Person and Performance
255 Kuh unimpressed with defense experts: Richard H. Kuh, *Foolish Figleaves? Pornography in—and out of—Court* (New York: MacMillan, 1967), p. 204.
256 "They took positions that were absurd": Richard Kuh, from an unaired outtake interview with Robert Weide for *Lenny Bruce: Swear to Tell the Truth* (Los Angeles: Whyaduck Productions, 1998) written and produced by Robert Weide.
256 Kuh's cross-examinations: Trial Transcript, *People v. Bruce, et al.* (New York City Criminal Court; Part 2B: County of New York), July 3, 1964, pp. 53–63 (Morrison's qualifications); July 9, 1964, pp. 116–8 (Gans's qualifications); July 3, 1964, pp. 107–113 (Dodson's qualifications).
256 Justice Murtagh sympathetic to Kuh's strategy: Trial Transcript, *People v. Bruce, et al.* (New York City Criminal Court; Part 2B: County of New York), July 6, 1964, pp. 145–6 (testimony of questionable value; err on side of openness); July 1, 1964, pp. 3–4 (Murtagh-Gilman exchange), pp. 9–11 (Murtagh-London exchange).
258 Kuh's cross-examinations: Trial Transcript, *People v. Bruce, et al.* (New York City Criminal Court; Part 2B: County of New York), July 6, 1964, p. 9 (Johnson qualifications); July 2, 1964, p. 75 (Lanier qualifications); July 6, 1964, p. 10 (Phipps re: morality), pp. 27–8 (Johnson on Fourth Commandment); July 1, 1964, pp. 21–2 (Kilgallen generalities); July 6, 1964, pp. 162–6 (Feiffer bias); July 2, 1964, pp. 3–9 (Hentoff bias); July 1, 1964, pp. 31–8 ("divide and conquer").
261 Fifteen hundred words: Leonard Harris, "Is It Art or Is It Obscenity?" *New York World-Telegram and Sun,* July 29, 1964, p. 16.

262 Wollenberg's cross-examination of Grover Sales: Lenny Bruce, *How to Talk Dirty and Influence People* (New York: Fireside, 1992) pp. 114–28.
262 Kuh's *compare and contrast* stratagem with Kilgallen: Trial Transcript, *People v. Bruce, et al.* (New York City Criminal Court; Part 2B: County of New York), July 1, 1964, pp. 48, 50–1, 54.
263 Bruce LPs: Judith Michaelson, "In for Hogan," *New York Post,* February 9, 1974, p. 22.
263 "Bruce of yore" and "inarticulate": Richard H. Kuh, *Foolish Figleaves? Pornography in—and out of—Court* (New York: MacMillan Co., 1967), pp. 176, 195.
263 Trial proceedings: Trial Transcript, *People v. Bruce, et al.* (New York City Criminal Court; Part 2B: County of New York), July 2, 1964, pp. 28–9 (Hentoff's "kaleidoscope"); July 3, 1964, p. 79 (Kuh question); July 1, 1964, p. 27 (Kuh question), pp. 84–5 (Kuh question to Kilgallen); July 9, 1964, pp. 36–7 (Creel question to Epstein); July 6, 1964, pp. 44–8 (Johnson: community standards).
266 D.A. staff: Stephanie Gervis Harrington, "How Many Four-Letter Words Can a Prosecutor Use?" *Village Voice,* July 16, 1964, p. 3; Nat Hentoff, "Burt Lancaster, Abraham Lincoln and Lenny Bruce," *New York Herald Tribune,* December 20, 1964, pp. 1, 16.
266 Example of Kuh cross-examination on gestures: Trial Transcript, *People v. Bruce, et al.* (New York City Criminal Court; Part 2B: County of New York), July 6, 1964, pp. 50–1.
266 Dorothy Kilgallen touches Bruce's arm: Lee Israel, *Kilgallen* (New York: Delacorte Press, 1979), p. 382.

8. COURT ADJOURNED: NEW YORK, PART III
Epigraph: Lenny Bruce, quoted in John Cohen, editor, *The Essential Lenny Bruce* (New York: Ballantine Books, 1967), p. 262.

Gifts From on High
269 Impact of *Jacobellis v. Ohio* on Bruce's Chicago conviction: "Highest State Court Annuls Two Decisions in Obscenity Cases," *Chicago Tribune,* July 9, 1964, sec. 1, p.15; Suggestions on Behalf of Lenny Bruce in Response to the Court's Order of July 7, 1964, in *People v. Bruce* (Supreme Court of Illinois No. 37902, November Term, 1963), pp. 2–3; Suggestions of the People of the State of Illinois, in *People v. Bruce* (Supreme Court of Illinois No. 37902, November Term, 1963), pp. 10–1.
270 Kuh's "clarification" of the withdrawal of Illinois Supreme Court opinion: Trial Transcript, *People v. Bruce, et al.* (New York City Criminal Court; Part 2B: County of New York), July 27, 1964, pp. 88–9.
271 *Fanny Hill: Larkin v. G.P. Putnam's Sons,* 14 N.Y.2d 399, 200 N.E. 2d 760 (N.Y. 1964); 14 N.Y. 2d at 406, 200 N.E. 2d at 764 (Desmond, C.J., dissenting); 14 N.Y. 2d at 407, 200 N.E. 2d at 765 (Scileppi, J., dissenting). *Fanny Hill* was finally legalized in New York. But the book would not be protected under the First Amendment within the entire United States for almost another two years, when the Supreme Court cleared the work of obscenity charges filed in Massachusetts. *Memoirs v. Massachusetts,* 383 U.S. 413 (1966).
271 *Tropic of Cancer: Grove Press, Inc. v. Gerstein,* 378 U.S. 577 (June 22, 1964).
271 "How can they continue this?": Lenny Bruce, quoted in Martin Garbus, *Ready for the Defense* (New York: Farrar, Strauss, Giroux), p. 123.
271 Kuh's comment at preliminary hearing: Trial Transcript, *People v. Bruce, et al.* (New York City Criminal Court; Part 2B: County of New York), June 30, 1964, p. 22.

A Cast of Critics
272 "All I can see": Lenny Bruce, quoted in Ralph Gleason, "The Sickness That Killed Lenny Bruce," *San Francisco Chronicle,* August 5, 1966.

272 "We have a good trial record": Letter from Ephraim London to Lenny Bruce, July 20, 1964.

272 Kuh's efforts to persuade Crowther, Trilling, and Green; "sort of reverse McCarthyism": Richard H. Kuh, *Foolish Figleaves? Pornography in—and out of—Court* (New York: MacMillan Co., 1967), pp. 204–6.

273 Justice Brennan opinion (joined by Goldberg): *Jacobellis v. Ohio*, 378 U.S. 184, 191 (1963).

273 Trial proceedings: Trial Transcript, *People v. Bruce, et al.* (New York City Criminal Court; Part 2B: County of New York), July 27, 1964, p. 40 (Potter: social value); July 28, 1964, pp. 9–10 (Fischer: social value).

274 Marya Mannes's testimony: Trial Transcript, *People v. Bruce, et al.* (New York City Criminal Court; Part 2B: County of New York), July 28, 1964, pp. 47–8, 59–60, 63–4, 68. The official trial transcript refers to her as Marian Mannes Clarkson.

276 Sylvester's testimony: Trial Transcript, *People v. Bruce, et al.* (New York City Criminal Court; Part 2B: County of New York), July 27, 1964, pp. 26–7 (Sylvester: community standards), pp. 22–3 (Creel questions Sylvester). Interestingly, on August 3, 1964, Lenny Bruce sent a letter to Justice Creel, asking whether there was "such a thing as hardcore vulgarity." Lenny answered his own question by emphasizing that such language was that of the working class, the unpolished masses. Such language was spoken virtually everywhere, except in the unreal realm of courtrooms, he argued. His highly inappropriate letter ended with a definition of "vulgarity" from *Webster's Third International Dictionary*. See Letter from Lenny Bruce to Justice James Randall Creel, dated August 3, 1964, Lawrence Schiller Papers, Woodland Hills, CA.

277 Trial proceedings: Trial Transcript, *People v. Bruce, et al.* (New York City Criminal Court; Part 2B: County of New York), July 28, 1964, p. 15 (Van den Haag: community standards); July 27, 1964, pp. 42–3 (Potter: community standards); July 28, 1964, pp. 38–9 (Fischer: unity), pp. 65–6 (Mannes: unity).

277 "Bruce, the accused": Richard H. Kuh, *Foolish Figleaves? Pornography in—and out of—Court* (New York: MacMillan Co., 1967), p. 209.

Censorship Debate and Courtroom Drama

278 *Open Mind* forum: "Censorship and the Open Society," *New York Post*, July 8, 1964, p. 26.

279 Ephraim London's cross-examinations: Trial Transcript, *People v. Bruce, et al.* (New York City Criminal Court; Part 2B: County of New York), July 28, 1964, pp. 16–24 (Van den Haag qualifications); July 27, 1964, pp. 44–5 (Potter qualifications), pp. 50–8, 80 ("*reductio ad absurdum*"), pp. 19–20 ("test of the petition").

283 Niebuhr endorsement: Thomas Buckley, "One Hundred Fight Arrest of Lenny Bruce," *New York Times*, June 14, 1964, p. 75.

283 Niebuhr letter: Richard H. Kuh, *Foolish Figleaves? Pornography in—and out of—Court* (New York: MacMillan Co., 1967), pp. 179–80.

287 Trial proceedings: Trial Transcript, *People v. Bruce, et al.* (New York City Criminal Court; Part 2B: County of New York), July 27, pp. 68–72, 82–6 (Kuh protest: Niebuhr letter), pp. 13–4, 28 (Sylvester: conversations and nightclub entertainment); July 28, 1964, p. 43 (Van den Haag redirect).

287 Bruce at end of trial: Trial Transcript, *People v. Bruce, et al.* (New York City Criminal Court; Part 2B: County of New York), July 28, 1964, pp. 46–52; "Bruce Clashes with Lawyers as Trial Ends," *New York Post*, July 29, 1964, p. 30.

287 London's advice: Nat Hentoff, "Burt Lancaster, Abraham Lincoln and Lenny Bruce," *New York Herald Tribune*, December 20, 1964, pp. 1, 18.

287 Bruce as "inept lawyer": Leonard Harris, "Is It Obscenity or Is It Art?" *New York World-Telegram and Sun*, July 29, 1964, p. 16.

287 Bruce as "inarticulate": Richard Kuh, from unaired outtake interview with Robert

Weide for *Lenny Bruce: Swear to Tell the Truth* (Los Angeles: Whyaduck Productions, 1998), written and produced by Robert Weide.

Playing the Court
288 Bruce's troubled relationship with London: Lenny Bruce, quoted in Allen G. Schwartz, "Lenny at the Bar," *Village Voice*, August 11, 1966, p. 23 ("I'll perform my act"); Nat Hentoff, "Burt Lancaster, Abraham Lincoln and Lenny Bruce," *New York Herald Tribune*, December 20, 1964, pp. 1, 16 ("see me work" and summer letters); Albert Goldman and Lawrence Schiller, *Ladies and Gentlemen, Lenny Bruce!!* (New York: Random House, 1974), pp. 482–3 (errors in transcript and hand-slapping).
288 Legislative history: Trial Transcript, *People v. Bruce, et al.* (New York City Criminal Court; Part 2B: County of New York), December 21, p. 5.
288 "Surprise ending": Leonard Harris, "Is It Obscenity or Is It Art?" *New York World-Telegram and Sun*, July 29, 1964, p. 16.
289 "Appellantophile": Interview with Lawrence Meyer, October 2, 2001 (recalling his 1965 interview with Bruce, during which Bruce gave Meyer a copy of a letter to London).
289 Letter to London and London's bill for services: Albert Goldman and Lawrence Schiller, *Ladies and Gentlemen, Lenny Bruce!!* (New York: Random House, 1974), pp. 483–5.
289 Letter to Judge Murtagh: Lenny Bruce, "A Letter to Judge Murtaugh (sic)," reprinted in David Meltzer, editor, *Tree*, vol. 4 (Winter, 1974), pp. 60–73 (footnotes omitted).
291 Trolley Ho appellate judgment: *People v. Bruce*, Unpublished Opinion of September 14, 1964, Appellate Division of the Superior Court of Los Angeles, No. CRA5912 (Trial Court No. 207444).
292 Bruce's request to be named counsel: "Bruce Dismisses Lawyers, Asks Reopening of Trial," *New York Times*, October 6, 1964, p. 30.
292 Clean-shaven: Nat Hentoff, "Burt Lancaster, Abraham Lincoln and Lenny Bruce," *New York Herald Tribune*, December 20, 1964, pp. 1, 16.
292 Crooks in suits bit: Lenny Bruce, quoted in Allen G. Schwartz, "Lenny at the Bar," *Village Voice*, August 11, 1966, p. 23.
293 Bruce's pleas: Trial Transcript, *People v. Bruce, et al.* (New York City Criminal Court; Part 2B: County of New York), November 4, 1964, pp. 2–16.
293 "Scathing, self-lascerating, jivey, *j'accusing*": "Bruce's Trial," *Newsweek*, June 20, 1964.
294 Judgment: Trial Transcript, *People v. Bruce, et al.* (New York City Criminal Court; Part 2B: County of New York), November 4, 1964, p. 17.
294 Press coverage: Jack Roth, "Lenny Bruce Act is Ruled Obscene," *New York Times*, November 5, 1964, p. 47; "Lennie Bruce Found Guilty of Obscene Show in Village," *Newsday*, November 5, 1964, sec. C, p. 2; Albin Krebs, "Bruce Club Act Ruled Obscene," *New York Herald-Tribune*, November 5, 1964, p. 17; "Lenny Bruce, Guilty on N.Y. Obscenity Charges, Faces Sentencing Dec. 16," *Variety*, November 11, 1964, p. 61; "Court Says No to Bruce, He Must See Psychiatrist," *Village Voice*, November 12, 1964, p. 1; "Profane Comedy," *Time*, November 13, 1964.
294 "Kafka novel": Lenny Bruce, quoted in Peter Hart, "Lenny Bruce Sets Return to Stage," *New York Times*, January 26, 1966, p. 24.
294 "Halls of Justice": Lenny Bruce, quoted in Allen G. Schwartz, "Lenny at the Bar," *Village Voice*, August 11, 1966, p. 23.

A Court Opinion Unfit to Be Printed
295 Definition of *censor*: *The New Shorter Oxford English Dictionary*, Lesley Brown, editor (Oxford, England: Clarendon Press, 1993), vol. I, p. 360.

295 Murtagh's attempt to ban published opinions: Jack Roth, "Criminal Court Judges Ordered Not to Issue Written Opinions," *New York Times*, November 15, 1963, p. 1.

295 *New York Law Journal:* James Randall Creel, "Notes and Views," *New York Law Journal*, November 24, 1964, p. 1; "The Lenny Bruce Case," *New York Law Journal*, December 4, 1964, p. 1.

296 *Per curiam* opinion: The majority opinion in favor of Bruce in the Illinois Supreme Court would likewise be *per curiam*. See *People v. Bruce*, 31 Ill. 2d 459, 202 N.E. 2d 497 (1964). To all appearances, whenever a court (trial or appellate) wrote about Lenny Bruce (favorably or otherwise), it wrote anonymously.

296 Prosecution's memo: Richard H. Kuh, *Foolish Figleaves?: Pornography in— and out of—Court* (New York: Macmillan, 1967) p. 184.

296 *Jacobellis v. Ohio*, 378 U.S.184 (1964).

296 *Larkin v. G.P. Putnam's Sons*, 14 N.Y. 2d 399, 200 N.E. 2d 760 (N.Y., 1964). *Larkin* held *Fanny Hill* to be nonobscene under New York law. "The end result of the *Fanny Hill* experience," Kuh complained shortly afterwards, "has been to suggest to New York police and prosecutors the utter futility of seeking action against the non-masochistic, non-sadistic written word, when offered for sale to adults." See Richard Kuh, "Obscenity: Prosecution Problems and Legislative Suggestions," *The Catholic Lawyer* 10 (Winter 1964), pp. 285, 290.

297 "Overruled": *People v. Fritch*, 13 N.Y. 2d 119, 192 N.E. 2d 713 (N.Y., 1963), overruled in *Larkin v. G.P. Putnam's Sons*, 14 N.Y. 2d 399, 200 N.E. 2d 760 (N.Y., 1964).

297 "The court did not declare the statute unconstitutional": *People v. Wendling*, 258 N.Y. 451, 454, 180 N.E. 169, 170 (N.Y., 1932) (emphasis added).

298 *Roth v. U.S.*, 354 U.S. 476, 488, note 20 (1957).

298 All references to the per curiam opinion are to the unpublished opinions (majority and dissenting) in *People v. Bruce, et al* (November 16, 1964: Criminal Court of the City of New York).

Victory in Illinois

301 Reversal of Bruce's Chicago obscenity charge: *People v. Bruce*, 31 Ill. 2d 459, 202 N.E. 2d 497 (1964); "Lenny Bruce '62 Obscenity Case Reversed," *Chicago Tribune*, November 25, 1964, p. 6; "Illinois Reverses a Bruce Conviction," *New York Times*, November 25, 1964, p. 44; "News of the Week in Law: Obscenity Cases," *New York Times*, December 20, 1964, sec. IV, part K, p. 7; Letter from Maurice Rosenfield to Lenny Bruce, dated November 24, 1965.

301 Appellate case of Bruce's New York codefendant, Howard Solomon: See *People v. Solomon*, 255 N.E. 2d 729 (N.Y. 1970).

Civil Rights and Uncivil Words

301 §1983 action: Trial Transcript, *People v. Bruce, et al.* (New York City Criminal Court: Part 2B: County of New York) December 21, 1964, p. 4.

302 *Monroe v. Pape*, 365 U.S. 167 (1961).

303 Second Circuit arguments: Martin Garbus, *Ready for the Defense* (New York: Farrar, Straus, & Giroux, 1971) pp. 137–8.

303 "More than a little nervous": Selma Rovinsky, quoted in Albert Goldman and Lawrence Schiller, *Ladies and Gentlemen, Lenny Bruce!!* (New York: Random House, 1974), p. 500.

304 Extraordinary circumstances: Mark Tushnet, *Making Constitutional Law: Thurgood Marshall and the Supreme Court, 1961–1991* (New York: Oxford University Press, 1997) p. 18.

304 Appellate court denial: "Lenny Bruce Plea Denied," *New York Times*, December 19, 1964, p. 28; Edward de Grazia, *Girls Lean Back Everywhere: The Law of Obscenity and the Assault on Genius* (New York: Random House, 1992), p. 452.

"The Jew Is Not Remorseful"
305 Court proceedings: Trial Transcript, *People v. Bruce, et al.* (New York City Criminal Court: Part 2B: County of New York) December 21, 1964, p. 4 (denial of motion to recuse), pp. 5–17 (legislative history).
306 "Deeper and deeper": Henry Paul, "Final Performance Nets Four Months at Hard Labor," *Village Voice*, December 24, 1964, pp. 1, 19.
306 Court proceedings: Trial Transcript, *People v. Bruce, et al.* (New York City Criminal Court: Part 2B: County of New York) December 21, 1964, p. 4 ("encouraging perjury"), pp. 33–4 (transcript errors), pp. 42–5 (Miller re: *Jacobellis* and mitigating circumstances), pp. 45–7 (Kuh re: competency), p. 47 (Hershman), pp. 48–9 (Rosenfield's letter and Murtagh's ruling), pp. 50–1 (Miller: mitigation).
308 Kuh's resignation: "Prosecutor to Resign to Make Study of Laws," *New York Times*, July 27, 1964, p. 16.
309 Village Theater performance: Albert Goldman and Lawrence Schiller, *Ladies and Gentlemen, Lenny Bruce!!* (New York: Random House, 1974), p. 498.
309 Advertisement for Village Theater, Thanksgiving 1964 show: *Village Voice*, November 26, 1964, p. 15.
309 Kuh's sentencing arguments: Trial Transcript, *People v. Bruce, et al.* (New York City Criminal Court: Part 2B: County of New York) December 21, 1964, pp. 52–3; Nat Hentoff, "The Onliest Lenny Bruce," *Village Voice*, February 5, 1991, pp. 22–3.
309 "I am a Jew": Lenny Bruce, quoted in Henry Paul, "Final Performance Nets Four Months at Hard Labor," *Village Voice*, December 24, 1964, pp. 1, 20; Trial Transcript, *People v. Bruce, et al.* (New York City Criminal Court: Part 2B: County of New York) December 21, 1964, pp. 53–4.
310 Obligation of criminal court: John M. Murtagh and Sara Harris, *Cast the First Stone* (New York: McGraw-Hill, 1957), p. 296.
310 Sentencing: Trial Transcript, *People v. Lenny Bruce, et al.* (New York City Criminal Court: Part 2B: County of New York) December 21, 1964, pp. 55, 57 (sentences), pp. 57–8 (Justice Creel's vote to suspend sentences); "Lenny Bruce Convicted, Sentenced to Four Months," *Cash Box*, January, 1965, p. 28; "Lenny Bruce Gets Four Months in Jail," *New York Times*, December 22, 1964, p 32.
310 Stay of execution: Trial Transcript, *People v. Bruce, et al.* (New York City Criminal Court: Part 2B: County of New York) December 21, 1964, pp. 56–60; Martin Garbus, *Ready for the Defense* (New York: Farrar, Straus & Giroux, 1971), p. 136; "Lenny Bruce is Released in $50 Bail Pending Appeal," *New York Times*, December 22, 1964, p. 10; "Lenny Bruce Wins Stay of Obscenity Conviction," *Variety*, December 30, 1964, p. 43.
311 Schwartz's suggestions of Patrick Wall: Letter from Allen Schwartz to Lenny Bruce, dated July 1, 1965, Lawrence Schiller Papers, Woodland Hills, California.

Island Retreat
312 Rikers Island: John C. Devlin, "Mayor Opens $9-Million Bridge to an Expanding Rikers Island," *New York Times*, November 23, 1966, p. 41 (history of Rikers Island); Charles G. Bennett, "Fare is in Danger, Patterson Warns," *New York Times*, October 18, 1960 (overcrowding); Jack Roth, "Prison Cook Held in Narcotics Case," *New York Times*, March 7, 1964, p. 19 (prisoner population); "City's New Prison Gets Bright Décor," *New York Times*, September 29, 1963, p. 65 (bright colors); Robert C. Doty, "Model City Prison Given a Preview," *New York Times*, February 14, 1964, p. 16 (completed Classification Center).
312 Selma Rovinsky: Letter from Selma Rovinsky to John Judnick, December 15, 1964, Albert Goldman Papers, Butler Library, Columbia University, New York, Box 7.

312 Marlton interview: James A. Wechsler, "On Lenny Bruce," *New York Post,* December 23, 1964, p. 24.
313 Editorial: "Lenny Bruce," *New York World Telegram and Sun,* December 28, 1964, p. 26.
313 Legal vindication: Lenny Bruce, quoted in "The Law: Obscenity," *Time,* March 1, 1968, p. 64.

9. The Path to Vindication
Epigraph: Phil Spector, quoted in Jan Wenner, "The Rolling Stone Interview," *Rolling Stone,* November 1, 1969, p. 23–24.

High Hopes, Painful Flops
317 "Ideas…imprisoned within me": Lenny Bruce, quoted in Edward de Grazia, *Girls Lean Back Everywhere: The Law of Obscenity and The Assault on Genius* (New York: Random House, 1992) p. 473 (from petition to NY Federal District Court, 1965).
318 "Constitution won't permit them": Lenny Bruce, *How to Talk Dirty and Influence People* (Chicago: Playboy Press, 1965), p. 149.
318 Bruce's fall out window: "Lenny's Painful Flop," *San Francisco Chronicle,* March 30, 1965, p. 2; "Lenny Bruce Injured in Fall," *New York Times,* March 30, 1965, p. 51; "DMT," alt.culture, at www.alt.culture.com/aentires/d/dmt.html (accessed November 17, 1999); Albert Goldman and Lawrence Schiller, *Ladies and Gentlemen, Lenny Bruce!!* (New York: Random House, 1974), p. 507 (DMT "jewels").
319 "Walls are closing in": Letter from Edward de Grazia to Ralph J. Gleason, dated April 9, 1965.
320 "If you appear": Letter from Ralph J. Gleason to Lenny Bruce, dated May 3, 1965.
320 Supreme Court's denial of certiorari: Petition for a Writ of Certiorari in *Bruce v. Hogan et al.,* U.S. Supreme Court Docket No. 1258 (October Term, 1964); *Bruce v. Hogan,* 381 U.S. 946 (1965); Letter from Edward de Grazia to Ralph J. Gleason, dated June 8, 1965; "Supreme Court Refuses Hearing to Lenny Bruce," *New York Times,* June 2, 1965, p. 41.
321 Dying for love of the law: Letter from Edward de Grazia to Ralph J. Gleason, dated April 9, 1965.

White Christmas
321 Kunstler: William M. Kunstler with Sheila Isenberg, *My Life as a Radical Lawyer* (New York: Carol Publishing Group, 1996 revised edition), pp. 167–9.
323 A swell of civil rights litigation: "Lennie Bruce Asks Court to Bar Police Harassment," *New York Times,* October 14, 1965, p. 56; Order for Denial of Order to Show Cause, *Bruce v. Sacramento County Executive Branch, et al.,* U.S. District Court for the Northern District of California, Northern Division, Civil No. 9538 (denied November 2, 1965; Thomas J. MacBride, J.). Additionally, on July 21, 1965, Lenny wrote a letter to Richard Marx, a Miami Beach lawyer, inquiring into the possibility of bringing a civil rights action against the sheriff of North Bay Village for harassing Marvin Dubin, the owner of Le B, where Lenny had performed. Apparently, the sheriff pressured Bruce to sign a document swearing that he would not use any "dirty words" during his club appearances. The police monitored the show with recording equipment. Letter of Lenny Bruce to Richard Marx, dated July 21, 1965, Lawrence Schiller Papers, Woodland Hills, California.
323 Sacramento state civil rights action: Complaint in *Bruce and Katsaros v. Misterly,* Superior Court of the State of California, County of Sacramento, No. 517226 (filed February 24, 1965).
323 Los Angeles §1983: Complaint in *Bruce v. Draeger et al.,* U.S. District Court for the Southern District of California, Central Division, Docket No. 65-669-TC (filed April 30, 1965).

323 San Francisco federal §1983: ; "Lenny Bruce Asks for Court Help," *San Francisco Chronicle,* October 14, 1965, p. 46.

323 "I'll pull your license": Norman Levy, quoted in Petition for a Writ of Certiorari in *Bruce v. Hogan et al.,* U.S. Supreme Court Docket No. 1258 (October Term, 1964), p. 17, note *.

323 Suspension and revocation proceedings at Trolley Ho and Booby Trap: Department of Alcoholic Beverage Control Accusation against Donald and James Duffin and the Trolley Ho, File No. 2116 (1964); Letter from the County of Los Angeles Public Welfare Commission to Davfly Inc., et al., February 17, 1965.

323 Clubs not hiring for fear of being closed down: Lenny Bruce, quoted in Peter Hart, "Lenny Bruce Sets Return to Stage," *New York Times,* January 26, 1966, p. 24.

324 Christmas party: William M. Kunstler with Sheila Isenberg, *My Life as a Radical Lawyer* (New York: Carol Publishing Group, 1996 revised edition), p. 168.

"For My Part, Go to Hell"

325 "Your appeal papers": Letter from William Schaap to Lenny Bruce, dated May 26, 1965.

325 Schwartz likewise urged him to proceed: Letter from Allen Schwartz to Lenny Bruce, dated July 1, 1965, Lawrence Schiller Papers, Woodland Hills, CA.

326 Cuccia's arguments: Affidavit in Opposition to the Defendant's Motion for an Extension of Time, *People v. Bruce,* Supreme Court of New York, Appellate Term: First Department, May 24, 1965.

327 Bruce's "mess": Letter from Maurice Rosenfield to Robert J. Landry, dated November 5, 1965.

327 Provisos: Letter from Jay H. Topkis to Lenny Bruce, dated November 19, 1965.

328 Embarrassment: Letter from Maurice Rosenfield to Jay H. Topkis, dated November 24, 1965.

329 "Go to hell": Letter from Maurice Rosenfield to Lenny Bruce, dated November 24, 1965.

329 "Leader in the sense department": Letter from William H. Schaap to Maurice Rosenfield, dated November 29, 1965.

330 Amicus curiae brief: Letter from Maurice Rosenfield to Jay H. Topkis, dated December 2, 1965; Letter from Jay H. Topkis to Maurice Rosenfield, dated December 9, 1965.

331 Marlton Hotel: Interview with Carl Montgomery, October 25, 1999.

The Specter of a Rebel

331 The Spector Bruce account: Mark Ribowsky, *He's a Rebel* (New York: E.P. Dutton, 1989), pp. 198–203, 226-8; Jan Wenner, "The Rolling Stone Interview," *Rolling Stone,* November 1, 1969, pp. 23, 24, 25; "Lenny Bruce Returns in 1-Man Talkathon; A 2-Wk. Run, Cops Willing," *Variety,* February 16, 1966, p. 50 (signed "Murf" a.k.a. Ralph Gleason); Peter Bart, "Lenny Bruce Sets Return to Stage," *New York Times,* January 26, 1966, p. 24; Stan Bertstein, "Lenny Bruce Returns but Few Come to Pay Homage," *Los Angeles Times,* February 14, 1966; *Lenny Bruce is Out Again* (Los Angeles, CA: Philles Records, 1965, No. PHLP-4010). In 1989, Spector filed a $30-million defamation action against Mark Ribowsky. "The suit charged that [his biography] contained 'false and defamatory statements.'" Apparently, "an out-of-court settlement was worked out under which certain passages [were] eliminated in any paperback edition of the book." Robert Hilburn, "Tearing Down the Wall of Silence," *Los Angeles Times,* November 10, 1991, Calendar, p. 6.

333 Sydney Irmas: Irmas, of the Los Angeles law firm Irmas and Rutter, had secured a dismissal of Bruce's prosecution for The Trolley Ho obscenity arrest in 1964, discussed in chapters 5, 6, and 8. Moreover, Irmas had represented Lenny successfully

before the California Supreme Court in a narcotics appeal. *People v. Bruce*, 64 Cal. 2d 55, 409 P. 2d 943 (CA, January 31, 1966). Bruce challenged Superior Court Judge William Munnell's order committing him to a narcotic addict's rehabilitation program in the state penitentiary. The opinion by Justice Burke for a unanimous state high court ruled that there was legally insufficient evidence to declare Bruce a drug addict and therefore remanded the matter to the superior court for further proceedings.

334 Philles Records released *Lenny Bruce Is Out Again*: Years after Lenny's death, Spector also released *The Law, Language, and Lenny Bruce* (Burbank, CA: Warner-Spector Records, 1974) (recorded in 1965).

"I'm Going to Die This Year"

336 "Self-destructive element": Hugh Hefner, from *A Toast to Lenny* (Montvail, NJ: Pioneer Artists Laserdisk, 1984, also aired on HBO).

336 "Spark of talent": Judge Benjamin Landis, quoted in "Lenny Bruce Is Sentenced to Probation in Heroin Case," *New York Times,* April 19, 1966, p. 39.

336 "He looked very, very sick": Mort Sahl, quoted in Charles Champlin, "Death of Lenny Bruce Raises Questions about His Talents," *Los Angeles Times,* August 5, 1966, p. 3.

336 Sally Marr: Jane Wollman, "Mother of Modern Comedy," *Newsday*, October 15, 1989, p. 21.

337 *Memoirs v. Massachusetts*, 383 U.S. 413, 419–20, note 7 (1966).

337 A prescient conversation: Lotus Weinstock, from *A Toast to Lenny* (Montvail, NJ: Pioneer Artists Laserdisk, 1984, also aired on HBO). When Weinstock first met Lenny in Los Angeles in 1965, she went by the name Maury Hayden.

337 "Six cans of Coca-Cola": Kitty Bruce, from *A Toast to Lenny* (Montvail, NJ: Pioneer Artists Laserdisk, 1984, also aired on HBO).

338 Fillmore concert: Bill Graham and Robert Greenfield, *Bill Graham Presents: My Life Inside Rock and Out* (New York: Delta Trade Paperbacks/Dell, 1993), pp. 156–9.

339 Press coverage of Bruce's death: "An Obituary for Lenny Bruce" (1964), republished in Paul Krassner, *The Winner of the Slow Bicycle Race: The Satirical Writings of Paul Krassner* (New York: Seven Stories Press, 1996); William E. Gold and Gene Youngblood, "Needle Found in Arm of Comic," *Los Angeles Herald Examiner,* August 4, 1966, p. 1; "Lenny Bruce Dies, Apparently from Overdose of Drugs," *Los Angeles Times,* August 4, 1966, p. 1; Charles Champlin, "Death of Lenny Bruce Raises Questions about His Talents," *Los Angeles Times,* August 5, 1966, p. 3; "New Test in Bruce Case Due," *Los Angeles Herald Examiner,* August 5, 1966, sec. A, p. 23; "Lenny Bruce Autopsy Fails to Show Cause of Death," *New York Times,* August 8, 1966, p. 31; "Morphine Overdose Ruled Cause of Bruce's Death," *New York Times,* August 16, 1966, p. 34.

340 "He died of an overdose of police": Phil Spector, "Talent," *Billboard,* August 20, 1966.

341 "The one of death": Ed Sherman, "George Crater Meets Lenny Bruce," *Down Beat's Music*, 1960, pp. 56, 57.

342 Cemetery: Interview with Frank Ray Perilli, January 25, 2000; Paul Krassner, "The Persecution of Lenny Bruce," *High Times,* February 2000, pp. 42, 46; Ralph J. Gleason, "Obituary," republished at members.aol.com/dcspohr/lenny/obgleas.htm (accessed November 16, 1998); *Lenny Bruce, Live at the Curran Theater* (Berkeley, CA: Fantasy Records, 1970) (cover photo of misspelled temporary grave marker).

The Wisdom of Solomon

342 Advertisement for Blood, Sweat and Tears: *Village Voice,* February 15, 1968, p. 45.

343 Hellerstein on Solomon's appeal: William Hellerstein, quoted in Edward de

Grazia, *Girls Lean Back Everywhere: The Law of Obscenity and the Assault on Genius* (New York: Random House, 1992) p. 479; Interview with William E. Hellerstein, June 9, 1999.

344 Appellate brief for the defense: Brief for Defendant-Appellant in *People v. Solomon*, Supreme Court Appellate Term, First Department, Docket No. Sept. #351; Robert E. Tomasson, "Appeals Court Voids Conviction in Lenny Bruce Obscenity Case," *New York Times,* February 20, 1968, p. 51; Memorandum Decision in *People v. Solomon,* Supreme Court Appellate Term, First Department, Docket No. Sept. #351, published in *New York Law Journal,* February 19, 1968.

346 Garbus would make the same mistake in his book: Martin Garbus with Stanley Cohen, *Tough Talk* (New York: Times Books, 1998), p. 42.

346 "While the performance presented": Order in *People v. Solomon*, Supreme Court Appellate Term, First Department, Docket No. Sept. #351, February 16, 1968.

346 The majority relied on the Illinois Supreme Court's opinion in *People v. Bruce* and the Supreme Court's opinion in *Roth v. U.S.*: Justice Hofstadter's dissent focused mainly on the state's power to regulate public conduct and argued that Bruce's monologues "contained little or no literary or artistic merit. They were merely a device to enable Bruce to exploit the use of obscene language."

347 H. Richard Uviller: Uviller was a seasoned attorney in the obscenity area, successfully having argued *Mishkin v. New York*, 383 U.S. 502 (1966), in which the Supreme Court (per Justice Brennan) held that sadomasochistic, fetishistic, and homosexual materials could be regulated if pruriently appealing to the relevant "deviant" groups.

347 Motions to amend order or hear reargument: Notice of Motion to Amend Order and Affidavit of H. Richard Uviller in Support of Motion to Amend Order in *People v. Solomon,* Supreme Court Appellate Term, First Department, Docket No. Sept. #351, March 8, 1968; Affidavit of William E. Hellerstein in Opposition to Motion to Amend Order in *People v. Solomon,* Supreme Court Appellate Term, First Department, Docket No. Sept. #351, March 22, 1968; Order Denying Motion to Amend Order in *People v. Solomon,* Supreme Court Appellate Term, First Department, Docket No. Sept. #351, April 25, 1968; Memorandum Decision Denying Motion to Amend Order in *People v. Solomon,* Supreme Court Appellate Term, First Department, Docket No. Sept. #351, published in *New York Law Journal,* April 24, 1968; Notice of Motion to Reargue the Motion to Amend the Order and Memorandum in Support of Motion in *People v. Solomon,* Supreme Court Appellate Term, First Department, Docket No. Sept. #351, May 3, 1968; Affidavit of William E. Hellerstein in Opposition to Motion to Reargue Motion to Amend the Order in *People v. Solomon,* Supreme Court Appellate Term, First Department, Docket No. Sept. #351, May 7, 1986; Memorandum Decision of Appellate Term Denying Reargument in *People v. Solomon,* Supreme Court Appellate Term, First Department, Docket No. Sept. #351, published in *New York Law Journal,* June 12, 1968; People-Appellant's Brief to the New York Court of Appeals in *People v. Solomon*, p. 2.

348 Chief Judge Stanley H. Fuld: Richard Kuh once described Judge Fuld as "New York's most permissive high court judge, at least in the area of alleged pornography…" See Richard Kuh, "Obscenity: Prosecution Problems and Legislative Suggestions," *Catholic Lawyer* 10 (Winter 1964), pp. 285, 286.

348 New York Court of Appeals oral arguments: Interview with William E. Hellerstein, June 9, 1999.

348 *People v. Solomon*, 26 N.Y. 2d 621, 255 N.E. 2d 729 (NY, 1970).

349 *Memoirs v. Massachusetts*, 383 U.S. 413, 419–20, n. 7 (1966).

349 "Finally all over": Letter from William E. Hellerstein to Howard L. Solomon, dated January 9, 1970.

349 "[T]he law is a beautiful thing": Lenny Bruce, quoted in John Cohen, editor, *The Essential Lenny Bruce* (New York: Douglas Books, 1970), p. 211.

10. THE RESURRECTION OF LENNY BRUCE: 1966–1974
Epigraph: Mort Sahl, quoted in John D. Weaver, "The Fault, Dear Bruce, Is Not In Our Stars, But In Ourselves," *Holiday*, vol. 44, November 10, 1968, p. 72 (Sahl statement dated as 1966).

Icon and Irony
353 "Death is the best publicity agent": Artie Shaw, quoted in Ralph J. Gleason, Liner Notes from *Lenny Bruce Live at the Curran Theater* (Berkeley, CA: Fantasy Records, 1972).
353 Bruce's memorial service: Dick Schaap, "The Last Show," *Playboy*, January 1967, p. 162; Tape of August 12, 1966 Judson Memorial Church service for Lenny Bruce: "Lenny Bruce Memorial," WBAI Radio (Pacifica Radio Archives), November 18, 1966; Howard Moody, "Memoriam," *Playboy*, January 1967, p. 254.
354 The *Time* obituary Krassner alluded to (August 12, 1966, p. 74) read, in part: "Bruce was never in tune with this world, and he soured totally after his beautiful blonde [sic] wife became a drug addict....From Manhattan to Hollywood, he viewed life as a four-letter word and, with gestures, commented blackly on it, never lacking for listeners and finding some curious champions....His path led ever lower after a Manhattan criminal court, in 1964, convicted him of being 'obscene, indecent, immoral and impure.'"
356 Kuh, the man who helped turn Lenny Bruce, the destroyer of icons, into an American icon: Something of the same point has been made by Frank Kofsky: "By compelling Bruce to become a martyr…his persecutors also helped make him a hero." Frank Kofsky, *Lenny Bruce: The Comedian as Social Critic and Secular Moralist* (New York: Monad Press, 1974), p. 61.

Essentially Yours
357 Carnegie Hall concert: "UA Issues New Lenny Bruce LP," *Cash Box*, April 1, 1967. In 1992, Don Friedman, who produced the 1961 performance, conducted auditions for a Lenny Bruce–like comedian to perform the Carnegie Hall performance anew. See Bruce Weber, "The Iconoclast as Icon: Filling Lenny's Shoes," *New York Times*, July 24, 1992, sec. B, p. 3.
357 Wrangling over Bruce's recordings: "Bruce's Mother: Use of Son's Tapes Illegal; Takes Action," *Billboard*, April 8, 1967, p. 4.
357 "I've lost a friend": Nico, "Eulogy to Lenny," *Chelsea* (New York: Verve & Polygram Records, 1967).
358 Magnuson film and "the basic thrust of the performance": *The Lenny Bruce Performance Film* (Santa Monica, CA: Rhino Home Video, 1992) produced by John Magnuson; Albert Goldman and Lawrence Schiller, *Ladies and Gentlemen, Lenny Bruce!!* (New York: Random House, 1974), pp. 519–21.
358 "A devastating recapitulation": Vincent Canby, "Lenny Bruce," *New York Times*, March 20, 1967, sec. L, p. 26.
358 "When Lenny Bruce died": John Cohen, editor, *The Essential Lenny Bruce* (New York: Ballantine Books, 1967) unnumbered introduction and pp. 307, 308.
359 "From all the Yippies": Abbie Hoffman, *Woodstock Nation: A Talk-Rock Album* (New York: Vintage Books, 1969).
359 A member of the radical honor roll: Robert S. Gold, editor, *The Rebel Culture* (New York: Dell Publishing, 1970).
359 His posthumous animated parable: "Thank You Mask Man," from *The Lenny Bruce Performance Film* (Rhino Home Video), produced by John Magnuson.

Making Book

360 "Hell in a handbasket": Richard Kuh, "Obscenity: Prosecution Problems and Legislative Suggestions," *The Catholic Lawyer* 10 (Winter 1964), pp. 285, 295.

360 "Important contribution": William F. Buckley. Jr., "Serious Proposals to Confront the Onslaught of Smut," *Washington Post,* Book World, February 18, 1968, p. 3.

360 Kuh's involvement with 1970 obscenity subcommittee, whose proposals were ultimately defeated by Church opposition describing the measures as "too lenient": "Obscenity Expert Asks Clearer Laws on Illegal Material," *New York Times,* March 6, 1970, p. 35; Paul L. Montgomery, "State Loses a Round in Pornography Fight," *New York Times,* November 26, 1972, p. 97.

360 Review of *Foolish Figleaves?:* Fred Graham, "Dirty Words and Fuzzy Laws," *New York Times Book Review,* December 10, 1967, p. 6. Nat Hentoff maintains that Kuh sent him a review copy of *Foolish Figleaves?* with the hope that the columnist might review the book. According to Hentoff, Kuh complained to the *Village Voice* that Hentoff had not reviewed the book even though Kuh had taken the trouble to send him a copy. "An autographed copy, it was," wrote Hentoff. "I did not review Mr. Kuh's book because I find him personally offensive, and so disqualified myself." See Nat Hentoff, "A Last One for Lenny," *Village Voice,* February 29, 1968, p. 5.

361 Role of prosecutor: Richard H. Kuh, *Foolish Figleaves?—Pornography in—and out of—Court* (New York: Macmillan, 1967), pp. 302, 303. Kuh, from an unaired out-take interview with Robert Weide for *Lenny Bruce: Swear to Tell the Truth* (Los Angeles: Whyaduck Productions, 1998) written and produced by Robert Weide.

361 Need for more "precise" obscenity laws: Richard H. Kuh, "Plan to Keep Pornography Away From Children," *Ladies Home Journal,* vol. 85 (September, 1968), p. 7.

361 "*Some* censorship": Richard H. Kuh, "Censorship *With* Freedom of Expression," in Harry M. Clor, editor, *Censorship and Freedom of Expression* (Chicago: Rand McNally College Publishing, 1971), pp. 132, 145 (emphasis in original).

362 Kuh's changing prescription for liberal censorship: Richard H. Kuh, "Obscenity Censorship," *Wilson Library Bulletin,* vol. 42, p. 902.

362 Kuh never mentioned the *Solomon* case at all: In an October 4, 1998 letter to the *New York Times* (Section AR, p. 4), Kuh wrote: "Ultimately, some appreciable time after the Bruce conviction, a divided appellate court vacated it, soundly attacking the constitutionality of New York's then existing anti-obscenity statutes." Actually, *two* New York appellate courts rendered favorable rulings in *Howard Solomon's* (not Bruce's) case. As to the applicable First Amendment obscenity law, it was not significantly different in 1964 when Bruce was convicted than it was in 1968 when the Solomon conviction was reversed.

363 Excessive prosecutorial zeal: Martin Garbus, *Ready for the Defense* (New York: Farrar, Straus & Giroux), pp. 135, 140, 123, 138, 82, 83.

The Play's the Thing

364 As if [Lenny] just had stepped down from his place on the cover of *Sgt. Pepper's* with its crowd of pop-culture heroes: Bruce's picture was included on the cover of the Beatles' *Sgt. Pepper's* album, reportedly because he was one of the "favorites of all the Beatles," especially John. See Beatles, *Sgt. Pepper's Lonely Hearts Club Band* (New York: EMI Records, 1967); Albert Goldman, *The Lives of John Lennon* (New York: William Morrow, 1988), pp. 80, 259.

365 Lines from the play: Julian Barry, *Lenny* (New York: Grove Press, 1971), p. 99 ("Geneva Conference"), p. 8 ("vibrators"), p. 113 ("six thousand words"), pp. 100–1 (Bruce-lawyer exchange). In 1971, an audio album of the play was released as a two-record LP (*Lenny,* Blue Thumb Records, 1971). Decades later, a remake of Julian Barry's *Lenny* opened in London (August 1999) at the Queens Theatre with Eddie Izzard starring as Lenny Bruce.

365 Dustin Hoffman: Patrick Agan, *Hoffman vs. Hoffman: The Actor and the Man* (London: Robert Hale, 1986), p. 66.
366 "Overriding significance": Richard H. Kuh, "Censorship *with* Freedom of Expression," in Harry M. Clor, editor, *Censorship and Freedom of Expression: Essays on Obscenity and the Law* (Chicago: Rand McNally College Publishing Co., 1971), p. 144.

Leaving London
366 No mention of Ephraim London: *Lenny Bruce Without Tears* (New York: Fred Baker Film & Video Co., 1992). As late as 1998, Kuh noted that Garbus was the "junior" lawyer in the New York obscenity trial; and, therefore, Garbus could not fairly claim, without qualification, to be the attorney who "defended" Lenny Bruce. Richard H. Kuh, Letter to the Editor, *New York Times*, October 4, 1998, sec. AR, p. 4. In fairness to Garbus, he did mention Ephraim London in two of his books, though he downplayed London's role.
366 Elgin Theater newspaper advertisement: *Village Voice*, July 6, 1972, p. 52.
367 Muggeridge, Tynan, Hentoff, Garbus, Krassner, Hogan, Cuccia, and Glenesk quotes: *Lenny Bruce Without Tears* (New York: Fred Baker Film & Video Co., 1992).
369 Jean Shepherd: John M. Whalen, "Jean Shepherd, Looking Life in the Eye and Laughing," *Washington Post*, October 21, 1999, sec. C, p. 1.
370 The documentary was fringe stuff: Fred Baker continued to create and host various Lenny Bruce events, such as his July 29, 1981 tribute to Lenny held at the Manhattan Punch Line Theater. Then, in October 1987, Baker hosted "The Lenny Bruce Revue" at the Harold Clurman Theater in Manhattan, which consisted of an arranged sequence of Bruce monologues performed by a nine-member ensemble and accompanied by dancers and slides.

Man of the Moment
370 Account of Kuh's appointment to and early days in the Manhattan District Attorney position: Laurie Johnston, "Idealistic Prosecutor," *New York Times*, February 6, 1974, p. 41; Tom Goldstein, "Kuh Appointed Manhattan Prosecutor: Scotti, Chagrined, Planning to Retire," *New York Times*, February 6, 1974, p. 41; Editorial, "New District Attorney," *New York Times*, February 6, 1974, p. 36; Judith Michaelson, "In For Hogan," *New York Post*, February 9, 1974, p. 22.
372 "Temporary," "interim": Nat Hentoff, "'The Idealistic (sic) Prosecutor,'" *Village Voice*, February 21, 1974, pp. 22, 23 ["(sic)" in original title].

"He Sees the Law as a Weapon"
373 "I think the staff realizes": The *Newsmakers*, WCBS, February 17, 1974 interview quoting Richard Kuh is cited in Nat Hentoff, "'The Idealistic (sic) Prosecutor' (3)," *Village Voice*, February 28, 1974, p. 9.
374 "He was too puritanical": "Three More to Quit over Kuh? They Deny It," *New York Post*, February 6, 1974, p. 34.
374 Nat Hentoff articles: Nat Hentoff, "'The Idealistic (sic) Prosecutor' (1)," *Village Voice*, February 14, 1974, pp. 9, 10, 12, 13; Nat Hentoff, "'The Idealistic (sic) Prosecutor' (2)," *Village Voice*, February 21, 1974, pp. 22, 23; Nat Hentoff, "'The Idealistic (sic) Prosecutor' (3)," *Village Voice*, February 28, 1974, pp. 9, 10, 14.

Old Foes, New Battles, and Artists
377 Vanden Heuvel, Garbus, and Morgenthau opposition: Thomas P. Ronan, "Kuh Faces Race to Retain Post," *New York Times*, March 3, 1974, p. 33.
377 Vanden Heuvel's record and Hogan's in-house supporters: Mike Pearl, *Mr. District Attorney: The Story of Frank S. Hogan and the Manhattan D.A.'s Office* (New York: Mason/Charter, 1977), pp. 228, 235–47.

377 Morgenthau vs. Kuh: *U.S. v. Winston,* 267 F. Supp. 555 (S.D. N.Y., 1967).
377 Morgenthau a candidate: Tom Goldstein, "Vanden Heuvel Bows Out of Manhattan D.A. Race," *New York Times,* March 21, 1974, p. 45; Frank Lynn, "Morgenthau Enters Democratic Contest for Manhattan D.A.," *New York Times,* March 15, 1974, p. 1.
377 Kuh "a prosecutor not a persecutor": Herbert Monte-Levy, Letter to the Editor, *New York Times,* March 6, 1974, p. 36.
378 Hogan's death: "Hogan, District Attorney Thirty-Two Years, Dies," *New York Times,* April 3, 1974, pp. 1, 32; Barry Cunningham with Mike Pearl, *Mr. District Attorney: The Story of Frank S. Hogan and the Manhattan D.A.'s Office* (New York: Mason/Charter, 1977), pp. 194–7, 240, 279; Laurie Johnston, "Three Hundred Pay Tribute to Hogan in Court," *New York Times,* April 4, 1974, p. 44; Paul Montgomery, "Thousand Pay Tribute to Hogan," *New York Times,* April 6, 1974, p. 35.
379 Paid political ad: "Lenny Bruce Arrested!" *New York Times,* April 3, 1974, p. 4 (emphasis in original).
379 Campaign against Kuh: Interviews with Carl R. Baldwin, July 21, 1999, and Tom Wesselmann, July 21, 1999. While Wesselmann, a noted pop culture artist, does not deny signing the ad and likewise being involved in the protest, he today curiously claims to lack any specific recollection of his 1974 involvement.

The Ghost of Lenny Bruce
381 "1974 will be a heavy year for the ghost of Lenny Bruce": Ralph J. Gleason, "The Ghost of Lenny Bruce," *San Francisco Chronicle,* January 6, 1974, p. 21.
381 *The World of Lenny Bruce: New York Times,* April 12, 1974, p. 16 (Speiser); Clive Barnes, "Theater: 'Lenny Bruce,'" *New York Times,* June 12, 1974, p. 39 (Speiser); *Village Voice,* July 11, 1974, p. 74 ("No Expletives Deleted!" ad). See also Douglas J. Keating, "Lenny Bruce and His Assault on the Limits of Free-Speech," *Philadelphia Inquirer,* October 30, 1998, p. 40. For a critical assessment of the Speiser play, see Nat Hentoff, "What's Left of Lenny?" *Village Voice,* June 13, 1974, p. 85 ("in no way does Speiser come anywhere near the *performer* Lenny was").
381 *Ladies and Gentlemen—Lenny Bruce!!:* Portions of the book—once tentatively titled *Lenny, Honey, and Sally—*were published, along with many photographs, in the September 3, 1971, issue of the *Los Angeles Free Press.* Albert Goldman, from the journalism of Lawrence Schiller, "A Day in the Life of Lenny Bruce," *Los Angeles Free Press,* September 3, 1971, pp. 33–5, 37–46, 48–52, 54–8, 60, 62.
381 Authorship of *Ladies and Gentlemen— Lenny Bruce!!:* Albert H. Goldman (1927–1994) was a contemporary jazz and rock music critic with a Ph.D. in English. Between 1963 and 1972, he taught as an adjunct professor of English at Columbia University. The Pennsylvania-born writer once described himself as "one-half New York intellectual and one-half Brooklyn-Broadway wiseguy." Goldman, a pop music columnist for *Life* (1970–1973), wrote for many publications, including the *New York Times Magazine, Commentary,* and *The New Republic.* For a critique of Goldman's methodology and biographical techniques, see Greil Marcus, *Dead Elvis: A Chronicle of a Cultural Obsession* (Cambridge, MA: Harvard University Press, 1991), pp. 47–59. Regarding Richard Warren Lewis, Goldman noted that he "deserves credit and recognition for his narratives of Lenny's Chicago and West Coast trials, which I have adapted." See Albert Goldman and Lawrence Schiller, *Ladies and Gentlemen, Lenny Bruce!!* (New York: Random House, 1974), p. 565. Lewis was a prolific writer who wrote for *TV Guide, Playboy, Life,* and the *Saturday Evening Post,* among other publications. He was also the author of *The Scavengers and Critics of the Warren Report* (New York: Dell Books, 1967) (based on investigative work by Lawrence Schiller). Lewis died in 1998. See Obituary, *Los Angeles Times,* March 14, 1998, Pt. A, p. 16. Lawrence Schiller, who lives in Southern California, has written books on the Sharon Tate

killing, the O.J. Simpson trial, and the JonBenét Ramsey murder. He worked with Norman Mailer on a biography of Marilyn Monroe. In 1966, Schiller edited and produced *Why Did Lenny Bruce Die?* (Capitol Records, No. SKAO2630).

382 "My books are a cold dose of reality": When Goldman died of a heart attack at age sixty-six, he was working on a biography of Jim Morrison. Earlier, he coedited a work on Richard Wagner and authored a book on Thomas De Quincy. He also wrote highly controversial, tome-like biographies of Elvis Presley and John Lennon. His other books included works on carnival life, marijuana, disco music, and two collections of essays.

382 Goldman's biographical profile of Lenny Bruce: Albert Goldman and Lawrence Schiller, *Ladies and Gentlemen, Lenny Bruce!!* (New York: Random House, 1974) (pagination in order of quotation in text), pp. 17, 162, 176, 184, 452, 195, 280, 480, 452, 451, 540, 452, 467, 451, 461, 448, 464.

382 Goldman's description of himself, his response to his critics, and his life and death: Nigel Leigh, "Pop Goes the Icons," *The Guardian,* April 4, 1974, p. 21; Obituary, *Los Angeles Times,* April 1, 1994, sec. A, p. 26; William Grimes, Obituary, *New York Times,* March 30, 1994, sec. D, p. 19.

382 "Factual errors": Nat Hentoff, "What's Left of Lenny?" *Village Voice,* June 13, 1974, p. 85.

383 Albert Goldman interviewed Kuh: Interview with Richard Kuh, September 30, 1999.

383 "Twitching of a damaged muscle": Richard H. Kuh, *Foolish Figleaves? Pornography in—and out of—Court* (New York: Macmillan, 1967), p. 176, quoting Albert Goldman, "The Trial of Lenny Bruce," *New Republic,* September 12, 1964, p. 13.

384 Morgenthau gains, "little visible Democratic organization," and Kuh Republican nomination: Frank Lynn, "Morgenthau in District Attorney Race," *New York Times,* May 21, 1974, p. 48.

384 New prosecutorial program: M.A. Farber, "Kuh Offers Charge in Small Methadone Sales," *New York Times,* June 19, 1974, pp. 1, 29.

384 "Almost from the moment of his appointment": Tom Buckley, "Manhattan D.A. Race Bears Imprint of the Past," *New York Times,* June 4, 1974, pp. 39, 61.

"Feminists Here Split Over an Endorsement of Kuh"

385 Feminists' support of Kuh: Steven R. Weisman, "Feminists Here Split Over an Endorsement of Kuh," *New York Times,* June 15, 1974, p. 33; Interview with Barbara Seaman, October 5, 1999 (Joyce Kuh and *Ladies Home Journal*); Stephanie Harrington, "Is Richard Kuh Really a Feminist Candidate?," *Village Voice,* July 18, 1974, pp. 5, 9.

386 *Miller v. California:* Susan Brownmiller, "Decision, Decision," *New York Times,* August 6, 1973, p. 31; *Miller v. California,* 413 U.S. 15 (1973).

387 "Patina of chic," "deliberate devaluation," and targeting ACLU-type liberals: Susan Brownmiller, *Against Our Will: Men, Women, and Rape* (New York: Simon & Schuster, 1975), pp. 392, 395.

387 Harrington's views on Kuh: Stephanie Harrington, "Is Richard Kuh Really a Feminist Candidate?" *Village Voice,* July 18, 1974, pp. 5, 6, 9.

388 "Long history of anti-obscenity laws": Gloria Steinem, "Obscene?" *Ms.,* October 1973, p. 21.

388 *Free and Female: The Sex Life of the Contemporary Woman* (New York: Coward, McCann & Geoghegan, 1972) once had been banned in some cities: See *New York Times,* August 29, 1983, sec. B, p. 3.

388 Susan Brownmiller was likewise sensitive to the problem: Susan Brownmiller, "Decision, Decision," *New York Times,* August 6, 1973, p. 31.

389 Consumer protection bureau: Gerald Gold, "Rivals for Consumers' Affection Pledge Cooperation for Kuh's New Bureau," *New York Times,* July 17, 1974, p. 41.

Tempers, Gentlemen

390 Kuh and Morgenthau square off: "Kuh Expects Funds for Sex-Crime Unit," *New York Times,* Aug. 29, 1974, p. 35; Marcia Chambers, "Kuh Assails Morgenthau As an Inept Administrator," *New York Times,* July 18, 1974, p. 39; "Morgenthau-Kuh Debate Flares into Accusatory Argument," *New York Times,* September 3, 1974, p. 37; "Kuh and Morgenthau State Positions on the Eve of Democratic Primary," *New York Law Journal,* September 9, 1974, pp. 1, 5; Deirdre Carmody, "Morgenthau Says Record Backs Him on Bruce Trial," *New York Times,* September 4, 1974, p. 31.

392 "Ugly stories about the Bruce case and my role in it": The debate continued on into the next day's paper. Pointing to the Bruce trial record, Kuh noted that he had not opposed Bruce's request for bail, but rather challenged the procedure by which the request had been presented to the Court. See Deirdre Carmody. "Morgenthau Says Record Backs Him on Bruce Trial," *New York Times,* September 4, 1974, p. 31.

393 Civil Liberties Union and Citizens Union: Deirdre Carmody, "Morgenthau, Kuh Faulted on Rights," *New York Times,* September 6, 1974, p. 38.

393 "Preferred candidate": Editorial, "District Attorney's Race," *New York Times,* September 5, 1974, p. 36.

393 WCBS-TV and Central Park: Peter Kihss, "Kuh Asks for Tighter Laws on Fifteen-Year-Olds," *New York Times,* September 9, 1974, p. 28.

Wide Margins

393 Morgenthau wins nomination. Donald Flynn, "Kuh Will Race Uphill After Win by Morgy," *New York Daily News,* September 12, 1974, p. 26 (story and photo); Peter Kihss, "Morgenthau Lead is Overwhelming," *New York Times,* September 11, 1974, pp. 1, 34; Peter Kihss, "Morgenthau-Kuh Contest to be Repeated on Nov. 5," *New York Times,* September 12, 1974, p. 32.

394 "I can't get worked up about politics": Lenny Bruce, quoted in John Cohen, editor, *The Essential Lenny Bruce* (New York: Ballantine Books, 1967), p. 76.

394 Kuh's new initiatives: Marcia Chambers, "Scrutinize Police, Kuh Orders Staff," *New York Times,* October 11, 1974, pp. 1, 20; Marcia Chambers, "Kuh Says Judge Lacked Candor," *New York Times,* October 22, 1974, p. 34; R.W. Apple Jr., "Kuh Points to Morgenthau and a Bugging," *New York Times,* October 26, 1974, p. 14; "Kuh Asks Morgenthau to Open Twenty-Year Old Wiretapping File," *New York Times,* October 28, 1974, p. 26.

395 "He had performed ably": Editorial, "The District Attorneys," *New York Times,* October 31, 1974, p. 40.

396 Landslide and no formal concession: Marcia Chambers, "Morgenthau Is Sworn In; Vows Fight on Violence," *New York Times,* January 5, 1975, p. 31.

Cinematic Justice

396 "Dustin Hoffman plays Lenny": Honey Bruce with Dana Benenson, *Honey: The Life and Loves of Lenny's Shady Lady* (Chicago: Playboy Press, 1976), pp. 4–5. Al Pacino almost got the Lenny role. See also Patrick Agan, *Hoffman vs. Hoffman: The Actor and the Man* (London: Robert Hale, 1986), p. 67.

397 Filming *Lenny*: Patrick Agan, *Hoffman vs. Hoffman: The Actor and the Man* (London: Robert Hale, 1986), pp. 67, 69, 70.

397 Quotes from movie: *Lenny* (United Artists, 1974), directed by Bob Fosse and produced by Marvin Worth.

397 Marvin Worth: Worth (1926–1998) was a noted writer and movie producer. The eclectic Worth was Sally Marr's manager in the early years. He then worked with Lenny and got him an audition on *The Arthur Godfrey Show*. For some time, he also managed Charlie Parker and Billie Holiday.

399 Book based on movie: Valerie Kohler Smith, *Lenny: The Real Story* (New York: Grove Press, 1974).
399 Soundtrack released: *Lenny* (motion picture soundtrack) (United Artists, 1974).
399 $11 million: Jeff Lenburg, *Dustin Hoffman: Hollywood's Anti-Hero* (New York: St. Martin's Press, 1983), p. 94.
399 "Disappointment": Andrew Kopkind, "Lenny Bruce: Resurrection of a Junkie Prophet," *Ramparts*, vol. 13, March 1975, pp. 45, 46.

11. EX OFFICIO JUDGMENTS

Epigraph: William M. Kunstler with Sheila Isenberg, *My Life as a Radical Lawyer* (New York: Citadel Press, 1996 updated edition), p. 167.

Lenny's Legacy
404 Companion case to Bruce's New York case: *People v. Solomon*, 26 N.Y. 2d 621, 255 N.E. 2d 720, 307 N.Y.S. 2d 464 (N.Y., 1970).

Outlaw?
405 Artist as outlaw: As modern pop culture would have it, Lenny Bruce has risen to the status of artist as outlaw—for his radical poetry, no less. See Alan Kaufman, *The Outlaw Bible of American Poetry* (New York: Thunders' Mouth Press, 1999), pp. 288–91, 650 (with a photo of the young Lenny).
405 Krim's comments on Bruce: Seymour Krim, *Shake It for the World, Smartass* (New York: Dial Press, 1970), p. 266 (from a 1963 editorial originally published in *Nugget* magazine). Still, Krim did believe (with some inconsistency?) that "to make Lenny the martyr for all the dirty mouths around is vindictive and unjust, even if at times he seems to desire a niche in history as a Copacabana Jesus" (p. 263). Krim, however, never explained why he thought it was "vindictive and unjust" to prosecute Lenny Bruce.
406 Joe Hill: Philip Foner, *The Case of Joe Hill* (New York: International Publishers, 1965).
406 Goldman's early articles on Lenny Bruce once were used by lawyers to defend the dissident comic: They were also used by Bruce's prosecutors. See, e.g., Richard H. Kuh, *Foolish Figleaves?* (New York: Macmillan Co., 1967), p. 176.
406 Goldman's analysis of Bruce's defense: Albert Goldman, *Freakshow: The Rocksoul-bluesjazzjewblackhumorsexpopsych Gig and Other Scenes from the Counter-Culture* (New York: Atheneum, 1971), pp. 203–6 (based on an article, "One Law for the Lion and Ox," that originally appeared in 1965 in *Censorship*).

Community Standards, Then and Again
409 Epigraph: William F. Buckley Jr., *Inveighing We Will Go* (New York: G.P. Putnam's Sons, 1972), p. 57 (quoting from 1970 *Playboy* interview).
409 Kuh quotes circa 1974: Laurie Johnston, "Idealistic Prosecutor," *New York Times*, February 6, 1974, p. 41.
410 Burger Court opinions: *Miller v. California*, 413 U.S. 15 (1973) and *Paris Adult Theatre I v. Slaton*, 413 U.S. 49 (1973).
410 "A self-styled expert": Nat Hentoff, "'The Idealistic (sic) Prosecutor' (1)," *Village Voice*, February 14, 1974, pp. 9, 10.
411 Kuh's prosecution of Bruce: Trial Transcript, *People v. Bruce, et al.* (New York City Criminal Court; Part 2B: County of New York), July 1, 1964 (afternoon), pp. 84–5 (Kuh question to Kilgallen); July 6, 1964, pp. 44–8 (Kuh question to Johnson).

"Perhaps It Has Been My Fault"
413 They relished quoting Brennan as support for their cases against the dirty dissident: For example, the brief prepared by Assistant State Attorney James R. Thompson for

presentation to the Illinois high court stated: "The opinion by Mr. Justice Brennan in *Roth* is...authority for the People's argument—not defendant's." Brief and Argument for Defendant in Error, *People v. Bruce* (November Term, 1963) (Ill. S. Ct.), p. 10.

414 Justice Brennan on obscenity jurisprudence: William J. Brennan Jr., quoted in Nat Hentoff, "The Constitutionalist," *The New Yorker,* March 12, 1990, p. 50; William J. Brennan Jr., quoted in Jeffrey T. Leeds, "A Life on the Court: Justice Brennan, at the Start of the Fall Term, Discusses His Life on and off the Court," *New York Times Magazine,* October 5, 1986, pp. 25, 79.

414 The seven obscenity cases are: *Roth v. U.S.,* 354 U.S. 476 (1957) (Brennan, J., for the Court), *Kingsley Books, Inc. v. Brown,* 354 U.S. 436 (1957) (Brennan, J., dissenting), *Smith v. California,* 361 U.S. 147 (1959) (Brennan, J., for the Court), *Marcus v. Search Warrant,* 367 U.S. 717 (1961) (Brennan, J., for the Court), *Bantam Books, Inc. v. Sullivan,* 372 U.S. 58 (1963) (Brennan, J., for the Court), *Jacobellis v. Ohio,* 378 U.S. 184 (1964) (Brennan, J., plurality opinion), and *Ginzburg v. United States,* 383 U.S. 463 (1966) (Brennan, J., for the Court).

414 But it was only a hint in a footnote: It is noteworthy that Bruce's legal problems were compounded by a Brennan footnote in *Roth v. United States* (1957). By the same token, Brennan later sought to diminish such problems by a footnote in his *Memoirs v. Massachusetts* (1966) opinion, which was handed down too late to be of much use to Bruce. See *Memoirs v. Massachusetts,* 383 U.S. 413, 419–20, note 7 (1966).

414 "After sixteen years": *Paris Adult Theatre I v. Slaton,* 413 U.S. 49, 83–4 (1973) (Brennan, J., dissenting).

415 "The protection given": *Roth v. U.S.,* 354 U.S. 476 (1957).

415 Flaws in *Roth:* Harry Kalven Jr., "The Metaphysics of the Law of Obscenity," *Supreme Court Review* (1960), p. 1; Interview with Maurice Rosenfield, September 30, 1999.

417 "We have very few really free spirits": Eileen Sheehan, Unpublished interview with Harry Kalven Jr., Fall 1974.

Taking the Fifth

417 Epigraph: Lenny Bruce, quoted in John Cohen, editor, *The Essential Lenny Bruce* (New York: Ballantine Books, 1967), p. 300.

418 John Lilburne and subsequent Fifth Amendment history: Leonard W. Levy, *Origins of the Fifth Amendment* (New York: Oxford University Press, 1968), pp. 266–432.

418 It was the first time that Lenny...took the Fifth to exclude audio evidence of [his] performance: A qualification is necessary here. In the Chicago trial, Lenny's co-counsel, Earle Warren Zaidins, invoked the Fifth Amendment when the State attempted to introduce the tape of Bruce's Gate of Horn performance. Of course, the motivation was to preserve the defense's control of the tape as its *own* evidence, for its *own* use. As it turned out, the defense later freely introduced the tape into evidence.

419 Fifth Amendment claims: Trial Transcript, *People v. Bruce, et al.* (New York City Criminal Court; Part 2B: County of New York), April 14, 1964, pp. 7, 20; April 28, 1964, p. 26.

419 Solomon's right to plead the Fifth: Asserted by Schwartz, Trial Transcript, *People v. Bruce, et al.* (New York City Criminal Court; Part 2B: County of New York), April 14, 1964, p. 12.

419 Kuh's reactions: Trial Transcript, *People v. Bruce, et al.* (New York City Criminal Court; Part 2B: County of New York), April 14, 1964, pp. 47, 52, 77; April 28, 1964, p. 27.

Who Killed Lenny Bruce?
421 Epigraph: Peter Hall, "Why I Love Lenny the Liberator," *The Guardian* (England), July 24, 1999, p. 3.
421 "Why do you think Lenny Bruce died?": In 1966, Capitol Records released *Why Did Lenny Bruce Die?* (Capitol, SKAO, 2630). The audio documentary was edited and produced by Lawrence Schiller and consisted of interviews with Bruce friends and family; there was even an interview with Arthur Schaefer, one of Lenny's San Francisco prosecutors.
421 "Delighted to speculate": Larry Josephson interview with Richard H. Kuh, WBAI Radio (Pacifica Radio), 1972.
421 "We drove him to poverty": Vincent Cuccia, quoted in Martin Garbus, *Ready for the Defense* (New York: Farrar, Straus, Giroux, 1971), p. 81.
421 "My only regret": Larry Josephson interview with Sherman Block, WBAI Radio (Pacifica Radio), 1989.
422 "Inner turmoil": Martin Garbus, *Ready for the Defense* (New York: Farrar, Straus, Giroux, 1971), p. 138.
422 "He [was] alive": Dick Schaap, "The Friends of Lenny Bruce," *Herald Tribune,* November 19, 1964, p. 19 (written *before* Bruce's death). See also Dick Schaap, "A Minority Report," *Herald Tribune,* July 2, 1964; Dick Schaap, "The Bruce Behind Bars," *Herald Tribune,* December 21, 1964.
422 "An overdose of police": Phil Spector, quoted in *Playboy,* January 1967, p. 163.
422 "Lenny OD'd deliberately": William M. Kunstler with Sheila Isenberg, *My Life as a Radical Lawyer* (New York: Citadel Press, 1994 updated edition), p. 168.
423 "He surrendered": Larry Josephson interview with Lotus Weinstock, WBAI Radio (Pacifica Radio), 1989.
423 "A heavy weight of destruction": Irving Howe, *World of Our Fathers* (New York, Galahad Books, 1976), p. 573.
423 Sahl's take on the "Who killed Lenny?" question: Robert Weide interview with Mort Sahl, aired on Larry Josephson, WBAI Radio (Pacifica Radio), 1989.
424 Spector's reaction to Sahl's view: Phil Spector, quoted in Jan Wenner, "The Rolling Stone Interview," *Rolling Stone,* November 1, 1969, p. 24.
425 Brennan quotation: *New York Times v. Sullivan*, 376 U.S. 254 (1964).

EPILOGUE: ONLY WORDS
Epigraph: Robert J. Landry, "Lenny Bruce's Taboo Defiance Cost: From $200,000 a Year to Ostracism," *Variety,* November 3, 1965, pp. 2, 70.

Free Speech Zones
429 The Cho account: Based on bits delivered at her February 22, 2001 8:30 P.M. performance at the Improv comedy club in Washington, D.C.. Variations of those bits are recounted in her subsequently published autobiography, *I'm the One That I Want* (New York: Ballentine Books, 2001), pp. 33-4 (Jeremy and Alan), p. 166 (telling the truth). Interview with Margaret Cho, February 23, 2001.
430 Great impact of comedy: Amelia David, "The Laughs, They Were A-Changin': Comedy Grows Up," *Back Stage,* December 15, 2000, sec. A, p. 24.
431 Observations about Lenny Bruce's impact on comedy: Ralph Gleason, quoted in Nat Hentoff, "The Onliest Lenny Bruce," *Village Voice,* February 15, 1991, p. 22; Lawrence Schiller, from *Why Did Lenny Bruce Die?* (Capitol Records, 1966, KAO 2630); Arthur Gelb, quoted in Liner Notes for *The Lenny Bruce Performance Film* (Santa Monica, CA: Rhino Home Video, 1992), produced by John Magnuson; Interview with George Carlin, May 20, 2001; Barry Sanders, *Sudden Glory: Laughter as Subversive History* (Boston: Beacon Press, 1995), p. 255; Joan Rivers with Richard Meryman, *Enter Talking* (New York: Delacorte Press, 1986), p. 308; Interview with Margaret Cho, February 23, 2001; Peter Hall, "Why I Love Lenny the

Liberator," *The Guardian,* July 24, 1999, Saturday Review, p. 3.

431 Comedy clubs have become free speech zones, public places where First Amendment freedom is virtually unrivaled: Something of the same can be said of live theater on public stages and, to a slightly lesser extent, of books, the Internet, and movies.

Coming Out of the Free Speech Closet

433 Transcription of Carlin monologue: Appendix to Opinion of the Court in *FCC v. Pacifica Foundation,* 438 U.S. 726.

433 Carlin's routine—"Filthy Words": The routine was recorded before a live audience at Circle Star Theater, San Carlos, California, and released in October 1973 as a cut on the album *Occupation: Foole* (Little David Records No. 1005). An earlier rendition was released in September 1972 on *Class Clown* (Little David Records No. 1004).

433 Carlin's purpose behind routine: Jim Mann and William J. Eaton, "Court Backs Ban on 'Dirty' Words on Radio and TV," *Los Angeles Times,* July 4, 1978, sec. I, pp. 1, 8.

433 Policemen and servicemen: *The O'Reilly Factor,* Fox News Network, April 30, 2001 (Bill O'Reilly interviewing George Carlin, Transcript # 043005cb.256).

434 Zeidler and Zeidler radio commercials: Albert Goldman and Lawrence Schiller, *Ladies and Gentlemen, Lenny Bruce!!* (New York: Random House, 1974), pp. 264–8.

434 Pacifica case: *Pacifica Foundation v. FCC,* 556 F. 2d 9, 13 (D.C. Cir., 1977) (emphasis in original); p. 69 (Bazelon, J., concurring), quoting *Times Film Corp. v. City of Chicago,* 365 U.S. 43, 77 (Warren, C.J., dissenting).

435 "There is no such thing as First Amendment punishment": Lenny Bruce, quoted in John Cohen, editor, *The Essential Lenny Bruce* (New York: Ballentine Books, 1967), p. 283.

436 The FCC was well within its power to silence Carlin's "seven dirty words" during the most popular listening hours: Justice Stevens provided two main reasons for the majority's decision. First, indecent words assault a captive audience in the privacy of the home or car, "where the individual's right to be let alone plainly outweighs the First Amendment rights to intrude." Second, offensive broadcasts may grab the attention of children, and "the government's interest in the 'well being of its youth'" justified regulation of even non-obscene but indecent expression. Four Justices, including Justice William Brennan, dissented from those lines of thinking. *FCC v. Pacifica Foundation,* 438 U.S. 726, 749 (1978).

436 Indecent words...are not entitled...to much constitutional protection: By contrast, in *Sable Communications, Inc. v. FCC,* 492 U.S. 115 (1989), the Supreme Court invalidated a federal law that banned indecent telephone "dial-a-porn." Writing for the Court, Justice Byron White declared: "Sexual expression which is indecent but not obscene is protected by the First Amendment." And such protection, the Court ruled, was entitled to considerable (not peripheral) First Amendment protection. Compare *Denver Area Educational Telecommunications Consortium, Inc. v. FCC,* 518 U.S. 727 (1996), which upheld and invalidated various regulations concerning indecent expression on cable television.

436 "Big Daddy": Lenny Bruce, quoted in John Cohen, editor, *The Essential Lenny Bruce* (New York: Ballentine Books, 1967), p. 280 .

437 Communications Decency Act of 1996: 47 U.S.C.A. §§223(a)(1)(B)(ii) (criminalizing the knowing transmission by computer of obscene or indecent messages to any person under 18 years of age), 223(d) (criminalizing the knowing sending or making available to any person under eighteen years of age any material that depicts or describes sexual or excretory activities or organs in a manner "patently offensive" according to contemporary community standards), 223(e)(5)(A) (providing

"affirmative defenses" to those who take "good faith" actions to restrict access by minors to the prohibited communications).

437 Potential effects of Communications Decency Act: Mike Godwin, *Cyber Rights: Defending Free Speech in the Digital Age* (New York: Time Books, 1998), p. 267.

437 *Reno v. ACLU*, 521 U.S. 844 (1997): p. 882 ("burning the house to roast the pig"), quoting *Sable Communications, Inc. v. F.C.C.*, 492 U.S. 115, 127 (1989); p. 878 (CDA covers any of the seven "dirty words"); pp. 867–9 (distinguishing *Pacifica Foundation*). Prior to authoring the opinion of the Court in *Reno v. ACLU*, Justice Stevens had conceded a partial retrenchment from his reasoning in *FCC v. Pacifica Foundation*. See John Paul Stevens, "The Freedom of Speech," 102 *Yale Law Journal* 1293, 1307 (1993), suggesting how the result in *Pacifica* might have been different.

438 Warnings and shopping items: www.georgecarlin.com (accessed August 20, 2001).

439 Justice Stevens's inclusion of Carlin's controversial words: One of the words from that routine, "cunt," had never previously appeared and has never subsequently appeared in the *U.S. Supreme Court Reports*.

440 Carlin's quotes: George Carlin, *Napalm and Silly Putty* (New York: Hyperion, 2001), p. 175 (joking about anything), p. 171 (Mother Teresa).

440 The "7 Dirty Words": *oyez.nwu.edu/cases/cases.cgi?case_id=120&command= show*, accessed August 20, 2001. On Northwestern University's Oyez site for the U.S. Supreme Court, an audiofile of the entire "7 Dirty Words" routine is readily available as a link from the *FCC v. Pacifica* case.

440 AOL: A.S. Berman, "Lenny Bruce Still Testing the Limits," *USA Today*, November 2, 2000, sec. D, p. 3.

"We Want It Stopped"

441 "Filth, vulgarity, sex, and violence": Ad, The Parents Television Council. The ad ran in the *Washington Post*, among other publications, on December 12, 1999, sec. B, p. 4, and on October 17, 1999, sec. B, p. 6.

441 "In today's Anything Goes culture": Steve Allen, "That's Entertainment?" *Wall Street Journal*, November 13, 1998, p. 17.

442 Bruce a "philosopher": Steve Allen, quoted in pamphlet accompanying *The Lenny Bruce Performance Film* (Santa Monica, CA: Rhino Home Video, 1992: CD and video box set), produced by John Magnuson.

442 Audio clips of Bruce's act: *Lenny Bruce: Swear to Tell the Truth* (San Fernando, CA: Whyaduck Productions, 1998), written and produced by Robert B. Weide and narrated by Robert De Niro, aired on HBO, August 1999.

443 Allen commenting on Lenny Bruce and the PTC decency campaign: Noel Holston, "Steve Allen Says TV is Stuck on the Wrong Channel," *Star Tribune* (Minneapolis), November 19, 1998, sec. E, p. 1; Steve Allen, *Vulgarians at the Gate: Trash TV and Raunch Radio* (New York: Prometheus Books, 2001), pp. 222, 313.

"I'm Not a Comedian, I'm Lenny Bruce"

444 Commenting on Allen's anxieties: Interview with Hugh Hefner, July 17, 2001.

445 Justice Anthony Kennedy: *United States v. Playboy Entertainment Group*, 120 S. Ct. 1878 (2000).

445 George Carlin was less idealistic: Interview with George Carlin, May 20, 2001.

446 "Offend *everybody*": *Steve Allen Show*, April 12, 1959, excerpted in *Lenny Bruce Without Tears* (New York: Fred Baker Film & Video Co., 1992), narration and continuity by John Parsons and narrated by Fred Baker.

446 "Experimented with extremes": Tony Hendra, *Going Too Far* (New York: Dolphin Doubleday, 1987) p. 119.

448 "I'm not a comedian, I'm Lenny Bruce": Lenny Bruce, quoted in Ralph J. Gleason, "Lenny Bruce: Obscene Language Pinch in Frisco after Philly Rap," *Variety*, October 11, 1961, pp. 61, 64.

448 "Pissing on the velvet": Lenny Bruce, quoted in John Cohen, editor, *The Essential Lenny Bruce* (New York: Ballantine Books, 1967), p. 118.

448 "Performers can work": Nat Hentoff, "The Onliest Lenny Bruce," *Village Voice,* February 15, 1991, p. 22.

448 "I like to find where the line is drawn": Interview with George Carlin, May 20, 2001.

449 Landry on Bruce: Robert J. Landry, "Lenny Bruce's Taboo Defiance Cost: From $200,000 a Year to Ostracism," *Variety,* November 3, 1965, pp. 2, 70.

449 "I don't want to end up like [Lenny Bruce], but I want to be like him": Interview with Margaret Cho, February 23, 2001.

BIBLIOGRAPHY

WORKS BY BRUCE

Books and Other Published Writings
Bruce, Lenny. *The Almost Unpublished Lenny Bruce*. Philadelphia: Running Press, 1984.
———. "Bruce Here." *Rogue Magazine*, January through December 1960 (series).
———. *The Essential Lenny Bruce*. John Cohen, ed. New York: Ballantine Books, 1967.
———. "The Fecalphiles." *The Realist*, November 1964, pp. 1, 10-2.
———. "How to Talk Dirty and Influence People: Part One of an Autobiography."
    Playboy, October 1963, p. 104.
———. "How to Talk Dirty and Influence People: Part Two of an Autobiography."
    Playboy, November 1963, p. 140.
———. "How to Talk Dirty and Influence People: Part Three of an Autobiography."
    Playboy, December 1963, p. 182.
    "How to Talk Dirty and Influence People: Part Four of an Autobiography."
    Playboy, January 1964, p. 68.
———. *How to Talk Dirty and Influence People*. Chicago: Playboy Press, 1965. Reprint,
    New York: Fireside Books, 1992.
———. "A Letter to Judge Murtaugh [sic]." *Tree*, Winter 1974, vol. 45, pp. 60-73.
———. "Obscenity, Narcotics and Me." *The Realist*, March 1964, p. 1.
———. "The Playboy Panel: Hip Comics and the New Humor." *Playboy*, March 1961,
    p. 25.
———. "Stamp Out Help: The Pot Smokers." *High Times*, October 1976,
    p. 43.

Movies
Bruce, Lenny. Phil Tucker, dir. *Dance Hall Racket*. N.P.: Psychotronic Film Society
    Archives, 1953.
———. *Dream Follies*. N.P., 1953.
———. *The Leather Jacket*. N.P., 1955-1957.

Recordings
Bruce, Lenny. *I'm Not A Nut, Elect Me*. "Togetherness." Berkeley, CA: Fantasy Records,
    1960. LP.
———. *The Law, Language, and Lenny Bruce*. Burbank, CA: Warner-Spector, 1974.
    LP.
———. *Lenny Bruce: American*. Berkeley, CA: Fantasy Records, 1962. LP.

———. *Lenny Bruce: Carnegie Hall.* Los Angeles, CA: United Artist Records, 1972. 2 LPs.

———. *Lenny Bruce's Interviews of Our Times.* Berkeley, CA: Fantasy Records, n.d. LP.

———. *Lenny Bruce Is Out Again.* Los Angeles CA: Philles Records, 1965. LP.

———. *Lenny Bruce, Live 1962: Busted!* N.P.: Viper's Nest Records, 1995. CD.

———. *Lenny Bruce, Live at the Curran Theater.* Berkeley, CA: Fantasy Records, 1972. 3 LPs. 1999 2-CD set.

———. *The Lenny Bruce Originals, Volume 1.* Berkeley, CA: Fantasy, 1991. CD.

———. *The Lenny Bruce Originals, Volume 2.* Berkeley, CA: Fantasy, 1991. CD.

———. *The Lenny Bruce Performance Film.* Santa Monica, CA: Rhino Home Video, 1992. Videocassette and CD.

———. *Lenny Bruce: The Berkeley Concert.* Burbank, CA: Reprise Records, 1969. LP.

———. *The Real Lenny Bruce.* Berkeley, CA: Fantasy Records, 1975. 2 LPs.

———. *Recording Submitted as Evidence in the San Francisco Obscenity Trial.* San Francisco, CA: produced by Lenny Bruce, 1962. LP.

———. *The Sick Humor of Lenny Bruce.* Berkeley, CA: Fantasy Records, 1959. LP.

———. *The Story of Lenny: What I Was Arrested For.* Los Angeles, CA: Casablanca Records, 1975. LP.

———. *Thank You Mask Man: The Real Lenny Bruce.* Berkeley, CA: Fantasy Records, 1972. LP.

———. *To Is a Preposition; Come Is a Verb.* Los Angeles, CA: Douglas Records, n.d. LP.

———. *Warning: Sale of this Album...* Los Angeles, CA: Privately pressed label, 1962. Lenny Bruce LB-9001/2. LP.

Published Interviews with Bruce
Interview by Pierre Berton, in *The Cool Crazy Committed World of the Sixties.* Toronto: McClelland & Stewart, 1966, pp. 87–96

Interview by Paul Krassner, in *Impolite Interviews.* New York: Lyle Stuart, 1961.

Interview by Lionel Olay, in "The Trials and Tribulations of L*nny Br*ce." *Cavalier,* October 1963, pp. 11–2, 82–4.

Interview by Studs Terkel, in Lenny Bruce *The Almost Unpublished Lenny Bruce.* Philadelphia: Running Press, 1984, pp. 15–21.

UNPUBLISHED CORRESPONDENCE BY OR ABOUT BRUCE

Bruce, Lenny. Letter to the American Civil Liberties Union. 23 March 1964.

———. Letter to Richard Marx. 21 July 1965.

———. Western Union telegram to Maurice Rosenfield. 18 November 1963.

———. Letter to John Stern. 16 March 1964.

Collier, Chet. Letter to Lenny Bruce. 13 March 1964.

Fried, Seymour. Letter to Ralph Gleason. 8 November 1961.

Friedman, Don. Telegram to Lenny Bruce. 8 June 1964.

Gleason, Ralph J. Letter to Lenny Bruce. 3 May 1965.

de Grazia, Edward. Letter to Ralph J. Gleason. 9 April 1965.

———. Letter to Ralph J. Gleason. 8 June 1965.

Hellerstein, William E. Letter to Howard L. Solomon. 9 January 1970.

London, Ephraim. Letter to Lenny Bruce. 20 July 1964.

Los Angeles County Public Welfare Commission. Letter to Davfly, Inc., et al., 17 February 1965.

Messinger, Sheldon L. Letter from Vice Chairman of the Center for Law and Society to Professor Harry Kalven, Jr. 25 April 1963.

Rosenfield, Maurice. Letter to Lenny Bruce. 24 November 1965.

———. Letter to Robert J. Landry. 5 November 1965.

———. Letter to Jay H. Topkis. 24 November 1965.

———. Letter to Jay H. Topkis. 2 December 1965.
———. Western Union telegram to Lenny Bruce. 18 November 1963.
Rovinsky, Selma. Letter to John Judnick. 15 December 1964.
Schaap, William H. Letter to Lenny Bruce. May 26, 1965.
———. Letter to Maurice Rosenfield. 29 November 1965.
Schwarz, Allen. Letter to Lenny Bruce. 1 July 1965.
Squadron, Howard M. Letter to Maurice Rosenfield. 13 November 1965.
Sullivan, Ed. Letter to Frank Ray Perilli. 26 November 1958.
Topkis, Jay H. Letter to Lenny Bruce. 19 November 1965.

LINER NOTES ON LENNY BRUCE (FROM RECORDS, CDs, AUDIOTAPES, AND VIDEOS)

Gleason, Ralph J. *The Best of Lenny Bruce.* Berkeley, CA: Fantasy Records, n.d. Audio cassette.
Goldman, Albert. *Lenny Bruce: Carnegie Hall.* Los Angeles: United Artist Records, 1972. LP.
Lenny Bruce: The Berkeley Concert. New York: Reprise Records, n.d. LP.
Live at the Curran Theater. Berkeley, CA: Fantasy Records, 1972. LP.
Sales, Grover. *Lenny Bruce Originals.* Vols. 1 and 2. Berkeley, CA: Fantasy Records, 1991. CD.
The Sick Humor of Lenny Bruce. Berkeley, CA: Fantasy Records, 1959. LP.

BOOKS AND RECORDINGS ON OR PARIALLY ABOUT BRUCE

Allen, Steve. *Funny People.* New York: Stein & Day, 1981.
Barry, Julian. *Lenny.* New York: Grove Press, 1971.
The Beat Generation. Santa Monica, CA: Rhino/Word Beat Records, 1992.
Belli, Melvin M. and Robert Blair Kaiser. *My Life on Trial: An Autobiography.* New York: William Morrow, 1976.
Bessie, Alvah. *One for My Baby.* New York: Holt Rinehart Winston, 1980.
Bookspan, Martin, and Ross Yockey. *André Previn: A Biography.* New York: Doubleday, 1981.
Bruce, Honey, and Dana Benenson. *Honey: The Life and Loves of Lenny's Shady Lady.* Chicago: Playboy Press, 1976.
Casey, George. *Lenny, Janis and Jimi.* New York: Pocket Books, 1975.
Cochran Jr., Johnnie L., and Tim Rutten. *Journey to Justice.* New York: One World/Ballantine, 1996.
Conrad, Barnaby. *Name Dropping: Tales From the Barnaby Coast Saloon.* New York: HarperCollins West, 1994.
Cunningham, Barry, and Mike Pearl. *Mr. District Attorney: The Story of Frank S. Hogan and the Manhattan D.A.'s Office.* New York: Mason/Charter, 1977.
Dylan, Bob. *Shot of Love.* "Lenny Bruce." London: Columbia Records, 1981. LP.
Fox-Sheinwold, Patricia. *Too Young to Die.* Baltimore: Ottenheimer Publishers, 1979.
Freedland, Michael. *André Previn.* London: Century, 1991.
Garbus, Martin. *Ready for the Defense.* New York: Farrar, Straus & Giroux, 1971.
Garbus, Martin and Stanley Cohen. *Tough Talk: How I Fought for Writers, Comics, Bigots, and the American Way.* New York: Times Books, 1998.
Gold, Robert S., ed. *The Rebel Culture.* New York: Dell Publishing, 1970.
Goldman, Albert. *Freakshow: The Rocksoulbluesjazzsickjewblackhumorsexpoppsych Gig and Other Scenes from the Counter-Culture.* New York: Atheneum, 1974.
Goldman, Albert from the journalism of Lawrence Schiller. *Ladies and Gentlemen, Lenny Bruce!!* New York: Random House, 1974.
Gordan, Max. *Live at the Village Vanguard.* Introduction by Nat Hentoff. New York: St. Martin's Press, 1980.
de Grazia, Edward. *Girls Lean Back Everywhere: The Law of Obscenity and the Assault on Genius.* New York: Random House, 1992.

Hendra, Tony. *Going Too Far*. New York: Dolphin/Doubleday, 1987.

Hentoff, Nat. *Free Speech for Me—But Not for Thee: How the Left and Right Relentlessly Censor Each Other*. New York: HarperCollins Publishers, 1992.

Hoffman, Abbie. *Woodstock Nation: A Talk-Rock Album*. New York: Vintage Books, 1969.

Israel, Lee. *Kilgallen*. New York: Delacorte Press, 1979.

King, Larry, and Peter Occhiogrosso. *Tell It to the King*. New York: Putnam's Sons, 1988.

Kofsky, Frank. *Lenny Bruce: The Comedian as Social Critic and Secular Moralist*. New York: Monad Press, 1974.

Krassner, Paul. *Confessions of a Raving, Unconfined Nut*. New York: Simon & Schuster, 1993.

———. *Paul Krassner's Impolite Interviews*. New York: Lyle Stuart, 1961.

———. "An Obituary for Lenny Bruce (1964)." *The Winner of the Slow Bicycle Race: The Satirical Writings of Paul Krassner*. New York: Seven Stories Press, 1996.

Krim, Seymour. *Shake It for the World, Smartass*. New York: Dial Press, 1970.

Kuh, Richard H. *Foolish Figleaves? Pornography in—and out of—Court*. New York: Macmillan, 1967.

———. "Censorship with Freedom of Expression." *Censorship and Freedom of Expression: Essays on Obscenity and the Law*. Clor, Harry M., ed. Chicago: Rand McNally College Publishing, 1971.

Kunstler, William M. and Sheila Isenberg. *My Life As a Radical Lawyer*. New York: Carol Publishing Group, 1996. Rev. Ed.

Landson, Jandesman. *Rebel Without Applause*. New York: Paragon House, 1987.

Lax, Eric. *Woody Allen: A Biography*. New York: Knopf, 1991.

Myerson, Michael. *These Are the Good Old Days: Coming of Age as a Radical in America's Late, Late Years*. New York: Grossman Publishers, 1970.

Nico. "Eulogy to Lenny." *Chelsea Girl*. New York: Verve & Polygram Records, 1967. LP.

Ribowsky, Mark. *He's a Rebel*. New York: E.P. Dutton, 1989.

Rivers, Joan, and Richard Meryman. *Enter Talking*. New York: Delacorte Press, 1986.

Rosen, Jeffrey. "We Hardly Know It When We See It: Obscenity and the Problem of Unprotected Speech." *Reason and Passion: Justice Brennan's Enduring Influence*. Rosenkranz, Joshua and Bernard Schwartz, eds. New York: W.W. Norton, 1997.

Sahl, Mort. *Heartland*. New York: Harcourt Brace Jovanovich, 1976.

Sales, Grover. *The Trial of Lenny Bruce*. (Performance based on Lenny Bruce's obscenity trial.) San Francisco, 1962. Audio cassette.

Sanders, Barry. *Laughter as Subversive History*. Boston: Beacon Press, 1995.

Schiller, Lawrence. *Why Did Lenny Bruce Die?* Capitol Records, 1966, KAO 2630.

Schumacher, Michael. *Dharma Lion: A Critical Biography of Allen Ginsberg*. New York: St. Martin's Press, 1992.

Sheehan, Eileen. Unpublished Interviw with Harry Kalven Jr. Fall 1974.

Simon and Garfunkel. "7:00 News/Silent Night." *Collected Works*. New York: Columbia Records, 1981. 2 CDs.

Smith, Valerie Kohler. *Lenny: The Real Story*. New York: Dell, 1974.

Sol, Saporta. *Society, Language, and the University: From Lenny Bruce to Noam Chomsky*. New York: Vantage Press, 1994.

Sukenick, Ronald. *Down and In: Life in the Underground*. New York: Beech Tree Books, 1987.

Thomas, William Karl. *Lenny Bruce: The Making of a Prophet*. New York: Archon Books, 1989.

MOVIES, VIDEOS, AND DOCUMENTARIES ON BRUCE

Abrams, Daniel L. prod. (A.J. Benza, nar.). *Mysteries and Scandals: Lenny Bruce*. Los Angeles: Cable TV/Entertainment Television, December 28, 1998. Videocassette.

Baker, Fred, prod. *Lenny Bruce, Without Tears*. WarnerVision Entertainment, 1992.

Videocassette.

Callner, Marty, prod. *A Toast to Lenny*. Montvale, N.J.: Pioneer Artists, 1984. Laser Disc.

CNN Larry King Live. "George Carlin Discusses 'Silly Putty and Napalm.'" eMediaMillWorks, June 8, 2001. Videocassette. Transcript No.06088CN.V22.

Cohen, Thomas A., dir. *The Hungry i Reunion*. Vid-America, 1981. Videocassette.

E! True Hollywood Story: Lenny Bruce. "Lenny Bruce." Los Angeles: Cable TV/Entertainment Television, July 16, 2001. Videocassette.

The Lenny Bruce Performance Film. Santa Monica, CA: Rhino Home Video, 1992. Videocassette and CD box set.

The O'Reilly Factor. "An Interview with George Carlin." News Network, April 30, 2001. Transcript No. 043005cb.256. Videocassette.

Sales, Grover, prod. *The Trial of Lenny Bruce*. Television script based on San Francisco obscenity trial, 1962.

Weide, Robert B., prod. (Robert De Niro, nar.). *Lenny Bruce: Swear to Tell the Truth*. San Fernando, CA: Whyaduck Productions, 1998. Videocassette. Aired HBO Television, August 1999.

Worth, Marvin, prod. *Lenny*. Los Angeles: United Artists, 1974.

RADIO PROGRAMS ON BRUCE

"Comedian in Transition." An interview with George Carlin. Interviewed by Alan Farley. Berkeley, CA: Pacifica Radio (KPFA), February 11, 1971. Audiocassette. Pacifica Radio Archive No. E2BB2893.

"The Conservative Viewpoint: An Interview with Richard Kuh." Interviewed by Larry Josephson. Berkeley, CA: Pacifica Radio (KPFA), 1970. Audiocassette. Pacifica Radio Archive, No. E2BB3842.01.

Francklyn, Lili, and Michael Yoshida, prod. "The Beat Poets of San Francisco." Berkeley, CA: Pacifica Radio (KPFA), 1979. Audiocassette. Pacifica Radio Archive No. E2AZ0250.

Goldman, Albert. "Lenny Bruce: A Profile." Berkeley, CA: Pacifica Radio (KPFA), March 18, 1963. Audiocassette. Pacifica Radio Archive No. E2BB0382.

Interview of Robert Weide and Mort Sahl. Interviewed by Larry Josephson. New York: Pacifica Radio (WBAI), 1989. Audiocassette.

Interview of Lotus Weinstock. Interview by Larry Josephson. New York: Pacifica Radio (WBAI), 1989. Audiocassette.

Josephson, Larry, prod. "Lenny Bruce: American." New York: Pacifica Radio (WBAI), 1972. Audiocassette. Pacifica Radio Archive No. E2BC0766a.

"Lenny Bruce." 89 min. documentary. Berkeley, CA: Pacifica Radio (KPFA), 1976. Audiocassette. Pacifica Radio Archive No. E2BC2998.

"Lenny Bruce Comes Clean." Berkeley, CA: Pacifica Radio (KPFA), November 11, 1963. Audiocassette. Pacifica Radio Archive No. E2BB1120.

"Lenny Bruce Memorial." New York: Pacifica Radio (WBAI), November 18, 1966. Audiocassette. Pacifica Radio Archive No. E2BB1235.

Miller, Jonathan. "Talk on Lenny Bruce." New York: Pacifica Radio (WBAI), April 1, 1963. Audiocassette. Pacifica Radio Archive No. E2BB4027.

Modern Times with Larry Josephson. An interview with Sherman Block. Santa Monica, CA: WBAI Radio, 1989. Audiocassette.

"Thank God for the Kike." Comments by Ralph Gleason, Albert Bendich, and Alexander Hoffman. Berkeley, CA: Pacifica Radio (KPFA), August 7, 1966. Audiocassette. Pacifica Radio Archive No. E2BB1271.

"Ready for the Defense." An interview with Martin Garbus. Interviewed by Mary Bess. Berkeley, CA: Pacifica Radio (KPFA), 1971. Audiocassette. Pacifica Radio Archive No. E2BC0903.

MAGAZINE AND JOURNAL ARTICLES ON LENNY BRUCE

Auchincloss, Douglas. "The Broken Taboo Breaker." *Time,* 7 June 1971, p. 62.

Babitz, Eve. "Honky Tonk Nights: The Good Old Days at L.A.'s Troubadour." *Rolling Stone,* August 1979, p. 36.

Brustein, Robert. "Lenny Bruce as Victim." *The New Republic,* 17 July 1971.

Edler, Peter. "The Arrest of Lenny Bruce." *The California Magazine,* April 1962, p. 14.

Ferlinghetti, Lawrence. "Horn on 'HOWL.'" *Evergreen Review,* 1957, vol. 1, no. 4, p. 145.

Gleason, Ralph J. "A Celluloid Ghost." *Rolling Stone,* 16 January 1975.

Goldman, Albert. "The Comedy of Lenny Bruce." *Commentary,* October 1963, p. 312.

———. "A Day in the Life of Lenny Bruce." *Los Angeles Free Press,* 3 September 1971, pp. 33–5, 37–46, 48–52, 54–8, 60.

———. "The Trial of Lenny Bruce." *New Republic,* 12 September 1964, p. 13.

Henkin, Louis. "Morals and the Constitution: The Sin of Obscenity." *Columbia Law Review,* 1963, vol. 63, p. 391.

Hentoff, Nat. "Burt Lancaster, Abraham Lincoln, and Lenny Bruce." *New York Herald Tribune: This Week,* 20 December 1964, pp. 1, 16.

———. "The Humorist as Grand Inquisitor." *Liberation,* May 1963, p. 27.

———. "Satire, Schmatire." *Commentary,* 7 July 1961, p. 376.

———. "Where Liberals Fear to Tread." *The Reporter,* 23 June 1960, vol. 22, p. 50.

Hill, Stanley. "Vice Cops Crack Down on World's Sickest 'Sick-Sick' Comic." *Vice Squad,* April 1963, vol. 3, no. 2, p. 18.

Kopkind, Andrew. "Lenny Bruce: Resurrection of a Junkie Prophet." *Ramparts,* March 1975, vol. 13, p. 45.

Krassner, Paul. "The Persecution of Lenny Bruce." *High Times,* February 2000, p. 42.

———. "Why Andrew Dice Clay Is No Lenny Bruce." *The Realist,* Fall 1990.

Kuh, Richard H. "Obscenity, Censorship and the Non-Doctrinaire Liberal." *Wilson Library Bulletin,* May 1968, vol. 42, p. 902.

———. "A Prosecutor Considers the Model Penal Code." *Columbia Law Review,* 1963, vol. 63, p. 608.

———. "Wake Up America: Plan to Keep Pornography Away From Children." *Ladies Home Journal,* September 1968, vol. 85, p. 70.

"Lenny Bruce: The Condemned," *Changes,* April 1970, p. 10.

Marine, Gene. "Lenny, You Meshugginah: You Can't Play the Hero!" *Ramparts,* June 1972, vol. 10, p. 58.

Miller, Jonathan. "The Sick White Negro." *Partisan Review,* Spring 1963, vol. 30, p. 149.

Moody, Howard. "Memoriam." *Playboy,* January 1967, p. 254.

Muggeridge, Malcolm. Review of *How to Talk Dirty and Influence People* by Lenny Bruce. *Esquire,* November 1965, p. 65.

Murray, Michael. "Media." *Commonweal,* 29 November 1974, vol. 101, p. 213.

Schaap, Dick. "The Last Show." *Playboy,* January 1967, p. 162.

Sherman, Ed. "George Crater Meets Lenny Bruce." *Down Beat's Music 1960,* May 1960, pp. 56–7.

Steinem, Gloria. "Obscene?" *Ms.,* October 1973, p. 21.

Waldman, Myron S. "Comic Left Reeling after Tale of the Tape." *Newsday,* 28 June 1964.

Weaver, John D. "The Fault, Dear Bruce, Is Not In Our Stars, But In Ourselves." *Holiday,* 10 November 1968, vol. 44, p. 72.

Weide, Bob. "Lotus and Lenny and Joan." *The Realist,* Spring 1998, no. 138, p. 9.

Zimmerman, Paul D. "Citizen Bruce." *Newsweek,* 18 November 1974, p. 103.

———. "Between the Lines." *New York* magazine, 1972, p. 4.

———. "Bruce's Trial." *Newsweek,* 20 July 1964, p. 76.

———. "Lenny Bruce: Foul Mouthed Nuisance or Rebel Saint?" *Man's World,* October 1964.

———. "Profane Comedy." *Time,* 13 November 1964, p. 88.

———. "Rebel With a Caustic Cause." *Playboy,* February 1959, p. 21.

———. "Regarding Opinion in *People v. Bruce.*" *New York Law Journal,* 4 December 1964, vol. 152, no. 108, p. 1.

———. "The Sickniks." *Time,* 13 July 1959, p. 42.

SELECTED NEWSPAPER ARTICLES, REVIEWS, AND LETTERS ON LENNY BRUCE OR OBSCENITY
Note: The vast majority of newspaper articles are not listed here but are cited in the endnotes to the book.

Allen, Steve. "That's Entertainment?" *Wall Street Journal,* 13 November 1998, p. 17.

Anspacher, Carolyn. "Dismissal for 'Howl' Clerk Indicated." *San Francisco Chronicle,* 23 August 1957, p. 4.

———. "'Howl' Trial Starts—Big Crowd." *San Francisco Chronicle,* 17 August 1957, pp. 1, 6.

"Barrage vs. Lenny Bruce Reflect N.Y. Dalies' New-Found Though Stance." *Variety,* 23 March 1960, vol. 22, p. 50.

Bell, Arthur. "The Intimate Lenny Bruce: Interview with Dustin Hoffman, Star of Lenny." *Village Voice,* 21 November 1974, p 132.

Berman, A.S. "Lenny Bruce Still Testing the Limits." *USA Today,* 2 November 2000, sec. D, p. 3.

Bess, Donovan. "Court Rules on Biblical Essays—1 Wins, 1 Loses." *San Francisco Chronicle,* 7 August 1957, p. 1.

"Bookmen Ask Mayor to Ban Cop Censors." *San Francisco Chronicle,* 16 August 1957, pp. 1, 4.

"Britain to Expel Bruce a Second Time." *New York Times,* 14 April 1963, p. 75.

"Bruce Free in Frisco." *Variety,* 20 March 1963, p. 86.

"Bruce to Ask Court Only for 2-Letter Word on LP—OK." *Weekly Variety,* 17 June 1964.

Buckley, William F. Review of *Foolish Figleaves? Pornography In—and Out Of Court* by Richard H. Kuh. *Washington Post Book World,* 18 February 1968, p. 5.

"Burton Marks, 57, Noted Criminal Trail Lawyer, Dies." *Los Angeles Times,* 6 June 1987, pt. 4, p. 7.

"Comedian Lenny Bruce Arrested." *Chicago American,* 5 December 1962, p. 3.

"Comic Turns Lawyer in Obscenity Hearing." *Chicago Sun-Times,* 19 February 1963, p. 42.

"Cops Nab Bruce for 'Obscenity' at Chi Gate of Horn." *Variety,* 12 December 1962, p. 53.

Cottman, Gail. "Bruce—He Knows Law; Law Knows Him." *UCLA College Times,* 10 November 1965. Reprinted in *The Unpublished Lenny Bruce.* Philadelphia: Running Press, 1984, pp. 120–3.

"Court Says No to Bruce, He Must See Psychiatrist." *Village Voice,* 12 November 1964, p. 1.

"Creative Writing in Horn's Court." *San Francisco Chronicle,* 8 August 1957, editorial and cartoon, p. 20.

David, Amelia. "The Laughs, They Were A-Changin': Comedy Grows Up." *Back Stage,* 15 December 2000, sec. A, p. 24.

Davis, Ross. "Lenny Bruce Speaks Out…on Everything." *Daily Bruin* (UCLA), 10 February 1966.

"England Bars Lenny Bruce in 'Public Interest.'" *Variety,* 10 April 1963, p. 2.

"Fear Lenny Bruce's Chi Obscenity Rap May Cue Tighter Show Biz Censorship." *Variety,* 20 March 1963, p. 2.

Fuller, John C. "Trade Winds: Ginsberg Trial." *The Saturday Review,* 5 October 1957, p. 24.

Garbus, Martin. Response to Letter to the Editor by Richard H. Kuh. *New York Times,* 4 October 1998, sec. A, p. 4.

———. "When the Censor Was in the Statehouse." *New York Times,* 20 September 1998, sec. 2, p. 27.

Gate of Horn press release. 5 December 1962.

Gleason, Ralph J. "A One-Dimensional Lenny." *Sunday Examiner and Chronicle,* 22 December 1974, This World, p. 19.

———. "Ann's 440." *Variety,* 9 April 1958, p. 111.

———. "Lenny Bruce's Obscene Language Pinch in Frisco after Philly Rap." *Variety,* 11 October 1961, p. 61.

———. "On the Town: Lenny Bruce Faces Kafka-esque Trial." *San Francisco Chronicle,* 14 April 1965, p. 45.

———. "The Sickness That Killed Lenny Bruce." *San Francisco Chronicle,* 5 August 1966, p. 47.

———. "The 'Symbol of Obscenity' Pin-Points Life's Paradoxes." *San Francisco Chronicle,* 12 December 1965, p. 43.

Goldman, Albert. "Comics." Review of *How to Talk Dirty and Influence People* by Lenny Bruce. *New York Review of Books,* 20 January 1966, p. 15.

Graham, Fred. Review of *Foolish Figleaves? Pornography In—and Out Of—Court* by Richard H. Kuh. *New York Times Book Review,* 10 December 1967, p. 6.

Gruson, Sydney. "Britain Bars Lenny Bruce in the 'Public Interest.'" *New York Times,* 9 April 1963, p. 75.

Hall, Peter. "Why I Love Lenny the Liberator." *The Guardian* (England), 24 July 1999, *Saturday Review*, p. 3.

Harrington, Stephanie Gervis. "City Puts Bomb Under Off-Beat Culture Scene." *Village Voice,* 26 March 1964, p. 1.

———. "DA Presses Bruce Case, as Fair Opening Nears." *Village Voice,* 16 April 1964, p. 2.

———. "How Many Four-Letter Words Can a Prosecutor Use?" *Village Voice,* 16 July 1964, p. 3.

———. "Is Richard Kuh Really a Feminist Candidate?" *Village Voice,* 18 July 1974, p. 5.

Harris, Gerald. "My Brief on Lenny Bruce." *New York Times,* 19 September 1990, sec. 1, p. 29.

Harris, Michael. "Lenny Bruce Acquitted In Smut Case." *San Francisco Chronicle,* 9 March 1962, p. 1.

Hentoff, Nat. "A Ballot from the Crypt." *Village Voice,* 21 November 1974, p. 34.

———. "Does Free Speech Include 'Fag'?" *Village Voice,* 27 May, 2 June 1998 (series), p. 18.

———. "The Idealistic (sic) Prosecutor." *Village Voice,* 14, 21, 28 February 1974 (series), p. 9, p. 22, p. 9.

———. "Lenny Bruce, Redeemed." *Washington Post,* 29 December 1990, sec. A, p. 19.

———. "Lenny: Redeeming the Memory of a Heretic." *New York Times,* 21 July 1972, sec. 2D, p. 17.

———. "The Onliest Lenny Bruce." *Village Voice,* 15 February 1991, p. 22.

———. "Only When it Hurts." Review of *How to Talk Dirty and Influence People*, by Lenny Bruce. *Washington Post,* 7 November 1965, Book World, p. 8.

———. "What's Left of Lenny?" *Village Voice,* 13 June 1974, p. 85.

———. "Will Morgenthau Do Justice?" *Village Voice,* 6 November 2001, p. 33.

Hilburn, Robert. "Tearing Down the Wall of Silence," *Los Angeles Times,* 10 November 1991, p. 6.

Hogan, William. "Between the Lines." *San Francisco Chronicle,* 19 May 1957, p. 34.

Holston, Noel. "Steve Allen Says TV Is Stuck On the Wrong Channel." *Star Tribune* (Minneapolis), 19 November 1998, sec. E, p. 1.

Houser, John G. "Lenny Bruce Blasts Off; Verbally, That Is." *Los Angeles Herald Examiner,* 23 May 1963.

"Howl Decision Landmark of Law." *San Francisco Chronicle,* 7 October 1957, p 18.

"Jurist Mario Clinco; Twice Judge of the Year." *Los Angeles Times,* 17 May 1986, pt. 3, p. 19.

Keating, Douglas. "Lenny Bruce and His Assault on the Limits of Free Speech." *Philadelphia Inquirer,* 30 October 1998, p. 40.

Krassner, Paul. "The Man Who Said Too Much." *Los Angeles Times,* 4 August 1996, sec. M, p. 3.

Kuh, Richard H. "Prosecuting Censorship." *New York Times,* October 4, 1998, sec. A, p. 4.

Landry, Robert J. "Lenny Bruce's Taboo Defiance Cost: From $200,000 a Year to Ostracism." *Variety,* 3 November 1965, pp. 2, 70.

Leigh, Nigel. "Pop Goes the Icons," *The Guardian,* 4 April 1974, p. 21.

"Law-Abiding Lenny Doesn't Go to Jail." *Buffalo Evening News,* 28 June 1964.

"Lenny Bruce Act Upheld by Court on 'Social Value.'" *Variety,* 21 February 1968, p. 60.

"Lenny Bruce Arrested Again for 'Obscenity.'" *Los Angeles Herald Examiner,* 24 May 1963, sec. A, p. 14.

"Lenny Bruce's Encore." *Variety,* 17 April 1963, p. 58.

"Lenny Bruce Gets One Year, Fined $1,000." *Chicago Sun-Times,* 15 March 1963, p. 11.

"Lenny Bruce Goes to Court May 31." *Los Angeles Times,* 25 May 1963, pt. III, p. 2.

"Lenny Bruce, Guilty on N.Y. Obscenity Charges, Faces Sentencing Dec. 16." *Variety,* 11 November 1964, p. 61.

"Lenny Bruce in Philly Alleges 10G 'Fix' Offer to Quash Narcotics Rap." *Variety,* 11 October 1962, p. 1.

"Lenny Bruce Jailed for Off-Color Nightclub Jokes." *Los Angeles Herald Examiner,* 13 February 1963, sec. A, p. 3.

"Lenny Bruce Trial Winds Up With Hung Jury." *Los Angeles Times,* 16 February 1963, sec. 3, p. 8.

"Lenny Bruce Rap Kayos Chi Gate's License 15 Days." *Variety,* 13 February 1963, p. 57.

"Lenny Bruce Wins Stay of Obscenity Conviction." *Variety,* 30 December 1964, p. 43.

Levy, Herbert M. Letter to the Editor. *New York Times,* 6 March 1974.

Mann, Jim and William J. Eaton. "Court Backs Ban on 'Dirty' Word on Radio and TV." *Los Angeles Times,* 4 July 1978, pt. 1, pp. 1, 8.

Miller, Jonathan. "On Lenny Bruce (1926–1966)." *New York Review of Books,* 6 October 1966, p. 10.

"Minneapolis Columnist Cried Over Death of Bruce." *Variety,* 10 August 1966, p. 59.

"New Test for Obscenity." *The Nation,* 9 November 1957.

"Now It's Obscenity Two Ways." *Los Angeles Herald Examiner,* 25 October, 1962, sec. A, p. 3.

Parents Television Council. Ad. *Washington Post,* 17 October 1999, sec. B, p. 6.

———. Ad. *Washington Post,* 12 December 1999, sec. B., p. 4.

Paul, Henry. "Final Performance Nets Four Months at Hard Labor." *Village Voice,* 12 December 1964, p. 1.

Perlman, David. "How Captain Hanrahan Made 'Howl' a Best-Seller." *The Reporter,* 12 December 1957, vol. 17, p. 37.

———. "'Howl' Not Obscene, Judge Rules." *San Francisco Chronicle,* 4 October 1957, p. 1.

Podhoretz, Norman. "A Howl of a Protest from San Francisco." *New Republic,* 16 September 1957, p. 20.

Pollack, Joe. "Non-Conformity Brings in 'The Bread,' Comic Says." *St. Louis Globe-Democrat,* 16 September 1959, sec 1, p. 16.

Reich, Kenneth. "Block Squares Off as Formidable Political Force." *Los Angeles Times,* 30 April 1994, pt. B, p. 3.

Robb, Inez. "Out of Step." *New York World Telegram,* 11 January 1965, p. 17.

Roberts, John G. "Juvenile Police Head Raids Bookshop in San Francisco." *National Guardian,* 6 August 1957.

———. "Westcoast Censorship Trial Draws Big Audiences in Support of Poem." *National Guardian,* 9 September 1957.

Ruark, Robert. "Let's Nix the Sickniks." *Saturday Evening Post,* 29 June 1963, pp. 38–9.

Schapp, Dick. "The Bruce Behind Bars." *Herald Tribune,* 21 December 1964.

———. "The Friends of Lenny Bruce." *Herald Tribune,* 19 November 1964, p. 19.

———. "A Minority Report." *Herald Tribune,* 2 July 1964.

"'Sick' Comedian Bruce 'Sicker' With New Arrest." *Los Angeles Herald-Examiner,* 25 October 1962, sec. A., p. 3.

Tallmer, Jerry. "Lenny Bruce: No Help Wanted." *New York Post,* 7 April 1964, p. 6.

———. "Village Salutes Lenny Bruce: A Farewell in Poetry and Music." *New York Post,* 1966.

Terry, Dickson. "Lenny Isn't 'Sick,' He's Just a Rebel." *St. Louis Post Dispatch,* 13 September 1959.

Van Hook, Perry. "Bruce Ponders Pornography." *Daily Bruin* (UCLA), 10 February 1966.

Weber, Bruce. "The Iconoclast as Icon: Filling Lenny's Shoes." *New York Times,* 24 July 1992, section B, p 3.

Wechsler, James. "On Lenny Bruce." *New York Post,* 23 December 1964, p. 24.

Williams, Martin. "The Comedy of Lenny Bruce." *Saturday Review,* 24 November 1962, vol. 45, p. 60.

Wilson, Earl. "Sick…Sicker…Rich!…" *New York Post,* 11 March 1960, p. 10.

Obituaries (partial listing)

Champlin, Charles. "Death of Lenny Bruce Raises Questions about His Talent." *Los Angeles Times,* 5 August 1966, p. 3.

Chodrov, Frank. "Lenny Bruce, R.I.P." *National Review,* 6 September 1966, p. 874.

"Doug Weston Dies at 72, Owned Influential L.A. Club." *Washington Post,* 16 February 1999, sec. B., p. 8.

"Jake Ehrlich, Criminal Lawyer Who Won Murder Cases, Dies." *New York Times,* 25 December 1971, p. 20.

"Lenny Bruce, 40, Takes Final 'Trip.'" *Variety,* 10 August 1966, p. 53.

"Lenny Bruce Dies, Apparently from Overdose of Drugs." *Los Angeles Times,* 4 August 1966, p. 1.

Miller, Jonathan. "On Lenny Bruce (1926–1966)." *New York Review of Books,* 6 October 1966, p. 10.

Obituary, Albert Goldman. *Los Angeles Times,* 1 April 1994, part A, p. 26

Obituary, Ephraim London. *New York Times,* 14 June 1990, sec. C, p. 19.

Obituary, Lenny Bruce. *Time,* 12 August 1966, p. 74.

Obituary, Richard Warren Lewis. *Los Angeles Times,* 14 March 1998, sec. A, p. 16.

Obituary, William Grimes. *New York Times,* 30 March 1994, sec. D, p. 19.

"Very First Person; Requiem for a Heavyweight; Sherman Block's Insatiable Desire to Lead Drove Him Until the Very End." *Los Angeles Times Magazine,* 20 December 1998, p. 18.

COURT OPINIONS, LEGAL BRIEFS, AND TRIAL TRANSCRIPTS
RELATED TO PEOPLE v. BRUCE

Published Opinions

Bruce v. Hogan, 381 U.S. 946 (1965) (denying certiorari).

Fantasy Records, Inc. v. Travelers Indemnity Co., 283 N.Y.S. 2d 473 (1967) (intellectual property).
Grove Press, Inc. v. Gerstein, 378 U.S. 577 (June 22, 1964) (granting certiorari).
Lenny Bruce Enterprises v. Fantasy Records, Inc., 243 N.Y.S. 2d 789 (1963) (intellectual property).
People v. Bruce, 31 Ill. 2d 459, 202 N.E. 2d 497 (1964) (monologue given by defendant at adult nightclub did not constitute an obscene performance where the monologue contained "some content of social importance").
People v. Bruce, 64 Cal. 2d 55, 409 P. 2d 943 (1966) (drug case).
People v. Solomon, 26 N.Y. 2d 621, 255 N.E.2d 720, 307 N.Y.S. 2d 464 (1970) (companion case to Bruce's New York cases).

Unpublished Opinions
Bruce v. Sacramento County Executive Branch, et al. (U.S. District Court for the Northern District of California, Northern Division, Civil No. 9538) (Thomas J. MacBride, J.)
———. Order for Denial of Order to Show Cause (denied November 2, 1965).
People v. Bruce (June 18, 1964) (Illinois Supreme Court).
People v. Bruce (September 14, 1964) (Appellate Division, Superior Court of Los Angeles) (No. CRA5912) (Trial Court No. 207444) (Trolley Ho appellate judgment)
People v. Bruce (November 4, 1964) (N.Y. Criminal Trial Court).
People v. Bruce (May 24, 1965) (Supreme Court of New York, Appellate Term: First Department)
———. Affidavit in Opposition to the Defendant's Motion for an Extension of Time.
People v. Solomon, Memorandum Decision (Supreme Court Appellate Term, First Department, Sept. Docket No. 351), published in New York Law Journal, February 19, 1968 (majority and dissenting opinions).
———. Order (February 16, 1968).
———. Notice of Motion to Amend Order and Affidavit of H. Richard Uviller in Support of Motion to Amend Order (March 8, 1968).
———. Affidavit of William E. Hellerstein in Opposition to Motion to Amend Order (March 22, 1968).
———. Memorandum Decision Denying Motion to Amend Order, published in New York Law Journal, April 24, 1968.
———. Order Denying Motion to Amend Order (April 25, 1968).
———. Notice of Motion to Reargue the Motion to Amend the Order and Memorandum in Support of Motion (May 3, 1968).
———. Affidavit of William E. Hellerstein in Opposition to Motion to Reargue Motion to Amend the Order (May 7, 1968).
———. Memorandum Decision of Appellate Term Denying Reargument, published in New York Law Journal, June 12, 1968.

Court Transcripts and Evidence
People v. Bruce, Trial Transcript (San Francisco Municipal Court: Dept. No. 10: County of San Francisco) (November 17, 1961).
People v. Bruce, Trial Transcripts (San Francisco City Municipal Court: Dept. No. 11: County of San Francisco) (March 5–8, 1962).
———. Recording Submitted as Evidence in the San Francisco Obscenity Trial, March 1962 (produced by Lenny Bruce) (LP).
People v. Bruce, Transcripts of Proceedings (Supreme Court of Illinois from the Municipal Court of Chicago: Gen. No. 62 MC 66009: First District, Criminal Court Branch 46) (February 18, 1963–March 14, 1963).
———. Appellant/Plaintiff in Error's Abstract of the Record (Illinois Supreme Court, Case No. 37902) (1963).
People v. Bruce, Trial Transcripts (Beverly Hills Municipal Court) (February 14, 1963).

————. Affidavit of Ben I. Shapiro (filed June 2, 1965).
People v. Bruce, et al., Trial Transcripts (New York City Criminal Court; Part 2B: County of New York) (April 13, 1964–December 21, 1964).
————. Dorothy Kilgallen testimony, July 1, 1964, portions reprinted in *American Jury Trials,* 1965, vol. 10, pp. 232–49.

Appellate Briefs and Legal Petitions and Complaints
Bruce and Katsaros v. Misterly, Complaint, Superior Court of the State of California, County of Sacramento, No. 517226 (filed February 24, 1965).
Bruce v. Draeger et al., Complaint, U.S. District Court for the Southern District of California, Central Division, Docket No. 65-669-TC (filed April 30, 1965).
Bruce v. Hogan et al., Petition for a Writ of Certiorari, U.S. Supreme Court Docket No. 1258 (October Term, 1964).
People v. Bruce, Appellant/Plaintiff in Error's Brief (Illinois Supreme Court, Case No. 37902) (1963).
————. Appellant/Plaintiff in Error's Reply Brief (1963).
————. Appellant/Plaintiff in Error's Suggestions on Behalf of Lenny Bruce (in response to the Court's order of July 7, 1964).
————. Brief and Argument for the State of Illinois (November Term, 1963).
————. Brief and Argument for Defendant Lenny Bruce (November Term, 1963).
People v. Solomon, Brief for Defendant-Appellant (Supreme Court Appellate Term, First Department, Docket No. Sept. No.351).
————. Defendant-Respondent's Brief to the New York Court of Appeals.
————. People-Appellant's Brief to the New York Court of Appeals.

COURT OPINIONS RELEVANT TO BRUCE CASES
A.C.L.U. v. Chicago, 3 Ill. 2d 334, 342, 121 N.E. 2d 585 (1954), (quoting with approval *Swearingen v. U.S.,* 161 U.S. 446 (1896) (vulgarity not alone obscene).
Adams Theatre Co. v. Keenan, 12 N.J. 267, 96 A.2d 519 (1953) (per Brennan, J.).
Bantam Books, Inc. v. Sullivan, 372 U.S. 58 (1963) (Rhode Island commission to suppress objectionable materials held to be a system of informal censorship violating the Fourteenth Amendment).
Burstyn v. Wilson, 343 U.S. 495, 497 (1952) (First Amendment bar to blasphemy prosecutions).
Butler v. Michigan, 352 U.S. 380, 382 (1957) (obscenity statute violates Fourteenth Amendment Due Process clause).
Chaplinsky v. New Hampshire, 315 U.S. 568 (1942) (holding New Hampshire statute prohibiting a person from addressing offensive, derisive, or annoying words to another lawfully in any public place, which by their utterance inflict injury or incite immediate breach of the peace, constitutional under the First Amendment).
Denver Area Educational Telecommunications Consortium, Inc. v. F.C.C., 518 U.S. 727 (1996) (upholding and invalidating various regulations concerning indecent expression on cable television).
Douglas v. California, 372 U.S. 353 (1963) (denial of equal protection of the laws where appellate court determines appointment of counsel would be of no value to an indigent defendant appealing conviction as a matter of right).
Douglas International Corp. v. Baker, 335 F. Supp. 282 (S.D.N.Y.1971) (intellectual property).
Faretta v. California, 442 U.S. 806, 819 (1975) (constitutional right to self-representation), 422 U.S. 836 (Burger, C.J., dissenting), 422 U.S. 846 (Blackmun, J., dissenting).
F.C.C. v. Pacifica Foundation, 438 U.S. 725 (1978) (the level of First Amendment protection is particular to the medium of expression).
Ginzburg v. United States, 383 U.S. 463 (1966) (although accused publications might

not themselves be obscene, conviction of defendant could be sustained in view of evidence of defendant's pandering in production, sale, and publicity with respect to publication of nonobscene materials).

Jacobellis v. Ohio, 378 U.S. 184 (1964) (Ohio conviction for possessing and exhibiting an allegedly obscene film was reversed as violative of the First and Fourteenth Amendments because the film was not found to be obscene under the *Roth* test).

In Re Duane J. Johnson, 59 Cal. 2d 644, 381 P.2d 643 (1963) (release of narcotics addicts).

Katz v. United States, 389 U.S. 347 (1967) (what a person knowingly exposes to the public, even in his own home or office, is not a subject of Fourth Amendment protection).

Kingsley Books, Inc. v. Brown, 354 U.S. 436 (1957) (New York statute authorizing injunction of sale and distribution of indecent written work does not amount to prior restraint of free speech and does not violate the Fourteenth Amendment).

Kingsley International Pictures Co. v. Regents of University of State of New York, 360 U.S. 684, 688 (1959) (First Amendment protection of motion pictures with adulterous subject matter).

Larkin v. G. P. Putnam's Sons, 14 N.Y. 2d 399, 200 N.E. 2d 760, 252 N.Y.S. 2d 71 (1964) (book recounting the life of a prostitute and containing erotic male photographs intended for homosexual audience could not be suppressed under a New York criminal procedure statute authorizing an injunction upon sale and distribution of books found to be obscene, lewd, lascivious, filthy, indecent, or disgusting, because the book was found to fall within the area of publications permissible under constitutional provisions guaranteeing freedom of the press). See *Memoirs v. Massachusetts,* 383 U.S. 413 (1966) (controversy involving same book in the State of Massachusetts).

Magnuson v. Video Yesteryear, 85 F. 3rd 1424 (9th Cir., 1996) (intellectual property).

Marcus v. Search Warrant, 367 U.S. 717 (1961) (due process violated by state procedure which leaves officers to make determination whether material is obscene).

Memoirs v. Massachusetts, 383 U.S. 413 (1966) (reversed state supreme court's holding that a book recounting the life of a prostitute and containing erotic male photographs intended for homosexual audience was obscene, indecent and impure erroneous under the *Roth* test). See *Larkin v. G. P. Putnam's Sons,* 14 N.Y. 2d 399, 200 N.E. 2d 760, 252 N.Y.S. 2d 71 (1964) (controversy involving same book in the State of New York).

Miller v. California, 413 U.S. 15 (1973) (sexually explicit work subject to state regulation where the work has no literary, artistic, political, or scientific value; rejection of "utterly without social value" as a constitutional standard for state regulation of sexually explicit work).

Monroe v. Pape, 365 U.S. 167 (1961) (complaint against Illinois police officers for violation of constitutional rights sufficient to state a cause of action under federal statute rendering every person who deprives a citizen of a constitutional right under color of any state law liable to the injured party).

New York Times v. Sullivan, 376 U.S. 254 (1964) (rule of libel law applied by Alabama courts was constitutionally deficient for failure to provide free speech safeguards required by the First and Fourteenth Amendments).

Pacifica Foundation v. F.C.C., 556 F.2d 9 (D.C. Cir., 1977) (FCC order banning radio broadcast of allegedly indecent language defining sexual or excretory activities in terms patently offensive by contemporary community standards for the broadcast medium, at times of the day when there is a reasonable risk that children may be in the audience, and specifically banning seven patently offensive words, constituted censorship under the Communications Act).

Paris Adult Theatre I v. Slaton, 413 U.S. 49 (1973) (Constitution does not preclude state regulation of obscene material shown at an adult theater provided the regulation comports with the First Amendment; state law regulating speech must be evaluated under the First Amendment).

People v. Doubleday & Co., 272 App. Div. 799, 71 N.Y.S. 2d 736 (1947), affirmed 297 N.Y. 687, 77 N.E. 2d 6 (1947), affirmed by an equally divided Court, sub nom, 335 U.S. 848 (1948) (Frankfurter, J., not participating) (unanimously affirming without opinion state conviction of publisher for sale of book found to be obscene within the meaning of state criminal obscenity statute).

People v. Fritch, 13 N.Y. 2d 119, 192 N.E. 2d 713 (1963) (new trial ordered on conviction of sale of obscene book).

People v. Richmond County News, 9 N.Y. 2d 578, 216 N.Y.S. 2d 369, 175 N.E. 2d 681 (1961) (reversal of a conviction under New York penal code for sale and distribution of an allegedly obscene magazine affirmed, because the magazine was held not to be obscene under the *Roth* test).

People v. Wendling, 258 N.Y. 451, 454, 180 N.E. 169 (1932) (profane and vulgar language not alone obscene).

Reno v. A.C.L.U., 521 U.S. 844 (1997) (under the First Amendment, indecent but nonobscene sexual expression addressed to adults may not be suppressed in the interest of protecting children from harmful materials on the Internet).

Roth v. United States, 354 U.S. 476 (1957) (setting forth the test for obscenity; "whether to the average person, applying contemporary community standards, the dominant theme of the material taken as a whole appeals to prurient interest," which requires that (a) the dominant theme of the material taken as a whole appeals to a prurient interest in sex; (b) the material is patently offensive because it affronts contemporary community standards relating to the description or representation of sexual matters; and (c) the material is utterly without redeeming social value).

Sable Communications, Inc. v. F.C.C., 492 U.S. 115 (1989) (sexual expression which is indecent but not obscene is protected by the First Amendment).

Smith v. California, 361 U.S. 147 (1959), rehearing denied 361 U.S. 950 (1960) (Los Angeles ordinance imposing strict criminal liability on booksellers possessing obscene material and dispensing entirely with element requiring booksellers' knowledge of contents of books held unconstitutional under the First Amendment because of its chilling effect upon protected expression).

Swearingen v. U.S., 161 U.S. 446, 450 (1895) (vulgarity versus obscenity; interpreting Comstock Act).

Times Film Corp. v. City of Chicago, 365 U.S. 43 (1961) (Chicago ordinance requiring examination of films by city officials prior to permission for their public exhibition, tantamount to a system of administrative licensing, is facially unconstitutional under the First and Fourteenth Amendments as prior restraint).

United States v. Klaw, 330 F.2d 115, 168 (2nd Cir., 1965) (First Amendment protection; publication found not obscene under *Roth* test).

United States v. Playboy Entertainment Group, 529 U.S. 803 (2000) (Telecommunications Act's "signal bleed" provision, requiring cable operators to scramble sexually explicit channels, held a restriction upon speech and subject to strict scrutiny under the First Amendment, because the provision was unconcerned with "signal bleed" from other types of channels and was directed only at channels primarily dedicated to sexually-oriented programming).

United States v. Winston, 267 F.Supp. 555 (S.D.N.Y., 1967) (district from which information was transmitted was the proper venue for illegal wagering prosecution).

Zeitlin v. Arnebergh, 59 Cal. 2d 901, 383 P.2d 152 (1963) (legislature in defining proscribed obscene material, requiring that it be utterly without redeeming social importance, intended to give legal sanction to all material relating to sex except that which was totally devoid of social importance, and did not indicate that, to escape proscription, social importance of material must outweigh its prurient appeal).

STATUTORY AND MUNICIPAL LAWS RELATED TO PEOPLE V. BRUCE
Federal
42 U.S.C. §1983 (Civil Action for Deprivation of Civil Rights) (1994).
47 U.S.C. §223 (Communications Decency Act) (1996).

State
California Penal Code §311.6.
Illinois Revised Statutes, 1961, chap. 38, par. 11–20.
New York Penal Code §1140-a (The Consolidated Laws of New York Annotated, Bk. 39, 1964) (Brooklyn, N.Y., Edward Thompson Co.).
San Francisco Municipal Code (Police Code), pt. II, ch. VIII, §176 (Jan. 19, 1953).
San Francisco Municipal Code (Police Code), pt. II, ch. VIII, §176 (Oct. 11, 1962).

PUBLICATIONS BY JUDGE INVOLVED IN PEOPLE V. BRUCE
Murtagh, John M. Preface to *Sisters of the Night: The Startling Story of Prostitution in New York Today* by Jess Stearn. New York: Gramercy Publishing, 1956.
Murtagh, John M., and Sarah Harris. *Cast the First Stone.* New York: McGraw Hill, 1957.

AUTHORS' INTERVIEWS
Arnebergh, Roger. Telephone interview. 22 June 2001.
Baldwin, Carl R. Telephone interview. 21 July 1999.
Bean, Orson. Telephone interview. 23 March 2000.
Bendich, Albert. Telephone interview. 22 April 1999.
———. In-person interview. Fantasy Studios, Berkeley, California. 27 August 2001.
Carlin, George. In-person interview. Las Vegas, Nevada. 20 May 2001.
Cho, Margaret. In-person interview. Washington, D.C. 23 February 2001.
Cohen, Herb. Telephone interviews. 4 April 2001, 7 April 2001, 6 June 2001.
D'Amore, Jo Jo. Telephone interviews. 16 May 2001, 18 May 2001.
Frawley, Thomas P. Telephone interview. 18 May 2001.
Fried, Seymour. Telephone interview. 6 June 2001.
Friedman, Don. Telephone interview. 9 March 2002.
Green, Shecky. Telephone interview. 15 May 2001.
Hall, Val. Telephone interview. 29 May 2001.
Hecht, Richard. Email interview. 9 April 2001.
———. Telephone interview. 9 June 2001.
———. In-person interview. Santa Monica, California. 16 July 2001.
Hefner, Hugh. In-person interview. Beverly Hills, California. 17 July 2001.
Hellerstein, William E. Telephone interview. 9 June 1999.
Horowitz, Sue. Telephone interview. 15 May 2001.
Ibrahimi, Ferozan. Telephone interview. 29 July 2001.
Irmas, Audrey M. Telephone interview. 15 May 2001.
Jones, Ken. Telephone interview. 23 May 2001.
Jurgensen, Randy. Telephone interview. 15 May 2001.
Kassal, Bently. Telephone interview. 18 March 1999.
Krassner, Paul. In-person interview. Desert Hot Springs, California. 25 July 2001.
Kuh, Richard. Telephone interview. 30 September 1999.
Lasher, Allan. Telephone interview. 17 May 2001.
Lesnick, Joel. Telephone interview. 25 May 2001.
Martin, William J. Telephone interview. 15 July 1999.
Meyer, Lawrence. Telephone interview. October 2001.
Montgomery, Carl. In-person interview. Marlton Hotel, New York. 25 October 1999.
Perilli, Frank Ray. Telephone interviews. 29 May 2001, 1 June 2001.
Rosenfield, Maurice. Telephone interviews. 12 May 1999, 18 May 1999, 8 June 1999,

30 September 1999, 3 July 2001.

———. In-person interview. Rancho Mirage, California. 20 December 1999.

Rosenfield, Maurice and Lois Rosenfield. Telephone interview. 20 December 1999.

Ross, Ronald. Telephone interview. 20 June 2001.

———. In-person interview. Palos Verdes, California. 24 July 2001.

Rothman, Ron. Telephone interviews. 4 June 2001, 6 June 2001.

Schayer, Gerald. Telephone interview. 22 May 2001.

Seaman, Barbara. Telephone interview. 5 October 1999.

Selber, Bernard S. Telephone interview. 6 June 2001.

Sloate, Maynard. Telephone interviews. 25 July 2001, 3 August 2001.

———. In-person interview. LasVegas, Nevada. 20 May 2001.

Sobel, Jack. Telephone interviews. 19 February 1999, 3 June 2001.

Solomon, Howard. Telephone interview. 24 August 1999.

———. In-person interview. Crestline, California. 25 July 2001.

Wesselmann, Tom. Telephone interview. 21 July 1999.

Zaidins, Earle Warren. Telephone interview. 14 May 1999.

RELATED BOOKS AND ARTICLES ON FREE SPEECH AND/OR COMEDY

Agan, Patrick. *Hoffman vs. Hoffman: The Actor and the Man.* London: Robert Hale, 1986.

Berger, Phil. *The Last Laugh: The World of the Stand-Up Comics.* New York: Limelight Editions, 1985.

Blackstone, William. *Commentaries on the Laws of England and of Public Wrongs.* Boston: Beacon Press, 1962.

Bollinger, Lee C. *The Tolerant Society: Freedom of Speech and Extremist Speech in America.* New York: Oxford University Press, 1986.

Brownmiller, Susan. *Against Our Will: Men, Women, and Rape.* New York: Simon & Schuster, 1975.

Buckley Jr., William F. *Inveighing We Will Go.* New York: G.P. Putnam's Sons, 1972.

Chafee Jr., Zachariah. *Free Speech in the United States.* New York: Antheneum, 1969.

Charters, Samuel. "Hipsters, Flipsters and Finer Poppin' Daddies: A Note on His Lordship, Lord Buckley, the Hippest of the Hipsters." In *Beat Down to Your Soul,* edited by Ann Charters. New York: Penguin Books, 2001.

Clark, Hunter R. *Justice Brennan: The Great Conciliator.* New York: Birch Lane Press, 1995.

Cochran Jr., Johnnie L., and Tim Rutten. *Journey to Justice.* New York: Ballentine Books, 1996.

Eisler, Kim Isaac. *A Justice for All: William J. Brennan, Jr. and the Decisions that Transformed America.* New York: Simon & Schuster, 1993.

Epstein, Lawrence J. *The Haunted Smile: The Story of Jewish Comedians in America.* New York: Public Affairs, 2001.

Erlich, J.W., ed. *HOWL of the Censor: The Four Letter Word on Trial.* San Carlos, CA: Nourse Publishing, 1956.

Ernst, Morris Leopold, and Alan U. Schwartz. *Censorship: Search for the Obscene.* New York: Macmillan, 1964.

Friedman, Leon, ed. *Obscenity: The Complete Oral Arguments before the Supreme Court in Major Obscenity Cases.* New York: Chelsea House, 1970.

Godwin, Mike. *Cyber Rights: Defending Free Speech in the Digital Age.* New York: Time Books, 1998.

Graham, Bill, and Robert Greenfield. *Bill Graham Presents: My Life Inside Rock and Out.* New York: Delta Trade Paperbacks/Dell, 1993.

Hendra, Tony. *Going Too Far.* New York: Dolphin Doubleday, 1987.

Hentoff, Nat. "The Constitutionalist." *The New Yorker,* March 12, 1990, p. 50.

———. *The Nat Hentoff Reader.* New York: DaCapo Press, 2001.

Hixson, Richard F. *Pornography and the Justices: The Supreme Court and the Intractable Obscenity Problem.* Carbondale, Ill.: Southern Illinois University Press, 1996.

Irons, Peter, ed. *May It Please the Court: The First Amendment.* New York: New Press, 1997.

Kuh, Richard H. "The Freedom Writ: The Expanding Use of Federal Habeas Corpus." *Harvard Law Review,* 1948, vol. 60, p. 657.

———. "Obscenity: Prosecution Problems and Legislative Suggestions." *Catholic Lawyer,* 1964, vol. 10, pp. 285–300.

———. "A Prosecutor Considers the Model Penal Code." *Columbia Law Review,* 1963, vol. 63, p. 608.

Leeds, Jeffrey T. "A Life on the Court: Justice Brennan, at the Start of the Fall Term, Discusses His Life on and off the Court." *New York Times Magazine,* October 5, 1986, p. 25.

Levy, Leonard W. *Blasphemy: Verbal Offense Against the Sacred, from Moses to Salman Rushdie.* Chapel Hill: University of North Carolina Press, 1993.

———. *Origins of the Fifth Amendment.* New York: Oxford University Press, 1968, pp. 266–432.

Lewis, Anthony. "Sex and the Supreme Court." *Esquire,* June, 1963, p. 82.

Lewis, Richard Warren. *The Scavengers and Critics of the Warren Report.* New York: Dell Books, 1967.

Lockhart, William B., and Robert C. McClure. "Censorship of Obscenity: The Developing Constitutional Standards." *Minnesota Law Review,* 1960, vol. 45, p. 5.

———. "Literature, the Law of Obscenity, and the Constitution." *Minnesota Law Review,* 1954, vol. 38, p. 295.

———. "Obscenity Censorship: The Core Constitutional Issue." *Utah Law Review,* 1961, vol. 7, p. 289.

Kalven Jr., Harry, and Maurice Rosenfield. "The Contemporary Function of the Class Suit." *University of Chicago Law Review,* 1941, vol. 8, p. 684.

———. "The Metaphysics of the Law of Obscenity." *Supreme Court Review,* 1960, vol. 1, p. 10.

Kluger, Richard. *Simple Justice.* New York: Knopf, 1976.

Margrath, C. Peter. "The Obscenity Cases: The Grapes of *Roth.*" *Supreme Court Review,* 1966, p. 7.

Markman, Stephen J., and Alfred S. Regnery. "The Mind of Justice Brennan: A 25-Year Tribute." *National Review,* 18 May 1984, p. 33.

Nowak, John, and Ronal Rotunda. *Constitutional Law.* St. Paul: 5th ed., 1955.

Rembar, Charles. *The End of Obscenity: The Trials of Lady Chatterley, Tropic of Cancer, and Fanny Hill by the Lawyer Who Defended Them.* New York: Harper & Row, 1968.

Sandero, Barry. *Sudden Glory: Laughter as Subversive History.* Boston: Beacon Press, 1995.

Schapp, Dick. *Flashing Before My Eyes: Fifty Years of Headlines, Deadlines and Punchlines.* New York: Harper Entertainment, 2001.

Schaumacher, Michael. *Dharma Lion: A Biography of Allen Ginsberg.* New York: St. Martin's Press, 1992.

Silesky, Barry. *Ferlinghetti: The Artist in His Time.* New York: Warner Books, 1990.

Stevens, John Paul. "The Freedom of Speech." *Yale Law Journal,* 1993, vol. 102, p. 1307.

Trager, Oliver. *Dig Infinity: The Life and Art of Lord Buckley.* Lanham, MD: Welcome Rain Press, 2001.

Tushnet, Mark. *Making Constitutional Law: Thurgood Marshall and the Supreme Court, 1961–1991.* New York: Oxford University Press, 1997.

Wenner, Jan. "The Rolling Stone Interview." *Rolling Stone,* November 1, 1969, p. 23.

MISCELLANEOUS PUBLICATIONS

Albert Goldman Papers. Butler Library, Columbia University. Multiple files. New York, multiple dates.

Allen, Steve. *Vulgarians at the Gate: Trash TV and Raunch Radio.* New York: Prometheus Books, 2001.

Arnold, Kenneth James. *California Courts and Judges Handbook.* San Francisco: California Law Book Co., 1968.

Brown, Lesly, ed. *The New Shorter Oxford English Dictionary.* Oxford, England: Clarendon Press, 1993.

Carlin, George. *Napalm and Silly Putty.* New York: Hyperion, 2001.

Charters, Ann, ed. *Beat Down to Your Soul.* New York: Penguin Books, 2001.

———. *The Portable Beat Reader.* New York: Penguin Books, 1992.

Cho, Margaret. *I'm the One that I Want.* New York: Ballantine, 2001.

DeMarco, Gordon. *A Short History of Los Angeles.* San Francisco: Lexikos, 1988.

Ginsberg, Allen. *Howl and Other Poems.* New York: HarperPerennial, 1995.

———. *Howl: Original Draft Facsimile, Transcript and Variant Versions,* ed Barry Miles. New York: Harper & Row, 1986.

———. *Deliberate Prose: Selected Essays, 1952-1995,* Bill Morgan, ed. New York: Perennial/HarperCollins, 2001.

Homer. *The Odyssey.* Translated by Richmond Latimore. New York: Harper Perennial, 1991.

Howe, Irving, and Kenneth Libo. *World of Our Fathers: The Journey of the East European Jews to America and the Life They Found and Made.* New York: Galahad Books, 1976.

Kerouac, Jack. *The Dharma Bums.* New York: Viking Press, 1958.

Lenburg, Jeff. *Dustin Hoffman: Hollywood's Anti-Hero.* New York: St. Martin's Press, 1983.

McClure, Michael. *Scratching the Beat Surface.* San Francisco: North Point Press, 1982.

McGilligan, Patrick. *Jack's Life: A Biography of Jack Nicholson.* New York: W.W. Norton, 1994.

Nicholson, Stuart. *Billie Holiday.* Boston: Northeastern University Press, 1995.

Nicosia, Gerald. *Memory Babe: A Critical Biography of Jack Kerouac.* Berkeley, CA: University of California Press, 1994 ed.

Parrish, Michael. *For the People: Inside the Los Angeles County District Attorney's Office 1850-2000.* Santa Monica, CA: Angel City Press, 2001.

Pennebaker, D.A. *Bob Dylan: Don't Look Back.* New York: Valentine Books, 1968.

Schumacher, Michael. *Dharma Lion: A Biography of Allen Ginsberg.* New York: St. Martin's Press, 1992.

Silesky, Barry. *Ferlinghetti: The Artist in His Time.* New York: Warner Books, 1990.

Souhami, Diana. *The Trials of Radclyffe Hall.* New York: Doubleday, 1999.

Watson, Steven. *The Birth of the Beat Generation.* New York: Pantheon, 2000.

WORLD WIDE WEB PUBLICATIONS

AOL Interview with Mort Sahl. www.geocities.com/TelevisionCity/3217/aol.html [cited 26 August 2001].

Australian press coverage of Lenny's September 1962 visit. www.freenetpages.co.uk/hp/lennybruce [cited 3 December 2001].

"DMT." www.alt.culture.com/aentires/d/dmt.html [cited 17 November 1999].

Dollarhide, Maya. "Lenny Bruce Unlocked Words for All Who Followed." www.freedomforum.org/speech/1999/8/24lennybruce.asp [cited 3 December 2001].

Gleason, Ralph J. "Obituary." members.aol.com/dcspohr/lenny/obgleas.htm [cited 3 December 2001].

Kehr, Dave. "The Whole 'Bruce' and Nothing but Bruce." *New York Daily News,* 21 October 1998. 152.52.15.131/1998-10-21/New_York_Now/Movies/a8520.asp [cited 19 December 1998].

Ladies and Gentlemen, Lenny Bruce! member.aol.com/dcspohr/lenny/lenny1.htm [cited 19 December 1998].

"Lenny Bruce Covers a Favorite Subject: Lenny Bruce in an Off-Broadway Club Date July 15, 1964, Comments on Censorship and Obscenity Laws." www.sonarchy.org/archives/lbruce.html [cited 3 December 2001].

"The Lenny Bruce FBI File." www.fadetoblack.com/foi/lennybruce [cited 3 December 2001].

Lenny Bruce Photographs. www.conceptimage.com/a_Pages/People/Lenny Bruce.html [cited 19 December 2001].

O'Brien, Ruth. "Martin Garbus: Not a First Amendment Absolutist." www.freedomforum.org/speech/1998/12/16garbus.asp [cited 3 December 2001].

Smith, Danile V. "The Complete Lenny Bruce." www.freenetpages.co.uk/hplennybruce [cited 3 December 2001].

Trilling, Lionel. "The Sad Fate of Lenny Bruce." *The New York Review of Books,* October 17, 1966. www.nybooks.com/articles/12295 [cited 3 December 2001].

Walton, Rob. "Enemies of the State: Interview with Hugh Hefner." www.playboy.com/movies-tv/features/lennybruce/index.html [cited 26 August 2001].

www.georgecarlin.com. [cited 20 August 2001].

www.oyez.nwu.edu. [cited 20 August 2001].

INDEX

CREDITS

by Daily News LP; Martin Garbus; Allen G. Schwartz; (John M. Murtagh) © 1950 The New York Times, reprinted with permission; XIII ("100 Fight Arrest") © 1964 The New York Times, reprinted with permission; (Edward de Grazia); © 1971 Attorney William Kunstler (photo credit: Jack Manning); Nat Hentoff © Meg Handler; XV ("Lenny Bruce Arrested") © 1974 The New York Times, reprinted with permission.

Page 351 (The Resurrection of Lenny Bruce) *Lenny* © 1974 United Artists Corporation, all rights reserved, courtesy of MGM CLIP+STILL; 401 (Ex Officio Judgments) © Kai Shuman/Michael Ochs Archives.

AUDIO CREDITS

"The Lie";"Axelrod's Warning"; and "The Crime I Committed" written and performed by Lenny Bruce, November 19, 1961. Originally from *Lenny Bruce Live at the Curran Theater*—Fantasy 34201. Under license from Fantasy, Inc.

"Religions, Inc." written and performed by Lenny Bruce; recorded in San Francisco, 1958. Originally from *The Sick Humor of Lenny Bruce*—Fantasy 7003. Licensed from *Lenny Bruce Originals, Vol. 1*—Fantasy 60-023. Under license from Fantasy, Inc.

"The Steve Allen Show" and "'What Offends Me'" audio appears under license from Meadowlane Enterprises, Inc. Copyright © 1990 Steve Allen. All rights reserved.

"To Is a Preposition, Come Is a Verb"; "A Pretty Bizarre Show"; and "Blah Blah Blah" used by permission of Douglas Records, © Douglas Music Corp.

"Christians and Jews" (Sex and God) used by permission of John Magnuson, © 1967 John Magnuson Assoc.

"Thank You Mask Man" used by permission of John Magnuson, © 1968 John Magnuson Assoc.

"A Comedy of Errors"; "Hauling Ass to Save Her Ass"; "Lenny Reads the Complaint"; and "Thurgood Marshall" from *The Lenny Bruce Performance Film*, used by permission of John Magnuson, © 1966 John Magnuson Assoc.

Ralph Gleason Interview used by permission of John Magnuson.

"Las Vegas Tits and Ass"; "Chicago Is So Corrupt, It's Thrilling"; and "Christ and Moses" excerpts from the legendary *Lenny Bruce: The Carnegie Hall Concert*, produced by Don Friedman on World Pacific Records, used by permission of and © Rora Music (UNI Network International Inc.).

Gate of Horn Intro; "Adolf Eichmann"; and "The Bust" from *Lenny Bruce: Busted* (1962 Gate of Horn concert) used by permission of Vipers Nest Records.

Martin Garbus Interview from the documentary film *Lenny Bruce: Swear to Tell the Truth*, used by permission of Robert Weide and Martin Garbus.

"Richard Kuh Cross-Examines Richard Gilman"; "Kuh Questions Dorothy Kilgallen"; and "Kuh Rails Against Rev. Forrest Johnson" from the New York trial tapes, used by permission of Chuck Harter.

Some audio segments have been edited for time.

The following interviews were conducted by the authors and appear on the CD with the permission of the interviewees:

Lawrence Ferlinghetti
Albert Bendich
Richard Hecht
Ronald Ross
George Carlin
Paul Krassner
Hugh Hefner
Margaret Cho

Nat Hentoff was recorded at National Video Center, New York, NY.

Audio restoration and editing by Mike Konopka, Thundertone Audio. Additional audio editing performed at Metro Mobile Recording.

ACKNOWLEDGMENTS

PERHAPS THE BEST part of publishing a book is the opportunity to honor those who made the journey possible. It is an undertaking that we relish. We begin at the beginning and reflect on all of the marvelous people who kindly assisted us along the way.

Without Nadine Strossen, our friend, *The Trials of Lenny Bruce* may not have come to pass. Years ago, she pointed us in the right direction. So to Nadine—the Queen of Civil Liberties—we tip our hats and open our arms in gratitude. Another Nadine also deserves special credit—Nadine Cohodas. Early on, she helped shape our book proposal, helped us to find a literary agent, and thereafter edited the manuscript at various stages. Nadine, a talented writer herself, has a way of making other writers look better than they otherwise would be. To Nadine: thanks for believing in us. One other person's help was essential at the beginning: Robert B. Weide, the producer of the award-winning documentary *Lenny Bruce: Swear to Tell the Truth*. On many occasions, Bob gave of himself freely so as to reveal his admiration of Lenny Bruce, his love of comedy, and his dedication to civil liberties. To Bob: thanks for lending a helping hand so often.

Now, onto Neeti Madan, our literary agent at Sterling Lord Literistic. Neeti surprised us at times, freaked us out at times, and ultimately delighted us. Throughout, she steered us ably, kindly, and successfully…and she continued to be supportive even *after* the book contract was signed. If it were not for Neeti, we may never have met our two editors at Sourcebooks: Deborah Werksman and Alex Lubertozzi. *Oy vei*, two editors working with two authors! Deb and Alex—real Lenny Bruce fans—helped us, tolerated us, edited us, fought for and with us, bugged us, and even befriended us in various and "sweet" ways. Thanks much, you two. Our gratitude goes, as well, to our attorney, Melvin Wulf, who kept us on the straight and narrow in matters of libel and copyright.

George Carlin. What a *mensch*! He gave of his time, mind, wit, and self in uncommon fashion. One of the true delights of writing this book was getting to know George—irreverent, insightful, and funny in ways all too human. Margaret Cho, another comedian with a big mind and heart, was her true self—kind in spirit, thoughtful in word, and so very supportive of all of the Lenny Bruces of this world. Hugh Hefner, like George and Margaret, was generous with his help. He stood with Lenny in the good times, bad times, unpopular times, and at all other times. He *believed* in Lenny in ways that speak volumes about his own faith in the First Amendment. Our thanks, as well, to his able and energetic publicity associate, Rob Hilburger.

We interviewed countless souls in the course of researching and writing *The Trials of Lenny Bruce*. Many were helpful, some impossible, and some very special. Al Bendich of Berkeley was one of the special ones. Over the years, Al has not received the credit due him for his remarkable role in *People v. Bruce*. In his own modest but vital way, he helped bring back to life the San Francisco story of Lenny's trials. Lenny Bruce owed a great debt to Al Bendich, as do we. We are happy to recognize that debt of sincere appreciation now. Thanks, as well, to the others who assisted us in piecing together the many parts of the San Francisco puzzle: Lawrence Ferlinghetti, owner of City Lights Bookstore; Seymour Fried, Lenny's lawyer at the first S.F. obscenity trial; and Grover Sales, who befriended Lenny and testified at the second obscenity trial in San Francisco.

Maurice Rosenfield of Illinois is another of the special ones. Years ago, he (and his friends Harry Kalven and Robert Ming) defended Lenny Bruce *sans* compensation. Without Maury's selfless and enlightened assistance, the Chicago chapter would have lacked much vital information. Maury: we thank you and salute you. Jamie Kalven, true to his father's kind spirit, shared Professor Kalven's Lenny Bruce papers with us. What a find! And without Earle Warren Zaidins, many of the hues surrounding the colorful Chicago obscenity trial would have been missing. Thanks Earle. The same to Burt Joseph, a Chicago lawyer, who always said "yes" and always helped us to find this or that soul we thought long dead.

The L.A. Story of this book owes much to eight men: Maynard Sloate (a onetime club owner), Herb Cohen (same), Gene Norman (owner of The Crescendo), Paul Krassner (Lenny's friend and editor), Jo Jo D'Amore (Lenny's inimitable cohort), Frank Ray Perilli (Lenny's pal and entertainment colleague), Richard Hecht (a former prosecutor), and Ronald Ross (same). In many ways, the lives, lifestyles, and values of those men are radically different. Yet in one way, so very helpful to us, they are all alike: namely, their remarkable abilities and willingness to tell the Lenny Bruce story as they knew and lived it. There are many others whose assistance was invaluable, and we thank them heartily: Roger Arnebergh, Judge Robert Feinerman, Shecky Green, Audrey Irmas, Satsimran Kaur, Allan Lasher, Paul McGuigan, Joyce Morita, Ron Rothman, and Judge Bernard Selber. Our appreciation, as well, to "the men in blue" (or in plainclothes) from the L.A. County Sheriff's Office: Thomas Frawley, Val Hall, Ken Jones, Joel Lesnick, and Gerald Schayer. All of these individuals made our expedition exciting as we unturned this or that leaf in Bruce's extraordinarily complex legal life in Los Angeles.

In researching and writing the long and unruly New York story (actually several stories), we benefited greatly from numerous people: Howard and Ella Solomon (the owners of the Café Au Go Go), Martin Garbus (one of Lenny's N.Y. trial lawyers), Bentley Kassal (one of Lenny's pretrial lawyers), Edward DeGrazia (Lenny's civil rights attorney), Allen G. Schwartz (the Solomons' trial lawyer), William E. Hellerstein (Howard Solomon's appellate lawyer), Dick Schapp (Lenny's friend who defended him in print), Jack Sobel (Lenny's agent), and Don Friedman (the man who made the Carnegie Hall performance possible—good luck, Don, on your forthcoming autobiography). Thanks, too, to Chuck Harter (a Lenny Bruce aficionado) for his welcomed assistance, and the best of fortune on your Lenny Bruce project.

Lawrence Schiller, whose incredible research buttressed *Ladies and Gentlemen, Lenny Bruce!*, kindly granted us access to his Bruce papers. We are indebted to him for giving us a copy of the trial transcript of the Troubadour case. We also benefited from being able to examine the papers of the late Albert Goldman (and those of others in the files) now archived at the Rare Book and Manuscript Library at Columbia University. We especially want to thank the library's staff: Patrick Lawlor and Jane Siegel, along with Tanya Chebotarev, Jennifer Lee, Henry Rowen, and Kevin O'Connor. Thanks, too, to Jamie Kalven and the librarians at the University of Chicago Law Library for granting us access to the archived papers of the late Professor Harry Kalven Jr. Charles E. Brown of the St. Louis Mercantile Library at the University of Missouri-St. Louis loved Lenny Bruce enough to help us track down some great St. Louis stories. Special thanks, as well, to Susan H. Kezele, Kelly Kunsch, Bob Menanteaux, and Brendan Starkey, the librarians at the Seattle University School of Law, who tolerated endless requests for interlibrary loans and computer searches. We are grateful, finally, to all those countless unnamed librarians at the Library of Congress who, for months on end, helped us to rediscover the life and legacy of Lenny Bruce.

The fabulous folks at Seattle University School of Law were supportive in countless ways. We are immensely grateful for the generous research and travel budget provided over the years by Deans James Bond and Rudy Hasl; for the unstinting administrative assistance given by Nancy Ammons (a *very* special lady); for the talented research assistance of Cliff Gilley, John Solberg, and Steve Trinen; for the tireless and successful efforts of our "copyright clearance king," Steve Mays, and his assistant Bree Kelly; for the intellectual property advice of our friend and colleague Robert Cumbow; and for the unceasing encouragement of our other professorial colleagues. Thanks to you all for paving the way for us at so many turns in the road.

The compact disc that accompanies this book could not have been possible without the help of Fantasy Records (Pamela Bendich), Douglas Records (Steven Saporta and Alan Douglas), Meadowlane Enterprises (Bill Allen), United Network (Don Friedman), Viper's Nest Records (Bernard Brightman), and John Magnuson. Their commitment to the First Amendment and freedom of information made this project a reality.

Philip Levy of Bridge Street Books (Washington, D.C.) is a Lenny Bruce junkie. He shared countless stories with us. Phillip—one of the most knowledgeable booksellers in the nation—was also kind enough to edit an early version of the manuscript. Our work is the better for it.

If we had our way, this book would have been titled *Comedy on Trial: Lenny Bruce's Struggles for Free Speech*. Not being sophisticated in the ways of commerce, we failed to consider a variety of marketing factors. Hence, we yielded (kicking!) to our publisher's promotional knowledge. Credit due, credit given.

COLLINS: Susan A. Cohen (the joy of my life) and Dylan Collins (my partner in play) had no hand in this book. But they love to see their names in print and I love to make them happy. Susan & Dyl: Fate willing, your books will come. At least I hope so. Meanwhile, thank you for giving me what this husband and father yearns for—love and laughter, comfort and care, and just enough independence to chronicle the lives of Lenny Bruce and other ranters.

Bunny Kolodner helped to prevent many a shipwreck. Her guidance—always caring, yet bordered—made the journey both possible and enjoyable. Bunny: the day this work is released I will dedicate a star to you. Promise.

Leonard W. Levy knows not of this book. Yet his influence has remained with me ever since that day in 1974 when he quizzed me about *The Origins of the Fifth Amendment*. Gladly, I passed the test, and have benefited greatly from his work ever since. Leonard: I just wanted that on the record.

Finally, there is David Skover. What *can* I say? He took me in out of the cold and threw me into the inferno. But what a time I've had! Oh, all the bridges we've burned, the fires we've ignited. Being devious has, however, cost us. Even so, I would not trade any of it for the calm that comes with a still life. David: Here's to the future...and all the wondrous hell that may come with it.

SKOVER: Sean Patrick O'Reilly, who is less a fan of Lenny Bruce than of the First Amendment, is the *sine qua non* for my artistry. His faith in me steeled my resolve and his love for me uplifted my spirits during the long trek in completing this work. Sean, may I do as much for you as you finish your first book, *Elements of Love*.

My cherished friend, Jill Wangsgard, put up with harrowing plane rides, crowded subway cars, and steaming summer days in New York to be my *aide de camp* during our research trip at the Rare Book and Manuscript Library at Columbia University. As you know all too well, Jill, I could never have done it without you. And Michael Rosenberg, Seattle's celebrated photographer, was also there for me in the pinch. Thanks, pal.

Finally, there is Ron Collins. How *can* I reply to him? He's become my brother in life, my partner in mind, and my comrade in crime. He is the only true "outlaw" free speech jurisprude with whom I've had the pleasures (and struggles) of intense collaboration. Ron: here's to the future...and the prospect of a heaven that we may be fortunate enough to glimpse.

ABOUT THE AUTHORS

RON COLLINS AND David Skover are friends.

Ron lives in the East, David in the West.

They have been writing together for well over a decade. Their work is a joint effort, with David manning the keys and Ron pacing.

This is their second book together, *The Death of Discourse* (1996, 2003) being the first.

Ron, who grew up in Southern California, is a First Amendment scholar at the Freedom Forum's First Amendment Center in Arlington, Virginia. David, who grew up in Wisconsin, is a law professor at Seattle University.

Both are law graduates. Ron went to law school at Loyola in Los Angeles, David at Yale in New Haven.

Both clerked for appellate judges—Ron for Justice Hans A. Linde of the Oregon Supreme Court (and later as a judicial fellow in the United States Supreme Court), and David for Judge Jon O. Newman of the United States Court of Appeals for the Second Circuit.

In a prior life, David sang in professional operatic and musical theater productions. He adores the works of Mozart, Verdi, Puccini, and Wagner, and admires the music of Stephen Sondheim.

Ron likes to probe Plato, Camus, Wittgenstein, and Simone Weil. He respects the thought of Louis Brandeis and admires the poetry of Allen Ginsberg, especially "Howl."

Both have written numerous scholarly articles (often together) in journals such as the Harvard, Stanford, Michigan, and Texas Law Reviews.

Ron has penned some 150 or so newspaper op-ed pieces, and edited *The Death of Contract* (1995) and *Constitutional Government in America* (1981). David coauthored (with Pierre Schlag) *Tactics of Legal Reasoning* (1986).

They are the founding coeditors of *Books-on-Law*, a monthly online journal dedicated to book reviews.